D1028852

The Ships of Canada's Naval Forces 1910-1981

A complete pictorial history of Canadian warships

The Ships of Canada's Naval Forces 1910~1981

A complete pictorial history of Canadian warships

Ken Macpherson
John Burgess

Foreword by Rear Admiral H. F. Pullen, OBE, CD

COLLINS
Toronto

First published 1981
by Collins Publishers
100 Lesmill Road, Don Mills, Ontario

Second printing, 1982

©1981 by Kenneth R. Macpherson and John Burgess

All rights reserved. No part of this publication may be reproduced, stored in a
retrieval system, or transmitted in any form or by any means, electronic,
mechanical, photocopying, recording, or otherwise, without prior written
permission of the publisher.

Design by Marg. Round

Canadian Cataloguing in Publication Data

Macpherson, Ken.
The ships of Canada's naval forces 1910-1981

Bibliography: p.
Includes index.
ISBN 0-00-216856-1

1. Warships — Canada — History — 20th century.
2. Canada. Royal Canadian Navy — Lists of vessels.
I. Burgess, John. II. Title.

VA400.M32   623.8'25'0971   C81-094988-1

Printed in Canada

Contents

Part Three   1945-1981

Appendices

Foreword

Here is the book for which a great many naval veterans have been waiting. In it they will find the details and illustrations of well remembered ships that were their "homes" for many tempestuous months in a most unfriendly environment under conditions of considerable danger. There is a brief outline of each ship's service and enough information to conjure up a host of memories: of commissionings and workups; of convoys and struggles with the worst the North Atlantic could produce, gales of wind, mountainous seas, fog, snow and ice; and for some, encounters with the enemy.

This is the definitive account of all those Canadian men-of-war that have served their sovereign and country both in peace and war for over seventy years, as "a security for such as pass on the seas upon their lawful occasions". Well and truly have they done so under the White Ensign and, latterly, the Canadian flag. This book is a record of loyal and faithful service, which it is hoped, will not be forgotten by succeeding generations.

The authors of this excellent book have made a significant contribution to Canadian history and are to be congratulated. I wish them every success in this most worthwhile undertaking.

H. F. Pullen,
Rear Admiral

Big Hill,
Chester Basin,
Nova Scotia

Preface

Our book is intended as a history, not so much of the Royal Canadian Navy and Maritime Command, as of the ships that have composed them over the past seventy-one years. Not every ship is pictured: obviously the hundreds of harbour craft could not be included, and for less obvious reasons the Fairmiles, MTBs and infantry landing craft are represented by one photograph typical of each class. We hope those who served in these craft will understand and excuse their omission, and that a majority of those who have served at sea will find in these pages the old, familiar outlines of the ships that were their homes.

The Ships of Canada's Naval Forces 1910-1981 is in a real sense the precocious offspring of **Canada's Fighting Ships** (1975), but its scope is vast by comparison. The meticulous research involved in producing it has made possible the correction of errors in the parent volume, particularly as respects service dates of individual ships, and the inclusion of a wealth of additional information.

The photographs are in every instance the best we could find, consistent with our wish that as few as possible should have been published before. Most are "official", but in a good many instances we were able to obtain better ones through the kindness of the individuals and institutions whose names appear on page 238.

We acknowledge with gratitude the assistance of Dr. W.A.B. Douglas, Head of the Directorate of History, CFHQ, and his staff, particularly Philip Chaplin and David Kealy; Mr. Simon Cox and Miss M. W. Thirkettle of the Naval Historical Branch, Ministry of Defence, UK; Don Gibson; Tony Grazebrook; Arnold Hague; Tom Lynch; Peter Robertson; and the many who lent photographs not used in the book but none the less much prized.

We are also indebted to the Ontario Arts Council for a grant which gave us much encouragement in the early stages of compiling our book.

A special word of thanks is due Rear Admiral H. F. Pullen and E. C. Russell, who long ago conceived the idea of producing a book similar to this but, fortunately for us, did not proceed with it. As Naval Historian, Ted Russell provided us with information which now, long afterward, appears in this book, and Admiral Pullen has kindly written a Foreword to it, as well as offering valuable suggestions on the text.

The Ships of Canada's Naval Forces 1910-1981 is affectionately dedicated to our wives, Mary Macpherson and Gwen Burgess, whose cheerful acceptance of solitary evenings and a diminishing share of house-room made it all possible.

KRM and JKB

Part One 1910~1939

Introduction

The Royal Canadian Navy (RCN) came into existence on May 4, 1910, when the Naval Service Act became law, and later that year its first ships were commissioned — two cruisers purchased from the Royal Navy (RN). Apart from two submarines acquired in 1914, *Niobe* and *Rainbow* were the only offensive warships to serve in the RCN during the First World War.

The Act provided, however, that the Department of Naval Service should incorporate the fishery patrol, hydrographic, tidal survey, and wireless telegraphic services of the Department of Marine and Fisheries. The ships associated with these services were the backbone of the young navy during most of the war. When not needed as naval vessels they carried on their regular peacetime duties, sometimes performing both roles simultaneously. There were also five former yachts and a number of ships commandeered from customs, post office, and navigational aids maintenance duties, as well as a host of tugs and motor launches. Information concerning their naval careers is now very scarce.

This motley assortment did a creditable job as patrol craft, minesweepers, and examination vessels, particularly off the east coast, the German threat in the Pacific having faded after Admiral Graf von Spee's defeat in December, 1914. In 1917 three classes of minesweeping trawlers and drifters began to make their appearance from a variety of yards on the Great Lakes and St. Lawrence River. Four of the trawlers were to be among the few ships the Navy could boast during the lean years between the wars.

Niobe and *Rainbow* went to the scrapyard in 1920, to be replaced by the modern cruiser *Aurora* and the destroyers *Patrician* and *Patriot*. Doomed by budget cuts, *Aurora* was retired in 1922 along with two submarines acquired in 1919. With the creation of the Department of National Defence in 1922 the miscellaneous government ships mentioned earlier ceased to be considered, even on paper, as naval vessels and were transferred back to the Department of Marine and Fisheries. *Patrician* and *Patriot* were replaced in 1928 by *Champlain* and *Vancouver*, so that from 1922 to 1931 the RCN consisted in its entirety of a destroyer and two trawlers on each coast.

In 1931 the destroyers *Saguenay* and *Skeena*, the first ships designed and built for the RCN, were commissioned; *Fraser* and *St. Laurent* were purchased from the RN in 1937 as replacements for *Champlain* and *Vancouver*, and a year later *Restigouche* and *Ottawa* joined them. These six destroyers will be found in Part Two 1939 — 1945 pp 34, 35 and 36, owing to their close kinship with the eight others of the River class. A class of four modern minesweepers was added in 1938, and the training schooner *Venture*, training ship *Skidegate*, and trawler *Armentières* made up the rest of the thirteen ships that constituted the RCN on the eve of the Second World War.

Rainbow

Niobe, 1907

RAINBOW

On August 4, 1910, at Portsmouth, England, *Rainbow* was commissioned the first unit of the infant RCN. One of a class of 20 "protected cruisers," she had served in the RN since 1893. *Rainbow* arrived at Esquimalt on November 7, 1910, and carried out training duties, ceremonial visits, and some fishery patrols until the end of 1912. She then lay largely idle until the outbreak of the First World War, during which, apart from two submarines, she was the sole defender of Canada's western seaboard.

The German threat in the Pacific ended with the defeat of Admiral Graf von Spee's squadron at the Battle of the Falkland Islands in December, 1914, and thereafter *Rainbow* patrolled the Pacific coast as far south as Panama. In 1916 and early 1917 she was used in the transporting of $140 million in Russian bullion between Esquimalt and Vancouver. By 1917 her crew was needed to man patrol vessels on the east coast, and on May 8 she was paid off. *Rainbow* was recommissioned on July 5 to serve as a depot ship at Esquimalt. Paid off again on June 1, 1920, she was sold to a Seattle shipbreaker.

NIOBE

A good deal more imposing than *Rainbow*, *Niobe* had served in the RN from 1898 to 1910, one of eight sisters of the *Diadem* class. She was commissioned in the RCN on September 6, 1910, at Devonport, and arrived at Halifax on October 21. *Niobe* was nearly lost during the night of July 30-31, 1911, when she went aground off Cape Sable, necessitating repairs that were not completed until the end of 1912. In the fall of 1914, after the ravages of two years' disuse had been made good, she joined the RN's 4th Cruiser Squadron on contraband patrol off New York.

Worn out, she returned to Halifax on July 17, 1915, never to put to sea again. She was paid off that September 6 and became a depot ship. Her upperworks were wrecked in the Halifax explosion of December 6, 1917, but she continued to serve as a depot ship until 1920, when she was sold for scrap. *Niobe* was broken up at Philadelphia two years later.

Aurora with *Patrician* and *Patriot* at Esquimalt, 1921

Patrician at Esquimalt, 1924

AURORA

One of the eight-ship Arethusa class, *Aurora* had served with the Grand Fleet from 1914 to 1916, and was the first British ship in action at the Battle of the Dogger Bank in 1915. She was on hand at the surrender of the German High Seas Fleet in November, 1918.

Aurora was presented to the RCN in 1920, along with two destroyers, and commissioned on November 1. After the three ships arrived in Halifax on December 21, they set out on a training cruise via the Caribbean to Esquimalt, returning to Halifax on July 30, 1921. A year later, drastic cuts in the naval budget made it necessary to pay off *Aurora*. Disarmed in 1922, she lay at Halifax in an increasingly embarrassing state of deterioration until 1927, when she was sold for breaking up.

PATRICIAN and PATRIOT

These sister ships, commissioned in 1916, served in the RN for the duration of the First World War. In 1920 *Patrician*, *Patriot*, and the cruiser *Aurora* were offered to Canada as replacements for the decrepit *Niobe* and *Rainbow*. The three were commissioned at Devonport on November 1, 1920, and left for Canada a month later.

When the naval budget was cut by a million dollars in 1922, the two destroyers became the only seagoing ships in the RCN. *Patrician* was ordered that autumn to the west coast, where she was to spend the next five years training officers and men of the naval reserve. *Patriot* performed the same function on the east coast. In September, 1921, she assisted Dr. Alexander Graham Bell, towing his experimental hydrofoil craft *HD-4* at high speed on Bras d'Or Lake near Baddeck, N.S. As perhaps the strangest assignment of her career, *Patrician* was detailed in November, 1924, to intercept a band of Nanaimo bank-robbers trying to reach the United States by motor launch. Both were sold for scrap in 1929, *Patriot* to be broken up at Briton Ferry, Wales, and *Patrician* at Seattle.

CHAMPLAIN and VANCOUVER

Initially named *Torbay* and *Toreador*, respectively, these sister ships were originally commissioned in the RN in 1919. They were lent to the RCN while replacements for *Patrician* and *Patriot* were being built in Britain, and the transfer took place at Portsmouth on March 1, 1928. (As there was already a *Vancouver* serving in the RN, she was renamed *Vimy* to free the name for the new Canadian ship.)

In May, 1928, *Champlain* arrived at Halifax and *Vancouver* at Esquimalt to provide reserve training, as did *Patrician* and *Patriot*, at opposite coasts. They were paid off at their respective bases on November 25, 1936, and sold for scrap the following year.

Patriot at Halifax, 1923

Champlain

CC 1 and CC 2

These submarines, originally named *Iquique* and *Antofagasta*, respectively, were built at Seattle for the Chilean government. However, the deal with the Chileans fell through, and on the eve of the First World War these submarines were purchased by the premier of British Columbia, Sir Richard McBride. The Dominion government ratified the purchase and on August 6 the two boats were commissioned as *CC 1* and *CC 2* because of their resemblance to the British "C" class submarines. After three years' cruising and training on the west coast they were ordered to Europe, and on June 21, 1917, set out for Halifax with their mother ship *Shearwater*. They were the first warships ever to transit the Panama Canal under the White Ensign. Unfit for a transatlantic crossing, they remained at Halifax until sold for scrap in 1920.

CH 14 and CH 15

As their nomenclature implies, these were Canadian members of the British "H" class, two of ten built during the First World War at Quincy, Mass. *H 14* and *H 15* were on their way to Britain when hostilities ended, and were rerouted to Bermuda. They were presented to the RCN in February, 1919, and commissioned at Halifax that June as *CH 14* and *CH 15*. Scarcely used, they were paid off on June 30, 1922, and sold for scrap five years later.

Vancouver

CC 1 (nearer) and CC 2 at Halifax, 1918

CH 14 and CH 15

Acadia

ACADIA

Acadia, a Dominion government hydrographic survey ship, was commissioned as a patrol vessel from January 16, 1917, to March, 1919, and carried out A/S patrol in the Bay of Fundy, off the south shore of Nova Scotia and in the Gulf of St. Lawrence. She then resumed survey duty until the outbreak of the Second World War when she was commissioned on October 2, 1939, first serving as training ship for HMCS Stadacona, later patrolling the Halifax approaches from May, 1940, to March, 1941. She also occasionally acted as close escort for small convoys between Halifax and Halifax Ocean Meeting Point. After refit in 1941, she served as a training ship at Halifax for A/A and DEMS (Defensively Equipped Merchant Ship) gunners and, in June, 1944, went to HMCS Cornwallis as gunnery training ship. Paid off on November 3, 1945, she was returned to the Dominion government. *Acadia* retired from service on November 28, 1969, to become a museum ship at the Bedford Institute in Dartmouth, N.S. On February 9, 1980, she was handed over to the Maritime Museum of the Atlantic.

ALGERINE

Built at Devonport Dockyard in 1895, this RN sloop was based at Esquimalt before the First World War. Her crew was sent east in 1914 to man *Niobe*, and *Algerine* was lent to the RCN in 1917 to serve for the duration of the war as a depot ship at Esquimalt. Sold in 1919 and converted for salvage work, *Algerine* was wrecked in Principe Channel, B.C., on October 13, 1923.

CANADA

A fishery patrol vessel built in 1904 along warship lines, *Canada* provided training for an embryo corps of Canadian naval officers before the creation of the RCN, and was commissioned as a naval patrol vessel from January 25, 1915 to November, 1919. Sold for commercial purposes in 1924, she was reported lost near Miami in 1926.

Algerine

Canada, 1918

CARTIER/CHARNY

A Dominion government hydrographic survey ship that served as an armed patrol vessel on the east coast during the First World War, *Cartier* reverted to government service between the wars, but was commissioned as a training ship at Halifax on September 18, 1939. She was renamed *Charny* on December 9, 1941. Paid off on December 12, 1945, she was reported derelict and sunk at Sydney, N.S. a dozen years later.

CONSTANCE and CURLEW

These oddly-shaped little sisters were built at Owen Sound in 1891 and 1892, respectively, for the Canadian government — *Constance* to serve the Customs department, and *Curlew*, the Dept. of Marine and Fisheries. Both were fitted for minesweeping in 1912 and promptly taken into naval service upon the outbreak of war. When required, they functioned as east-coast patrol craft throughout the war, otherwise performing their regular duties. *Curlew* was sold in 1921, *Constance* in 1924.

A third sister, *Petrel*, was built as a fishery patrol vessel at Owen Sound in 1892, but did not see salt water until 1905. Between 1914 and 1918 she was employed frequently as a patrol or examination vessel on the east coast. After the war she reverted briefly to her fishery patrol duties before being sold in 1923.

Charny (ex-Cartier), 1940

Constance

Curlew

Florence before she joined the navy

FLORENCE

Originally named *Czarina*, then *Emeline*, this American-built yacht was bought and renamed by John Eaton, who brought her to Toronto in 1910. He presented *Florence* to the RCN, which commissioned her on July 19, 1915, and for most of the ensuing year she served as guardship at Saint John, N.B. and patrol vessel in the Bay of Fundy. However, she proved to be unsuitable and was paid off in August, 1916. Later that year *Florence* was sold to buyers in Martinique and is said to have been lost in the Caribbean in January, 1917.

GALIANO

Built in Dublin, Ireland, as a fishery patrol craft for the Dominion government, *Galiano* was sister to *Malaspina* (p. 19). Although *Galiano* apparently was not commissioned until December 15, 1917, she alternated civil duties with those of a naval patrol and examination vessel throughout the war. She foundered with all hands in Barkley Sound, B.C., on October 30, 1918.

GRILSE

Formerly the yacht *Winchester*, she was purchased in the U.S. in June, 1915, fitted with a torpedo tube, and commissioned July 15 as a torpedo boat. Since she was unsuited for winter service in Canadian waters, *Grilse* left Halifax on December 11, 1916, for the Caribbean and was reported lost in a storm. She turned up at Shelburne, N.S. three days later, however. After several months' refit *Grilse* resumed her patrol duties until she was paid off on December 10, 1918. An effort was made to sell her in 1920, but no adequate bid was received, and during 1921-22 she was attached to a youth training establishment in Halifax dockyard. In 1922 she was sold to Solomon Guggenheim, who renamed her *Trillora*, and was still in his possession when, on September 21, 1938, she foundered in a hurricane on Long Island Sound.

Galiano

Grilse

Gulnare

Hochelaga

GULNARE

Gulnare was purchased by the Canadian government in 1902 for fishery protection work. From 1918 to 1919 she served as a contraband control vessel on the east coast, returning after the war to government duties which included hydrographic survey. She was sold to Marine Industries Ltd. about 1938, and broken up about ten years later.

HOCHELAGA

An armed yacht formerly named *Waturus*, *Hochelaga* was purchased in the U.S. in 1914. She served as a patrol vessel from August 13, 1915 to 1920, and from then until 1923 took up coastguard duties. She then spent many years as a Pictou-Charlottetown ferry and was sold in 1942, to reappear briefly four years later when she was seized by the RN as an illegal Israeli immigrant ship.

Lady Evelyn

LADY EVELYN

Built on the Mersey for a Blackpool firm and originally named *Deerhound*, she was acquired and renamed by the Postmaster-General's department in 1907. *Lady Evelyn's* new function was to meet transatlantic mail steamers in the Gulf of St. Lawrence and take off the mail for transfer to trains. She was commissioned in the RCN as a patrol vessel from June, 1917 to 1919, and survived in commercial service on the west coast until shortly before the Second World War.

LAURENTIAN

The Yorkshire-built *King Edward* was acquired in 1911 by Canada Steamship Lines and renamed *Laurentian*. She was sold to the RCN six years later and served as a patrol vessel from May, 1917 to January, 1919. Later transferred to the Department of Marine and Fisheries, she served as a lighthouse supply vessel and buoy tender until sold for scrap in 1947.

Laurentian

Malaspina

MALASPINA

Like her sister *Galiano*, she joined the Canadian government fleet as a west-coast fishery patrol vessel in 1913. With the outbreak of the war *Malaspina* took up a part-time career as a patrol vessel, but from December 1, 1917 to March 31, 1920, was commissioned solely for contraband control in the Strait of Juan de Fuca. Between the wars she served the Department of Transport, but on September 6, 1939 was again commissioned by the RCN for patrol and examination work. She was later taken over by HMCS Royal Roads as a training vessel. *Malaspina* was paid off on March 31, 1945, sold for scrap the following year, and broken up at Victoria.

MARGARET

Margaret had scarcely been delivered to the Canadian Customs department when, in August, 1914, she was taken up by the RCN for patrol work, chiefly in the St. Lawrence River and Gulf of St. Lawrence. She was commissioned from February 3, 1915 to April 3, 1919, and soon afterward returned to the Dominion government. Sold to the Brazilian Navy about 1935 and renamed *Rio Branco*, she was discarded in 1958.

NEWINGTON

Originally a fishing trawler, *Newington* was purchased in 1908 by the Dominion government for use as a lighthouse tender. In 1914 she was crudely fitted as a minelayer to lay a defensive minefield in Johnstone Strait, should need arise. She served the RCN on the west coast as a patrol vessel during the First World War, then reverted to government service until 1937, when she was sold. When she sank in Burrard Inlet, B.C., on August 26, 1959, she was 60 years old.

Margaret

Newington, May 2, 1944

P.V. I-VII

These seven New England-built menhaden trawlers made up a patrol and minesweeping flotilla based at Sydney, N.S. Purchased in the U.S., they served in the RCN between March, 1917 and April, 1919, subsequently reverting to their former names and occupation. Each was armed with a 12-pounder gun.

RESTLESS

This innocuous-looking little ship was employed throughout the First World War as an examination vessel on the west coast. Built in 1906, she was purchased for fishery patrol two years later. She served as a training ship at the Royal Naval College of Canada, Esquimalt, from 1918 to 1920, when she was donated to the Navy League of Canada for sea cadet training. She was sold in 1927, but remained in commercial service until about 1950, when she was destroyed by fire in Saanichton Bay, B.C.

SHEARWATER

Stationed at Esquimalt, the sloops *Shearwater* and *Algerine* were, in 1914, the last remnants of the vanished RN Pacific Squadron. *Shearwater's* two 4-inch guns were put ashore to defend Seymour Narrows when the First World War broke out, and her crew was sent to Halifax to man HMCS *Niobe*. The Admiralty agreed to lend *Shearwater* to the RCN, and on September 8, 1914, she was commissioned as a tender to the newly acquired submarines *CC 1* and *CC 2*. In the summer of 1917 she sailed with her charges via the Panama Canal to Halifax. She was paid off June 13, 1919, and in 1924 sold into mercantile hands and renamed *Vedas*. Her register was closed in 1937.

P.V. II

	Former Name	Where Built	Launch Date	Displ.	Dimensions
P.V. I	William B. Murray	Rockland, Me.	1912	390	151.6' x 24.1' x 13'
P.V. II	Amagansett	Rockland, Me.	1912	390	151.6' x 24.1' x 13'
P.V. III	Herbert N. Edwards	Rockland, Me.	1911	323	155.6' x 23.1' x 12.9'
P.V. IV	Martin J. Marran	Rockland, Me.	1911	323	155.6' x 23.1' x 12.9'
P.V. V	Rollin E. Mason	Essex, Mass.	1911	323	155.6' x 23.1' x 12.9'
P.V. VI	Leander Wilcox	Noank, Conn.	1903	205	126' x 22.3' x 9.2'
P.V. VII	Rowland H. Wilcox	Noank, Conn.	1911	247	132' x 22.3' x 10.7'

Restless

Shearwater

STADACONA

Originally named *Columbia*, this large yacht was purchased from her New York owner and commissioned on August 13, 1915, for patrol duty out of Halifax. She was also for a time flagship at Halifax of Vice-Admiral Sir Charles Kingsmill. Early in 1919, *Stadacona* was sent round to the west coast and, after brief service as a dispatch vessel, paid off March 31, 1920. After a few years' employment as a fishery patrol and hydrographic survey vessel, she was sold in 1924. She then achieved a degree of notoriety as a rumrunner's depot ship under the name *Kuyakuzmt*. In 1929 she was rebuilt at Vancouver and once again became a yacht, successively named *Lady Stimson* and *Moonlight Maid*. In 1941 she became a towboat, and served the U.S. government as such for a time in 1942. She was burned for salvage at Seattle in January, 1948.

TUNA

This former yacht was built as *Tarantula* for W. K. Vanderbilt, Jr., and acquired by the RCN in 1914. Converted into a torpedo boat by the addition of two tubes, *Tuna* was commissioned on December 5, 1914. She was paid off on May 10, 1917, as a result of irreparable engine-mount fracture. Her hull, sold in June, 1918, and stripped for salvage, still lay in Halifax's Northwest Arm in the 1930s.

TR 1-60

These large minesweeping trawlers were copies of the RN's Castle class. It seems impossible to determine how many were actually commissioned, but the number is likely about 45. *TR 37, 39, 40, 51, 55, 56,* and *58-60* were lent to the USN from November, 1918 until sometime in 1919. Little used, the TRs found willing buyers as replacements for fishing tonnage lost during the war, and a good many were absorbed into the RN as auxiliary minesweepers during the Second World War. Two of them appear in the 1940s roster of the RCN as *Andrée Dupré* and *Macsin*.

	Builder
TR 1-6, 37-44	Port Arthur Shipbuilding Co. Ltd.
TR 7-12	Collingwood Shipbuilding Co. Ltd.
TR 13-14	Thor Iron Works, Toronto, Ont.
TR 15-18	Polson Iron Works, Toronto, Ont.
TR 19-20, 54-57	Kingston Shipbuilding Co.
TR 21-31	Canadian Vickers Ltd., Montreal, Que.
TR 32-34, 51-53	Government Shipyards, Sorel, Que.
TR 35-36, 45-50	Davie Shipbuilding Co. Ltd., Lauzon, Que.
TR 58-60	Tidewater Shipbuilding Co., Trois Rivières, Que.

Stadacona

Tuna

TR 9

C.D. 1-100

These wooden-hulled drifters were built along the same general lines as those of the RN. All were launched during 1917, and 37 are supposed to have been commissioned before the end of the war. They were intended for minesweeping and patrol duty, and 14 served at Gibraltar, 6 at Bermuda and 5 in West Africa from 1918 to 1919. A further 18 were lent to the USN during the same period. Like the TRs, they found ready employment as fishing vessels after the war, and a few served in the RN from 1939 to 1945. Three of the drifters, unnumbered, were destroyed incomplete by fire at the Canada Steamship Lines plant at Sorel on June 19, 1917.

	Builder
C.D. 1-50	Davie Shipbuilding Co. Ltd., Lauzon, Que.
C.D. 51-53	Government Shipyards, Sorel, Que.
C.D. 54-59	Sorel Shipbuilding & Coal Co., Que.
C.D. 60-61, 68-70	H.H. Sheppard & Sons, Sorel, Que.
C.D. 62-67	LeClaire & Sons, Sorel, Que.
C.D. 71-96	Canadian Vickers Ltd., Montreal, Que.
C.D. 97-100	Harbour Commissioners, Montreal, Que.

C.D. 27

Battle Class Trawlers

ARLEUX

Built at Montreal and commissioned on June 5, 1918, *Arleux* saw only brief service before being handed over to the Department of Marine and Fisheries, though in common with several sisters she remained nominally a naval vessel until June 30, 1922. As a fishery patrol vessel she frequently acted as mother ship to the winter haddock-fishing fleet off the east coast. Taken up again by the RCN, she was commissioned September 13, 1939, and in 1940 designated *Gate Vessel 16* at Halifax. She was sold for commercial use on February 15, 1946, and foundered August 19, 1948 off White Head Bay, N.S.

ARMENTIÈRES

Commissioned from June 5, 1918 to October 28, 1919, *Armentières* re-entered naval service in 1923 only to be sunk in Pipestem Inlet, B.C., on September 2, 1925. Refloated on October 26, she was recommissioned the following year and continued in service, primarily as a training ship, but with occasional intervals on fishery patrol. In the spring *Armentières* used to escort the fur seals en route to their breeding grounds in the Pribilof Islands, to protect them from illegal hunting procedures. From 1934 until the outbreak of the Second World War she was the only one of her class still in naval service. She served as an examination vessel at Prince Rupert throughout most of the war, and after being paid off on February 8, 1946, was sold to become SS *A. G. Garrish*. Two changes of name later, she still existed in 1962 as the *Laforce*. She was sold to an American buyer in 1972.

Arleux as gate vessel, Halifax, 1940

Armentières, December 9, 1940

ARRAS

Built at Kingston, *Arras* was in commission from July 8, 1918 to 1919, when she became a fishery protection vessel. As such, she frequently served as hospital ship to the Grand Banks fishing fleet. Taken up again by the RCN, she was in service from September 11, 1939 to April 1, 1946. Initially stationed at Halifax, from mid-1941 she was employed at Sydney, N.S., as *Gate Vessel 15*, and was extensively damaged by fire in November, 1943. She was broken up at Halifax in 1957.

Arras, 1940

FESTUBERT

Built at Toronto, *Festubert* was commissioned on November 13, 1917, and after brief service was laid up until May 1, 1923. She was then recommissioned for training and other duties on the east coast until once more placed in reserve in 1934. From 1939 to August 17, 1945, she was again in service as *Gate Vessel 17* at Halifax. *Festubert* was sold in 1946 for commercial use and renamed *Inverleigh*. She was scuttled off Burgeo, Nfld., on June 30, 1971.

GIVENCHY

Built at Montreal, *Givenchy* was commissioned on June 22, 1918, and paid off on August 12, 1919, at Esquimalt. She then entered the service of the Department of Marine and Fisheries as a fishery protection vessel, but was returned to the RCN on April 15, 1939. Though her principal function was that of accommodation ship (notably to the Fishermen's Reserve), she was actually in commission from June 25, 1940 to December 7, 1943. Sold on September 19, 1946, *Givenchy* is thought to have been broken up in the U.S. in 1953.

Festubert, November 12, 1943

Givenchy

LOOS

Launched at Kingston on September 27, 1917, *Loos* was in commission between August 1, 1918 and 1920. In 1922 she entered the service of the Department of Marine and Fisheries as a lighthouse supply ship. About 1937 she was sold out of government service, but was taken up again by the RCN on December 12, 1940. By June, 1941, she had been converted to *Gate Vessel 14* and served as such for a time at Shelburne. In 1945 she was returned to her previous owner, Marine Industries Ltd., and broken up in 1949.

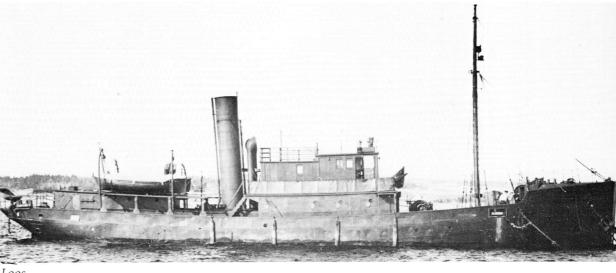

Loos

Messines fitting out at Toronto, astern of *Ypres*, 1917

MESSINES

Launched at Toronto on June 16, 1917 along with three sisters, *Messines* began a short commission on November 13, and in 1920 was handed over to the Department of Marine and Fisheries to become a lightship. Eventually designated *Lightship No. 3*, she was scrapped in 1962.

ST. ELOI

Built at Toronto, *St. Eloi* was commissioned on November 13, 1917. Like *Messines*, she was turned over to the Department of Marine and Fisheries in 1920 for conversion and ultimately designated *Lightship No. 20*. The RCN recovered her in 1940 and she became *Gate Vessel 12* for the duration of the war, spending at least part of that time at Shelburne. The Department of Transport, successor to the Department of Marine and Fisheries, took her back in June, 1945 and she was not finally disposed of until 1962.

ST. JULIEN

Built at Toronto and commissioned on November 13, 1917, *St. Julien* was transferred to the Department of Marine and Fisheries in 1920, and was known by 1934 as *Lightship No. 22*. Sold out of government service in 1958, she was renamed *Centennial*, and still existed as recently as 1978.

St. Eloi

St. Julien fitting out at Toronto, 1917

Thiepval

THIEPVAL

Launched in 1917 at Kingston, *Thiepval* was in commission between July 24, 1918 and March 19, 1920, when she was turned over to the Department of Marine and Fisheries as a patrol vessel. Taken back into the RCN, she was commissioned April 1, 1923, for service on the west coast. In February, 1924, she was detailed to proceed across the north Pacific to Hakodate, Japan, to deposit fuel and lube "dumps" for the round-the-world flight of Maj. Stuart MacLaren. Travelling over 11,000 miles in the process, *Thiepval* also salvaged what remained of the aircraft after it was wrecked at Nikolski, USSR, on August 3. The trawler herself was wrecked on an uncharted rock in Barkley Sound, B.C., on February 27, 1930.

VIMY

The Toronto-built *Vimy* was in commission from November 13, 1917 to November 30, 1918, seeing even less service than the dates would indicate. In 1922 she was transferred to the Department of Marine and Fisheries for conversion, and eventually known as *Lightship No. 5*. She is thought to have been broken up about 1958.

YPRES

Built at Toronto and in commission from November 13, 1917 to 1920, *Ypres* was recommissioned as a training ship on May 1, 1923. She was placed in reserve in November, 1932, but emerged from a 1938 refit as *Gate Vessel 1* of Halifax boom defence. On May 12, 1940, she was run down and sunk at Halifax by HMS *Revenge*, fortunately without loss of life.

Vimy fitting out at Toronto, 1917

Ypres, 1924

Fundy Class Minesweepers

COMOX

Commissioned on November 23, 1938, *Comox* was stationed at Esquimalt at the outbreak of the war, and carried out local patrol duties until March, 1940, when, with *Nootka*, she was ordered to the east coast. Arriving at Halifax in April, she spent the entire war on local minesweeping duties with Halifax Local Defence Force. On January 15, 1945, with *Fundy*, she rescued survivors from the U.S. liberty ship *Martin van Buren*, torpedoed off Halifax. She was paid off July 27, 1945, sold for commercial purposes in 1946 and converted to a tug, the *Sung Ming*.

FUNDY

Commissioned at Collingwood on September 1, 1938, she was at Halifax when the war began, and served almost continuously as a member of Halifax Local Defence Force on local minesweeping duties. In July, 1942, her one change of occupation occurred when she escorted one convoy to Boston and another back to Halifax. On January 15, 1945, with *Comox*, she rescued survivors of the torpedoed *Martin van Buren*. *Fundy* was paid off at Halifax on July 27, 1945, and sold two years later to Marine Industries Ltd.

GASPÉ

Commissioned at Quebec on October 21, 1938, *Gaspé* was at Halifax when hostilities broke out. Throughout the war she served with Halifax Local Defence Force on local minesweeping duties. She was paid off at Halifax on July 23, 1945, and sold into mercantile service in 1946, becoming the Shanghai tug *Sung Li*.

Comox, June, 1942

Fundy, 1944

Gaspé, 1940

Nootka, September 23, 1942

Skidegate, January, 1941

Venture

NOOTKA/NANOOSE

Commissioned on December 6, 1938, at Esquimalt, Nootka was based there when the war began. She performed local patrol duty until March, 1940, when, with *Comox*, she was transferred to Halifax. Arriving there in April, she was assigned to Halifax Local Defence Force with which she remained throughout the war. On April 1, 1943, she was renamed *Nanoose* so that her original name could be allotted to a Tribal class destroyer. She was paid off at Halifax on July 29, 1945, and, like two of her sisters, sold in 1946 to become a tug. Her Chinese owners renamed her *Sung Ling*.

SKIDEGATE

Named *Ochecac* before her purchase, this diminutive vessel was commissioned on July 25, 1938, for training purposes in connection with the Fishermen's Reserve, formed that year on the west coast. Of declining use as the war progressed, *Skidegate* was paid off on February 18, 1942, finally sold into mercantile service in 1946 and renamed *Santa Rosa*.

VENTURE

The only sailing vessel among the thirteen ships serving in the RCN on the eve of the Second World War, this three-masted schooner was built at Meteghan, N.S., and commissioned on October 25, 1937, as a training ship. With war imminent, *Venture* was paid off on September 1, 1939, to become an accommodation vessel at Halifax for ratings on the staff of the Rear Admiral, 3rd Battleship Sqdn., RN. In November, 1941, she was recommissioned as guardship at Tuft's Cove, at the entrance to Bedford Basin. She gave up her name on May 13, 1943, to the former yacht *Seaborn* and thereafter was known as *Harbour Craft 190*. She was sold on December 10, 1945, to a Halifax firm and renamed *Alfred & Emily*. Engaged first in the sealing trade and then in carrying coal, she was lost by fire at sea in 1951.

Part Two 1939~1945

Introduction

During the Second World War the RCN grew from 13 ships to some 450, excluding the smaller auxiliaries. The majority were engaged in the Battle of the Atlantic, fought throughout most of the war around several series of convoys running between North America and the United Kingdom. This battle was fundamental to Britain's survival, and the importance of the RCN's role in it can hardly be exaggerated.

This introduction presents the activities of the RCN against the background of that Atlantic struggle, which an anonymous Admiralty historian has divided into eight phases. Much of the missing detail will be found in the histories of the ships themselves and in the appendix on convoys.

September 3, 1939 to June 9, 1940

During this period the U-boats found most of their victims in the southwest approaches to the British Isles — about as far as they could handily operate from their home bases. Transatlantic convoys were initiated almost immediately on the outbreak of war. They were escorted by battleships, cruisers, or armed merchant cruisers, as the greatest threat at the time was the surface raider. Eastbound convoys were given a local escort of one or two Canadian destroyers which would accompany the convoy to a point south of St. John's, Nfld. The first such convoy, HX.1, was escorted out of Halifax by *Saguenay* and *St. Laurent* on September 16, 1939, six days after Canada had declared war on Germany. Passive defences in the form of A/S nets were completed at Esquimalt in October and at Halifax in November.

The four destroyers based on the west coast had joined their sisters in Halifax by the end of the year, and the small force was augmented in November by the arrival of HMCS *Assiniboine*, transferred from the RN. The only other notable ships added to the RCN in this period were the three small "Prince" class liners, for conversion to armed merchant cruisers. Orders for 64 corvettes and 18 Bangor class minesweepers were placed with 15 Canadian shipyards in 1940. In April the Germans overran Denmark and Norway, and four of Canada's destroyers were ordered to the U.K.

June 10, 1940 to March 17, 1941

Italy entered the war on June 10 and soon afterward France collapsed. The Canadian destroyers found themselves engaged in the melancholy business of evacuating troops from France, and in the process *Fraser* was rammed and sunk by HMS *Calcutta* on June 25.

Able now to operate from bases in France and Norway, the U-boats could stay at sea longer and range farther out into the Atlantic. In the face of this threat, as well as that posed by E-boats and the Luftwaffe to

Channel traffic, convoys ceased in July to use the southwestern approaches and were routed north of Ireland instead. The remaining three Canadian destroyers now served as local escorts in those waters. The newly acquired HMCS *Margaree* was lost in collision in convoy on October 22 with most of her ship's company, many of them survivors of *Fraser*.

From July to October the U-boats wreaked havoc with the weakly defended shipping, and the German "aces" came into prominence. They favoured attacking on the surface and by night, and toward the end of the year introduced the "wolf pack" attack.

The destroyer shortage caused by losses and damage during the Norwegian campaign and the evacuation of France was to some extent made good through the agreement of September 2, 1940, whereby sites for military bases were leased by Britain in return for 50 overage U.S. destroyers. Six of these were commissioned into the RCN that month and two more later. Corvette production was in full swing both in Britain and in Canada, whose first 18 were commissioned during this period. The period ended with the loss of U-boats commanded by three of the German "aces" in attacks on convoys between March 7 and 17.

March 18, 1941 to January 11, 1942
Faced with a growing number of convoy escorts in what had been so happy a hunting ground, the U-boats moved their patrols farther into the Atlantic. It was now imperative that continuous escort be provided across the ocean, and to this end Britain began basing escorts at Hvalfjord, Iceland, in April. In June, 1941, an RCN base was established at St. John's, Nfld., and Canadian ships overseas were withdrawn to become part of what was called the Newfoundland Escort Force (NEF). Canada accepted responsibility for ocean escort of convoys to the meeting point south of Iceland as from the end of May.

In May the cast of the ongoing drama were upstaged by those engaged in the hunt for the German battleship *Bismarck*, finally sunk on May 27. The victory was dearly bought, HMS *Hood* having been sunk by *Bismarck* three days earlier.

On September 10 the corvettes *Chambly* and *Moose Jaw* had barely arrived to reinforce the Canadian escort of a beleaguered eastbound convoy when they attacked and sank *U 501*. HMCS *Lévis* was torpedoed and sunk nine days later with another convoy, not far away, and on December 7 *Windflower* was lost in a collision. She had been the first Canadian corvette launched.

A German long-range bomber, the F.W. 200 Kondor, became a serious menace to transatlantic shipping during this period, both as an attacker and as a spotter for U-boats. A countermeasure in the form of naval auxiliaries called fighter catapult ships was introduced in April, and in May the first of 26 mercantile counterparts called CAM (catapult aircraft merchant) ships went to sea. The types were alike in that they could not recover the Hurricane fighter, whose pilot had to "ditch" and hope for rescue. HMS *Audacity*, which entered service in June, remedied this defect. A German freighter captured by HMCS *Assiniboine* and HMS *Dunedin*, and later fitted with a flight deck, she was the precursor of the escort carriers — mostly U.S.-built — that would appear in growing numbers as the Battle of the Atlantic progressed.

Among decisions made at the meeting of Roosevelt and Churchill at Argentia, Nfld., in August, 1941, was one permitting U.S. warships to escort convoys to and from the Mid-Ocean Meeting Point. This arrangement was initiated the following month, and was to cost the USN its first war casualty when, on October 31, USS *Reuben James* was torpedoed and sunk in convoy HX.156.

Toward the end of the year an appreciable number of U-boats were withdrawn to serve in the Mediterranean and its western approaches, so that the Atlantic convoys had a comparatively quiet time until mid-January. During this period 50 new corvettes were commissioned, including the first 4 with extended fo'c's'les. The first 19 Bangor class minesweepers and the first 13 Fairmiles also entered service.

January 12 to July 31, 1942
Four days after Pearl Harbor, Hitler declared war on the U.S., and in mid-January a large force of U-boats made their appearance off the eastern seaboard and in the Caribbean. In these waters they took a staggering toll of merchant shipping, especially tankers, as no convoy system had been established for coastwise traffic. This was finally remedied in May, and by July the system was effective enough that the U-boats returned to mid-ocean waters.

March, 1942 saw the first use by the Germans of "milch cow" U-boats to refuel and replenish their smaller sisters at sea, nearly doubling the latters' endurance. Not to be outdone, the RN devised a method of refuelling escorts at sea from ordinary merchant tankers, which went into practice that summer. About the same time high-frequency direction-finding (HF/DF or "Huff-Duff") was perfected for shipboard installation. It had been used since the beginning of the war by shore stations to obtain cross-bearings on U-boat wireless transmissions and "fix" their location at sea. Convoys could thus be warned of U-boats in their paths or aircraft directed to attack them. In time all destroyers, frigates and convoy rescue ships were equipped with this device which, though largely unsung in histories of the sea war, played a very significant part in the defeat of the U-boats.

The RCN by now formed the backbone of the western Atlantic escort force, with 13 destroyers and 67 corvettes in commission and, by the autumn of 1942, bore almost half the burden of escorting North Atlantic convoys. Base facilities had been completed at Londonderry, Ireland, and in February, 1942, Canadian mid-ocean escorts inaugurated the "Newfie-Derry run," seldom thereafter calling at Iceland. An escort of one of the earliest convoys on that run, HMCS *Spikenard* was torpedoed and sunk on the way across, on February 10.

In May two ships were sunk in the Gulf of St. Lawrence, leading to the formation of a St. Lawrence Escort Force based at Gaspé. This typically consisted of two corvettes, five Bangor minesweepers, and some of the Fairmile motor launches that had begun entering service the previous fall. In August and September U-boats were again active in the Gulf and the St. Lawrence River itself, and the armed yacht *Raccoon* and the corvette *Charlottetown* were torpedoed and sunk on September 7 and 11, respectively. On the other side of the ledger, the period ended with the sinking of *U 90* by *St. Croix* on July 24, and of *U 588* by *Skeena* and *Wetaskiwin* on July 31 in mid-Atlantic.

August 1, 1942 to May 21, 1943
This period began with a renewed effort by the U-boats against North Atlantic convoys, especially in what the Germans called the "black pit," a gap north of the Azores out of reach of land-based air cover. The wolf packs were larger than ever before, and they were steadily refining their methods of intercepting convoys and calling in their comrades for the kill. Losses were appallingly heavy and U-boat sinkings disproportionately small. Canadian ships sank, or assisted in sinking, four U-boats in the Atlantic, three in the Mediterranean, and one in the Caribbean. HMCS *Ottawa* was torpedoed and sunk on September 13, corvettes *Louisburg* and *Weyburn* on February 6 and 22, 1943. That the latter two were lost in the Mediterranean is explained by their being among 16 Canadian corvettes assigned to convoys supplying Allied forces in North Africa after Operation "Torch," the invasion of November, 1942.

An important development during this period was the formation in September, 1942, of the first support groups — groups of ships that could be dispatched to bolster the escorts of threatened convoys, and which could now afford the luxury of hunting U-boats to death rather than merely "putting them down" and rejoining the convoy. Their effective use was, however, delayed by the needs of the North African campaign.

In February, 1943, Dönitz, who had succeeded the less forceful Raeder as Grand Admiral of the Kriegsmarine, won Hitler's approval to mount an all-out onslaught on the North Atlantic sea-lanes. Allied fortunes there sank to an unsurpassed low, U-boats sinking 171 ships in February and March. One of the deadliest attacks of the war was that delivered against the combined convoys HX.229/SC.122 in March by 44 U-boats, which sank 21 ships for the loss of only one of their own.

At this inauspicious-seeming juncture, on April 30, the RCN assumed control of the northwest Atlantic. Seven corvettes lent to the USN for Caribbean convoy duty were now returned, as were the 14 from the Mediterranean. In addition six of the RN's veteran destroyers were to be transferred to the RCN. Commissioned between March, 1943 and February, 1944, they received the names of Canadian rivers. Canadian ocean escort groups were further reinforced at this time by the allocation to them of three RN frigates and six RN corvettes. In addition, six RN A/S trawlers were lent to bolster the escort force in the Gulf of St. Lawrence. Brief accounts of these fifteen ships will be found in Appendix One.

Through April the tide of battle began almost imperceptibly to turn in the Allies' favour, and May proved as disastrous for the U-boats as March had been for the convoys. The 42-ship convoy ONS.5 lost only 13 ships despite having 41 U-boats deployed against it, not to mention sinking 7 of the attackers and damaging 5, while SC.130 lost none despite the efforts of a wolf pack of 32. In all, 41 U-boats were sunk that month, and on May 24 Dönitz recalled most of the others. The Battle of the Atlantic had two years to run, but the Kriegsmarine lost the initiative in May, 1943, and was never to regain it.

The U-boats were defeated by a combination of factors: improved intelligence, more and experienced convoy escorts, continuous air cover, and support groups. Each of five of the support groups contained one of the newly commissioned U.S.-built escort aircraft carriers. These, together with shore-based Liberators, provided vital air cover across the "black pit," while elsewhere the U-boats were subjected to increasingly effective attacks by long-range aircraft from bases in Newfoundland, Greenland, Iceland, and Britain. Two new weapons also made their appearance: The first, the Hedgehog, threw its 24 projectiles ahead of the ship, enabling the operator of the Asdic, a submarine-detecting device, to maintain contact with his quarry until the moment of firing. The second was the airborne rocket projectile, such as those with which a Swordfish from the aircraft carrier *Archer* sank *U 752* on May 23. The RCN's first two Tribal class destroyers, *Athabaskan* and *Iroquois*, were completed during this period.

May 22 to September 18, 1943

At the end of May the first of 19 MAC (merchant aircraft carrier) ships went into service. These differed from U.S.-built escort carriers in that they carried regular cargoes — most of them oil, some of them wheat — as well as aircraft.

There were no attacks on North Atlantic convoys in June, but land-based bombers launched a devastating assault on U-boats transiting the Bay of Biscay en route to or from their bases in western France. Sixteen were sunk there in July alone, whereas merchant ship losses were negligible during the rest of the period. At the same time, U.S. hunter/killer groups incorporating escort carriers were systematically annihilating the "milch cows" south and west of the Azores. During this period the RCN's second pair of Tribals, *Haida* and *Huron*, were commissioned, as were its first five frigates and first Algerine class minesweeper.

September 19, 1943 to June 6, 1944

The expected renewal of U-boat attacks on North Atlantic convoys began with a wolf pack attack on ON.202, September 19-23. One of the first victims was HMCS *St. Croix*. The attack was notable as the first in which the U-boats were armed with acoustic torpedoes, which tracked their targets by the sound of their propellers. It was also one of the earliest occasions on which a homing torpedo was used against a U-boat by an aircraft, *U 238* being sunk by this means. HMCS *Chedabucto* was accidentally lost on October 21 in the St. Lawrence River.

Despite a determined effort throughout the autumn, the U-boats accomplished little in the North Atlantic and suffered heavy losses. During this period Capt. F. J. Walker's group of RN sloops enjoyed its greatest success, sinking 11 U-boats. One of these, *U 264*, was the first operational boat fitted with a Schnorchel — a 26-foot tube which enabled the boat to run on diesels while submerged and to refresh the air in the boat without surfacing. By autumn few boats went on patrol without it, and the device was to occasion a sharp decline in sinkings, especially by aircraft.

Another unsuccessful effort early in 1944 was abandoned in March, leaving only a couple of weather-reporting U-boats in the North Atlantic. All serviceable boats were now being held ready against the anticipated invasion of northern Europe. During this period RCN ships assisted in the destruction of seven U-boats. HMCS *Valleyfield* was lost south of Newfoundland on May 7.

During the last quarter of 1943 the RCN Tribals were used extensively on convoys to Russia, then early in 1944 took part in a series of attacks on German shipping off the coast of Norway. Prior to D-Day three of them participated in strikes against German shipping in the Channel; *Athabaskan* was lost in one of these strikes on April 29.

While still committed to its duties in the North Atlantic, the RCN was deeply involved in preparations for the invasion. Early in 1944, 16 Bangors and 19 corvettes made the passage to the U.K., the former to be equipped for minesweeping and the latter to help escort the ships massing for D-Day. The 9 remaining River class destroyers were withdrawn from the Atlantic for service in the Channel, and 11 frigates were formed into two escort groups for U-boat hunting, under operational control of Western Approaches Command. As well, the RCN now manned two flotillas of motor torpedo boats, which took part in a variety of operations in the Channel before, during, and after D-Day.

During the night of June 5-6, RCN Bangors swept a safe channel in to Omaha Beach where American troops were to land, and on and after D-Day itself (June 6) 16 Canadian corvettes escorted shipping and artificial harbour components across the Channel. Two new RCN destroyers, *Algonquin* and *Sioux*, provided inshore fire support during the landings, in which 30 RCN-manned infantry landing craft took part. *Prince David* and *Prince Henry* were also on hand in their new role as infantry landing ships.

June 7, 1944 to May 8, 1945

With the Normandy beachhead secure, the British-based RCN ships shared with their RN sisters the task of defending the Channel approaches from Biscay-based U-boats, and of harrassing German shipping both in the Channel and in the Bay of Biscay itself. The A/S sweeps were carried out principally by the frigates and River class destroyers, which sank four U-boats in August and September.

The Tribals specialized in dramatic night actions, *Haida* and *Huron* sinking a large German destroyer in one of these forays. The Bangors meanwhile busied themselves clearing German mines from the Channel and from liberated ports, a task that was to occupy them for some months.

The anticipated U-boat onslaught against post-invasion traffic failed to materialize; instead, attempts began almost immediately to resume operations in British coastal waters. These attempts increased toward the end of the year as the Biscay boats, driven from their bases, reorganized themselves in Norway for an effort that continued almost until the end of the war. They achieved little success while suffering heavy losses, but HMC ships *Regina*, *Alberni*, *Trentonian*, and *Guysborough* were among their victims. At the end of 1944, RCN ships made up 14 of the 37 escort groups based at Londonderry, whose primary duty was to counter the enemy's inshore campaign, and Canadian ships sank 6 of his U-boats.

No longer needed in the Channel, *Algonquin* and *Sioux* returned to Scapa Flow, and until early in 1945 escorted Russian convoys and assisted in strikes against German shipping off the Norwegian coast. On August 22 the Canadian-manned escort carrier *Nabob* was torpedoed while taking part in an air strike against the battleship *Tirpitz* in her Norwegian lair. *Algonquin*, one of the screening destroyers, took off 203 of *Nabob's* crew as a precaution, but the carrier struggled back to Scapa Flow.

In mid-September, 1944, the North Atlantic convoys resumed the Western Approaches route south of Ireland, which they had been forced to abandon four years earlier. There were still a few U-boats on patrol in the northwest Atlantic, and toward the end of the year there were five or six off Halifax and in the Gulf of St. Lawrence. *Shawinigan* and *Clayoquot* fell prey to two of these, and *Esquimalt* to another in April, 1945. That month the first operational Type XXI U-boat left her Norwegian base on patrol. She and her class represented the ultimate in submarine development; they had no need to surface while at sea, and had an underwater speed about equal to that of a frigate. Had they come into production a year earlier the course of the war would have been dramatically changed. As it was, they accomplished nothing.

On May 4, 1945, Dönitz ordered his U-boats to cease hostilities, and on May 8, to surface and surrender. *U 190*, which had sunk HMCS *Esquimalt*, complied on May 12 and a day later *U 889* followed suit, the only two U-boats to be surrendered to the RCN.

The Pacific

The RCN's involvement in the war against the Japanese was negligible. A small force of seven corvettes and seven minesweepers, based at Esquimalt and Prince Rupert, was maintained for escort and A/S duties on the west coast. Apart from isolated Japanese submarine attacks off the California and Oregon coasts — in December, 1941, June-July, 1942, and October, 1942 — no threat to west-coast shipping materialized, and no ship was attacked in Canadian waters. Five of the seven corvettes were therefore transferred to the east coast in October, 1942, to release a number of more experienced Halifax-based corvettes for Operation "Torch."

The three Canadian armed merchant cruisers, together with the corvettes *Dawson* and *Vancouver*, left Esquimalt on August 20, 1942, to support the U.S. Aleutians campaign, remaining in those waters for a little over two months. The corvettes later returned to Alaskan waters for escort duties from February to June, 1943.

The only RCN ship to see active service against the Japanese was the cruiser *Uganda*, which served with the British Pacific Fleet between April and July, 1945, in operations against Truk and the Japanese home islands.

When the Pacific war ended in August, 1945, the newer, war-built destroyers and a majority of the frigates were undergoing tropicalization and refit in Canadian yards for service in the Pacific, but were never required.

Cruisers

UGANDA/QUEBEC

As HMS *Uganda*, the name-ship of her class, she was completed January 3, 1943, at Vickers-Armstrong Ltd., Newcastle-on-Tyne. After working up with the Home Fleet she joined Plymouth Command in April for operations in the Bay of Biscay and the English Channel, and in July joined the 15th Cruiser Squadron, Mediterranean Fleet, as part of Force "K." She was badly damaged by a German glider bomb on September 13, 1943, while supporting the Allied landings at Salerno, Italy, and arrived at Charleston, S.C., in November for a year of repair work.

Presented to the RCN, the ship was commissioned HMCS *Uganda* on October 21, 1944, at Charleston, and in November returned to the U.K. for further modifications. She left in January, 1945, for the Pacific via the Suez Canal, to join the 4th Cruiser Squadron, British Pacific Fleet. In April she joined Task Force 57 in the Okinawa area, and was thereafter principally employed in screening the Fleet's aircraft carriers operating against Japanese airfields in the Ryukyu Islands. On June 14 she participated in the bombardment of Truk, and in July supported carriers operating against Tokyo. She left the Fleet late in July and arrived at Esquimalt on August 10 for refit.

Uganda spent the rest of her career as a training ship, having been renamed *Quebec* on January 14, 1952. Paid off on June 13, 1956, she arrived at Osaka, Japan, on February 6, 1961, to be broken up.

ONTARIO

Laid down by Harland and Wolff, Belfast, as HMS *Minotaur*, she was presented to the RCN and, on April 26, 1945, commissioned at Belfast as HMCS *Ontario*. She was completed on May 25, and after trials and workups, left the Clyde River on July 2 for the Pacific via the Mediterranean and the Suez Canal. *Ontario* joined the 4th Cruiser Squadron, British Pacific Fleet, too late to see war service, but was employed in a variety of duties which took her to Hong Kong, Manila, and Japan. She arrived at Esquimalt on November 27 for refit.

Ontario spent the remainder of her career as a training ship, and was paid off October 15, 1958. She arrived in tow for breaking up at Osaka, Japan, on November 19, 1960.

Armed Merchant Cruisers

PRINCE DAVID

Formerly a three-funnelled Canadian National Steamships liner, she was purchased on December 19, 1939, and after very extensive conversion commissioned at Halifax on December 28, 1940, as an armed merchant cruiser. After working up at Bermuda in January and February, 1941 *Prince David* was assigned to the RN's America and West Indies Station for the rest of the year. That December she was transferred to Esquimalt and in May, 1942, after refit at Esquimalt and Vancouver, joined Esquimalt Force. From August to November she served under USN control in the Aleutian campaign. She then resumed her former duties out of Esquimalt until the beginning of March, 1943, when she was paid off for conversion to an infantry landing ship. The rebuilding, which took place at Esquimalt and Vancouver, was

Continued on p. 156

Quebec, March 7, 1952

Ontario, 1945

Prince David at Taranto, Italy, 1944, as converted to infantry landing ship

Prince Henry, August 6, 1941, as originally fitted as armed merchant cruiser

Prince Robert at Gibraltar, 1943, fitted as A/A ship

Nabob, January 25, 1944

PRINCE HENRY

Originally a Canadian National liner but latterly Clarke Steamship's *North Star*, she was bought on March 11, 1940, and given back her maiden name. Like her two sisters, *Prince Henry* was converted to an armed merchant cruiser, commissioning at Montreal on December 4, 1940. She arrived at Bermuda on January 15, 1941, to work up, afterward transiting the Panama Canal to take up patrol off Callao, Peru. On April 1 she intercepted the German freighters *München* and *Hermonthis*, which scuttled themselves. In May she arrived at Esquimalt and engaged in patrols off the west coast until August 24 when she left for Halifax via Bermuda. In January, 1942, after brief employment at St. John's as depot ship for Newfoundland Escort Force, she was assigned to patrol duties in the West Indies but was soon again ordered to Esquimalt. Arriving May 7, she served with Esquimalt Force until

Continued on p. 156

PRINCE ROBERT

The third of the C.N. sisters, *Prince Robert* was purchased in December, 1939, and fitted out as an AMC, commissioning at Vancouver July 31, 1940. She left in mid-September for patrol off Mexico and Peru, and on September 25 intercepted and captured the German freighter *Weser*. On December 15 she left Callao, Peru for Australia to act as escort to a Canada-bound troop convoy, and in May, 1942 returned to the South Pacific for three months' escort and patrol duties under RN control on the New Zealand Station. She left Auckland on July 28, 1941 for Easter Island to investigate reports of a Japanese supply ship in the area, and arrived at Esquimalt on August 24 for a short refit. In November she escorted a shipload of ill-fated Canadian troops to Hong Kong and on her return rejoined Esquimalt Force. In August, 1942, *Prince Robert* was placed under USN control for duty in the Aleutians, arriving back at Esquimalt on November 4.

She was paid off on January 2, 1943, for

Continued on p. 156

Aircraft Carriers

NABOB

Laid down as the merchant vessel *Edisto*, but converted to an aircraft carrier while building, she was commissioned HMS *Nabob* at Tacoma, Wash., on September 7, 1943. After working up, she entered Burrard drydock at Vancouver on November 1 for modification to RN standards, completing January 12, 1944. About this time it was arranged that she and a near-sister *Puncher*, should be manned largely by Canadians while remaining RN ships. In February she embarked 852 Squadron (FAA) of Avengers at San Francisco and sailed for the U.K. via New York, where she took aboard a flight-deck cargo of Mustangs for the RAF. She joined the British Home Fleet at Scapa Flow on August 1, and that month took part in two operations off the Norwegian coast, the second being an attack on the *Tirpitz*. On August 22 *Nabob* was torpedoed by *U 354* in the Barents Sea, resulting in a hole some 32 feet square abaft the engine room and below the waterline. Amazingly, she made Scapa under her own power on August 27, but was not considered worth repairing and was paid off at Rosyth on October 10. She left there in 1947 to be broken up in Holland, but was resold and converted for merchant service, emerging in 1952 as the German MV *Nabob*. Sold Panamanian in 1967 and renamed *Glory*, she was broken up in Taiwan in 1978.

PUNCHER

Begun as MV *Willapa*, she was commissioned HMS *Puncher* at Tacoma, Wash., on February 5, 1944, and arrived at Vancouver on March 15 for modification to RN standards. She left Esquimalt in June for Norfolk, Va., en route ferrying motor launches from New Orleans to New York. In July she left Norfolk for Casablanca with a cargo of 40 USAAF aircraft, returning to Norfolk to load the Corsairs of 845 (RN) Squadron and a deckload of U.S. aircraft for the U.K. On February 1, 1945, she joined the Home Fleet, and following VE-Day was used for several months for deck landing training. In September she was partially converted to serve as a troop carrier and employed the rest of the year repatriating Canadian troops from Britain. In 1946 she left Halifax for Norfolk and was paid off there January 16 for return to the USN. Converted for merchant service, she became the British *Muncaster Castle* in 1949, later to be renamed *Bardic* in 1954 and *Bennevis* in 1959. She was broken up in Taiwan in 1973.

Puncher, 1944

Destroyers

It has already been told how the RCN entered the Second World War with an offensive force consisting solely of six destroyers. *Saguenay* and *Skeena*, essentially copies of the RN's "A" class, had been the first ships built to Canadian order. In 1937 and 1938 they were joined by *Fraser, St. Laurent, Restigouche,* and *Ottawa,* "C" class sisters purchased from the RN and given the names of Canadian rivers. A few weeks after the war broke out the "C" class flotilla leader was acquired and renamed *Assiniboine.*

Soon known as the River class, these were joined in 1940 by the ill-fated *Margaree* and, in 1943 and 1944, by *Chaudière, Gatineau, Kootenay, Qu'Appelle, Ottawa* (2nd), and *Saskatch-*

ewan, representatives of four fairly homogeneous RN classes.

In September, 1940, the RCN was given 6 of the 50 overage U.S. destroyers transferred to Britain in return for the use of British bases. Those serving in the RN were called the Town class because of their names, and their RCN sisters received the same epithet despite being named for U.S.-Canadian border rivers: *Columbia, Niagara, St. Clair, St. Croix,* and *St. Francis. Annapolis* was an exception to the rule. Two more of this class were acquired later, *Hamilton* in 1941 and *Buxton* in 1943.

In 1942 and 1943 Canada's first four Tribal class destroyers were commissioned: *Athabas-*

kan, Haida, Huron, and *Iroquois.* Another four entered service shortly after the war: *Athabaskan* (2nd), *Cayuga, Micmac,* and *Nootka.* The last destroyers acquired before hostilities ended were two of the RN's "V" class, renamed *Algonquin* and *Sioux.* Had the Pacific war continued longer, Canada would also have received a flotilla of eight "C" class destroyers to replace her aging Rivers, but only two were transferred, late in 1945, becoming HMCS *Crescent* and *Crusader.* The Tribals, "C," and "V" class units were the only Canadian destroyers whose careers extended more than a few months into the postwar period.

River Class

SAGUENAY

Saguenay and her sister, *Skeena,* were the first ships built for the RCN. *Saguenay* was commissioned on May 22, 1931, at Portsmouth and made her maiden arrival at Halifax on July 3. With the outbreak of the Second World War she escorted local convoys until late September, when she was assigned to the America and West Indies Station, and based at Kingston, Jamaica. On October 23, 1939, in the Yucatan Channel, she intercepted the German tanker *Emmy Friederich,* which scuttled herself. She returned to Halifax in mid-December to resume local escort duty until October 16, 1940, when she sailed for the U.K. to join EG 10, Greenock. On December 1, 1940, while escorting convoy HG.47, she was torpedoed by the Italian submarine *Argo* 300 miles west of Ireland. With her bows wrecked and 21 dead, *Saguenay* made Barrow-in-Furness largely under her own power, and was under repairs until May 22, 1941. She left Greenock on May 23, and arrived on June 7 at St. John's, where she joined the NEF, which was then forming. On November 15, 1942, she was rammed by the Panamanian freighter *Azra,* south of Cape Race, Nfld., and lost her stern when her depth charges exploded. The ship was docked at Saint John, N.B., where her stern was sealed off, then taken to Cornwallis in October, 1943, to serve as a training ship. Paid off July 30, 1945, she was broken up in 1946.

Saguenay

Skeena arriving at Plymouth, May 31, 1940

Fraser, 1938

Ottawa, September, 1940

SKEENA

Commissioned at Portsmouth on June 10, 1931, she arrived at Halifax with *Saguenay* on July 3 and proceeded to Esquimalt the following month. *Skeena* returned to Halifax in April, 1937, and with the outbreak of war engaged in local escort duties until ordered to the U.K. On her arrival at Plymouth, on May 31, 1940, she was assigned to Western Approaches Command, taking part in the evacuation of France and escorting convoys in British waters. She returned to Halifax on March 3, 1941, for refit, then joined Newfoundland Command, Mid-Ocean Escort Force (MOEF). In April, 1943, she became a member of EG C-3. During this period she saw continuous convoy duty and on July 31, 1942, while escorting convoy ON.115, shared with *Wetaskiwin* in the sinking of *U 588*. In May, 1944, she was assigned to EG 12 for invasion duties, and was present on D-Day. That September she was transferred to EG 11 and, on October 25, dragged her anchors in a storm and was wrecked on Videy Island, near Reykjavik. Sold in June, 1945, to a local resident, she was refloated and later broken up.

FRASER

Built in 1932 as HMS *Crescent* and purchased by the RCN five years later, *Fraser* was commissioned on February 17, 1937, at Chatham, U.K. She arrived at Esquimalt on May 3 and was stationed on the west coast until the outbreak of the war. Ordered to Halifax, she arrived on September 15 and, like her sisters, was put to work as local escort to ocean convoys out of Halifax. In November *Fraser* was transferred to operational control of the RN's America and West Indies Station, but continued to be based at Halifax until ordered in March, 1940, to join Jamaica Force for Caribbean patrol service. On May 26 she left Bermuda for the U.K., arriving at Plymouth on June 3. A participant in the evacuation of France, she was returning to Plymouth from St. Jean de Luz when, on June 25, she was sunk in collision with the British cruiser *Calcutta* in the Gironde River estuary, losing 47 of her complement.

OTTAWA

Completed in 1932 as HMS *Crusader*, she was purchased by the RCN and commission as *Ottawa* on June 15, 1938 at Chatham, U.K. She arrived at Esquimalt that November 7 and, the war intervening, left for Halifax almost exactly a year later. Though assigned to the RN's America and West Indies Station, she remained based at Halifax as a local escort to eastbound convoys. She left Halifax for the Clyde August 27, 1940, and on arrival was assigned to EG 10, Greenock, until the formation of Newfoundland Command in June, 1941. *Ottawa* then shifted her base to St. John's and was employed as a mid-ocean escort from June, 1941 onward, joining EG C-4 in May 1942. While escorting convoy ON.127, she was torpedoed and sunk by *U 91* in the North Atlantic, September 13, 1942, and 114 of her ship's company were lost.

RESTIGOUCHE

Completed in 1932 as HMS *Comet*, she was purchased at the same time as *Ottawa* and commissioned as *Restigouche* at Chatham, U.K., the same day. Like her sister, she arrived at Esquimalt November 7, 1938, and left for Halifax November 15, 1939. She performed local escort duties from that port until May 24, 1940, when she left for Plymouth. Upon arriving there on May 31 *Restigouche* was assigned to Western Approaches Command. While assisting in the evacuation of French ports she rescued survivors of *Fraser*. She left Liverpool at the end of August for a brief refit at Halifax, returning to the U.K. in January, 1941. In June, 1941, "Rustyguts" was allocated to Newfoundland Command, and in April, 1943, became a member of EG C-4, in the interval toiling ceaselessly as a mid-ocean escort. On December 13, 1941, she suffered storm damage en route to join convoy ON.44, and extensive repairs were carried out at Greenock. She was allocated to EG 12 in May, 1944, for invasion duties, including

Continued on p. 156

Restigouche, 1941

ST. LAURENT

Completed in 1932 as HMS *Cygnet*, she was purchased for the RCN and commissioned at Chatham on February 17, 1937 as *St. Laurent*. She arrived in Halifax on April 8 and soon afterward sailed for Esquimalt. Shortly after war was declared she returned to the east coast, arriving at Halifax on September 15, and for several months escorted convoys on the first leg of the transatlantic journey. *St. Laurent* left Halifax for the U.K. on May 24, 1940, and on arrival at Plymouth on May 31, was assigned to Western Approaches Command, playing a brief role in the evacuation of France. On July 2, 1940, she rescued 860 survivors of the torpedoed liner *Arandora Star*. She returned to Halifax on March 3, 1941, for refit, on completion of which she joined Newfoundland Command as a mid-ocean escort, serving continuously for the following three years. In April, 1943, she became a member of EG C-1. During this period "Sally" assisted in the destruction of two U-boats: *U 356* on December 27, 1942, while escorting convoy ONS.154; and *U 845* on March 10, 1944, while with convoy SC.154. In May, 1944, she was transferred to EG 11 for invasion duties, remaining with the group on patrol and support duties until the end of November, when she returned to Canada for major repairs at Shelburne, N.S. She afterward remained in Canadian waters as a member of Halifax Force and after VE-Day was employed in transporting troops from Newfoundland to Canada. She was paid off on October 10, 1945, at Sydney and broken up in 1947.

St. Laurent

ASSINIBOINE

Completed in 1932 as HMS *Kempenfelt*, she was transferred to the RCN at Devonport on October 19, 1939, and arrived in Halifax on November 17. Assigned to the America and West Indies Station, she left for Jamaica on December 5 to carry out Caribbean patrols. While so employed *Assiniboine* assisted in the capture of the German freighter *Hannover* in the Mona Passage and towed her into Kingston, Jamaica. She returned to Halifax on March 31, 1940, and was employed there as a local escort until January 15, 1941, when she sailed for the U.K. to join EG 10, Greenock. With the formation of Newfoundland Command in June, 1941, "Bones" was allocated to it for mid-ocean escort service. While thus employed with convoy SC.94, on August 6, 1942, she rammed and sank *U 210*, necessitating repairs at Halifax from August 29 to December 20. Not long after her return to service, while on

Assiniboine, December, 1940

Diana (later Margaree), 1933

Chaudière, August 25, 1944

Gatineau, February, 1945

passage to Londonderry on March 2, 1943, she attacked a U-boat with depth charges set too shallow, causing serious damage to her stern. Repairs were effected at Liverpool from March 7 to July 13, 1943, when she joined EG C-1 of MOEF. In April, 1944, she returned to Canada for refit at Shelburne, N.S., and on August 1 arrived at Londonderry to become a member of EG 12 and, a few weeks later, EG 11. In December she was loaned to EG 14, Liverpool, and remained with it until VE-Day. She returned to Canada in June, 1945, and, after brief employment as a troop transport, was paid off August 8, 1945. On November 10, 1945, en route for scrapping at Baltimore, *Assiniboine* broke her tow and was wrecked near East Point, P.E.I. Her remains were broken up *in situ* in 1952.

MARGAREE

Completed in 1932 as HMS *Diana*, she was serving on the China Station when the war broke out, and transferred to the Mediterranean for a short time before returning to Britain to join the Home Fleet. In May, 1940, she took part briefly in the Norwegian campaign and in mid-July commenced refit at Albert Docks, London. There she was transferred to the RCN to replace the lost *Fraser*, commissioning as *Margaree* on September 6, 1940. On October 20 she left Londonderry for Canada with a five-ship convoy, OL.8, and two days later was lost in collision with the freighter *Port Fairy*. 142 of her ship's company were lost, many of them survivors of *Fraser*.

CHAUDIÈRE

Completed in 1936 as HMS *Hero*, she saw extensive service in the Second World War, including the second Battle of Narvik, April, 1940; the evacuation of Greece and Crete, April and May, 1941; and the Syrian invasion, June, 1941. As a unit of the Mediterranean Fleet, she also took part in the second Battle of Sirte in March, 1942, and, in May and October of the same year, shared in the sinking of two U-boats. In April, 1943, she returned to the U.K. for a major refit at Portsmouth, and there was transferred to the RCN on November 15, 1943, becoming HMCS *Chaudière*. In January, 1944, she became a member of EG C-2, MOEF, and on March 6 shared in the destruction of *U 744*. In May she was assigned to EG 11, Western Approaches Command, for invasion support duty, and was present on D-Day. On August 20 and 28, respectively, she assisted in the sinking of *U 984*, west of Brest, and of *U 621* off La Rochelle. During the next three months she was employed in patrol and support duties in the North Atlantic, Bay of Biscay, and English Channel. She returned to Halifax at the end of November for repairs, and a major refit begun at Sydney two months later was still incomplete on VE-Day. *Chaudière* was paid off August 17, 1945 to reserve at Sydney, and broken up there in 1950.

GATINEAU

Completed in 1934 as HMS *Express*, she saw strenuous war service with the RN. She was the second last ship to leave Dunkirk, having made six trips and evacuated 3,500 troops. On August 31, 1940, while laying a defensive minefield off the Dutch coast, she was herself extensively damaged by a German mine. Repairs carried out at Hull, U.K., took more than a year, and included fitting a complete new fore end. She went to the Far East late in 1941, and on December 10 was on hand to rescue nearly 1,000 survivors of HMS *Prince of Wales*, sunk by Japanese bombs off Malaya. After long service with the Eastern Fleet she returned to Liverpool in February, 1943, for refit, and in the process was transferred to the RCN. She was commissioned there as *Gatineau* on June 3, 1943, and joined EG C-3, MOEF. On March 6, 1944, while escorting convoy HX.280, she assisted in the sinking of *U 744*. That May she transferred to EG 11, Londonderry, for invasion duties, and was present on D-Day. She proceeded to Canada in July, 1944, for major refit at Halifax, then sailed in March, 1945, for workups at Tobermory. No longer needed after VE-Day, she returned to Canada in June and two months later went round to the west coast. She was paid off January 10, 1946, into reserve at Esquimalt, and is believed to have been scuttled at Royston, B.C. in 1948, as part of a breakwater.

KOOTENAY

She was completed in 1933 as HMS *Decoy*, and at the outbreak of the war was with the 21st Destroyer Flotilla, East Indies Fleet. The flotilla was transferred later that month to the Mediterranean and in January, 1940, to the South Atlantic. *Decoy* was reassigned in May, 1940, to the Mediterranean Fleet, and on November 13 was damaged by bombs at Alexandria, requiring ten weeks' repairs at Malta. While in the Mediterranean she took part in the evacuation of Greece and Crete, and in the supply run to Tobruk. Then assigned to the Eastern Fleet in February, 1942, she returned to Britain that September for a major refit at Jarrow-on-Tyne. There, on April 12, 1943, she was transferred to the RCN as *Kootenay*, and after working up at Tobermory, was assigned to EG C-5, MOEF. In

Continued on p. 156

OTTAWA (2nd)

Completed in 1936 as HMS *Griffin*, she took part in the evacuation of Namsos, Norway, in May, 1940, before transferring in August to Force 'H' at Gibraltar and in November to the 14th Destroyer Flotilla in the Mediterranean. She subsequently took part in the evacuation of Greece and Crete, embarking 720 troops on one trip from Suda Bay. She also escorted a relief convoy to Malta. Transferred to the Eastern Fleet in February, 1942, she returned to the U.K. that October for major refit at Portsmouth and Southampton, toward the end of which, on March 20, 1943, she was commissioned at Southampton as HMCS *Griffin*. On April 10, despite the objections of her captain, she was renamed HMCS *Ottawa*. She joined EG C-5, based at St. John's, as a mid-ocean escort, but was removed from this duty in May, 1944, to take part in the invasion with EG 11. During post-invasion patrols in the Channel and the Bay of Biscay she took part with *Kootenay* (p. 156) in the destruction of three U-boats. *Ottawa* returned to Canada in October, 1944, for refit at Saint John, N.B., remaining in Canadian waters until paid off November 1, 1945, at Sydney. She was broken up in 1946.

QU'APPELLE

Completed in 1935 as HMS *Foxhound*, she was a member of the 8th Flotilla, Home Fleet, on the outbreak of war, and on September 14, shared in the sinking of *U 39* off the Hebrides — the first U-boat "kill" of the war. In April, 1940, she took part in the second Battle of Narvik and that November was transferred to Force 'H' at Gibraltar. On June 18, 1941, she shared in the sinking of *U 138* west of Cadiz, and she took one convoy to Malta. From January, 1942 to May, 1943, she served with the Eastern Fleet, then transferred to West Africa Command, Freetown. In September, 1943, she returned to the

Kootenay, February, 1944

Ottawa (2nd), May, 1943

Foxhound (later Qu'Appelle)

Saskatchewan, October 1, 1945

U.K. for an extensive refit on the Humber, and on February 8, 1944, was commissioned there as HMCS *Qu'Appelle*. She served on D-Day with EG 12, and afterward took part in Biscay and Channel patrols, latterly with EG 11. She arrived at Halifax for the first time on November 29, 1944, and proceeded to Pictou, N.S., for refit. Completing this refit on March 31, 1945, she served as a troop transport between Greenock and Halifax from August to October. She was paid off on October 11 to serve as a stationary training ship attached to the Torpedo School at Halifax. Removed from service in June, 1946, *Qu'Appelle* was sold in 1947 for scrapping at Sydney, N.S.

SASKATCHEWAN

Completed in 1935 as HMS *Fortune*, she was serving with the 8th Flotilla, Home Fleet when the war broke out, and took part in the Norwegian campaign and the occupation of Iceland in May, 1940. She also shared in the sinking of *U 27*, *U 44*, and the Vichy French submarine *Ajax*. On May 10, 1941, while escorting a Malta convoy, she was badly damaged by bombs and spent six months under repairs at Chatham, U.K. In February, 1943, following two years' service with the Eastern Fleet, *Fortune* returned to the U.K. for major refit at London, and there on May 31, 1943, was transferred to the RCN as *Saskatchewan*. She was assigned to EG C-3, MOEF, until May, 1944, then transferred to EG 12 for invasion duties. She proceeded to Canada in August, 1944, to refit at Shelburne, N.S., returning to the U.K. in January, 1945, first as a unit of EG 14, and then EG 11. She returned to Canada the month after VE-Day and, after employment as a troop transport, was paid off January 28, 1946, at Sydney and broken up.

Annapolis, September 11, 1944

Town Class

ANNAPOLIS

As USS *Mackenzie*, she served three years with the U.S. Pacific Fleet before being laid up in reserve at Mare Island, California, in 1922. Briefly commissioned again during the first year of the Second World War, she arrived at Halifax on September 20, 1940 and there, four days later, was transferred to the RCN. A month later she burned out her No. 4 boiler and as a result lost her aftermost funnel. Owing to reduced endurance, *Annapolis* never crossed the Atlantic, but spent her entire RCN career with Western Local Escort Force (WLEF). In June, 1943, she became a member of EG W-8 and later, for a short time, W-10. In April, 1944, she was relegated to training duties at HMCS Cornwallis, also functioning as escort to RN submarines between Halifax and Digby, N.S. Paid off at Halifax, June 4, 1945, she left later that month in tow for Boston, where she was broken up.

BUXTON

Commissioned as USS *Edwards* in 1919, she saw brief service with the USN in Europe before being placed in reserve at San Diego in 1922. Recommissioned in December, 1939, she was given an overhaul, and from April to September, 1940, was on Neutrality Patrol in the Gulf of Mexico and off the east coast of the U.S. On October 8 she was commissioned HMS *Buxton* at Halifax and assigned to local duties, since serious defects prevented her crossing the Atlantic. Following a major refit at Boston from July to September, 1941, she made her first transatlantic crossing in October, only to undergo further repairs at Chatham, U.K., which kept her

Continued on p. 156

Buxton, May 10, 1944

COLUMBIA

As USS *Haraden* she served in the Adriatic Sea during part of 1919 before returning to the U.S. for training out of Norfolk, Va. Placed in reserve at Philadelphia in 1922, she emerged in December, 1939, to take part in the Neutrality Patrol, and was transferred to the RCN as *Columbia* on September 24, 1940, at Halifax. At first employed on local escort duty, she left Halifax January 15, 1941, for the U.K., where she was assigned to EG 4, Greenock. In June, 1941, she joined the newly formed NEF, and in March, 1942, following repairs at Halifax, transferred to WLEF. In January, 1943, she went to the aid of her RN sister, HMS *Caldwell*, adrift without propellers southeast of Cape Breton, and successfully towed her 370 miles to Halifax. Following a major refit at Saint John from February 1 to May 20, 1943, she rejoined WLEF, becoming a member of EG W-4 at the end of June and of W-10 in December. On February 25, 1944, owing to a combination of fog and faulty radar, she rammed a cliff in Motion Bay, Nfld. without so much as touching bottom. Repairs only sufficient to make her watertight were carried out at Bay Bulls, though not until May. That September she was taken to Liverpool, N.S., to serve as an ammunition storage hulk for ships refitting there. Paid off on June 12, 1945, into reserve at Sydney, she was sold for scrap later that year.

Columbia, December, 1943

HAMILTON

As USS *Kalk* she served the USN in European waters during 1919, returning to the U.S. to perform training duties for a few months before being laid up at Philadelphia in 1922. Recommissioned in June, 1940, she served briefly with the Neutrality Patrol in the Atlantic before being transferred to the RN at Halifax on September 23, 1940. Commissioned as HMS *Kalk*, she was renamed *Hamilton* (for Hamilton, Bermuda) at St. John's where, on her arrival on October 1, she was damaged in collision with her sister HMS *Georgetown*. She was taken to Saint John, N.B., for repairs and, while being undocked there on October 26, ran aground and received damage sufficient to lay her up for half a year. She was therefore offered to the RCN, recommissioned at Saint John as an RCN ship on July 6, 1941, and assigned to WLEF. After escorting one convoy, she was in collision with the Netherlands submarine *O-15* at Halifax. After repairs she again took up local escort duties, and in June, 1943, became a member of WLEF's EG W-4. She still had not made a transatlantic passage when in August, 1943, she was allocated to HMCS Cornwallis as a training ship. She was paid off on June 8, 1945, at Sydney and broken up at Baltimore the same year.

Hamilton

NIAGARA

Completed in 1919 as USS *Thatcher*, she served with the Pacific Fleet until 1922, when she was placed in reserve at San Diego. Briefly recommissioned and overhauled in 1940, she was transferred to the RCN as HMCS *Niagara* at Halifax on September 24, 1940, and sailed for the U.K. on November 30. There, in March, 1941, she was assigned to EG 4, Greenock, but in June joined the newly formed NEF. On August 28 she was on hand to take aboard the crew of *U 570*, which had surrendered to a Coastal Command aircraft south of Iceland. In March, 1942, she joined WLEF, that June becoming a member of its EG W-9 and, in October, of W-10. In common with the other "Towns," she required major refits on a number of occasions and on March 2, 1944, following one of these, she became a torpedo-firing ship for training Torpedo Branch personnel at Halifax. She was paid off at Sydney on September 15, 1945, and broken up in 1947.

Niagara

St. Clair, November 9, 1942

St. Croix, June 28, 1942

St. Francis, May, 1942

ST. CLAIR

Completed in 1918 as USS *Williams*, she served with the Pacific Fleet until 1922, when she was laid up at San Diego. Recommissioned in 1940, she served briefly with the Neutrality Patrol before being transferred to the RCN at Halifax on September 24, 1940, as HMCS *St. Clair*. Assigned to EG 4, Greenock, she arrived in the Clyde on December 11 to undertake escort duty for Western Approaches Command. On May 27, 1941, in company with three RN destroyers, she was attacked by five German bombers west of Galway, Ireland. HMS *Mashona* was capsized by bombs, and *St. Clair* sank the hulk after picking up survivors. Assigned to NEF, she collided with the oiler *Clam* on June 17, 1941, shortly after her arrival at St. John's, and remained under repairs until December 2. In March, 1942, she joined WLEF and in June, 1943, was assigned to its EG W-2. Except for two-months' absence that summer, attached to HMCS Cornwallis, she remained with the group until December, when she was ordered to St. Margaret's Bay to serve as a depot ship for RN submarines used in A/S training. In May, 1944, she was taken to Halifax for repairs, remaining there until paid off August 23. She was then reduced to a firefighting and damage control training hulk in Bedford Basin, where her remains still lay as late as 1950.

ST. CROIX

Completed in 1919, she operated with the Atlantic Fleet as *USS McCook* until placed in reserve at Philadelphia in 1922. Recommissioned in December, 1939, she again served with the Atlantic Fleet prior to being transferred to the RCN at Halifax as HMCS *St. Croix* on September 24, 1940. She sailed for the U.K. via St. John's on November 30, but ran into a hurricane and had to return. Arriving at Halifax on December 18, she remained under repair until mid-March 1941, when she took up the role of local escort. In August, 1941, she joined NEF, escorting convoys to Iceland. In May, 1942, following six months' refit at Saint John, N.B., she escorted her first convoy, SC.84, to the U.K., and was thereafter employed constantly on the "Newfie-Derry" run. In April, 1943, she was assigned to EG C-1, and in June to C-5. During this period she sank *U 90* while escorting convoy ON.113 on July 24, 1942, and on March 4, 1943, while accompanying convoy KMS.10 from Britain to Algeria, she assisted HMCS *Shediac* in destroying *U 87*. In August, 1943, *St. Croix* was allocated to support group EG 9 for an offensive against U-boats crossing the Bay of Biscay, but the group was diverted to the assistance of a series of convoys beset by U-boats in the Atlantic. While thus engaged, with convoy ON.202, *St. Croix* was torpedoed and sunk by *U 305* on September 20, south of Iceland. Five officers and 76 men were rescued by HMS *Itchen*, but only one of these survived the loss of *Itchen* two days later.

ST. FRANCIS

As USS *Bancroft*, her career almost exactly paralleled that of her sister, USS *McCook*, and she was turned over to the RCN at Halifax on the same day, becoming HMCS *St. Francis*. She spent the remainder of the year based at Halifax, and on November 5 searched for the *Admiral Scheer* following the latter's attack on convoy HX.84. She left Halifax January 15, 1941, for the Clyde, where she was assigned to EG 4 of Western Approaches Command, Greenock. On the formation of Newfoundland Command in June, 1941, she was based at St. John's and continuously employed as a mid-ocean escort until early December, 1942, when she began a major refit at Halifax. On completion of her refit

Continued on p. 156

Tribal Class

ATHABASKAN

Commissioned on February 3, 1943 at New-castle-on-Tyne and assigned to the British Home Fleet, *Athabaskan* left on March 29 to patrol the Iceland-Faeroes Passage for blockade runners. Stress of weather caused hull damage that required five weeks' repairs at South Shields, U.K., following which, in June, 1943, she took part in Operation Gearbox III, the relief of the garrison at Spitsbergen. On June 18 she collided with the boom defence vessel *Bargate* at Scapa Flow, occasioning a month's repairs at Devon-port. In July and August she was based at Plymouth, carrying out A/S patrols in the Bay of Biscay, and on August 27 was hit by a glider bomb off the Spanish coast. She managed to reach Devonport, where she remained under repair until November 10. Returning to Scapa Flow in December, she escorted convoy JW.55A to Russia, but in February, 1944, rejoined Plymouth Command and was assigned to the newly formed 10th Destroyer Flotilla. On April 26 she assisted in the destruction of the German torpedo boat *T 29* in the Channel off Ushant, and three days later was sunk by a torpedo from *T 24* north of the Île de Bas. Her captain and 128 men were lost, 83 taken prisoner, and 44 rescued by *Haida*.

HAIDA

Commissioned on August 30, 1943, at New-castle-on-Tyne, *Haida* was assigned to the British Home Fleet and during the first three months of her career made two trips to North Russia as a convoy escort. In January, 1944, she joined the 10th Flotilla at Plymouth, and for the next eight months was engaged in sweeps and patrols in the Channel and the Bay of Biscay. She was present on D-Day. During this period she took part in the sinking of several enemy vessels, including torpedo boat *T 29*, on April 26 off Ushant; *T 27*, on April 29 off Ushant; destroyer *Z 32*, on June 9 off Île de Bas; *U 971*, on June 24 off Land's End; and minesweeper *M 486*, on August 6 off Île d'Yeu. In September she sailed for Canada to refit at Halifax, returning to Plymouth in January, 1945. In March she returned to Scapa Flow and escorted another convoy to Murmansk, as well as carrying out strikes against German shipping off the Norwegian coast. She returned to Halifax on June 10 to begin tropicalization refit, but with the surrender of Japan this was cancelled and she was paid off on March 20, 1946. She was recommissioned at Halifax in 1947 and for the next three years took part in training and NATO exercises, then in July, 1950, began extensive modernization. *Haida* was re-commissioned on March 11, 1952, to prepare for service in Korean waters. Between 1952 and 1954 she did two tours of duty in that theatre, then resumed her training role until she was paid off for the last time on October 11, 1963, at Sydney. Purchased by a private group of citizens, she arrived at Toronto in tow on August 25, 1964, to become a floating memorial, and in 1970 was accorded a berth at Ontario Place.

HURON

Commissioned July 19, 1943, at Newcastle-on-Tyne, she was assigned, like *Haida*, to the 3rd Destroyer Flotilla of the British Home Fleet. She made a trip in October to Murmansk with technical personnel and special naval stores, and for the rest of the year escorted convoys to and from North Russia. In February, 1944, after one more such trip, she joined the 10th Flotilla at Plymouth for invasion duties, spending the next seven months in the Channel and the Bay of Biscay. She was present on D-Day. *Huron*

Continued on p. 156

Athabaskan

Haida, July 4, 1944

Huron, 1944

Iroquois on trials, 1942

IROQUOIS

The first of the Canadian Tribals to commission,
she did so at Newcastle-on-Tyne, on November
30, 1942. *Iroquois* was assigned to the 3rd
Flotilla, Home Fleet, but proved to have struc-
tural flaws and was not fully operational until
January 30, 1943. On a quick round trip to
Canada in March, she incurred weather damage
that kept her under repairs at Plymouth until
early June, following which she was employed
on Gibraltar convoys. In July three troopships
she was escorting to Freetown were attacked by
German aircraft 300 miles off Vigo, Spain, and
two were sunk, *Iroquois* rescuing 628 survivors
from the *Duchess of York*. *Iroquois* then spent
several months escorting Russian convoys. In
February, 1944, she arrived at Halifax for a refit,
returning to Plymouth early in June to join the
10th Flotilla for invasion duties. After D-Day she
carried out patrols in the Channel and the Bay of
Biscay, and for some months escorted capital
ships and troopships in U.K. coastal waters. She

Continued on p. 156

"V" Class

ALGONQUIN

Not a "Tribal" despite her name, she was laid
down as HMS *Valentine* but commissioned on
February 17, 1944, at Glasgow as HMCS *Algonquin*. Assigned to the 26th Destroyer Flotilla of
the British Home Fleet, she left Scapa Flow on
March 31 to help escort a carrier attack on the
Tirpitz. In April she escorted a similar attack on
German shipping off the Lofoten Islands, Norway, and on May 28 left Scapa for D-Day
operations. On June 6 she bombarded shore
targets on the Normandy coast. At the end of
June she returned to Scapa, from whence she
carried out attacks on German convoys off
Norway and, at year's end, escorted convoys
JW.63 and RA.63 to and from Murmansk. On
August 22, 1944, she took off 203 of *Nabob*'s
ship's company when the latter was torpedoed in
the Barents Sea. She returned to Halifax in
February, 1945, for refit, leaving on August 12
via Malta to join the British Pacific Fleet, but
was recalled on VJ-Day and left Alexandria for
Esquimalt on November 3. There she was paid
off into reserve on February 6, 1946, but was
recommissioned on February 25, 1953, after
very extensive modernization, and sailed for the
east coast that summer. After fourteen years'
service with Atlantic Command, she returned to
the west coast in March, 1967, and was paid off
for the last time on April 1, 1970, to be broken
up in Taiwan in 1971.

Algonquin, August 10, 1953

SIOUX

Laid down as HMS *Vixen*, she was commissioned HMCS *Sioux* at Cowes, Isle of Wight, on
Feb. 21, 1944, and assigned to the 26th Flotilla
of the British Home Fleet. She took part in escorting carrier attacks against the *Tirpitz* and
against German shipping off Norway, and on
May 28 left Scapa for Portsmouth for D-Day
duties. Returning to Scapa Flow in July, she
resumed her previous occupation and also escorted three convoys each way to and from
Murmansk. She left the U.K. on April 6, 1945,
for her first trip to Canada and, upon arrival,
underwent a major refit at Halifax. In November
Sioux was transferred to Esquimalt, where she
was paid off into reserve on February 27, 1946.
After some modernization she was recommissioned in 1950, and did three tours of duty in
Korean waters, from 1951 to 1955. Afterward
she resumed her training role until paid off at
Halifax on October 13, 1963. She was broken up
in 1965 at La Spezia, Italy.

Sioux, 1944

Frigates

At first called "twin-screw corvettes," this type was designed for the RN by the same William Reed who had designed the original corvette, and was intended to remedy the latter's shortcomings as an ocean escort. The name "frigate" was adopted by the Admiralty at the suggestion of Vice-Admiral Percy Nelles, Canada's Chief of Naval Staff. A far more habitable ship than the smaller corvette, it was also faster and had twice the endurance — 7,200 sea miles at 12 knots. The RN frigates were named for rivers and, hence, known as the River class; the RCN units were named for towns and cities.

The first of 60 frigates built in Canada for the RCN, HMCS *Waskesiu* was commissioned in June, 1943. A further 10 were built for Britain on a lease-lend arrangement with the U.S., which in the end kept 2 of them, and these are said to have been the basis from which the U.S. destroyer escort was developed. In 1944, 7 RN frigates, identifiable by their river names, were transferred to the RCN, along with 3 of the Loch class, a slightly larger model designed for prefabrication. Most of the RCN frigates were fitted with twin 4-inch guns, the only Canadian escort ships so armed except the Tribals.

Many of the frigates were retained or recommissioned after the war to provide sea training for officer cadets and naval reservists. Between 1953 and 1958 the remaining 21 of the class underwent conversion to a flush-decked configuration, the once vast quarterdeck enclosed to house two Squid A/S mortars. The bridge was also greatly enlarged and the funnel heightened. Known as Prestonian class ocean escorts, all but *Victoriaville* had passed from the scene by 1968, and she had been renamed *Granby* two years earlier on assuming the duties of a diving tender.

River Class, 1942-1943 Programme

BEACON HILL

Commissioned May 16, 1944, at Esquimalt, *Beacon Hill* arrived at Halifax on July 11, having escorted *Puncher* from New Orleans to New York en route, and proceeded to Bermuda to work up. On her return to Halifax she left in September to join EG 26, an RCN support group based at Londonderry, but for varying periods was detached to Plymouth and Portsmouth. She remained in U.K. waters for the balance of the European war, leaving Greenock for home on May 28, 1945. Intended for Pacific service, she underwent tropicalization refit at Liverpool, N.S., from June to November, and sailed from Shelburne for Esquimalt on December 22. She was paid off at Esquimalt on February 6, 1946, but recommissioned in the summer of 1949 for cadet training. She was again paid off in 1954 for conversion to a Prestonian class ocean escort, was commissioned as such on December 21, 1957, and served on the west coast until finally paid off on September 15, 1967. She was broken up in 1968 at Sakai, Japan.

CAP de la MADELEINE

Commissioned September 30, 1944, at Quebec City, she arrived at Halifax October 20, and soon afterward sailed for Bermuda to work up. Returning in December, she was allocated to EG C-7, MOEF, based at St. John's. She left that port December 28, 1944, to accompany convoy HX.328 eastward, but was detached on January 3 to the westbound convoy ONS.39, as she had to return for repairs. These were carried out successively at St. John's, Halifax, and Quebec, and completed on May 7, 1945. She then began tropicalization refit at Lauzon, but this was cancelled in August owing to termination of hostilities, and the ship was paid off November 25 at Shelburne. She was sold to Marine Industries Ltd., but later reacquired by the RCN and converted to a Prestonian class unit. Recommissioned on December 7, 1954, she served on the east coast until paid off on May 15, 1965. She was broken up the following year at La Spezia, Italy.

Beacon Hill in characteristic west-coast camouflage, June 5, 1944

Cap de la Madeleine off Quebec City, 1944

CAPE BRETON

Commissioned at Quebec City on October 25, 1943, *Cape Breton* arrived at Halifax on November 28 and worked up in St. Margaret's Bay in January, 1944. Assigned to EG 6, a support group based at Londonderry, she left Halifax for the U.K. on February 24. She operated at various times from 'Derry, Portsmouth and Plymouth, and in April, 1944, sailed to North Russia, returning with convoy RA.59. She was also on hand on D-Day. She returned to Canada late in 1944, arriving on November 6 at Shelburne for a major refit. This was completed in April and she was then sent to Bermuda to work up. Assigned to EG 9, she left St. John's on May 9 with convoy HX.354, and later that month sailed from 'Derry direct to Vancouver. A tropicalization refit begun on June 26 was cancelled before completion and the ship was paid off January 26, 1946, after several months in reserve at Esquimalt. She was sold in 1947 and expended as a breakwater in 1948, reportedly at Kelsey Bay, B.C.

Cape Breton off Quebec City, 1943

CHARLOTTETOWN (2nd)

Commissioned at Quebec City on April 28, 1944, *Charlottetown* visited her namesake city en route to Halifax on May 22. She arrived in Bermuda on June 18 for a month's working-up, and on her return to Halifax was assigned to EG 16. She left Halifax on March 7, 1945, for Londonderry, the group having been transferred there, and was also briefly based at Portsmouth. In May she escorted two convoys to Gibraltar and two back, and in mid-June left 'Derry for Sydney, N.S. There she commenced a tropicalization refit that was completed at Halifax on February 28, 1946, and on March 3 left for Esquimalt. She spent the rest of the year training cadets and new entries, and on March 25, 1947, was paid off at Esquimalt. She was sold the same year, and her hull expended as a breakwater at Oyster Bay, B.C.

Charlottetown (2nd), June, 1944

CHEBOGUE

Chebogue was commissioned at Esquimalt on February 22, 1944, and sailed for Halifax on March 15, arriving on April 12. After working up in Bermuda in May she returned to Canada and was assigned to EG C-1. After visiting Yarmouth, N.S., from June 12 to 14, she left St. John's on June 23 for Britain as part of the escort of convoy HXF.296. On her second return trip, this time as Senior Officer's ship of EG C-1 escorting convoy ONS.33, she was torpedoed by *U 1227* on October 4, 800 miles west of the British Isles. She had made some 900 miles under tow, successively, of HMCS *Chambly*, HMS *Mounsey*, HMCS *Ribble*, and the ocean tug HMS *Earner* when, on October 11, the towline parted in a gale and *Chebogue* drove ashore in Swansea Bay, Wales. She was refloated the following day, taken to Port Talbot and placed in reserve. In December she was moved to Newport, Wales, to be made ready for a transatlantic crossing under tow, but instead was taken to Milford Haven and paid off on September 25, 1945. She was broken up locally in 1948.

Chebogue, March 17, 1944

DUNVER

The name represents an odd effort to honour Verdun, Quebec, without duplicating the name of the destroyer HMS *Verdun*. The first frigate launched for the RCN, *Dunver* was commissioned at Quebec City on September 11, 1943 and arrived at Halifax on October 3, having escorted a Sydney-Halifax convoy en route. After working up at Pictou she was allocated to EG C-5, and served continuously on North Atlantic convoys until October, 1944. That July she had been Senior Officer's ship while escorting HXS.300, the largest convoy of the war with 167 merchant ships. On September 9, she and HMCS *Hespeler* sank *U 484* near convoy ONF.202, south of the Hebrides. In October, 1944, she commenced refitting at Pictou, completing on December 27, and in April, 1945, joined EG 27, based at Halifax, for the rest of the European war. In June she went to the west coast for tropicalization, but this was discontinued in August and she was laid up at Esquimalt. Paid off January 23, 1946, *Dunver* was sold and her hull expended as part of a breakwater at Royston, B.C., in 1948.

Dunver, November, 1943. Her unusually low number, K03, was a bequest from HMS Heliotrope, *transferred to the USN in 1942.*

EASTVIEW

Commissioned at Montreal on June 3, 1944, *Eastview* arrived at Halifax on June 26 and proceeded to Bermuda to work up. On her return in August she was attached to EG C-6 as Senior Officer's ship, and on September 18 left St. John's with her first convoy, HXF.308. For the balance of the European war she was continuously on Atlantic convoy duty, and was one of the escort of HX.358, the last HX convoy of the war, leaving St. John's May 27, 1945. That July she went to the west coast and had barely commenced tropicalization refit when work was stopped and the ship laid up in reserve at Esquimalt. She was paid off on January 17, 1946, and sold in 1947, and her hull made part of a breakwater at Oyster Bay, B.C., the following year.

GROU

She was named for a French martyr of 1690 in lieu of the name Pointe-aux-Trembles, Que., the latter being considered overly long. Commissioned at Montreal on December 4, 1943, she arrived at Halifax later that month, worked up in St. Margaret's Bay and in March, 1944, was assigned to EG 6, Londonderry. In April she went to Kola Inlet and returned as escort to convoy RA.59 from North Russia. Based at various times at 'Derry, Portsmouth, and Plymouth, she was present on D-Day on A/S patrol. *Grou* left for home with convoy ON.285 on February 17, 1945, and on March 4 began a six-month tropicalization refit at Dartmouth, N.S. In October she left for the west coast, where she was paid off into reserve at Esquimalt on February 25, 1946. She was broken up at Victoria in 1948.

Eastview, 1944

Grou

Joliette, 1945

Jonquière off Quebec City, 1944

Kirkland Lake off Quebec City, 1944

JOLIETTE

Commissioned at Quebec City on June 14, 1944, *Joliette* left on July 1 for Halifax, whence she proceeded to Bermuda to work up. Returning to St. John's in August, she became a member of EG C-1 but on reaching Londonderry the following month was reassigned to EG 25. Returning to 'Derry on November 22 from her first round trip to Halifax, she ran aground in Lough Foyle, receiving extensive bottom damage. Repairs were effected at Belfast from December 5, 1944 to April 5, 1945, after which *Joliette* went to Tobermory to work up. She then returned to Londonderry, but sailed for Canada in June. On November 19, she was paid off at Sydney and laid up at Shelburne. In 1946 she was sold to the Chilean Navy, to serve as *Iquique* until disposed of in 1968.

JONQUIÈRE

Commissioned at Quebec City on May 10, 1944, she arrived at Halifax on June 5 and proceeded from there to Bermuda to work up. Returning in August, *Jonquière* was assigned to EG C-2 and after three Atlantic crossings was transferred to EG 26 at Londonderry. She was also based from time to time at Portsmouth and Plymouth, remaining in U.K. waters on A/S patrol until May 27, 1945, when she sailed with ON.305, the last westbound convoy. She was paid off December 4 at Shelburne and later taken to Lauzon for conversion to a Prestonian class ocean escort, recommissioning September 20, 1954. She was finally paid off on September 12, 1966, and broken up at Victoria in 1967.

KIRKLAND LAKE

Commissioned at Quebec City on August 21, 1944, she arrived at Halifax on September 10 and left on November 20 for Bermuda to work up. On her return to Halifax in December *Kirkland Lake* was assigned to EG 16, leaving on March 8 for Londonderry when the group was transferred there. She was based at various times at 'Derry and Portsmouth, and in May, 1945, escorted two convoys to Gibraltar and two back. She returned to Canada in June for tropicalization refit at Quebec City, and when this was completed on November 5, returned to Halifax. She was paid off December 14, 1945, to maintenance reserve in Bedford Basin and broken up at Sydney, 1947-48.

KOKANEE

Commissioned at Esquimalt on June 6, 1944, *Kokanee* arrived at Halifax on July 24 and left for Bermuda in August to work up. On arrival at St. John's in September she was assigned to EG C-3 as Senior Officer's ship, and spent the rest of the European war on Atlantic convoy duty. She left Londonderry for the last time on May 25, 1945, with convoy ON.304, and soon after arriving left for the west coast. On October 4 she completed tropicalization refit, but as VJ-Day had intervened she was paid off into reserve on December 21. She was sold to Canadian brokers in 1947, but resold in 1948 to the government of India for conversion to a pilot vessel for the Hooghly River and renamed *Bengal* in 1950.

LA HULLOISE

Commissioned at Montreal on May 20, 1944, *La Hulloise* arrived at Halifax in June. She proceeded to Bermuda in July to work up, and on returning was assigned to EG 16 at Halifax. In October she was reassigned to EG 25, and transferred with it to Londonderry in November, 1944. She spent the remainder of the war in U.K. waters, based variously at 'Derry and Rosyth. On March 7, 1945, with *Strathadam* and *Thetford Mines*, she took part in sinking *U 1302* in St. George's Channel. Late in May she sailed for Canada to undergo tropicalization refit at Saint John. Work was completed October 19, but the Pacific war had ended and she was paid off at Halifax on December 6. Recommissioned for cadet and new entry training in 1949, *La Hulloise* was largely operational from then until November 23, 1953, when she was paid off for conversion to a Prestonian class ocean escort. She was commissioned as such on October 9, 1957, and remained in service until paid off July 16, 1965. She was broken up at La Spezia, Italy, in 1966.

LONGUEUIL

Commissioned on May 18, 1944, at Montreal, she arrived June 30 in Bermuda to work up. In July she became a member of EG C-2, and on August 7 left St. John's for Londonderry with convoy HXF.302. She spent her entire wartime career on convoy duty and for varying periods was Senior Officer's ship of her group. Returning to Canada in June, 1945, she proceeded to Vancouver for tropicalization refit, but this was cancelled and the ship paid off December 31 at Esquimalt. She was sold in 1947 and, reportedly, expended as part of a breakwater at Kelsey Bay, B.C., in 1948.

Kokanee, June 23, 1944

La Hulloise in a U.K. port

Longueuil, Bermuda, July, 1944

MAGOG

After commissioning at Montreal on May 7, 1944, *Magog* arrived at Halifax on May 28 and worked up briefly in St. Margaret's Bay before sailing for Bermuda to complete the process in July. She then returned to Montreal for repairs, subsequently completing these at Halifax in August. There she joined EG 16, performing A/S duty in the Halifax, Gaspé, and Sydney areas. On October 14, 1944, while escorting convoy GONS.33 (the Gulf section of ONS.33), she was torpedoed and badly damaged by *U 1223* in the St. Lawrence River off Pointe des Monts. Lacking 60 feet of her stern, she was towed to Quebec and there adjudged a constructive total loss. Paid off December 20 to care and maintenance, she was sold in 1945 to Marine Industries Ltd., Sorel, who scrapped her in 1947.

Magog

MATANE

Commissioned at Montreal on October 22, 1943, *Matane* arrived at Halifax November 13 and began working up in St. Margaret's Bay, completing the process at Pictou. In April, 1944, she joined EG 9, Londonderry, as Senior Officer's ship, thereafter serving mainly on escort and patrol duty in U.K. waters. She was present on D-Day. On July 20 she was hit by a German glider bomb off Brest and towed, badly damaged, to Plymouth by HMCS *Meon*. In April, 1945, she completed eight and one-half months' repairs at Dunstaffnage, Scotland, worked up at Tobermory and, on May 13, sailed from Greenock to escort convoy JW.67 to North Russia. She was detached on May 16, however, to help escort 14 surrendered U-boats from Trondheim to Loch Eriboll. In June, after one round trip to Gibraltar as convoy escort, she left Londonderry for Esquimalt via Halifax. She arrived at Esquimalt in July and on Februay 11, 1946, was paid off into reserve there. She was sold in 1947 and her hull sunk in 1948 as part of a breakwater at Oyster Bay, B.C.

MONTREAL

Commissioned on November 12, 1943, at Montreal, she arrived at Halifax on November 29, worked up locally and on February 25 left St. John's for Londonderry to join EG C-4. She was employed continuously on convoy duty until late September, 1944, when she joined EG 26, then forming at 'Derry. On December 17, 1944, she rescued survivors of *U 1209*, wrecked on Wolf Rock southwest of Land's End. *Montreal* remained in U.K. waters, and for short periods early in 1945 was based at Portsmouth and at Plymouth. She left 'Derry for the last time on March 12, 1945 as escort to convoy ON.290. Arriving at Shelburne, N.S., on March 31, she completed tropicalization refit there at the end of August, then performed odd jobs out of Halifax until paid off October 15 to reserve in Bedford Basin. Sold in 1947, she was broken up at Sydney.

Matane, January, 1944, typical of the first 15 RCN frigates, with single 4-inch forward and no clinker screen to her stack

Montreal

NEW GLASGOW

Commissioned on December 23, 1943, at Esquimalt, New Glasgow arrived at Halifax on February 17, 1944, and then proceeded to Bermuda to work up. On her return late in April she joined EG C-1. She left St. John's with her first convoy, HXS.291, on May 15, and for the next five months was steadily employed on convoy duty. Late in September she was allocated to EG 26, then forming at Londonderry, and for the remainder of the European war served in U.K. waters, based for short periods at Portsmouth and at Plymouth early in 1945. On March 21, 1945, she rammed and fatally damaged U 1003 off Lough Foyle, and was herself laid up for repairs at Rosyth until June 5. She then proceeded via Londonderry to Halifax and thence to Shelburne, where she was paid off to reserve on November 5. Rebuilt in the long interval as a Prestonian class ocean escort, she was recommissioned on January 30, 1954, and served in a training capacity until January 30, 1967, when she was paid off at Esquimalt. She was broken up in Japan that year.

New Glasgow, 1944

NEW WATERFORD

Commissioned on January 21, 1944, at Victoria, she arrived at Halifax on March 9 and in Bermuda on April 22 to work up. Returning to Halifax, she was assigned to EG 6 as a replacement for the damaged HMCS *Teme*, and sailed for Londonderry on June 19. She remained with the group until the end of the European war, detached for short periods to Portsmouth and Plymouth, and in April, 1945, returned home for tropicalization refit at Liverpool, N.S. This was completed in November, and New Waterford left in January, 1946, for the west coast, where she was paid off to reserve at Esquimalt on March 7. Briefly recommissioned in 1953, she later underwent conversion to a Prestonian class ocean escort, commissioning as such on January 31, 1958. She was paid off for the last time on December 22, 1966, and broken up the following year at Savona, Italy.

ORKNEY

Commissioned on April 18, 1944, at Victoria, *Orkney* arrived at Halifax June 8. After working up in Bermuda she returned to Halifax in August to join EG 16, but was transferred as Senior Officer's ship to EG 25 at Londonderry, sailing late in October with eastbound convoy HX.317. She remained on duty in U.K. waters until February 13, 1945, when she collided with SS *Blairnevis*, which sank, and was herself under repairs at Dunstaffnage, Scotland, until mid-April. Following a week's workups at Tobermory, *Orkney* returned briefly to 'Derry, then sailed late in May for home and tropicalization refit at Louisbourg. This was completed on October 20, after which she served locally until paid off January 22, 1946, to reserve in Bedford Basin. Sold in 1947, she was renamed *Violetta* and served for a time as an Israeli immigrant ship before joining the Israeli Navy as *Mivtakh*. Sold in turn to the Sinhalese (Sri Lanka) Navy in 1959 as *Mahasena*, she was broken up at Singapore in 1964.

New Waterford, 1944

Orkney, 1944

Outremont, 1945, fitted with U.S.-type SU radar

Port Colborne, December 5, 1943

Prince Rupert wearing the funnel emblem of EG C-3

OUTREMONT

Commissioned at Quebec City on November 27, 1943, *Outremont* arrived at Halifax on December 13 and carried out working-up exercises in St. Margaret's Bay. She left St. John's on February 17, 1944, to join EG 6, Londonderry, and served mainly on escort and patrol duties in U.K. waters. She was present on D-Day. She left the U.K. on November 30 for tropicalization refit at Sydney, which kept her idle until August 20, 1945, only to be paid off November 5 and sold to Marine Industries Ltd. Later reacquired by the RCN and converted to a Prestonian class ocean escort, she was recommissioned September 2, 1955, and served in a training role until finally paid off June 7, 1965, and broken up at La Spezia, Italy, the following year.

PORT COLBORNE

Commissioned at Victoria on November 15, 1943, *Port Colborne* arrived at Halifax January 9, 1944, and proceeded to Bermuda to work up in February. Late in April she sailed for Londonderry to join EG 9, which was based there. She remained on patrol and escort duty in U.K. waters, including participation on D-Day, except for a round trip to North Russia in December, 1944, with convoys JW.62 and RA.62. She left 'Derry for Halifax February 21, 1945, and on September 24 completed tropicalization refit at Liverpool, N.S. On November 7 she was paid off at Halifax and laid up in reserve in Bedford Basin, and in 1947 was broken up at Sydney.

PRINCE RUPERT

Commissioned at Esquimalt on August 30, 1943, she arrived at Halifax October 21, worked up at Pictou and, in January, 1944, joined EG C-3 as Senior Officer's ship. *Prince Rupert* left St. John's on January 3 to join her maiden convoy, SC.150, and was thereafter continuously employed as an ocean escort until late that year. On March 13, with U.S. naval units and U.S. and British aircraft, she assisted in sinking *U 575* in the North Atlantic. In November, 1944, she began a refit at Liverpool, N.S., and on its completion in March, 1945, joined EG 27, Halifax. In June *Prince Rupert* sailed for Esquimalt, where she was paid off January 15, 1946. She was sold in 1947, and her hull expended as a breakwater at Royston, B.C., the following year.

ST. CATHARINES

Commissioned on July 31, 1943, at Esquimalt, *St. Catharines* arrived at Halifax on October 4 and in November sailed for the U.K. as a member of EG C-2. She was continuously employed on convoy duty until October, 1944, and from February to September of that year was Senior Officer's ship. With six other escorts of convoy HX.280, she took part in the destruction of *U 744* on March 6, 1944. After refitting at Shelburne from October to December, 1944, she went to Bermuda to work up and, on her return to Halifax, commenced tropicalization refit there. By the time this was completed in August, 1945, the war was over and the ship was paid off on November 18. In 1947 she was sold to Marine Industries Ltd. and laid up at Sorel, but was reacquired in 1950 and converted to a weather ship. Now owned by the Department of Transport, she was taken round to the west coast to be stationed in the North Pacific as of July, 1952. Replaced in March, 1967, by CGS *Vancouver*, she was broken up in Japan in 1968.

SAINT JOHN

Commissioned on December 13, 1943, at Montreal, she arrived at Halifax on December 20 and in January, 1944, was sent to Bermuda to work up. On her return in February she was based for a short time at Halifax, but April joined EG 9 in Londonderry. She was present on D-Day. On September 1, 1944, she and *Swansea* sank *U 247* off Land's End, and on February 16, 1945, *Saint John* destroyed *U 309* in Moray Firth. In December, 1944, she escorted convoys JW.62 and RA.62 on the North Russia run, to and from Kola Inlet. She arrived at Cardiff for repairs on February 27, 1945, and, when these were completed in April, proceeded home for tropicalization refit at Saint John, from May to October. She was paid off November 27, 1945, at Halifax and placed in reserve in Bedford Basin until sold in 1947 for scrapping at Sydney.

SPRINGHILL

Commissioned on March 21, 1944, at Victoria, she arrived at Halifax on May 12 and left in mid-June for three weeks' working up in Bermuda. In August *Springhill* joined EG 16, Halifax, as Senior Officer's ship. She left on March 7, 1945, for Londonderry, the group having been transferred there, but returned in April for tropicalization refit at Pictou. This occupied her from May to October, and on December 1 she was paid off at Halifax and laid up in reserve in Bedford Basin. She was broken up in 1947 at Sydney.

St. Catharines

Saint John, May, 1944

Springhill, April 17, 1944

52

Stettler, January, 1966, as modernized in the 1950s

Stormont being disarmed for disposal, September 28, 1945

Swansea, 1949

STETTLER

Stettler was commissioned May 7, 1944, at Montreal, and arrived at Halifax on May 28. She carried out workups in Bermuda in July. On her return to Halifax she was assigned to EG 16. On March 7, 1945, she left for Londonderry, EG 16's new base, and was thereafter employed in U.K. waters except for two round trips to Gibraltar in May and June, 1945. She left 'Derry for home on June 16, the last Canadian warship to do so, and began tropicalization refit at Shelburne. Work was suspended in August and the ship was paid off November 9, 1945. She was sold but later recovered and converted to a Prestonian class ocean escort, being recommissioned on February 27, 1954. She subsequently moved to the west coast, and was finally paid off there on August 31, 1966. She was broken up in 1967 at Victoria.

STORMONT

Commissioned at Montreal on November 27, 1943, *Stormont* arrived at Halifax in December, worked up in St. Margaret's Bay and in mid-March, 1944 sailed for Londonderry to join EG 9. She was present on D-Day, and in July, 1944 assisted the damaged HMCS *Matane* toward Plymouth. In October she escorted a convoy to Gibraltar and, in December, escorted convoy JW.62 to Kola Inlet and RA.62 back. She left 'Derry on December 19, 1944, for Halifax and tropicalization refit at Shelburne. The latter, begun in June, was discontinued on August 20 and the ship was paid off November 9, 1945. She was sold in 1947 to a Montevideo buyer for conversion to a merchant ship, but was resold in 1951. Converted at Kiel, 1952-54, to a luxury yacht for Aristotle Onassis, she was renamed *Christina*.

SWANSEA

Commissioned at Victoria on October 4, 1943, *Swansea* arrived at Halifax on November 16 and worked up off Pictou and in St. Margaret's Bay. Assigned to EG 9, Londonderry, she made her passage there with convoy SC.154, incidentally taking part in the sinking of *U 845* on March 10. On April 14 she repeated the process in company with HMS *Pelican*, the victim this time being *U 448*. She was present on D-Day, and for the next four months patrolled the Channel in support of the ships supplying the invasion forces. While thus employed, she and *Saint John* sank *U 247* off Land's End on September 1. She left Londonderry on November 5 for a major refit at Liverpool, N.S., from December, 1944 to July, 1945. It was the first tropicalization of a frigate for Pacific service, and on VJ-Day *Swansea* was assessing the results in the Caribbean. She was paid off November 2, 1945 to reserve in Bedford Basin, but was twice recommissioned for training cadets and new entries between April, 1948 and November, 1953. She was rebuilt, from 1956 to 1957, as a Prestonian class ocean escort, serving on the east coast until finally paid off October 14, 1966. She was broken up in 1967 at Savona, Italy.

THETFORD MINES

Commissioned on May 24, 1944, at Quebec City, *Thetford Mines* arrived in Bermuda on July 12 to work up, returning to Halifax on August 16. Soon afterward assigned to EG 25, she was transferred with the group to Londonderry in November, and served in U.K. waters from then until VE-Day, working out of 'Derry and for a time out of Rosyth. On March 7, 1945, she helped sink *U 1302* in St. George's Channel, and on May 11 arrived in Lough Foyle as escort to eight surrendered U-boats. She returned home late in May, was paid off November 18 at Sydney and laid up at Shelburne. In 1947 she was sold to a Honduran buyer who proposed converting her into a refrigerated fruit carrier.

VALLEYFIELD

Commissioned December 7, 1943, at Quebec City, she arrived at Halifax on December 20 and commenced working up in St. Margaret's Bay, completing the process in Bermuda. She left Halifax at the end of February, 1944, to join EG C-1 and sailed for the U.K. with convoy SC.154, but was detached to Horta en route, escorting a tug and its tow, the rescue ship *Dundee*. Her next assignment was to escort the damaged HMCS *Mulgrave*, in tow from Horta for the Clyde. The three left the Azores on March 14 and joined convoy SL.151 (from Sierra Leone) three days later. *Valleyfield* made one return trip to Canada, and on her next trip left Londonderry on April 27 with convoy ONM.234. She parted company on May 7 for St. John's and shortly afterward was torpedoed and sunk by *U 548*, 50 miles southeast of Cape Race, with the loss of 125 lives. She was the only RCN ship of her class to be lost.

WASKESIU

The first frigate completed on the west coast, *Waskesiu* was commissioned at Victoria on June 16, 1943, and left for Halifax on July 8. She worked up in Bermuda the following month, returning to Halifax on September 11, and late in October left for Londonderry to join EG 5, renumbered EG 6 on November 21. *Waskesiu* served chiefly in U.K. waters, but early in 1944 supported Gibraltar and Sierra Leone convoys. On February 24, while escort to SC.153, she sank *U 257*, and in April made a trip to North Russia to bring back convoy RA.59. She was present on D-Day. On September 14 she left 'Derry with ONF.253 for Canada, and soon after arriving began an extensive refit at Shelburne. On its completion in March, 1945, she proceeded to Bermuda to work up, following which she sailed for Londonderry via Horta. She left 'Derry for Canada late in May, proceeding to Esquimalt in June to commence tropicalization refit, but work was suspended in August and she was paid off into reserve on January 29, 1946. She was sold to the Indian government in 1947 for conversion to a pilot vessel, and renamed *Hooghly* in 1950.

Thetford Mines

Valleyfield, 1943

Waskesiu

Wentworth

WENTWORTH

Wentworth was commissioned on December 7, 1943, at Victoria and arrived at Halifax January 25, 1944. She left for Bermuda to work up, but defects forced her to return and the working-up exercises were carried out in St. Margaret's Bay. In June she joined EG C-4, becoming Senior Officer's ship in August, and remained continuously on convoy duty until February, 1945, when she commenced a major refit at Shelburne, from March 7 to August 9. She was paid off on October 10, 1945, to reserve in Bedford Basin, and broken up in 1947 at Sydney.

River Class, 1943-1944 Programme

ANTIGONISH

Commissioned at Victoria on July 4, 1944, she arrived at Halifax on August 22 and, after undergoing minor repairs, sailed for Bermuda in mid-October to work up. On her return to Halifax on November 2, she joined EG 16, transferring with the group to Londonderry in March, 1945. During the next three months *Antigonish* was employed on patrol and support duty, including two round trips to Gibraltar. She left Londonderry in mid-June and on July 3 began tropicalization refit at Pictou, completing November 17. On December 22 she left for Esquimalt and there, on February 5, 1946, was paid off into reserve. She recommissioned for training on April 26, 1947, and was paid off on January 15, 1954. The ship was converted, 1956-57, to a Prestonian class ocean escort, and again took up her training role until finally paid off on November 30, 1966. She was broken up in Japan in 1968.

Antigonish, July 27, 1944

BUCKINGHAM

Commissioned on November 2, 1944, at Quebec City, she proceeded to the east coast and sailed from Halifax on December 18 for Bermuda to work up. She returned in mid-January 1945, and in February was assigned to EG 28, as a member of which she carried out escort and patrol duty out of Halifax until VE-Day. In May she arrived at Shelburne, escorting the surrendered *U 889*. In June she began a tropicalization refit at Liverpool, N.S., continuing it at Shelburne until August 20, when it was suspended. *Buckingham* was paid off on November 16 at Sydney and placed in reserve at Shelburne until 1946, when she was sold to Marine Industries Ltd. Reacquired by the RCN, she was converted to a Prestonian class ocean escort, 1953-54, and recommissioned for training purposes. Further modified by the addition of a helicopter landing deck aft, she carried out, October-December, 1956, trials preliminary to the design of the destroyer helicopter carriers. She was paid off for the last time on March 23, 1965, and broken up the following year at La Spezia, Italy.

Buckingham, October 29, 1956, fitted with experimental landing pad

CAPILANO

Commissioned at Victoria on August 25, 1944, *Capilano* arrived at Halifax on October 20. Following workups begun in St. Margaret's Bay and completed in Bermuda in November, she joined EG C-2 in St. John's, Nfld., and was continuously on North Atlantic convoy duty until VE-Day. She left Londonderry for the last time on May 30, 1945, and on June 10 began tropicalization refit at Shelburne. The work was completed on October 13, and on November 24, 1945, the ship was paid off at Halifax and placed in reserve in Bedford Basin. She was sold for mercantile use in 1947, and in 1948 she appeared under Jamaican registry as *Irving Francis M.* She foundered in 1953 off the Cuban coast while en route from Jamaica to Miami in tow of *Bess Barry M.,* the former HMCS *St. Boniface.*

CARLPLACE

Carlplace was commissioned on December 13, 1944, at Quebec City, the last RCN frigate to enter service. En route to Halifax, she suffered serious ice damage to her hull, necessitating several weeks' repairs at Halifax and Philadelphia. She then proceeded to Bermuda to work up, returning to Halifax on March 24, 1945. In April she was allocated to EG 16, Londonderry, and sailed for the Clyde via the Azores, escorting an RN submarine homeward bound from refit in the U.S. She finally arrived at Londonderry on April 23 and left on May 5 to escort convoys to and from Gibraltar. Late that month she returned to Canada for tropicalization refit at Saint John, N.B. Begun on June 2 and continued at Shelburne, N.S., on July 10, the work was called off on August 20, and on November 13, 1945, the ship was paid off at Halifax and laid up at Shelburne. Sold to the Dominican Republic in 1946 for conversion to a presidential yacht, she was renamed *Presidente Trujillo* and, in 1962, *Mella.*

COATICOOK

Commissioned on July 25, 1944, at Quebec City, *Coaticook* proceeded to Bermuda in mid-September for three weeks' working up. She was then assigned to EG 27 with which she served on A/S and support duties out of Halifax for the balance of the war. In June, 1945, *Coaticook* sailed to Esquimalt, where she was paid off into reserve on November 29. In 1949 her stripped hull was sunk for a breakwater at Powell River, but was refloated in 1961. On December 14, 1961, while in tow for Victoria to be broken up, the hull was found to be structurally unsound and instead scuttled off Race Rock.

Capilano, September 9, 1944

Carlplace

Coaticook, December, 1944

FORT ERIE

Commissioned at Quebec City on October 27, 1944, she did not arrive at Halifax until December. She worked up in Bermuda in mid-January and, on her return to Halifax, was assigned to EG 28, an RCN support group based on Halifax, for the duration of the European war. Tropicalization refit, begun June 2, 1945, at Pictou, was cancelled on August 20 and *Fort Erie* was paid off on November 22, to be laid up at Shelburne. She was sold in 1946 to Marine Industries Ltd., but reacquired by the RCN and rebuilt in 1954 and 1955 as a Prestonian class ocean escort. Recommissioned April 17, 1956, she was generally in service as a training ship until finally paid off on March 26, 1965 at Halifax. She was broken up at La Spezia, Italy, in 1966.

Fort Erie, November 8, 1944

GLACE BAY

Commissioned on September 2, 1944, at Lévis, she arrived at Halifax September 23. She carried out workups in Bermuda in mid-October and on her return was assigned to EG C-4, Londonderry. She left St. John's for that port on November 17, escorting a number of U.S.- built subchasers destined for the Russian Navy. *Glace Bay* was employed continuously on convoy duty until VE-Day, and early in June, 1945, left 'Derry for the last time to spend several months at a variety of tasks off the east coast of Canada. In October she made a round trip to Bermuda, and on her return was paid off on November 17 at Sydney. She lay in reserve at Shelburne until sold in 1946 to the Chilean Navy and renamed *Esmeralda* and then, in 1952, *Bacquedano*. She was broken up in 1968.

Glace Bay

HALLOWELL

Commissioned on August 8, 1944, at Montreal, *Hallowell* arrived at Halifax on September 3 and left a month later for Bermuda to work up. Returning early in November, she was allocated to EG C-1 and was Senior Officer's ship from December onward, remaining with the group until the end of the European war. She left St. John's November 28 to join convoy HX.322, and was thereafter continuously employed escorting North Atlantic convoys. Early in June, 1945, she left Greenock for home, and in July and August was engaged in transporting troops from St. John's to Canada. She was paid off at Sydney on November 7 and placed in reserve at Shelburne. Sold to Uruguayan interests in 1946, she was resold to a Palestinian firm in 1949 for conversion to a short-service Mediterranean ferry and renamed *Sharon*. In 1952 she was acquired by the Israeli Navy, reconverted to a warship and renamed *Misnak*. In 1959 she was again sold, this time to the Sinhalese (Sri Lanka) Navy and renamed *Gajabahu*. She was discarded in 1978.

Hallowell

INCH ARRAN

Commissioned on November 18, 1944, at Quebec City, *Inch Arran* left for Halifax on December 3, visiting Dalhousie en route. In January she proceeded to Bermuda to work up, and on her return to Halifax on February 4, she was assigned to EG 28. She served for the rest of the war on A/S and support duties out of Halifax, and on May 13 escorted the surrendered *U 889* into Shelburne. Tropicalization refit, commenced on June 6 at Sydney, was suspended on August 20, and the ship was paid off on November 28, 1945. Placed in reserve at Shelburne, she was sold in 1946 to Marine Industries Ltd., but reacquired in 1951 by the RCN for conversion to a Prestonian class ocean escort at Saint John. She was recommissioned on August 23, 1954, serving on the east coast as a training ship until finally paid off on June 23, 1965. She was then acquired by the Kingston Mariners' Association for conversion to a nautical museum and youth club, but was eventually scrapped in 1970.

LANARK

Commissioned on July 6, 1944, at Montreal, *Lanark* arrived at Halifax on July 28. She carried out workups in Bermuda in September and, returning to Halifax in October, was assigned to the newly formed EG C-7, Londonderry. She spent the balance of the European war on convoy duty, most of that time as Senior Officer's ship, and early in June, 1945, sailed for home. In mid-July she began tropicalization refit at Liverpool, N.S., but this was called off on August 31 and the ship was paid off at Sydney on October 24. She was then placed in reserve at Shelburne, but was sold to Marine Industries Ltd. in 1946. Later repurchased by the RCN, she was converted to a Prestonian class ocean escort, 1954-55, and on April 26, 1956, commissioned for training purposes on the east coast. She was paid off for the last time on March 16, 1965, and broken up at La Spezia, Italy, the following year.

LASALLE

Commissioned on June 29, 1944, at Quebec City, she arrived in Bermuda on August 31 to carry out working-up exercises. She left on October 1 for Halifax, there to become a member of the newly formed EG 27, and spent the remainder of the war in that area on A/S patrol and support duty. In June, 1945, *Lasalle* sailed for the west coast and was paid off on December 17 at Esquimalt. She was dismantled in 1947 and her hull expended as a breakwater in 1948 at Kelsey Bay, B.C.

Inch Arran, November, 1944

Lanark, May 30, 1960

Lasalle, February 20, 1945

Lévis (2nd), July 5, 1944

Lauzon, December 16, 1953

LAUZON

Commissioned on August 30, 1944, at Quebec City, *Lauzon* arrived at Halifax in mid-October and in November spent three weeks working up in Bermuda. She arrived at St. John's November 30 to join EG C-6, and was continuously employed as a mid-ocean escort until VE-Day. She left Londonderry June 13 for the last time, and that summer was employed as a troop-carrier between St. John's and Quebec City. Paid off on November 7, 1945, she was laid up in reserve at Shelburne, N.S. until purchased in 1946 by Marine Industries Ltd. The RCN reacquired her in 1951 for conversion to a Prestonian class ocean escort. She was recommissioned on December 12, 1953, and assumed a training role on the east coast until finally paid off on May 24, 1963. She was sold the following year to a Toronto buyer, presumably for scrap.

LÉVIS (2nd)

Commissioned at Quebec City on July 21, 1944, she arrived in Bermuda at the end of August to work up, and a month later left for Halifax to join the newly formed EG 27. She spent the balance of the war with the group, on patrol and escort duty out of Halifax, and on June 4 commenced tropicalization at Lunenburg, N.S. The work was completed November 26 and she sailed a month later for Esquimalt, arriving January 30, 1946. Paid off on February 15 to reserve there, she was sold in 1947 and her hull expended the following year as part of a break-water at Oyster Bay, B.C.

PENETANG

Commissioned on October 19, 1944, at Quebec City, she left on November 6 for Halifax and in December proceeded to Bermuda to work up. Returning northward in January, 1945, *Penetang* joined convoy HX.331 at New York as local escort. She was allocated in February to EG C-9, and made the crossing to the group's Londonderry base as an escort to SC.168. She spent the rest of the war as a mid-ocean escort, returning to Canada in June, 1945, to be employed as a troop carrier between St. John's and Quebec City. One of the few frigates not taken in hand for tropicalization, she was paid off on November 10 and laid up at Shelburne. She was sold in December to Marine Industries Ltd., but later reacquired and converted to a Prestonian class ocean escort, recommissioning on June 1, 1954. Again paid off on September 2, 1955, she was lent to the Norwegian Navy on March 10, 1956 and renamed *Draug*. Transferred outright three years later, she served until 1966 and was then broken up.

Penetang

POUNDMAKER

Poundmaker was commissioned on September 17, 1944, at Montreal, arrived at Halifax in October and worked up in Bermuda in November. In mid-December she arrived at St. John's to join EG C-8, serving as a mid-ocean escort for the rest of the war. She left Londonderry for the last time on May 11, 1945, to escort convoy ONS.50 westward, and on May 31 began tropicalization refit at Lunenburg. Work was completed on August 20, and on November 25 she was paid off at Sydney and taken to Shelburne for disposal. She was sold to the Peruvian Navy in 1947 and renamed *Teniente Ferre* and, in 1963, *Ferre*. She was broken up in 1966.

PRESTONIAN

Commissioned September 13, 1944 at Quebec City, *Prestonian* arrived at Halifax the following month in need of repairs, and it was early January, 1945, before she could go to Bermuda to work up. On her return to Canada she was assigned to EG 28, based at Halifax, and employed locally until VE-Day. She then underwent tropicalization at Halifax, completing August 20, and on November 9 was paid off and sold to Marine Industries Ltd. Later reacquired by the RCN, she was rebuilt to become the name-ship of the Prestonian ocean escort class. She was recommissioned on August 22, 1953, and finally paid off on April 24, 1956, having been lent to the Norwegian Navy. Renamed *Troll*, she was transferred outright in 1959, and in 1965 reclassified as a submarine depot ship and renamed *Horten*. She was discarded in 1972.

ROYALMOUNT

Royalmount was commissioned at Montreal on August 25, 1944, arrived at Halifax on September 8 and carried out working-up exercises in Bermuda later that month. She arrived at St. John's on November 15 to join EG C-1, and spent the remainder of the war with the group as a mid-ocean escort. She left Liverpool April 21, 1945 and escorted convoy ONS.48 on her homeward passage to refit, from May 26 to October 5, at Sydney. She was paid off at Halifax on November 17, 1945, and placed in reserve in Bedford Basin until 1947, when a New York buyer purchased her for scrap.

Poundmaker

Prestonian completing at Lauzon, September 9, 1944

Royalmount

Runnymede, December, 1944

St. Pierre, 1944

St. Stephen, August 14, 1944

RUNNYMEDE

Runnymede was commissioned on June 14, 1944, at Montreal and arrived in Bermuda for workups toward the end of July. On August 21 she returned to Halifax to become Senior Officer's ship of EG C-5, and was to wear its barber pole stripes the rest of her wartime career. She left Londonderry toward the end of May, 1945, and made her passage home as escort to convoy ON.305. She left Halifax on June 20 for Esquimalt, arriving July 18, and early in August commenced tropicalization refit at North Vancouver. Work was soon suspended and she sailed for Esquimalt to be placed in reserve, though not paid off until January 19, 1946. Sold in 1947, she is reported to have been expended as part of a breakwater at Kelsey Bay, B.C., in 1948.

ST. PIERRE

Commissioned on August 22, 1944, at Quebec City, she arrived at Halifax in October and spent more than four months under repair. She carried out workups in Bermuda in March, 1945 and on April 5 left for Londonderry via the Azores, having been assigned to EG 9. From Horta she picked up convoy SC.172, arriving at 'Derry on April 21. On May 13 she left Greenock to escort JW.67 to North Russia, but was detached three days later to accompany a number of surrendered U-boats bound from Trondheim to Loch Eriboll. She left the U.K. late that month for Canada, and on June 4 commenced tropicalization refit at Lauzon. The job was called off on August 20 and the ship paid off November 22 at Sydney, to be placed in reserve at Shelburne. In 1947 she was sold to the Peruvian Navy and renamed *Teniente Palacios,* shortened to *Palacios* in 1953. She was broken up in 1966.

ST. STEPHEN

Commissioned on July 28, 1944, at Esquimalt, *St. Stephen* arrived at Halifax on September 28 and in October proceeded to Bermuda to work up. Returning in mid-November, she joined EG C-5 and spent the balance of the war as a mid-ocean escort. She left Barry, Wales, on May 27, 1945, to take passage home with convoy ON.305, and early in June began tropicalization refit at Dartmouth, N.S. This was cancelled in August and on January 30, 1946, the ship was paid off at Halifax and laid up in Bedford Basin. On September 27, 1947, she was recommissioned, having undergone alterations to fit her as a weather ship. She was stationed between Labrador and Greenland until August, 1950, when she sailed to Esquimalt to be paid off on August 31 and lent to the Department of Transport. Retained primarily as a "spare" in the event of a mishap to *St. Catharines* or *Stone Town,* she was purchased by the Department in 1958. Ten years later she was sold to a Vancouver buyer, purportedly for conversion to a fish factory ship.

STE. THÉRÈSE

Commissioned on May 28, 1944, at Lévis, she arrived at Halifax early in July and, after preliminary workups in St. Margaret's Bay, proceeded to Bermuda to complete the process. Returning in mid-August, *Ste. Thérèse* left Halifax in late October to join convoy HX.317 for passage to Londonderry. There she joined EG 25 and served with it in U.K. waters until February, 1945, when she was reassigned to EG 28, Halifax. She served locally with EG 28 until the end of the war, and on November 22 was paid off at Sydney and placed in reserve at Shelburne. She recommissioned on January 22, 1955, after conversion to a Prestonian class ocean escort, finally being paid off at Esquimalt on January 30, 1967. She was broken up in Japan that year.

SEA CLIFF

Sea Cliff was commissioned on September 26, 1944, at Quebec, and arrived at Halifax October 20, proceeding to Bermuda in November to work up. On completion she sailed to St. John's to become a member of EG C-3, and left December 23 to join her first convoy, HX.237. She spent the remainder of the war on North Atlantic convoy duty, and on May 21, 1945, left Londonderry for the last time, to join ON.304 on her passage to Canada. She began tropicalization refit at Liverpool, N.S., on June 10, but work was halted August 28 and the ship was paid off November 28 at Halifax. She was placed in reserve at Shelburne until 1946, when she was sold to the Chilean Navy and renamed *Covadonga*. She was broken up in 1968.

STONE TOWN

Commissioned at Montreal on July 21, 1944, *Stone Town* arrived at Halifax on August 13, and on September 3 commenced a month's workups in Bermuda. On her return to Canada she was assigned to newly formed EG C-8 as Senior Officer's ship, and spent the balance of the war as a mid-ocean escort. She sailed from Londonderry on May 12, 1945, as escort to convoy ONS.50 on her way home, and on July 22 commenced tropicalization refit at Lunenburg. Work was stopped on August 24 and the ship was paid off on November 13 at Lunenburg, to be laid up in reserve at Shelburne. Sold to the Department of Transport for a weather ship, she was modified for the purpose at Halifax in 1950, and sailed that October for Esquimalt. In October, 1957, after 15 years on station in the North Pacific, she was replaced by CGS *Quadra* and sold in 1968 to a Vancouver buyer, purportedly for conversion to a fish factory ship.

Ste. Thérèse, August, 1945

Sea Cliff

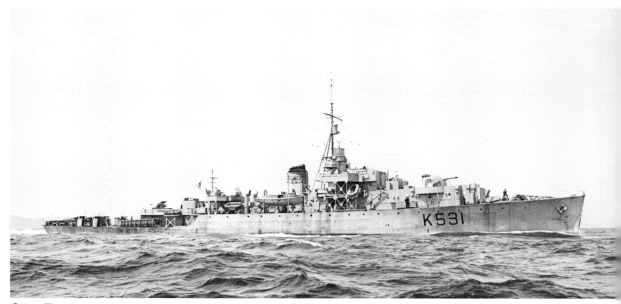

Stone Town, June, 1945

STRATHADAM

Commissioned on September 29, 1944, at Victoria, she arrived at Halifax on November 21 and left a month later for Bermuda to work up. Returning to Halifax, she was assigned to EG 25, Londonderry, and sailed from St. John's on February 2, 1945. Except for one trip late that month to Gibraltar, *Strathadam* was employed in U.K. waters until VE-Day. On March 7, with *La Hulloise* and *Thetford Mines*, she took part in the sinking of *U 1302* in St. George's Channel, and on April 11 she was carrying out another attack when a Hedgehog projectile exploded prematurely, killing six of her crew. She returned to Canada at the end of May, and in July commenced tropicalization refit. This was cancelled August 20 and the ship was paid off at Halifax on November 7, to be laid up at Shelburne. She was sold to Uruguayan interests in 1947 but acquired by the Israeli Navy in 1950 and renamed *Misgav*. She was broken up in 1959.

Strathadam, October 27, 1944

SUSSEXVALE

The last frigate launched for the RCN, *Sussexvale* was commissioned on November 29, 1944, at Quebec City, and arrived at Halifax on December 16. She left on January 8, 1945, for a month's workups in Bermuda, on completion of which she was assigned to EG 26. She arrived in Londonderry to join the group on March 6 and spent the remainder of the war in U.K. waters, based primarily at Portsmouth. She returned home in May to begin tropicalization refit at Shelburne, but this was called off and the ship was paid off at Sydney on November 16. Placed in reserve at Shelburne, she was subsequently sold to Marine Industries Ltd., but reacquired by the RCN and converted to a Prestonian class ocean escort. Recommissioned March 18, 1955, she served as a training ship until paid off on November 30, 1966. She was scrapped in Japan in 1967.

TORONTO

Commissioned on May 6, 1944, at Lévis, she arrived at Halifax on May 28, leaving on June 18 for a month's working-up in Bermuda. In August *Toronto* was allocated to EG 16, Halifax, but for the next few weeks operated principally from Sydney. Following repairs in November she joined Halifax Force and was employed locally until May, 1945, when she began five months' training duty at HMCS Cornwallis. Paid off on November 27, she was placed in reserve at Shelburne, but was recommissioned on March 26, 1953, after conversion to a Prestonian class ocean escort. She was paid off for the last time on April 14, 1956, having been lent to the Norwegian Navy, which renamed her *Garm*. She was permanently transferred in 1959, and reclassed in 1964 as a torpedo boat depot ship. Simultaneously renamed *Valkyrien*, she served a further 13 years before being disposed of.

Sussexvale in the Channel, 1945

Toronto, May 31, 1945

VICTORIAVILLE

Commissioned on November 11, 1944, at Quebec City, she arrived at Halifax on December 3 and late that month proceeded to Bermuda to work up. In February, 1945, she was assigned to EG C-9, leaving Halifax on February 27 to join convoy SC.168 for her passage to Londonderry, where the group was based. *Victoriaville* spent the balance of the war on North Atlantic convoy duty. She left Barry, Wales, on May 2 to pick up convoy ON.300 on her way home to Canada, and on May 12 escorted the surrendered *U 190* into Bay Bulls, Nfld. She began tropicalization refit at Saint John, N.B., on May 24, but work was stopped on August 20, and on November 17 the ship was paid off at Sydney and laid up at Shelburne. Subsequently sold to Marine Industries Ltd., she was reacquired by the RCN and recommissioned on September 25, 1959, following conversion to a Prestonian class ocean escort. On December 21, 1966, she assumed the name and duties of the retiring diving tender *Granby*, but was paid off December 31, 1973, and sold for scrap the following year.

River Class, ex-RN

ANNAN

Named after a river in Scotland, she was transferred newly built from the RN to the RCN at Aberdeen on June 13, 1944. On completion of workups at Tobermory, she joined EG 6, Londonderry, for patrol and escort duties in U.K. waters. On October 16, 1944, while on A/S patrol south of the Faeroes, she sank *U 1006*, rescuing 46 survivors. In April, 1945, EG 6 was transferred to Halifax, but *Annan* sailed for the U.K. on May 29 and was handed back to the RN at Sheerness on June 20. That November she was sold to the Danish Navy and renamed *Niels Ebbesen*. She was broken up at Odense, Denmark, in 1963.

ETTRICK

Named after a river in Scotland, *Ettrick* was completed in July, 1943, as an RN ship and assigned to EG C-1, a Canadian escort group. On January 29, 1944, while undergoing a refit in Halifax, she was transferred to the RCN, and on completion of the refit on May 6 she was assigned to EG C-3. She arrived in Bermuda on September 30 for a month's working-up, and on her return made two round trips to Londonderry with EG C-3 before being transferred in October to EG 27, Halifax. She was employed locally until VE-Day, and on May 30, 1945, returned to the RN at Southampton. She was then converted to a combined operations H.Q. ship, though never employed as such, and in April, 1946, was laid up at Harwich. In 1953 she was broken up at Grays, Essex.

Victoriaville, May 2∈, 1960

Annan, May 30, 1945. The goose-neck whaler davits were characteristic of the ex-RN frigates.

Ettrick, December, 1944

MEON

Named after an English river, *Meon* was completed in December, 1943, at Glasgow and sailed on January 16, 1944, with convoy ON.220 for Canada. She was commissioned in the RCN at Halifax on February 7, and in April worked up in St. Margaret's Bay. In May she was assigned to EG 9 and sailed with convoy HXM.289 to join EG 9 in Londonderry. For the next five months she was employed in U.K. coastal waters, and was present on D-Day. She was then transferred to the EG 27, Halifax, as Senior Officer's ship, arriving there on October 19. Employed locally until March 31, 1945, she then left Halifax to join convoy HX.347 on passage to Britain, and was returned to the RN at Southampton on April 23. Like *Ettrick*, she was converted to a combined operations H.Q. ship but was never used as such, and lay idle at Harwich for 20 years before being broken up at Blyth in 1966.

Meon, May, 1944

MONNOW

Named after an English river, she was transferred newly built to the RCN at Bristol on March 8, 1944. Following workups at Tobermory in April *Monnow* joined EG C-2 in May and served with that group until August, when she was reassigned to EG 9, Londonderry. She served throughout her career in U.K. waters except for a round trip to Gibraltar in October, 1944, and to Kola Inlet with convoys JW.62 and RA.62 in November and December. On May 13, 1945, she left Greenock to pick up JW.67 for North Russia but was detached three days later to escort surrendered U-boats en route from Trondheim to Loch Eriboll. She left Londonderry on May 25 for Sheerness, where on June 11 she was paid off and returned to the RN. That October she was sold to the Danish Navy and renamed *Holger Danske*. She was broken up at Odense, Denmark in 1959. *Monnow* was one of two among the larger RCN warships that never saw a Canadian port.

Monnow. The unusually thick stanchions just ahead of the bridge support a "split" Hedgehog.

NENE

Named for an English river, *Nene* was completed in April, 1943, as an RN ship but assigned to Canadian EG 5 based at St. John's. The group was renumbered EG 6 in November, 1943, to avoid confusion with EG C-5. On November 20 *Nene*, with *Calgary* and *Snowberry*, sank *U 536* north of the Azores while escorting the combined convoys MKS.30 and SL.139. From February, 1944, onward *Nene* was Senior Officer's ship of EG 6. She was transferred to the RCN at Halifax on April 6, 1944, immediately prior to a refit at Dartmouth, N.S., that was not completed until mid-July. She then proceeded to Bermuda to work up, and in August joined EG C-5. After escorting three transatlantic convoys she was transferred in October, 1944, to EG 9, Londonderry. Except for a trip to North Russia with convoy JW.62, *Nene* served in U.K. waters until the end of the war, based at various times at Londonderry, Plymouth, Rosyth, and Portsmouth. She left Greenock May 13, 1945, to join JW.67 for North Russia but was detached on May 16 to escort 14 surrendered U-boats bound from Trondheim to Loch Eriboll. She arrived at Sheerness on May 27 and was handed back on June 12 to the RN, which placed her in reserve at Southampton. She was broken up at Briton Ferry, Wales, in 1955.

Nene at St. John's

RIBBLE

Named for an English river, *Ribble* was built for the RN but commissioned in the RCN as a new ship at Blyth, U.K., on July 24, 1944. After workups at Tobermory she arrived at Londonderry on September 4 to join the newly formed EG 26 the following month. She spent her whole career with this group, based much of the time at Portsmouth and Plymouth, and from October 7 to 9, 1944, towed the damaged HMCS *Chebogue* toward Swansea, Wales. She was paid off at Sheerness on June 11, 1945, and returned to the RN, and after 12 years in reserve at Harwich was broken up in 1957 at Blyth.

TEME

Named after a river on the English-Welsh border, she was commissioned in the RCN at Middlesbrough on February 28, 1944. After working up, *Teme* was assigned in May to EG 6, Londonderry, and spent her whole career with this group. She was present on D-Day, and on June 10 was rammed in the Channel by the escort carrier HMS *Tracker*, and cut almost in half abaft the bridge. She was towed by *Outremont* 200 miles to Cardiff, where she remained under repair until Christmas. In January, 1945, she went to Tobermory to work up, returning to Londonderry on February 9 to rejoin her group. On March 29, while escorting a coastal convoy, BTC.111, in the Channel off Falmouth, she was torpedoed by *U 246*, losing 60 feet of her stern. Surveyed at Falmouth, she was declared a constructive total loss, paid off on May 4 and handed back to the RN. She was broken up at Llanelly, Wales, in 1946.

Loch Class

LOCH ACHANALT

Commissioned on July 31, 1944, at Leith, Scotland, she worked up at Tobermory and joined EG 6 in September at Londonderry. *Loch Achanalt* served with the group until VE-Day on A/S patrol and support duty in U.K. waters, based for brief periods at Portsmouth and Plymouth. When the group was transferred to Halifax in April, 1945, she accompanied it, but left Halifax on May 29 for Sheerness and there was paid off on June 20 and returned to the RN. She remained in reserve at Sheerness until 1948, when she was sold to the Royal New Zealand Navy and renamed *Pukaki*. She was broken up at Hong Kong in 1966.

Ribble, 1944

Teme, March 8, 1944

Loch Achanalt, August, 1944

Loch Alvie, 1944

LOCH ALVIE

Commissioned on August 10, 1944, at Dalmuir, Scotland, she carried out workups at Tobermory and joined EG 9, Londonderry, in September. Briefly based at Portsmouth and Plymouth, *Loch Alvie* served in U.K. waters for the duration of the war, except for a trip to Gibraltar in October and to Iceland in March, 1945. She left Greenock May 13, 1945, to escort convoy JW.67 to North Russia, but was detached 3 days later to escort 14 surrendered U-boats bound from Trondheim to Loch Eriboll. Like *Monnow,* she never saw a Canadian port. She was paid off at Sheerness on June 11 and returned to the RN, which laid her up in reserve there. She was later recommissioned for service in Far Eastern waters, following which she was laid up at Singapore. After being cannibalized for parts, she was broken up there in 1965.

LOCH MORLICH

Commissioned on July 17, 1944, at Wallsend-on-Tyne, she joined EG 6 at Londonderry in September after working up at Tobermory. *Loch Morlich* remained with the group in U.K. waters until the end of the war, based for short periods at Portsmouth and Plymouth. In April, 1945, the group was transferred to Halifax and *Loch Morlich* went along, but left on May 29 for Sheerness where, with *Loch Achanalt,* she was paid off on June 20 for return to the RN. She lay in reserve at Sheerness until 1949, when she was sold to the Royal New Zealand Navy and renamed *Tutira.* She was broken up at Hong Kong in 1966.

Loch Morlich, 1944

Corvettes

The corvette was designed by William Reed of Smith's Dock Co., near Middlesbrough, Yorkshire, and patterned after his firm's whale-catcher, *Southern Pride*, of 1936. The proposed class name, "patrol vessel, whaler type," was not to Winston Churchill's liking, and he dubbed it "corvette" instead.

Impressed with the design, the Canadian Naval Staff ordered 64 corvettes early in 1940. Owing to their short length they could negotiate the St. Lawrence canal system, and many were to be built in Great Lakes shipyards. Ten, originally intended for the RN, were lent to Canada and manned by RCN crews. Like their RN sisters, they bore the names of flowers, whereas the Canadian units were named for towns and cities. The ten were commissioned incomplete in Canada as RN ships, and sailed to U.K. yards for completion. There, on May 15, 1941, they were all formally commissioned as RCN ships.

Sixteen more corvettes were ordered under the 1940-41 Programme, the first six identical to those built earlier but the remainder somewhat larger and of an improved design. In the original version the break in the fo'c's'le was located just ahead of the bridge, making the ship's low waist very wet in rough weather. In the improved design, the fo'c's'le was extended halfway aft and the bows given greater sheer and flare. All but 12 of the earlier corvettes had their fo'c's'les lengthened as the war progressed.

The last 27 corvettes built in Canada differed little externally from the older ones but had twice the endurance — 7,400 sea miles at 10 knots — owing to increased fuel capacity. An additional four of these were acquired from the RN in exchange for Canadian-built mine-sweepers.

The corvette was originally designed as a coastal escort, but shortage of ocean escorts forced it into the latter role throughout the worst years of the war. It met the challenge admirably, and in the process became the quintessential ship of the wartime RCN.

In 1944 a dozen Castle class corvettes were acquired, again in exchange for minesweepers. Originally named for British castles, they received town names in accordance with RCN practice. They were much larger than the Flowers, hence far more comfortable. They and the Loch class frigates were the only British ships of the period to be armed with the Squid, a triple-barrelled mortar which threw its projectiles ahead of the ship.

Unlike the frigates, the corvettes were nearly all disposed of at the war's end — most of them for scrap, some to minor navies, others to various mercantile pursuits including that of whale-catching.

Flower Class, 1939-1940 Programme

AGASSIZ

Commissioned at Vancouver on January 23, 1941, *Agassiz* arrived at Halifax on April 13 and left on May 23 for St. John's to join the newly formed NEF. She sailed early in June with a convoy for Iceland and was thereafter in continuous service as an ocean escort until the end of 1943. In September, 1941 she took part in a major battle around convoy SC.44, rescuing survivors of her torpedoed sister, HMCS *Lévis*. She was also part of the escort of the hard-pressed convoy ON.115 in July, 1942. On January 5, 1943, she commenced a major refit at Liverpool, N.S., completing in mid-March, and in April was assigned to newly designated EG C-1. She arrived at New York on December 16 for another major refit, including extension of her fo'c's'le, completing March 4, 1944. After working up in St. Margaret's Bay in April, she joined EG W-2 of WEF, transferring in August to W-7. She spent the remainder of the war with W-7, being paid off on June 14, 1945, at Sydney, and was broken up in 1946.

ALBERNI

Commissioned at Esquimalt on February 4, 1941, she arrived at Halifax on April 13 with *Agassiz*, and the two left on May 23 for St. John's to join the recently formed NEF. *Alberni* left the following month with a convoy for Iceland, serving as a mid-ocean escort until May, 1942, when she was taken out of service to have a new boiler installed. In September, 1941, she had taken part in the defence of convoy SC.42, which lost 18 ships to as many U-boats. Assigned to duties in connection with the invasion of North Africa, she sailed for the U.K. in October with convoy HX.212, and until February, 1943, escorted convoys between the U.K. and the Mediterranean. She returned to Halifax in March, 1943 and served briefly with WLEF before transferring to Quebec Force in May. For the next five months she escorted Quebec-Labrador convoys, leaving Gaspé on November 6 to undergo repairs at Liverpool, N.S. With repairs completed early in February, she proceeded to Bermuda to work up, and on her return to Halifax joined EG W-4. On April 24 she sailed for the U.K. for duties connected with the coming invasion, and was still engaged in these when, on August 21, 1944, she was torpedoed and sunk by *U 480*, southeast of the Isle of Wight. Fifty-nine of her ship's company lost their lives.

Agassiz, May, 1944

Alberni, May, 1941

Algoma

Amherst, July 17, 1941. A classic example of an early corvette in the original configuration of short fo'c's'le, foremast ahead of bridge, mainmast still fitted, and minesweeping gear aft.

Arrowhead, September 27, 1942

ALGOMA

Commissioned at Montreal on July 11, 1941, *Algoma* arrived at Halifax July 18. She escorted her first convoy to Iceland in September, and was thereafter employed as an ocean escort until the end of May 1942. During this period she was involved in two major convoy actions: ONS.67 (February 1942) and ONS.92 (May 1942). In July 1942, after six weeks' repairs at Liverpool, N.S., she joined WLEF. In October, allocated to duties connected with the invasion of North Africa, she left for Britain with convoy SC.107, which lost fifteen ships to U-boat attacks. *Algoma* served under RN orders the next few months, escorting convoys between Britain and the Mediterranean. In February 1943 she was based at Bône, Algeria, but returned in April to St. John's via the U.K. She served briefly with Western Support Force which, based at St. John's, existed only during May 1943, and with WLEF, before joining Quebec Force in June. *Algoma* escorted Quebec-Labrador convoys until mid-November, when she was lent to EG C-4 for one round trip to the U.K. She arrived at Liverpool, N.S., late in December for a major refit, which included extending her fo'c's'le and was not completed until mid-April 1944. In May she joined EG C-5 and arrived in Bermuda on June 1 to work up. Returning to St. John's on June 27, she made three round trips to the U.K. before joining EG 41 (RN), Plymouth Command, in September. She was employed on patrol and escort duties in the Channel until the end of May 1945, when she returned to Canada and was paid off July 6 for disposal at Sydney. In 1946 she was sold to the Venezuelan Navy, being renamed *Constituçion*, and was not discarded until 1962.

AMHERST

Commissioned on August 5, 1941 at Saint John, N.B., she arrived at Halifax on August 22 and after working up, joined Newfoundland command in October. She was steadily employed as an ocean escort for the succeeding three years, during which time she was involved in two particularly hard-fought convoy battles: ON.127 (August, 1942) and SC.107 (October, 1942). She had joined EG C-4 in August, 1942. Her only real respite was between May and November, 1943, when she underwent a major refit at Charlottetown, including the extension of her fo'c's'le. After workups at Pictou, N.S., she returned to the North Atlantic grind until September, 1944, when she began another long refit, this time at Liverpool, N.S. Following workups in Bermuda in January, 1945, she joined Halifax Force, but in March was lent to EG C-7 for one round trip to the U.K. She was paid off July 16, 1945 at Sydney, and placed in reserve at Sorel. Sold in 1946, she served in the Venezuelan Navy as *Federaçion* until broken up in 1956.

ARROWHEAD

Commissioned at Sorel on November 22, 1940, she arrived at Halifax on December 3, carried out workups and sailed on January 21, 1941, with convoy HX.104 for Sunderland. There she was in dockyard hands for the two months' work required to complete her fully. After working up at Tobermory *Arrowhead* joined EG 4, Iceland Command (RN), and in June transferred to the newly formed NEF. For the rest of 1941 she escorted convoys between St. John's and Iceland, proceeding early in December to Charleston, S.C. for refit. Returning to Halifax in February, 1942, she made one round trip to Londonderry before joining WLEF. In July she transferred to Gulf Escort Force, escorting

Continued on p. 156

ARVIDA

Commissioned at Quebec City on May 22, 1941, *Arvida* arrived at Halifax on June 6. She joined Sydney Force in July, acting as escort to local sections of transatlantic convoys until September, when she joined Newfoundland Command. She left Sydney on September 5 to join her maiden ocean convoy, SC.43, and was thereafter in almost continuous service as an ocean escort until the end of 1943. In June, 1942, she became a member of EG C-4 and, in May, 1943, of C-5. While escorting convoy ON.188 in mid-June, 1943, she was damaged by her own depth charges and arrived at Iceland on June 16 for repairs that took a week to complete. Three of *Arvida*'s convoys received particularly rough handling by U-boats: ONS.92 (May, 1942), ON.127 (September, 1942), and SC.107 (November, 1942). While with ON.127 she rescued survivors of the torpedoed HMCS *Ottawa* on September 13. She had major refits at Saint John (January to April, 1942); Lunenburg/Saint John (December, 1942 to March, 1943); and Baltimore, Md. (January to April, 1944). While at Baltimore she was given her extended fo'c's'le, afterward joining EG W-7 of WLEF. In mid-May, 1944, she was sent to Bermuda to work up, returned to Halifax on June 9, and in August joined EG W-2. In December she transferred to W-8, remaining with that group until the end of the war. *Arvida* was paid off on June 14, 1945, at Sorel and later sold for commercial use, entering service in 1950 as the Spanish-flag *La Ceiba*.

BADDECK

Commissioned at Quebec City on May 18, 1941, *Baddeck* arrived at Halifax on May 29. She again left Quebec City late in June for Halifax, escorting SS *Lady Rodney*, but had to return to her builder's at Lauzon owing to an engine breakdown. In September the two set out from Halifax for Jamaica, but again *Baddeck*'s engine failed, and she reached her destination only with difficulty. When further repairs had been completed, she was assigned to Newfoundland Command, leaving Sydney on October 5 for Iceland as ocean escort to convoy SC.48, which lost nine ships to U-boats. Engine repairs kept her at Hvalfjord, Iceland, until mid-December but failed to cure the problem and she was in dock at Halifax for the first six months of 1942. She worked up at Pictou in July, 1942, then

Continued on p. 156

BARRIE

Commissioned at Montreal on May 12, 1941, *Barrie* arrived at Halifax on May 24 and was initially employed as a local escort out of Sydney. On September 5 she left Sydney to join convoy SC.43 for Iceland, but defects necessitated her sailing on to Belfast for two months' refit. She served as a mid-ocean escort until May, 1942, when she was assigned to WLEF on her return from Londonderry with ON.91, and she remained with this force until the end of the war. When individual escort groups were formed by WLEF in June, 1943, she became a member of EG W-1, and continued so except for brief service with EG W-8 in the fall of 1944. In mid-March, 1944, she commenced a long refit, including fo'c's'le extension, at Liverpool, N.S., working up at Bermuda afterward in August. On May 19, 1945, she left New York with HX.357, her last convoy, and was paid off on June 26 at Sorel. Sold for merchant service in 1947, she became the Argentinian *Gasestado* but was taken over by the Argentinian Navy in 1957 as a survey vessel and renamed *Capitan Canepa*. She was broken up in 1972.

Arvida, November 22, 1943, sporting the funnel band of the "Barber Pole" EG C-5

Baddeck, June 10, 1944

Barrie, 1945

Battleford, October 5, 1943

BATTLEFORD

Commissioned at Montreal on July 31, 1941, she arrived at Halifax on August 4, remaining there for six weeks while undergoing repairs, radar installation, and workups. Briefly a member of Sydney Force, *Battleford* transferred to NEF and left Sydney on November 28 to escort convoy SC.57 to Iceland. Returning to Halifax on January 7, 1942, she went to Liverpool, N.S., for a refit that kept her idle until the end of March. Arriving in the U.K. with a convoy early in May, she completed further repairs at Cardiff in mid-June, then carried out workups at Tobermory. From July, 1942 to May, 1943 she was a member of EG C-1, and in December was escort to convoy ONS.154, which was badly mauled, losing 14 ships. She participated with other RCN escorts in the destruction of *U 356* on December 27. Arriving at Halifax on April 23, 1943, with her last ocean convoy, ONS.2, she commenced a two-month refit at Liverpool, N.S., joining EG W-4 of WLEF in mid-June. Early in April, 1944, she commenced a long refit at Sydney, including fo'c's'le extension, following which she proceeded to Bermuda to work up. Returning to Halifax, she was employed for the balance of the war as a local escort with EG W-3 and was paid off at Sorel July 18, 1945. Sold to the Venezuelan Navy in 1946 and renamed *Libertad*, she was wrecked April 12, 1949.

BITTERSWEET

Built at Sorel, *Bittersweet* was towed to Liverpool, N.S. for completion so as not to be icebound. She was commissioned January 23, 1941 at Halifax, and on March 5 left with convoy HX.113 for the Tyne. There, from April 1 to June 6, the finishing touches were carried out, and after working up at Tobermory she left for Iceland on June 27, having been assigned to Newfoundland Command. She was continuously employed as an ocean escort until December 31, 1941, when she arrived at Charleston, S.C., for refit, resuming her duties in March. *Bittersweet* served with EG C-5 and C-3 until October 1943, one of her most strenuous convoys being ONS.192, which lost seven ships. She underwent a refit at Baltimore, Md., from October to November 1943, which included the extension of her fo'c's'le, then proceeded to Pictou to work up. She then resumed her convoy duties, leaving Londonderry late in October, 1944 to join her last convoy, ON.262. Upon arriving in Canada she went to Pictou to commence a refit that was completed at Halifax February 10, 1945. She was then assigned briefly to Halifax Force before transferring in April to Sydney Force, with which she remained until the end of the war. She was returned to the RN at Aberdeen on June 22, 1945, and broken up at Rosyth the following year.

Bittersweet about to be taken in tow by Skeena, May, 1943

BRANDON

Commissioned at Quebec City on July 22, 1941, *Brandon* arrived at Halifax August 1. She joined Newfoundland Command in September after working up and left St. John's September 26 for her first convoy, SC.46. She served as an ocean escort to and from Iceland until December, when she arrived in the U.K. for three months' repairs at South Shields. From mid-March, 1942, after three weeks' workups at Tobermory, she served on the "Newfie-Derry" run almost continuously until September, 1944. From December, 1942, onward, she served with EG C-4, helping defend the hard-pressed convoy HX.224 in February, 1943, and in the following month escorting convoys to and from Gibraltar. In August, 1943, she had a three-month refit at Grimsby, England,

Brandon

Continued on p. 156

BUCTOUCHE

Commissioned at Quebec City on June 5, 1941, *Buctouche* arrived at Halifax on June 12. After working up, she joined Newfoundland Force at St. John's on July 28. On August 26 she left St. John's for Iceland with convoy SC.41, and thereafter escorted convoys to and from Iceland until January, 1942, when Londonderry became the eastern terminus. In June, 1942, she was transferred to WLEF, with which she was to remain until the end of the war except for two months in the summer of 1944, when she was attached to Quebec Force. On June 28, 1944, she was damaged by grounding in Hamilton Inlet, Labrador, but made Pictou on her own for two months' repairs. After the formation of escort groups by WLEF in June, 1943, *Buctouche* served principally with EG W-1. In October, 1943, she commenced a four-month refit at Saint John, in the process acquiring an extended fo'c's'le. She was paid off at Sorel on June 15, 1945, and broken up at Hamilton, Ont., in 1949.

CAMROSE

Commissioned at Sorel on June 30, 1941, *Camrose* arrived at Halifax on July 6. She was assigned to Halifax Force after working up, but in October joined Newfoundland Command, leaving St. John's on October 8 for Iceland with convoy SC.48. She was employed as ocean escort to and from Iceland until February, 1942, when she commenced a major refit at Lunenburg. Upon completion in May she resumed her mid-ocean escort duties for one round trip to Londonderry, but was assigned in June to WLEF. In October *Camrose* was allocated to duties connected with the invasion of North Africa. She left Halifax on October 20 for the U.K., and for the next five months escorted convoys between Britain and the Mediterranean. In April, 1943, she proceeded to Pictou, N.S. for a refit lasting five and one-half months, including fo'c's'le extension, after which she worked up and was assigned to EG 6. She left St. John's early in December for Londonderry, where she was based for the next four months in support of convoys, especially to and from Freetown and Gibraltar. While so employed, she shared with HMS *Bayntun* the sinking of *U 757* in the North Atlantic on January 8, 1944, while with combined convoy OS.64/KMS.38. In May she joined Western Approaches Command, Greenock, for invasion duties, escorting convoys to staging ports and to and from the Normandy beaches. She left the U.K. on September 2 for another refit at Pictou, followed by workups in Bermuda, returning in January, 1945, to become a member of EG 41, Plymouth. She served with this group until VE-Day, afterward participating in the reoccupation of St. Helier, in the Channel Islands, *Camrose* left Greenock for home early in June, 1945, and was paid off at Sydney on July 22. She was broken up at Hamilton, Ont., in 1947.

CHAMBLY

Commissioned at Quebec City on December 18, 1940, *Chambly* arrived at Halifax on December 24. After working up she joined Halifax Force, and on May 23, 1941, left Halifax as one of the original seven corvettes forming NEF. She served continuously as an ocean escort between St. John's and Iceland until December 8, when she returned to Halifax for refit. During this period she took part in two major convoy battles: HX.133 (June, 1941), which lost six ships; and SC.42 (September, 1941), which lost 18. In the latter case she had left St. John's on September 5 with *Moose Jaw* for exercises, and when SC.42 came under attack, they received permission to

Continued on p. 156

Buctouche

Camrose, November, 1943

Chambly, January, 1945

Chicoutimi, September 6, 1944

CHICOUTIMI

Commissioned at Montreal on May 12, 1941, *Chicoutimi* arrived at Halifax on May 17. She carried out workups and then joined Sydney Force, escorting ocean convoys on the first leg of their eastward journey. In September she joined Newfoundland Command and left Sydney on September 29 to escort convoy SC.47 to Iceland. She was employed for the next five months as an ocean escort between St. John's and Iceland and, later, Londonderry. Reassigned to WLEF, she left 'Derry on February 27, 1942, to meet convoy ON.71. She served with WLEF until August, 1944 (from June, 1943, on with EG W-1), when she was transferred to HMCS Cornwallis as a training ship. In April, 1945, she went to Sydney Force and, on June 16, was paid off at Sorel for disposal. She was broken up at Hamilton, Ont., in 1946. A credit to her builders, Canadian Vickers, *Chicoutimi* required only three short refits during her active career, and she was one of the few corvettes to survive the war with a short fo'c's'le.

CHILLIWACK

Commissioned at Vancouver on April 8, 1941, she arrived at Halifax on June 19, was assigned to Newfoundland Command in July, and for the rest of the year escorted convoys between St. John's and Iceland. Early in February *Chilliwack* escorted SC.67, her first transatlantic convoy, and was thereafter employed almost continuously as an ocean escort until November, 1944. From June, 1942, onward she was a member of EG C-1, and during this period escorted three convoys around which epic battles were fought: SC.94 (August, 1942), ONS.154 (December, 1942), and ON.166 (February, 1943). In addition, she assisted in sinking two U-boats: *U 356* (when escort to ONS.154, December 27, 1942); and *U 744* (when escort to HX.280, March 6, 1944). In the course of a major refit from April to October, 1943, at Dartmouth, N.S., she acquired her long fo'c's'le. Assigned on December 4 to EG W-8, WEF, she left for a month's workups in Bermuda. Reassigned in April, 1945, to Halifax Force, she was temporarily lent to EG C-1 the following month for one final round trip to Londonderry. Paid off July 14 and laid up at Sorel, she was broken up at Hamilton, Ont., in 1946.

Chilliwack, June, 1942

COBALT

Built at Port Arthur and commissioned there on November 25, 1940, *Cobalt* was taken to Halifax in advance of completion to beat the St. Lawrence freeze-up, arriving December 24. Completing early in January, 1941, she worked up and joined Halifax Force, but left on May 23 with the other six corvettes that first formed NEF. For the next six months she operated as an ocean escort between St. John's and Iceland, proceeding in mid-November to Liverpool, N.S., for three months' refit. Following completion she made two round trips to Londonderry before being assigned in May, 1942, to WLEF, with which she was to spend the balance of the war. She served with EG W-6 from June, 1943; with W-5 from April, 1944; and with W-7 from February, 1945. During the second of two other extensive refits at Liverpool, N.S., from April to July 20, 1944, her fo'c's'le was lengthened. She was paid off at Sorel on June 17, 1945, and subsequently sold for conversion to a whale-catcher, entering service in 1953 as the Dutch *Johanna W. Vinke*. She was broken up in South Africa in 1966.

Cobalt, May, 1941

COLLINGWOOD

The first RCN corvette to enter service, *Collingwood*, was commissioned on November 9, 1940, at Collingwood, arrived at Halifax December 4, and joined Halifax Force in January, 1941. She sailed on May 23 as one of the seven corvettes that were charter members of Newfoundland Command, and in June commenced six months' employment as an escort between St. John's and Iceland. Early in December she began a two-month refit at Halifax, following which she resumed mid-ocean escort duties between St. John's and Londonderry. These duties continued, with time off for three minor refits, until the end of 1944. From December, 1942, onward she was a member of EG C-4. *Collingwood* was involved in one major convoy battle, that of HX.133 in June, 1941, when eight ships were torpedoed and six sunk. During her refit at New York City from October to December, 1943, she received her extended fo'c's'le. She left Londonderry on November 16, 1944, for the last time, refitted briefly at Liverpool, N.S., then went to Digby to serve as a training ship from April to June, 1945. Paid off on July 23, 1945, and laid up at Sorel, she was broken up at Hamilton, Ont., in 1950.

Collingwood, September, 1943

DAUPHIN

Commissioned at Montreal on May 17, 1941, *Dauphin* arrived at Halifax on May 24. She joined Sydney Force late in June and in September transferred to Newfoundland Command. She left Sydney on September 5 to join her maiden convoy, SC.43, continuing on to the U.K. for further workups at Tobermory and returning to mid-ocean service in mid-October. *Dauphin* was almost continuously employed as an ocean escort until August, 1944, after December, 1942 as a member of EG A-3, (redesignated C-5 in June, 1943). She escorted three particularly strenuous convoys: SC.100 (September, 1942), ON.166 (February, 1943), and SC.121 (March, 1943). In the course of a major refit at Pictou from April to September, 1943, her fo'c's'le was lengthened. *Dauphin* left Londonderry for the last time on August 11, 1944, underwent refit at Liverpool, N.S., then proceeded to Bermuda to work up. Returning in January, 1945, she was assigned to EG W-7, Western Escort Force, for the balance of the war. She was paid off at Sorel on June 20, 1945, and sold for conversion to a merchant ship, entering service in 1949 as the Honduran *Cortes*. She became the Ecuadorean *San Antonio* in 1955, and apparently still exists.

Dauphin, 1941

DAWSON

Built at Victoria, *Dawson* was commissioned on October 6, 1941 and, after working up, joined Esquimalt Force for local patrol duty. On August 20, 1942, she arrived at Kodiak, Alaska, to take part in the Aleutian campaign under U.S. operational control, returning to Esquimalt November 4. She resumed her duties with Esquimalt Force until February 1943, when she again proceeded to Alaskan waters to work with U.S. naval units until the end of May. In September she commenced a major refit, including fo'c's'le extension, at Vancouver, worked up following its completion January 29, 1944, and on February 14 left for Halifax. Arriving there March 25, she joined EG W-7, WEF. Early in January, 1945, she began a refit at Dartmouth, on completion of which in April she went to Bermuda to work up. The European war had ended by the time she returned, and she was paid off June 19 at Sorel. Sold for scrap, she foundered at Hamilton on March 22, 1946 but was raised and broken up.

Dawson, November 10, 1944

Drumheller

Dunvegan, August 7, 1943

Edmundston, Bermuda, August-September, 1944

DRUMHELLER

Commissioned at Montreal on September 13, 1941, *Drumheller* arrived at Halifax on September 25. She joined Sydney Force in November after completing workups, but soon afterward transferred to Newfoundland Command, and left St. John's on December 11 to join her first convoy, SC.59, for Iceland. *Drumheller* was employed for two months on that convoy run, but on February 6, 1942, arrived at Londonderry — one of the first Canadian ships to do so. She left for St. John's the following week, but developed mechanical defects en route and returned to the U.K. to refit at Southampton. On completion of the repairs she arrived at Tobermory on March 22 to work up, resuming ocean escort service at the end of April as a member of EG C-2. She served with the group until April, 1944, with respite only from mid-November, 1943 to mid-January, 1944, while undergoing a refit, including fo'c's'le extension, at New York City. Her most hectic convoy was the combined ON.202/ONS.18 of September, 1943, which lost six merchant vessels and three escorts. On May 13, 1943, while escorting HX.237 she, HMS *Lagan*, and a Sunderland aircraft collaborated in sinking *U 456*. In April, 1944 *Drumheller* was allocated to Western Approaches Command, Greenock, for invasion duties, transferring in September to Portsmouth Command and in November to Nore Command. She served with the latter until the end of the war, escorting convoys in U.K. coastal waters, and returned to Canada in mid-May, 1945. Paid off on July 11, 1945, at Sydney, she was broken up in 1949 at Hamilton, Ont.

DUNVEGAN

Named for a village in Nova Scotia, *Dunvegan* was commissioned at Sorel on September 9, 1941, and arrived at Halifax a week later. She joined Sydney Force after working up, but in mid-November was transferred to Newfoundland Command, leaving St. John's on November 18 as ocean escort to convoy SC.55 as far as Iceland. On her return she underwent repairs at Halifax, and on their completion in January, 1942, was assigned briefly to WLEF. Resuming her duties as ocean escort with Newfoundland Command, she arrived at Londonderry on March 10. In succeeding weeks she made two more round trips to 'Derry, leaving that port for the last time in mid-June, 1942. On reaching Halifax, she was assigned to WLEF and, in June, 1943, to its EG W-8. In October, 1943, she proceeded to Baltimore, Md., for a refit which included fo'c's'le extension and lasted until the end of the year. She then carried out workups off Norfolk, Va., completing the process in Bermuda after some repairs at Halifax. On her return she resumed her duties with WLEF, from April, 1944 onward as a member of EG W-6. On May 7, 1945, she left Halifax as local escort to convoy SC.175, but was detached on May 10 to act, with HMCS *Rockcliffe*, as escort to the surrendered *U 889*. She was paid off on July 3, 1945, at Sydney and sold in 1946 to the Venezuelan Navy, serving as *Indepencia* until broken up in 1953.

EDMUNDSTON

Commissioned at Esquimalt on October 21, 1941, *Edmundston* was assigned after workups to Esquimalt Force. On June 20, 1942, she rescued 31 crew members of SS *Fort Camosun*, disabled by a torpedo from the Japanese submarine *I-25* off the coast of Washington. She left Esquimalt for the Atlantic on September 13, arriving at Halifax on October 13, and was

Continued on p. 157

EYEBRIGHT

Commissioned at Montreal on November 26, 1940, she arrived incomplete at Halifax on December 11 and, after working up, left on January 21, 1941, with convoy HX.104 for Sunderland. There she completed on April 16, and proceeded to Tobermory to work up. In May *Eyebright* was allocated to EG 4 (RN), based at Iceland, whence she sailed on June 12 to join convoy OB.332 for Halifax. She joined New-foundland Command in June, and for the next five months was employed as escort to convoys between St. John's and Iceland. In November she began a refit at Charleston, S.C., resuming escort duty late in January, 1942, and arrived at Londonderry with her first transatlantic convoy, SC.66, on February 6. In January, 1943, she joined EG C-3, and that July commenced two months' refit at Baltimore, Md., including fo'c's'le extension. Following repairs at Pictou and workups at Bermuda in the summer of 1944, she joined EG W-3, WLEF, and saw continuous service in the western Atlantic until the end of the war, with one further round trip to London-derry as a temporary member of EG C-5. *Eyebright* was returned to the RN at Belfast on June 17, 1945, and sold in 1947 for conversion to a whale-catcher. She entered service in 1950 as the Dutch *Albert W. Vinke*, last appearing in Lloyd's list for 1964-65.

FENNEL

Built at Sorel, she was towed in December, 1940, to Liverpool, N.S., for completion and commis-sioned there on January 16, 1941. She left Halifax on March 5 with convoy HX.113 for the U.K., and while there received finishing touches at Greenock. Following workups at Tobermory in June *Fennel* was assigned to NEF, first serving as an ocean escort between St. John's and Iceland, then between St. John's and Londonder-ry. In June, 1942, she commenced a year's service with the newly formed WLEF. She underwent a refit at New York from mid-July to late Septem-ber, 1942. In June, 1943, she was detached to EG C-2 for one round trip to 'Derry, and on returning she went to Baltimore, Md., for a refit which included the extension of her fo'c's'le, completing on September 6. After working up at Pictou she resumed her ocean escort duties with C-2, and on March 6, 1944, was one of seven escorts of HX.280 that hounded *U 744* to its death. In August she had two months' refit at Pictou, followed by three weeks' workups in Bermuda, and at year's end transferred to EG C-1 for the duration of the war. *Fennel* arrived at Greenock May 29, 1945, from one of the last convoys, and was returned to the RN at Lon-donderry on June 12. She was sold in 1946 for conversion to a whale-catcher, entering service in 1948 as the Norwegian *Milliam Kihl*. She was broken up at Grimstad, Norway, in 1966.

GALT

Commissioned on May 15, 1941, at Montreal, *Galt* arrived at Halifax June 6. She was assigned in July to NEF and left St. John's on August 25 with SC.41, her first convoy, for Iceland. She was to serve on that route until January, 1942. In February, 1942 she commenced a refit at Liver-pool, N.S., which was completed on May 11, and after working up in June was assigned to EG C-3. She arrived at Londonderry for the first time on June 5 with convoy HX.191, and served on the "Newfie-Derry" run for the balance of the year. She arrived January 4, 1943, at Liverpool, N.S., for another refit which was completed at Halifax in mid-April, worked up in St. Marga-ret's Bay and, in June, joined EG C-1. She left Halifax March 13, 1944, for New York for yet

Continued on p. 157

Eyebright

Fennel, April, 1945

Galt, August, 1944

Hepatica

HEPATICA

Commissioned on November 12, 1940, at Quebec City, *Hepatica* arrived at Halifax on November 17 and left on December 18 with convoy HX.97, armed with a dummy 4-inch gun. The real thing was installed, and other deficiencies remedied, at Greenock, completing on March 6, 1941. After working up in April, she joined EG 4, Greenock. In June, after brief service as a U.K.-Iceland escort, she was assigned to NEF for the rest of the year, escorting convoys between Iceland and St. John's. Late in January, 1942, she escorted SC.64, the inaugural "Newfie-Derry" convoy, and for the next three months served on that run. In June she joined the Tanker Escort Force, operating from Halifax, for one round trip to Trinidad and then, late in July, joined Gulf Escort Force as a Quebec-Sydney convoy escort. In October she was reassigned to Halifax Force, escorting Quebec-Labrador convoys and, in December, to WLEF. She was to serve with WLEF for the remainder of the war, from June, 1943 as a member of EG W-5 and from April, 1944, with W-4. During this period *Hepatica* had two extensive refits from February 11 to April 1, 1943 and March 20 to June 8, 1944 both at New York. The latter refit included the lengthening of her fo'c's'le, and was followed by three weeks' workups in Bermuda. She left St. John's May 27, 1945, as escort to HX.358, and on June 27 was handed over to the RN at Milford Haven. She was broken up at Llanelly, Wales, in 1948.

KAMLOOPS

Commissioned at Victoria on March 17, 1941, *Kamloops* arrived at Halifax on June 19 and was assigned to Halifax Force, serving as a local escort until the end of the year. In January, 1942, she commenced a year's duty as A/S training ship at Halifax and Pictou. In mid-February, 1943, she completed a three-month refit at Liverpool, N.S., and after working up at Halifax, joined WLEF in March. She transferred in June to EG C-2, Newfoundland Command, and served with this group as an ocean escort for the remainder of the war. In September, 1943, she was with combined convoy ON.202/ONS.18, which lost six merchant ships and three of its escort. In mid-December she began a refit at Charlottetown, completed on April 25, 1944, in the course of which her fo'c's'le was extended. Following workups in Bermuda in June she rejoined EG C-2. She was paid off at Sorel on June 27, 1945, and sold for scrap that October.

Kamloops

KAMSACK

Commissioned at Montreal on October 4, 1941, *Kamsack* arrived at Halifax on October 13. She joined Sydney Force the following month but shortly transferred to Newfoundland Command, and on January 19, 1942, left St. John's to pick up convoy SC.65 for Londonderry. In June, after three round trips, she was reassigned to WLEF, then forming, and served in it for the rest of the war. From June, 1943, she was a member of EG W-4, and from April, 1944, a member of EG W-3. During this period she had two extensive refits: the first, begun at Liverpool, N.S., on November 12, 1942, was completed at Halifax on January 18, 1943; the second, in the course of which her fo'c's'le was extended, was carried out at Baltimore, Md., between late December, 1943 and mid-March, 1944. *Kamsack* was paid off on July 22, 1945, at Sorel and sold to the Venezuelan Navy. Renamed *Carabobo*, she was wrecked on passage to Venezuela in December, 1945.

Kamsack, May, 1944

KENOGAMI

Commissioned at Montreal on June 29, 1941, *Kenogami* arrived at Halifax on July 4. She served briefly with Halifax Force before arriving at St. John's on August 24 to join Newfoundland Command. She sailed on September 1 to join convoy SC.42 for Iceland, but remained with the convoy all the way to the U.K., as it lost 18 ships in what proved to be one of the worst convoy battles of the war. In February, 1942, after five months' ocean escort duty between St. John's and Iceland, she made her first trip to Londonderry, joining WLEF on her return. She received an extensive refit at Halifax through June and July, and in October resumed her ocean escort duties with EG C-1. The following month she took part in another fierce convoy battle, that of ONS.154, which lost 14 ships. In March, 1943, she made one round trip to Gibraltar, escorting follow-up convoys to the invasion of North Africa. On May 11 she left 'Derry for the last time, attached to EG B-4 (RN) with convoy ON.183. After a two-month refit at Liverpool, N.S., and workups at Pictou, she joined WLEF's EG W-8. In April, 1944, she transferred to W-4, but in December rejoined W-8 for the balance of the war. During this period she underwent a major refit at Liverpool, N.S., between June and October, 1944, including fo'c's'le extension, followed by three weeks' workups in Bermuda. She was paid off on July 9, 1945 at Sydney and broken up at Hamilton in 1950.

LETHBRIDGE

Commissioned at Montreal on June 25, 1941, *Lethbridge* arrived at Halifax on July 4. She served briefly with Sydney Force before joining NEF and leaving Sydney on October 11 with convoy SC.49 for Iceland. She was employed between St. John's and Iceland until February, 1942, and thereafter on the "Newfie-Derry" run. On June 20, 1942, she left Londonderry for the last time, and on her return to Halifax joined Gulf Escort Force to escort Quebec-Sydney convoys. After refitting at Liverpool, N.S., from September 10 to October 22, and working up at Pictou, she arrived at New York on November 18 to be placed under U.S. control as escort to New York-Guantanamo convoys. In March, 1943, she returned to Halifax to join WLEF for the remainder of the war, from June, 1943, as a member of EG W-3 and from April, 1944, as a member of W-5. She acquired her extended fo'c's'le during a refit at Sydney from January to March, 1944, which was followed by three weeks' working-up at Bermuda in April. She was paid off on July 23, 1945, at Sorel and sold to Marine Industries Ltd., who resold her in 1952 for conversion to a whale-catcher. The conversion at last completed in 1955, she entered service under the Dutch flag as *Nicolaas Vinke*. She was broken up at Santander, Spain, in 1966.

LÉVIS

Commissioned on May 16, 1941, at Quebec City, *Lévis* arrived at Halifax on May 29, worked up there and in June, 1941, joined NEF. On September 13, 1941, after one round trip to Iceland, she left St. John's as ocean escort to convoy SC.44. On September 19 she was torpedoed by *U 74*, 120 miles east of Cape Farewell, Greenland, resulting in the loss of 18 lives. During the several hours she remained afloat, the remainder of her ship's company were taken off by her sisters *Mayflower* and *Agassiz*.

Kenogami

Lethbridge

Lévis about to sink, September 20, 1941

LOUISBURG

Built at Quebec City and commissioned there on October 2, 1941, *Louisburg* arrived at Halifax on October 15. She was assigned to Sydney Force until mid-January, 1942, when she was transferred to Newfoundland Command. On February 1 she left St. John's for Londonderry as escort to convoy SC.67, another of whose escorts, HMCS *Spikenard*, was lost. After a long refit at Halifax, from March 27 to June 27, 1942, *Louisburg* made two more round trips to 'Derry before being assigned to duties in connection with Operation "Torch," the invasion of North Africa. She arrived at Londonderry on September 23, then proceeded to the Humber for fitting of extra A/A armament. This work was completed on October 18, the day before the accompanying photograph was taken. On December 9, 1942, while anchored at Londonderry, she was accidentally rammed by HMS *Bideford*, necessitating five weeks' repairs at Belfast. *Louisburg* had scarcely commenced her "Torch" duties when, on February 6, 1943, she was sunk by Italian aircraft east of Oran while escorting a convoy from Gibraltar to Bône, Algeria. Thirty-eight of her ship's company were lost.

Louisburg, October 19, 1942

LUNENBURG

Commissioned on December 4, 1941, at Quebec City, she arrived at Halifax on December 13 and after working up did escort duty between Halifax and St. John's. In July, 1942, she was transferred to Halifax Force as escort to Quebec City-Hamilton Inlet (Labrador) convoys. *Lunenburg* arrived at Sydney on August 31 to join Gulf Escort Force, but two weeks later was detached for Operation "Torch" duties. Arriving at Londonderry on September 27, she proceeded to Liverpool for extra A/A armament and in November began a four-month stint escorting convoys between the U.K. and the Mediterranean. At the end of March, 1943, she returned to Liverpool for a major refit, including fo'c's'le extension, completing on August 17. After a brief sojourn in Canadian waters she was assigned to EG 6, Western Approaches Command, arriving at Plymouth late in November to join. For the next five months she operated in support of convoys between the U.K. and Gibraltar, and between Londonderry and other U.K. ports, as well as patrolling the Northwestern Approaches from her Londonderry base. When the group's corvettes were replaced with frigates in April, 1944, *Lunenburg* went to Western Approaches Command, Greenock, to be based at Portsmouth for invasion duties. For the next five months she was employed primarily in the English Channel. She left Londonderry on September 23 for a refit begun at Saint John, N.B., but completed at Halifax in mid-January, 1945. Following work-ups in Bermuda she returned to the U.K. via the Azores, to serve with Plymouth Command until the end of the war. In May, 1945, she visited St. Helier during the reoccupation of the Channel Islands. She left Greenock in mid-June for Halifax, was paid off at Sorel on July 23, and broken up at Hamilton in 1946.

Lunenburg

MATAPEDIA

Commissioned at Quebec City on May 9, 1941, *Matapedia* arrived at Halifax on May 24. She was assigned to Sydney Force as a local escort until late September, when she was transferred to Newfoundland Command for ocean escort work between St. John's and Iceland. On her first trip, she left Sydney on September 29 for Iceland with convoy SC.47. After three round trips she left St. John's on February 6, 1942, with SC.68 for Londonderry, returning in March with ON.70. It

Continued on p. 157

Matapedia, 1941

MAYFLOWER

Commissioned at Montreal on November 28, 1940, she arrived at Halifax on December 11 to work up and complete stores. On February 9, 1941, *Mayflower* left with convoy HX.108 for the U.K., fitted, like her sister *Hepatica*, with a dummy gun. This and other shortcomings were looked after on the Tyne River, where she was pronounced complete on May 5, and she left Loch Ewe as a member of EG 4 with convoy OB.332 for Iceland on June 10. Later that month she joined Newfoundland Command, and for the remainder of the year served between Iceland and St. John's as an ocean escort. During this period she took part in the battle of convoy SC.44, when four merchant ships and HMCS *Lévis* were lost, *Mayflower* taking off survivors of the latter. After a major refit at Charleston, S.C., from December 9, 1941 to February 9, 1942, *Mayflower* resumed her mid-ocean role on the "Newfie-Derry" run until April, 1944. In April, 1942, she became a member of EG A-3, transferring to C-3 in February, 1943. She underwent two further long refits: from October 29, 1942 to January 11, 1943, at Pictou; and from November 29, 1943 to February 14, 1944, at Norfolk, Va. She received her extended fo'c's'le during the latter, following which she worked up in St. Margaret's Bay, then sailed on April 21 for the U.K. to join Western Approaches Command, Greenock, for invasion duties. She left Oban on May 31, to escort blockships for Normandy and arrived off the beaches on the day after D-Day. For the remainder of the war she operated in U.K. waters, and on May 31, 1945, was paid off for return to the RN. Laid up at Grangemouth, Scotland, she was broken up at Inverkeithing in 1949.

MONCTON

Commissioned at Saint John, N.B., on April 24, 1942, she arrived at Halifax on May 12. She was the last of the RCN's initial Flower class programme to complete, owing to heavy demands on her builder, the Saint John Dry Dock Co., for repair work to war-damaged ships. After working up she joined WLEF, Halifax, and when the force was divided into escort groups in June, 1943, she became a member of EG W-5. She remained in this service until transferred to the west coast in January, 1944, proceeding there via Guantanamo, Cristobal, Balboa, and San Pedro, Cal. Upon arrival she was assigned to Esquimalt Force, of which she remained a member until VJ-Day. In the course of an extensive refit at Vancouver from May 5 to July 7, 1944, her fo'c's'le was extended. She was paid off at Esquimalt on December 12, 1945, and sold for conversion to a whale-catcher at Kiel. She entered service in 1955 as the Dutch-flag *Willem Vinke* and was broken up at Santander, Spain, in 1966.

MOOSE JAW

Built at Collingwood, she was commissioned at Montreal on June 19, 1941, and arrived at Halifax on June 27 for final fitting-out. After working up, she arrived at St. John's on August 25 to join Newfoundland Command, and on September 5 sailed with *Chambly* for exercises. The two were ordered to reinforce the beleaguered convoy SC.42, which lost 18 ships, and just before joining on September 10, they surprised and sank *U 501* astern of the convoy. *Moose Jaw*, which had rammed the U-boat, required ten days' repairs at Greenock, following which she arrived at Tobermory on October 1 to work up. For the next four months she operated between St. John's and Iceland, but in January, 1942, she arrived at Londonderry from SC.64,

Continued on p. 157

Mayflower, May, 1943

Moncton, November, 1943. The protective rails spanning her quarterdeck show she has been equipped to act, if required, as a fleet tug.

Moose Jaw, June, 1942

MORDEN

Commissioned at Montreal on September 6, 1941, *Morden* arrived at Halifax on September 16. She joined Newfoundland Command and left St. John's November 23 to escort SC.56, her first convoy, to Iceland. She continued on to the U.K., however, to carry out two months' refit and repairs at Southampton. She left the Clyde on March 5, 1942, to pick up westbound convoy ON.73, and was thereafter continuously in service as an ocean escort until the fall of 1943 — from August, 1942, as a member of EG C-2. After a brief refit at Lunenburg in June, 1943, and workups at Pictou, she sailed for Plymouth to join EG 9. She left Devonport on September 15 to join the group on patrol south of the Scilly Islands, but the group was ordered to the assistance of combined convoy ONS.18/ ON.202 which lost six merchant ships and three of its escort. In October *Morden* rejoined EG C-2 and was given an extensive refit at Londonderry between late November, 1943 and the end of January, 1944. The work done included the lengthening of her fo'c's'le. She left 'Derry for the last time on November 14, 1944. In May, 1945, on completion of a long refit at Sydney and Halifax, she joined EG W-9 of WLEF and left New York on May 23 as local escort to HX.358, the last HX convoy. Paid off on June 29, 1945, at Sorel, she was broken up at Hamilton in 1946.

Morden off Port Arthur on builder's trials, 1941

NANAIMO

Commissioned at Esquimalt on April 26, 1941, *Nanaimo* arrived at Halifax on June 27 and for the next three months carried out local duties. In October she was assigned to Newfoundland Command, leaving Halifax on October 11 to join convoy SC.49 for Iceland, her first trip as an ocean escort. After three round trips to Iceland, she escorted SC.68 to Londonderry in February, 1942. Her return trip with ON.68 was to be her last Atlantic crossing, for in March she was reassigned to WLEF. With the formation of escort groups in June, 1943, she became a member of EG W-9, transferring to W-7 in April, 1944. In November, 1944, she was allocated to Pacific Coast Command, arriving at Esquimalt on December 7. There she underwent a refit that lasted until February 21, 1945 but left her one of the few corvettes to survive the war with a short fo'c's'le. She was paid off for disposal at Esquimalt on September 28, 1945, and subsequently sold for mercantile use. Converted to a whale-catcher at Kiel in 1953, she entered service as the Dutch-flag *Rene W. Vinke*, finally being broken up in South Africa in 1966.

Nanaimo

NAPANEE

Commissioned at Montreal on May 12, 1941, *Napanee* arrived at Halifax on May 17. She was assigned initially to Sydney Force but transferred in September to Newfoundland Command, leaving Sydney for Iceland with convoy SC.47 on September 29. She served on that route until January, 1942, when she sailed with SC.65, the first of many "Newfie-Derry" convoys she would escort until August, 1944. The worst of them was ONS.154, which lost 14 ships in December, 1942, but *Napanee* assisted in sinking one of its attackers, *U 356*, on December 27. In March, 1943, she made a side trip to Gibraltar with EG C-1, which she had joined in September, 1942. She arrived at Montreal May 22, 1943, for a five-month refit, including fo'c's'le extension, afterward working up at Pictou and joining EG C-3. She left 'Derry for the last time on August 3, 1944, refitted again at Pictou, then carried out three weeks' workup in Bermuda. On her return she joined EG W-2 on the "triangle run" until the end of the war. Paid off July 12, 1945, at Sorel, she was broken up at Hamilton in 1946.

Napanee

OAKVILLE

Commissioned at Montreal on November 18, 1941, she arrived at Halifax ten days later and joined Halifax Force on her arrival. On its formation in March, 1942, she transferred to WLEF. In July she returned to Halifax Force to escort Halifax-Aruba convoys and, on her second arrival at Aruba late in August, was diverted to reinforce convoy TAW.15 (Aruba-Key West section). The convoy was attacked August 28 in the Windward Passage, losing four ships, but *Oakville* sank the seasoned *U 94*, in part by ramming. After temporary repairs at Guantanamo she arrived at Halifax on September 16 and there completed repairs on December 1. She then joined the U.S. Eastern Sea Frontier Command to escort New York-Guantanamo convoys until March 22, 1943, when she arrived at Halifax to join WLEF. She served with three of its escort groups: W-7 from June, 1943; W-8 from December, 1943; and W-6 from April, 1944. In mid-December she began a major refit at Galveston, Texas, which included fo'c's'le extension, and was completed on March 29, 1944. After minor repairs at Halifax, she proceeded to Bermuda for workups in May, thereafter returning to her duties with EG W-6. A refit begun at Lunenburg early in April, 1945, was discontinued in June and the ship was paid off at Sorel on July 20. She was sold to the Venezuelan Navy in 1946 and renamed *Patria*, serving until 1962.

ORILLIA

Commissioned November 25, 1940, at Collingwood, she arrived at Halifax on December 11 for completion and was assigned to Halifax Local Defence Force until May 23, 1941. *Orillia* sailed that day for St. John's to become one of the seven charter members of the NEF, and for the balance of the year escorted convoys between St. John's and Iceland. In September, 1941, she was escort to convoy SC.42, which lost 18 ships. She arrived at Halifax December 24 for a refit, upon completion of which on March 22, 1942, she joined EG C-1, leaving St. John's April 3 with SC.77 for Londonderry. On her arrival she was sent to Tobermory for three weeks' workups, then returned to the "Newfie-Derry" run until January, 1944. *Orillia* took part in major battles around convoys SC.94, which lost 11 ships in August, 1942, and ON.137 that October, which lost only 2 ships despite being heavily attacked. She was a member of EG C-2 from November, 1942 to May, 1944, when she joined EG C-4 following two months' refit at Liverpool, N.S. She left Londonderry for the last time on January 16, 1944, to commence a long refit, again at Liverpool, which included the lengthening of her fo'c's'le. This refit was completed on May 3, but further repairs were completed at Halifax late in June. She arrived in Bermuda on June 29 for three weeks' workups, on her return joining EG W-2, Western Escort Force, for the duration of the war. Paid off on July 2, 1945, at Sorel, she was broken up at Hamilton in 1951.

PICTOU

Commissioned at Quebec City on April 29, 1941, *Pictou* arrived at Halifax on May 12. She joined Newfoundland Command and left St. John's on June 6 with HX.131 for Iceland, one of the first two corvettes to escort an HX convoy. She remained on the St. John's-Iceland run for the rest of the year. After brief repairs at Halifax she returned to St. John's, where breakdowns forced her to turn back from three successive convoys. She finally crossed with HX.180 in March, 1942, to Londonderry, carried out further repairs at Liverpool and, on completion early in June, joined EG C-4. On August 5, while

Continued on p. 157

Oakville, 1945

Orillia

Pictou, January, 1942

Prescott on trials off Kingston, June, 1941

Quesnel, May, 1945

Rimouski, July, 1945

PRESCOTT

Commissioned at Montreal on June 26, 1941, *Prescott* arrived at Halifax on July 4 and was attached briefly to Halifax Force before arriving at St. John's on August 31 to join Newfoundland Command. She spent the rest of the year escorting convoys between St. John's and Iceland, but early in 1942 experienced mechanical difficulties requiring two months' repairs at Liverpool, N.S. Resuming her mid-ocean duties on April 21, she made two round trips to Londonderry before being transferred to WLEF in July. In September she was assigned to duties in connection with Operation "Torch", returning to Canada on April 4, 1943. Late that month she began a six-month refit at Liverpool, N.S., including extension of her fo'c's'le. After work-ups at Pictou she sailed from St. John's on December 19 for the U.K. to join EG 6, Londonderry. She served with the group, principally as escort to U.K.-Gibraltar/Freetown convoys, until April, 1944, when its corvettes were replaced with frigates, then joined Western Approaches Command, Greenock, for invasion duties. In September she returned to Liverpool, N.S., for another refit and, after working up, went back to the U.K. to serve with Nore Command until the end of the war. Returning to Halifax late in May, 1945, she was paid off at Sorel July 20 and broken up in 1951 at Hamilton.

QUESNEL

Named for a B.C. village, she was commissioned on May 23, 1941 at Esquimalt, and for the next year patrolled off the west coast as a member of Esquimalt Force. In June, 1942, she towed the torpedoed SS *Fort Camosun* into Victoria. Transferred to the east coast to replace an Operation "Torch" nominee, she arrived at Halifax on October 13 and was assigned to WLEF until June, 1944. With the division of the force into escort groups in June, 1943, she became a member of EG W-1. During this period she underwent a refit, including fo'c's'le extension, from early September to December 23, 1943, at Pictou. This refit was followed by workups in St. Margaret's Bay and Bermuda. In June, 1944, *Quesnel* joined Quebec Force and spent five months escorting Labrador-Quebec convoys. In November she was transferred to Halifax Force, going to Sydney for refit and, on completion late in January, 1945, to Bermuda for workups. She resumed escort duty late in March, temporarily attached to EG W-5 and W-8 of WLEF until the end of the war. She was paid off on July 3, 1945, at Sorel and broken up in 1946 at Hamilton.

RIMOUSKI

Commissioned on April 26, 1941 at Quebec City, *Rimouski* arrived at Halifax on May 12 and was assigned to Newfoundland Command. She shared with *Pictou* the honour of being one of the first two corvettes to escort an HX convoy (HX.131, in June, 1941). On January 20, 1942, after three months' refit at Halifax, she left St. John's to join convoy SC.65 for Londonderry. After three round trips, she joined WLEF in June, 1942. In the course of a five-month refit at Liverpool, N.S., begun March 24, 1943, she received her extended fo'c's'le. Upon completion she was assigned to EG C-1, MOEF, transferring to C-3 in December. In April, 1944, while at Londonderry, she was allocated to Western Approaches Command, Greenock, for invasion duties, and left Oban on May 31, to escort blockships for Normandy. She was employed until August as escort to Channel and coastal convoys, then returned to Canada, where she served briefly as a Halifax-based training ship. A refit begun at Louisbourg early in November was

Continued on p. 157

ROSTHERN

Commissioned on June 17, 1941 at Montreal, *Rosthern* arrived at Halifax on June 26. She joined Newfoundland Command and left St. John's for Iceland on October 7 as ocean escort to convoy SC.48. She proceeded on to the Clyde, where mechanical defects kept her for two months, and arrived at Halifax on December 28 for further repairs, not resuming service until mid-February, 1942. She left Argentia, Nfld., on February 27 with HX.177 for Londonderry, and was thereafter employed continuously on North Atlantic convoys until June, 1944. In April, 1942 she became a member of EG A-3, re-numbered C-5 in May. *Rosthern* took part in three major convoy battles: SC.100 (September, 1942); ON.166 (February, 1943); and SC.121 (March, 1943). She left Londonderry for the last time on May 27, 1944, and on her return to Canada became a training ship at Halifax for navigation and ship-handling, attached at first to WLEF and then, from December onward, to Halifax Force. She carried out workups at Bermuda in December, escorting HMCS *Provider* on the homeward trip. *Rosthern* had no long refits during the war, and never did have her fo'c's'le lengthened. Paid off on July 19, 1945, at Sorel, she was broken up at Hamilton in 1946.

SACKVILLE

Commissioned on December 30, 1941, at Saint John, N.B., *Sackville* arrived at Halifax on January 12, 1942. She joined NEF after working up, and on May 26 left St. John's to escort HX.191 as part of the newly formed EG C-3. In April, 1943, she transferred to C-1, and that September briefly joined EG 9 in support of the beleaguered combined convoy ONS.18/ON.202, which lost six merchant vessels and three escorts. In October *Sackville* transferred to C-2 for the balance of her war career. She underwent two major refits: at Liverpool, N.S., and Halifax, from January 14 to May 2, 1943; and at Galveston, Texas, from late February to May 7, 1944, when her fo'c's'le was extended. Upon her return from working up in Bermuda, in June, 1944, she made a crossing to Londonderry. Soon after leaving for the westward journey she split a boiler and had to return to 'Derry for repairs. She again left on August 11, to limp home as escort to ONS.248, refitted at Halifax and, in September, briefly became a training ship at HMCS Kings. In October she began, at Halifax, refit and reconstruction to a loop-laying vessel, and work was still in progress by VE-Day. The ship was paid off on April 8, 1946, but recommissioned August 4, 1950, as depot ship, reserve fleet. She was refitted in 1950 but remained inactive until 1953, when, as a Canadian Naval Auxiliary Vessel (CNAV), she began a survey of the Gulf of St. Lawrence that was to last several years. She also carried out a number of cruises to the Baffin Island-Greenland area. Extensive modification in 1968 reflected *Sackville*'s new status as a research vessel, and she is currently operated by the Department of National Defence on behalf of the Bedford Institute of Oceanography. The Maritime Museum of the Atlantic hopes ultimately to acquire her for reconversion to her original appearance, as the last surviving corvette.

SASKATOON

Commissioned at Montreal on June 9, 1941, *Saskatoon* arrived at Halifax on June 22. She joined Halifax Force after working up and in August made a trip to the Bahamas, returning at the end of September. She remained on local escort duty until March, 1942, then joined WLEF on its formation. She served with this force on

Continued on p. 157

Rosthern

Sackville

Saskatoon, March, 1945

Shawinigan, June 23, 1942

SHAWINIGAN

Commissioned on September 19, 1941, at Quebec City, *Shawinigan* arrived at Halifax on October 27. She joined Sydney Force in November but on January 13, 1942, arrived at St. John's to join Newfoundland Command. She left January 25 to escort convoy SC.66 to Londonderry, the first of three round trips. In mid-May she left 'Derry for the last time, and in June was assigned to Halifax Force as escort to Quebec-Labrador convoys. She joined WLEF that November, almost immediately commencing a refit at Liverpool, N.S. This refit was completed in mid-March, 1943, and in June *Shawinigan* joined the recently established EG W-3. In April, 1944, while undergoing another refit at Liverpool, she was transferred to W-2 and, on completion of the refit in mid-June, proceeded to Bermuda to work up. On November 25, while on independent A/S patrol out of Sydney, she was torpedoed in the Cabot Strait by *U 1228* and lost with all hands.

SHEDIAC

Commissioned at Quebec City on July 8, 1941, *Shediac* arrived at Halifax on July 18. She served briefly with Halifax Force and Sydney Force before joining Newfoundland Command in October, leaving Sydney October 5 to escort convoy SC.48 to Iceland. After three round trips there, she accompanied SC.67 to Londonderry in January, 1942, again the first of three return trips. Following a six-week refit at Liverpool, N.S., she joined WLEF in July, returning in October to the "Newfie-Derry" run as a member of EG C-1. She took part in two major convoy battles: ONS.92 (May, 1942); and ONS.154 (December, 1942). On March 4, 1943, while escorting KMS.10, a U.K.-Gibraltar convoy, she assisted in the destruction of *U 87* west of the Azores. She left Londonderry for the last time on March 28, 1943, underwent refit at Liverpool, N.S., from April 27 to July 1, then joined WLEF's EG W-8. Transferred to the west coast, she left Halifax April 3, 1944, and arrived at Esquimalt May 10. She refitted at Vancouver from mid-June to mid-August, 1944, in the process receiving her extended fo'c's'le. She was paid off at Esquimalt on August 28, 1945 and sold in 1951 for conversion to a whale-catcher, entering service as the Dutch-flag *Jooske W. Vinke* in 1954. She was broken up at Santander, Spain, in 1965.

Shediac

SHERBROOKE

Commissioned at Sorel on June 5, 1941, *Sorel* arrived at Halifax on June 12. She joined Halifax Force later that month but transferred in September to Newfoundland Command and left Sydney on September 29 to escort convoy SC.47 as far as Iceland. After two round trips to Iceland, she left St. John's on January 14, 1942, to join SC.64, the first "Newfie-Derry" convoy, and was thereafter employed as an ocean escort on that run, principally with EG C-4. She took part in two particularly hard-fought convoy battles: ON.127 (August, 1942); and HX.229 (March, 1943). Her westbound trip after the latter convoy was her last; after a major refit at Lunenburg from April to June, 1943, and work-ups at Pictou, she joined EG W-2 of WLEF, transferring in April, 1944, to W-7 and in October, 1944, to W-1. Late in May, 1944, she underwent a refit at Liverpool, N.S., that included fo'c's'le extension, followed by a month's repairs at Halifax and three weeks' workups in Bermuda in October. She was paid off at Sorel on June 28, 1945, and broken up at Hamilton in 1947.

Sherbrooke, July, 1943

SNOWBERRY

Commissioned at Quebec City on November 26, 1940, she arrived at Halifax on December 13 for further work and sailed February 9, 1941, with convoy HX.108 for the U.K. There she completed fitting out at Greenock, completing April 3, and worked up at Tobermory before joining Western Approaches Command, Greenock, in May. She left Aultbea early in June to join convoy OB.332, arriving at Halifax on June 23 to join Newfoundland Command. From July to October she made three round trips to Iceland, and on December 8 arrived at Charleston, S.C., for six weeks' refit. On February 12, 1942, she left St. John's to escort SC.69 to Londonderry. In March she joined the newly formed WLEF, shifting in June to Halifax Tanker Escort Force for one round trip to Trinidad and two round trips to Aruba with tanker convoys. In September she was placed under U.S. control, escorting New York-Guantanamo convoys until March, 1943, when she arrived at Charleston, S.C., for refit, including fo'c's'le extension. On completion in mid-May, and after workups at Pictou, she joined the newly established EG 5 (later EG 6) and returned to U.K. waters in August. While serving with this support force on November 20, 1943, as escort to a U.K.-Gibraltar/Freetown convoy, she took part in the sinking of *U 536* north of the Azores. When the group replaced its corvettes with frigates in March, 1944, *Snowberry* proceeded to Baltimore, Md., for five weeks' refit, afterward returning to Halifax. She went to Bermuda to work up in July, and on returning was briefly assigned to WLEF but left St. John's in mid-September for the U.K. There she joined Portsmouth Command for the balance of the war. She was handed back to the RN at Rosyth on June 8, 1945, and used the following year as a target ship off Portsmouth. Her remains were broken up in 1947 at Thornaby-on-Tees.

SOREL

Commissioned at Sorel on August 19, 1941, *Sorel* arrived at Halifax on August 30. She joined Sydney Force in October but transferred in November to Newfoundland Force, leaving St. John's on November 18 to escort convoy SC.55 to Iceland. On her next trip, mechanical defects forced her to go on to the U.K., and she arrived at Leith, Scotland, January 17, for ten weeks' repairs. She left Londonderry on April 23 to join convoy ON.88, and in May joined WLEF. Between October 19, 1942, and February, 1943, she underwent refit, including fo'c's'le extension, successively at Liverpool, N.S., Pictou, and Halifax. In February she entered service as a training ship, first at Digby, then at St. Margaret's Bay, and at Pictou. In September, 1943, she was temporarily allocated to EG C-3 for one round trip to Londonderry, and on her return underwent refit at Halifax and Dartmouth. This refit completed on March 31, 1944, she proceeded to Bermuda for workups and on her return was assigned to WEF's EG W-4 for the rest of the war. She was paid off on June 22, 1945, and broken up.

SPIKENARD

Commissioned on December 6, 1940, at Quebec City, she arrived at Halifax five days later to complete fitting out and working up. She left Halifax on January 21, 1941, escorting convoy HX.104 to the U.K., where she received her finishing touches at South Shields, Tyne, from February 4 to April 21. She arrived at Tobermory on April 22 to work up, and on June 10 left Aultbea to escort convoy OB.332. Arriving at Halifax on June 25, she joined Newfoundland

Continued on p. 157

Snowberry, May, 1942. Her Type 271 radar is housed in a very early lantern.

Sorel, July, 1943

Spikenard leaving Halifax

Sudbury, November, 1944

Summerside, July, 1942

The Pas, 1941

SUDBURY

Commissioned October 15, 1941, at Montreal, *Sudbury* arrived at Halifax on October 26. She joined Sydney Force as local escort to ocean convoys but in January, 1942, joined Newfoundland Command, making one round trip to Londonderry. On her return she transferred to the newly formed WLEF and in June, to Halifax Tanker Escort Force. In the following three months she made two round trips to Trinidad and one to Aruba, escorting tankers both ways. That September *Sudbury* was placed under U.S. control, escorting New York-Guantanamo convoys. She arrived at Liverpool, N.S., on December 26, for two months' refit, worked up at Halifax and then joined WLEF, in June, 1943, becoming a member of EG W-9. That September she was lent to EG C-5 for her second transatlantic trip, afterward resuming service with W-9 until New Year's Day, 1944, when she left for the west coast. She arrived at Esquimalt on February 3, 1944, and later that month commenced refit, including fo'c's'le extension, at Vancouver. On completion on May 10, she joined Esquimalt Force for the duration of the war, being paid off on August 28, 1945, at Esquimalt. After the war *Sudbury* was sold and converted for use as a salvage tug, entering service in 1949 under her original name. She was broken up at Victoria in 1967.

SUMMERSIDE

Commissioned at Quebec City on September 11, 1941, *Summerside* arrived at Halifax on September 25. She was assigned to local escort duty out of Halifax and later Sydney but left St. John's on December 11 as ocean escort to SC.59 for Iceland, returning with ON.50. It was to be her only trip there. She left St. John's on January 25, 1942, for convoy SC.66 to Londonderry, returning with ON.71 to join WLEF in March. In July she was transferred to Gulf Escort Force until, earmarked for duties in connection with Operation "Torch," she left Halifax on October 19 for the U.K. For the next four months she was employed on U.K.-Mediterranean convoys, returning to Canada in mid-March, 1943, for a major refit at Saint John from April 11 to September 25. Her fo'c's'le was extended in the process. After working up at Halifax she joined EG C-5 and in April, 1944, after seven transatlantic trips, was assigned at Londonderry to Western Approaches Command for invasion duties. She was employed in U.K. waters until returning to Canada for two months' refit at Liverpool, N.S., commencing in mid-October. After further repairs at Halifax were completed on January 18, 1945, she proceeded to Bermuda for three weeks' workups. In March she sailed for the U.K. to serve with EG 41 (RN) out of Plymouth until the war's end. She returned to Canada at the end of May, was paid off at Sorel on July 6 and broken up at Hamilton in 1946.

THE PAS

Commissioned at Montreal on October 21, 1941, *The Pas* arrived at Halifax on November 4. She joined Halifax Force as a local escort, but in March, 1942, was reassigned to WLEF, then forming. In June she was transferred to Halifax Tanker Escort Force, and during the next three months made three round trips between Halifax and Trinidad-Aruba. In September she came under U.S. control as escort to New York-Guantanamo convoys but arrived at Liverpool, N.S., on November 27, for two months' refit. Following workups locally, she rejoined WLEF and, on its division into escort groups in June, 1943, became a member of EG W-4. The ship was badly damaged in collision with the Ameri-

Continued on p. 157

TRAIL

Commissioned at Vancouver on April 30, 1941, she left Esquimalt May 31 for the east coast, arriving at Halifax on June 27. In August she joined Newfoundland Command, departing St. John's on August 23 to escort convoy HX.146 as far as Iceland. During the year she made four round trips there, and on January 20, 1942, left St. John's to join SC.65 for the first of two round trips to Londonderry. She returned to Halifax on April 2 and, after a brief refit at Liverpool, N.S., joined Halifax Force for Northern Waters in June. Between July and November she was employed escorting convoys between Labrador and Quebec City, also calling at Gaspé and Hamilton Inlet. She arrived at Halifax in November to join WLEF for the balance of the war, as a member successively of escort groups W-6 (from June, 1943); W-5 (from April, 1944); and W-4 (from December, 1944). She underwent a refit at Lunenburg from mid-July to September 3, 1943, followed by workups at Pictou, and a further refit at Liverpool, N.S., between mid-July and October 23, 1944. Following the latter, which included extension of her fo'c's'le, she underwent additional repairs at Halifax and then proceeded to Bermuda to work up in December. She left there on January 7, 1945, for Boston to resume service with WLEF until paid off on July 17 at Sorel. In 1950 the ship was broken up at Hamilton.

TRILLIUM

Commissioned at Montreal on October 31, 1940, *Trillium* arrived at Halifax on November 14 and in the Clyde on December 20 for final fitting out at Greenock, which was completed on March 3, 1941. In April, after three weeks' workups at Tobermory, she joined EG 4 (RN), Greenock, for outbound North American convoys. She left Aultbea on June 10 with OB.332 for St. John's to join Newfoundland Command. After two round trips to Iceland she arrived at Halifax on August 28 for three months' refit there and at Lunenburg. On completion of the refit in December she made one further round trip to Iceland and, on January 20, 1942, left St. John's for convoy SC.65 to Londonderry. After two return trips on the "Newfie-Derry" run she went to Galveston, Texas, for refit from April 16 to June 23. Following workups at Pictou, she resumed mid-ocean service with EG A-3 from August, 1942 until April, 1943, when she

Continued on p. 157

WETASKIWIN

Commissioned at Esquimalt on December 17, 1940, she was the first west coast-built corvette to enter service. On patrol out of Esquimalt until she left on March 17, 1941, for the Atlantic, she arrived at Halifax on April 13 and left on May 23 for St. John's to become one of the founding members of NEF. In June she escorted her first convoy, HX.130, to Iceland, and during the next eight months made six round trips there with eastbound convoys. She returned to Halifax on January 24, 1942, and in February commenced a major refit at Liverpool, N.S. After working up in May she joined EG C-3, arriving in Londonderry on June 5 for the first time from convoy HX.191. During this period *Wetaskiwin* participated in two major convoy actions: SC.42 (September, 1941); and SC.48 (October, 1941). On July 31, 1942, while escorting ON.115, she shared with *Skeena* the sinking of *U 588*. In mid-January, 1943 she arrived at Liverpool, N.S., for refit, which was completed on March 9 and followed by further repairs at Halifax. In May, 1943, she joined EG C-5, and that December went to Galveston, Texas, for a long refit, including extension of her fo'c's'le. Following its com-

Trail, May 12, 1944

Trillium, Febuary 23, 1943, rescuing survivors of three ships sunk in convoy ON.166.

Wetaskiwin

pletion on March 6, 1944, she returned briefly to Halifax before proceeding to Bermuda for work-ups late in April. Returning northward, she re-joined C-5, leaving Londonderry on September 23 for the last time to join EG W-7, WLEF, for the remainder of the war. She was paid off at Sorel on June 19, 1945, and sold in 1946 to the Venezuelan Navy, which renamed her *Victoria*. She was discarded in 1962.

WEYBURN

Commissioned at Montreal on November 26, 1941, she arrived at Halifax on December 6 and joined Halifax Force for local escort work, but was soon in need of repairs. These were carried out at Halifax during March and April, following which she joined WLEF. In July she transferred to Gulf Escort Force for Quebec City-Sydney con-voys but in September was allocated to duties in connection with Operation "Torch." She arrived at Londonderry on September 27 from convoy SC.100, and at Liverpool on October 2 for fitting of Oerlikon A/A guns. The work was completed on October 21 and in November *Weyburn* began four months' employment as escort to U.K.-Mediterranean convoys. On Feb-ruary 22, 1943, she struck a mine laid off Gibraltar three weeks earlier by *U 118*, and was lost with seven of her ship's company.

WINDFLOWER

Commissioned on October 20, 1940, at Quebec City, she arrived at Halifax on October 31 and left on December 6 with convoy HX.94 for the U.K. There, at Scotstoun, she completed fitting out on March 2, 1941, following which she went to Tobermory to work up. Later in March she was assigned to EG 4 (RN), Greenock, escorting convoys between the U.K. and Iceland. She left Aultbea on June 10 for St. John's with OB.332, and on arrival transferred to Newfoundland Command. After two round trips between St. John's and Iceland, she arrived at Liverpool, N.S., on August 29 for a short refit, resuming her ocean escort duties in mid-October. She made one more round trip to Iceland, and on December 7, 1941, while making her second trip, was rammed and sunk in convoy SC.58 by the Dutch freighter *Zypenberg* in dense fog off the Grand Banks. Twenty-three of her complement were lost.

Flower Class, 1940-1941 Programme

BRANTFORD

Commissioned on May 15, 1942, at Montreal, she arrived at Halifax on May 30. After working up at Pictou, she joined WLEF in July. When this force was divided into escort groups in June, 1943, she became a member of EG W-3, trans-ferring to W-2 in April, 1944. Lent in June, 1944, to EG C-3 for one round trip to Londonderry, she left Halifax on June 2 with convoy HX.294 and returned at the end of the month with ONS.242. *Brantford* underwent two refits during her career: the first at Quebec City during the summer of 1943; the second at Sydney, completing September 12, 1944, following which she was assigned to HMCS Cornwallis for training duties until the end of the war. Her fo'c's'le was never lengthened. She was paid off on August 17, 1945, at Sorel, sold for conver-sion to a whale-catcher and, in 1950, entered service as the Honduran *Olympic Arrow*. Sold into Japanese hands, she was renamed *Otori Maru No. 11* in 1956, last appearing in Lloyd's list for 1962-63.

Windflower in one of the earliest photographs (December, 1940) of a corvette released. She is not yet armed.

Brantford, October 11, 1944

Weyburn, May, 1942

DUNDAS

Built at Victoria and commissioned on April 1, 1942, she joined Esquimalt Force after working up, and in August made a round trip as convoy escort to Kodiak, Alaska, in support of the Aleutian campaign. On September 13 she sailed for the east coast to replace an Operation "Torch" nominee, joining WLEF upon arrival at Halifax on October 13. She served with EG W-7 from June, 1943, with W-5 from September, 1943, and with W-4 from April, 1944. In the course of a major refit at Montreal from June 13 to November 19, 1943, *Dundas* acquired her extended fo'c's'le. She commenced another long refit early in January, 1945, at Liverpool, N.S., resuming service in April. Paid off on July 17 at Sorel, she was sold later that year and broken up in 1946 at Hamilton, Ont.

MIDLAND

Commissioned at Montreal on November 17, 1941, she arrived at Halifax on November 30 and spent her entire career with WLEF, from June, 1943, as a member of EG W-2. She underwent two extensive refits: the first at Liverpool, N.S., from November 30, 1942 to April 14, 1943; the second at Galveston, Texas, from mid-March to May 25, 1944. The latter refit included the extension of her fo'c's'le. Upon its completion she returned briefly to Halifax before leaving on July 1 for three weeks' working-up in Bermuda. She was paid off at Sydney on July 15, 1945 and broken up the following year at Fort William, Ont.

NEW WESTMINSTER

Built at Victoria, she was commissioned there January 31, 1942, and assigned to Esquimalt Force until the threat of Japanese invasion had abated. Ordered to Halifax to release an east-coast corvette for Operation "Torch" service, she arrived there on October 13, a month after leaving Esquimalt. Assigned to WLEF, she operated on the "triangle run" until May, 1943, when she began a major refit at Sydney. This refit included fo'c's'le extension and was not completed until December 10. The ship was then made a part of EG C-5, and in July, 1944, sailed with HXS.300, the largest convoy of the war. She left Londonderry on December 14, 1944, for the last time, returning home to refit at Saint John until early March, 1945. Allocated to Sydney Force until the end of hostilities, she was paid off at Sorel on June 21, 1945, and in 1947 sold for commercial purposes. She served under various names, the last being the Bahamian *Azua*, from 1954 to 1966, when she arrived at Tampa for breaking up.

Dundas, April 11, 1942

Midland

New Westminster

TIMMINS

Commissioned at Esquimalt on February 10, 1942, *Timmins* served with Esquimalt Force until transferred to the east coast. Upon arrival at Halifax on October 13, she was assigned to WLEF. With its division into escort groups in June, 1943, she became a member of EG W-6, transferring to W-2 in April, 1944. She commenced a two-month refit at Liverpool, N.S., late in June, 1943, followed by workups at Pictou. A second refit, again at Liverpool, was carried out between late June and mid-October, 1944. It included the extension of her fo'c's'le and three weeks' working-up in Bermuda followed. *Timmins* was paid off on July 15, 1945, at Sorel, and sold later that year for commercial use. She entered service in 1948 as the Honduran-flag *Guayaquil* and, ironically, foundered at Guayaquil, Ecuador, on August 3, 1960.

Timmins, February, 1942

VANCOUVER

Commissioned at Esquimalt on March 20, 1942, she joined Esquimalt Force and, on June 20, escorted the torpedo-damaged SS *Fort Camosun* to Victoria. In August she left for Kodiak, Alaska, to perform escort service for several weeks in support of the Aleutian campaign. On February 24, 1943, she again arrived at Kodiak to serve under U.S. control until the end of May. In mid-September she emerged from three months' refit at Vancouver with an extended fo'c's'le. Reassigned in February, 1944, to WLEF, she arrived at Halifax on March 25. After serving briefly with escort groups W-3 and W-1, she was transferred in June to Quebec Force as escort to Quebec City-Goose Bay convoys for three months. Late in November, after a month's refit at Charlottetown, she proceeded to Bermuda to work up, and on her return rejoined W-1 for the balance of hostilities. She was paid off June 26, 1945, at Sorel and broken up at Hamilton, Ont. in 1946.

Vancouver (2nd) oiling at sea, June, 1945

Revised Flower Class, 1940-1941 Programme

CALGARY

Commissioned at Sorel on December 16, 1941, *Calgary* arrived at Halifax on December 28. She served with WLEF until November, 1942, when she was assigned to duties in connection with Operation "Torch." She arrived at Londonderry on November 3 but proved to have mechanical defects that precluded her intended use on U.K.-Mediterranean convoys. Instead, she had to undergo three months' repairs at Cardiff, completing at the end of March, 1943, and in April returned to Canada and rejoined WLEF. In June, 1943, she was transferred to EG 5, Western Support Force, and sailed for the U.K. with convoy SC.133. For the next few months she was employed in support of Atlantic convoys and, on November 20, shared in sinking *U 536* north of the Azores. *Calgary* returned to Canada early in 1944 for refit at Liverpool, N.S., completing on March 17. After working up at Halifax, she left on May 1 for the U.K. to join Western Approaches Command, Greenock, for invasion duties. Initially based at Sheerness, she was moved to Nore Command in September for the duration of the war. Returning home late in May, 1945, she was paid off at Sorel on June 19 and broken up at Hamilton in 1951.

Calgary, May, 1944

CHARLOTTETOWN

Commissioned at Quebec City on December 13, 1941, *Charlottetown* arrived at Halifax on December 18. She was a member of WLEF until mid-July, 1942, when she was transferred to Gulf Escort Force owing to increased U-boat activity in the Gulf of St. Lawrence, She was employed as escort to Quebec-Sydney convoys until September 11, 1942, when she was torpedoed and sunk by *U 517* in the St. Lawrence River near Cap Chat, Que. Nine of her ship's company were lost. She had earlier delivered convoy SQ.35 to Rimouski and was en route back to Gaspé, her base, at the time.

FREDERICTON

Commissioned on December 8, 1941, at Sorel, *Fredericton* arrived at Halifax on December 18. She was assigned to WLEF until July, 1942, when she joined Halifax Force (Aruba Tanker Convoys). In September, after one round trip to Aruba, she was placed under U.S. operational control to escort New York-Guantanamo convoys. She arrived in New York for the last time on February 21, 1943, rejoining WLEF in March. After a major refit at Liverpool, N.S., from June 9 to October 10, 1943, and workups at Pictou, she joined EG C-1 and for the next ten months was employed as an ocean escort. She left Londonderry on September 30, 1944, for convoy ON.256 and, upon arriving in Canada, went to Saint John, N.B., for two months' refit. This was completed in mid-December and, in January, 1945, the ship proceeded to Bermuda for three weeks' workups. In February she joined EG C-9, with which she was to spend the balance of the war as ocean escort. *Fredericton* was paid off on July 14, 1945, at Sorel and broken up in 1946.

HALIFAX

Commissioned on November 26, 1941, at Montreal, *Halifax* was the first RCN corvette to be completed with a long fo'c's'le. Assigned to WLEF on her arrival at Halifax on December 18, she was transferred in July, 1942, to Halifax Force (Aruba Tanker Convoys). On August 14 she arrived at Aruba with HA.3, her third tanker convoy, and was assigned to escort TAW.15, a Trinidad-Aruba-Key West convoy which developed into the only major convoy battle of the war in those waters. Arriving in New York on September 14, she was placed under U.S. control for New York-Guantanamo convoys until March, 1943, when she joined WLEF. Between May 2 and October 15 she underwent an extensive refit at Liverpool, N.S., followed by workups at Pictou. On New Year's Day, 1944, she arrived at St. John's to join EG C-1, leaving Londonderry on August 11 for two weeks' refit at Lunenburg. This refit was followed by three weeks' further repairs at Halifax and, late in December, workups in Bermuda. In January, 1945, she briefly joined Halifax Force, transferring in February to EG C-9 for the rest of the war. Paid off on July 12 at Sorel, she was sold for conversion to a salvage vessel.

Charlottetown

Fredericton, July 25, 1942

Halifax, Bermuda, December, 1944

Kitchener at Milford Haven, May, 1945

KITCHENER

Commissioned at Quebec City on June 28, 1942, *Kitchener* arrived at Halifax on July 16 and carried out six weeks' workups at Pictou before briefly joining WLEF in September. It may have been during this unusually long workup that she starred in the film *Corvette K-225* with Randolph Scott. In October she was assigned to duties in connection with Operation "Torch," and arrived at Londonderry on November 3. For the next four and one-half months she escorted U.K.-Mediterranean convoys, returning to Canada in mid-April, 1943, with convoy ONS.2. In May she joined Western Support Force but in June transferred to EG C-5, MOEF, and during the following four months made three round trips to Londonderry. A major refit, commenced in October at Liverpool, N.S., was completed on January 28, 1944, followed by two weeks' working-up in Bermuda. In mid-April she arrived at Londonderry, where she was assigned to invasion duties with Western Approaches Command, based at Milford Haven. She arrived off the beaches on D-Day escorting a group of landing craft. From August until the end of the war she served with EG 41, Plymouth, returning home late in May, 1945, to be paid off at Sorel July 11. She was broken up at Hamilton in 1949.

La Malbaie, June, 1942

La MALBAIE

Commissioned at Sorel on April 28, 1942, *La Malbaie* arrived at Halifax on May 13 and, after working up there and at Pictou, joined WLEF late in June. After undergoing mechanical repairs at Halifax from August 11 to December 20, she was assigned to EG C-3, arriving at Londonderry for the first time on January 12, 1943, from HX.221. She served with C-3 until her final departure from 'Derry on October 26, 1944. During this period she underwent a major refit at Liverpool, N.S., mid-September to mid-December, 1943. Late in December, 1944, she joined Halifax Force for the duration of hostilities, was paid off on June 28, 1945, at Sorel, and broken up in 1951 at Hamilton. A pre-launching photo of *La Malbaie* served as the model for the 20¢ Canadian stamp of 1942.

PORT ARTHUR

Commissioned on May 26, 1942, at Montreal, she arrived at Halifax on June 10 and was allocated to WLEF at the end of July. In September she was appointed to Operation "Torch" duties, arriving at Londonderry on November 1 from convoy SC.105, and during the next four months escorted U.K.-Mediterranean convoys. On January 19, 1943, while so employed, *Port Arthur* sank the Italian submarine *Tritone* off Bougie, Algeria. She arrived at Halifax on March 23, 1943, and, after brief repairs there, joined Western Support Force at St. John's. Early in August she began a major refit at Liverpool, N.S., completing on December 31. After working up at Halifax, she joined EG W-9, WEF. In April, 1944, she was assigned to Western Approaches Command for invasion duties and left St. John's on April 24 for Londonderry. During the following four months she was occupied as a convoy escort in support of the invasion, and in September joined Portsmouth Command. In February, 1945, she returned to Canada, where VE-Day found her still under refit at Liverpool, N.S. She was paid off July 11 at Sorel and broken up at Hamilton in 1948.

Port Arthur

REGINA

Regina arrived at Halifax on January 6, and was commissioned on January 22, 1942. She served with WLEF from mid-March until September, when she was reassigned to Operation "Torch." Crossing as escort to convoy SC.108, she arrived at Belfast on November 22 for refit, following which she was employed as escort to U.K.-Mediterranean convoys. While thus engaged on February 8, 1943, she sank the Italian submarine *Avorio* in the western Mediterranean, north of Phillipville, Algeria. Returning to Canada late in March, she briefly rejoined WLEF before commencing a refit at Sydney on June 9. The work was completed at Pictou in mid-December and workups carried out there, followed by further repairs at Halifax and Shelburne. *Regina* joined EG C-1 in February, 1944, and at the beginning of March left Argentia to escort SC.154 to the U.K., but was detached in mid-ocean with *Valleyfield* to escort an RN tug towing the convoy rescue ship *Dundee* toward Horta. She left Horta on March 14, this time escorting the damaged HMCS *Mulgrave*, under tow for the Clyde. Arriving at Londonderry toward the end of March, *Regina* was assigned to Western Approaches Command for invasion duties. She was employed as an escort to Channel and coastal convoys until August 8, 1944, when she was torpedoed and sunk off Trevose Head, Cornwall, by *U 667*. Thirty of her ship's company were lost.

VILLE de QUÉBEC

Commissioned on May 24, 1942, at Quebec City, she arrived at Halifax on June 12, having escorted Quebec-Sydney convoy QS.7 en route. Late in July, after working up at Pictou, she was assigned to WLEF and used almost exclusively as an escort to convoys between Boston and Halifax. In September *Ville de Québec* was allocated to Operation "Torch," arriving at Londonderry on November 10, and for the succeeding four months was employed on U.K.-Mediterranean convoys. On January 13, 1943, she sank *U 224* west of Algiers. She returned to Canada in April, carried out brief repairs at Halifax, then arrived at Gaspé on May 12 to join Quebec Force, escorting Quebec-Sydney and Quebec-Labrador convoys. In September she returned to Halifax and later that month joined EG W-2, WLEF. In mid-January, 1944, she began an extensive refit at Liverpool, N.S., completing early in May, and on May 22 left for a month's workups in Bermuda. On her return she joined EG C-4 for one round trip to Londonderry, transferring in September to EG 41, Plymouth. Based at Milford Haven, she served with that group for the balance of the war, returning to Canada late in May, 1945, to be paid off on July 6 at Sorel. Sold for mercantile use in 1946, she was last noted as the Panamanian *Medex* and removed from Lloyd's Register in 1952.

WOODSTOCK

Commissioned on May 1, 1942, at Montreal, she arrived at Halifax on May 23 and, after working up at Pictou, joined WLEF. Assigned to Operation "Torch," she arrived on September 23 at Londonderry from convoy HX.207 and proceeded to the Humber for six weeks' refit, including extra A/A armament. While serving as escort to U.K.-Mediterranean convoys, on January 1, 1943, she sank *MTB 105* 250 miles northwest of the Azores, after the merchant ship carrying it had been sunk. *Woodstock* returned to Canada in March, and in April, after repairs at Halifax, joined EG C-1 for one round trip to the U.K. In June she was transferred to EG 5, Western Support Force, at St. John's, but later that month was reassigned to EG C-4 at Londonderry. She escorted only one convoy as a member of that

Regina

Ville de Québec

Woodstock, October 2, 1943

Atholl, 1944

Cobourg, May, 1944

Fergus, Bermuda, January, 1945

group before commencing refit late in June at Liverpool, N.S. Completed at Halifax in mid-September, the refit was followed by three weeks' workups at Pictou, the ship then rejoining C-4. In April, 1944, while at Londonderry, she was allocated to Western Approaches Command for invasion duties, and was so employed for the next three months. She left 'Derry for the last time on August 3, 1944, for two months' refit at Liverpool, N.S. She left Halifax on October 18 for the west coast, arriving at Esquimalt a month later to join Esquimalt Force. On January 27, 1945, she was paid off there for conversion to a loop-layer but upon recommissioning on May 17 was employed as a weather ship until finally paid off on March 18, 1946. Sold in 1948 for conversion to a whale-catcher, she entered service in 1951 as the Honduran-flag *Olympic Winner*. She passed into Japanese ownership in 1956, was renamed *Otori Maru No. 20*, and in 1957, *Akitsu Maru*. She was broken up at Etajima in 1975.

Revised Flower Class, I.E., 1942-1943 Programme

ATHOLL

Commissioned on October 14, 1943, at Quebec City, *Atholl* arrived at Halifax in November and returned there in mid-December for two months' repairs after working up at Pictou. In February, 1944, she was assigned to EG 9, Londonderry, and made her passage there in March as escort to convoy HX.281. She had scarcely arrived when it was decided that the group should consist only of frigates, and she returned to Canada in April with ONM.231, joining EG C-4 at St. John's. She served the rest of the war as a mid-ocean escort except for time out under refit at Sydney and Halifax from December, 1944 to April, 1945. Early in June, 1945, she left Londonderry for the last time, and was paid off on July 17 at Sydney and laid up at Sorel. She was broken up at Hamilton, Ont., in 1952.

COBOURG

Commissioned at Midland on May 11, 1944, she arrived at Halifax June 17, having paid a visit to her namesake port en route. She arrived in Bermuda in mid-July for three weeks' workups and on her return was allocated to EG C-6, St. John's. *Cobourg* served with the group as a mid-ocean escort for the duration of the war, leaving Londonderry on March 27, 1945, to join convoy ON.293 for her last trip westward. She arrived at Halifax May 2 for refit and was paid off June 15 at Sorel to await disposal. Sold into mercantile service in 1945, she began her new career in 1947 under the name of *Camco*. In 1956 she assumed the name *Puerto del Sol* under Panamanian flag, and on July 1, 1971, burned and sank at New Orleans. She was later raised and scrapped.

FERGUS

Commissioned at Collingwood on November 18, 1944, *Fergus* was the last corvette launched for the RCN. She arrived at Halifax in mid-December, and early in January, 1945, proceeded to Bermuda to work up. Arriving at St. John's on February 2, she joined EG C-9, with which she was to serve on North Atlantic convoy duty until VE-Day. She left Greenock early in June for return to Canada, was paid off on July 14 at Sydney and placed in reserve at Sorel. Sold for mercantile use in November, she was renamed *Camco II* and, in 1948, *Harcourt Kent*. She was wrecked on Cape Pine, Nfld., November 22, 1949.

FRONTENAC

Frontenac was commissioned at Kingston on October 26, 1943, arrived at Halifax in mid-December, and carried out working-up exercises in St. Margaret's Bay in January, 1944. She was then assigned to EG 9, Londonderry, and made the crossing in March as escort to convoy SC.154. It was decided, however, that EG 9 should be made up only of frigates, and *Frontenac* returned to St. John's, where in May she joined EG C-1. She left Belfast December 19 to escort ON.273, her last westbound convoy, and early in January, 1945, commenced three months' refit at Liverpool, N.S. On completion she was assigned to Halifax Force and sent to Bermuda to work up, but saw little further service before being paid off at Halifax on July 22. She was then taken to Sorel, but was sold in October to the United Ship Corp. of New York.

GUELPH

Commissioned at Toronto on May 9, 1944, *Guelph* arrived at Halifax early in June and left on July 2, escorting the ancient RN submarines *P.553* and *P.554* to Philadelphia. She then proceeded to Bermuda for workups, leaving there on August 2 for New York, where she joined EG W-3. She served with this group as a local escort until late September, when she was transferred to EG C-8 which, although forming in Londonderry, was to be based at St. John's. She made her passage eastward as escort to convoy HXF.310. On her final transatlantic trip she left Belfast on April 9, 1945, to be based at Halifax until paid off on June 27 at Sorel. On October 2 she was sold to a New York buyer, retaining her name under Panamanian flag. She was last noted in Lloyd's Register for 1964-65 as *Burfin*, a name she had borne since 1956.

HAWKESBURY

Commissioned at Quebec City on June 14, 1944, *Hawkesbury* arrived at Halifax in mid-July and proceeded to Bermuda on August 6 for three weeks' working-up. On September 18 she left St. John's to join convoy HXF.308 for passage to Londonderry, where she was to join EG C-7, then forming. She served the remainder of her career on North Atlantic convoy duty, leaving Londonderry early in June, 1945, for Canada, and was paid off on July 10 at Sydney. Taken to Sorel, she was later sold for mercantile purposes, entering service after conversion in 1950 to the Cambodian-owned *Campuchea*. She was broken up at Hong Kong in 1956.

Frontenac, December, 1944

Guelph while a member of EG C-8

Hawkesbury, 1944

Lindsay, 1944

Louisburg (2nd) *celebrating VE-Day*

Norsyd

LINDSAY

Commissioned at Midland on November 15, 1943, *Lindsay* arrived at Halifax in December and late in January, 1944, sailed to Bermuda for three weeks' workups. Upon her return she was briefly attached to EG W-5, but left Halifax on April 23 to join Western Approaches Command at Londonderry. For the next four months she served in U.K. waters as an unallocated unit, in September joining the RN's EG 41, Plymouth Command, for service in the Channel. On January 22, 1945, she was damaged in collision with HMS *Brilliant* southwest of the Isle of Wight. Following temporary repairs at Devonport from January 22 to February 19, she sailed for Canada via Londonderry, arriving at Halifax early in March. She left there on March 15 for Saint John, where she was under refit until June 22, then proceeded to Sydney and was paid off on July 18. She was sold for mercantile use in 1946 and renamed *North Shore*, later passing into Greek registry for Mediterranean passenger service under the name of *Lemnos*.

LOUISBURG (2nd)

Commissioned at Quebec City on December 13, 1943, she was sailed to Halifax in advance of completion in order to escape the freeze-up, arriving late in December, and was not ready for service until February, 1944. Late in March she went to Bermuda for workups and upon returning to Halifax was assigned as an unallocated unit to Western Approaches Command, Londonderry. She sailed for the U.K. on April 23 and spent the next four months on escort duties associated with the invasion. That September she was allocated to EG 41, Plymouth, and late in March, 1945, returned home for refit at Saint John. Upon completion of this refit she was paid off at Sorel on June 25 and placed in reserve there. She was sold in 1947 to the Dominican Navy and renamed *Juan Alejandro Acosta*. Deleted from the active list in 1978, she was driven ashore in a hurricane on August 31, 1979.

NORSYD

The name is a contraction of North Sydney. *Norsyd* was commissioned at Quebec City on December 22, 1943 and, en route to Halifax, was diverted to Indiantown, N.B., for fitting-out that was not completed until mid-March. She arrived in Bermuda later that month to work up, and on her return was assigned to EG W-7, WEF. She served with W-7, escorting local convoys, until November, 1944, when she was transferred to EG C-2, St. John's, taking her first convoy, HX.323, eastward early in December. On May 27, 1945, she began a refit at Halifax and soon after its completion, on June 25, was paid off and laid up at Sorel. She was sold into mercantile service in 1948 as *Balboa*, but acquired by the Israeli Navy in 1950 and reconverted to a warship. Renamed *Haganah*, she served until broken up in 1956.

NORTH BAY

Commissioned on October 25, 1943, at Collingwood, *North Bay* arrived at Halifax on November 29, and in December carried out workups in St. Margaret's Bay. On completion of these she was assigned to EG 9, Londonderry, making her passage there as escort to convoy SC.154 early in March, 1944. When EG 9 became a frigates-only group, *North Bay* returned to St. John's in April and became a member of EG C-4. From December 11 to mid-February, 1945, she underwent a refit at Sydney and proceeded to Bermuda to work up. On completing this exercise she sailed directly to St. John's to join EG C-2, but later in April she was transferred to C-3 and, on April 30, left St. John's to join convoy SC.174 for a final trip to Londonderry. She returned in May with ON.304 and was paid off on July 1 and laid up at Sorel. In 1946 she was sold for mercantile use, becoming the Bahamian-registered *Kent County II*.

North Bay at Montreal, November, 1943

OWEN SOUND

Commissioned at Collingwood on November 17, 1943, *Owen Sound* arrived at Halifax on December 13, worked up in St. Margaret's Bay in January, 1944, and in February was assigned to EG 9, Londonderry. On March 10, while acting as escort to convoy SC.157, she assisted HMCS *St. Laurent* and HMS *Forester* in the destruction of *U 845*. In May she transferred to EG C-2 at Londonderry and, in October, to newly formed C-7. She left 'Derry February 6, 1945 for her last westward trip, as escort to ON.283 and, on arrival at Halifax, commenced refit. On completion of the refit in mid-May she sailed for Bermuda for three weeks' working up and on her return was paid off on July 19 and placed in reserve at Sorel. Later that year she was sold to the United Ship Corp. of New York, to become the Greek-flag merchant ship *Cadio*, last appearing in Lloyd's list for 1967-68.

RIVIÈRE du LOUP

Commissioned at Quebec City on November 21, 1943, she arrived at Halifax on December 18 requiring a month's repairs. She carried out working-up exercises in Bermuda early in February, returning on February 18 to complete the exercises in St. Margaret's Bay. Continuing mechanical problems necessitated further repairs, which continued at Halifax until early in August. Having lost most of her original crew during this period, she had to return to Bermuda to work up again. Early in September, 1944, *Rivière du Loup* returned to Halifax and joined EG W-3, WEF. In October she was assigned to EG C-3 and left St. John's on November 13 to pick up her first transatlantic convoy, HX.319. On arrival in the U.K., still dogged by troubles, she underwent a month's repairs at Belfast. Her career as a mid-ocean escort ended with her arrival at Halifax late in May, 1945, from convoy ON.304, and she was paid off on July 2 and placed in reserve at Sorel. In 1947 she was sold to the Dominican Navy and renamed *Juan Bautista Maggiolo*. She was broken up in 1972.

Owen Sound, 1945

Rivière du Loup, November 1, 1944

St. Lambert

ST. LAMBERT

Commissioned at Quebec City on May 27, 1944, she arrived at Halifax on June 19 and in July sailed for Bermuda to work up. On her return in mid-August *St. Lambert* was assigned to EG C-6, Londonderry, and left St. John's September 18 to join convoy HXF.308 for her passage there. She served on North Atlantic convoys for the rest of her career, leaving St. John's on May 27, 1945, as escort to HX.358, the last HX convoy of the war. In mid-June she sailed from Londonderry on her final trip homeward and was paid off on July 20 and laid up at Sorel for disposal. Sold in 1946 for conversion to a merchant ship, she became the Panamanian *Chrysi Hondroulis* and, in 1955, the Greek-flag *Loula*, last noted in Lloyd's Register for 1957-58.

TRENTONIAN

Commissioned at Kingston on December 1, 1943, *Trentonian* arrived at Halifax late in December and, after further fitting-out at Liverpool, N.S., and Halifax, left the latter port for Bermuda on February 18, 1944, to work up. Returning at the beginning of March, she was assigned to Western Approaches Command and left for Londonderry on April 23 to join. For three months she carried out escort duty in connection with the invasion and on June 13, while escorting the cable vessel *St. Margaret* off Normandy, she was shelled in error by a U.S. destroyer. The shell, fortunately a dud, passed through her engine room and did little damage. Late in August she transferred to EG 41 (RN) and, based at different times at Plymouth and at Milford Haven, escorted Channel convoys. While so engaged on February 22, 1945, she was torpedoed and sunk near Falmouth by *U 1004*, with the loss of six lives.

WHITBY

Commissioned at Midland on June 6, 1944, she did not arrive at Halifax until August 16, owing to a layover en route at Shelburne for repairs. Following workups in Bermuda in September she sailed direct to St. John's, arriving on September 30, and was assigned to EG C-4. She left St. John's on October 5 for Londonderry to join the group, with which she was to serve for the balance of the war. *Whitby* left Londonderry for Canada in mid-June, 1945, and was paid off on July 16 and placed in reserve at Sorel. She was sold in 1946 for merchant service and reportedly renamed *Bengo*.

Trentonian, Bermuda, February, 1944

Whitby in Georgian Bay, 1944

**Revised Flower Class I.E.,
1943-1944 Programme**

ASBESTOS

Commissioned at Quebec City on June 16, 1944, she arrived at Halifax on July 9 and later that month proceeded to Bermuda to work up. *Asbestos* left Bermuda on August 21 for St. John's, where she joined EG C-2, and left on September 10 for HXF.307, her maiden convoy to Britain. For the rest of the war she was steadily employed as a North Atlantic escort and left Londonderry for the last time at the beginning of June, 1945. Paid off on July 8, she was laid up at Sorel for disposal. In 1947 she was sold to the Dominican Republic but was wrecked on the Cuban coast en route there. She was later salved and taken to New Orleans for scrapping.

BEAUHARNOIS

Commissioned at Quebec City on September 25, 1944, *Beauharnois* arrived at Halifax on October 20 and left for Bermuda on November 6 to work up. On November 30 she sailed from Bermuda for St. John's, where she joined EG C-4, leaving on December 9 to pick up her first convoy, HX.324. She was employed on North Atlantic convoys for the next few months, the last one being ONS.45, for which she left Londonderry on March 23, 1945. Among her last duties was acting as escort to the cable vessel *Lord Kelvin* off Cape Race in May. She was paid off on July 12 and laid up at Sorel. Sold for mercantile purposes in 1946, she was renamed *Colon*, but became a warship again in 1950, when she was acquired by the Israeli Navy and renamed *Wedgewood*. She was broken up in Israel in 1956.

BELLEVILLE

Commissioned at Kingston on October 19, 1944, she visited the Ontario port for which she was named before leaving for Halifax, where she arrived early in November. *Belleville* continued fitting out at Halifax until mid-January, then sailed to Bermuda for a month's working-up. Further repairs followed on her return, after which she was allocated to EG C-5, leaving St. John's on March 28 to join her first convoy, HX.346. She made three Atlantic crossings before the war's end, leaving Londonderry for the last time at the beginning of June, 1945. She was paid off on July 5, 1945, and placed in reserve at Sorel until 1947, when she was sold to the Dominican Republic and renamed *Juan Bautista Cambiaso*. She was broken up in 1972.

Asbestos, 1944

Beauharnois in the St. Lawrence, September 25, 1944

Belleville, October 23, 1944, on the occasion of a visit to her namesake city

LACHUTE

Commissioned at Quebec City on October 26, 1944, *Lachute* arrived at Halifax in mid-November and left for Bermuda on December 2 for three weeks' workups. Assigned on her return to EG C-5 at St. John's, she left there on January 5, 1945, to escort her first convoy, SC.164. She served the remainder of her career as a mid-ocean convoy escort, leaving Londonderry on May 26 to join ON.305, the last westbound convoy of the war. On July 10 she was paid off and placed in reserve at Sorel. In 1947 she was sold to the Dominican Republic and joined its navy as *Colon*. Deleted from the active list in 1978, she was driven ashore in a hurricane on August 31, 1979.

MERRITTONIA

She was named for Merritton, Ont., the modification having been suggested by the town council. Commissioned at Quebec City on November 10, 1944, she arrived at Halifax in mid-December and sailed to Bermuda for a month's workups. On her return *Merrittonia* was assigned to EG C-7 and left St. John's on February 7 to meet the group, which was westbound with convoy ON.283 from Britain. Thereafter continuously employed on North Atlantic convoy duty, she left Londonderry for the final time at the beginning of June, 1945. She was paid off on July 11 and laid up at Sorel for disposal. Purchased by K.C. Irving Ltd., Moncton, on November 16, 1945, she was wrecked on the Nova Scotia coast on November 30.

PARRY SOUND

Commissioned at Midland on August 30, 1944, *Parry Sound* arrived at Halifax late in September and left in October for three weeks' working-up in Bermuda. From Bermuda she sailed direct to St. John's, arriving on November 11, and was assigned to EG C-7. As the group was in Londonderry at the time, she sailed on November 17, in company with several U.S.-built Russian sub-chasers, to join. Her first convoy was ONS.39, which she picked up at the end of the year. She left St. John's on January 17, 1945, for convoy HX.332 but developed defects and had to turn back. It was mid-March before repairs were completed, and *Parry Sound* returned to convoy duty on April 7. She departed Londonderry for the last time early in June and was paid off at Sydney on July 10. Sold for conversion to a whale-killer, she entered service in 1950 as the Honduran-flag *Olympic Champion*. In 1956 she was sold to Japanese owners and renamed *Otori Maru No. 15*, last noted in Lloyd's list for 1962-63.

Lachute, March, 1945

Merrittonia, Bermuda, January, 1945

Parry Sound, Georgian Bay, 1944

PETERBOROUGH

Commissioned at Kingston on June 1, 1944, she arrived at Halifax on June 26 and in Bermuda on July 17 to work up. *Peterborough* left Bermuda on August 7 for St. John's, where, in September, she joined EG C-6 and sailed for her first convoy, HXF.308, on September 18. Continuously employed as a mid-ocean escort for the rest of her career, she left St. John's on May 27, 1945, to join convoy HX.358, the last HX convoy of the war. In mid-June she left Londonderry for home, where she was paid off on July 19 and laid up at Sorel. She was sold to the Dominican Republic in 1947 and renamed *Gerardo Jansen*, serving until disposed of for scrap in 1972.

SMITHS FALLS

Commissioned at Kingston on November 28, 1944, she was the last RCN corvette to enter service. She arrived at Halifax late in December and remained there fitting out until February 10, 1945, then proceeded to Bermuda for workups. On her return *Smiths Falls* was assigned to EG C-2, Londonderry, and made her passage there as escort to convoy SC.171 early in April, the first of three crossings before the end of hostilities. She left Londonderry early in June for the last time, and was paid off July 8 and placed in reserve at Sorel for disposal. Sold for conversion to a whale-killer, she entered service in 1950 as the Honduran-flag *Olympic Lightning*, but was sold to Japanese owners in 1956 and renamed *Otori Maru No. 16*. She last appeared in Lloyd's list for 1962-63.

STELLARTON

Commissioned at Quebec City on September 29, 1944, *Stellarton* arrived at Halifax late in October and sailed for Bermuda early in November to work up. She left Bermuda on December 4 for St. John's, where she joined EG C-3 and on January 4, 1945, sailed to pick up her first convoy, HX.329. She was employed for the rest of the war as a mid-ocean escort, and left Londonderry for the last time on May 21 to join ON.304. On July 1 she was paid off and placed in reserve at Sorel until 1946, when she joined the Chilean Navy as *Casma*. She was broken up in 1969.

Peterborough

Smiths Falls, February 1945

Stellarton, 1945

STRATHROY

Commissioned at Midland on November 20, 1944, *Strathroy* arrived at Halifax in December and immediately escorted her first convoy, HF.147, to Saint John, N.B. She arrived there on December 18 for completion of fitting-out that could not be done at the builder's prior to freeze-up. She then carried out workups in Bermuda, and on completing these joined Halifax Force in April, 1945, for local escort duties. On July 12 she was paid off and laid up at Sorel for disposal. Purchased in 1946 by the Chilean Navy and renamed *Chipana*, she was broken up in 1969.

THORLOCK

Thorlock was commissioned at Midland on November 13, 1944, and arrived at Halifax on December 16. On January 7, 1945, she left for Bermuda to work up, setting out on February 1 for the return journey northward. Later that month she was allocated to EG C-9 and on February 26 left Halifax to pick up her first convoy, SC.168. She served for the remainder of the war as an ocean escort, making five transatlantic trips. On May 12, 1945, when on the final leg of an Atlantic crossing with convoy ON.300 from the U.K., she was diverted, along with HMCS *Victoriaville*, to accept the surrender of *U 190* and escort the U-boat to Bay Bulls, Nfld. She was paid off on July 15, 1945, and placed in reserve at Sorel. Sold in 1946, she served in the Chilean Navy as *Papudo* until disposed of for scrap in 1967.

WEST YORK

Commissioned at Collingwood, Ont., on October 6, 1944, *West York* arrived at Halifax in mid-November and left a month later for Bermuda to work up. In February, 1945, she joined EG C-5 at St. John's, leaving February 16 to rendezvous with her maiden convoy, HX.338. She made three round trips across the Atlantic before the end of her career, the last one as escort to ON.305, which she joined from Londonderry at the end of May, 1945. Paid off on July 9, and laid up at Sorel, she was sold later that year for commercial use. As SS *West York*, she was towing the decommissioned HMCS *Assiniboine* when the towline parted and the destroyer was wrecked on Prince Edward Island, November 7, 1945. The former *West York* sailed under a variety of names and flags, returning to Canadian registry in 1960 as *Federal Express*. She sank at Montreal on May 5, 1960, after being in collision, and her after section was raised and broken up later that year.

Strathroy, Bermuda, March, 1945

Thorlock, Bermuda, January, 1945

West York, May, 1945

Revised Flower Class I.E., ex-RN

FOREST HILL

Named for a village absorbed by Toronto, *Forest Hill* was laid down as HMS *Ceanothus* but was transferred to the RCN and commissioned on December 1, 1943 on the Clyde, Scotland. Following workups at Tobermory she joined EG C-3 at Londonderry, leaving on January 29, 1944, to join her first convoy, ONS.28. She served as an ocean escort until late in December, when she arrived at Liverpool, N.S., for an extended refit, on the completion of which, two months later, she sailed for Bermuda to work up. Returning in April, 1945, she joined Halifax Force for local duties. Paid off on July 9 and laid up at Sorel, she was broken up at Hamilton in 1948.

GIFFARD

Named for a Quebec village, she was originally laid down as HMS *Buddleia* but was transferred to the RCN and commissioned on November 10, 1943, at Aberdeen. After working-up at Tobermory *Giffard* joined EG C-1 at Londonderry and on February 15, 1944, sailed to join her first convoy, ON.224. On May 7 she rescued 49 survivors of the torpedoed *Valleyfield*, and the following week resumed her duties as an ocean escort until November 27, when she left Halifax for Liverpool, N.S., to undergo a major refit. Completed in March, 1945, this was followed by workups in Bermuda, when she arrived in St. John's on April 15, to be employed locally until her departure on May 13 with convoy HX.355 for the U.K. *Giffard* left Greenock early in June on her final westward voyage, was paid off on July 5 and laid up at Sorel to await disposal. She was broken up in 1952 in Hamilton.

LONG BRANCH

Named for a village absorbed by Toronto, she was originally laid down as HMS *Candytuft* but was transferred to the RCN and commissioned on the Clyde on January 5, 1944. In April, following a month's workups at Tobermory, *Long Branch* joined EG C-5 at Londonderry, and sailed to pick up her maiden convoy, ONS.233. She developed mechanical defects on the crossing and was under repair at St. John's for six weeks. She left St. John's June 14 to resume her duties, but returned from her next westbound convoy with the assistance of HM tug *Tenacity*. Repaired, she left St. John's a week later to join HXS.300, the largest convoy of the war, and continued as an ocean escort until her final departure from 'Derry on January 27, 1945. Arriving at Halifax on February 11, she commenced a refit on completion of which, in April, she was assigned to Halifax Force for local duties. On June 17 she was paid off at Sorel for disposal. Sold for commercial use in 1947, she was renamed *Rexton Kent II* (later dropping the "II") and finally scuttled off the east coast in 1966.

Forest Hill, 1943

Giffard

Long Branch, December, 1944

Mimico, 1944

MIMICO

Named after a town now part of Toronto, *Mimico* was laid down as HMS *Bulrush* but was transferred to the RCN and commissioned on February 8, 1944 at Sunderland, U.K. On April 18, after working up at Stornoway, she arrived at Oban, Scotland, where she was assigned to Western Approaches Command for escort duty in connection with the invasion. She arrived off the Normandy beaches with a convoy on the day after D-Day. She remained on escort duty in the Channel, assigned briefly in September to Portsmouth Command and, in October, to Nore Command, based at Sheerness. In February and March, 1945, she refitted at Chatham, then returned to Sheerness and resumed her previous role until late in May, when she left the U.K. for the last time. She was paid off on July 18, 1945, and laid up at Sorel. Sold for use as a whale-killer, she entered service in 1950 as *Olympic Victor* but passed into Japanese hands in 1956 and was renamed *Otori Maru No. 12*. She was last noted in Lloyd's Register for 1962-63.

Castle Class

ARNPRIOR

Laid down as HMS *Rising Castle*, she was transferred to the RCN and commissioned at Belfast on June 8, 1944. After working up at Tobermory she joined EG C-1 at Londonderry in August, leaving on August 19 to join her first convoy, ONM.249. *Arnprior* was continuously employed as an ocean escort for the balance of the war. At the beginning of June, 1945, she left Greenock for St. John's, where she underwent a two-month refit, and from September was based at Halifax. She was paid off there on March 14, 1946, and sold later that year to the Uruguayan Navy, which renamed her *Montevideo* and operated her as a training ship until 1975.

BOWMANVILLE

Laid down as HMS *Nunney Castle*, she was transferred to the RCN and commissioned at Sunderland, U.K., on September 28, 1944. Following workups at Tobermory *Bowmanville* joined EG C-4 at Londonderry, sailing on November 24 to join her first convoy, ON.268. She served continuously as an ocean escort for the rest of the war. Early in June, 1945, she left Londonderry for the last time, and was based at Halifax until paid off on February 15, 1946. She was sold into mercantile service in 1947 under the Chinese flag and first renamed *Ta Shun*, then *Yuan Pei*. In 1949 she was taken over by the Chinese Communist government, rearmed and renamed *Kuang Chou*.

Arnprior, 1944

Bowmanville, October, 1944, fitted with Type 277 radar

COPPER CLIFF

Laid down as HMS *Hever Castle*, she was
transferred to the RCN and commissioned at
Blyth, U.K., on July 25, 1944. After working up
at Tobermory in August she was assigned to EG
C-6 but in fact joined EG C-7 then forming at
Londonderry, in October. She left Londonderry
to pick up her first convoy, ONS.266, on
November 16, and was thereafter continuously
employed as an ocean escort. *Copper Cliff* left
Londonderry for her final westward crossing
early in June, 1945, and later that month sailed
from Halifax for Esquimalt. There, on November
21, she was paid off into reserve. In 1946 she
became the Chinese-flag merchant ship *Ta Lung*,
soon afterward renamed *Wan Lee*, and was
taken over by the Chinese Communist government in 1949.

HESPELER

Laid down as HMS *Guildford Castle*, she was
transferred to the RCN and commissioned on
February 28, 1944 at Leith. Following workups
at Tobermory she arrived at Londonderry in
April to become a member of EG C-5. *Hespeler*
sailed on April 21 to meet her first convoy,
ONS.233, and for the next 11 months was
employed as an ocean escort. On July 23, 1944,
she left St. John's with EG C-5 to escort the
largest convoy of the war, HXS.300, and on
September 9, while temporarily on patrol duty
south of the Hebrides, she sank *U 484* in
co-operation with *Dunver*. She left 'Derry for the
last time on March 8, 1945, to escort ON.289
westward, and upon arriving at Halifax began a
refit, completing it at Liverpool, N.S., in July.
She then sailed for the west coast and on
November 15 was paid off into reserve at
Esquimalt. Sold in 1946 to the Union Steamship
Co., Vancouver, she was converted to a coastal
passenger ship, SS *Chilcotin*. In 1958 she became
the Liberian-flag *Stella Maris* and in 1965, the
Greek *Westar*. Sold later that year to a Canadian
buyer, she was gutted by fire on January 28,
1966, in the Mediterranean and broken up at La
Spezia, Italy.

HUMBERSTONE

Laid down as HMS *Norham Castle*, she was
transferred to the RCN and commissioned at
Glasgow on September 6, 1944. After working
up at Tobermory she arrived in October at
Londonderry to join EG C-8, then forming. She
left 'Derry October 22 to join convoy ON.261
for her first Atlantic crossing and continued in
service as an ocean escort for the remainder of
the war. *Humberstone* left Londonderry May 12,
1945, for her last convoy, ONS.50, and in June
sailed to Esquimalt, where she was paid off on
November 17. She was sold to Chinese owners
in 1946 and converted for merchant service as
Taiwei, subsequently undergoing five more
name-changes before becoming the Korean
South Ocean in 1954. She was broken up at
Hong Kong in 1959.

Copper Cliff, 1944

Hespeler, 1944

Humberstone

Huntsville

Kincardine, 1944

Leaside, June, 1945

HUNTSVILLE

Laid down as HMS *Woolvesey Castle*, she was transferred to the RCN and commissioned on June 6, 1944, on the Clyde. She worked up at Stornoway early in July and joined EG C-5 at Londonderry later that month, leaving on August 11 for ONS.248, her first convoy. In November *Huntsville* missed a convoy while under repair at Halifax and acted as local escort to one convoy from St. John's to New York — seemingly the only ship of her class to visit there. Rejoining the Atlantic convoy cycle in December, she left Londonderry for the last time on April 16, 1945, to meet ON.297. In May she commenced refit at Halifax, completed in August, and in September was placed in reserve. She was paid off for disposal on February 15, 1946, and sold that year, entering service in 1947 as SS *Wellington Kent*. Renamed *Belle Isle II* in 1951, she was sunk in collision off Trois-Rivières on August 19, 1960.

KINCARDINE

Laid down as HMS *Tamworth Castle*, she was transferred to the RCN and commissioned at Middlesbrough on June 19, 1944. After working up at Tobermory and Stornoway she arrived at Londonderry late in August to join EG C-2 but had to return to her builder's for repairs. Returning to Londonderry in mid-September, she remained on local duties until October 2, when she left to join ON.257, her first convoy. *Kincardine* served as an ocean escort for the remainder of the war, leaving 'Derry for the last time at the beginning of June, 1945. Briefly allocated to HMCS Cornwallis for training in July, she then underwent a minor refit at Liverpool, N.S. Placed in maintenance reserve at Halifax in October, she was paid off there on February 27, 1946. Later that year she was sold to the French government and resold in 1947 to Moroccan interests, to be renamed *Saada*.

LEASIDE

Laid down as HMS *Walmer Castle*, she was transferred to the RCN and commissioned on August 21, 1944, at Middlesbrough. Following workups at Tobermory in September *Leaside* arrived at Londonderry early in October to join EG C-8, then forming. She sailed on October 22 to meet ON.261, her first convoy, and served the rest of the war as an ocean escort. On May 11, 1945, she made her last departure from 'Derry to join ONS.50. She left St. John's in June for Esquimalt, where she was paid off for disposal on November 16. Sold in 1946 to the Union Steamship Co., Vancouver, she was converted to a coastal passenger vessel and renamed *Coquitlam*. In 1950 she was renamed *Glacier Queen* and in 1970 stripped in anticipation of becoming a floating restaurant. The hulk sank in Cook Inlet, Alaska, on November 8, 1978, but was raised, towed to sea and scuttled in January, 1979.

ORANGEVILLE

Laid down as HMS *Hedingham Castle*, she was transferred to the RCN and commissioned at Leith on April 24, 1944. After working up at Tobermory in May she joined EG C-1 at Londonderry, leaving on June 4 to meet ONS.239, her first convoy. She spent the remainder of the war on North Atlantic convoy duty, leaving 'Derry for the last time on April 21, 1945, to escort ONS.48. After refitting at Liverpool, N.S., from May to August, *Orangeville* was placed in maintenance reserve at Halifax and finally paid off on April 12, 1946. She was sold later that year for conversion to mercantile use under the Chinese flag and renamed *Ta Tung*. In 1951 she was taken over by the Nationalist Chinese government, rearmed and renamed *Te-An*.

PETROLIA

Laid down as HMS *Sherborne Castle*, she was transferred to the RCN and commissioned on June 29, 1944, at Belfast. Following workups at Tobermory, she joined EG C-4 at Londonderry in August, leaving on September 2 for her first convoy, ONS.251. An ocean escort for the rest of the war, she left Londonderry for the last time early in June, 1945. In August *Petrolia* underwent a refit at Charlottetown and was placed in maintenance reserve at Halifax in October. Paid off at Liverpool, N.S., on March 8, 1946, she was sold not long afterward to a New York buyer and renamed *Maid of Athens*. In 1947 she was transferred to Indian registry and renamed *Bharat Laxmi*, serving as such until broken up at Bombay in 1965.

ST. THOMAS

Laid down as HMS *Sandgate Castle*, she was transferred to the RCN and commissioned at Middlesbrough on May 4, 1944. In June *St. Thomas* carried out workups at Tobermory, leaving later that month for Londonderry where, in July, she became part of EG C-3. She sailed on August 3 to join ONF.247, her first convoy, and was employed as an ocean escort for the rest of the war. On December 27, 1944, while escorting HX.327, she sank *U 877* in the North Atlantic. She left Londonderry for the last time on April 11, 1945, commencing refit on arrival at Halifax April 30. Following completion of the refit in July she sailed for the west coast and was paid off at Esquimalt on November 22. In 1946 she was sold to the Union Steamship Co., Vancouver, converted to a coastal passenger vessel, and renamed *Camosun*. She was renamed *Chilcotin* in 1958 and, later that year, *Yukon Star*. After several years of idleness, she was broken up at Tacoma in 1974.

Orangeville, 1944

Petrolia in St. John's narrows, June, 1945

St. Thomas

Tillsonburg, 1944

TILLSONBURG

Laid down as HMS *Pembroke Castle*, she was transferred to the RCN and commissioned on the Clyde on June 29, 1944. Following working-up at Stornoway *Tillsonburg* arrived at Londonderry on August 19, sailing a week later for St. John's to join EG C-6, then forming. Unlike her sisters, therefore, she first escorted an eastbound convoy, HXF.308, leaving St. John's on September 18 to join it. An ocean escort for the balance of the war, she left Londonderry for her last crossing in mid-June, 1945. Briefly based at St. John's, Sydney, and Halifax, she was paid off at Halifax on February 15, 1946, and later that year was sold to Chinese owners for mercantile service. Initially named *Ta Ching*, she was renamed *Chiu Chin* in 1947. In 1951 she was taken over by the Nationalist Chinese government, rearmed and renamed *Kao-An*.

A/S Trawlers

Western Isles Class

Sixteen anti-submarine trawlers of the Isles class were built in Canada for the RN, which lent eight of them to the RCN for the duration of the war, as escorts for coastal convoys were in short supply at the time of their completion in 1942. They were not, however, commissioned in the RCN, and were manned by RN crews. These ships were given names of Canadian islands and therefore known as the Western Isles class.

Anticosti

ANTICOSTI

Commissioned at Collingwood on August 10, 1942, *Anticosti* arrived at Halifax on September 7 and was assigned to Saint John, N.B. Force. Except for a few months' service with Sydney Force during the first half of 1944, she operated out of Saint John until the end of the war. Boiler defects kept her out of service between May 11 and July 21, 1943, and she underwent a long refit at Louisbourg from July to October, 1944, on completion of which she went to Bermuda to work up. The ship was returned to the RN on June 17, 1945, at Plymouth, was sold the following year to Norwegian owners and renamed *Gulöy*. Renamed twice subsequently, she still existed as late as 1968 as the Ethiopian-flag *Giuseppina*.

BAFFIN

Commissioned at Collingwood on August 26, 1942, she arrived at Halifax on October 2 but was under repair with a defective crankshaft until mid-January, 1943. After working up she was temporarily assigned to Halifax Local Defence Force, then to Sydney Force, with which she remained until VE-Day. She underwent a refit at Louisbourg from March to April, 1944, after which she worked up in Bermuda during the first three weeks of May. *Baffin* was returned to the RN on the Clyde, August 20, 1945, and in 1947 sold for conversion to a cargo vessel. She retained her original name until 1952 when she became the German *Niedermehnen*, and last appeared in Lloyd's Register for 1965-66.

Baffin, April 15, 1944

CAILIFF

Commissioned at Collingwood on September 17, 1942, *Cailiff* appears to have been named for New Brunswick's Cailiff Rocks. She arrived at Halifax on November 7, escorting a Quebec-Sydney convoy en route. Allocated initially to Halifax Local Defence Force, she was transferred to Newfoundland Force in December, 1943, and remained a member of this force until the end of the war. She then sailed for the U.K., where she was returned to the RN on June 10, 1945. Sold for mercantile use in 1947, she is still in service as the Norwegian *Borgenes*.

IRONBOUND

Named for an island off La Have, N.S., *Ironbound* was commissioned at Kingston on October 16, 1942. She arrived at Halifax on November 23, having escorted a Quebec-Sydney convoy on passage. Late in February, 1943, she was assigned to Halifax Local Defence Force and served with it until May, 1945. Returned to the RN at Plymouth on June 17, 1945, she was sold for mercantile use, and in 1948 hoisted the Norwegian flag as *Turöy*. In 1954 she was sold to Finnish owners and renamed *Korsö*. She became a belated casualty of the war on November 5, 1957, when she was sunk by a drifting mine west of Cape Mondego, Portugal.

LISCOMB

Named for an island off the Nova Scotia coast, *Liscomb* was commissioned on September 8, 1942, at Kingston. She arrived at Halifax October 20, and was assigned to Halifax Local Defence Force. In February, 1944, she was transferred to Sydney Force, remaining in its service until the end of the war except for two months' absence from mid-October to mid-December, 1944, when she went to Bermuda to work up. Returned to the RN at Plymouth on June 17, 1945, *Liscomb* was sold in 1946 to Norwegian owners and renamed *Aalesund*. She was last noted in Lloyd's list for 1968-69.

Cailiff

Ironbound, 1944

Liscomb

Magdalen

MAGDALEN

Commissioned at Midland, Ont., on August 24, 1942, she arrived at Sydney on October 9 and proceeded to Pictou for workups, arriving at Halifax on November 13. With the exception of the period from February to June, 1944, when she served with Sydney Force, *Magdalen* spent her wartime career as a member of the Saint John, N.B. Force. She was returned to the RN at Plymouth on June 17, 1945, and in 1946 became the Norwegian-flag *Maröy*. Though she became the Italian-owned *Cinzia* in 1951, and disappeared as such from Lloyd's Register after 1958, she has been reported wrecked near Marsala, Sicily, on December 10, 1961, under the name *Sabina*.

MANITOULIN

Commissioned at Midland on September 27, 1942, *Manitoulin* arrived at Halifax on November 30, and was assigned briefly to Sydney Force in February, based at Port-aux-Basques, Nfld., but on April 4 arrived at Halifax to join Halifax Local Defence Force. She was returned to the RN at Plymouth on June 17, 1945, and sold to a Norwegian buyer who renamed her *Ran* in 1947. She was last noted in Lloyd's list for 1964-65 as the Canadian-registered *Blue Peter II*.

MISCOU

Named for an island in the Gulf of St. Lawrence, she was commissioned at Collingwood on October 17, 1942, as *Bowell* but renamed on November 5 at Montreal. She arrived at Halifax on November 24, and in February, 1943, was assigned to Sydney Force. Except for the period between February and July, 1944, when she was detached to Saint John, N.B. Force, *Miscou* remained with Sydney Force for the duration of the war. She underwent an extended refit at Liverpool, N.S., between early February and the end of May, 1944, then worked up in Bermuda in June. She was returned to the RN at Plymouth on June 17, 1945, and entered merchant service in 1948 as the Norwegian *Cleveland*. Renamed *Sigurd Hund* in 1950, she last appears in Lloyd's Register for 1964-65.

Manitoulin, 1942

Miscou

Minesweepers

The RCN had four minesweepers in 1939, Canadian-built copies of the RN's Basset class, and consideration was being given to building more of these when the Naval Staff learned of the RN's newer Bangor class. The Bangor was larger and faster, had much greater endurance, and burned oil unlike the coal-burning Bassets. Accordingly, 28 Bangors were ordered in 1940 and 20 more under subsequent programmes. Another six, built at Vancouver for the RN, were lent to the RCN for the duration of the war. Ten Bangors of the first programme were of a smaller, diesel-engined variety and one of these, *Granby*, survived until 1966. Most of the Bangors were named after Canadian towns and cities, the rest after bays.

Like the corvettes, the Bangors were small enough to be produced at shipyards on the Great Lakes, and 16 were built at Toronto and Port Arthur. The Toronto yard turned out six others of the class for the RN.

As enemy mines were laid only once (1943) in Canadian waters, the Bangors were used principally as escorts to coastal shipping or as local escorts to ocean convoys. Sixteen of them, however, assisted in sweeping the approaches to Normandy before D-Day, and stayed to help clear German and Allied minefields in the Channel for some months afterward.

The Bangors were bluff-bowed ships, very wet in a head sea, and arguably less comfortable even than corvettes in rough weather. These faults were eliminated in the Algerine class, all 12 RCN units of which were built at Port Arthur.

They were intended by the RCN as convoy escorts, hence not fitted with minesweeping gear. Although they were larger than corvettes, the latter outperformed them as ocean escorts, the Algerines finding particular favour as Senior Officers' ships in Western Local groups. Most found employment for many years after the war on hydrographic survey duties or as training ships for reservists. Forty-one of this class were built at Toronto, and 11 at Port Arthur, for the RN.

Two classes of wooden-hulled ships were built in Canada for magnetic minesweeping, the Llewellyn and Lake classes. None of the latter class had been commissioned by VJ-Day, and the ten most nearly complete were turned over to the USSR.

Bangor Class, 1939-1940 Programme

BELLECHASSE

Named for a county in Quebec, *Bellechasse* was built at Vancouver and commissioned there December 13, 1941. She spent her entire career on the west coast, alternating between Prince Rupert Force and Esquimalt Force. Paid off on October 23, 1945, at Esquimalt, she was sold the following year to the Union Steamship Co., Vancouver, but her intended conversion for mercantile service was not carried out.

BURLINGTON

Burlington was commissioned at Toronto on September 6, 1941, and arrived at Halifax on September 30. After working up, she made Halifax her base, and in March, 1942, was assigned to WLEF, transferring in May to Gulf Escort Force. Late in December she commenced refitting progressively at Halifax, Lunenburg, and Dartmouth. Following completion of the work in May, 1943, she worked up at Pictou and was assigned in June to EG W-9 of WLEF. In February, 1944, she was transferred to Halifax Local Defence Force, and in September sent to Bermuda for a month's workup. On her return she joined Newfoundland Force, based at St. John's, and served there until June 8, 1945, when the Command was disbanded. She then engaged in miscellaneous duties until paid off on October 30, 1945, and was sold to a New Jersey buyer in 1946.

Bellechasse, November 30, 1944

Burlington, July, 1942

Chedabucto, 1941

Chignecto, July 19, 1944

Clayoquot, July, 1943

CHEDABUCTO

Built at Vancouver and commissioned there on September 27, 1941, *Chedabucto* left Esquimalt for the Atlantic on November 11, arriving at Halifax on December 17. On April 10, 1942, she sank the British SS *Trongate*, afire at Halifax with a cargo of explosives. Assigned briefly to WLEF, she transferred in June, 1942 to Gulf Escort Force, escorting convoys between Quebec City and Sydney. In September, 1942, she was assigned to Sydney Force and then, in January, 1943, reassigned to WLEF. Soon afterward she underwent a lengthy refit at Lunenburg and Halifax, on completion of which in June, 1943, she worked up at Pictou and was allocated to Gaspé Force. On October 21, 1943, *Chedabucto* was involved in a night collision with the cable vessel *Lord Kelvin*, and sank 30 miles from Rimouski with the loss of one officer.

CHIGNECTO

Commissioned at Vancouver on October 31, 1941, *Chignecto* spent her whole career on the west coast, alternating between Esquimalt Force and Prince Rupert Force. She was paid off on November 3, 1945, at Esquimalt and sold in 1946 to the Union Steamship Co., Vancouver, for conversion to a coastal merchant ship. The conversion was not proceeded with, and she has proved impossible to trace beyond 1951, when an offer to purchase her was received from a San Francisco firm.

CLAYOQUOT

Named after Clayoquot Sound, Vancouver Island, she was commissioned at Prince Rupert on August 22, 1941. After working up, she left Esquimalt on October 10 for Halifax, arriving November 14. Initially assigned to Halifax Local Defence Force, she was transferred in March, 1942, to WLEF and in May to Gulf Escort Force. While serving with Gulf Escort Force she rescued 55 survivors of HMCS *Charlottetown*, torpedoed and sunk near Cap Chat on September 11, 1942. In October *Clayoquot* joined Sydney Force. She arrived at Halifax on December 29 for a major refit, which was progressively carried out there and at Liverpool and Pictou, N.S. Completing her refit in May, 1943, she rejoined Sydney Force in July after working up. In January, 1944, she was transferred to HMCS Cornwallis for officers' training in A/S warfare, and in October was reassigned to Halifax Force. On December 24, while taking station on convoy XB.139, she was torpedoed and sunk three miles from Sambro Light Vessel by *U 806*, losing eight of her crew.

COWICHAN

Commissioned at Vancouver on July 4, 1941, she sailed from Esquimalt for Halifax on August 6, arriving on September 10. After working up in Bermuda she was initially assigned to Halifax Local Defence Force, but was transferred in January, 1942, to Newfoundland Force and in September to WLEF. With WLEF's division into escort groups in June, 1943, *Cowichan* became a member of EG W-6. She remained with the group until February, 1944, when she was ordered to the U.K. for invasion duties. She left Halifax on February 19 with *Caraquet, Malpeque* and *Vegreville* via the Azores for Plymouth, arriving on March 13. Assigned to the 31st Minesweeping Flotilla, she was present on D-Day. *Cowichan* returned to Canada for refit late in February, 1945, but resumed her duties overseas in June. Proceeding home in September, she was paid off on October 9, 1945, and placed in reserve at Shelburne. Sold in 1946 to a New York buyer and converted for mercantile purposes under Greek flag, she still existed in 1956 under her original name.

GEORGIAN

Commissioned at Toronto on September 23, 1941, *Georgian* arrived at Halifax on October 13. On completing workups she was assigned to Sydney Force, but in January, 1942, she joined Newfoundland Force and remained with it until February, 1944. Through a tragic error on June 12, 1942, she rammed and sank the British submarine *P.514* off Newfoundland. Nominated for duties in connection with the invasion of Europe, she left Halifax on February 18, 1944, with *Bayfield, Mulgrave* and *Thunder* for Plymouth via the Azores, arriving on March 7. Assigned to a series of minesweeping flotillas, particularly the 14th, she was present on D-Day. She returned to Canada in January, 1945, for refit at Lunenburg, N.S., then returned to the U.K. for service with the 31st Flotilla in April. That fall she sailed again for Canada, where she was paid off at Sydney on October 23 and laid up at Shelburne until sold for scrap.

MAHONE

Commissioned at Vancouver on September 29, 1941, she left Esquimalt on November 11 for Halifax, where upon her arrival on December 17, she was assigned to WLEF. Between May, 1942 and January, 1943, she served with Halifax Force, then underwent a major refit at Liverpool, N.S., from January 19 to April 3. She was then transferred to Gaspé Force because of U-boat activity in the St. Lawrence, but returned to Halifax Force in November, 1943, and soon afterward went to Sydney Force. On January 29, 1944, she was rammed by SS *Fort Townshend* off Louisbourg, N.S., and after temporary repairs was sent to Halifax for further repair work which lasted four months. Early in July she proceeded to Bermuda to work up, returning to Halifax a month later. *Mahone* was paid off at Halifax on November 6, 1945, and laid up at Shelburne. In 1946 she was placed in strategic reserve at Sorel until 1951, when she was reacquired by the RCN, which kept her in reserve at Sydney until March 29, 1958. That day marked her transfer to the Turkish Navy as *Beylerbeyi*, and she remained in service until discarded in 1972.

Cowichan, July 11, 1941

Georgian, March, 1944

Mahone, 1944

Malpeque, February 25, 1944

MALPEQUE

Commissioned at Vancouver on August 4, 1941, *Malpeque* left for Halifax on September 13, arriving on October 19. She was briefly assigned to Sydney Force, then to Newfoundland Force, with which she served until February 19, 1944, when, with *Caraquet*, *Cowichan* and *Vegreville*, she sailed for the U.K. via the Azores for invasion duties. Arriving at Plymouth on March 13, she was assigned to the 31st Minesweeping Flotilla, and was present on D-Day. She proceeded to Canada in April, 1945, for refit at Liverpool, N.S., but returned to the U.K. in June and remained there until September. She then returned home and was paid off on October 9, 1945, to reserve at Shelburne. Taken to Sorel in 1946 and placed in strategic reserve, she was reacquired by the RCN in 1952 and laid up at Sydney. Never recommissioned, she was sold for scrap in February, 1959.

MINAS

Named for Minas Basin in the Bay of Fundy, she was built at Vancouver and commissioned there August 2, 1941. She sailed for Halifax on September 13, arriving on October 19. After brief service with Sydney Force, she was assigned in January, 1942, to Newfoundland Force. That November she transferred to WLEF, and when WLEF was divided into escort groups in June, 1943, she became a member of EG W-7. That December she was reassigned to W-4. On February 1, 1943, she collided with HMS *Liscomb* outside Halifax, necessitating a month's repairs. *Minas* left Halifax for the U.K. on February 20, 1944, with *Blairmore*, *Fort William* and *Milltown*, via the Azores. On arrival in the U.K. on March 8, she was assigned to the 31st Minesweeping Flotilla for invasion duties, and was on hand on D-Day. In September she proceeded to Canada to refit at Dartmouth, N.S., returning to Plymouth in January, 1945. There she rejoined the 31st Flotilla until she sailed again for Canada on September 4. She was paid off into reserve at Shelburne on October 6, 1945, and later moved to Sorel, but was reacquired by the RCN in 1952 and recommissioned on March 15, 1955 for training on the west coast. Paid off on November 7, 1955, she was sold in August, 1958, and broken up at Seattle the following year.

Minas, March, 1944

MIRAMICHI

Commissioned at Vancouver on November 26, 1941, *Miramichi* spent her entire service career on the west coast, alternating between Esquimalt Force and Prince Rupert Force. In the summer and fall of 1943, while serving with Esquimalt Force, she was used occasionally for training purposes. She was paid off at Esquimalt on October 24, 1945, and is thought to have been broken up at Vancouver in 1949, having been purchased in 1946 by the Union Steamship Co. for conversion that was never proceeded with.

Miramichi, June 22, 1944

NIPIGON

Commissioned at Toronto on August 11, 1941, *Nipigon* arrived at Halifax on September 5. She was the first of the Bangor class to join Sydney Force, on October 3, and remained with it until her return to Halifax on January 17, 1942. She was then assigned for varying periods to WLEF, Halifax Force, and Newfoundland Force. She was again attached to WLEF when, in June, 1943, that force was divided into escort groups, and she became a member of EG W-1. Early in 1944 she underwent a major refit at Lunenburg and Liverpool, N.S., on completion of which she sailed in May to work up in Bermuda. Returning in mid-June, she was assigned to Halifax Force until it was disbanded a year later, afterward performing various duties on the Atlantic coast. *Nipigon* was paid off at Sydney on October 13, 1945, and laid up at Shelburne. She was placed in strategic reserve at Sorel in 1946 but was reacquired and refitted in 1952, though not again commissioned. Transferred to the Turkish Navy on November 29, 1957, she served as *Bafra* until 1972.

OUTARDE

Named for Outarde Bay, Que., she was commissioned at Vancouver on December 4, 1941. *Outarde* spent her whole career on the west coast, alternately serving with the Prince Rupert and Esquimalt Forces. She was paid off November 24, 1945, at Esquimalt, sold in 1946 for conversion to a merchant ship, and renamed *Ping Hsin* by her Shanghai owners. She vanished from Lloyd's Register after 1950.

QUATSINO

Named for Quatsino Sound, Vancouver Island, she was built at Prince Rupert and commissioned on November 3, 1941. *Quatsino* spent her entire service life on the west coast, alternately a member of the Prince Rupert and Esquimalt Forces. She was paid off at Esquimalt on November 26, 1945, and converted for commercial purposes in 1947, to be renamed *Chen Hsin* and domiciled at Shanghai. She vanished from Lloyd's Register after 1950.

Nipigon

Outarde, September 3 1942

Quatsino, April 28, 1944. The "jigsaw" camouflage was peculiar to west-coast Bangors.

QUINTE

Commissioned at Vancouver on August 30, 1941, *Quinte* left Esquimalt October 10 for Halifax, arriving on November 14. She was assigned at first to WLEF, and then, in June, 1942, to Halifax Force. On November 30, 1942, after completing a six-week refit at Lunenburg, she ran aground at the entrance to St. Peter's Canal, Cape Breton, causing extensive damage to her bottom, and had to be beached. Salvage work continued throughout most of the winter, and on April 25, 1943, she arrived at Pictou in tow for repairs, which were not completed until June, 1944. She was then sent to HMCS Cornwallis as a training ship, arriving at Digby on August 21, and remained there until the end of 1945. In 1946 she was employed with the Naval Research Establishment at Halifax until paid off on October 25. *Quinte* was broken up at Sydney in 1947.

THUNDER

Commissioned at Toronto on October 14, 1941, *Thunder* arrived at Halifax October 30. After working up, she joined Sydney Force, but in January, 1942, was transferred to WLEF and subsequently to Halifax Local Defence Force, Shelburne Force, Halifax Force, and back to Sydney Force. She sailed with *Bayfield, Georgian* and *Mulgrave* from Halifax on February 18, 1944, for Plymouth via the Azores. Arriving on March 13, she was allocated to the 32nd Minesweeping Flotilla as Senior Officer's ship but was later transferred to the 4th Flotilla, and was present on D-Day. *Thunder* returned to Canada in August, 1944, to refit at Sydney but was back at Plymouth in late November, assigned to the 31st Flotilla. In May, 1945, in the Bay of Biscay, she accepted the surrender of the German auxiliary minesweeper FGi 07. She sailed for Canada in September, 1945, to be paid off on October 4 at Halifax, and was broken up at Sorel in 1947.

UNGAVA

Commissioned at Vancouver on September 5, 1941, *Ungava* left on October 10 for Halifax, arriving on November 14. Initially assigned to Halifax Force, she was transferred in May, 1943, to Gaspé Force, then back to Halifax Force that December. In May, 1944, she joined Sydney Force, returning again to Halifax Force in February, 1945. Following a refit from April to May, 1945, at Liverpool, N.S., she went to Bermuda to work up, and on her return after VE-Day she was assigned miscellaneous duties until paid off on April 3, 1946. She was sold later that year to a New Jersey buyer, presumably for scrap.

Quinte as training ship at Cornwallis

Thunder, February 25, 1944

Ungava, September 20, 1941

WASAGA

The first of the RCN Bangors, *Wasaga* was commissioned at Vancouver on June 30, 1941. She left Esquimalt on August 6 for Halifax, arriving on September 10. Sent to Bermuda for working-up, she was assigned to Halifax Force on her return. In March, 1942, she was transferred to Newfoundland Force and, in January, 1944, to Sydney Force. Ordered to the U.K. for invasion duties, she sailed from Halifax on February 21, 1944, for Plymouth via the Azores, in company with *Canso*, *Guysborough* and *Kenora*. Arriving at Plymouth early in March, she was assigned at first to the 32nd and then to the 31st Minesweeping Flotilla, and was on hand on D-Day. She sailed for Canada on September 30, 1944, to refit at Charlottetown, returning to Plymouth on February 4, 1945. That September she returned to Canada and was paid off at Halifax on October 6, to be laid up at Shelburne until sold for scrap in 1947.

Bangor Class, ex-RN

BAYFIELD

Named for the village of Bayfield, N.S, she was built at Vancouver for the RN but transferred to the RCN for manning, and commissioned on February 26, 1942. After working up, *Bayfield* joined Esquimalt Force in May but was transferred to Prince Rupert Force in November, returning to Esquimalt in March, 1943, for reassignment to the east coast. She left Esquimalt on March 18, arriving at Halifax on April 30 and, after a major refit at Baltimore, Md., joined Halifax Force until ordered to the U.K. for invasion duties. On February 18, 1944, with *Georgian*, *Mulgrave* and *Thunder*, she left Halifax for Plymouth via the Azores, arriving on March 7. Allocated to the 31st Minesweeping Flotilla, she was present on D-Day, and she remained with Plymouth Command until paid off on September 24, 1945. Returned to the RN, she was placed in reserve at Sheerness until 1948, when she was broken up at Gateshead.

CANSO

Built for the RN but transferred to the RCN for manning, *Canso* was commissioned at Vancouver on March 6, 1942. After working up, she was assigned to Esquimalt Force from May, 1942 to July, 1943, when nominated for service in the Atlantic. She left Esquimalt on July 8, 1943, arriving at Halifax on August 19, and was allocated to Halifax Force. On February 21, 1944, with *Guysborough*, *Kenora*, and *Wasaga*, she sailed from Halifax via the Azores for Plymouth, arriving on March 8. She was allocated in turn to the 32nd, 16th, and 31st Minesweeping Flotillas, and was on hand on D-Day. In August she returned briefly to Canada for a refit at Saint John, N.B., and in November resumed her task of clearing German minefields. She was paid off on September 24, 1945, and returned to the RN at Sheerness, to be broken up at Sunderland in 1948.

Wasaga, March, 1944

Bayfield, March, 1944

Canso, March, 1944

Caraquet leaving Baltimore after refit, September, 1943

CARAQUET

Named for a New Brunswick bay, she was built for the RN but transferred to the RCN for manning and commissioned April 2, 1942, at Vancouver. In May she joined Esquimalt Force and in September was transferred to Prince Rupert Force, but she returned to Esquimalt in March, 1943, with orders to proceed to the east coast. She left Esquimalt for Halifax on March 17, arriving on May 2, and was allocated to WLEF, transferring in July to Halifax Force and in December to Newfoundland Force. During this period she underwent a six-week refit at Baltimore, Md., from mid-July, 1943. On February 19, 1944, with *Cowichan*, *Malpeque* and *Vegreville*, she left for Plymouth via the Azores, arriving on March 13. She was assigned to the 31st Minesweeping Flotilla for invasion duties and was present on D-Day. *Caraquet* proceeded to Canada at the end of September to refit at Lunenburg, returning to Plymouth in March, 1945, for further mine-clearance work. Paid off on September 26 and returned to the RN at Sheerness, she was sold to the Portuguese Navy in 1946 and renamed *Almirante Lacerda*. She remained in service as a survey vessel until 1975.

GUYSBOROUGH

Built at Vancouver for the RN but transferred to the RCN for manning, she was commissioned on April 22, 1942, and assigned to Esquimalt Force. On March 17, 1943, she left for Halifax, arriving on April 30. After brief service with WLEF, she joined Halifax Force. In mid-September *Guysborough* underwent six weeks' refit at Baltimore, Md. On February 21, 1944, with *Canso*, *Kenora* and *Wasaga*, she left Halifax for the Azores en route to Plymouth, where she arrived on March 8. She was assigned to the 14th Minesweeping Flotilla and was present on D-Day. That December she returned to Canada for refit at Lunenburg, after which, bound again for Plymouth, she was torpedoed and sunk on March 17, 1945, by *U 878* off Ushant in the Channel. Fifty-one of her complement lost their lives.

Guysborough, March, 1944

INGONISH

Built at Vancouver for the RN but transferred to the RCN for manning, *Ingonish* was commissioned on May 8, 1942. She saw her first service with the Esquimalt and Prince Rupert Forces. She left Esquimalt March 17, 1943, for Halifax where, after her arrival on April 30, she was allocated briefly to Western Local Defence Force and then, in June, to Halifax Force. In mid-November she had a nine-week refit at Baltimore, Md. In May, 1944, she was transferred to Sydney Force and in February, 1945, back again to Halifax Force. Following an extensive refit at Saint John she went in May to work up in Bermuda and in June sailed for the U.K. She was returned to the RN at Sheerness on July 2, 1945, and placed in reserve until taken to Dunston-on-Tyne for scrapping in 1948.

Ingonish, March, 1944

LOCKEPORT

Built for the RN at Vancouver but transferred to the RCN for manning, she was commissioned on May 27, 1942, and served with Esquimalt Force until March 17, 1943, when she left for Halifax. On her arrival there on April 30 she was assigned briefly to WLEF and, in June, to Halifax Force. In November and December, 1943, she was lent to Newfoundland Force but was withdrawn owing to engine trouble. On January 9, 1944, while en route to Baltimore for refit, her engines broke down in a storm, and she made 190 miles under improvised sail before being towed the rest of the way to her destination. Upon her return to Halifax in April, *Lockeport* was ordered to Bermuda to work up, and on the homeward journey she escorted the boats of the 78th Motor Launch Flotilla. Returning to Sydney Force in May, 1944, she was frequently an escort to the Port-aux-Basques/Sydney ferry. She left Canada on May 27, 1945, for the U.K., and was returned to the RN at Sheerness on July 2, to be broken up three years later.

Bangor Class, 1940-1941 Programme

COURTENAY

Commissioned at Prince Rupert on March 21, 1942, *Courtenay* spent her whole career on the west coast, serving alternately with the Esquimalt and Prince Rupert Forces. She was paid off on November 5, 1945, at Esquimalt and sold in 1946 to the Union Steamship Co., Vancouver, for use as a merchant ship. However, she was not converted to this use, and has proved impossible to trace beyond 1951, when a purchase offer was made by a San Francisco firm.

DRUMMONDVILLE

Commissioned at Montreal on October 30, 1941, she arrived at Halifax on November 11 and served at various times with WLEF, Gulf Escort Force, Halifax Local Defence Force, and Sydney Force before joining Newfoundland Force in February, 1944. Following a major refit at Louisbourg, she proceeded to Bermuda in mid-August to work up, returning to St. John's early in October. The Newfoundland Force was disbanded in June, 1945, and from then until Octo-

Lockeport, April, 1944

Drummondville, St. John's, March, 1942

Courtenay, June 8, 1944

ber *Drummondville* was employed at miscellaneous duties on the east coast. She was paid off at Halifax on October 29, 1945, and in 1946 placed in strategic reserve at Sorel. Reacquired by the RCN in 1952, she was placed in reserve at Sydney but never recommissioned, and in 1948 she was sold for conversion to a merchant ship. As SS *Fort Albany* she was sunk by collision near Sorel on December 8, 1963, and raised and broken up there the following year.

GANANOQUE

Commissioned at Toronto on November 8, 1941, *Gananoque* arrived at Halifax on November 23. She was assigned to Halifax Local Defence Force and subsequently for brief periods to Halifax Force, St. John's Local Defence Force, Gulf Escort Force, and Sydney Force. In January, 1943, she was assigned to WLEF, returning to Halifax Force in July of the same year, and to Sydney Force once again in May, 1944. During this period she had the distinction of twice refitting at other than Atlantic coast ports: in May, 1943, she underwent a six-week refit at Quebec City, and in July, 1944, an eight-week refit at Charlottetown. In February, 1945, she was allocated to Newfoundland Force, based at St. John's, until the force was disbanded in June, whereupon she went to Atlantic Coast Command. *Gananoque* was paid off at Sydney on October 13, 1945, and laid up at Shelburne. Placed in strategic reserve at Sorel in 1946, she was reacquired by the RCN in 1952 but not recommissioned, and in February, 1959, she was sold for scrap.

Gananoque

GODERICH

Commissioned at Toronto on November 23, 1941, *Goderich* arrived at Halifax on December 6. She spent her whole career based at Halifax as a member, alternately, of Halifax Local Defence Force and Halifax Force. She was damaged on November 18, 1942, in a collision with the tanker *Iocoma* in Halifax harbour, which necessitated three weeks' repairs there. *Goderich* saw almost continuous service, undergoing only one major refit at Liverpool, N.S., from March 5 to May 15, 1943. On January 29, 1943, she rescued survivors from the after section of the U.S. tanker *Brilliant*, which had broken in half during a storm. She was paid off at Halifax on November 6, 1945, and in 1946 placed in strategic reserve at Sorel. In 1951 she was reacquired by the RCN and underwent modernization at Lauzon. Never recommissioned, however, she lay in reserve at Sydney until sold in February, 1959 for scrap.

Goderich

GRANDMÈRE

Grandmère was commissioned at Montreal on December 11, 1941. En route to Halifax she broke down in the Gulf of St. Lawrence on December 21, and was towed to Sydney by HMCS *Kamsack*. Later that month, while alongside at Sydney undergoing repairs, she suffered serious damage to her No. 2 boiler, and was taken to Pictou for repairs, which were not completed until May, 1942. She finally arrived at Halifax, her original destination, on May 5. She served for varying periods with WLEF, Sydney Force, Halifax Force, and Halifax Local Defence Force. On October 11, 1942, while with Sydney Force, she rescued 101 survivors of the passenger ferry *Caribou*, torpedoed in the Cabot Strait. In July, 1943, she had a seven-week refit at Louisbourg and underwent a second major refit at Sydney and Halifax in September, 1944, following which she worked up in Bermuda in February, 1945. The ship was paid off at Sydney on October 23, 1945, and placed in reserve at Shelburne. Sold in 1947, she was modified for use as a yacht, first renamed *Elda* and later, *Jack's Bay*.

Grandmère, May, 1942

KELOWNA

Commissioned on February 5, 1942, at Prince Rupert, *Kelowna* spent her entire career on the west coast, alternately a member of Prince Rupert Force and Esquimalt Force. She was paid off at Esquimalt on October 22, 1945, and sold the following year for commercial purposes, first renamed *Condor* and later, in 1950, *Hung Hsin*. Owned in Shanghai, she disappeared from Lloyd's Register after 1950.

MEDICINE HAT

Commissioned at Montreal on December 4, 1941, she arrived at Halifax on December 13 and was allocated to WLEF and then, in June, 1942, to Sydney Force. In January, 1943, she returned to WLEF but was transferred to Halifax Force in June, and there remained until May 1944, apart from a brief absence from November to December, 1943, when she was lent to Newfoundland Force. In May, 1944, she returned to Sydney Force until January, 1945, when she was transferred to Newfoundland Force until VE-Day. She was thereafter employed at miscellaneous duties on the Atlantic coast until November 6, 1945, when she was paid off at Halifax and laid up at Shelburne. In 1946 *Medicine Hat* was placed in strategic reserve at Sorel until reacquired in 1951 and taken to Sydney. She remained in Sydney until she was transferred to the Turkish Navy on November 29, 1957. Renamed *Biga*, she remained in service until 1963.

RED DEER

Commissioned at Montreal on November 24, 1941, *Red Deer* arrived at Halifax on December 3. She was assigned to WLEF, later serving at various times with Halifax Local Defence Force, Gulf Escort Force, and Sydney Force. On January 12, 1942, she rescued survivors from the British SS *Cyclops*, which was torpedoed 125 miles southeast of Cape Sable, the first victim of the epic U-boat campaign off the U.S. east coast. In May, 1944, she began a refit at Liverpool, N.S., and was sent to Bermuda to work up late in July. In February, 1944, she had been allocated to Newfoundland Force, and she continued a member of this force until VE-Day. She was paid off at Halifax on October 30, 1945, and laid up at Shelburne, later being placed in strategic reserve at Sorel. Reacquired by the RCN in 1952, she was never recommissioned, and was sold in February, 1959, for breaking up at Sorel.

Kelowna, October 4, 1944

Medicine Hat, October, 1943

Red Deer, August 17, 1943

Swift Current, May, 1944

SWIFT CURRENT

Commissioned at Montreal on November 11, 1941, she arrived at Halifax on November 24 and was based there for A/S training. In May, 1942, *Swift Current* was moved to Pictou in the same capacity, and continued in this role until February, 1943, when she was transferred to Halifax Force. She went to Gaspé Force in June, 1943, but returned to Halifax Force in November. In February, 1944, following a major refit at Lunenburg, she was transferred to Newfoundland Force, remaining there until June, 1945. Miscellaneous duties occupied her until she was paid off at Sydney on October 23, 1945, and laid up at Shelburne. *Swift Current* was placed in strategic reserve at Sorel the following year, but reacquired by the RCN in 1951 owing to the Korean emergency. However, she was not recommissioned and was handed over to the Turkish Navy on March 29, 1958. Renamed *Bozcaada*, she remained in Turkish service until 1971.

VEGREVILLE

Commissioned at Montreal on December 10, 1941, *Vegreville* arrived at Halifax on December 18 and was assigned to WLEF. She was reassigned to Gulf Escort Force in June, 1942, and transferred that September to Newfoundland Force. In January, 1944, she was assigned to invasion duties, and sailed on February 19 from Halifax for Plymouth via the Azores, in company with *Caraquet, Cowichan,* and *Malpeque.* Arriving at Plymouth on March 13, *Vegreville* was assigned successively to the 32nd, 14th, and 31st Minesweeping Flotillas, and was present on D-Day. In September, 1944, she proceeded to Canada to refit at Sydney, returning to Plymouth on February 4, 1945. On April 23, while operating off the French coast, she sustained severe damage to her port engine. Dockyard survey at Devonport indicated that she was not worth repairing at that stage of the war, and she was laid up at Falmouth in June. Paid off on June 6, 1945, she was broken up at Hayle, U.K., in 1947.

Vegreville, October, 1943

Bangor Class, 1940-1941 Programme (Diesel)

BROCKVILLE

Commissioned on September 19, 1942, at Sorel, she arrived at Halifax on October 20 in need of two weeks' repairs, having grounded at Rimouski en route. After working up, she was assigned briefly to WLEF and then to Halifax Force. In March she was transferred back to WLEF and when that force was divided into escort groups in June, she became a member of EG W-3. In May, 1944, *Brockville* returned to Sydney Force, remaining with it until June, 1945. She had two wartime refits: one at Dalhousie, N.B., lasting seven weeks in August and September, 1943; the other a three-month refit at Lunenburg at the end of 1944, followed by workups in Bermuda in March, 1945. On August 28, 1945, she was paid off at Halifax, transferred to the marine section of the RCMP and renamed *Macleod*. *Brockville* was reacquired by the RCN in 1950 and recommissioned on April 5, 1951. After modernization at Lauzon in 1952 she was assigned to Point Edward naval base at Sydney and later transferred to the west coast. She was paid off into reserve at Esquimalt on October 31, 1958, and broken up three years later.

Brockville, July 15, 1955

DIGBY

Commissioned at Quebec City on July 26, 1942, she arrived at Halifax on August 15, and after completing workups at Pictou, was assigned to WLEF. When WLEF was divided into escort groups in June, 1943, *Digby* became a member of EG W-5. In April, 1944, she arrived at Lunenburg to commence a refit that continued at Shelburne and at Halifax and was completed on August 7. She then proceeded to Bermuda for workups. On returning she was allocated to Sydney Force and, in February, 1945, to Newfoundland Force. She was paid off on July 31, 1945, and placed in reserve at Sydney. *Digby* was proposed for transfer to the marine section of the RCMP in 1945, to be renamed *Perry*, but was not taken over. She lay in strategic reserve at Sorel until reacquired by the RCN in 1951 and refitted for training duties. She was recommissioned on April 29, 1953, finally being paid off on November 14, 1956 and scrapped.

Digby, July 4, 1955

ESQUIMALT

Commissioned at Sorel on October 26, 1942, *Esquimalt* arrived at Halifax on November 21. Chronically plagued by mechanical troubles, she underwent repairs there until March 27, 1943, and again throughout most of May. She was then assigned to Newfoundland Force until September, 1944, when she was transferred to Halifax Local Defence Force. Late in September she underwent a three-month refit at Halifax. While on A/S patrol on April 16, 1945, she was torpedoed and sunk by *U 190* five miles off Chebucto Head, near Halifax, with the loss of 39 of her ship's company.

Esquimalt, May, 1944

Granby working up off Pictou, July, 1943

Lachine, October, 1943

Melville

GRANBY

Commissioned at Quebec City on May 2, 1942, *Granby* arrived at Halifax on May 13. She completed working up and was assigned first to Sydney Force and then to Western Local Defence Force. In June, 1943, when the latter was divided into escort groups, she became a member of EG W-3 until May, 1944, when she returned to Sydney Force. During this period she had an extensive refit at Lunenburg from June to October, 1944, afterward proceeding to Bermuda to work up. She returned in November and was assigned to Shelburne Force in February, 1945. In April she was transferred to Halifax Force and remained under repair at Halifax until paid off on July 31, 1945. Although allocated to the marine section of the RCMP as *Col. White*, she was not actually taken over. She was recommissioned on May 23, 1953 for conversion to a deep-diving tender, and served as such until finally paid off on December 15, 1966, and sold.

LACHINE

Commissioned at Quebec City on June 20, 1942, *Lachine* arrived at Halifax on July 4 and, after repairs and workups, was assigned to Sydney Force in September. In October she was transferred to WLEF, and in June, 1943, became a member of EG W-6, one of the force's newly created escort groups. She served with Halifax Force from June, 1944 until VE-Day, and on July 31, 1945, was paid off at Shelburne. During the war she underwent two refits: the first, at Dalhousie, N.B., from October to November, 1943; the second, at Lunenburg, from December, 1944 to March, 1945, followed by workups in Bermuda. An intended transfer to the marine section of the RCMP as *Starnes* did not materialize, and *Lachine* was sold in 1945 for conversion to a salvage tug.

MELVILLE

The first of the diesel-engined Bangors, *Melville* was commissioned at Quebec City on December 4, 1941. She arrived at Halifax on December 13, worked up, and was assigned to WLEF. In May, 1942, she was transferred to Shelburne Force, returning to WLEF that September. On February 3, 1943, she arrived at Lunenburg for refit and proceeded to Halifax to continue it. She did not resume service until July 8, when she joined WLEF's recently created EG W-5. In March, 1944, she underwent further repairs at Lunenburg, following which, on June 6, she sailed from Bermuda to work up. Returning to Halifax July 2, she was assigned to Sydney Force until June, 1945. *Melville* was paid off at Sydney on August 18, 1945, and handed over to the marine section of the RCMP. Renamed *Cygnus*, she was broken up in 1961.

NORANDA

Commissioned at Quebec City on May 15, 1942, *Noranda* arrived at Halifax on May 30, and after working up at Pictou was assigned to Halifax Force. In February, 1943, she was transferred to WLEF and, on its division into escort groups that June, became a member of EG W-9. *Noranda* went to Sydney Force in May, 1944, and after a major refit at Lunenburg from September to December, proceeded to Bermuda to work up. Returning to Halifax on February 2, 1945, she served briefly with Halifax Force before rejoining Sydney Force. She was paid off at Halifax on August 28, 1945, and transferred to the marine section of the RCMP as *Irvine*. Sold in 1962 for use as a yacht and renamed *Miriana*, she sank at Montego Bay, Jamaica, in May, 1971.

TRANSCONA

Built at Sorel and commissioned there on November 25, 1942, *Transcona* was the last Bangor class minesweeper to join the RCN. She arrived at Halifax on December 19, having escorted HMCS *Provider* en route, and remained in shipyard hands there from December 22 to March 6, 1943, owing to engine defects. Following workups at Halifax, she was assigned April, 1943, to WLEF and, in June, to newly created EG W-2. In May, 1944, she joined Halifax Force, remaining until June, 1945, after which she performed various local tasks until she was paid off at Sydney on July 31, 1945. During this period she was under refit and repair at Lunenburg from February to May, 1945. On September 1 *Transcona* was transferred to the marine section of the RCMP and renamed *French*. She was sold for scrap at La Have, N.S., in 1961.

TROIS-RIVIÈRES

Built at Sorel and commissioned there on August 12, 1942, she arrived at Halifax on August 29 and, after working up at Pictou, was assigned to WLEF. In November, 1942, she was transferred to Newfoundland Force, serving until the Command was disbanded in June, 1945. She was under repair at Dalhousie, N.B., Halifax and Saint John between October, 1943 and January, 1944, and had a major refit at Lunenburg from February to May, 1945, followed by workups in Bermuda. *Trois-Rivières* was paid off on July 31, 1945, and handed over later that year to serve the RCMP as *MacBrien*. She was sold for scrap in 1960.

Noranda, 1942

Transcona

Trois-Rivières, 1942

126

TRURO

Commissioned at Quebec City on August 27, 1942, she arrived at Halifax on September 15 and was allocated to WLEF. In June, 1943, she became a member of newly created EG W-4. In May, 1944, she was transferred to Sydney Force, and from December, 1944 to February, 1945, underwent a major refit at Lunenburg. *Truro* was then assigned briefly to Halifax Force before returning to Sydney Force until June, 1945. Paid off on July 31 at Sydney, she was handed over to the RCMP later that year and renamed *Herchmer*. She was sold for mercantile use in 1947 and, as *Gulf Mariner*, was abandoned ashore in the Fraser River after plans to convert her to a suction dredge had fallen through. She was broken up in 1964.

Bangor Class, 1941-1942 Programme

BLAIRMORE

Commissioned at Port Arthur on November 17, 1942, *Blairmore* arrived at Halifax on December 24, and after working up was assigned to WLEF. Upon the division of the force into escort groups in June, 1943, she became a member of EG W-4 and remained with the group until February, 1944. Transferred to the U.K. for invasion duties, she left Halifax on February 20 in company with *Fort William*, *Milltown* and *Minas* for Plymouth via the Azores, arriving on March 8. Assigned to the 31st Minesweeping Flotilla, she was present on D-Day and continued with Plymouth Command until September 21, 1945, when she sailed for Canada. During this period she returned to Canada for a refit at Halifax in April, 1945, returning to Plymouth in July.

Blairmore was paid off at Sydney, N.S., on October 16, 1945, sold to Marine Industries Ltd., and placed in strategic reserve at Sorel in 1946. She was reacquired by the RCN in July, 1951, owing to the Korean crisis, and converted to a "coastal escort." Again placed in reserve at Sydney, she was transferred to the Turkish Navy as *Beycoz* on March 29, 1958, remaining in service until 1971.

FORT WILLIAM

Commissioned at Port Arthur on August 25, 1942, *Fort William* arrived at Halifax on September 24 with a good many defects, and did not commence working up until mid-October. A month later she was assigned to Halifax Force for local convoys. On January 11, 1943, she suffered considerable damage in collision with the government vessel *Lisgar* at Halifax, and was under repair there for a month. In June, 1943, she was transferred to Newfoundland Force. She returned to Halifax in February, 1944, for a short refit, and on February 20 left with *Blairmore*, *Milltown* and *Minas* for Plymouth via the Azores, arriving on March 8. Assigned to the 31st Minesweeping Flotilla, she was present on D-Day. *Fort William* refitted at St. John's March, 1945, rejoining the 31st Flotilla in July and remaining until September 21, when she left Plymouth for Canada. She was paid off on October 23, 1945, at Sydney and was placed in strategic reserve at Sorel in 1946. Reacquired in June, 1951, and extensively modernized, she lay in reserve at Sydney until November 29, 1957, when she was transferred to the Turkish Navy and renamed *Bodrum*. She was removed from service in 1971 and broken up.

Truro

Blairmore in the Channel, March 17, 1944

Fort William, March, 1944

KENORA

Commissioned on August 6, 1942, at Port Arthur, she arrived at Halifax on September 7 and proceeded to Pictou for workups. She was then assigned to WLEF and in June, 1943, became a member of EG W-8. She left Halifax on February 21, 1944 with *Canso*, *Guysborough* and *Wasaga* via the Azores for Plymouth, arriving on March 8. *Kenora* was assigned to the 14th Minesweeping Flotilla, with which she was present on D-Day, and in October returned to Canada for a refit at Liverpool, N.S. She proceeded to the U.K. again in February, 1945, and was assigned to the 31st Flotilla until September 4, when she left Plymouth for Canada. *Kenora* was paid off at Halifax on October 6, 1945, and placed in reserve at Shelburne. In 1946 she went into strategic reserve at Sorel until reacquired by the RCN in 1952 and moved to Sydney. On November 29, 1957, she was transferred to the Turkish Navy as *Bandirma*. She was removed from service in 1972.

Kenora, March, 1944

KENTVILLE

Commissioned at Port Arthur on October 10, 1942, *Kentville* arrived at Halifax on November 15, having escorted a Quebec-Sydney convoy en route. After working up, she was assigned to Halifax Force in January, 1943. With the exception of the period between May and November, 1943, when she served with Sydney Force, she spent her entire career based at Halifax. In May, 1944, she underwent a refit at Charlottetown, on completion of which in July she proceeded to Bermuda for working up, returning to Halifax in mid-August. *Kentville* was paid off at Sydney on October 28, 1945, and went into reserve, first at Shelburne and then, in 1946, at Sorel. She was reacquired by the RCN in 1952, refitted and placed in reserve at Sydney, and was again in commission during the summer of 1954. Transferred on November 29, 1957 to the Turkish Navy and renamed *Bartin*, she remained in service until 1972.

Kentville, 1945

MILLTOWN

Commissioned on September 18, 1942 at Port Arthur, *Milltown* arrived at Halifax on October 27 and, after working up, joined Halifax Force in December. In March, 1943, she transferred to WLEF and in June, to Gaspé Force. In November, 1943, she returned to Halifax Force until February 20, 1944, when, with *Blairmore*, *Fort William* and *Minas*, she sailed via the Azores for Plymouth, arriving on March 8. She was present on D-Day with the 31st Minesweeping Flotilla. She returned to Canada to refit at Saint John, N.B., from March to June, 1945, leaving Halifax June 23 for Plymouth via the Azores. She left Plymouth for home on September 21 and was paid off on October 16 at Sydney and laid up at Shelburne. *Milltown* was placed in strategic reserve at Sorel in 1946, but reacquired by the RCN in 1952 and kept in reserve at Sydney until February, 1959, when she was sold for scrap.

Milltown, March, 1944

Mulgrave, March, 1944

Port Hope visiting her namesake town, August, 1942

Sarnia, October, 1943

MULGRAVE

Commissioned at Port Arthur on November 4, 1942, *Mulgrave* arrived at Halifax on November 30 and was assigned to Halifax Force for the first quarter of 1943. She then transferred to WLEF, becoming a member of newly created EG W-2 in June, 1943. On February 18, 1944, with *Bayfield*, *Georgian* and *Thunder*, she left Halifax for Plymouth via the Azores. On February 29, when entering Horta, *Mulgrave* suffered grounding damage and had to be towed to Greenock, Scotland. After repairs at Ardrossan she finally made Plymouth on April 24 to commence training and exercises. She was temporarily assigned to the 32nd Minesweeping Flotilla, then in June to the 31st, with which she was present on D-Day. On October 8, 1944, the unlucky *Mulgrave* was damaged by a ground mine near Le Havre and had to be beached. On November 3 she left Le Havre in tow for Portsmouth, where she was declared a constructive total loss. Placed in reserve at Falmouth in January, 1945, with a reduced complement, she was formally paid off on June 7 and scrapped at Llanelly, Wales, two years later.

PORT HOPE

Commissioned at Toronto on July 30, 1942, *Port Hope* arrived at Halifax on August 29 and on completion of workups, joined Halifax Force. In May, 1943, owing to U-boat activity in the Gulf of St. Lawrence, she was transferred to Gaspé Force, but returned to Halifax Force in November. In January, 1944, she was transferred to Newfoundland Force. That October she underwent an extensive refit at Saint John and Halifax, on completion of which went to Bermuda to work up. Returning, *Port Hope* served a short further stint with Halifax Force from April to June, 1945, then performed miscellaneous duties on the east coast until paid off at Sydney on October 13, 1945. She lay in strategic reserve at Sorel until 1952, when the RCN reacquired her, but was not recommissioned, and was sold in February, 1959, for breaking up at Sorel.

SARNIA

Commissioned at Toronto on August 13, 1942, *Sarnia* arrived at Halifax on September 22, having escorted a Quebec-Sydney convoy en route, and was assigned to Newfoundland Force. In September, 1944, she underwent a major refit at Lunenburg, and on completion went to Bermuda in November to work up. On her return to Canada she was assigned to Halifax Force and, later, to Halifax Local Defence Force until June, 1945. On April 15, 1945, she rescued survivors of HMCS *Esquimalt*, torpedoed outside Halifax. She then performed miscellaneous duties until paid off on October 28, 1945, at Sydney and laid up at Shelburne. In 1946 she was placed in strategic reserve at Sorel and in 1951 reacquired by the RCN and extensively refitted. She did not recommission, however, and on March 29, 1958 was transferred to the Turkish Navy to serve until 1972 as *Buyukdere*.

STRATFORD

Commissioned at Toronto on August 29, 1942, *Stratford* arrived at Halifax on September 22 and was assigned to Newfoundland Force. She remained with this force as a convoy escort throughout her wartime career, and saw continuous service. She did not require a major refit until December, 1944, when this was done at Dartmouth, N.S. On its completion she carried out workups in Bermuda from February 15 to March 8, 1945. Returning from Bermuda, she was involved in a collision with HMCS *Ottawa* in the Halifax approaches on March 11, receiving extensive damage to her fo'c's'le. Though inactive thereafter, she was not paid off until January 4, 1946, and was then sold for scrap.

WESTMOUNT

Commissioned at Toronto on September 15, 1942, *Westmount* arrived at Halifax on October 10 and proceeded to Pictou to work up. Following this, she underwent engine repairs at Halifax from November 20 to February 2, 1943. She was then assigned to Halifax Local Defence Force and, later, to Halifax Force. In May, 1943, she was transferred to Sydney Force, but returned to Halifax Force in January, 1944. In February, 1945, she commenced a major refit at Lunenburg and, after this was completed late in April, proceeded to Bermuda to work up. Upon her return to Halifax on May 30 she was assigned to miscellaneous duties until paid off at Sydney on October 13, 1945, and laid up at Shelburne. In 1946 she was placed in strategic reserve at Sorel until reacquired by the RCN in 1951. On March 29, 1958, she was transferred to the Turkish Navy, serving as *Bornova* until 1972.

Algerine Class

BORDER CITIES

Commissioned at Port Arthur on May 18, 1944, *Border Cities* arrived at Halifax in mid-June, and on July 8 proceeded to Bermuda to work up. Returning to Halifax on August 3, she was assigned as Senior Officer's ship to EG W-2 of WLEF. In June, 1945, she was assigned to Atlantic Coast Command and, in August, placed temporarily in maintenance reserve at Sydney. On November 10 she left, with four sisters, for the west coast, and on January 15, 1946, was paid off into reserve at Esquimalt. She was sold for scrap in 1948 and broken up at Victoria soon afterward.

Stratford

Westmount

Border Cities, July, 1944

FORT FRANCES

Commissioned at Port Arthur on October 28, 1944, she arrived at Halifax on November 26, and sailed for Bermuda in January, 1945 to work up. Returning to Halifax, *Fort Frances* served briefly with escort groups W-8 and W-9 of Western Escort Force before being paid off into maintenance reserve on August 3, 1945. She was again in commission from October 23, 1945 to April 5, 1946, and in 1948 was handed over to the Department of Mines and Technical Surveys as a hydrographic survey ship. In 1958 she reverted to naval service as a civilian-manned oceanographic research vessel. She was sold for breaking-up in 1974.

Fort Frances, March 28, 1945

KAPUSKASING

Commissioned at Port Arthur on August 17, 1944, *Kapuskasing* arrived at Halifax early in September and on October 1 proceeded to Bermuda to work up. She returned to Halifax in mid-November and was assigned as Senior Officer's ship to EG W-1 of Western Escort Force. When the force was disbanded in June, 1945, she was placed temporarily in maintenance reserve at Sydney, then taken to Halifax for refit in November. On completion of the refit she was paid off into reserve on March 27, 1946. In 1949 she was lent to the Department of Mines and Technical Surveys and converted for hydrographic survey work. Returned to the navy in 1972, she was expended as a target on October 3, 1978.

Kapuskasing, June, 1945

MIDDLESEX

Middlesex was commissioned at Port Arthur on June 8, 1944, arrived at Halifax in mid-July and sailed for Bermuda in August to work up. Assigned to EG W-3 of Western Escort Force, she joined the group in New York on August 30, direct from Bermuda. *Middlesex* was principally engaged as southern local escort to U.K.-bound convoys out of New York. She was Senior Officer's ship from mid-November, 1944, until the force was disbanded in June, 1945, whereupon she refitted at Halifax and was placed in maintenance reserve there. In March, 1946, she returned to service as emergency ship at Halifax. On December 2, 1946, en route to assist the fishing vessel *Ohio*, she ran ashore on Half Island Point, near Halifax, and was declared a total loss.

Middlesex, August, 1944

NEW LISKEARD

Commissioned at Port Arthur on November 21, 1944, *New Liskeard* arrived at Halifax on December 15 and proceeded to Bermuda for workups in March, 1945. Upon her return in April she was assigned to EG W-8 of Western Escort Force. When EG W-8 was disbanded in June she was allocated to HMCS Cornwallis as a training ship from July to September. She then was placed in maintenance reserve, first at Sydney and then at Halifax, until the end of the year. Refitted at Halifax, she was recommissioned on April 9, 1946, as a training ship for cadets. On April 22, 1958, she was paid off for conversion to an oceanographic research vessel, serving as such until May 1, 1969. Later that year she was taken to Dartmouth Cove, N.S., for breaking up.

OSHAWA

Commissioned at Port Arthur on July 6, 1944, she arrived at Halifax on August 18. She worked up in Bermuda in September, and on her return was allocated to EG W-6 of Western Escort Force as Senior Officer's Ship. The group was disbanded in June, 1945, and *Oshawa* was paid off into maintenance reserve at Sydney on July 28. She was recommissioned on October 24, and in November sailed for Esquimalt. She arrived there December 21, and on February 26, 1946, was paid off into reserve. During one more commission from April 11, 1956 to November 7, 1958, she was extensively converted for oceanographic research, in which role she continued, civilian-manned, until sold and broken up at Victoria in 1966.

PORTAGE

Named for Portage la Prairie, Man., she was commissioned at Port Arthur on October 22, 1943, and arrived at Halifax on November 28. After working up in St. Margaret's Bay *Portage* was assigned to EG W-2 of Western Escort Force as Senior Officer's ship, late in January, 1944. In mid-April she was transferred, still as S.O., to W-3, and continued as such until late October, when she underwent an extensive refit at Liverpool, N.S. She then proceeded to Bermuda for workups, rejoining W-3 in March, 1945. The group was disbanded in June and *Portage* was placed in maintenance reserve at Sydney and then at Halifax, where she was paid off on July 31, 1946. She was reactivated for training purposes during the summers of 1947 and 1948, and spent most of the period between 1949 and 1959 in the same role, much of the time on the Great Lakes. She was finally paid off on September 26, 1958, and scrapped at Sorel three years later.

New Liskeard at Port Arthur, November 20, 1944

Oshawa, 1944

Portage

ROCKCLIFFE

Commissioned at Port Arthur on September 30, 1944, *Rockcliffe* arrived at Halifax on October 30 and proceeded to Bermuda to work up. Upon returning to Halifax in mid-December she was assigned to EG W-6 until June, 1945. She escorted the surrendered *U 889* part of the way to Shelburne, N.S., on May 10, 1945. Paid off to reserve at Sydney on July 28, 1945, she was recommissioned for passage to Esquimalt, where she arrived on December 21, 1945. On January 14, 1946, she was again paid off into reserve, but was recommissioned on March 3, 1947, to serve as a training ship. She was finally paid off on August 15, 1950, and scrapped ten years later.

ST. BONIFACE

Commissioned at Port Arthur on September 10, 1943, *St. Boniface* arrived at Halifax late in October, and worked up at Pictou from November to December. She was then assigned as Senior Officer's ship to EG W-5 of Western Escort Force until mid-April, 1944. She then transferred to W-4, again as S.O., until early December when, following minor repairs at Halifax, she proceeded to Bermuda to work up. Upon returning to Canada, she rejoined W-4 until the group was disbanded in June, 1945. On April 18, 1945, *St. Boniface* was in collision with SS *Empire Chamois* in the Halifax approaches, as the freighter's convoy, SC. 173, was forming up for passage to the U.K. *St. Boniface* suffered extensive damage to her bows, but made Halifax under her own power and was under repair there for three months. In August, 1945, she became a training ship at HMCS Cornwallis until January, 1946, when she was placed in reserve at Halifax. She was finally paid off on September 25, 1946, and sold for mercantile use. She was last noted under Panamanian flag as *Bess Barry M.* in 1954.

SAULT STE. MARIE

Commissioned at Port Arthur on June 24, 1943, this was the first Algerine class ship to join the RCN. Originally intended to be named *The Soo*, she was renamed owing to objections from her namesake city. *Sault Ste. Marie* arrived at Halifax on August 8, 1943, and proceeded to Bermuda for workups in September. On her return she joined EG W-9 of Western Escort Force, serving as Senior Officer's ship until mid-April, 1945. She then transferred as S.O. to W-7 until the group was disbanded in June. After a short period in reserve at Sydney she was ordered to the west coast, arriving at Esquimalt on December 12. She was paid off into reserve on January 12, 1946, but recommissioned for reserve training on May 7, 1949. The ship returned to the east coast in mid-December 1955, and spent the summers of 1956 to 1958 on the Great Lakes. She was paid off on October 1, 1958, and broken up in 1960 at Sorel.

Rockcliffe, March, 1945

St. Boniface

Sault Ste. Marie, August, 1943

WALLACEBURG

Commissioned at Port Arthur on November 18, 1943, she arrived at Halifax on December 13, and after working up was assigned to EG W-8, Western Escort Force, in February, 1944. In April, *Wallaceburg* was transferred to EG W-6 as Senior Officer's ship, but returned in December to W-8. During July and August, 1945, she was attached to HMCS Cornwallis for training, then placed in reserve, first at Sydney and then at Halifax. She was paid off on October 7, 1946, but recommissioned on November 1, 1950 for cadet training. *Wallaceburg* spent the summers of 1956 and 1957 on the Great Lakes and was paid off on September 24, 1957. On July 31, 1959, she was transferred to the Belgian Navy, to serve as *Georges Lecointe* until she was discarded in 1969.

Wallaceburg

WINNIPEG

Commissioned at Port Arthur on July 29, 1943, she arrived at Halifax in mid-September and, after working up at Pictou, was assigned to EG W-7 of Western Escort Force. That December she was transferred to W-6, acting as Senior Officer's ship from February to April, 1944. *Winnipeg* then joined W-5, again as S.O., and served with that group until it was disbanded in June, 1945. In August she was placed in reserve at Sydney, but was reactivated for passage to Esquimalt, where she arrived on December 21. She was paid off into reserve there on January 11, 1946, but in 1956 she was brought around to the east coast and, on August 7, 1959, handed over to the Belgian Navy as *A.F. Dufour*. She was broken up in 1966.

Winnipeg, November 8, 1944

Llewellyn Class

Llewellyn represents her class of ten 105-foot wooden minesweepers, as photographs could not be found for all of them. The first two were completed at Quebec City in 1942; the other eight on the west coast in 1944. The two east-coast ships, *Llewellyn* and *Lloyd George*, were commissioned at Quebec City on August 24, 1942, and arrived at Halifax on September 5, having escorted a Quebec-Sydney convoy en route. Their names reflect the fact they were equipped with "double-L" magnetic minesweeping gear, but ingenuity seems to have failed when

it came to naming the rest of the class. They were assigned to Halifax Local Defence Force, and spent their wartime careers on precautionary sweeps of the Halifax approaches. *Llewellyn* served after the war as guardship for the reserve fleet at Halifax until she was paid off on June 14, 1946. She was recommissioned in 1949 for use as a tender at Saint John, and finally was paid off on October 31, 1951. *Lloyd George* also served as guard vessel, but was paid off on July 16, 1948, to spend many years in reserve at Halifax.

The other eight ships of the class were employed on the west coast, alternating between Esquimalt Force and Prince Rupert Force until the end of 1945, when all were paid off. *Revelstoke* alone was recommissioned for passage to Halifax where, like her east-coast sisters, she acted as guardship for a time. She was recommissioned in the summer and fall of 1952 and 1953 for use as a tender at St. John's, and was finally paid off on October 23, 1953, for transfer to the Department of Indian Affairs.

Llewellyn Class

Displ.	Dimensions
228	119' 4'' x 22' x 8' 8''

Speed	Crew	Armament
12	3/20	4-.5'' m.g. (2 xII)

Name	Pt.No.	Builder	When Commissioned	Where Commissioned	Paid Off	Remarks
Coquitlam	J364	Newcastle S/B Co. Ltd., Nanaimo, B.C.	25/7/44	Nanaimo	30/11/45	Sold, 1946
Cranbrook	J372	Star Shipyards Ltd., New Westminster, B.C.	12/5/44	New Westminster	3/11/45	Sold, 1947
Daerwood	J357	Vancouver Shipyards Ltd., Vancouver, B.C.	22/4/44	Vancouver	28/11/45	Sold, 1947
Kalamalka	J395	A.C. Benson Shipyard Ltd., Vancouver, B.C.	2/10/44	Vancouver	16/11/45	Sold, 1947
Lavallee	J371	A.C. Benson Shipyard Ltd., Vancouver, B.C.	21/6/44	Vancouver	27/12/45	Sold, 1947
Llewellyn	J278	Chantier Maritime de St. Laurent, Ile d'Orléans, Que.	24/8/42	Quebec City	31/10/51	Sold, 1959
Lloyd George	J279	Chantier Maritime de St. Laurent, Ile d'Orléans, Que.	24/8/42	Quebec City	16/7/48	Sold, 1959
Revelstoke	J373	Star Shipyards Ltd., New Westminster, B.C.	4/7/44	New Westminster	23/10/53	Sold, 1956
Rossland	J358	Vancouver Shipyards Ltd., Vancouver, B.C.	15/7/44	Vancouver	1/11/45	Sold, 1946
St. Joseph	J359	Newcastle S/B Co. Ltd., Nanaimo, B.C.	24/5/44	Nanaimo	8/11/45	Sold, 1947

Llewellyn, April 12, 1950

Name	Pt.No.	Builder	Completed	Remarks
Alder Lake	J480	Midland Boat Works, Midland, Ont.	22/9/45	To USSR, 20/9/45, as *T-196*
Ash Lake	J481	Midland Boat Works, Midland, Ont.	/45	To Dept. of Mines as *Cartier*
Beech Lake	J482	Vancouver Shipyards Ltd., Vancouver, B.C.	8/2/46	To USSR, 5/2/46, as *T-200*
Birch Lake	J483	Port Carling Boat Works Ltd., Port Carling, Ont.	—	Completed as MV *Aspy III*
Cedar Lake	J484	J.J. Taylor & Sons Ltd., Toronto, Ont.	4/11/45	To USSR, 1/11/45, as *T-197*
Cherry Lake	J485	J.J. Taylor & Sons Ltd., Toronto, Ont.	—	Cancelled 22/10/45
Elm Lake	J486	Mac-Craft Corp., Sarnia, Ont.	18/11/45	To USSR, 17/11/45, as *T-193*
Fir Lake	J487	Mac-Craft Corp., Sarnia, Ont.	/47	Completed as mission ship *Regina Polaris*
Hickory Lake	J488	Grew Boat Works Ltd., Penetanguishene, Ont.	14/8/45	To USSR, 15/8/45, as *T-194*
Larch Lake	J489	Grew Boat Works Ltd., Penetanguishene, Ont.	2/11/45	To USSR, 2/11/45, as *T-198*
Maple Lake	J490	Clare Shipbuilding Co., Meteghan, N.S.	—	Cancelled 18/9/44
Oak Lake	J491	Clare Shipbuilding Co., Meteghan, N.S.	—	Cancelled 18/9/44
Pine Lake	J492	Port Carling Boat Works Ltd., Port Carling, Ont.	22/9/45	To USSR, 20/9/45, as *T-195*
Poplar Lake	J493	Star Shipyards, New Westminster, B.C.	9/1/46	To USSR, 9/1/46, as *T-199*
Spruce Lake	J494	Star Shipyards, New Westminster, B.C.	19/3/46	To USSR, 19/3/46, as *T-202*
Willow Lake	J495	Newcastle Shipbuilding Co. Ltd., Nanaimo, B.C.	11/3/46	To USSR, 11/3/46, as *T-201*

Lake Class

These were copies of the Admiralty type, 126-foot wooden-hulled minesweepers, of which 24 were completed in east-coast yards for the RN. Of the 16 for which orders were placed by the RCN, only 10 were completed as warships, VJ-Day having intervened, and these were transferred to the USSR. The 3 on which work was stopped were completed for civilian use. The remaining 3 were apparently never begun.

Lake Class

Displ.	Dimensions	Armament
360	140' x 27' 11'' x 12' 6''	2-20 mm

Pine Lake in Georgian Bay, 1945

Armed Yachts

Although empowered to requisition British-registered craft of any description from private owners, the RCN failed to turn up vessels with any real potential for A/S use in 1939. A discreet survey of the U.S. yacht market showed promise, but purchase seemed impossible without contravening neutrality regulations. It was accordingly arranged for a sufficient number of Canadian yachts, however inadequate, to be requisitioned from their owners, who then replaced them with yachts purchased in the U.S. These replacements had, of course, already been selected with care by the RCN, which, "discovering" that the replacements were better than the yachts originally requisitioned, took over the replacements instead. By the spring of 1940, 14 large yachts had been acquired in this somewhat questionable fashion, armed, and given animal names. They ranged in age from 7 to 39 years, and five of them (*Beaver*, *Cougar*, *Grizzly*, *Renard* and *Wolf*) had served in the USN as auxiliary patrol craft from 1917 to 1919.

Two other large yachts were acquired in 1940. One of them, *Sans Peur*, had belonged to the Duke of Sutherland; the other, *Ambler*, was the only Canadian-registered yacht considered to be worth taking up. Both retained their own names while in naval service.

Makeshift though the yachts were, they shouldered the responsibility for local A/S defence until the summer of 1941, when corvettes began to be available to replace them, and afterward proved their worth as training vessels and guardships.

AMBLER

The only yacht acquired from a Canadian owner, *Ambler* was commisssioned on May 6, 1940, at Midland. She was converted and armed at Quebec City, leaving on July 20 for Rivière du Loup, where she was to be based for patrol duties on the St. Lawrence River. In October, 1941, she was transferred to Halifax as tender to HMCS Stadacona and, in 1942, to HMCS Cornwallis as a training ship. She was paid off to reserve at Sydney on July 20, 1945, and sold into Greek registry in 1947.

BEAVER

The oldest of her type, *Beaver* had reached the age of 39 when she was commissioned on April 1, 1941, at Halifax and assigned to Halifax Local Defence Force. She was employed much of the time as a radar training ship but served briefly, first with Saint John, N.B. Force and then with Sydney Force, toward the end of 1942, returning to Halifax on December 27 to refit. On July 29, 1943, she arrived at Digby to become a training ship for DEMS (Defensively Equipped Merchant Ship) gunners, and was later used for seamanship training. *Beaver* was paid off on October 17, 1944, sold in 1946, and resold ten years later for scrap.

CARIBOU

Commissioned on May 27, 1940, at Halifax, *Caribou* left the following day for Quebec City for conversion and arming. On completion of this, in mid-November, 1940, she returned to Halifax and was employed until August, 1941, as guardship at the entrance to Bedford Basin. Early in October, 1941, following refit, she had her first taste of patrol duty, but a serious galley fire on November 19 put her out of action until February, 1942, while repairs were made at Lunenburg. In March she was transferred to Saint John, N.B. Force. On July 31 she arrived at Halifax for survey and was declared unfit for active patrol duty. Relegated to training service at HMCS Cornwallis, she had been transferred to Saint John in the same capacity by September, 1943 and, in April, 1944, to Digby again. She remained there until the war's end and was paid off on July 20, 1945 and sold for commercial use the following year.

Ambler, May 16, 1944

Beaver, April, 1941

Caribou, May 13, 1944

Cougar, July 17, 1942

COUGAR

Commissioned on the west coast on September 11, 1940, *Cougar* was employed initially on A/S patrol from Esquimalt, then transferred in May, 1942, to Prince Rupert Force. In June, 1944 she returned to Esquimalt as an examination vessel and was paid off on November 23, 1945. Sold to a California buyer in 1946, she resumed her original name, *Breezin' Thru*, for a time before sinking in a hurricane at Kingston, Jamaica, in September, 1950.

ELK

Elk left Halifax for Pictou on June 21, 1940, for conversion and arming, after which she was commissioned at Halifax on September 10 and transferred to America and West Indies Station. She arrived in Bermuda on September 23, returning to Halifax on May 13, 1941. Following a major refit there, she sailed for Trinidad on December 2. On May 11, 1942, she returned to Halifax and was assigned to Sydney Force, serving extensively as escort to Sydney-Corner Brook convoys. In February, 1943, she was sent to Halifax for repairs, and in May transferred to Digby as a training ship. A month later, however, she was moved to Shelburne, remaining there until November and then returning to Digby, where she was to be based until the end of the war. She served almost continuously as escort to the ancient British training submarine *L.23*. *Elk* was paid off on August 4, 1945, and sold. After long service as a short-haul passenger ferry, *Grand Manan III*, she was sold in 1968 for breaking up.

GRIZZLY

Grizzly was commissioned on July 17, 1941, on the west coast, but the condition of her engines made it impractical for her to function effectively. She was therefore towed to Prince Rupert in July for use as a stationary guardship and examination vessel. In the spring of 1944 she was taken to Victoria, where her hull was found to be in poor condition. Paid off on June 17, she was broken up at Victoria the following year.

Elk

Grizzly, September 4, 1942

HUSKY

Husky left Halifax on May 30, 1940, for conversion and arming at Quebec City. Commissioned at Halifax on July 23, she was assigned to Sydney Force for A/S patrol duty. She was transferred that December to Trinidad, but returned to join Saint John, N.B. Force on September 24, 1941. A year later she returned to Halifax Local Defence Force for a few months before being reassigned in March, 1943, to training duties at HMCS Cornwallis (then located at Halifax). She moved with that establishment to Digby, and for the remainder of the war exercised with RN submarines in the Bay of Fundy. Paid off to reserve at Sydney on August 3, 1945, she was sold into mercantile service in 1946. After a term as the inspection vessel *Good Neighbor* for the Port of New Orleans, she was sold in 1968 for use as a sport-diving tender in Honduran waters but has since returned to New Orleans to become a floating restaurant.

Husky, February 17, 1944

Lynx at Lévis, August 13, 1940

LYNX

Lynx left Halifax with *Husky* on May 30, 1940, for conversion and arming at Quebec City. On her return she was commissioned at Halifax on August 26 and allocated to Sydney Force. She returned at year's end to Halifax for the winter, and in July, 1941, was assigned to Gaspé Force. The ship was plagued by mechanical troubles, however, and spare parts proved unobtainable. She was accordingly transferred to Halifax on November 25. On January 18, 1942, *Lynx* rescued the passengers and crew of SS *Empire Kingfisher*, which had sunk off Cape Sable. Soon afterward condemned for further sea duty, she was paid off on April 23, 1943, and offered for sale, but no buyer was forthcoming until July, 1943. For some years a banana trader in the Caribbean, she was finally lost near Sydney, Australia, under the name *Rican Star*.

MOOSE

Moose left Halifax on June 3, 1940, for conversion and arming at Quebec City, where she was commissioned on September 8. She was then assigned to Halifax Local Defence Force until May, 1942, transferring then to Sydney, where by September, 1943, she was employed as training ship and examination vessel under control of HMCS Cornwallis. *Moose* was paid off on July 20, 1945, and sold the following year to Marine Industries Ltd., who renamed her

Moose, 1940

Otter arriving at Halifax under the Red Ensign as *Conseco. No photo of her as a naval vessel has been found.*

Raccoon

Reindeer, December 9, 1944

Renard, March, 1941

Fraternité. Sold to a U.S. buyer in 1956, she became *Ottelia*, and is apparently still in service in the Mediterranean.

OTTER

Otter accompanied *Moose* to Quebec City for conversion and arming, returning to Halifax on October 2, 1940, to be commissioned two days later for service with Halifax Local Defence Force. She was destroyed by accidental explosion and fire off Halifax Lightship on March 26, 1941, with the loss of two officers and 17 men.

RACCOON

Raccoon left Halifax on October 18, 1940, for Pictou, where she was converted and armed. She returned to Halifax at the end of the year and was commissioned, probably on December 31, for service with Halifax Local Defence Force. In July, 1941, she became a member of Gaspé Force, but returned to HLDF on February 1, 1942. On May 25, 1942, she returned to Gaspé to join the Gulf Escort Force, with which she saw extensive service as escort to Quebec-Sydney convoys. On September 7, 1942, while escorting convoy QS.33, she was torpedoed and sunk by *U 165* in the St. Lawrence River. There were no survivors.

REINDEER

Reindeer accompanied *Husky* and *Lynx* to Quebec City for conversion and arming in the summer of 1940. She was commissioned at Halifax on July 25 for service with Sydney Force, returning to Halifax on December 26 for the winter. She joined Gaspé Force in July, 1941, but by year's end was back again with Halifax Local Defence Force. In May, 1942, she moved to Sydney Force, and that November, to Saint John, N.B. Force. On December 24, 1942, *Reindeer* was assigned as training ship to HMCS Cornwallis, then located at Halifax, transferring with the establishment to Digby in 1943. She was employed there on A/S training with RN submarines until the end of the war, except for a stint at Saint John, N.B., during the first half of 1944. She was paid off to reserve at Sydney on July 20, 1945, and sold later that year.

RENARD

In her prime, *Renard* had shown a turn of speed to match her destroyer-like appearance, but she was 24 years old when commissioned on May 27, 1940, at Halifax. She left the following day for Quebec City for conversion and arming, returning on December 3 to Halifax, where she was assigned to Halifax Local Defence Force. In April, 1942, she began a long refit at Liverpool, N.S., and Pictou, on completion of which in July she became a torpedo and gunnery training ship attached to HMCS Cornwallis, with torpedo tubes fitted for the purpose. She moved with the establishment to Digby in July, 1943, but returned that November to Halifax to serve as a torpedo-firing ship. Surveyed in 1944 and found not to be worth repairing, she was paid off on August 1. She was sold in 1945, purportedly to become a floating power plant for a Cape Breton mine, but was derelict at Sydney in 1955.

SANS PEUR

This large yacht, the property of the Duke of Sutherland, was requisitioned in 1939 at Esquimalt and commissioned for patrol service on March 5, 1940. From May, 1942, *Sans Peur* served the dual function of patrol vessel and training vessel, but after November was used for training alone. Originally chartered, the ship was purchased in 1943. Following an extensive refit at Esquimalt, she left on January 24, 1944 for Halifax, arriving late in February. In March she was sent to HMCS Cornwallis, where she carried out A/S training in conjunction with RN submarines, and after February, 1946, she was a training ship at Halifax. Paid off on January 31, 1947, she was sold to Maple Leaf Steamships of Montreal, but on resale the following year she reverted, under Panamanian flag, to her original name, *Trenora*. Later refitted by her builders at Southampton, she resumed her career as a yacht for Italian owners, but by 1975 was in use as VIP accommodation at Okinawa, Japan.

VISON

Vison left Halifax on June 23, 1940, for Pictou, where she was to be converted and armed. She returned to Halifax on October 2 and was commissioned three days later. She was then assigned to the base at Gaspé, but returned to Halifax that November when the base was closed for the winter. In December, 1940, she was sent southward, operating out of Trinidad and Bermuda until her return to Halifax on May 13, 1941. In July she became a member of Gaspé Force, proceeding to Halifax for passage to Trinidad in December, 1941. She rejoined Halifax Local Defence Force in April, 1942, but was transferred to Sydney Force in July. In February, 1943, *Vison* returned to Halifax as a training ship attached to HMCS Cornwallis and moved with the establishment to Digby in April. She remained there until the end of the war as a seamen's training ship, exercising with RN submarines in the Bay of Fundy, and was paid off for disposal on August 4, 1945.

WOLF

Aged 25 years at the time of her commissioning on October 2, 1940, *Wolf* spent the entire war as a member of Esquimalt Force, at first on training and patrol duty and then, from September, 1943, as an examination vessel. Paid off on May 16, 1945, she was sold in 1946 to become the merchant vessel *Gulf Stream*. She was wrecked off Powell River, B.C., on October 11, 1947.

Sans Peur

Vison, April 27, 1943

Wolf, June 1, 1943

Motor Torpedo Boats

CMTB-1

A prototype MTB, she was shipped to Canada in 1940 by the British Power Boat Co., which had contracts for 12 of the type to be built at Montreal. *CMTB-1* arrived on July 16, 1940, was rebuilt to RCN specifications and sent to Halifax as a training vessel that fall. She arrived there on December 17 after a trip fraught with difficulties owing to ice and weather, and had been aground for a time near Richibucto, N.B. on November 27. She was at some point designated *V-250*. The boat returned to Montreal for refit in August, 1941, following which she was turned over to the RN as *MTB 332*. She seems to have been the only one of the twelve to serve, however briefly, in the RCN. The others became *MTBs 333-343* (RN) in 1941.

MTB-1

S-09

This was one of six U.S. PT boats acquired by the RN under Lend Lease in 1941. Numbered *PT-3, 4, 5, 6, 7,* and *9,* they were subsequently lent by the RN to the RCN. *PT-9* was redesignated S-09, while her five sisters served the RCAF as crash boats from 1941 to 1945. Alone of the group, *S-09* was built in Britain, by the British Power Boat Co. at Hythe, in 1939, for the Elco Boat Co. of New Jersey. She was handed over to the RCN without engines, arriving in tow at Montreal on August 23, 1941. There the Canadian Power Boat Co. fitted her with two 500 HP engines that enabled her to make only 22 knots. Commissioned on September 25, 1942, she served out of Halifax, Gaspé, and Quebec before proceeding to Toronto in May, 1944, to serve as firing range patrol vessel off Frenchman's Bay. She was turned over to the British Naval Liaison Officer at New York in June, 1945.

S-09

"D" and "G" Class Motor Torpedo Boats

The proposal, made in 1942, that the RCN should form a British-based flotilla of motor craft was not acted upon because Canada had no such boats. A year later, however, the Admiralty offered to supply and maintain boats if the RCN would man them. Two flotillas were accordingly formed early in 1944: the 29th, equipped with 72-foot "G" type motor torpedo boats (MTBs 459 — 466, 485, 486 and 491); and the 65th, with 115-foot Fairmile "D" boats (MTBs 726, 727, 735, 736, 743 — 748, and 797). These flotillas took part in a variety of pre-invasion operations off the coast of France, and in protect-

MTB 462, May 22, 1944

ing the flank of the invasion forces. After D-Day they helped prevent E-boats (their German counterparts) and larger craft from attacking cross-Channel traffic replenishing the beachhead. 29th Flotilla *MTBs 460* and *463* fell prey to mines on July 1 and 7, 1944, and five others — *MTBs 459, 461, 462, 465,* and *466* — were destroyed by fire at Ostend, Belgium, on February 14, 1945.

MTB 726, May, 1944

Motor Launches

The versatile 112-foot "B" class motor launch was designed in England by the Fairmile Company and the boats were accordingly known as Fairmiles. Eighty were built in Canada, 59 of them in Great Lakes boatyards. Fourteen of the remainder were built on the west coast and seven at Weymouth, N.S. They were numbered Q 050 to 129.

The Fairmiles played a vital role as escorts in the St. Lawrence River and the Gulf of St. Lawrence, and as escorts to convoys between Newfoundland and the mainland. They also carried out A/S patrol, port defence and rescue duties, releasing larger escort craft urgently needed elsewhere.

In 1942 it was decided to send two flotillas for the winter to the Caribbean, where the U-boats were enjoying great success owing to a shortage of U.S. escorts. The 72nd and 73rd Flotillas, of six boats each, left Halifax in mid-December for Trinidad via Boston and other east coast ports. Stress of weather en route forced the 72nd Flotilla to return home after reaching Savannah, Georgia, but the boats of the 73rd Flotilla operated until the following spring out of Miami and Key West under the (U.S.) Commander, Gulf Sea Frontier.

Their "mother ship," HMCS *Provider*, was stationed at Key West. She also acted as base ship for the 70th and 78th Flotillas in Bermuda during the winter of 1943-44. Early in June, 1943, *ML 053* distinguished herself by recovering, intact, two mines of a barrage laid by *U 119* in the Halifax approaches on June 1. *MLs 052, 062,* and *063* were transferred to the Free French Forces in February, 1943, and stationed at St. Pierre and Miquelon under operational control of the Flag Officer, Nfld.

Most of the Fairmiles were sold at war's end, but half a dozen remained in service as training ships on the Great Lakes in the 1960s: *Beaver (ML 106), Cougar (ML 104), Moose (ML 111), Raccoon (ML 079), Reindeer (ML 116),* and *Wolf (ML 062).* A seventh, *Elk (ML 124),* served on the west coast. The animal names, recalling those of the armed yachts whose duties the Fairmiles had taken over, were bestowed in 1954.

ML 067

Infantry Landing Craft

Twenty-four of these were lent to Canada by the USN expressly for the Normandy invasion, and RCN crews manned a further six previously on loan to the RN. Built in three New Jersey shipyards in 1943, all were commissioned between December, 1943 and March, 1944. These 158-foot craft could carry 155 troops below deck, landing them in shallow water via gangways on either bow.

Formed into three flotillas, the Canadian LCI(L)s shared to the full the hazards of the D-Day landings. Sandy beaches were seldom encountered, and many of the craft suffered damage from rocks, man-made obstacles, and limpet mines. The majority, however, continued to ferry Allied personnel to and from the beaches until well into August, 1944. By the end of September all of the craft had been paid off for return to the USN.

1st Canadian (260th RN) Flotilla: *LCI(L) 117, 121, 166, 177, 249, 266, 277, 285, 298, 301*
2nd Canadian (262nd RN) Flotilla: *LCI(L) 115, 118, 135, 250, 252, 262, 263, 276, 299, 306*
3rd Canadian (264th RN) Flotilla: *LCI(L) 125, 255, 270, 271, 288, 295, 302, 305, 310, 311*

LCI(L) 115, 1944

Auxiliaries

ADVERSUS

Built as an RCMP patrol craft in 1931, *Adversus* served the RCN in a similar capacity on the east coast until December 20, 1941, when she was lost aground in a blizzard on McNutt's Island, near Shelburne, N.S.

ALACHASSE

Sister to *Adversus*, *Alachasse* was taken over from the RCMP early in the war for patrol duty on the east coast. She was paid off on November 28, 1945, and sold to Marine Industries Ltd., in whose service she remained until 1957.

Adversus, 1940

Alachasse, April 3, 1944

ANDRÉE DUPRÉ

Originally a Sorel-built naval trawler of the TR class, she was sold for commercial use after the First World War and renamed *Napoléon L*. Again renamed and in the hands of Marine Industries Ltd. as a tug, she was taken up by the RCN in 1939 for use as an examination vessel at Halifax. Sold after the war, she resumed her former occupation as a tug, renamed *Remorqueur 16*, at Bordeaux, France.

BRAS d'OR

The New York shipowner for whom this trawler was ordered at Sorel went bankrupt soon after her launching in 1919, and she and five sisters were sold incomplete. She was completed in 1926 for service with the Department of Marine and Fisheries as *Lightship No. 25*. Requisitioned on September 15, 1939 as an auxiliary minesweeper and renamed *Bras d'Or*, she patrolled the Halifax approaches from 1939 to 1940. She joined the St. Lawrence Patrol in June, 1940, based at Rimouski, and on June 10 intercepted and seized the Italian freighter *Capo Noli*. On the night of October 18-19, 1940, while keeping the Roumanian freighter *Ingener N. Vlassopol* under surveillance in the Gulf of St. Lawrence, *Bras d'Or* disappeared.

DUNDALK

Commissioned on November 13, 1943, at Walkerville, Ont., this small tanker was used to deliver fuel oil from Halifax refineries to bases on the east coast and in Newfoundland. Occasionally *Dundalk* served as a lighter. She was paid off on April 9, 1946, and subsequently served as a CNAV until November 13, 1959.

Andrée Dupré, November, 1940

Bras d'Or, 1940

Dundalk, April 12, 1950

DUNDURN

Commissioned on November 25, 1943, at Walkerville, Ont., *Dundurn* performed the same duties as her sister, *Dundalk*. She was transferred to Esquimalt in 1946 and, on January 2, 1947, was paid off to serve as a CNAV.

EASTORE and LAYMORE

Originally built in Georgia for the U.S. Army, *Eastore* was commissioned on December 7, 1944, as a supply vessel, and served on the east coast until paid off on April 8, 1946, to become a CNAV. She was sold on July 30, 1964.

Laymore, a sister ship, was built at Kewaunee, Wis., and commissioned in the RCN on June 12, 1945. While stationed on the east coast she performed a variety of functions, including those of transport, boom defence, and laying moorings. She was paid off on April 17, 1946, to become a CNAV, and that summer was transferred to the west coast, becoming an oceanographic research vessel in 1966. She was offered for sale in 1977. A third sister, intended to be named *Westore*, was not acquired.

FLEUR de LIS

This triple-screw RCMP vessel was commissioned on November 16, 1939, as a patrol craft at Halifax. *Fleur de Lis* operated from Shelburne in 1942 and in 1943 joined Sydney Force for examination service in the Gut of Canso, based at Mulgrave, N.S. In November, 1945, she was paid off and acquired by Marine Industries Ltd., who still had her in 1953 when her register was closed.

Dundurn, September 14, 1959

Eastore, April 6, 1964

Fleur de Lis, 1940

FRENCH

A former RCMP vessel, she was commissioned at Halifax on September 18, 1939, for local patrol work. By the spring of 1942 *French* was based at Mulgrave, N.S., as an examination vessel, and that December was transferred to Saint John N.B. Force. In May, 1943, she joined Sydney Force and returned to examination service work in the Gut of Canso, based once more at Mulgrave. In January, 1944, she rejoined Halifax Local Defence Force, but after completing a major refit at Lunenburg that July she returned again to Mulgrave. Sold to commercial interests after the war, *French* was operating out of Halifax as *Le Français* as recently as 1953. On August 15 of that year she was badly damaged in a hurricane off Cape May, N.J., and abandoned to the underwriters.

JALOBERT

Built as *Polana* in 1911 for the Department of Agriculture, she later became a quarantine patrol vessel for the Department of Health. In 1923 she was acquired by the Department of Marine and Fisheries as a pilot vessel and renamed *Jalobert*, commemorating one of Jacques Cartier's master mariners. She served as an examination vessel in the St. Lawrence during the Second World War, and then returned to the Department of Transport. Sold out of government service in 1954, she served until 1980 as *Macassa* and later as *Queen City*.

LAURIER

Formerly an RCMP patrol vessel, she was commissioned in 1939 at Halifax for local A/S duties, and occasionally served as escort to the Sydney sections of Halifax convoys (SHX). By 1943 she was a member of Sydney Force, based at Mulgrave, N.S., for examination and patrol duty in the Gut of Canso. In February *Laurier* returned to Halifax Local Defence Force, but rejoined Sydney Force that September. Paid off on March 25, 1946, she was returned to the RCMP.

French, 1940

Jalobert, October 24, 1944

Laurier, August, 1940

MACDONALD

Like her sister, *Laurier*, *Macdonald* was a former RCMP vessel. She was commissioned on October 11, 1939, for patrol duty out of Halifax. Paid off on January 28, 1945, she was turned over to the Fisheries Department in 1946 and renamed *Howay*. She is still in service.

MACSIN

A sister to *Andrée Dupré* and, like her, a TR class naval trawler built at Sorel in 1918, *Macsin* was sold into commercial hands postwar and renamed *Gedéon L*. She was later renamed and acquired by Marine Industries Ltd., from whom the RCN took her over in 1940. She served throughout the Second World War as an examination vessel, and later was sold to the French government to serve as a tug at St. Nazaire.

MARVITA

This wooden-hulled craft saw service as a rum-runner during the early 1930s but was in the employ of the Newfoundland government when the RCN chartered her in 1941. *Marvita* served as an examination vessel until 1945, returning to her previous owners in 1946. She was transferred to the federal Department of Revenue in 1949, and was lost on Cape Ballard, Nfld., on July 15, 1954.

Macdonald, June 6, 1941

Macsin, August 28, 1941

Marvita, May, 1941

MASTADON

Formerly Department of Public Works *Dredge No. 306*, she was taken over by the RCN and converted to an auxiliary tanker for use on the west coast. Commissioned on December 9, 1942, *Mastadon* delivered oil to naval storage tanks and occasionally assisted in the distribution of commercial oil products as well. She was paid off on March 12, 1946, and entered mercantile service, being noted under Peruvian flag in the 1950s.

MONT JOLI

Mont Joli was chartered on July 5, 1940, for use as an examination vessel and purchased on June 29, 1943. An east coast auxiliary, she was paid off on March 29, 1946, and shortly afterward sold for commercial use. She still existed under the same name as late as 1966, when she was destroyed by fire.

MOONBEAM

Formerly the Department of Transport *Hopper Barge No. 1*, she was acquired by the RCN in December, 1940, and converted to a fuel oil carrier for use on the east coast and at St. John's, Nfld. *Moonbeam* was paid off on November 13, 1945, and sold the following year to become *Oakbranch* and, about 1960, *B.L.L. 24*. Her register was closed in 1971, the ship having been broken up.

MURRAY STEWART

Built in 1918, she was purchased in 1922 by the Department of Transport, which lent her to the RCN in 1942. *Murray Stewart* served most of the war as an examination vessel at Saint John, N.B., and was paid off on August 22, 1945. Sold in 1946, she was in service by 1951 as *David Richard* at her native Port Arthur, and in 1979 was renamed *Georgian Queen*.

Mastadon, February 25, 1943

Mont Joli, April, 1942

Murray Stewart, 1939

Moonbeam, April, 1941

148

Nitinat

NITINAT

A newly built fishery patrol vessel, *Nitinat* was chartered in September, 1939, for patrol and examination duties on the west coast. She was returned to her owners in June, 1945, to finish her career by fire in the Fraser River on February 1, 1977.

NORSAL

A vessel hired from the Powell River Co. for miscellaneous duties, *Norsal* returned to commercial service after the war, to be renamed *Maui Lu* in 1973.

PRESERVER

Commissioned on July 11, 1942 at Sorel, she arrived at Halifax on August 4, having escorted a Quebec-Sydney convoy en route. She was assigned to Newfoundland Force as a Fairmile base supply ship, arriving at St. John's on September 18 but transferring almost immediately to Botwood, Nfld. She returned to St. John's in mid-December, staying until the end of July, 1943, when she moved to Red Bay. Back at St. John's in November, she returned to Red Bay in mid-June, 1944, and at the beginning of September, moved to Sydney. After a refit at Halifax at the beginning of 1945, *Preserver* returned once more to St. John's but was transferred to Shelburne, N.S. in June. Paid off on November 6, 1945, at Shelburne, she was sold to the Peruvian Navy in 1946 and renamed *Mariscal Castilla*, then *Cabo Blanco*. She was broken up in 1961.

Norsal, January, 1941

Preserver, June 27, 1942

PROVIDER

Sister to *Preserver*, she was commissioned at Sorel on December 1, 1942, and arrived at Halifax on December 14. Two flotillas of Fairmiles were to proceed to the Caribbean to alleviate a shortage of escorts there, and *Provider* was ordered south to be their base supply ship. She accordingly sailed on January 19, 1943, but had to return owing to storm damage and sailed again ten days later, arriving at Trinidad on February 20. One Fairmile flotilla, the 73rd, joined her at Guantanamo, Cuba, proceeding with her in March to a new base at Key West. Returning to Halifax on April 23, she was then assigned to Gaspé Force, arriving on May 22, and subsequently transferred to Sept Îles, where she remained from June 29 until November. At the end of 1943 she proceeded to Halifax and thence to Bermuda to serve as base ship for the 70th and 78th Flotillas. *Provider* returned to Halifax on July 31, 1944, but sailed again that September for Bermuda, where she was attached to the recently established base HMCS Somers Isle, until May, 1945. She then went to Halifax as base supply ship until she was paid off on March 22, 1946, to be sold later that year to Peruvian owners and renamed *Maruba*. Subsequently acquired by the Peruvian Navy, she served as *Orgenos* until disposed of for scrap in 1961.

RAYON d'OR

Requisitioned on September 11, 1939, this former fishing trawler became an auxiliary minesweeper based at Halifax. Her duties also included loop-laying and maintenance. Early in 1943, following a winter refit, *Rayon d'Or* was assigned to Sydney Force and remained in that service until February, 1944, when she rejoined the Halifax Local Defence Force. Paid off in 1945, she resumed her commercial career until 1954.

REO II

A former rum-runner, *Reo II* was chartered by the RCN on July 30, 1940, and commissioned on January 23, 1941, as an auxiliary minesweeper. She also served as an examination vessel and coil skid towing vessel. Declared surplus on October 19, 1945, she was paid off and in 1946 sold for mercantile purposes. She still existed in 1981, in the hands of the Lunenburg Marine Museum Society.

Provider, January 17, 1943

Rayon d'Or, 1940

Reo II, April 24, 1941

ROSS NORMAN

A wooden-hulled coaster chartered on June 19, 1940, *Ross Norman* served successively as auxiliary minesweeper, coil skid towing craft and mobile deperming craft with Halifax Local Defence Force. She was purchased on August 26, 1943. Paid off on April 8, 1946, she was sold in 1947 and, as *Chicoutimi Trader*, was lost by stranding on Grindstone Island, Que., on November 18, 1952.

SANKATY

Formerly a Stamford-Oyster Bay, Mass., ferry, *Sankaty* was commissioned on September 24, 1940, at Halifax as a minelaying, loop-laying and maintenance vessel. She was paid off on August 18, 1945, and became a Prince Edward Island ferry under the name of *Charles A. Dunning*. Sold for scrap in 1964, she sank on October 27 en route to Sydney.

SHULAMITE

Another one-time rum-runner and sister to *Marvita*, she was acquired by the RCN from the Newfoundland government to be used as an examination vessel. Returned to her previous owners in August, 1945, she was later sold and renamed *Norsya* in 1950. She foundered off Matane, Que., on September 19, 1953.

Ross Norman

Sankaty, March, 1941. Note mines on quarterdeck.

Shulamite, April 26, 1944

STANDARD COASTER

Hired on July 31, 1940, and commissioned on February 11, 1942, this wooden-hulled coaster was based at Halifax, functioning primarily as a coil skid towing vessel. She was paid off on March 25, 1946 and returned to merchant service. She was broken up at Saint John, N.B., and her register closed in 1957.

STAR XVI

Left homeless by the fall of Norway, the whale-catcher *Star XVI* was chartered in August, 1941, from the Norwegian government-in-exile, and by early 1942 was a member of St. John's Local Defence Force. She transferred in June, 1942, to Sydney Force, with which she remained until the war's end, and was returned to her owners after being paid off on August 31, 1945.

SUDERØY IV

Like *Star XVI*, *Suderöy IV* and her two sisters were stranded overseas when the Germans over-ran Norway, and were chartered by the RCN in June, 1940. Commissioned in June, 1941, she served with Halifax Local Defence Force until paid off on August 31, 1945, and returned to her owners.

Standard Coaster, April 21, 1944

Star XVI

Suderoy IV

Suderöy V

SUDERÖY V

Chartered in 1940 and commissioned on June 2, 1941, *Suderöy V* joined St. John's Local Defence Force. From June, 1942 until she was paid off on August 7, 1945, she was a member of Sydney Force. After the war she resumed her occupation as a whale-catcher.

SUDERÖY VI

Chartered in 1940 and commissioned on March 19, 1941, this whale-catcher had been the British *Southern Gem* before her sale to Norwegian owners. She served with Halifax Local Defence Force throughout the war as an auxiliary minesweeper. Paid off on August 31, 1945, she was returned to her owners.

NOTE: Evidence received from Dr. Robert Stark, at one time C.O. of *Suderöy VI*, raises the probability of some or all of these ships having been misidentified in the first printing.
It would appear that, contrary to logic, *Suderöys IV, V* and *VI* bore pendant numbers J03, J04 and J05. Accordingly, this second printing presents new photographs of *Suderöys IV* and *V*, while the photo earlier thought to represent *Suderöy V* now illustrates *Suderöy VI*.

SUNBEAM

Formerly the Department of Transport *Hopper Barge No. 4*, she was acquired by the RCN in 1940 and converted to a fuel oil carrier. *Sunbeam* was commissioned on November 11, 1940, and served as a lighter at Halifax and St. John's, and occasionally as a transport. Paid off on December 13, 1945, and sold into commercial service, she was renamed *Birchbranch* in 1949. Her register was closed in 1968, as she had been broken up.

Suderöy VI, July 1943

Sunbeam

VENCEDOR

This rather bizarre-looking vessel was built in Britain in 1913 as the three-masted topsail schooner *Exmouth II*, tender to the Thames River training ship *Exmouth*. She was renamed after her sale in 1927 to the Lieutenant-Governor of British Columbia. Used by the RCN as a miscellaneous auxiliary on the west coast, she was sold after the war and was still in service in 1981.

VENOSTA

She was commissioned on November 17, 1939, as a gate vessel and auxiliary minesweeper at Halifax, and later employed at Sydney. She had served in the RN as a minesweeper during the First World War. *Venosta* is said to have been paid off on January 22, 1942, and designated *C.Y. 509*. Sold postwar, she was still in service under her original name in 1953, but was later known progressively as *Reyneld V*, *Fort Prevel* and *Michel P*. She was broken up and her register closed in 1972.

VENTURE II

Formerly the U.S. yacht *Seaborn*, she had been acquired in 1939 by Northumberland Ferries Ltd. and renamed *Charles A. Dunning* just in time to be taken over for naval service and revert to her former name. On December 7, 1939, she was commissioned as HMS *Seaborn*, flagship of the Rear Admiral, 3rd Battleship Squadron, Halifax. At the end of September, 1941, she became HMCS *Sambro*, depot ship at Halifax for destroyers and auxiliaries, and on March 6, 1943 was again renamed *Venture II* as depot ship for Fairmiles. When the sailing yacht *Venture* was redesignated in May, 1943, *H.C. 190*, the depot ship dropped her Roman suffix and remained plain *Venture* until paid off on January 14, 1946. Sold for commercial purposes, she still existed in 1953 under Panamanian flag.

VIERNOE

A near-sister to *Venosta*, she also served with the RN from 1915 to 1919. *Viernoe* was commissioned in the RCN on October 11, 1939, and in 1941 was serving as a boom defence vessel at Sydney. She is said to have been paid off on January 22, 1942, and designated *C.Y. 512* (sig-

Vencedor, July 27, 1945

Venosta, 1940

Venture II

Viernoe, 1940

nificance unknown). Subsequently sold for mercantile use, she was broken up and her register closed in 1954.

WHITETHROAT

A controlled minelayer converted from an Isles class trawler, *Whitethroat* was commissioned at Beverley, Yorkshire, on December 7, 1944. She made her passage to Canada with convoy ONS.42 in February, 1945, to replace HMCS *Sankaty*. She assisted in the dismantling of harbour defences until May 6, 1946, when she was paid off to become a CNAV, and was employed in 1947 making repairs to submarine telegraph cables. In 1950, she carried out oceanograph work for the Naval Research Establishment, but on April 17, 1951, was recommissioned to provide mine- and loop-laying training in the Korean emergency. She remained with Seaward Defence until September 30, 1954, when she again became a CNAV. Transferred to the west coast in March, 1955, she was attached to the Pacific Naval Laboratory until sold in 1967.

Whitethroat, April 10, 1963

The Fishermen's Reserve

The Fishermen's Reserve was formed in 1938 because of the growing likelihood of war. By October, 1941, it comprised 17 ships and, until the advent of the first corvettes, was the only naval force available on the west coast. The ships were mostly fishing craft of various kinds, many of them seiners like *Santa Maria*. In December, 1941, 5 more ships joined, and shortly thereafter 20 more, seized from their Japanese-Canadian owners following Pearl Harbor.

The force performed a valuable inshore patrol service, as their skippers were thoroughly familiar with the intricacies of the British Columbia coastline. It remained, however, very much an *ad hoc* organization until August, 1942, when officialdom took a hand, and formal training of its personnel was begun at Esquimalt in an establishment called Givenchy II. Personnel had increased rapidly since Pearl Harbor, and it was envisaged that they might better be used as crews for landing craft in Combined Operations exercises with the army.

The danger of Japanese attack on the west coast failed to materialize, however, and through 1943 and 1944 Fishermen's Reserve personnel were discharged or siphoned off into the RCNVR. By the end of 1944 the force had ceased to exist, the only five of its ships still in service now manned by the RCNVR at Prince Rupert.

There no longer seems to be an official list of the ships that composed the Fishermen's Reserve, but the following are probably all the likely candidates:

Allaverdy	Fifer	Ripple II
B.C. Lady	Flores	San Tomas
Barkley Sound	Foam	Santa Maria
Billow	Howe Sound I	Seiner
Bluenose	Joan W. II	Signal
Camenita	Johanna	Smith Sound
Canfisco	Kuitan	Spray
Cape Beale	Leelo	Springtime V
Cancolim	Loyal I	Stanpoint
Capella	Loyal II	Surf
Chamiss Bay	Maraudor	Takla
Combat	Margaret I	Talapus
Comber	Meander	Tordo
Crest	Merry Chase	Valdes
Dalehurst	Mitchell Bay	Vanisle
Departure Bay	Moolock	West Coast
Early Field	Moresby II	Western Maid
Ehkoli	Nenamook	

Santa Maria

PRINCE DAVID

completed that December, and shortly after recommissioning she left for the U.K. via Cristobal and New York.

Upon arrival in the Clyde in February, 1944, *Prince David* joined Combined Operations Command, and landed troops in Normandy on D-Day. In July she left for the Mediterranean to take part in Operation "Dragoon," the invasion of southern France, on August 15. She saw extensive service in the Mediterranean until damaged by a mine on December 10, 1944, off Aegina Island, Greece. Repaired at Ferryville, North Africa, she left in March, 1945, to refit at Esquimalt, but saw no further service and was paid off in June. Sold in 1948 for mercantile purposes and renamed *Charlton Monarch*, she was broken up in 1951.

PRINCE HENRY

the following March, except for the months of September and October, 1942, when she served under USN control in the Aleutians. On March 6, 1943, she commenced rebuilding into an infantry landing ship, was recommissioned on January 6, 1944, and left immediately for the U.K. She was present on D-Day as a member of Combined Operations Command and, like *Prince David*, next took part in the invasion of southern France. She remained in the Mediterranean until March, 1945, then proceeded to London to refit in East India Dock. During the refit, on April 15, she was paid off, and used afterward by the RN as an accommodation ship first at Portsmouth and later at Falmouth. Sold to the Ministry of Wartime Transport in 1946, she was renamed *Empire Parkeston* and employed as a troopship between Harwich and the Hook of Holland. She was broken up in 1962 at La Spezia, Italy.

PRINCE ROBERT

conversion to an auxiliary A/A ship, and was recommissioned on June 7 at Vancouver, leaving Esquimalt 12 days later for the Clyde via Bermuda. In November she was assigned to Gibraltar Command, Mediterranean Fleet, and employed as A/A escort to U.K.-Sierra Leone and U.K.-Mediterranean convoys. Though reassigned to Plymouth Command in January, 1944, she remained at the same duties, and from June to August escorted Mediterranean convoys. In September *Prince Robert* left Plymouth for Esquimalt, and upon arrival underwent a refit that lasted until June, 1945. She left Esquimalt July 4, 1945, for service with the British Pacific Fleet, arriving at Sydney, Australia on August 10. On August 31 *Prince Robert* entered Hong Kong, where her commanding officer had the honour to represent Canada at the surrender ceremonies, September 16. On October 20 she arrived at Esquimalt with repatriated Canadian prisoners from Hong Kong, and on December 10 was paid off and laid up in Lynn Creek, B.C. Sold in 1948, she became the merchant vessel *Charlton Sovereign* and, in 1952, the Italian-flag *Lucania*.

RESTIGOUCHE

D-Day, and afterward carried out Channel and Biscay patrols from her base at Plymouth. She returned to Canada in September, 1944, for a major refit at Saint John, N.B. and Halifax, and upon completion proceeded to Bermuda for working up. Returning to Halifax on February 14, 1945, she performed various local duties, and after VE-Day was employed for three months bringing home military personnel from Newfoundland. Paid off on October 5, 1945, she was broken up the following year.

KOOTENAY

May, 1944, she became a member of EG 11 and was present on D-Day. In succeeding months she carried out patrols in the Channel and the Bay of Biscay, and while thus engaged took part in the sinking of *U 678*, July 6, south of Brighton; *U 621*, August 18, off La Rochelle; and *U 984*, August 20, west of Brest. She sailed for Shelburne, N.S., in mid-September, 1944, for a major refit, returning to the U.K. in the spring of 1945. Following workups at Tobermory she operated out of Plymouth until the end of May, then returned to Canada, where she made six round trips as a troop transport between Newfoundland and Quebec City. She was paid off into reserve at Sydney on October 26, 1945, and in 1946 sold for scrapping.

BUXTON

idle from December, 1941 to April, 1942. Returning to Canadian waters that August, she was assigned to WLEF, but her defects persisted and she was taken to Boston in December for further repairs. These repairs completed, she arrived at St. John's on March 30, 1943, to rejoin WLEF, three months later becoming part of its newly formed EG W-1. Continuing sickly, *Buxton* was offered to the RCN for training purposes and arrived at Digby in December, having been commissioned on November 4, 1943 at Halifax. She continued as a stationary training ship until paid off June 2, 1945, at Sydney, and was broken up the same year at Boston.

ST. FRANCIS

in April, 1943, she returned to the MOEF, but by November was again urgently in need of repairs, which were carried out at Shelburne, N.S. In February, 1944, she was allocated to HMCS Cornwallis as a training ship. She was paid off at Sydney on June 11, 1945, and sold for scrap. In tow for Philadelphia, *St. Francis* sank off Rhode Island on July 14, 1945, after colliding with the American SS *Winding Gulf*.

HURON

assisted *Haida* in sinking torpedo boat *T 29* and destroyer *Z 32*, and in August made her first visit to Canada for refit at Halifax. In November she returned to the U.K. to carry out escort duties in the Western Approaches and to make one further trip to Russia. She returned to Halifax with *Haida* and *Iroquois* on June 10, 1945, and began tropicalization refit, but this was discontinued owing to VJ-Day and she was paid off on March 9, 1946. She was recommissioned at Halifax for training purposes in 1950, but sailed on January 22, 1951 on the first of two tours of duty in Korean waters, the second being carried out 1953-54. She then reverted to her peacetime role until she was finally paid off on April 30, 1963, at Halifax. She was broken up at La Spezia, Italy, in 1965.

IROQUOIS

rejoined the Home Fleet at Scapa Flow in March, 1945, escorted one more convoy to Russia and, following D-Day, sailed to Oslo as an escort to Crown Prince Olaf, who was returning to liberated Norway. Shortly afterward she visited Copenhagen, whence she escorted the German cruisers *Prinz Eugen* and *Nürnberg* to Kiel for their formal surrender. On June 4 she left Greenock with *Haida* and *Huron* for home. The end of the Pacific war brought a halt to her tropicalization refit, and *Iroquois* was paid off on February 22, 1946. The following year she began a long refit and on June 24, 1949, was recommissioned as a cadet training ship. In 1952 and 1953 she did two tours of duty in the Korean theatre, following which she returned to

ARROWHEAD

Quebec/Gaspé-Sydney convoys, and in October joined Halifax Force and for two months escorted Quebec-Labrador convoys. On November 30 she rejoined WLEF at Halifax, to remain with it until August, 1944. When this escort force was divided into escort groups in June, 1943, *Arrowhead* became a member of EG W-7, transferring to W-1 that December. During this period she underwent two major refits: at Charleston, S.C., in the spring of 1943, and at Baltimore, Md., a year later. During the latter refit her fo'c's'le was extended. In September, 1944, she joined Quebec Force and was again employed escorting Quebec-Labrador convoys. In December she transferred to EG W-8, WEF, and served on the "triangle run" (Halifax, St. John's, New York/Boston) for the balance of the war. On May 27, 1945, *Arrowhead* left St. John's to join convoy HX.358 for passage to Britain, where she was paid off and returned to the RN on June 27, at Milford Haven. Sold in 1947 for conversion to a whale-catcher and renamed *Southern Larkspur*, she was finally broken up at Odense, Denmark, in 1959.

BADDECK

joined WLEF until allocated to duties in connection with the invasion of North Africa, arriving at Londonderry on November 1. For the next four months she escorted U.K.-Mediterranean convoys, returning to Halifax on April 4, 1943. Later that month *Baddeck* was assigned to EG C-4 for two round trips to Londonderry, then in mid-July went to EG W-2, WLEF. In August she underwent a major refit at Liverpool, N.S., including fo'c's'le extension and, after working up in St. Margaret's Bay in January, 1944, sailed in March to join EG 9, Londonderry. In April she transferred to Western Approaches Command for invasion escort duties, based at Portsmouth, and on June 13 beat off an attack by motor torpedo boats while so employed. In September she was transferred to Nore Command, based at Sheerness, escorting local convoys until her departure for home on May 24, 1945. She was paid off at Sorel on July 4 and sold for mercantile purposes in 1946, and renamed *Efthalia*. After a number of name-changes, she was lost ashore near Jeddah as the Greek-flag *Evi* on March 11, 1966.

BRANDON

including fo'c's'le extension. She left Londonderry September 2, 1944, to join her last transatlantic convoy, ONS.251, and, after two months' refit at Liverpool, N.S., worked up in Bermuda. On February 5, 1945, she arrived at St. John's to join EG W-5, Western Escort Force, in which she served until the end of the war. Paid off at Sorel on June 22, 1945, she was broken up at Hamilton, Ont. in 1945.

CHAMBLY

join the convoy off Greenland in support. Just before joining on September 10, they came upon *U 501* trailing the convoy, and sank her. *Chambly* served as a mid-ocean escort to Iceland for the balance of 1941, then underwent repairs at Halifax from December 8, 1941 to February 22, 1942. She then made a round trip to Londonderry as an escort in March, 1942 and, on her return to St. John's on March 28, was based there to reinforce ocean escorts in the western Atlantic, doubling as a training ship. In

156

September she resumed regular mid-ocean escort duties, with time out for refit at Liverpool, N.S., from November 26, 1942 to February 13, 1943. From March to August, 1943 she was a member of EG C-2, then briefly joined the newly formed EG 9 at St. John's and, in September, EG 5. In December she returned to Liverpool, N.S., for three months' refit, including fo'c's'le extension. After workups in St. Margaret's Bay she resumed mid-ocean duties, this time with C-1, until her final departure from Londonderry on March 11, 1945. She was refitting at Louisbourg when the war ended, and was paid off and laid up at Sorel on June 20. Sold in 1946 for conversion to a whale-catcher, she entered service in 1952 under the Dutch flag as *Sonja Vinke*, and was broken up at Santander, Spain, in 1966.

EDMUNDSTON

assigned to WLEF. On January 4, 1943, she commenced a five-month refit at Halifax, including fo'c's'le extension, carried out workups at Pictou, then joined EG 5 at St. John's. For the next ten months she was employed in support of North Atlantic, Gibraltar, and Sierra Leone convoys. She underwent a refit at Liverpool, N.S., from May to July, 1944, worked up in Bermuda in August and, in October, joined the newly formed EG C-8. She served the remainder of the war as an ocean escort, leaving Londonderry on May 11, 1945, for the last time. She was paid off at Sorel on June 16 and sold for mercantile use, entering service in 1948 as *Amapala*, last noted under Liberian flag in Lloyd's list for 1961-62.

GALT

another refit, this one including fo'c's'le extension, completing early in May, and a month later left Halifax for Bermuda to work up. On her return she was allocated for the balance of the war to EG W-5, WEF. *Galt* was paid off June 21, 1945 at Sorel, and broken up at Hamilton in 1946.

MATAPEDIA

was to be her only trip to the U.K., as she joined WLEF on her return and, with the exception of a stint with Gaspé Force from November to December, 1944, remained with WLEF until the end of the war. She underwent a major refit at Pictou from May 8 to July 21, 1942, and in June, 1943, became a member of EG W-5. On September 8, 1943, she was rammed amidships in a thick fog off Sambro Lightship by SS *Scorton*, and seriously damaged. After temporary repairs at Dartmouth from September 10 to October 12, she was towed to Liverpool, N.S., for full repairs and refit, including fo'c's'le extension. This was completed early in February, 1944, and a month later she proceeded to Bermuda for two weeks' workups, on her return joining EG W-4 for the balance of the war. She underwent one further major refit from February 15 to April 28, 1945, at Halifax, again followed by workups in Bermuda, but the war was now over and she was paid off at Sorel on June 16. *Matapedia* was broken up at Hamilton in 1950.

MOOSE JAW

the inaugural "Newfie-Derry" convoy. On February 19, 1942, she ran aground on the south entrance of St. John's harbour en route to join convoy HX 176, and, although refloated soon afterward proved to be holed and leaking in several places. Temporary repairs were carried out at St. John's from February 20 to March 5, and permanent repairs at Saint John, N.B., from March 15 to June 25. Briefly assigned to WLEF, she was detached in September for duties in connection with Operation "Torch", and made

her passage to the U.K. with convoy SC.107, which lost 15 ships to U-boats. During the next five months *Moose Jaw* was employed escorting U.K.-Mediterranean convoys, returning to Halifax on April 20, 1943. Refitted there, she joined Quebec Force at the end of May for escort duties in the Gulf of St. Lawrence, later transferring to Gaspé Force. She underwent a major refit, including fo'c's'le extension, at Liverpool, N.S., from December 19, 1943 to March 23, 1944. After working up in St. Margaret's Bay she left Halifax on May 1 for the U.K., to join Western Approaches Command, Greenock, for invasion duties. She served in the Channel until September, 1944, when she joined EG 41, Plymouth, and escorted coastal convoys from her base at Milford Haven until the end of the war. She left for home in May, 1945, was paid off at Sorel on July 8 and broken up at Hamilton in 1949.

PICTOU

escorting convoy ON.116, she was rammed in a fog near St. John's by the Norwegian SS *Hindanger*, suffering severe damage to her stern. After completing repairs at Halifax on September 20, she joined EG C-2. On her return from the U.K. with ON.149 in December, 1942, she required further repairs at Halifax, followed immediately by refit at Liverpool, N.S. In May, 1943, she joined EG C-3, and on December 17 left Londonderry for the last time. From early January to March 31, 1944, she was refitting at New York, incidentally receiving her extended fo'c's'le. She then proceeded to Bermuda for three weeks' working-up, returning in mid-June to join EG W-5, Western Escort Force. Paid off on July 12, 1945, at Sorel, she was sold for conversion to a whale-catcher, entering service in 1950 as the Honduran-flag *Olympic Chaser*. Again sold in 1956, she served as *Otori Maru No. 7* until converted to a barge in 1963.

RIMOUSKI

completed at Liverpool and Halifax in February, 1945. After working up, she returned to the U.K., to be based at Milford Haven as a member of EG 41, Plymouth, for the duration of the war. Returning to Canada in June, 1945, she was paid off at Sorel on July 24 and broken up in 1950 at Hamilton.

SASKATOON

the "triangle run" until the end of the war, becoming a member of EG W-8 when it was established in June, 1943, and transferring to W-6 in April, 1944. During her career she had two major refits: at Halifax from August 11 to November 17, 1942; and at Pictou from mid-December, 1943 to April 1, 1944. Following the latter, which included fo'c's'le extension, she worked up for three weeks at Pictou and another three in Bermuda. She was paid off on June 25, 1945, at Sorel and soon afterward sold for conversion to a whale-catcher. She began her new career in 1948, successively named *Tra los Montes*, *Olympic Fighter* in 1950, and *Otori Maru No. 6* in 1956, last appearing as such in Lloyd's list for 1962-63.

SPIKENARD

Command, and between July, 1941 and January, 1942, made three round trips to Iceland as ocean escort. On February 1, 1942, she left St. John's for convoy SC.67 on the recently inaugurated "Newfie-Derry" run, and on February 10 was torpedoed and sunk south of Iceland by *U 136*. There were only eight survivors.

THE PAS

can SS *Medina* in the western Atlantic on July 21, 1943, while escorting convoy ON.192, and was under repair at Halifax and Shelburne until early October. She then returned to her duties with WLEF until September, 1944 (from April as a member of EG W-3), when she underwent a refit at Sydney and, on completion of this late in November, joined HMCS Cornwallis as a training ship for the balance of the war. *The Pas* never did receive an extended fo'c's'le. She was paid off on July 24, 1945, at Sorel and broken up at Hamilton the following year.

TRILLIUM

arrived at Boston for a refit that included the extension of her fo'c's'le. This was completed on June 10, after which she worked up at Pictou before joining EG C-4. Late in April, 1944 she returned to Pictou for a two-month refit, followed by additional repairs at Halifax, and early in August went to Bermuda to work up. She arrived at St. John's September 2, 1944, to join EG C-3. On January 14, 1945, while escorting the Milford Haven section of ON.278, she sank a coaster in collision and required five weeks' repairs, afterward resuming mid-ocean service until the end of the war. This ship was unique in that she spent her entire career as a mid-ocean escort, participating in three major convoy battles: SC.100 (September, 1942); ON.166 (February, 1943); and SC.121 (March, 1943). She left St. John's on May 27, 1945, for the U.K., where she was returned to the RN at Milford Haven on June 27. Sold in 1947 for conversion to a whale-catcher, she entered service in 1950 as the Honduran-registered *Olympic Runner*, and in 1956 became the Japanese *Otori Maru No. 10*. She last appeared in Lloyd's list for 1959-60.

Part Three 1945~1981

Introduction

Reverting with astonishing speed from a wartime to a peacetime footing, the RCN had fewer ships in commission at the end of 1946 than at the outbreak of the war: an aircraft carrier, two cruisers, two new Tribal class destroyers, a frigate, a minesweeper, and a former U-boat. These were, of course, wholly inadequate even as a training force, and in succeeding years many ships — especially frigates — were brought out of retirement and given major refits. Among them were three diesel Bangors, three Algerines, and two motor minesweepers.

The outbreak of the Korean War in 1950 accelerated this process, although only 2 of the 18 Bangors recovered in this emergency were recommissioned. Eight of our 11 destroyers, now all once again in commission, served with distinction in the Korean theatre. The aircraft carrier *Warrior* was replaced in 1948 by *Magnificent* and she by *Bonaventure* in 1957.

Twenty-one of the frigates were radically rebuilt as "ocean escorts" from 1953 to 1958 and in 1955 *St. Laurent*, the first of 20 destroyer escorts of novel design, was commissioned. The building programmes of 1950 and 1951 produced the only other large class of ships, the 20 Bay class coastal minesweepers. Six of these were transferred to the French Navy in 1954 but replaced by six of new construction bearing the same names. The latter six were all that remained of the class by 1964, and serve still on the west coast.

Two former U.S. submarines were acquired, one in 1961 and the other in 1968. They have since been disposed of and replaced by three submarines built to order in Britain and commissioned from 1965 to 1967. These submarines provide the A/S ships with friendly opponents against whom to test their skills.

All but two of the frigates had been discarded by 1967, and in 1970 the last two of the older destroyers were sold for scrap, along with *Bonaventure*. Since then the navy has been, as it was at the outbreak of war 42 years ago, an A/S force. Its duties, apart from training officer cadets and new-entry ratings, consist of upholding Canada's maritime commitment to NATO, enforcing fishery regulations, and generally "showing the flag" (which, incidentally, ceased to be the White Ensign as of 1965). The only major craft, apart from destroyer escorts and submarines, to enter service have been three large operational support ships, commissioned from 1963 to 1970.

The seven St. Laurent class DDEs were rebuilt from 1962 to 1966 to carry helicopters, but they and the Restigouche class are growing old, and four ships from these classes have been retired since 1973. Apart from these there remain, at time of writing, four somewhat newer Mackenzie class DDEs, two Annapolis class DDHs, and four modern "280" class DDHs. Consideration is being given to a programme of six new frigates, however, the first to be completed late in 1987.

Aircraft Carriers

Active consideration of an expanded role for
Canada in the Pacific war began as early as May,
1944, and it was agreed that larger ships would
be required than any then serving in the RCN.
The Canadian Naval Staff favoured returning
the escort aircraft carriers *Nabob* and *Puncher*,
then on loan from the RN, and taking over light
fleet carriers in their place.

Two of these, *Warrior* and *Magnificent*, were
offered on loan (with option to purchase) in
January, 1945, and arrangements were concluded
in May, but neither ship had been completed by
VJ-Day. *Warrior* was finally commissioned at
Belfast on January 24, 1946, arriving at Halifax
on March 31 with the Seafires and Fireflies of
803 and 825 Squadrons. Unsuited for an eastern
Canadian winter, she was transferred to Esquimalt in November.

Reductions in defence spending soon made it
evident that the RCN would be able to afford
only one carrier, and it was decided to exchange
Warrior for the slightly larger *Magnificent*. *Warrior* accordingly returned in February, 1947, to
the east coast, where she was engaged most of
the year in sea training and, latterly, in preparations for her return to the RN. In February, 1948,
she arrived at Belfast, where she transferred
stores to *Magnificent* and, on March 23, was
paid off. She served in the RN until 1958, when
she was sold to Argentina and renamed
Independencia.

Magnificent, a near-sister to *Warrior*, had been
launched at Belfast six months after her, in November, 1944. She was commissioned on April
7, 1948, and spent the ensuing nine years in an
unceasing round of training cruises and exercises,
visiting such far-flung ports as Oslo, Havana,
Lisbon, and San Francisco, and taking part in
large-scale NATO manoeuvres such as "Main-
brace" and "Mariner" in 1952 and 1953. On
December 29, 1956, she left Halifax for Port
Said, carrying a deckload of 233 vehicles as well
as 406 army personnel and stores — Canada's
contribution to the UN Emergency Force in the
Middle East. "Maggie" sailed from Halifax for
the last time on April 10, 1957, to be paid off at
Plymouth on June 14. After being laid up for
eight years there she arrived at Faslane, Scotland,
in July, 1965, for breaking up. When the Suez
crisis erupted, *Magnificent* had just completed
landing stores for her successor, a more modern
carrier whose construction had been suspended
in 1946. The successor's name was to have been
HMS *Powerful*, but the RCN decided to rename
her *Bonaventure* after the bird sanctuary in the
Gulf of St. Lawrence. Work on this ship had
stopped three months after her launching in February, 1945, with the result that when construction resumed in 1952, improvements could be
built into her. The most notable of these was the
angled flight deck, which provided a longer landing run without sacrificing forward parking
space, and permitted the removal of the unpopu-
lar crash barrier. Also noteworthy were a steam
catapult and a mirror landing sight, the latter
going far toward eliminating human error in
landing.

"Bonnie" was commissioned at Belfast on
January 17, 1957, and arrived at Halifax on June
26, carrying on deck an experimental hydrofoil
craft that was to serve in the development of
HMCS *Bras d'Or*. Unlike her predecessors, *Bonaventure* had Banshee jet fighters and Tracker A/S
aircraft as her complement. Like them, she enjoyed a busy career of flying training and participation in A/S and tactical exercises with ships of
other NATO nations. What was expected to be
her mid-life refit, carried out from 1966 to 1967,
took 16 months and cost over $11 million. In-
comprehensibly, she was paid off on July 1,
1970, and sold for scrap.

Warrior, 1945

Magnificent

Bonaventure, 1968

Destroyers

Tribal Class

ATHABASKAN (2nd)

The last of her class to be completed, "Athabee" was commissioned at Halifax on January 20, 1948, and sailed in mid-May for the west coast, where she trained new entries and officer cadets until the outbreak of the Korean War. She sailed from Esquimalt on July 5, 1950, for the first of three tours of duty in Korean waters, returning December 11, 1953, from the last of them. In October, 1954, she emerged from an extensive conversion classed as a destroyer escort, and resumed her training role until January, 1959, when she left for the east coast to become part of a homogeneous Tribal class squadron. After five more years of training cruises and NATO exercises she was placed in reserve at Halifax and, on April 21, 1966, paid off for disposal. She was broken up at La Spezia, Italy, in 1970.

Athabaskan (2nd), April 7, 1961

CAYUGA

Commissioned at Halifax on October 19, 1947, she sailed on February 4, 1948, for Esquimalt, her assigned base. She left there July 5, 1950, as Senior Officer's ship of the first three Canadian destroyers to serve in Korean waters. She carried out three tours of duty there, the last in 1954 after the armistice. In 1952, between the second and third tours, she was rebuilt as a destroyer escort. For four years after her return from Korea in mid-December, 1954, *Cayuga* carried out training on the west coast, transferring to the east coast in January, 1959, for five more years in the same capacity. Paid off at Halifax on February 27, 1964, she was broken up at Faslane, Scotland, the following year.

Cayuga

MICMAC

Micmac was commissioned at Halifax on September 18, 1945. Alone of her class, she never fired a shot in anger but spent her entire career as a training ship. On July 16, 1947, she collided in fog with SS *Yarmouth County* off Halifax, suffering very extensive damage to her bows. While under repair she was partially converted to a destroyer escort, returning to her duties early in 1950. Her conversion was completed during 1952 and she was recommissioned on August 14, 1953. At the end of 1963, after ten further strenuous years of training, NATO exercises, and "showing the flag", she was declared surplus and, on March 31, 1964, paid off at Halifax. She was broken up at Faslane, Scotland, in 1965.

Micmac

NOOTKA (2nd)

Commissioned on August 7, 1946, at Halifax, *Nootka* served as a training ship on the east coast and in the Caribbean until her conversion to a destroyer escort in 1949 and 1950. Earmarked for Korean duty, she transited the Panama Canal in December, 1950, for the first of two tours of duty in that theatre of war. Returning to Halifax via the Mediterranean at the end of 1952, she became the second RCN ship to circumnavigate the globe. During 1953 and 1954 she underwent further conversion and modernization, afterward resuming her original training duties. In 1963, with *Haida*, she toured the Great Lakes in the course of a summer's cruising. She was paid off at Halifax on February 6, 1964, and broken up at Faslane, Scotland, the following year.

"C" Class

CRESCENT
CRUSADER

In January, 1945, after a year's discussion, the British Admiralty agreed to lend the RCN a flotilla of "C" Class destroyers for use against the Japanese. The Pacific war ended, however, before any of the eight ships had been completed, and only two were transferred. The previous ships to bear their names, *Crescent* and *Crusader*, had been lost during the war as HMC ships *Fraser* and *Ottawa*; this time they retained their names although the transfer was made permanent in 1951.

Crescent and *Crusader* were virtually identical to *Algonquin* and *Sioux*, differing principally in having only one set of torpedo tubes and in being armed with 4.5-inch guns instead of 4.7-inch. Both ships were commissioned on the Clyde in 1945, *Crescent* on September 10 and *Crusader* on November 15.

Crescent arrived at Esquimalt in November, 1945, and *Crusader* in January, 1946, both having made the journey via the Azores and the West Indies. *Crusader* was almost immediately paid off into reserve, a state in which she was to spend several years, while *Crescent* carried out training duties until taken in hand for major conversion. She emerged in 1956 as a "fast A/S frigate," following an RN pattern which entailed stripping her to deck level, extending the fo'c's'le right aft, erecting new superstructure, and fitting completely new armament. She was now a near-sister to *Algonquin*, which had undergone similar transformation earlier.

While her sister was being rebuilt, *Crusader* carried out two tours of duty in the Korean theatre, the first between June, 1952 and June, 1953, the second after the armistice, from November, 1953 to August, 1954. Reverting then to her former training role, she was paid off on January 15, 1960, at Halifax. She had earlier served as a test vehicle for a prototype VDS (variable depth sonar) outfit, a more permanent installation of which was made in *Crescent* in 1960.

Crusader was sold for scrapping in 1963, but *Crescent* remained longer in service, being paid off at Esquimalt on April 1, 1970. She left Victoria with *Algonquin* on April 21, 1971, for Taiwan, to be broken up.

Nootka (2nd), May 21, 1960

Crescent, January 16, 1958, showing the transfiguration completed in 1956

Crusader, December, 1945

Assiniboine (2nd), December 13, 1967

Destroyer Escorts

St. Laurent Class

HMCS *St. Laurent*, launched in 1951, was the first A/S vessel designed and built in Canada. She and her six sisters, classed as destroyer escorts (DDEs), were originally armed with two twin 3-inch guns and two Limbo A/S mortar mounts, the latter located in a well beneath the quarterdeck. From 1962 to 1966 all seven were extensively rebuilt as destroyer helicopter escorts (DDHs), emerging with a hangar and flight deck. Space for the hanger was made by twinning the original single stack, while the flight deck necessitated the removal of one gun and one Limbo mount. The stern was rebuilt to accommodate equipment for handling variable depth sonar, a Canadian development that overcomes the problem of water layers at varying depths, which confuse fixed sonar systems.

ASSINIBOINE (2nd)

Assiniboine was the first ship delivered postwar to the RCN by Marine Industries Ltd., Sorel. She was commissioned on August 16, 1956, and recommissioned on June 28, 1963, following the year's work required for conversion to a destroyer helicopter carrier (DDH). She completed her Destroyer Life Extension (DELEX) programme at Canadian Vickers Ltd., Montreal, in November, 1979. The ship, a member of the 1st Canadian Destroyer Squadron, is based at Halifax and commanded by CDR R. Moore.

FRASER (2nd)

Built by Burrard's, Vancouver, *Fraser* was commissioned on June 28, 1957 and paid off on July 2, 1965 for conversion to a DDH. She was recommissioned on October 22, 1966, following this transfiguration. She is slated for DELEX refit at Canadian Vickers Ltd., Montreal, in the fall of 1981. *Fraser*, a member of the 5th Canadian Destroyer Squadron, is based at Halifax under the command of CDR G. Gadd.

MARGAREE (2nd)

A product of Halifax Shipyards Ltd., *Margaree* was commissioned on October 5, 1957, and paid off on September 29, 1964 for conversion to a DDH. she was recommissioned on October 15, 1965, in her new guise. Her DELEX refit was begun at Canadian Vickers Ltd., Montreal, but when it seemed likely that she would be ice-bound there, she was towed to Halifax in December, 1980, for completion of the work. A member of the 1st Canadian Destroyer Squadron, she is based at Halifax and commanded by CDR P. J. Stow.

Fraser (2nd), September 10, 1969

Margaree (2nd), September 10, 1969, in a photo graphically portraying the changed appearance of the class after conversion to DDHs. They were originally near-sisters to the Restigouche class.

163

OTTAWA (3rd)

Built at Montreal, *Ottawa* was commissioned on November 10, 1956. Converted to a DDH, she was recommissioned on October 21, 1964. She is to return to her builder, Canadian Vickers Ltd., in 1982 for DELEX refit. The ship, a member of the 1st Canadian Destroyer Squadron, is based at Halifax under the command of LCDR E. J. M. Young.

SAGUENAY (2nd)

Built by Halifax Shipyards Ltd., *Saguenay* was commissioned at Halifax on December 15, 1956. She was paid off on August 22, 1963, for conversion to a DDH, and not recommissioned until May 14, 1965. Her DELEX refit was completed at Montreal in May, 1980. A member of the 5th Canadian Destroyer Squadron, she is based at Halifax and commanded by CDR A. G. Schwartz.

ST. LAURENT (2nd)

The first ship of her design to be launched, *St. Laurent* was built by Canadian Vickers Ltd. at Montreal. She was commissioned four years later, on October 29, 1955, and recommissioned on October 4, 1963, following conversion to a DDH. She was paid off to reserve on June 14, 1974, at Halifax, and gradually cannibalized on behalf of her still-operating sisters. In October, 1979, she was sold for scrap, and on New Year's day, 1980, left in tow for Brownsville, Texas, to be broken up. On January 12, however, she capsized and sank in a gale off Cape Hatteras.

SKEENA (2nd)

Built by Burrard's at Vancouver, *Skeena* was commissioned on March 30, 1957, and recommissioned on August 14, 1965, following conversion to a DDH. She underwent DELEX refit at Montreal in 1981. A member of the 1st Canadian Destroyer Squadron, she is based at Halifax under the command of CDR J. G. R. Boucher.

Ottawa (3rd), June 12, 1965

Saguenay (2nd)

St. Laurent (2nd), 1955, shortly before she was commissioned

Skeena (2nd)

Chaudière (2nd), May 26, 1967

Restigouche Class

A second class of seven DDEs, the Restigouche class, entered service between 1958 and 1959. They approximated very closely the original *St. Laurent* design, but four of them were rebuilt, from 1967 to 1972, with an A/S rocket (ASROC) launcher aft in place of the after turret, a disproportionately tall mast, and a stern redesigned to accommodate VDS. None of the four rebuilt carries a helicopter. The three not rebuilt, *Chaudière, Columbia,* and *St. Croix,* were reduced to Category 'C' reserve in 1974. *St. Croix* serves as a harbour training ship at Halifax; the other two lie at Esquimalt.

CHAUDIÈRE (2nd)

Built by Halifax Shipyards Ltd., *Chaudière* was commissioned on November 14, 1959. Although the youngest of her class, she was paid off into Category 'C' reserve at Esquimalt on May 23, 1974, and will likely be disposed of in the near future.

COLUMBIA (2nd)

Built by Burrard's, Vancouver, *Columbia* was commissioned on November 7, 1959. Like *Chaudière,* she has lain in Category 'C' reserve at Esquimalt since February 18, 1974, and will probably be disposed of in 1982.

GATINEAU (2nd)

Gatineau, the first contribution of the Davie Shipbuilding Co., Lauzon, to the postwar RCN, was commissioned on February 17, 1959. She was extensively rebuilt, 1969-71, to accommodate ASROC and VDS, and is slated for DELEX refit in 1983. A member of the 2nd Canadian Destroyer Squadron, she is based at Esquimalt and commanded by CDR D. M. Robison.

Columbia (2na)

Gatineau (2nd), September 15, 1959

KOOTENAY (2nd)

First of her class to be launched, *Kootenay* was built by Burrard's, Vancouver, and commissioned on March 7, 1959. While on an overseas cruise in 1969, she suffered an engine room explosion on October 23 and was towed part of the way to Plymouth by *Saguenay*. She arrived at Halifax, still in tow, for repairs on November 27. Like three of her sisters, she underwent extensive modification, 1970-72, and she is scheduled for DELEX refit in 1984. A member of the 2nd Canadian Destroyer Squadron, she is based on the west coast and commanded by CDR B. H. Beckett.

RESTIGOUCHE (2nd)

Restigouche was damaged in collision, November 27, 1957, in the St. Lawrence River while still in the hands of her builder, Canadian Vickers Ltd. She was commissioned on June 7, 1958, and substantially rebuilt, 1970-72, to accommodate new weaponry. She is to receive her DELEX refit in 1986. A member of the 2nd Canadian Destroyer Squadron, she is based at Esquimalt under the command of CDR D. A. Henderson.

ST. CROIX (2nd)

Built by Marine Industries Ltd., Sorel, she was commissioned on October 4, 1958, and served until November 15, 1974, when she was paid off into Category 'C' reserve. She serves as a stationary training ship at Halifax pending her disposal.

Kootenay (2nd), *November 4, 1964*

Restigouche (2nd), *September 21, 1968*

St. Croix (2nd), *June, 1967*

Terra Nova, November 15, 1968

TERRA NOVA

Built by Victoria Machinery Depot, *Terra Nova* was commissioned on June 6, 1959. Like some others of her class, she was rebuilt, 1967-68, to accommodate ASROC and VDS. She is scheduled for DELEX refit in 1985. A member of the 2nd Canadian Destroyer Squadron, she is stationed on the west coast and commanded by CDR G. J. Eldridge.

Mackenzie Class

The four Mackenzie class DDEs, which entered service between 1962 and 1963, essentially repeat the original *Restigouche* design, while the two Nipigon class DDHs of 1964 incorporated from their launching the design elements of the rebuilt *St. Laurents*, and carry helicopters.

MACKENZIE

The lead ship of her class, *Mackenzie* was built by Canadian Vickers Ltd. at Montreal and commissioned on October 6, 1962. She is slated for DELEX refit in 1985. Currently a member of Training Group Pacific, she is commanded by CDR T. C. Milne.

QU'APPELLE (2nd)

Built by the Davie Shipbuilding Co., Lauzon, *Qu'Appelle* was commissioned on September 14, 1963, and is scheduled for DELEX refit in 1982. A member of Training Group Pacific, she is commanded by CDR R. J. Luke.

Mackenzie, June, 1967

Qu'Appelle (2nd), July 21, 1965

SASKATCHEWAN (2nd)

Built by Victoria Machinery Depot, *Saskatchewan* was commissioned on February 16, 1963, and is slated for DELEX refit in 1984. A member of Training Group Pacific, she is under the command of CDR J. D. Sine.

YUKON

Built by Burrard's, Vancouver, *Yukon* was commissioned on May 25, 1963, and is to undergo DELEX refit in 1983. A member of Training Group Pacific, she is commanded by CDR C. J. Crow.

Annapolis Class

ANNAPOLIS (2nd)

Built at Halifax Shipyards Ltd., *Annapolis* was commissioned on December 19, 1964. She underwent a major overhaul, 1978-79, and is to be given her DELEX refit in 1984. A member of the Halifax-based 5th Canadian Destroyer Squadron, she is under the command of CDR J. Nethercott.

Saskatchewan (2nd), October 19, 1965

Yukon, February 27, 1974

Annapolis (2nd), May 23, 1962

Nipigon (2nd), April 18, 1972

NIPIGON (2nd)

Built by Marine Industries Ltd., Sorel, *Nipigon* was commissioned on May 30, 1964, and was given a major overhaul in 1977=78. She is due for DELEX refit in 1982. A member of the 5th Canadian Destroyer Squadron, she is based on the east coast and commanded by CDR D. E. Gibb.

Iroquois Class

The four much larger "280," or Iroquois, class DDHs carry two helicopters and are armed with a 5-inch gun, a Mark X A/S mortar, and a Sea Sparrow A/S missile launcher. The last of these was commissioned in 1973. Apart from the hydrofoil *Bras d'Or* they are the only Canadian warships to be powered by gas turbine engines.

ALGONQUIN (2nd)

Built at Lauzon by the Davie Shipbuilding Co., *Algonquin* was commissioned on November 3, 1973. She is based at Halifax as a member of the 1st Canadian Destroyer Squadron, and is commanded by CDR D. E. Pollard

ATHABASKAN (3rd)

Another Davie Shipbuilding Co. product, *Athabaskan* was commissioned on September 30, 1972. She is a Halifax-based member of the 1st Canadian Destroyer Squadron, and is commanded by CDR J. W. McIntosh.

Algonquin (2nd), September, 1973

Athabaskan (3rd), October 11, 1972

HURON (2nd)

Built by Marine Industries Ltd., Sorel, *Huron* was commissioned on December 16, 1972. She represented Canada at the Silver Jubilee naval review at Spithead on June 28, 1977, and in 1981 carried Governor-General Edward Schreyer on a tour of five Scandinavian ports. A member of the 5th Canadian Destroyer Squadron, she is based at Halifax, and commanded by CDR R. J. Deluca.

IROQUOIS (2nd)

First of the "280" class, *Iroquois* was built by Marine Industries Ltd., Sorel, and commissioned on July 29, 1972. A member of the Halifax-based 5th Canadian Destroyer Squadron, she is commanded by CDR L. G. Mason.

DELEX

With a view to prolonging the lives of the 16 older destroyers, the Destroyer Life Extension Project (DELEX) was introduced in December, 1979. The procedure, which will be carried out by civilian ship repairers, is expected to take about 10 months per ship. In this way it is hoped, by 1987, that 12 years will have been added to the life expectancy of the Nipigon class and 8 years to that of the others.

On December 8, 1980, it was announced that Saint John Shipbuilding & Dry Dock Co. and Scan Marine of Longueuil, Que., will compete in the contract definition phase of the Canadian Patrol Frigate Programme. Initiated in 1977, this programme should result in the replacement of the six *St. Laurents* with six new frigates, the first to be completed late in 1987.

Fast Hydrofoil Escort

BRAS d'OR

In 1919 a hydrofoil craft developed by Alexander Graham Bell and F. W. Baldwin attained the unheard-of speed of 60 knots in trials on Cape Breton's Bras d'Or Lake. It was powered by two aircraft engines and air propellers. The potential of such a craft as an A/S vessel was finally considered in the early 1950s, when a small test vessel was built in Britain to Naval Research establishment specifications. It arrived at Halifax aboard HMCS *Bonaventure* in 1957, and its performance led to the awarding of a contract to De Havilland Aircraft of Canada in 1963.

HMCS *Bras d'Or*, named for the scene of the first tests and designated a fast hydrofoil escort (FHE), was commissioned in 1968. When "hull-borne" at low speeds, the craft is driven by a 2400-BHP diesel engine, but at about 23 knots the foils lift the hull clear of the water, and propulsion is taken over by a 30,000-SHP gas turbine engine powering twin screws. Trial speeds as great as 63 knots were attained.

Despite the evident success of the prototype FHE, she was laid up in 1971 and, at time of writing, efforts are being made to find her a home in a museum.

Huron (2nd), *November 22, 1972*

Iroquois (2nd), *June, 1972*

Bras d'Or (2nd) *at about 45 knots, January 14, 1971*

Submarines

U 190 and U 889

On May 12 and 13, 1945, *U 190* and *U 889* formally surrendered at sea to units of the RCN, hostilities having ended a few days earlier. Both were of the large IX C type, built at Bremen in 1942 and 1944. They were almost immediately commissioned in the RCN for testing and evaluation, following which, on January 12, 1946, *U 889* was turned over to the USN. She was expended in torpedo tests off New England the following year. *U 190* was paid off on July 24, 1947, and on October 21 she was sunk by Canadian naval aircraft near the position where she had sunk HMCS *Esquimalt* in April, 1945.

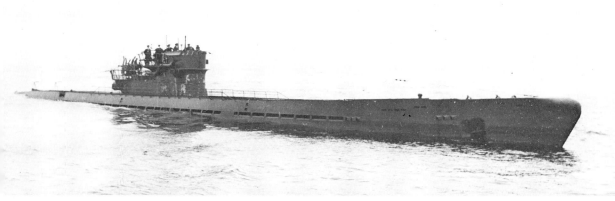

U 190, October 20, 1947

GRILSE (2nd)

During and after the war it had been the custom of the RN to provide "tame" submarines for A/S training in Nova Scotia waters. By 1961, with a growing fleet of new A/S ships based at Esquimalt, it had become desirable to have a submarine stationed there as well.

USS *Burrfish* was accordingly borrowed and commissioned as HMCS *Grilse* on May 11, 1961, at New London, Ct. *Burrfish*, launched in 1943, had carried out six war patrols in the Pacific between 1944 and 1945. Converted to a radar picket submarine, she resumed service with the USN, including three tours with the Mediterranean Fleet from 1950 to 1956. She was paid off by the RCN on October 2, 1969, and returned to her owners.

U 889, May, 1945

RAINBOW (2nd)

Purchased from the USN, HMCS *Rainbow* was commissioned on December 2, 1968. As USS *Argonaut*, she had been launched in 1944, in time to carry out one war patrol from Pearl Harbor in June, 1945. After the war she operated out of New London, Ct., from 1946 to 1955, undergoing modification in 1952 to what the USN calls Guppy configuration. She served in the RCN until December 31, 1974.

Grilse (2nd), October 17, 1961

Rainbow (2nd), March 18, 1969

"O" Class

OJIBWA
OKANAGAN
ONONDAGA

On September 23, 1965, HMCS *Ojibwa* was commissioned at Chatham, U.K., the first submarine built to RCN order. Two sisters, *Onondaga* and *Okanagan*, followed, commissioning on June 22, 1967 and June 22, 1968, respectively. Built at Chatham Dockyard, they are duplicates of the RN's Oberon class, its latest conventionally powered submarines.

All three are members of the 1st Canadian Submarine Squadron, based at Halifax. *Ojibwa* is commanded by LCDR N. P. Nicholson, *Okanagan* by LCDR F. Scherber, and *Onondaga* by LCDR A. B. Dunlop.

Ojibwa, August 25, 1965

Okanagan, September 28, 1968

Onondaga

Cordova, July 14, 1953

Minesweepers

CORDOVA

One of hundreds of motor minesweepers built for the USN during the Second World War, *Cordova* was launched as *YMS.420* in 1944 at Chicago. She was purchased by the RCN on December 3, 1951, and commissioned from August 9, 1952 to April 12, 1957, serving primarily as tender to the Vancouver Naval Reserve Division.

Bay Class

In 1951 and 1952, 14 replacements were laid down for the aging minesweepers of wartime construction. Six were transferred to the French Navy in 1954, but were replaced by six of the same name in 1956-57. The latter are all that survive, providing ship-handling experience for junior officers, on a rotating basis, as members of Training Group Pacific.

CHALEUR (1st)

Built by the Port Arthur Shipbuilding Co., she was commissioned on June 18, 1954, and paid off on September 30. She was transferred on October 9, 1954, to the French Navy, which renamed her *La Dieppoise*.

Chaleur being handed over to the French Navy, October 9, 1954

CHALEUR (2nd)

Built by Marine Industries Ltd., Sorel, she was commissioned on September 12, 1957, and, with her five surviving sisters, is a member of Training Group Pacific.

CHIGNECTO (2nd)

Built by Marine Industries Ltd., Sorel, she was commissioned on December 1, 1953, and paid off on March 31, 1954, the day of her transfer to the French Navy. She was renamed *La Bayonnaise*.

CHIGNECTO (3rd)

Built by G. T. Davie & Sons, Lauzon, she was commissioned on August 1, 1957, and with her five remaining sisters, forms part of Training Group Pacific.

Chaleur (2nd), *November 7, 1959*

Chignecto (2nd), *December 16, 1953*

Chignecto (3rd)

COMOX (2nd)

Built by Victoria Machinery Depot, she was commissioned on April 2, 1954, and paid off on September 11, 1957. On March 31, 1958, she was transferred to the Turkish Navy, which renamed her *Tirebolu*.

Comox (2nd), May 11, 1956

Cowichan (2nd), March 3, 1954

Cowichan (3rd), February 14, 1958

COWICHAN (2nd)

Built by the Davie Shipbuilding Co., Lauzon, she was commissioned on December 10, 1953, and on March 31, 1954, paid off and transferred to the French Navy. She was renamed *La Malouine*.

COWICHAN (3rd)

Built by Yarrows Ltd., Esquimalt, she was commissioned on December 12, 1957, and serves still on the west coast as part of Training Group Pacific.

FORTUNE

Built by Victoria Machinery Depot, she was commissioned on November 3, 1954, and paid off on February 28, 1964. Sold for commercial purposes in 1966, she figured, as *Greenpeace Two*, in an unsuccessful effort to hinder a nuclear test in the Aleutians in November, 1971. She is currently registered as *Edgewater Fortune*.

Fortune, February 14, 1968

FUNDY (2nd)

Built by the Saint John Dry Dock Co., she was commissioned on March 19, 1954, and paid off March 31, the date of her transfer to the French Navy, which renamed her *La Dunkerquoise*.

FUNDY (3rd)

Built by the Davie Shipbuilding Co., Lauzon, she was commissioned on November 27, 1956, and serves with her five remaining sisters as a member of Training Group Pacific.

GASPÉ (2nd)

Built by the Davie Shipbuilding Co., Lauzon, she was commissioned on December 5, 1953, and paid off on August 22, 1957. She was transferred to the Turkish Navy, which renamed her *Trabzon*, on March 31, 1958.

Fundy (2nd), March 9, 1954

Fundy (3rd), February 26, 1962

Gaspé (2nd), January 14, 1954

James Bay, March 6, 1957

JAMES BAY

Built by Yarrows Ltd., Esquimalt, she was commissioned on May 3, 1954, and paid off on February 28, 1964. She was subsequently sold for use in offshore oil exploration.

MIRAMICHI (2nd)

Built by the Saint John Dry Dock Co., she was commissioned on July 30, 1954, and paid off on October 1. On October 9, 1954, she was transferred to the French Navy, to be renamed *La Lorientaise*.

MIRAMICHI (3rd)

Built by Victoria Machinery Depot, she was commissioned on October 29, 1957, and still serves on the west coast as a member of Training Group Pacific.

Miramichi (2nd), August 2, 1954

Miramichi (3rd), November 14, 1957

QUINTE (2nd)

Built by the Port Arthur Shipbuilding Co., she was commissioned on October 15, 1954, paid off on February 26, 1964, and declared surplus the following year.

RESOLUTE

Built by Kingston Shipyards Ltd., she was commissioned on September 16, 1954, paid off on February 14, 1964 and declared surplus the following year.

THUNDER (2nd)

Built by Canadian Vickers Ltd., Montreal, she was commissioned on December 15, 1953, and paid off on March 31, 1954, the day of her transfer to the French Navy. She was renamed *La Paimpolaise*.

Quinte (2nd)

Resolute, February 26, 1962

Thunder (2nd) celebrating Christmas, 1953, at Halifax

THUNDER (3rd)

Built by the Port Arthur Shipbuilding Co., she was commissioned on October 3, 1957, and serves still as a member of Training Group Pacific.

TRINITY

Built by G. T. Davie & Son, Lauzon, she was commissioned on June 16, 1954, and paid off on August 21, 1957, for transfer to the Turkish Navy. The transfer took place on March 31, 1958, and the ship was renamed *Terme*.

UNGAVA (2nd)

Built by the Davie Shipbuilding Co., Lauzon, she was commissioned on June 4, 1954, and paid off on August 23, 1957. She was transferred on March 31, 1958, to the Turkish Navy, which renamed her *Tekirdag*.

Thunder (3rd), June 16, 1958

Trinity

Ungava (2nd), May 4, 1955

Patrol Craft

BLUE HERON
CORMORANT
LOON
MALLARD

The Bird Class "seaward defence patrol craft" were launched 1954-56 at four Ontario boat-yards. They were intended to replace the remaining Fairmile motor launches, and their principal peacetime functions were Reserve and cadet training and air/sea rescue. *Blue Heron* served on loan to the RCMP, 1957-68. All were paid off in the 1960s and sold 1970-71.

Blue Heron, September 25, 1956

Cormorant, May 23, 1962

Loon, February 29, 1962

Escort Maintenance Ships

CAPE BRETON
CAPE SCOTT

These modified Fort type cargo ships were launched at Vancouver in 1944 as HMS *Beachy Head* and *Flamborough Head*. The latter continued in service with the RN after the war, but *Beachy Head* was turned over to the Royal Netherlands Navy in 1947 as repair ship *Vulkaan*. In 1950 she was returned to the RN and resumed her original name until 1952, when she was transferred to the RCN and, in 1953, renamed *Cape Scott*. She lay alongside her sister, *Cape Breton*, at Halifax for some years, providing supplementary workshop and classroom facilities until *Cape Breton* was transferred to the west coast in 1958. After refit at Saint John, *Cape Scott* was at last commissioned on January 28, 1959, to serve at Halifax until paid off into reserve on July 1, 1970. In 1972 she was redesignated Fleet Maintenance Group (Atlantic), but was sold when the group moved ashore in 1975 and left under tow in 1978 to be broken up in Texas.

Flamborough Head was also acquired from the RN in 1952, and renamed *Cape Breton* upon commissioning on January 31, 1953. She served at Halifax until August 25, 1958, as repair ship and training establishment for technical apprentices. Converted to escort maintenance ship at Esquimalt, she was commissioned there on November 16, 1959, for service on the west coast. On February 10, 1964, *Cape Breton* was paid off into reserve, but since 1972 she has functioned as a towed mobile support facility and accommodation vessel at Esquimalt, designated Fleet Maintenance Group (Pacific).

Mallard, June 4, 1960

Cape Breton, January 22, 1960

Cape Scott, December 15, 1959

Operational Support Ships

PROVIDER (2nd)
PRESERVER (2nd)
PROTECTEUR

The first of this type, *Provider*, was commissioned on September 28, 1963, at Lauzon, Que. Originally designated as a fleet replenishment ship, she was the largest ship ever built in Canada for the RCN. She enabled RCN ships to remain at sea for extended periods, as well as greatly increasing their mobility and range. She has stowage space for some 12,000 tons of fuel oil, diesel oil, and aviation gas, in addition to spare parts, ammunition and missiles, general stores and food.

Experience with *Provider* led to significant changes in the design of the next two operational support ships, *Protecteur* and *Preserver*, commissioned at Saint John, N.B., on August 30, 1969 and July 30, 1970, respectively. Though similar in size to the tanker-like *Provider*, they have a higher freeboard, massive bridges, and paired funnels that make possible a single, much wider hangar door. Unlike *Provider*, the newer pair are also armed with a twin 3-inch "bow chaser" gun.

All three ships can refuel other fleet units at 20 knots, with automatic tensioning equipment to compensate for the ships' motion as fuel oil is transferred at 25 tons per minute. Each can carry three A/S helicopters as spares for the fleet or for transferring pallet loads of solid stores.

Provider (2nd)

Preserver (2nd)

Protecteur

Arctic Patrol Vessel

LABRADOR

HMCS *Labrador* was built in recognition of the growing strategic importance of Canada's Arctic region, and with a view to the assertion of her sovereignty there. The design was adapted from that of the U.S. Coast Guard's Wind class of icebreakers. Like them, she was built for power rather than speed, her six diesel-electric engines driving her at 16 knots maximum. Heeling tanks connected by reversible-propeller type pumps enable water ballast to be hurled from side to side at 40,000 gallons a minute, so that she can rock herself free when trapped by ice. She carries two helicopters.

Commissioned on July 8, 1954, *Labrador* sailed that summer on the first of four voyages she would make to the Arctic as a naval vessel. On that initial voyage she became the first warship to negotiate the Northwest Passage across the top of the continent and, returning to Halifax via the Panama Canal, the first to circumnavigate North America. On her second voyage, in 1955, she transported personnel and equipment for the construction of the eastern portion of the Distant Early Warning (DEW) Line. That summer and next, she also carried out extensive hydrographic surveys in the eastern Arctic, spending five and one-half months there in 1956 alone. A departure from custom in 1957 found her paying visits to Portsmouth, Oslo, and Copenhagen, and on November 22 she was paid off for refit.

She was fated not to fly the White Ensign again, for it was decided to transfer her to the Department of Transport. As CCGS *Labrador*, she is now primarily used for icebreaking in the lower St. Lawrence, but still on occasion embarks scientists for summer studies in the Arctic.

Labrador

Auxiliaries

Gate Vessels

PORTE DAUPHINE
PORTE de la REINE
PORTE QUÊBEC
PORTE ST. JEAN
PORTE ST. LOUIS

Their names, appropriately, are those of gates in the French fortifications at Quebec City and Louisbourg. Though designed specifically to operate the gates in anti-submarine booms, these craft serve primarily as training vessels in peacetime. *Porte St. Jean* and *Porte St. Louis* are based at Halifax, with summer forays into the Great Lakes, the others at Esquimalt. *Porte Dauphine* wore a coat of bright red paint, 1958-74, while on loan to the Dept. of Transport as an environmental research ship on the Great Lakes.

Porte Dauphine, May 11, 1953

Porte de la Reine

Porte Québec, July 14, 1953

Porte St. Jean, June 8, 1961

Porte St. Louis at Kingston, 1953

Survey Vessel
CEDARWOOD

Launched in 1941 at Lunenburg, N.S., as MV *J. E. Kinney*, this ship was taken up for war service with the Royal Canadian Army Service Corps and renamed *General Schmidlin*. Her function seems to have been that of supplying army detachments at scattered harbours in the Maritimes and Nfld. She was comissioned in the RCN on September 22, 1948, for oceanographic survey duties on the west coast, and renamed *Cedarwood*. Paid off on October 19, 1956, she was fitted in 1958 with artificial paddle-wheels and other dummy fittings in order to play the role of the steamer *Commodore* during B.C.'s centennial celebration.

Diving Support Vessel
CORMORANT

Formerly the Italian-flag stern trawler *Aspa Quarto*, built in 1965, she was purchased for Maritime Command in July, 1975, and converted, principally at Lauzon, Quebec, to her new purpose. She was commissioned there November 10, 1978, and arrived at Halifax December 1 to take up her duties. She serves as mother ship to an SDL-1 submersible capable of reaching a depth of 2000 feet, and boasts among her complement the first female personnel assigned to a Canadian naval vessel.

Cedarwood, June 14, 1949

Cormorant (2nd), 1978

Appendix I

RN Ships under RCN Control

During the Second World War a number of RN ships served alongside ships of the RCN, some of them under RCN control as members of Canadian escort groups. Nine of these ships — three frigates and six corvettes — spent most of their war careers in this fashion, and paid a disproportionately heavy price. Two frigates and two corvettes were lost, and the third frigate was irreparably damaged.

FRIGATES

HMS *Itchen* was completed on December 28, 1942, at Paisley, Scotland. After workups at Tobermory and a brief refit on the Clyde, she joined EG C-1 in March, 1943, as Senior Officer's Ship. She escorted eight North Atlantic convoys with C-1, but was transferred in August 1943 at Londonderry to an RCN support group, EG 9. On September 19 this group was ordered to the assistance of combined convoy ON.202/ONS.18 and, on September 22, *Itchen* was torpedoed and sunk by *U 666*, south of Greenland. Ironically, she had on board 80 survivors of

Itchen

HMCS *St. Croix*, sunk two days earlier, and all but one of these lost their lives.

HMS *Lagan* was completed at South Bank-on-Tees, December 2, 1942, and joined EG C-2 early in January, 1943. She escorted eleven North Atlantic convoys, and in March, 1943, made a round trip from Britain to Gibraltar in support of Operation "Torch" convoys. On September 20, 1943, while escorting convoy ON.202, she was torpedoed by *U 270* in the North Atlantic but managed to reach Liverpool. Subsequently declared a constructive total loss, she was broken up at Troon in May, 1946.

HMS *Tweed* was completed on April 28, 1943, at Glasgow and, after working up at Tobermory, joined an RCN support group, EG 5, in June. From then until December she served with the group in support of North Atlantic convoys, operating from Londonderry and St. John's. On January 7, 1944, while on blockade-runner patrol northwest of Spain, she was torpedoed and sunk by *U 305*.

CORVETTES

HMS *Celandine* was completed at Grangemouth, Scotland, on April 30, 1941. After working up she joined Newfoundland Command as an ocean escort. On June 27, 1941, she shared with *Gladiolus* and *Nasturtium* the sinking of *U 556*. In February, 1942, she became a member of TU 24.1.11, predecessor of EG C-1, making one round trip to Londonderry before proceeding to Norfolk, Va., for two months' refit. On completion of the refit in July, 1942, she joined EG C-4 and served with it until March, 1943, when she underwent another refit, this time at Liverpool, U.K. Following this, she returned to C-1 in August, 1943. *Celandine* left St. John's for the last time on February 1, 1944, to escort convoy HX.277, and spent the balance of the war in U.K. waters under RN command. She was broken up at Portaferry in October, 1948.

HMS *Dianthus* was completed at Leith, Scotland, on March 17, 1941, and, after working up, briefly joined EG 7 (RN) at Liverpool. In June, 1941, she was allocated to Newfoundland Command, arriving at Halifax on June 26. In February, 1942, she became a member of TU 24.1.11, predecessor of EG C-1, serving as an ocean escort until that August, when she commenced two months' refit at Bristol, U.K. Refit completed, she joined EG A-3 and served with it and its successor, C-5,

Celandine

until January, 1944. She left St. John's for the last time with convoy HX.274, and spent the balance of the war in U.K. waters under RN command. In 1949 she was sold for conversion to a whale-catcher.

HMS *Gladiolus*, completed on April 6, 1940, at South Bank-on-Tees, was the first corvette launched. After working up at Portland, she joined Western Approaches Command, Liverpool and, later, EG 1 and EG 2 at Londonderry. In June 1941 she was allocated to the recently formed Newfoundland Command, and in July joined its EG 25. In October she was transferred to Task Unit 4.1.15, and on October 16, while escorting convoy SC.48, was torpedoed and sunk by *U 558* in the North Atlantic. During her short career, *Gladiolus* sank *U 26* and *U 65*, and shared a third kill, *U 556*, with *Celandine* and *Nasturtium*.

HMS *Nasturtium* was completed on September 26, 1940, at South Bank-on-Tees and, after working up, joined EG 7, Western Approaches Command, Liverpool, as a North Atlantic escort. On June 27, 1941, with *Gladiolus* and *Celandine*, she took part in the sinking of *U 556*. In July, 1941, she joined Newfoundland Command and, in June, 1942, EG C-1, following refits at Mobile, Ala., and Liverpool. In August, 1942, after four Atlantic crossings with EG C-1, she transferred to A-3 for two further crossings. She returned to the U.K. in September, 1942, having been assigned to duties in connection with Operation "Torch". In June, 1943, on completion of a two-month refit at Belfast, *Nasturtium* was allocated to EG C-4. She left St. John's for the last time on March 18, 1944, as escort to convoy HX.283, and spent the remainder of the war in U.K. waters under RN command. She was sold in 1948 for conversion to a merchant ship.

HMS *Polyanthus* was completed at Leith, Scotland, on April 23, 1941, and after workups joined Newfoundland Command, which assigned her to EG 17. In May, 1942, following a refit at Galveston, Texas, she joined EG C-2, and was still a member of the group when, on September 20, 1943, she was torpedoed and sunk in convoy ON.202 by *U 963*.

HMS *Primrose* was completed on July 15, 1940, at Renfrew, Scotland, and after working up joined EG 6, Liverpool and then, in February, 1941, EG 7. In June, 1941, she joined newly formed Newfoundland Command and, in October, 1942, EG C-2, serving with this group as an ocean escort until August, 1943. Following a refit at Corpach, Scotland, *Primrose* remained in U.K. waters until January, 1945, when she returned to mid-ocean duties with EG B-2 until the end of the war. She was sold for conversion to a whale-catcher in 1949.

RN A/S TRAWLERS

It was expected that the spring of 1943 would bring renewed U-boat

Ayrshire

activity in the Gulf of St. Lawrence, and there was concern over the shortage of suitable RCN escorts for the area. The RN accordingly lent the RCN six of its ocean-going anti-submarine trawlers, complete with crews. Formerly large fishing trawlers, they were named: *Ayrshire*, *Cape Argona*, *Cape Mariato*, *Lord Middleton*, *Paynter*, and *St. Kenan*. With the exception of *Cape Argona*, which arrived at Halifax on May 7, all arrived in Canadian waters in mid-April. For the remainder of the month they were assigned to Halifax Force while undergoing repairs, and early in May they joined Sydney Force. *Cape Argona*, meanwhile, did escort work between St. Pierre and Halifax, joining the rest at Sydney May 31. The six trawlers performed an important role in the escort of Quebec-Sydney convoys and patrols in Cabot Strait during the remainder of 1943, then returned to the U.K.

Name	Pt. No.	Builder	Date	Displ.	Dimensions
Ayrshire	FY.225	Smith's Dock, Middlesbrough, U.K.	1938	540	176'x28'x15'
Cape Argona	FY.190	Cochrane & Sons, Selby, U.K.	1936	494	166'x27'x14'
Cape Mariato	4.172	Cochrane & Sons, Selby, U.K.	1936	497	170'x27'x14'
Lord Middleton	FY.219	Cochrane & Sons, Selby, U.K.	1936	464	161'x26'x14'
Paynter	FY.242	Cochrane & Sons, Selby, U.K.	1937	477	167'x28'x14'
St. Kenan	FY.264	Cook, Welton & Gemmell, Beverley, U.K.	1936	565	172'x29'x14'

Appendix 2

North Atlantic Convoys

The practice of sailing merchant ships in company for mutual protection or, if possible, escorted by warships, is centuries old. It was reintroduced during the First World War, but not until 1917 when the number of merchant ships sunk by U-boats became critical. The Germans had commenced unrestricted submarine warfare in February, 1917, and by April merchant ship losses had reached the stage where, during that month alone, 169 were sunk by enemy action.

The Admiralty made no very widespread use of convoys even so, but they were introduced on some of the Atlantic and Mediterranean routes. Various ports of assembly were chosen for ships proceeding to the U.K., and Sydney and Halifax were those used for convoys originating in Canada. The first trade convoy (as distinct from troop convoy) sailed from Sydney, N.S., on July 10, 1917, escorted by the cruiser HMS *Highflyer*. Trade convoys continued until the end of the war, but the RCN played a negligible role in escorting them.

Convoys were again introduced immediately on the outbreak of the Second World War and the first, HX.1, left Halifax for the U.K. on September 16, 1939. Around these convoys was fought the Battle of the Atlantic, the longest in history. Beginning on September 3, 1939 and ending on May 8, 1945, it was a battle in which the RCN was to play a crucial role.

Early convoys were small, comprising thirty to fifty ships, but they grew gradually larger as the war progressed. The largest, HXS.300, comprised 167 ships. It left New York for the U.K. on July 17, 1944, with an RCN mid-ocean escort (C-5) of one frigate and six corvettes. "Fast" convoys maintained a speed of about nine knots and averaged 13-14 days between Halifax and the U.K., while "slow" convoys made about seven knots and averaged 16-17 days on the crossing.

A typical convoy of forty ships might be ten columns wide, with four ships in each column. As a U-boat generally attacked from ahead, or on the bow, the ships in the outside column were the most likely targets. These usually carried bulky, inert cargoes such as lumber or wheat, while ammunition ships, valuable cargo ships and tankers were positioned in the middle of the convoy. If the convoy had six escorts, one (the Senior Officer's ship, usually a destroyer) would be positioned ahead of the convoy by day and astern by night. The other escorts would be stationed one on each bow, one on each beam of the convoy and one astern.

In September, 1940, the Germans introduced "wolf pack" tactics, attacking convoys at night with a number of U-boats. They would sink a ship in an outside column and then, when an escort fell out to rescue survivors, slip into the convoy between the columns. It might thus happen that half the escort would be carrying out rescue work and the other half hunting an attacker—leaving the convoy virtually unprotected. In January, 1941, specially equipped merchant ships called convoy rescue ships were introduced, and one assigned where possible to each convoy. This left the escorts free to pursue their designed role.

As the war progressed and more escorts became available, the RN and later the RCN were able to create "support groups" which could go to the aid of endangered convoys or convoys under heavy attack. This had become general practice by May, 1943, the height of the Atlantic battle.

CONVOY ORGANIZATION

There were seven series of convoys associated with the transatlantic crossing, as summarized in the accompanying chart. Westbound convoys were at first escorted to 12/13°W and then dispersed, but soon afterward this was extended to 15°W. In July, 1940, it was extended to 17°W and by October, 1940, convoys were dispersed at 19°W, some 400 miles west of Ireland. In April, 1941, with the acquisition of a fuelling base in Ireland, the dispersal point was shifted to 35°W, more than halfway across the Atlantic. By June, 1941, with the formation of Newfoundland Force, it was possible to provide continuous escort across the Atlantic. Convoys were escorted to approximately 61°N:25°W (south of Iceland), whence a group from Iceland escorted the ships to a dispersal point south of Newfoundland. The RCN supplied a majority of the escorts for the latter part of the voyage.

In February, 1942, coincident with the arrival of U-boats off the east coast of Canada and the U.S., the organization of westbound convoys was again changed. Eastern Local escorts brought feeder convoys from various U.K. ports to Oversay, the collection point, where transatlantic convoys were taken over by mid-ocean escort groups based at Londonderry or Liverpool. These in turn would hand over their convoys to Western Local escort groups off Newfoundland, then proceed to St. John's. The Western Local escort took the convoy to Halifax or, later, to New York. This pattern continued until the end of the war.

Eastbound convoys followed the same general pattern. HX convoys were at first provided with an ocean escort of an RN armed merchant cruiser or, occasionally, a battleship. The earlier SC convoys were escorted by RN sloops. In addition the convoys were, for the first few months of the war, escorted by RCN destroyers to 52°W (south east of Newfoundland). The convoys were met west of the U.K. by an escort turning homeward from an outbound ON or ONS convoy.

With the formation of the Newfoundland Force it was possible to provide continuous escort across the Atlantic. The first convoy so protected was HX.129, which left Halifax on May 27, 1941. An eastbound convoy was now provided with a local escort to 52°W, whence an escort group from St. John's took it to MOMP (Mid-Ocean Meeting Point) at 35°W. There it was met by a group from Iceland, which escorted the convoy on its final leg to the U.K. This pattern was changed in February, 1942, to a reverse version of the westbound convoy system.

WESTBOUND CONVOYS

Convoy Code	No. of Convoys	Route	First Convoy Sailed	Last Convoy Sailed	Remarks
OA	228	Thames outward via English Channel	7/9/39	24/10/40	At beginning, ran every two days. Both fast and slow convoys.
OB	349	Liverpool outward	7/9/39	22/7/41	As above. Replaced By ON and ONS convoys.
ON	221	U.K.-Halifax Later U.K.-New York	28/7/41	26/5/45	ONS.1 to ONS.171 as a general rule alternately slow and fast. Starting with ON.172, which sailed 10/3/43, all were fast. Last ON convoy was ON.305. All had continuous A/S protection.
ONS	84	U.K.-Halifax (former OB slow convoy)	29/7/41	6/3/43	As above. Slow convoys.
ONS	51	U.K.-Halifax New series.	15/3/43	21/5/45	Slow convoys. All had continuous A/S protection.
Total	933				

EASTBOUND CONVOYS

HX	358	Halifax-U.K.	16/9/39	23/5/45	HX.1 to HX.207 originated in Halifax; HX.208 to HX.358 in New York. Fast convoys.
SC	177	Sydney-U.K. Later Halifax-U.K.	15/8/40	26/5/45	57 sailed from Sydney, 97 from Halifax, and 23 from New York. Suspended between 17/5/44 and 4/10/44. Slow convoys.
Total	535				

THE ESCORTS

At the start of the war convoy escorts consisted of whatever ships were available, and the Allies paid a high price in losses for the lack of trained escort groups. This deficiency was not overcome until after May, 1941, when sufficient ships finally became available.

A typical escort group might consist of two or three destroyers and five or six corvettes, later adding a frigate. Generally, however, one-third of the ships were refitting or under repairs at any given time, so that the typical escort group at sea usually numbered about six ships. Newfoundland Command, responsible at the time for the western North Atlantic (convoys between Iceland and Newfoundland), formed twelve escort groups—EG 14 to 25, inclusive—in July, 1941. EG 14 consisted of seven RN and RCN destroyers, while each of the others was made up of one destroyer and three corvettes, a mixture of RN, RCN, and Free French ships.

These groups proved too small and were disbanded in November, 1941, the USN having taken over control of convoys in the western Atlantic on September 16. The escort groups of NEF came under the Commander, Task Force Four, USN, with headquarters at Argentia, Nfld. The mid-ocean escort groups were organized under Task Group 4.1, renumbered 24.1 in March, 1942. Subsequent re-designations are set forth in the table below:

RCN Escort Group	Date Formed	Renumbered 3/42 as	Renumbered 4/43 as	Convoys Escorted	Remarks	Group Disbanded
4.1.11	9/41	24.1.11	C-1*	66		6/45
4.1.12	''	24.1.12	C-2*	65		''
4.1.13	''	24.1.13	C-3*	68		''
4.1.14	''	24.1.14	C-4*	67		''
4.1.15	''	—	—	8		2/42
4.1.16	''	—	—	4		12/41
4.1.17	12/41	—	—	3		2/42
4.1.18	2/42	—	—	1		''
4.1.1	9/41	24.1.1	—	4		5/42
4.1.2	''	24.1.2	—	4		''
4.1.3	''	24.1.3	A-3*	60	Renumbered C-5, 30/4/43	6/45
C-6	8/44	—	—	13	Formed at Halifax	''
C-7	10/44	—	—	12	Formed at Londonderry	''
C-8	10/44	—	—	11	''	''
C-9	2/45	—	—	5	Formed at Halifax	''

Were semi-officially known by these designations as early as April, 1942, though still officially numbered as 24.1 groups.

Appendix 3

Special Assignments

CARIBBEAN SEA, 1942

By May, 1942, shortage of oil, both at Halifax and in the U.K., made necessary the initiation of fast tanker convoys between Halifax and Trinidad, and shortly afterward between Halifax and Aruba. Most of the escorts were provided by the RCN's Halifax Force, and seven corvettes were involved.

	Convoys Escorted			
Name	May, 1942	June, 1942	July, 1942	August, 1942
Fredericton			HA.2	AH.2
Halifax			HA.1 AH.1	HA.3 TAW.7 TAW.15
Hepatica		HT.2 TH.3		
Oakville			HA.1 AH.1	HA.3 TAW.7 TAW.15
Snowberry		HT.2 TH.3	HA.1 AH.1	HA.3 TAW.15
Sudbury	HT.1	TH.2 HT.3	TH.4 HA.2	AH.2
The Pas	HT.1	TH.2 HT.3	TH.4 HA.2	AH.2

*Convoy designations: AH Aruba-Halifax TH Trinidad-Halifax
HA Halifax-Aruba HT Halifax-Trinidad
TAW Trinidad-Aruba-Key West (Fla.)*

GUANTANAMO CONVOYS, 1942 — 1943

In August, 1942, the USN asked for the loan of corvettes to escort convoys between New York City and Guantanamo, Cuba (designated as NG or GN convoys, according to destination). The RCN provided seven corvettes, which were placed under the control of the Commander, Eastern Sea Frontier, USN.

Name	Arrived N.Y. to join	Period of Service
Fredericton	29/8/42	9/42-2/43
Halifax	14/9/42	9/42-3/43
Lethbridge	18/11/42	11/42-3/43
Oakville	7/12/42	12/42-2/43
Snowberry	7/9/42	9/42-3/43
Sudbury	29/8/42	9/42-12/42
The Pas	29/8/42	9/42-12/42

OPERATION NEPTUNE (THE INVASION OF NORTHERN FRANCE, JUNE, 1944). RCN SHIPS ENGAGED

Name	Command or Group	Name	Command or Group
2 LSI (M)		Qu'Appelle	EG 12
Prince David	Combined Operations (RN)	Restigouche	EG 12
		St. Laurent	EG 11
Prince Henry		Saskatchewan	EG 12
13 Destroyers		Sioux	26th DF (RN)
Algonquin	26th DF (RN)	Skeena	EG 12
Chaudière	EG 11	**11 Frigates**	
Gatineau	EG 11	Cape Breton	EG 6
Haida	10th DF (RN)	Grou	EG 6
Huron	10th DF (RN)	Matane	EG 9
Kootenay	EG 11	Meon	EG 9
Ottawa (2nd)	EG 11		

Continued

Name	Command or Group	Name	Command or Group
Outremont	EG 6	Regina	
Port Colborne	EG 9	Rimouski	
Saint John	EG 9	Summerside	
Stormont	EG 9	Trentonian	
Swansea	EG 9	Woodstock	
Teme	EG 6	**16 Minesweepers**	
Waskesiu	EG 6	Bayfield	31st MF
19 Corvettes	(all with Western Approaches Command, Greenock)	Blairmore	31st MF
		Canso	16th MF (RN)
Alberni		Caraquet	31st MF
Baddeck		Cowichan	31st MF
Calgary		Fort William	31st MF
Camrose		Georgian	14th MF (RN)
Drumheller		Guysborough	14th MF (RN)
Kitchener		Kenora	14th MF (RN)
Lindsay		Malpeque	31st MF
Louisburg		Milltown	31st MF
Lunenburg		Minas	31st MF
Mayflower		Mulgrave	31st MF
Mimico		Thunder	4th MF (RN)
Moose Jaw		Vegreville	14th MF (RN)
Port Arthur		Wasaga	31st MF
Prescott			

NOTE: The above table does not include minor vessels such as MTBs and LCI(L)s

OPERATION TORCH (NORTH AFRICAN LANDINGS), NOVEMBER, 1942

In August, 1942, the Admiralty requested the loan of a number of corvettes to support this operation. The RCN lent 16 of its own corvettes and 1 RN corvette from RCN EG C-1. All served in the Mediterranean or escorted U.K.-Gibraltar convoys in support of Operation Torch.

Name	Left Halifax for the U.K.	Transit Convoy	Returned to Halifax or St. John's	Transit Convoy	Remarks
Alberni	23/10/42	HX.212	23/3/43	ON.172	
Algoma	30/10/42	SC.107	4/4/43	ON.179	Returned to St. John's
Baddeck	18/10/42	SC.105	4/4/43	ON.174	
Calgary	23/10/42	SC.106	30/4/43	ON.179	Returned to St. John's
Camrose	22/10/42	SC.106	18/4/43	ONS.2	
Kitchener	23/10/42	SC.106	19/4/43	ONS.2	
Louisburg	15/9/42	HX.207			Lost, 6/2/43
Lunenburg	16/9/42	SC.100	20/9/43	ON.201	
Moose Jaw	30/10/42	SC.107	19/4/43	ONS.2	
Port Arthur	18/10/42	SC.105	23/3/43	ON.172	
Prescott	15/9/42	HX.207	4/4/43	ON.174	
Regina	30/10/42	SC.108	4/4/43	ON.174	
Summerside	23/10/42	HX.212	23/3/43	ON.172	
Ville de Québec	23/10/42	HX.212	22/4/43	ONS.2	
Weyburn	16/9/42	SC.100			Lost, 22/2/43
Woodstock	15/9/42	HX.207	24/3/43	ON.172	
Nasturtium (HMS)	16/9/42	SC.100	16/7/43	ONS.12	Return delayed by refit in U.K.

MURMANSK CONVOYS, 1943-45

The following RCN ships escorted convoys to North Russia between November, 1943 and May, 1945.

Name	No. of Round Trips	Convoys Escorted (See Key Below)
Destroyers		
Algonquin	1	M N
Athabaskan	1	C D
Haida	3	A B E F Q R
Huron	4	A B E F G H Q R
Iroquois	3	A B E F Q R
Sioux	2	M N O P
Frigates - EG 6		
Cape Breton	1	*J
Grou	1	*J
Outremont	1	*J
Waskesiu	1	*J
Frigates - EG 9		
Loch Alvie	2	K L S T
Monnow	2	K L S T
Nene	2	K L S T
Port Colborne	1	K L
Saint John	1	K L
Stormont	1	K L
Matane	1	S T
St. Pierre	1	S T

*Group sailed independently to Kola Inlet

Key

Code	Convoy	Sailed Loch Ewe	Arrived Kola Inlet
	Northbound to Russia		
A	JW.54A	15/11/43	24/11/43
C	JW.55A	12/12/43	20/12/43
E	JW.55B	20/12/43	29/12/43
G	JW.56B	22/1/44	1/2/44
K	JW.62	29/11/44	7/12/44
M	JW.63	30/12/44	8/1/45
	Sailed Clyde		
O	JW.65	11/3/45	21/3/45
Q	JW.66	16/4/45	25/4/45
S	JW.67	12/5/45	20/5/45

Code	Convoy	Sailed Archangel	Arrived Loch Ewe
	Southbound to U.K.		
B	RA.54B	26/11/43	9/12/43
	Sailed Kola Inlet		
D	RA.55A	23/12/43	1/1/44
F	RA.55B	31/12/43	8/1/44
H	RA.56	3/2/44	11/2/44
J	RA.59	28/4/44	6/5/44
	Arrived Clyde		
L	RA.62	10/12/44	20/12/44
N	RA.63	11/1/45	23/1/45
P	RA.65	23/3/45	1/4/45
R	RA.66	29/4/45	8/5/45
T	RA.67	23/5/45	31/5/45

Appendix 4

Commanding Officers

SUB/LT — Sub-Lieutenant

LT — Lieutenant

LCDR — Lieutenant-Commander

CDR — Commander

CAPT — Captain

COM — Commodore

SKPR — Skipper

SKPR/LT — Skipper-Lieutenant

CH/SKPR — Chief Skipper

A/ — Acting Rank

Acadia

LT	J. O. Boothby, RCN	20/2/40	— 1/4/40
LCDR	H. G. Shadforth, RCNR	12/4/40	—
LT	S. Henderson, RCNR	29/4/41	— 11/11/41
LCDR	J. L. Diver, RCNR	12/11/41	— 19/9/43
LCDR	R. V. Campbell, RCNR	20/9/43	— 15/12/43
LCDR	J. C. Littler, RCNR	16/12/43	— 30/3/44
LCDR	R. A. S. MacNeil, RCNR	31/3/44	— 6/6/44
SKPR/LT	F. W. Durant, RCNR	7/6/44	— 4/3/45
SKPR/LT	C. C. Clattenburg, RCNR	5/3/45	—

Agassiz

LCDR	B. D. L. Johnson, RCNR	23/1/41	— 14/3/43
A/LCDR	E. M. More, RCNR	15/3/43	— 13/3/44
A/LCDR	F. E. Burrows, RCNVR	14/3/44	— 8/1/45
LT	J. P. Jarvis, RCNVR	9/1/45	—

Alberni

LCDR	G. O. Baugh, OBE, RCNR	4/2/41	— 4/4/42
LT	A. W. Ford, RCNR	5/4/42	— 11/10/42
A/LCDR	I. H. Bell, RCNVR	12/10/42	— 21/8/44

Algoma

LT	J. Harding, RCNR	11/7/41	— 30/8/43
A/LCDR	J. P. Fraser, RCNR	1/9/43	— 10/10/43
A/LCDR	J. Harding, RCNR	11/10/43	— 3/2/44
LT	E. R. Hammond, RCNVR	17/3/44	— 26/3/44
LT	S. B. Kelly, RCNVR	27/3/44	— 5/4/44
LT	L. F. Moore, RCNR	6/4/44	— 9/8/44
LT	W. Davenport, RCNR	10/8/44	— 24/8/44
LT	J. N. Finlayson, RCNR	25/8/44	— 6/7/45

Algonquin

LCDR	D. W. Piers, DSC, RCN	17/2/44	— 19/4/45
LCDR	P. E. Haddon, RCN	20/4/45	— 6/2/46
CDR	P. F. X. Russell, RCN	25/2/53	— 27/8/54
CAPT	R. L. Hennessy, DSC, RCN	28/8/54	— 10/5/56
CAPT	D. W. Piers, DSC, RCN	11/5/56	— 6/7/56
LCDR	R. B. Hayward, RCN	7/7/56	— 28/7/57
LCDR	E. M. Jones, RCN	29/7/57	— 28/11/57
CAPT	D. G. King, DSC, RCN	29/11/57	— 23/9/58
CAPT	P. F. X. Russell, RCN	24/9/58	— 26/11/59
CAPT	A. F. Pickard, OBE, RCN	27/11/59	— 5/7/61
CAPT	A. D. McPhee, RCN	6/7/61	— 2/7/62
LCDR	D. C. Edwards, RCN	3/7/62	— 29/10/62
CDR	P. C. Berry, RCN	30/10/62	— 14/7/64
CDR	J. W. Mason, RCN	15/7/64	—

Algonquin (2nd)

CDR	R. L. McClean, RCN	3/11/73	— 7/5/76
CDR	H. M. D. MacNeil, RCN	8/5/76	— 10/8/77
CDR	J. Harwood, RCN	11/8/77	— 19/3/78
CDR	L. C. A. Westrop, RCN	20/3/78	— 24/7/80
CDR	D. E. Pollard, RCN	25/7/80	—

Ambler

A/LT	R. S. Kelley, RNVR	6/5/40	— 29/5/40
A/CDR	H. W. S. Soulsby, RCN	30/5/40	— 23/7/40
LCDR	E. G. M. Donald, RCN	24/7/40	— 11/10/40
LCDR	T. H. Beament, RCNVR	12/10/40	— 17/11/40
LCDR	L. L. Atwood, RCNVR	10/3/41	— 28/9/41
CH/SKPR	A. C. A. Chouinard, RCNR	29/9/41	— 18/5/42
LT	A. H. Rankin, RCNVR	19/5/42	— 26/7/42
LT	W. J. Kingsmill, RCNVR	27/7/42	— 26/10/42
LCDR	J. E. Mitchell, RCNVR	27/10/42	— 29/11/42
LT	A. M. Kirkpatrick, RCNVR	30/11/42	— 8/3/43
LT	W. T. Cook, RCNVR	9/3/43	— 5/5/43
LT	R. Montpetit, RCNVR	6/5/43	— 25/2/45
LT	E. K. Forbes, DSC, RCNVR	26/2/45	— 2/4/45
LT	S. T. Jagger, RCNVR	3/4/45	— 20/7/45

Amherst

LCDR	A. K. Young, RCNR	5/8/41	— 20/11/41
LT	H. G. Denyer, RCNR	21/11/41	— 19/9/42
A/LCDR	L. C. Audette, RCNVR	20/9/42	— 24/5/44
LT	D. M. Fraser, RCNVR	25/5/44	— 16/12/44
LT	K. W. Winsby, RCNVR	17/12/44	— 11/7/45

Annan

A/LCDR	C. P. Balfry, RCNR	13/6/44	— 26/5/45

Annapolis

A/CDR	H. Kingsley, RCN	24/9/40	— 10/10/40
CDR	C. D. Donald, RCN	11/10/40	— 28/3/41
LCDR	F. C. Smith, RCNR	29/3/41	— 1/7/42
A/LCDR	G. H. Davidson, RCN	2/7/42	— 4/10/42
LCDR	R. F. Harris, RCNR	5/10/42	— 14/10/42
A/LCDR	G. H. Davidson, RCN	15/10/42	— 3/12/42
LCDR	A. G. Boulton, RCNVR	4/12/42	— 2/3/44
LCDR	H. C. Walmesley, RCNR	3/3/44	— 15/4/45
SKPR/LT	C. C. Clattenburg, RCNR	16/4/45	— 4/6/45

Annapolis (2nd)

CDR	R. C. K. Peers, RCN	19/12/64	— 6/9/66
CDR	D. N. Mainguy, RCN	6/9/66	— 18/12/67
CDR	D. Ross, RCN	4/1/68	— 21/8/69
CDR	A. G. Lowe	21/8/69	— 20/2/71
CDR	A. P. Campbell	1/4/71	— 8/9/72
CDR	J. Drent	8/9/72	— 18/7/75
CDR	R. A. Wilson	8/8/75	— 14/5/77
CDR	A. R. H. Wood	14/5/77	— 16/4/79
CDR	W. P. Dumbrille	16/4/79	— 1/10/80
CDR	J. C. Braconnier	1/10/80	—

Antigonish

LCDR	R. D. Barrett, RCNR	4/7/44	— 4/5/45
A/LCDR	J. A. Dunn, RCNVR	5/5/45	— 22/7/45
A/LCDR	G. G. K. Holder, RCNVR	13/8/45	— 28/10/45
A/CDR	A H. G. Storrs, DSC & Bar, RCN	29/10/45	— 6/2/46
A/LCDR	J. E. Wolfenden, RCN(R)	26/4/47	— 16/8/47
LCDR	C. A. Law, DSC, RCN	17/8/47	— 3/12/48
LCDR	W. S. T. McCully, RCN	4/12/48	— 27/9/50
LCDR	R. Phillips, RCN	28/9/50	— 3/8/52
LCDR	H. R. Beck, RCN	4/8/52	— 15/1/54
LCDR	R. W. J. Cocks, RCN	12/10/57	— 16/8/60
LCDR	G. M. DeRosenroll, RCN	17/8/60	— 8/8/61
LCDR	E. M. Jones, RCN	9/8/61	— 27/8/63
LCDR	H. J. Wade, RCN	28/8/63	— 26/4/64
LCDR	P. L. McCulloch, RCN	27/4/64	— 2/9/65
LCDR	J. I. Donald, RCN	3/9/65	— 30/11/66

Armentières

LT	T. MacDuff, RCNR	1/9/39	—
LT	A. H. G. Storrs, RCNR	31/3/41	—
CH/SKPR	G. Billard, RCNR	29/7/41	—
CH/SKPR	W. E. Eccles, RCNR	2/3/42	—
CH/SKPR	J. D. McPhee, RCNR	14/12/42	—
SKPR/LT	G. F. Cassidy, RCNR	20/9/43	—
CH/SKPR	J. G. A. Grandmaison, RCNR		—
SKPR/LT	H. R. H. Stratford, RCNR	24/6/44	—
SKPR/LT	W. E. Eccles, RCNR	9/12/44	—
SKPR/LT	H. R. H. Stratford, RCNR		—
SKPR/LT	J. Craig, RCNR	7/8/45	—

Arnprior

A/LCDR	S. D. Thom, RCNVR	8/6/44	— 27/8/45
A/LCDR	T. B. Edwards, RCNR	28/8/45	— 14/3/46

Arras

LT	R. R. Kennedy, RCNR	4/5/40	—
LT	A. H. Cassivi, RCNR	28/1/41	—
LT	J. Willis, RCNR	1/5/41	—
LT	W. S. Arsenault, RCNR		—
LT	J. Willis, RCNR	17/4/43	—
SKPR/LT	A. Currie, RCNR	26/4/45	—
LT	W. S. Arsenault, RCNR	/ /45	—

Arrowhead

LT	V. Torraville, RCN	22/11/40	— 17/1/41
CDR	E. G. Skinner, RCNR	18/1/41	— 19/4/43
SKPR/LT	L. A. Hickey, RCNR	20/4/43	— 10/2/44
LT	W. P. Wickett, RCNVR	11/2/44	— 4/3/44
LT	R. H. Sylvester, RCNVR	5/3/44	— 15/4/44
SKPR/LT	L. A. Hickey, RCNR	16/4/44	— 21/10/44
LT	R. H. Sylvester, RCNVR	22/10/44	— 27/6/45

Arvida

LT	A. I. MacKay, RCNR	22/5/41	— 20/9/42
A/LCDR	D. G. King, RCNVR	21/9/42	— 15/3/44
LT	D. W. G. Storey, RCNVR	16/3/44	— 19/11/44
SKPR/LT	E. S. N. Fleasance, RCNR	20/11/44	— 4/12/44
LT	D. W. G. Storey, RCNVR	5/12/44	— 30/12/44
LT	J. C. P. Desrochers, RCNVR	31/12/44	— 17/1/45
LT	D. W. G. Storey, RCNVR	18/1/45	— 14/6/45

Asbestos

A/LCDR	J. Cuthbert, RCNR	16/6/44	— 8/7/45

Assiniboine

CDR	E. R. Mainguy, RCN	19/10/39	— 2/4/40
COM	G. C. Jones, RCN	3/4/40	— 15/9/40
CAPT	C. R. Taylor, RCN	16/9/40	— 29/10/40
COM	L. W. Murray, RCN	30/10/40	— 11/2/41
A/LCDR	J. H. Stubbs, RCN	12/2/41	— 1/10/42
LT	R. Hennessy, DSC, RCN	2/10/42	— 1/12/42
CDR	E. P. Tisdall, RCN	2/12/42	— 10/2/43
CDR	K. F. Adams, RCN	11/2/43	— 8/6/43
A/LCDR	R. P. Welland, DSC, RCN	9/6/43	— 7/7/43
CDR	K. F. Adams, RCN	8/7/43	— 30/9/43
A/LCDR	R. P. Welland, DSC, RCN	1/10/43	— 13/10/44
A/LCDR	R. Hennessy, DSC, RCN	14/10/44	— 21/2/45
CDR	E. L. Armstrong, RCN	22/2/45	— 8/8/45

Assiniboine (2nd)

CDR	E. P. Earnshaw, RCN	16/8/56	— 23/5/58
CDR	J. R. Coulter, RCN	24/5/58	— 19/2/59
CAPT	J. C. Pratt, RCN	19/2/59	— 17/8/60
CAPT	J. A. Charles, RCN	17/8/60	— 18/8/61
CDR	V. Browne, RCN	18/8/61	— 30/4/62
CDR	E. A. Wiggs, RCN	30/4/62	— 22/6/62
CDR	W. S. Blandy, RCN	28/6/62	— 15/1/66
CDR	T. L. Hebbert, RCN	15/1/66	— 15/7/67
CDR	G. L. Edwards, RCN	15/7/67	— 6/7/70
LCDR	E. Cullwick	6/7/70	— 18/8/70
CDR	L. J. Cavan	18/8/70	— 10/1/72
LCDR	H. Kieran	10/1/72	— 17/7/72
CDR	T. S. Hayward	17/7/72	— 20/11/72
CDR	G. G. Freill	20/11/72	— 22/12/72
LCDR	R. Thomas	22/12/72	— 14/4/73
CDR	R. Corneil	14/4/73	— 20/5/74
LCDR	R. Thomas	20/5/74	— 10/6/74
CDR	M. Taylor	10/6/74	— 16/7/75
CDR	E. K. Kelly	16/7/75	— 27/6/77
CDR	M. Duncan	27/6/77	— 31/7/79
CDR	G. Braithwaite	31/7/79	— 10/8/81
CDR	R. Moore	10/8/81	—

Athabaskan

CAPT	G. R. Miles, OBE, RCN	3/2/43	— 5/11/43
LCDR	J. H. Stubbs, DSO, RCN	6/11/43	— 29/4/44

Athabaskan (2nd)

CDR	J. S. Davis, RCN	20/1/48	— 28/10/48
LCDR	G. H. Davidson, RCN	29/10/48	— 25/11/48
CDR	M. A. Medland, RCN	26/11/48	— 14/9/49
LCDR	G. A. Powell, RCNR	15/9/49	— 14/1/50
LCDR	T. S. R. Peacocke, RCN	15/1/50	— 12/3/50
CDR	R. P. Welland, DSC, RCN	13/3/50	— 2/7/51
CDR	D. G. King, RCN	3/7/51	— 23/7/52
LCDR	H. Shorten, RCN	24/7/52	— 24/9/52
CDR	J. C. Reed, DSC, RCN	25/9/52	— 20/12/53
LCDR	H. Shorten, RCN	21/12/53	— 15/2/54
LCDR	C. E. Richardson, RCN	25/10/54	— 15/1/56
CDR	P. S. Booth, RCN	16/1/56	— 5/9/57
CDR	D. S. Boyle, RCN	6/9/57	— 1/3/59
CDR	J. H. G. Bovey, DSC, RCN	2/3/59	— 10/8/59
CDR	D. R. Saxon, DSC, RCN	11/8/59	— 24/5/61
CAPT	G. C. Edwards, RCN	25/5/61	— 15/3/62
CDR	A. E. Fox, RCN	16/3/62	— 3/1/63
LCDR	S. Dee, RCN	4/1/63	— 19/7/64
CDR	J. Y. Clarke, RCN	12/8/64	— 21/4/66

Athabaskan (3rd)

CDR	R. D. Yanow CD	30/9/72	— 6/9/74
CDR	G. L. Edwards CD	6/9/74	— 29/3/76
CDR	J. C. Slade CD	29/3/76	— 7/7/78
CDR	J. B. O'Reilly CD	7/7/78	— 7/7/80
CDR	J. W. McIntosh CD	7/7/80	—

Atholl

LT	W. D. H. Gardiner, RCNVR	14/10/43	— 16/9/44
LT	W. G. Garden, RCNVR	17/9/44	— 17/7/45

Aurora

CAPT	H. G. H. Adams, CBE, RN	1/11/20	— 1/7/22

Baddeck

LT	A. S. Easton, RCNR	18/5/41	— 5/4/42
LT	W. E. Nicholson, RCNR	6/4/42	— 20/4/42
LT	L. G. Cumming, RCNVR	21/4/42	— 5/10/42
LT	J. Brock, RCNVR	6/10/42	— 17/10/43
LT	G. C. Brown, RCNVR	18/10/43	— 19/4/44
A/LCDR	F. G. Hutchings, RCNR	20/4/44	— 23/7/44
LT	C. L. Campbell, RCNVR	24/7/44	— 14/10/44
LT	D. H. Tozer, RCNVR	15/10/44	— 4/7/45

Barrie

LT	R. M. Mosher, RCNR	12/5/41	— 9/1/42
CH/SKPR	G. N. Downey, RCNR	10/1/42	— 28/3/42
A/LCDR	R. M. Mosher, RCNR	29/3/42	— 13/3/43
LT	H. O. Magill, RCNVR	14/3/43	— 8/10/43
LT	D. R. Watson, RCNR	9/10/43	— 18/3/44
LT	H. O. Magill, RCNVR	19/3/44	— 15/6/44
LT	W. D. Stokvis, RCNVR	16/6/44	— 26/6/45

Battleford

LT	R. J. Roberts, RCNVR	31/7/41	— 5/10/42
LT	F. A. Beck, RCNVR	6/10/42	— 5/7/43
LCDR	A. H. Easton, RCNR	6/7/43	— 20/8/43
LT	F. A. Beck, RCNVR	21/8/43	— 7/5/44
LT	H. H. Turnbull, RCNVR	8/5/44	— 19/6/44
LT	P. A. F. Langlois, RCNVR	20/6/44	— 23/5/45
LT	F. D. Wickett, RCNVR	24/5/45	— 18/7/45

Bayfield

LT	D. W. Main, RCNR	26/2/42	— 3/11/42
LT	A. H. Gosse, RCNR	4/11/42	— 31/12/42
LT	D. W. Main, RCNR	1/1/43	— 19/1/44
LT	S. Pierce, RCNR	20/1/44	— 15/10/44
LT	J. C. K. McNaught, RCNVR	16/10/44	— 22/12/44
LT	F. A. Cunningham, RCNVR	23/12/44	— 1/9/45
LT	J. G. Kingsmill, RCNVR	2/9/45	— 24/9/45

Beacon Hill

A/CDR	E. T. Simmons, DSO, DSC, RCNVR	16/4/44	— 12/8/45
LCDR	H. L. Quinn, DSC, RCNVR	13/9/45	— 5/2/46
LT	J. E. Korning, RCN	16/5/49	— 15/9/49
LCDR	R. W. Murdoch, RCN	15/4/50	— 23/9/51
LCDR	J. W. McDowall, RCN	24/9/51	— 20/9/53
CDR	G. A. LaRue, RCN	21/9/53	— 4/1/54
LCDR	P. F. Wilson, RCN	21/12/57	— 14/11/58
LCDR	F. G. Henshaw, RCN	15/11/58	— 1/12/58

LCDR	W. S. Blandy, RCN	2/12/58	— 18/8/59
LCDR	A. G. Kilpatrick, RCN	19/8/59	— 24/8/61
LCDR	J. L. Fanabaker, RCN	25/8/61	— 17/5/62
LCDR	A. C. McMillin, RCN	18/5/62	— 15/9/63
LCDR	K. M. Young, RCN	16/9/63	— 27/10/64
LCDR	W. A Hughes, RCN	28/10/64	—
LCDR	G. V. Hartman, RCN		— 1/5/66
LCDR	P. E. Simard, RCN	2/5/66	— 11/9/66
LCDR	S. C. Gould, RCN	12/9/66	— 15/9/67

Beauharnois

A/LCDR	E. C. Smith RCNVR	25/9/44	— 20/5/45
LT	J. M. Pretty, RCNVR	21/5/45	— 12/7/45

Beaver

	(Not Known)	30/9/40	— 16/3/41
LCDR	G. H. Griffiths, RCN	17/3/41	— 31/7/41
A/CDR	R. I. Swansburg, RCNR	1/8/41	— 15/10/42
LT	J. F. Watson, RCNR	16/10/42	— 4/12/42
LCDR	J. S. Wilson, RCNR	5/12/42	— 28/12/42
LT	J. F. Watson, RCNR	29/12/42	— 3/1/43
LT	D. Davis, RCNVR	4/1/43	— 16/1/43
LT	J. F. Watson, RCNVR	17/1/43	— 19/9/43
A/LCDR	H. C. Walmseley, RCNR	20/9/43	— 5/3/44
LCDR	C. G. Williams, RCNR	6/3/44	— 7/8/44
LCDR	C. G. Williams, RCNR	23/9/44	— 13/3/45
SKPR/LT	I. E. Abbott, RCNR	14/3/45	— /6/45

Bellechasse

LT	H. H. Rankin, RCNR	13/12/41	— 2/5/43
LT	R. J. Roberts, RCNR	3/5/43	— 16/12/43
LT	H. H. Rankin, RCNR	17/12/43	— 5/1/44
LCDR	W. Redford, RCNR	6/1/44	— 22/3/45
LCDR	J. S. Cunningham, RCNVR	23/3/45	— 17/4/45
LT	J. M. MacRae, RCNVR	18/4/45	— 24/8/45

Belleville

LT	J. E. Korning, RCN	19/10/44	— 6/5/45
LCDR	R. M. Powell, RCNVR	7/5/45	— 5/7/45

Bittersweet

A/LCDR	J. A. Woods, RCNR	23/1/41	— 30/11/42
LCDR	F. B. Brooks-Hill, RCNVR	1/12/42	— 9/7/44
LT	F. W. Bogardus, RCNVR	10/7/44	— 7/12/44
SKPR/LT	F. C. Smith, RCNR	17/12/44	— 22/6/45

Blairmore

A/LCDR	W. J. Kingsmill, RCNVR	17/11/42	— 24/10/43
LT	J. C. Marston, RCNVR	25/10/43	— 14/6/45
SKPR/LT	H. V. Mossman, RCNR	15/6/45	— 16/10/45

Bonaventure

CAPT	H. V. W. Groos, RCN	17/1/57	— 14/1/58
CAPT	W. M. Landymore, OBE, RCN	15/1/58	— 11/9/59
CAPT	J. C. O'Brien, RCN	12/9/59	— 29/8/61
CAPT	F. C. Frewer, RCN	30/8/61	— 6/8/63
CAPT	R. W. Timbrell, DSC, RCN	7/8/63	— 1/4/65
CAPT	H. A. Porter, RCN	2/4/65	— 31/7/66
CDR	A. T. Bice, RCN	1/8/66	— 20/11/66
CAPT	R. H. Falls, RCN	21/11/66	— 8/4/69
CAPT	J. M. Cutts, RCN	9/4/69	— 8/1/70
CDR	H. W. Vondette, RCN	9/1/70	— 1/7/70

Border Cities

LCDR	B. P. Young, MBE, RCNR	18/5/44	— 23/7/45
LT	J. Butterfield, RCNR	24/10/45	— 15/1/46

Bowmanville

LCDR	M. S. Duffus, RCNVR	28/9/44	— 3/4/45
LT	A. D. Ritchie, RCNVR	4/4/45	— 20/4/45
LCDR	M. S. Duffus, RCNVR	21/4/45	— 24/8/45
LT	W. J. Ransom, RCNVR	25/10/45	— 15/2/46

Brandon

A/LCDR	J. C. Littler, RCNR	22/7/41	— 19/8/42
LT	R. J. G. Johnson, RCNVR	20/8/42	— 20/9/42
A/LCDR	J. C. Littler, RCNR	21/9/42	— 24/11/42
LT	H. E. McArthur, RCNVR	25/11/42	— 25/5/44
LT	J. F. Evans, RCNVR	26/5/44	— 26/4/45
LT	P. J. Lawrence, RCNR	27/4/45	— 22/6/45

Brantford

LT	W. D. F. Johnston, RCNR	15/5/42	— 26/4/43
LT	J. A. R. Allan, RCNVR	27/4/43	— 1/5/44
LT	R. C. Eaton, RCNVR	2/5/44	— 28/9/44
LT	J. P. Kieran, RCNR	29/9/44	— 27/4/45
LT	R. M. Smillie, RCNVR	28/4/45	— 17/8/45

Bras d'Or

LT	A. K. Young, RCNR	9/10/39	— 25/4/40
LT	C. A. Hornsby, RCNR	26/4/40	— 19/10/40

Bras d'Or (2nd)

CDR	C. Cotaras, RCN	19/7/68	— 6/7/70
CDR	G. L. Edwards	6/7/70	— 1/5/72

Brockville

LT	C. Peterson, RCNR	19/9/42	— 13/3/43
LT	R. C. Chenoweth, RCNVR	14/3/43	— 17/7/43
LT	C. Peterson, RCNR	18/7/43	— 23/7/43
LT	B. P. Young, RCNR	24/7/43	— 17/9/43
LT	F. K. Elles, RCNVR	18/9/43	— 2/8/44
LT	M. G. McCarthy, RCNVR	3/8/44	— 17/12/44
LT	J. R. Bell, RCNVR	18/12/44	— 7/2/45
LT	J. O. L. Lake, RCNR	8/2/45	— 14/5/45
LT	H. R. Knight, RCNR	15/5/45	— 24/5/45
LT	J. O. L. Lake, RCNR	25/5/45	— 16/7/45
LT	E. E. MacInnis, RCNR	30/7/45	— 28/8/45
LCDR	J. H. Maxner, RCN	1/11/50	— 21/4/54
LCDR	R. D. Hayes, RCNR	22/4/54	— 11/11/55
LCDR	E. S. Cassels, RCN	12/1/55	— 12/12/56

LCDR	L. I. Jones, RCN	29/8/58	— 31/10/58

Buckingham

A/LCDR	M. H. Wallace, RCNR	2/11/44	— 7/11/45
LT	R. M. Montague, RCNVR	8/11/45	— 16/11/45
LCDR	J. W. Roberts, RCN	25/6/54	— 7/9/55
LCDR	T. E. Connors, RCN	8/9/55	— 30/9/57
LCDR	D. M. MacLennan, RCN	6/5/58	—
LCDR	T. L. Hebbert, RCN	14/12/59	—
LCDR	R. F. Choat, RCN	15/9/62	— 7/6/63
LCDR	C. E. Leighton, RCN	8/6/63	— 31/3/64
LCDR	N. S. Jackson, RCN	1/4/64	— 10/1/65
LT	E. G. A. Bowkett, RCN	11/1/65	— 15/1/65
LT	J. T. Stuart, RCN	16/1/65	— 23/3/65

Buctouche

LT	W. W. Hackney, RCNR	5/6/41	— 6/5/42
SKPR/LT	G. N. Downey, RCNR	7/5/42	— 28/4/44
SKPR/LT	H. E. Young, RCNR	29/4/44	— 4/12/44
SKPR/LT	E. S. N. Pleasance, RCNR	5/12/44	— 1/1/45
SKPR/LT	H. E. Young, RCNR	2/1/45	— 15/6/45

Burlington

LCDR	W. J. Fricker, RCN	6/9/41	— 1/5/42
LT	M. Russell, RCNR	2/5/42	— 31/12/43
SKPR/LT	J. B. Cooper, RCNR	1/1/44	— 22/1/44
LT	J. W. Golby, RCNVR	23/1/44	— 6/2/44
LT	J. M. Richardson, RCNVR	7/2/44	— 3/1/45
LT	K. G. Clark, RCNVR	3/1/45	— 6/5/45
LT	P. P. Jefferies, RCNVR	7/5/45	— 12/8/45
LT	S. W. McEvenue, RCNVR	13/8/45	— 4/9/45
SKPR/LT	J. E. Vezina, RCNR	5/9/45	— 30/10/45

Buxton

LT	J. F. Watson, RCNR	4/11/43	—

Calgary

LT	G. Lancaster, RCNR	16/12/41	— 19/6/42
A/LCDR	H. K. Hill, RCNVR	20/6/42	— 17/3/44
LT	A. A. R. Dykes, RCNR	18/3/44	— 15/9/44
LT	L. D. M. Saunders, RCNVR	16/9/44	— 25/5/45
LT	G. M. Orr, RCNVR	26/5/45	— 19/6/45

Camrose

A/LCDR	L. R. Pavillard, RCNR	30/6/41	— 7/11/44
LT	J. B. Lamb, RCNVR	8/11/44	— 18/7/45

Canso

LT	H. S. MacFarlane, RCNR	6/3/42	— 3/2/43
LT	J. Kincaid, RCNR	4/2/43	— 23/5/43
LT	H. H. Rankin, RCNR	24/5/43	— 5/6/43
LT	J. Kincaid, RCNR	6/6/43	— 4/10/44
A/LCDR	J. M. Gracey, RCNVR	5/10/44	— 24/9/45

Cap de la Madeleine

LCDR	R. A. Judges, RCNVR	30/9/44	— 18/10/45
LCDR	W. O. O. Barbour, RCNR	19/10/45	— 25/11/45
LCDR	C. A. Gray, RCN	20/5/59	— 27/12/60
CDR	K. E. Grant, RCN	28/12/60	— 8/1/61
LCDR	D. R. White, RCN	9/1/61	— 6/2/61
CDR	K. E. Grant, RCN	7/2/61	— 25/10/62
LT	G. R. Ferguson, RCN	26/10/62	— 18/2/63
CDR	R. A. Beach, RCN	19/2/63	— 8/3/64
LCDR	F. J. French, RCN	27/11/64	— 15/5/65

Cape Breton

LCDR	A. M. McLarnon, RCNR	25/10/43	— 3/12/44
A/LCDR	J. C. L. Annesley, RCN	5/1/45	— 24/9/45

Cape Breton (2nd)

CDR	E. N. Clarke, RCN	31/1/53	— 21/3/54
CDR	D. H. Fairney, RCN	22/3/54	— 8/3/56
CAPT	J. S. Ross, RCN	9/3/56	— 2/7/56
CDR	F. Harley, RCN	3/7/56	— 31/7/57
LCDR	K. W. Salmon, RCN	1/8/57	— 26/8/57
CDR	J. C. Chauvin, RCN	27/8/57	— 11/6/58
CDR	H. R. Beck, RCN	12/6/58	— 1/8/58
LCDR	R. P. LeMay, RCN	2/8/58	— 25/8/58
CDR	M. F. Oliver, RCN	16/11/59	— 24/7/62
CDR	I. A. McPhee, RCN	25/7/62	— 10/2/64

Cape Scott

CDR	F. J. Jones, RCN	28/1/59	— 23/8/60
CDR	A. H. Rankin, RCN	24/8/60	— 10/5/64
CDR	C. A. Law, RCN	11/5/64	— 10/4/66
CAPT	H. H. Smith, RCN	11/4/66	—

Capilano

LCDR	H. E. McArthur, RCNVR	25/8/44	— 12/8/45
LT	C. B. Hermann, RCNVR	13/8/45	— 26/8/45

Caraquet

LT	A. A. R. Dykes, RCNR	2/4/42	— 3/11/43
CDR	A. H. G. Storrs, RCNR	4/11/43	— 18/9/44
LT	G. W. Leckie, RCNVR	13/11/44	— 26/9/45

Caribou

LT	A. K. Young, RCNR	27/5/40	—
LT	J. H. Marshall, RCNR	19/9/41	— 25/3/42
LT	J. Evelyn, RCNR	26/3/42	— 18/9/42
Mate	J. M. Moncrieff, RCNR	19/9/42	— 10/2/43
LT	D. Davis, RCNVR	11/2/43	— 11/8/43
LT	R. K. Bythell, RCNVR	12/8/43	— / /44
LT	J. C. Fritz, RCNVR	/8/44	— 20/7/45

Carlplace

A/LCDR	C. E. Wright, RCNVR	13/12/44	— 2/9/45

Cartier/Charny

LCDR	J. J. DesLauriers, RCNR	18/9/39	—
LT	A. B. Taylor, RCNR	21/8/40	— 21/10/41
LT	E. R. Shaw, RCNR	22/10/41	— 8/5/42

LT	F. E. Grubb, RCN	9/5/42	— /11/42
LT	C. L. Campbell, RCNVR	/11/42	— 4/4/43
LCDR	C. G. Williams, RCNR	5/4/43	— 3/3/44
LT	L. J. Wallace, RCNVR	4/3/44	— 31/10/44
LT	R. D. Brown, RCNVR	1/11/44	— 6/4/45
LT	L. J. Wallace, RCNVR	7/4/45	— 20/4/45
LT	R. D. Brown, RCNVR	21/4/45	— 16/11/45
SKPR/LT	P. Perrault, RCNR	17/11/45	— 12/12/45

Cayuga

CDR	O. C. S. Robertson, GM, RCN	20/10/47	— 1/1/49
CDR	M. A. Medland, RCN	15/9/49	— 4/7/50
CAPT	J. V. Brock, DSO, DSC, RCN	5/7/50	— 24/5/51
CDR	J. Plomer, OBE, DSC, RCN	25/5/51	— 18/6/52
LT	F. Little, RCN	18/6/52	— 14/7/52
LCDR	W. P. Hayes, RCN	23/2/53	— 31/12/54
CDR	G. H. Davidson, RCN	1/1/55	— 16/10/56
CDR	P. C. Benson, RCN	17/10/56	— 16/4/58
LCDR	G. A. Hoyte, RCN	17/4/58	— 23/6/58
CDR	M. H. E. Page, RCN	24/6/58	— 1/3/59
CDR	E. Petley-Jones, RCN	2/3/59	— 13/12/60
LCDR	F. J. Dunbar, RCN	14/12/60	— 2/8/61
CDR	A. H. MacDonald, RCN	3/8/61	— 1/2/62
CDR	W. M. Beckett, RCN	2/2/62	— 27/2/64

Chaleur

LT	M. A. Martin, RCN	18/6/54	— 30/9/54

Chaleur (2nd)

LCDR	R. Carle, RCN	12/9/57	— 27/6/59
LCDR	K. D. Lewis, RCN	28/6/59	— 29/3/61
CDR	R. B. Hayward, RCN	30/3/61	— 23/7/63
CDR	W. H. Willson, RCN	24/7/63	— 20/3/64

Chambly

A/LCDR	F. C. Smith, RCNR	18/12/40	— 25/3/41
CDR	J. D. Prentice, RCN	26/3/41	— 13/11/42
A/LCDR	A. F. Pickard, RCNR	14/11/42	— 26/1/44
LT	S. D. Taylor, RCNR	27/1/44	— 22/6/44
LT	H. A. Ovenden, RCNR	23/6/44	— 20/7/44
A/LCDR	S. D. Taylor, RCNR	21/7/44	— 13/5/45
LCDR	J. B. B. Shaw, RCNVR	14/5/45	— 20/6/45

Champlain

CDR	C. T. Beard, RCN	1/3/28	— 20/5/28
LCDR	J. C. I. Edwards, RCN	21/5/28	— 26/12/29
CDR	V. G. Brodeur, RCN	27/12/29	— 26/12/30
LCDR	A. R. Pressey, RCN	27/12/30	— 27/8/31
LCDR	G. B. Barnes, RCN	28/8/31	— 15/10/31
LCDR	A. R. Pressey, RCN	16/10/31	— 22/5/32
LCDR	V. S. Godfrey, RCN	23/5/32	— 23/5/34
LCDR	W. B. Creery, RCN	24/5/34	— 10/12/35
LCDR	R. E. S. Bidwell, RCN	11/12/35	— 25/11/36

Charlottetown

LT	J. W. Bonner, RCNR	13/12/41	— 11/9/42

Charlottetown (2nd)

LCDR	J. Harding, RCNR	28/4/44	— 23/4/45
A/CDR	W. C. Halliday, RCNR	24/4/45	— 9/7/45
A/CDR	W. C. Halliday, RCNR	19/9/45	— 5/10/45
LCDR	S. W. Howell, RCNR	6/10/45	—
LCDR	J. E. Wolfenden, RCNR	13/4/46	—

Chaudière

A/LCDR	C. P. Nixon, DSC, RCN	15/11/43	— 21/3/45
A/LCDR	W. Davenport, RCNR	22/3/45	— 20/6/45
LCDR	G. M. Kaizer, RCNR	2/8/45	— 12/8/45

Chaudière (2nd)

CDR	V. J. Wilgress, RCN	14/11/59	— 25/4/61
CDR	P. J. Pratley, RCN	24/4/61	— 11/4/63
CDR	R. H. Falls, RCN	11/4/63	— 25/8/64
CDR	G. R. Macfarlane, RCN	25/8/64	— 17/1/66
CDR	J. I. Manore, RCN	17/1/66	— 26/8/67
LCDR	W. G. Brown, RCN	26/8/67	— 24/11/67
LCDR	J. L. Woodbury, RCN	24/11/67	— 8/12/67
LCDR	P. G. Bissell, RCN	8/12/67	— 20/1/70
CDR	H. Rusk	20/1/70	— 30/6/71
LCDR	D. R. Donaldson	30/6/71	— 23/5/73
LCDR	J. G. Comeau	24/5/73	— 23/5/74

Chebogue

LCDR	T. MacDuff, RCNR	22/2/44	— 23/7/44
A/LCDR	M. F. Oliver, RCNR	24/7/44	— 21/1/45
LT	D. F. McElgunn, RCNVR	22/1/45	— 25/9/45

Chedabucto

LT	J. H. B. Davies, RCNR	27/9/41	— 31/10/43

Chicoutimi

LT	W. Black, RCNR	12/5/41	— 10/5/42
A/LCDR	H. G. Dupont, RCNR	11/5/42	— 15/2/43
LCDR	J. F. Stairs, RCNVR	16/2/43	— 7/5/44
LT	F. Cross, RCNR	8/5/44	— 3/9/44
LT	A. E. Giffin, RCNVR	4/9/44	— 16/11/44
SKPR/LT	C. C. Clattenburg, RCNVR	17/11/44	— 26/11/44
LT	A. E. Giffin, RCNVR	27/11/44	— 14/4/45
LT	R. A. Wyllie, RCNVR	15/4/45	— 16/6/45

Chignecto

LT	L. F. McQuarrie, RCNR	31/10/41	— 8/8/43
LT	H. H. Rankin, RCNR	9/8/43	— 29/8/43
LT	L. F. McQuarrie, RCNR	30/8/43	— 28/6/44
SKPR/LT	G. F. Cassidy, RCNR	29/6/44	— 1/3/45
LT	R. C. Eaton, RCNVR	2/3/45	— 23/9/45
	(Not Known)	24/9/45	— 3/11/45

Chignecto (2nd)

LCDR	C. J. Benoit, DSC, RCN	1/12/53	— 2/2/54

LCDR	E. J. Semmens, RCN	3/2/54	— 31/3/54
Chignecto (3rd)			
LCDR	R. C. K. Peers, RCN	1/8/57	— 10/3/58
LCDR	C. D. Gillis, RCN	11/3/58	— 3/11/59
LCDR	J. I. Manore, RCN	4/11/59	— 10/9/61
LCDR	D. G. Wales, RCN	11/9/61	— 25/7/63
LCDR	E. A. Makin, RCN	26/7/63	—
Chilliwack			
A/LCDR	L. F. Foxall, RCNR	8/4/41	— 25/5/43
LCDR	C. R. Coughlin, RCNVR	26/5/43	— 11/4/44
A/LCDR	D. R. Watson, MBE, RCNR	12/4/44	— 14/7/45
Clayoquot			
A/LCDR	G. A. Thomson, RCNR	22/8/41	— 18/11/41
A/LCDR	R. B. Campbell, RCNR	19/11/41	— 13/4/42
LT	H. E. Lade, RCNR	14/4/42	— 7/4/43
LT	C. L. Campbell, RCNVR	8/4/43	— 5/3/44
LT	D. R. Baker, RCNVR	6/3/44	— 11/4/44
LT	C. L. Campbell, RCNVR	12/4/44	— 15/6/44
LT	M. Smith, RCNR	.Q	— 28/7/44
A/LCDR	A. C. Campbell, RCNVR	29/7/44	— 24/12/44
Coaticook			
LCDR	L. C. Audette, RCNVR	25/7/44	— 3/6/45
LCDR	L. R. Hoar, RCNVR	4/6/45	— 22/7/45
A/LCDR	J. W. Golby, RCNVR	6/8/45	— 19/8/45
Cobalt			
A/LCDR	R. B. Campbell, RCNR	25/11/40	— 19/5/41
LT	C. J. Angus, RCNR	20/5/41	— 3/1/43
LT	M. F. Oliver, RCNR	4/1/43	— 6/2/43
LT	C. J. Angus, RCNR	7/2/43	— 5/5/43
A/LCDR	R. A. Judges, RCNVR	6/5/43	— 3/3/44
LT	A. A. R. Dykes, RCNR	4/3/44	— 17/3/44
A/LCDR	R. M. Wallace, RCNVR	26/6/44	— 17/6/45
Cobourg			
LT	G. H. Johnson, RCNVR	11/5/44	— 15/6/45
Collingwood			
LT	N. G. W. Bennett, RCNR	9/11/40	— 16/4/41
A/LCDR	W. Woods, RCNR	17/4/41	— 9/12/42
LT	D. W. Groos, RCN	10/12/42	— 5/6/43
A/LCDR	R. J. C. Pringle, RCNVR	6/6/43	— 4/7/44
LT	H. R. Knight, RCNR	5/7/44	— 2/5/45
LT	E. B. Pearce, RCNVR	3/5/45	— 17/6/45
SKPR/LT	J. D. Burnham, RCNR	18/6/45	— 23/7/45
Columbia			
LCDR	S. W. Davis, DSC, RCN	24/9/40	— 13/5/42
LCDR	G. H. Stephen, RCNR	14/5/42	— 17/3/43
LCDR	B. D. L. Johnson, RCNR	18/3/43	— 23/11/43
LCDR	R. A. S. MacNeil, OBE, RCNR	24/11/43	— 30/3/44
LT	T. A. G. Staunton, RCNVR	31/3/44	— 22/5/44
LT	M. L. Devaney, RCNVR	23/5/44	— 18/6/44
LCDR	F. O. Gerity, RCNR	19/6/44	— 30/6/44
LT	M. L. Devaney, RCNVR	1/7/44	— 22/7/44
LT	J. G. Hughes, RCNR	23/7/44	— 1/3/45
Columbia (2nd)			
CDR	W. P. Hayes, RCN	7/11/59	— 25/4/61
CDR	D. W. Knox, RCN	25/4/61	— 4/9/64
CDR	P. R. Hinton, RCN	4/9/64	— 15/9/65
CDR	A. C. McMillin, RCN	15/9/65	— 20/2/67
CDR	R. D. Okros, RCN	20/2/67	— 31/8/68
CDR	T. C. Shuckburg, RCN	31/8/68	— 23/7/70
CDR	E. A. Makin	23/7/70	— 6/8/72
CDR	R. F. Choat	7/8/72	— 18/2/74
Comox			
LCDR	H. W. S. Soulsby, RCNR	23/11/38	— 26/5/40
A/LCDR	D. C. Wallace, RCNR	27/5/40	— 27/7/40
A/CDR	S. H. Soulsby, RCN	28/7/40	— 9/10/40
LT	R. R. Kenny, RCNR	10/10/40	— 22/6/41
A/LT	T. Gilmour, RCNR	23/6/41	— 2/8/41
Mate	J. R. Biggs, RCNR	29/9/41	— 25/3/42
LT	F. G. Hutchings, RCNR	26/3/42	— 3/8/42
LT	J. P. A. Duggan, RCNR	4/8/42	— 13/4/44
LT	J. E. N. Vezina, RCNR	14/4/44	— 27/7/45
Comox (2nd)			
CDR	J. V. Steele, GM, RCN	2/4/54	— 9/8/55
LCDR	C. G. Smith, RCN	10/8/55	— 5/5/57
LCDR	P. S. Cox, RCN	6/5/57	— 11/9/57
Copper Cliff			
LCDR	F. G. Hutchings, RCNR	25/7/44	— 3/12/44
A/LCDR	F. W. Bogardus, RCNVR	4/12/44	— 11/1/45
LCDR	F. G. Hutchings, RCNR	12/1/45	— 25/7/45
LT	W. M. Combe, RCNR	20/8/45	— 20/9/45
Coquitlam			
LT	G. J. McNamara, RCNVR	25/7/44	— 3/7/45
Cordova			
LCDR	A. F. Rowland, RCN	13/1/55	— 31/5/55
LT	R. Freeman, RCN	1/6/55	— 12/4/57
Cormorant (2nd)			
LCDR	J. G. Morrison	24/7/78	— 17/8/81
LCDR	J. W. Alexander	17/8/81	—
Cougar			
LT	T. M. W. Golby, RCNR	20/8/40	— 1/1/41
LT	H. G. Denyer, RCNR	2/1/41	— 11/5/41
CH/SKPR	G. F. Cassidy, RCNR	12/5/41	— 5/11/42
CH/SKPR	R. W. Sparks, RCNR	6/11/42	— 7/2/43
SKPR/LT	E. W. Suffield, RCNR	8/2/43	— 22/2/43
CH/SKPR	R. W. Sparks, RCNR	23/2/43	— 23/11/43
SKPR	D. J. Smith, RCNR	24/11/43	— 12/1/44
SKPR/LT	G. F. Cassidy, RCNR	13/1/44	— 22/6/44
SKPR/LT	K. Bennett, RCNR	23/6/44	— 15/9/44
SKPR/LT	K. Bennett, RCNR	3/10/44	— 15/5/45
SKPR/LT	W. R. Chaster, RCNR	16/5/45	— 22/6/45
Courtenay			
A/LCDR	A. R. Ascah, RCNR	21/3/42	— 7/2/43
LT	A. H. Gosse, RCNR	8/2/43	— 1/3/43
A/LCDR	A. R. Ascah, RCNR	2/3/43	— 4/3/45
LT	W. M. Black, RCNVR	5/3/45	— 2/9/45
Cowichan			
LT	Ronald Jackson, RCNR	4/7/41	— 1/12/41
LT	Richard Jackson, RCNR	2/12/41	— 14/2/42
A/LT	J. R. Kidston, RCNVR	15/2/42	— 25/10/42
A/LCDR	K. W. N. Hall, RCNR	26/10/42	— 22/4/45
SKPR/LT	H. W. Stone, RCNR	23/4/45	— 9/10/45
Cowichan (2nd)			
LCDR	P. H. Cayley, RCN	10/12/53	— /12/53
LCDR	A. H. Slater, RCN	/12/53	— 15/3/54
LT	J. M. Cutts, RCN	16/3/54	— 31/3/54
Cowichan (3rd)			
LCDR	G. W. S. Brooks, RCN	12/12/57	— 27/8/59
LCDR	W. C. Wilson, RCN	28/8/59	— 30/8/61
LCDR	R. D. Okros, RCN	31/8/61	— /8/63
LT	A. P. Howard, RCN	/8/63	— /2/64
Cranbrook			
LT	C. G. Trotter, RCNVR	12/5/44	— 2/10/44
LT	R. Stark, RCNVR	3/10/44	— 17/10/44
LT	C. G. Trotter, RCNVR	18/10/44	— 3/5/45
SKPR/LT	J. R. Smith, RCNR	4/5/45	— 14/6/45
SKPR/LT	K. Bennett, RCNR	15/6/45	— 3/11/45
Crescent			
LCDR	C. P. Nixon, DSC, RCN	10/9/45	— 17/12/46
LCDR	J. C. O'Brien, RCN	18/12/46	— 4/1/48
LCDR	J. A. Charles, RCN	5/1/48	— 15/11/48
LCDR	D. W. Groos, DSC, RCN	16/11/48	— 1/12/49
LCDR	G. H. Hayes, DSC, RCN	26/9/50	— 24/9/51
LT	J. K. H. Mason, MBE, RCN	25/9/51	— 12/10/51
CDR	J. C. Littler, RCN	13/10/51	— 14/9/52
LCDR	J. R. Coulter, RCN	15/9/52	— 15/2/53
LCDR	D. L. Davies, RCN	16/2/53	— 25/2/53
CAPT	P. D. Taylor, DSC, RCN	31/10/55	— 10/3/57
CAPT	M. G. Stirling, RCN	11/3/57	— 17/5/57
LCDR	L. I. Jones, RCN	18/5/57	— 15/8/57
CAPT	M. G. Stirling, RCN	16/8/57	— 20/6/58
CAPT	J. C. Pratt, RCN	21/6/58	— 18/2/59
CDR	J. R. Coulter, RCN	19/2/59	— 14/9/59
CAPT	R. W. Murdock, RCN	15/9/59	— 11/6/61
CDR	P. H. Cayley, RCN	12/6/61	— 11/7/62
CAPT	A. D. McPhee, RCN	12/7/62	— 11/4/63
CDR	V. J. Murphy, RCN	12/4/63	— 22/10/64
CDR	H. C. LaRose, RCN	23/10/64	— 12/8/66
Crusader			
A/LCDR	M. G. Stirling, RCN	15/11/45	— 1/2/46
CDR	H. V. W. Groos, RCN	2/4/51	— 2/4/52
LCDR	J. H. G. Bovey, RCN	3/4/52	— 7/7/53
LCDR	J. Husher, RCN	8/7/53	— 20/7/53
LCDR	H. H. Smith, RCN	21/7/53	— 28/8/53
LCDR	W. H. Willson, DSC, RCN	29/8/53	— 12/9/54
LCDR	R. H. Leir, RCN	13/9/54	— 17/3/55
LCDR	J. Butterfield, RCN	18/3/55	— 31/5/55
CDR	L. B. Jenson, RCN	1/6/55	— 5/7/56
CDR	N. S. C. Dickinson, RCN	6/7/56	— 14/7/57
CDR	F. W. H. Bradley, RCN	15/7/57	— 14/12/58
LCDR	A. J. Tanner, RCN	15/12/58	— 11/8/59
LCDR	C. G. Pratt, RCN	12/8/59	— 15/1/60
Daerwood			
LCDR	E. S. McGowan, RCNVR	22/4/44	— 29/10/44
SKPR/LT	J. Craig, RCNR	30/10/44	— 13/11/44
LCDR	E. S. McGowan, RCNVR	14/11/44	— 14/2/45
SKPR/LT	W. E. Eccles, RCNR	2/4/45	— 9/8/45
LT	T. A. Mulhern, RCNVR	10/8/45	— 28/11/45
Dauphin			
LCDR	R. A. S. McNeil, OBE, RCNR	17/5/41	— 17/1/43
A/LCDR	M. H. Wallace, RCNR	18/1/43	— 10/10/44
LT	E. R. O'Kelly, RCNVR	11/10/44	— 20/6/45
Dawson			
A/LCDR	A. H. G. Storrs, RCNR	6/10/41	— 7/6/43
A/LCDR	T. P. Ryan, OBE, RCNR	8/6/43	— 30/3/44
SKPR/LT	J. B. Cooper, RCNR	31/3/44	— 19/6/45
Digby			
A/LCDR	S. W. Howell, RCNR	26/7/42	— 9/7/43
SKPR/LT	J. W. Sharpe, RCNR	10/7/43	— 6/4/44
LT	E. O. Ormsby, RCNVR	7/4/44	— 1/7/45
LCDR	E. G. T. Fisher, RCN	29/4/53	— 7/12/54
LCDR	E. T. Coggins, RCN	8/12/54	— 28/9/55
LCDR	A. F. Rowland, RCN	29/9/55	— 14/11/56
Drumheller			
A/CDR	G. H. Griffiths, RCN	13/9/41	— 15/10/42
LT	L. P. Denny, RCNR	16/10/42	— 20/8/43
LCDR	A. H. G. Storrs, RCNR	21/8/43	— 26/9/43
LT	L. P. Denny, RCNR	27/9/43	— 7/12/43
LT	H. R. Beck, RCNR	28/12/43	— 11/7/45
Drummondville			
LT	J. P. Fraser, RCNR	30/10/41	— 16/1/42
LT	J. P. Fraser, RCNR	5/2/42	— 12/1/43
LT	D. M. Stewart, RCNR	13/1/43	— 1/3/43
LT	J. P. Fraser, RCNR	2/3/43	— 9/5/43
LT	H. C. Hatch, RCNVR	10/5/43	— 7/4/44
SKPR/LT	F. W. M. Drew, RCNR	8/4/44	— 9/4/45
LT	G. E. Cross, RCNVR	10/4/45	— 23/6/45
Dundalk			
SKPR/LT	J. S. G. Ascah, RCNR	6/10/43	— 9/7/45
SKPR/LT	B. W. Allen, RCNR	10/7/45	—
Dundas			
A/LCDR	R. W. Draney, RCNR	1/4/42	— 17/5/43
LT	R. W. Hart, RCNVR	18/5/43	— 11/4/44
LT	R. B. Taylor, RCNVR	12/4/44	— 17/2/45
LT	D. E. Howard, RCNVR	18/2/45	— 17/7/45
Dundurn			
SKPR/LT	A. J. Porter, RCNR	25/11/43	— 2/4/44
LCDR	R. M. Mosher, RCNR	3/4/44	— 10/6/45
SKPR/LT	J. Blackmore, RCNR	11/6/45	—
Dunvegan			
LT	J. A. Tullis, RCNR	9/9/41	— 5/2/43
LT	J. E. Hastings, RCNR	6/2/43	— 30/6/43
LT	J. A. Tullis, RCNR	1/7/43	— 5/7/44
LT	J. A. Rankin, RCNR	6/7/44	— 11/3/45
LT	R. L. B. Hunter, RCNVR	12/3/45	— 3/7/45
Dunver			
LCDR	W. Woods, OBE, RCNR	11/9/43	— 6/5/44
LT	W. Davenport, RCNR	7/5/44	— 9/8/44
A/CDR	G. H. Stephen, RCNR	10/8/44	— 24/8/44
A/LCDR	W. Davenport, RCNR	25/8/44	— 26/3/45
A/CDR	St. C. Balfour, RCNVR	27/3/45	— 26/5/45
LCDR	C. P. Balfry, DSC, RCNR	27/5/45	— 2/9/45
Eastore			
CDR	J. E. McQueen, RCNVR	7/12/44	— 1/1/45
SKPR/LT	J. A. MacLeod, RCNR	2/1/45	— 14/10/45
SKPR/LT	A. R. Hallett, RCNR	15/10/45	— 8/4/46
Eastview			
LCDR	A. M. Kirkpatrick, RCNVR	3/6/44	— 16/9/44
LT	W. D. M. Gardiner, RCNVR	17/9/44	— 26/10/44
LT	R. E. Pare, RCNVR	27/10/44	— 28/11/44
LT	F. W. Bogardus, RCNVR	29/11/44	— 3/12/44
LT	R. E. Pare, RCNVR	4/12/44	— 7/12/44
A/LCDR	R. C. G. Merriam, RCNVR	8/12/44	— 11/8/45
LCDR	J. Morrison, RCNR	24/10/45	—
Edmunston			
A/LCDR	R. D. Barrett, RCNR	21/10/41	— 21/5/44
LT	J. Lecky, RCNVR	22/5/44	— 20/4/45
LT	A. D. Ritchie, RCNVR	21/4/45	— 27/5/45
LT	J. Lecky, RCNVR	28/5/45	— 16/6/45
Elk			
LCDR	N. V. Clark, RCNR	10/9/40	— 24/6/41
LT	R. Hocken, RCNR	14/7/41	— 17/8/41
LT	T. Gilmour, RCNR	18/8/41	— 31/10/41
LT	T. B. Edwards, RCNR	1/11/41	— 11/12/42
LT	J. A. Dunn, RCNVR	12/12/42	— 14/4/43
SKPR/LT	W. K. S. Hines, RCNR	15/4/43	— 18/6/45
Esquimalt			
LT	F. J. L. Davies, RCNR	16/10/42	— 5/2/43
LT	P. D. Taylor, RCNVR	6/2/43	— 12/3/44
LT	J. M. S. Clark, RCNVR	13/3/44	— 14/12/44
LCDR	W. McIsaac, RCNVR	29/12/44	— 1/2/45
LT	R. C. MacMillan, DSC, RCNVR	2/2/45	— 16/4/45
Ettrick			
A/LCDR	W. R. Stacey, RCNR	29/1/44	— 20/2/44
LCDR	E. M. More, RCNR	16/3/44	— 28/4/45
Eyebright			
LT	E. Randell, RCNR	26/11/40	— 24/6/41
LCDR	H. C. R. Davis, RCNR	25/6/41	— 6/2/43
LT	H. L. Quinn, RCNVR	7/2/43	— 1/9/44
LT	R. J. Margesson, RCNVR	2/9/44	— 17/6/45
Fennel			
LCDR	J. N. Smith, RCNR	16/1/41	— 31/10/41
LT	J. M. Gillison, RCNR	1/11/41	— 26/5/42
LCDR	R. B. Warwick, RCNVR	27/5/42	— 5/9/43
A/LCDR	W. P. Moffat, RCNVR	6/9/43	— 15/5/44
LCDR	K. L. Johnson, RCNVR	16/5/44	— 12/6/45
Fergus			
A/LCDR	H. F. Farncomb, RCNVR	18/11/44	— 14/7/45
Fleur de Lis			
Mate	A. Currie, RCNR	16/11/39	— 20/4/40
LT	R. J. Herman, RCNR	21/4/40	—
Mate	A. Currie, RCNR		— 10/3/42
LT	J. W. Dowling, RCNR	11/3/42	— 5/7/42
LCDR	M. G. G. Stanton, RCNVR	6/7/42	— 13/4/43
SKPR/LT	A. Currie, RCNR	14/4/43	— /11/45
Forest Hill			
A/LCDR	E. U. Jones, RCNVR	1/12/43	— 17/9/44
LT	F. R. Brebner, RCNVR	18/9/44	— 9/7/45
Fort Erie			
A/LCDR	A. W. Ford, RCNR	27/10/44	— 20/2/45
A/LCDR	E. F. Piper, RCNVR	21/2/45	— 5/8/45
A/LCDR	R. C. Chenoweth, RCN	6/8/45	— 4/11/45
CDR	W. W. MacColl, RCN	17/4/56	— 17/1/58
LCDR	H. C. LaRose, RCN	3/7/58	— 17/9/59
CDR	J. R. Coulter, RCN	18/9/59	— 10/8/60
CDR	L. B. Jenson, RCN	11/8/60	— 30/9/62
CDR	W. C. Spicer, RCN	4/10/62	— 12/8/63
CDR	E. Petley-Jones, RCN	12/8/63	—

Fort Frances

LT	D. E. Ryerson, RCNVR	28/10/44	— 25/7/45
LT	L. F. Horne, RCNVR	19/10/45	—
LCDR	W. O. O. Barbour, RCNR	6/3/46	— 5/4/46

Fort William

LT	H. Campbell, RCNR	25/8/42	— 29/6/43
LT	S. D. Taylor, RCNR	30/6/43	— 4/10/43
A/LCDR	H. Campbell, DSC, RCNR	5/10/43	— 18/5/45
LT	G. E. Kelly, DSC, RCNR	19/5/45	— 23/10/45

Fortune

LCDR	J. B. Young, RCN	3/11/54	— 23/8/55
LCDR	P. R. Hinton, RCN	24/8/55	— 21/3/57
LCDR	C. G. Smith, RCN	22/3/57	— 13/8/57
LCDR	S. G. Moore, RCN	14/8/57	— 15/2/59
LCDR	D. M. Waters, RCN	16/2/59	— 9/1/62
LCDR	A. B. Torrie, RCN	10/1/62	— 28/2/64

Fraser

CAPT	V. G. Brodeur, CB, CBE, RCN	17/2/37	— 24/3/37
CDR	H. E. Reid, CB, RCN	25/3/37	— 31/8/38
CDR	W. B. Creery, CBE, RCN	1/9/38	— 25/6/40

Fraser (2nd)

CDR	R. Phillips, RCN	28/6/57	— 3/1/59
CDR	D. L. MacKnight, RCN	3/1/59	— 4/1/61
CDR	D. J. Sheppard, RCN	4/1/61	— 6/9/62
CAPT	G. H. Hayes, RCN	6/9/62	— 3/10/62
CDR	R. C. Thurber, RCN	3/10/62	— 5/8/64
CDR	R. Carle, RCN	5/8/64	— 2/7/65
CDR	J. F. Watson, RCN	22/10/66	— 4/7/68
CDR	F. W. Crickard, RCN	4/7/68	— 17/11/69
CDR	R. G. Guy	17/11/69	— 30/6/71
CDR	C. M. Thomas	30/6/71	— 12/4/73
CDR	L. I. MacDonald	11/3/74	— 15/8/76
CDR	P. W. Cairns	15/8/76	— 12/8/77
CDR	H. R. Waddell	12/8/77	— 18/12/78
CDR	J. B. Elson	18/12/78	— 26/1/81
CDR	J. Nethercott	26/1/81	—

Fredericton

A/LCDR	J. H. S. MacDonald, RCNR	8/12/41	— 1/7/42
LCDR	J. E. Harrington, RCNVR	2/7/42	— 20/7/44
LT	J. C. Smyth, RCN	21/7/44	— 14/7/45

French

LT	J. W. Bonner, RCNR	18/9/39	— 26/2/41
LT	D. W. Main, RCNR	27/2/41	— 22/7/41
SKPR/LT	K. W. N. Hall, RCNR	23/7/41	— 22/10/42
SKPR/LT	W. G. Kent, RCNR	23/10/42	— 20/9/46

Frontenac

A/LCDR	E. T. F. Wennberg, RCNVR	26/10/43	— 15/3/45
LT	D. R. Baker, RCNVR	16/3/45	— 22/7/45

Fundy

LCDR	J. W. R. Roy, RCN	2/9/38	— 14/12/38
LCDR	A. R. Pressey, RCN	15/12/38	— 26/12/39
LCDR	O. C. S. Robertson, RCNR	27/8/39	— 22/2/40
A/LCDR	A. G. Stanley, RCNR	23/2/40	— 7/3/41
LT	A. Moorhouse, RCNVR	8/3/41	— 2/8/41
LT	A. M. McLarnon, RCNR	3/8/41	— 17/8/41
LT	A. Moorhouse, RCNVR	18/8/41	— 28/10/41
Mate	J. B. Raine, RCNR	29/10/41	— 9/3/42
SKPR/LT	F. A. Heckman, RCNR	10/3/42	— 27/7/45

Fundy (2nd)

LCDR	A. Slater, RCN	19/3/54	— 31/3/54

Fundy (3rd)

LCDR	R. C. Thurber, RCN	18/12/56	— 10/2/58
LCDR	N. St. C. Norton, RCN	18/2/58	— 18/8/59
LCDR	J. Butterfield, RCN	19/8/59	— 2/1/62
LT	R. J. Luke, RCN	3/1/62	— 7/2/64

Galiano

LT	R. M. Pope, RCNVR	15/12/17	— 30/10/18

Galt

LT	A. D. Landles, RCNR	15/5/41	— 10/3/43
LT	A. M. Kirkpatrick, RCNVR	11/3/43	— 30/3/44
LT	E. P. Taylor, RCNVR	31/3/44	— 24/4/45
LT	J. G. Lorriman, RCNVR	25/4/45	— 19/6/45
LT	E. P. Taylor, RCNVR	20/6/45	— 21/6/45

Gananoque

LT	E. M. More, RCNR	8/11/41	— 15/3/43
LCDR	W. Woods, RCNR	16/3/43	— 28/3/43
SKPR/LT	E. S. N. Pleasance, RCNR	29/3/43	— 2/11/43
SKPR/LT	J. B. Cooper, RCNR	3/11/43	— 27/11/43
SKPR/LT	E. S. N. Pleasance, RCNR	28/11/43	— 24/5/44
LCDR	A. P. Duke, RCNVR	25/5/44	— 23/6/45
LT	G. E. Cross, RCNVR	24/6/45	— 10/8/45

Gaspé

LCDR	H. N. Lay, RCN	12/1/39	— 17/8/39
A/LCDR	H. D. Mackay, RCNR	3/9/39	— 11/4/41
LT	R. T. Ingram, RCNR	12/4/41	— 2/8/41
LT	T. Gilmour, RCNR	3/8/41	— 17/8/41
LT	R. T. Ingram, RCNR	18/8/41	— 26/10/41
CH/SKPR	G. A. Myra, RCNR	27/10/41	— 2/8/42
LT	W. S. Bryant, RCNR	3/8/42	— 24/6/43
SKPR/LT	A. J. Burke, RCNR	25/6/43	— 7/1/45
SKPR/LT	R. A. Doucette, RCNR	8/1/45	— 23/7/45

Gaspé (2nd)

LCDR	H. B. Carnall, RCN	26/11/53	— 17/10/55
CDR	W. S. T. McCully, RCN	18/10/55	— 4/6/57
LCDR	H. C. LaRose, RCN	5/6/57	— 22/8/57

Gatineau

CDR	P. W. Burnett, RN	3/6/43	— 9/11/43
LT	E. M. Chadwick, RCN	10/11/43	— 22/11/43
LCDR	H. V. W. Groos, RCN	23/11/43	— 10/9/44
A/LCDR	R. L. Hennessy, DSC, RCN	11/9/44	— 29/9/44
LCDR	J. A. Bryant, RCNVR	30/9/44	— 9/11/44
LCDR	G. H. Davidson, RCN	10/11/44	— 14/7/45
A/LCDR	P. D. Budge, DSC, RCN	15/7/45	— 26/11/45

Gatineau (2nd)

CAPT	H. L. Quinn, DSC, RCN	17/2/59	— 14/9/59
CAPT	F. B. Caldwell, RCN	15/9/59	— 27/1/61
LCDR	R. A. Shimmin, RCN	28/1/61	— 24/5/61
LCDRT	H. C. MacRedy, RCN	25/5/61	— 24/8/61
CDR	A. H. McDonald, RCN	25/8/61	— 21/8/62
CDR	J. W. Roberts, RCN	22/8/62	— 28/4/64
CDR	W. G. Kinsman, DSO, RCN	29/4/64	— 11/8/65
CDR	J. A. Fulton, RCN	12/8/65	— 8/9/66
CDR	W. A. Hughes, RCN	8/9/66	— 29/9/69
CDR	T. S. Murphy	14/4/71	— 3/7/71
LCDR	J. C. Slade	3/7/71	— 11/7/75
CDR	L. G. Temple	11/7/75	— 11/11/77
CDR	J. B. McKenzie	11/11/77	— 26/7/79
CDR	C. D. E. Cronk	26/7/79	— 11/6/81
CDR	D. M. Robison	11/6/81	—

Georgian

A/LCDR	A. G. Stanley, RCNR	23/9/41	— 21/9/42
LCDR	W. Redford, RCNR	22/9/42	— 7/12/42
LT	P. M. Crawford, RCNVR	8/12/42	— 21/1/43
LT	G. H. Johnson, RCNVR	22/1/43	— 25/1/43
A/LCDR	H. A. Boucher, RCNVR	26/1/43	— 26/6/44
A/LCDR	D. W. Main, RCNR	27/6/44	— 23/3/45
LT	T. C. McLaughlin, RCNR	24/3/45	— 23/10/45

Giffard

A/LCDR	C. Peterson, RCNR	10/11/43	— 9/5/44
LT	G. H. Matheson, RCNR	10/5/44	— 5/7/45

Glace Bay

A/CDR	J. H. S. MacDonald, RCNR	2/9/44	— 23/2/45
A/LCDR	F. W. Bogardus, RCNVR	24/2/45	— 2/7/45
LT	D. B. D. Ross, RCNVR	3/7/45	— 10/8/45
LT	P. W. Lee, RCNVR	11/8/45	— 26/8/45
LT	S. L. Slade, RCN	27/8/45	—

Goderich

LT	R. R. Kenny, RCNR	23/11/41	— 20/8/42
LT	J. H. Hughes, RCNR	21/8/42	— 7/9/42
LT	R. R. Kenny, RCNR	8/9/42	— 6/4/43
LT	J. C. Pratt, RCNVR	7/4/43	— 6/3/44
LT	W. P. Wickett, RCNVR	7/3/44	— 21/3/44
LT	J. E. Taylor, RCNVR	22/3/44	— 15/8/45
LT	R. C. Hayden, RCNVR	16/8/45	— 22/8/45

Granby

Mate	J. R. Biggs, RCNR	2/5/42	— 7/2/43
LCDR	H. C. R. Davis, RCNR	8/2/43	— 16/3/43
A/LT	J. R. Biggs, RCNR	17/3/43	— 10/10/43
LT	G. G. K. Holder, RCNVR	11/10/43	— 9/5/44
LT	D. A. P. Davidson, RCNVR	10/5/44	— 30/7/44
LT	A. M. Brodie, RCNVR	31/7/44	— 24/4/45
LT	E. S. Turnill, RCNVR	25/4/45	— 27/5/45
LT	A. M. Brodie, RCNVR	28/5/45	— 18/6/45
LT	E. S. Turnill, RCNVR	19/6/45	— 7/8/45
LCDR	G. G. K. Holder, RCN	23/5/53	— 2/3/54
LCDR	G. A. Hoyte, RCN	3/3/54	— 13/5/54
LCDR	D. Brownlow, RCN	14/5/54	— 30/9/54
LCDR	W. E. Williams, RCN	1/10/54	— 11/10/56
LCDR	C. S. Smedley, RCN	12/10/56	— 16/8/59
LCDR	W. W. Palmer, RCN	17/8/59	—

Grandmère

LT	J. Cuthbert, RCNR	11/12/41	— 20/4/44
LT	N. W. Winters, RCNVR	21/4/44	— 20/7/45
LT	R. C. Hayden, RCNVR	23/8/45	— 23/10/45

Grilse

LT	J. K. L. Ross, RNCVR	15/7/15	— 15/7/16
LT	W. Wingate, RNCVR	16/7/16	— 10/1/17
CDR	J. T. Shenton, RCN	10/5/17	— 25/5/17
LCDR	W. T. Walker, RCN	26/5/17	— 16/12/17
LT	H. H. D. Wood, RNCVR	17/12/17	— 16/1/18
Mate	T. C. M. Cotton, RNCVR	17/1/18	— 11/2/18
LCDR	W. T. Walker, RCN	12/2/18	— 5/5/18
LT	A. F. Thomas, RNCVR	6/5/18	— 10/12/18

Grilse (2nd)

LCDR	E. G. Gigg, RCN	11/5/61	— 2/12/62
LCDR	G. C. McMorris, RCN	3/12/62	— 27/9/64
LCDR	J. Rodocanachi, RCN	28/9/64	— / /66
LCDR	M. Tate, RCN	/ /66	—

Grou

LCDR	H. G. Dupont, RCNR	4/12/43	— 2/7/45
A/CDR	B. D. L. Johnson, RCNR	9/8/45	— 14/11/45
LCDR	R. D. Barrett, RCNR	15/11/45	—

Guelph

LT	G. H. Hayes, DSC, RCN	9/5/44	— 14/5/45
LT	F. D. Wickett, RCNVR	15/5/45	— 20/5/45
LT	D. H. Smith, RCNVR	15/6/45	— 27/6/45

Guysborough

LT	B. T. R. Russell, RCNR	22/4/42	— 17/3/45

Haida

CDR	H. G. DeWolf, DSO, DSC, RCN	30/8/43	— 18/12/44
LCDR	R. P. Welland, DSC, RCN	19/12/44	— 2/9/45
LCDR	F. B. Caldwell, RCN	3/3/47	— 11/12/47
LCDR	A. F. Pickard, OBE, RCN	12/12/47	— 15/5/49
LCDR	E. T. G. Madgwick, RCN	16/5/49	— 12/1/50
CDR	R. A. Webber, DSC, RCN	13/1/50	— 31/12/51
CDR	D. Lantier, RCN	1/1/52	— 28/10/53
CAPT	J. A. Charles, RCN	29/10/53	— 15/12/54
CDR	V. Browne, RCN	16/12/54	— 10/7/56
CDR	H. R. Beck, RCN	11/7/56	— 6/4/58
CDR	J. Husher, RCN	7/4/58	— 2/9/60
CDR	G. S. Clark, RCN	3/9/60	— 2/8/61
CDR	D. C. Rutherford, RCN	3/8/61	— 19/7/62
CDR	W. H. Atkinson, DSC, RCN	20/7/62	— 22/9/63
LCDR	D. K. Gamblin, RCN	23/9/63	— 11/10/63

Halifax

LCDR	C. Copelin, OBE, RCNR	26/11/41	— 6/2/43
LT	M. F. Oliver, RCNR	7/2/43	— 21/6/44
A/LCDR	R. M. Hanbury, RCNVR	22/6/44	— 3/9/44
LT	L. E. Horne, RCNVR	4/9/44	— 12/7/45

Hallowell

SKPR/LT	E. S. N. Pleasance, RCNR	8/8/44	— 18/10/44
LCDR	R. H. Angus, RCNVR	19/10/44	— 4/8/45
LT	D. Davis, RCNVR	5/8/45	— 7/11/45

Hamilton

LCDR	N. V. Clark, RCNR	6/7/41	— 19/7/43
LCDR	D. G. Jeffrey, RCNR	20/7/43	— 18/1/44
CDR	F. Poole, RCNR	19/1/44	— 22/4/45
SKPR/LT	J. D. Burnham, RCNR	23/4/45	— 8/6/45

Hawkesbury

A/LCDR	W. G. Curry, RCNVR	14/6/44	— 10/7/45

Hepatica

LT	C. Copelin, RCNR	12/11/40	— 31/10/41
LCDR	T. Gilmour, RCNR	1/11/41	— 11/4/43
LT	H. E. Lade, RCNR	12/4/43	— 5/9/43
LT	J. A. Ferguson, RCNR	6/9/43	— 4/11/44
LT	E. M. Lutes, RCNVR	5/11/44	— 27/6/45

Hespeler

LCDR	N. S. C. Dickinson, RCNVR	28/2/44	— 13/11/44
LT	G. P. Manning, RCNVR	14/11/44	— 24/8/45

Humberstone

LCDR	H. A. Boucher, RCNVR	6/9/44	— 15/10/44
LT	C. L. Campbell, RCNVR	16/10/44	— 26/11/44
LCDR	H. A. Boucher, RCNVR	27/11/44	— 15/6/45
A/LCDR	J. W. Golby, RCNVR	19/8/45	— 14/10/45

Huntsville

A/LCDR	C. B. Hermann, RCNVR	6/6/44	— 20/7/45
LT	C. F. Usher, RCNVR	21/7/45	— 9/9/45

Huron

LCDR	H. S. Rayner, DSC, RCN	19/7/43	— 22/9/44
LCDR	H. V. W. Groos, RCN	23/9/44	— 24/10/45
LT	E. P. Earnshaw, RCN	24/10/45	— 21/2/46
LT	J. C. L. Annesley, RCN	22/2/46	— 20/3/46
LCDR	E. T. G. Madgwick, RCN	28/2/50	— 23/3/50
LCDR	T. C. Pullen, RCN	24/3/50	— 6/4/50
LCDR	E. T. G. Madgwick, RCN	7/4/50	— 23/9/51
CDR	J. C. Littler, RCN	24/9/51	— 12/10/51
CDR	R. C. Chenoweth, MBE, RCN	18/11/52	— 20/9/53
CDR	T. C. Pullen, RCN	21/9/53	— 24/6/54
CDR	L. P. McCormack, RCN	25/6/54	— 9/8/54
LCDR	E. D. Robbins, RCN	10/8/54	— 16/8/54
CDR	J. C. Pratt, RCN	17/8/54	— 7/8/55
CDR	R. A. Webber, DSC, RCN	8/8/55	— 27/1/57
CDR	N. Cogdon, RCN	28/1/57	— 1/8/57
CDR	W. H. Howe, RCN	28/3/58	— 6/12/59
CDR	H. H. Smith, RCN	7/12/59	— 3/11/61
CDR	W. C. Spicer, RCN	3/11/61	— 4/10/62
CDR	D. S. Bethune, RCN	4/10/62	— 9/4/63

Huron (2nd)

CDR	R. I. Hitesman	14/12/72	— 25/7/75
CDR	L. J. Cavan	25/7/75	— 15/7/77
CDR	M. H. D. Taylor	15/7/77	— 22/7/78
CDR	J. D. Spalding	22/7/78	— 24/7/81
CDR	R. J. Deluca	24/7/81	—

Husky

LT	H. Freeland, RCNR	23/7/40	— 5/9/41
LT	W. E. Harrison, RCNR	6/9/41	— 18/10/41
LT	A. H. Rankin, RCNVR	19/10/41	— 30/4/42
LT	J. P. Kieran, RCNR	1/5/42	— 29/9/44
LT	W. E. Jolliffe, RCNVR	30/9/44	— 12/11/44
LT	E. B. Pearce, RCNVR	13/11/44	— 30/4/45
LT	R. C. Hayden, RCNVR	1/5/45	— 12/6/45
SKPR/LT	C. C. Clattenburg, RCNR	13/6/45	— 3/8/45

Inch Arran

A/LCDR	J. W. E. Hastings, RCNR	18/11/44	— 15/3/45
LCDR	F. A. Beck, RCNVR	16/3/45	— 23/3/45
A/LCDR	J. W. E. Hastings, RCNR	24/3/45	— 20/6/45
LT	T. S. Dobson, RCNVR	21/6/45	— 7/8/45
LCDR	L. P. Denny, RCNR	8/8/45	— 28/11/45
LCDR	P. C. H. Cooke, RCN	25/11/59	— 11/9/61
LCDR	B. A. Mitchell, RCN	9/9/61	— 24/7/63
LCDR	C. R. Manifold, RCN	24/7/63	— 23/6/65
LCDR	E. A. Makin, RCN	23/6/65	—

Ingonish

A/LCDR	T. P. Ryan, OBE, RCNR	8/5/42	— 2/5/43
LT	F. E. Burrows, RCNVR	3/5/43	— 12/3/44
SKPR/LT	G. B. McCandless, RCNR	13/3/44	— 4/4/44
LT	R. C. G. Merriam, RCNVR	5/4/44	— 15/9/44

LT	H. V. Shaw, RCNVR	16/9/44	— 19/12/44
LT	P. W. Lee, RCNVR	20/12/44	— 25/2/45
LT	H. V. Shaw, RCNVR	26/2/45	— 26/3/45
LT	C. D. Chivers, RCNVR	27/3/45	— 2/7/45

Iroquois

CDR	W. B. L. Holms, RCN	30/11/42	— 29/7/43
CDR	J. C. Hibbard, DSC, RCN	30/7/43	— 7/2/45
CDR	K. F. Adams, RCN	8/2/45	— 2/7/45
CDR	E. W. Finch-Noyes, RCN	3/7/45	— 10/11/45
LT	C. G. Smith, RCN	11/11/45	— 30/1/46
LT	A. H. McDonald, RCN	31/1/46	— 22/2/46
LT	D. Adamson, RCNR	27/5/46	— 23/12/46
LCDR	J. Plomer, DSC, RCN	1/3/47	— 1/6/47
LCDR	J. S. Davis, RCN	2/6/47	— 13/11/47
LCDR	B. P. Young, MBE, RCN	14/11/47	— 2/5/49
LCDR	T. C. Pullen, RCN	24/6/49	— 30/9/49
CDR	W. M. Landymore, RCN	21/10/51	— 31/10/53
LCDR	S. G. Moore, RCN	1/11/53	— 22/3/54
CDR	M. F. Oliver, RCN	23/3/54	— 7/8/55
CDR	D. L. Hanington, DSC, RCN	8/8/55	— 23/5/57
LCDR	M. W. Mayo, RCN	24/5/57	— 19/11/57
CDR	W. D. F. Johnston, RCN	17/10/58	— 7/9/60
CDR	H. W. Moxley, RCN	8/9/60	— 19/3/62
CAPT	G. C. Edwards, RCN	20/3/62	— 30/9/62
LCDR	W. D. Munro, RCN	1/10/62	— 24/10/62

Iroquois (2nd)

CDR	D. N. MacGillivray	29/7/72	— 24/3/75
CDR	G. G. Freill	24/3/75	— 4/5/77
CDR	R. E. George	4/5/77	— 30/6/79
CDR	E. K. Kelly	1/7/79	— 16/4/81
CDR	L. G. Mason	16/3/81	—

James Bay

LCDR	G. R. Smith, RCN	3/5/54	— 4/10/55
LCDR	J. J. Coates, RCN	5/10/55	— 22/7/58
LT	I. C. S. Inglis, DSC, RCN	23/7/58	— 6/9/60
LT	R. A. Orton, RCN	7/9/60	— 3/7/62
LCDR	J. E. Hobbs, RCN	4/7/62	— 28/2/64

Joliette

A/LCDR	G. N. Downey, RCNR	14/6/44	— 2/2/45
LCDR	W. E. Harrison, RCNR	3/2/45	— 19/6/45
A/LCDR	K. W. N. Hall, RCNR	20/6/45	— 19/11/45

Jonquière

LCDR	J. R. Kidston, RCNVR	10/5/44	— 12/3/45
A/LCDR	A. Marcil, RCNVR	13/3/45	— 16/6/45
LT	J. H. Lincoln, RCNVR	17/6/45	— 4/8/45
LCDR	D. M. MacDonald, RCNVR	5/8/45	— 18/8/45
LCDR	H. R. Tilley, RCN	20/9/54	— 24/7/56
LCDR	C. D. Gibson, RCN	25/7/56	— 15/6/58
LCDR	E. V. P. Sunderland, RCN	16/6/58	— 8/9/59
LCDR	H. V. Clark, RCN	9/9/59	— 28/11/61
LCDR	R. L. Hughes, RCN	29/11/61	— 24/8/63
LCDR	A. P. Campbell, RCN	7/9/63	— 14/9/65
LCDR	D. R. Donaldson, RCN	15/9/65	— 23/9/66

Kalamalka

LT	C. J. Henrickson, RCNVR	2/10/44	— 20/7/45
LT	E. L. MacDonald, RCNVR	21/7/45	— 20/9/45

Kamloops

LT	J. M. Gillison, RCNR	17/3/41	— 31/10/41
LT	P. J. B. Watts, RCNR	1/11/41	— 4/2/42
LT	I. W. McTavish, RCNR	5/2/42	— 27/3/42
A/LCDR	J. H. Marshall, RCNVR	28/3/42	— 22/8/42
LT	N. S. C. Dickinson, RCNVR	23/8/42	— 10/1/43
LCDR	J. H. S. MacDonald, RCNR	17/2/43	— 1/3/43
LT	D. M. Stewart, RCNR	2/3/43	— 5/11/43
LT	S. D. Taylor, RCNR	6/11/43	— 20/12/43
A/LCDR	D. M. Stewart, RCNR	21/12/43	— 27/6/45

Kamsack

LT	E. Randell, RCNR	4/10/41	— 17/5/43
LCDR	W. C. Halliday, RCNR	18/5/43	— 8/2/44
LT	J. F. Carmichael, RCNR	9/2/44	— 10/5/45
LCDR	R. F. Wilson, RCNVR	11/5/45	— 22/7/45

Kapuskasing

LCDR	A. H. Rankin, OBE, RCN	17/8/44	— 2/9/45
LT	G. M. Kennelly, RCNVR	22/10/45	—

Kelowna

LT	W. Davenport, RCNR	5/2/42	— 4/8/43
SKPR/LT	E. W. Suffield, RCNR	5/8/43	— 21/11/43
LCDR	R. B. Campbell, RCNR	22/11/43	— 11/1/44
SKPR/LT	E. W. Suffield, RCNR	12/1/44	— 22/10/45

Kenogami

LCDR	R. Jackson, RCNVR	29/6/41	— 21/11/42
LT	J. L. Percy, RCNVR	22/11/42	— 23/2/44
LT	R. G. McKenzie, RCNVR	24/2/44	— 9/7/45

Kenora

A/LCDR	F. R. F. Naftel, RCNVR	6/8/42	— 14/9/43
LT	D. W. Lowe, RCNVR	15/9/43	— 7/2/45
A/LCDR	R. M. Meredith, RCNR	8/2/45	— 6/10/45

Kentville

LT	J. G. Hughes, RCNR	10/10/42	— 21/3/44
LT	W. J. Gilmore, RCNVR	22/3/44	— 28/4/44
LT	J. G. Hughes, RCNR	29/4/44	— 21/7/44
LT	F. G. Rainsford, RCNVR	22/7/44	— 14/12/44
LT	J. R. Brown, RCNVR	15/12/44	— 3/2/45
LT	F. G. Rainsford, RCNVR	4/2/45	— 8/7/45
LT	P. W. Lee, RCNVR	9/7/45	— 10/8/45

LT	W. G. Hunt, RCN	10/5/54	— 30/9/54

Kincardine

A/LCDR	R. P. Brown, RCNVR	19/6/44	— 27/8/45
A/LCDR	A. E. Gough, RCNR	28/8/45	— 13/9/45
SKPR/LT	A. H. Campbell, RCNR	4/10/45	—

Kirkland Lake

LT	J. A. Tullis, RCNR	21/8/44	— 13/11/44
A/CDR	N. V. Clark, OBE, RCNR	14/11/44	— 2/10/45
LCDR	F. H. Pinfold, RCNVR	3/10/45	—

Kitchener

LCDR	W. Evans, RCNVR	28/6/42	— 16/1/44
LT	J. E. Moles, RCNVR	17/1/44	— 11/7/45

Kokanee

LCDR	J. H. Marshall, RCNVR	6/6/44	— 14/12/44
LCDR	F. W. Lucas, RCNVR	15/12/44	— 31/1/45
A/LCDR	W. J. Kingsmill, RCNVR	1/2/45	— 14/3/45
LCDR	F. W. Lucas, RCNVR	15/3/45	— 19/8/45
LT	L. H. Reid, RCNVR	3/11/45	—

Kootenay

A/LCDR	K. L. Dyer, DSC, RCN	12/4/43	— 28/3/44
A/LCDR	W. H. Willson, DSC, RCN	29/3/44	— 26/10/45

Kootenay (2nd)

CDR	R. J. Pickford, RCN	7/3/59	— 11/7/60
CDR	H. Shorten, RCN	11/7/60	— 19/9/62
CDR	D. H. Ryan, RCN	19/9/62	— 15/1/65
CDR	C. G. Pratt, RCN	15/1/65	— 1/6/66
CDR	W. P. Rikely, RCN	1/6/66	— 1/7/67
CDR	G. C. McMorris, RCN	1/7/67	— 15/11/68
CDR	M. Tremblay, RCN	15/11/68	— 21/3/69
CDR	N. St. C. Norton	21/3/69	— 14/1/70
CDR	J. L. Creech	12/1/72	— 17/2/73
CDR	R. H. Kirby	17/2/73	— 14/6/74
CDR	J. Spalding	14/6/74	— 16/7/76
CDR	B. P. Moore	16/7/76	— 27/6/78
CDR	B. Johnston	27/6/78	— 11/8/80
CDR	B. H. Beckett	11/8/80	—

La Hulloise

LCDR	J. Brock, RCNVR	10/4/44	— 16/8/45
LT	J. C. Walker, RCNVR	17/8/45	— 2/10/45
LT	J. A. Wyatt, RCNVR	3/10/45	— 6/12/45
LCDR	M. J. A. T. Jette, RCN	24/6/49	— 31/12/49
CDR	R. A. Webber, DSC, RCN	1/1/50	— 13/1/50
CDR	T. C. Pullen, RCN	1/6/50	— 22/9/51
LT	A. H. McDonald, RCN	23/9/51	— 27/11/52
LCDR	H. A. Porter, RCN	28/11/52	— 6/11/53
LT	E. J. Hyman, RCN	7/11/53	— 23/11/53
LCDR	R. M. S. Greene, RCN	9/10/57	— 18/11/58
LCDR	F. P. R. Saunders, RCN	19/11/58	— 9/9/60
LCDR	W. J. H. Stuart, RCN	9/9/60	— 8/2/61
LCDR	A. H. Gracy, RCN	8/2/61	— 11/9/62
LCDR	A. G. Lowe, RCN	11/9/62	— 11/8/64
LCDR	E. A. Makin, RCN	11/8/64	— 16/7/65

La Malbaie

LT	I. W. McTavish, RCNR	28/4/42	— 11/2/43
A/LCDR	J. S. Davis, RCNVR	12/2/43	— 7/6/44
LT	E. F. Piper, RCNVR	8/6/44	— 21/2/45
LT	T. H. Dunn, RCNVR	22/2/45	— 28/6/45

Labrador

CAPT	O. C. S. Robertson, GM, RCN	8/7/54	— 29/10/55
CDR	J. M. Leeming, RCN	29/10/55	— 30/11/55
CAPT	O. C .S. Robertson, GM, RCN	1/12/55	— 12/2/56
CAPT	T. C. Pullen, RCN	13/2/56	— 3/11/57
CDR	C. A. Law, DSC, RCN	4/11/57	— 22/11/57

Lachine

LT	B. P. Young, RCNR	20/6/42	— 8/5/43
LT	L. F. Moore, RCNR	9/5/43	— 3/4/44
LT	F. R. Spindler, RCNVR	4/4/44	— 18/2/45
LT	F. M. Travers, RCNVR	22/3/45	— 23/4/45
LT	G. F. Pipe, RCNVR	24/4/45	— 31/7/45

Lachute

LT	R. G. Hatrick, RCNVR	26/10/44	— 10/7/45

Lanark

LCDR	J. F. Stairs, RCNVR	6/7/44	— 5/4/45
A/CDR	B. D. L. Johnson, OBE, RCNR	6/4/45	— 9/5/45
LCDR	J. F. Stairs, RCNVR	10/5/45	— 20/10/45
CDR	W. M. Kidd, RCN	26/4/56	— 9/11/56
LCDR	P. H. Cayley, RCN	10/11/56	— 11/6/58
LCDR	W. L. D. Farrell, RCN	12/6/58	— 11/7/58
LCDR	R. W. Leslie, RCN	12/7/58	— 15/9/60
LCDR	C. H. P. Shaw, RCN	16/9/60	— 28/8/62
LCDR	J. M. Reid, RCN	29/8/62	— 22/4/64
LCDR	F. J. P. French, RCN	23/4/64	— 26/11/64
LT	R. L. Clarke, RCN	27/11/64	— 15/12/64
LT	D. M. Swim, RCN	16/12/64	— 15/1/65
LT	J. T. Stuart, RCN	16/1/65	— 19/3/65

Lasalle

LCDR	F. A. Beck, RCNVR	29/6/44	— 2/7/45
LCDR	R. D. Barrett, RCNR	3/7/45	— 14/11/45

Laurier

LT	R. A. S. MacNeil, RCNR	12/4/40	— 10/4/41
SKPR/LT	D. E. Freeman, RCNR	11/4/41	— 30/6/45
SKPR/LT	J. W. G. Ascah, RCNR	1/7/45	— 4/11/45
SKPR/LT	A. Smith, RCNR	3/12/45	— 6/1/46
SKPR/LT	N. H. Pentz, RCNR	1/2/46	— 25/3/46

Lauzon

LCDR	W. Woods, OBE, RCNR	30/8/44	— 29/3/45
LCDR	D. G. Jeffrey, DSO, RCNR	30/3/45	— 10/4/45
A/LCDR	J. B. Graham, RCNVR	11/4/45	— 29/6/45
SKPR/LT	F. W. M. Drew, RCNR	30/6/45	— 3/11/45
LT	N. M. Stewart, RCNVR	4/11/45	— 7/11/45
LCDR	H. A. Porter, RCN	12/12/53	— 4/1/54
CDR	M. J. A. T. Jette, RCN	5/1/54	— 17/7/55
LCDR	J. C. Carter, RCN	18/7/55	— 12/4/57
LCDR	D. O. Campfield, RCN	13/4/57	— 3/10/58
LCDR	W. G. Kinsman,DSC, RCN	5/6/59	—

Lavallee

SKPR/LT	A. Miller, RCNR	21/6/44	— 20/3/45
SKPR/LT	J. R. Smith, RCNR	21/3/45	— 3/5/45
A/LCDR	C. G. Trotter, RCNVR	4/5/45	— 18/6/45
SKPR/LT	J. Craig, RCNR	19/6/45	— 15/7/45
A/LCDR	C. G. Trotter, RCNVR	16/7/45	— 20/8/45
SKPR/LT	J. E. Moore, RCNR	14/11/45	— 18/12/45

Laymore

SKPR/LT	F. H. Anderson, RCNR	12/6/45	—
SKPR/LT	G. Collier, RCNR	26/11/45	—

LCI(L)

115	LT	V. D. Ramsay, RCNVR
117	LT	R. L. Gordon, RCNVR
118	LT	C. R. Bond, RCNVR
121	LT	D. H. Botly, RCNVR
125	LT	C. R. Parker, DSC, RCNVR
135	LT	J. D. Kell, RCNVR
166	LT	G. M. Oliver, RCNVR
177	LT	W. C. Gardner, RCNVR
249	LT	J. E. O'Rourke, RCNVR
250	LT	H. M. Harrison, RCNVR
252	LT	R. E. St. J. Wakefield, RCNVR
255	LT	H. E. Trenholme, RCNVR
262	LT	P. R. Hinton, RCNVR
263	LT	J. B. B. Shaw, RCNVR
266	LT	J. G. Wenman, RCNVR
270	LT	A. C. Clark, RCNVR
271	LT	W. R. Sinclair, RCNVR
276	LT	A. A. Wedd, DSC, RCNVR
277	LT	W. H. M. Ballantyne, RCNVR
285	LT	H. S. Square, RCNVR
288	LT	W. E. Charron, RCNVR
295	LT	P. G. R. Campbell, RCNVR
298	LT	J. S. Monteith, RCNVR
299	LT	W. B. McGregor, RCNVR
301	LT	D. M. Smith, RCNVR
302	LT	J. M. Ruttan, DSC, RCNVR
305	LT	C. B. MacKay, RCNVR
306	LT	A. K. Stephens, RCNVR
310	LT	L. Williams, RCNVR
311	LT	D. J. Lewis, RCNVR

Leaside

LT	G. G. K. Holder, RCNVR	21/8/44	— 15/6/45
LT	H. Brynjolfson, RCNVR	16/6/45	— 30/8/45
LCDR	C. P. Balfry, RCNR	1/9/45	— 16/11/45

Lethbridge

LT	W. Mahan, RCNR	25/6/41	— 13/8/41
LT	R. Hocken, RCNR	14/8/41	— 2/9/41
LT	R. J. Roberts, RCNR	3/9/41	— 7/9/41
A/LCDR	H. Freeland, RCNR	8/9/41	— 20/10/42
LCDR	R. S. Kelly, RCNR	21/10/42	— 21/4/43
LCDR	W. Woods, RCNR	22/4/43	— 15/6/43
A/LCDR	St. C. Balfour, RCNVR	16/6/43	— 26/12/43
LT	F. H. Pinfold, RCNVR	15/3/44	— 19/8/44
LT	J. Roberts, RCNVR	20/8/44	— 30/9/44
LT	F. H. Pinfold, RCNVR	1/10/44	— 14/4/45
LT	J. Holland, RCNVR	8/5/45	— 23/7/45

Lévis

LT	C. W. Gilding, RCNR	16/5/41	— 19/9/41

Lévis (2nd)

LCDR	P. C. Evans, RCNR	21/7/44	— 6/9/44
LT	P. T. Molson, RCNVR	7/9/44	— 17/9/44
LCDR	P. C. Evans, RCNR	18/9/44	— 19/9/45
LCDR	P. C. Evans, RCNR	23/10/45	—

Lindsay

A/LCDR	G. A. V. Thomson, RCNVR	15/11/43	— 18/7/45

Llewellyn

CH/SKPR	A. Currie, RCNR	24/8/42	— 14/9/42
LT	J. A. MacKinnon, RCNR	15/9/42	— 24/9/43
SKPR/LT	W. H. Crocker, RCNR	25/9/43	— 11/10/43
LT	J. A. MacKinnon, RCNR	12/10/43	— 26/2/45
LT	F. W. Anderson, RCNVR	27/2/45	— 29/3/45
LT	J. A. MacKinnon, RCNR	30/3/45	— 11/4/45
LT	F. W. Anderson, RCNVR	12/4/45	— 19/8/45
LT	F. W. Anderson, RCNVR	8/9/45	—
CDR	E. W. Briggs, RCNR	25/7/49	— 21/8/49
LT	J. C. Marston, RCNR	22/8/49	— 31/10/51

Lloyd George

CH/SKPR	W. H. Crocker, RCNR	24/8/42	— 23/8/43
LT	G. F. Crosby, RCNVR	24/8/43	— 11/10/43
CH/SKPR	W. H. Crocker, RCNR	12/10/43	— 7/11/43
CH/SKPR	W. H. Crocker, RCNR	26/11/43	— 23/2/45
LT	J. F. Stevens, RCNVR	24/2/45	— 8/5/45
SKPR/LT	C. K. Darrach, MBE, RCNR	9/5/45	— 6/1/46
Bos'n	J. R. Addison, BEM, RCN	7/1/46	— 7/5/47

LT	L. J. MacGregor, RCN(R)	8/5/47	— 21/6/48
LT	K. A. Stone, RCN	22/6/48	— 16/7/48
Loch Achanalt			
A/LCDR	R. W. Hart, RCNVR	31/7/44	— 26/5/45
LT	D. M. Saunders, RCNVR	27/5/45	— 20/6/45
Loch Alvie			
LCDR	E. G. Old, RCNR	10/8/44	— 11/6/45
Loch Morlich			
LCDR	L. L. Foxall, RCNR	17/7/44	— 25/5/45
A/CDR	T. Gilmour, RCNR	26/5/45	— 20/6/45
Lockeport			
LT	D. Trail, RCNR	27/5/42	— 11/8/42
LCDR	A. T. Morrell, RCNR	12/8/42	— 18/8/42
LT	D. Trail, RCNR	19/8/42	— 21/8/43
LT	R. M. Wallace, RCNVR	22/8/43	— 23/6/44
LT	C. A. Nicol, RCNR	24/6/44	— 2/7/45
Long Branch			
A/LCDR	W. J. Kingsmill, RCNVR	5/1/44	— 21/1/44
CDR	E. G. Skinner, DSC, RCNVR	22/1/44	— 2/2/44
A/LCDR	A. B. Taylor, RCNR	3/2/44	— 14/3/44
A/LCDR	W. J. Kingsmill, RCNVR	15/3/44	— 16/4/44
LCDR	R. J. G. Johnson, RCNVR	17/4/44	— 7/10/44
A/LCDR	J. B. O'Brien, RCNVR	8/10/44	— 21/2/45
LT	K. B. Culley, RCNVR	22/2/45	— 14/6/45
Longueuil			
LCDR	M. J. Woods, RCNVR	18/5/44	— 18/7/45
Loos			
CH/SKPR	N. H. Pentz, RCNR	3/12/40	—
SKPR	E. T. Coggins, RCNR	15/5/41	—
SKPR	J. A. D. Anthony, RCNR	1/5/42	—
SKPR	J. Cossar, RCNR	22/6/42	—
Louisburg			
LCDR	W. F. Campbell, RCNVR	2/10/41	— 6/2/43
Louisburg (2nd)			
LT	J. B. Elmsley, RCNVR	13/12/43	— 10/2/45
LT	M. W. Knowles, RCNVR	11/2/45	— 25/6/45
Lunenburg			
LT	W. E. Harrison, RCNR	4/12/41	— 13/10/43
LT	D. L. Miller, DSC, RCNVR	14/10/43	— 19/7/44
LT	D. H. Smith, RCNVR	20/7/44	— 22/12/44
LT	W. S. Thomson, RCNVR	23/12/44	— 23/7/45
Lynx			
CDR	J. R. Prudence, RCNR	25/5/40	—
LT	J. L. A. Levesque, RCNR	26/8/40	— 24/5/42
LCDR	A. D. MacLean, RCNVR	25/5/42	— /9/42
Macdonald			
LT	A. R. Ascah, RCNR	11/10/39	— 1/3/42
CH/SKPR	G. Billard, RCNR	2/3/42	— 4/11/42
CH/SKPR	E. W. Suffield, RCNR	5/11/42	— 17/12/43
SKPR/LT	K. Bennett, RCNR	18/12/43	— 26/5/44
CH/SKPR	R. W. Sparkes, RCNR	27/5/44	— 28/1/45
Mackenzie			
CDR	A. B. German, RCN	6/10/62	— 29/5/64
CDR	H. J. Wade, RCN	29/5/64	— 17/1/66
LCDR	R. D. Okros, RCN	17/1/66	— 7/3/66
CDR	G. M. De Rosenroll, RCN	7/3/66	— 11/8/67
LCDR	W. J. Draper, RCN	11/8/67	— 22/11/67
CDR	O. J. Cavenagh, RCN	22/11/67	— 24/7/69
CDR	R. L. McLean	24/7/69	— 20/1/71
CDR	G. G. Armstrong	20/1/71	— 6/8/72
LCDR	R. J. Deluca	6/8/72	— 11/9/72
CDR	R. H. Kirby	11/9/72	— 23/1/73
CDR	R. D. C. Sweeny	23/1/73	— 17/9/74
CDR	R. L. Donaldson	17/9/74	— 21/5/76
CDR	J. Chouinard	21/5/76	— 14/1/77
CDR	J. W. McIntosh	14/1/77	— 31/12/78
CDR	H. R. Waddell	31/12/78	— 27/8/81
CDR	T. C. Milne	27/8/81	—
Magnificent			
COM	H. G. DeWolf, CBE, DSO, DSC, RCN	7/4/48	— 29/8/48
COM	G. R. Miles, OBE, RCN	30/8/48	— 28/6/49
CDR	A. G. Boulton, DSC, RCN	29/6/49	— 6/9/49
COM	K. F. Adams, RCN	7/9/49	— 28/10/51
CAPT	K. L. Dyer, DSC, RCN	29/10/51	— 10/3/53
COM	H. S. Rayner, DSC & Bar, RCN	11/3/53	— 29/1/55
CAPT	A. H. G. Storrs, DSC & Bar, RCN	30/1/55	— 2/8/56
CAPT	A. B. F. Fraser-Harris, DSC & Bar, RCN	3/8/56	— 14/6/57
Magog			
LT	L. D. Quick, RCNR	7/5/44	— 20/12/44
Mahone			
LT	D. M. Stewart, RCNR	29/9/41	— 3/12/42
LT	W. J. Gilmore, RCNVR	4/12/42	— 9/1/44
LT	W. Turner, RCNR	10/1/44	— 28/3/44
LT	L. R. Hoar, RCNVR	5/6/44	— 25/3/45
LT	N. R. Chappell, RCNVR	26/3/45	— 20/8/45
Malaspina			
LT	H. Newcombe, RNCVR	1/12/17	— 31/3/20
LCDR	W. Redford, RCNR	6/9/39	—
LT	G. S. Hall, RCNR	14/11/40	—
CH/SKPR	W. R. Chaster, RCNR	17/4/41	—
CH/SKPR	J. M. Richardson, RCNR	21/11/41	—
CH/SKPR	A. W. Ogden, RCNR	28/1/42	—
LCDR	J. S. Cunningham, RCNVR	8/3/43	—
Malpeque			
A/LCDR	W. R. Stacey, RCNR	4/8/41	— 5/8/42
LT	J. G. McQuarrie, RCNR	6/8/42	— 13/9/42
A/LCDR	W. R. Stacey, RCNR	14/9/42	— 12/8/43
LT	J. A. Dunn, RCNVR	13/8/43	— 13/9/43
A/LCDR	W. R. Stacey, RCNR	14/9/43	— 24/10/43
LT	D. Davis, RCNVR	25/10/43	— 25/4/45
LT	O. R. Archibald, RCNVR	26/4/45	— 9/10/45
Margaree			
CDR	J. W. R. Roy, RCN	6/9/40	— 22/10/40
Margaree (2nd)			
CDR	J. E. Korning, RCN	5/10/57	— 10/11/59
CDR	E. V. P. Sunderland, RCN	10/11/59	— 17/8/60
CDR	J. H. Maclean, RCN	17/8/60	— 22/5/62
CDR	J. L. Panabaker, RCN	22/5/62	— 26/9/64
CDR	R. C. MacLean, RCN	15/10/65	— 3/7/67
CDR	P. M. Birch-Jones, RCN	4/7/67	— 23/8/68
CDR	R. I. Hitesman, RCN	23/8/68	— 25/7/70
CDR	J. K. Kennedy	25/7/70	— 24/1/72
LCDR	D. Nugent	24/1/72	— 5/4/72
CDR	R. G. Campbell	5/4/72	— 4/1/74
CDR	R. E. George	4/1/74	— 18/12/75
CDR	R. J. Lancashire	18/12/75	— 10/8/77
CDR	P. W. Cairns	10/8/77	— 13/7/78
CDR	R. A. Rutherford	13/7/78	— 12/8/80
CDR	P. J. Stow	12/8/80	—
Mastadon			
CH/SKPR	H. R. H Stratford, RCNR	9/12/42	— 5/1/44
LT	H. H. Rankin, RCNR	6/1/44	— 12/3/46
Matane			
LCDR	A. H. Easton, DSC, RCNR	22/10/43	— 3/4/44
A/CDR	A. F. C. Layard, DSO, RN	4/4/44	— 26/7/44
A/LCDR	F. W. T. Lucas, RCNVR	27/7/44	— 19/9/44
LT	J. M. Ruttan, RCNVR	20/9/44	— 3/2/45
LCDR	W. R. Stacey, RCNVR	4/2/45	— 28/3/45
A/LCDR	F. J. Jones, RCNVR	29/3/45	— 19/7/45
LCDR	P. D. Taylor, RCNVR	20/7/45	— 27/11/45
Matapedia			
LT	R. J. Herman, RCNR	9/5/41	— 26/4/43
LT	J. D. Frewer, RCNVR	27/4/43	— 12/5/44
LT	C. F. Usher, RCNVR	13/5/44	— 16/6/45
Mayflower			
A/LCDR	G. H. Stephen, RCNR	28/11/40	— 12/5/42
A/LCDR	V. Browne, RCNVR	13/5/42	— 2/3/44
LT	D. S. Martin, RCNR	3/3/44	— 31/5/45
Medicine Hat			
LT	J. Bevan, RCNR	4/12/41	— 1/5/43
LT	J. E. Heward, RCNVR	2/5/43	— 20/12/43
LT	A. A. R. Dykes, RCNR	21/12/43	— 10/1/44
LT	J. E. Heward, RCNVR	11/1/44	— 28/8/44
LT	R. J. Keelan, RCNVR	29/8/44	— 7/5/45
LT	K. G. Clark, RCNVR	8/5/45	— 11/6/45
CDR	A. M. McLarnon, RCNR	12/6/45	— 18/7/45
LT	W. R. Aylwin, RCNVR	19/7/45	—
Melville			
LT	R. T. Ingram, RCNR	4/12/41	— 19/6/42
A/LCDR	E. R. Shaw, RCNR	20/6/42	— 13/10/43
SKPR/LT	J. B. Cooper, RCNR	8/11/43	— /12/43
LT	J. E. Taylor, RCNVR		— 17/1/44
LT	J. S. Foster, RCNR	18/1/44	— 25/1/44
LT	W. N. Winters, RCNVR	26/1/44	— 20/4/44
LT	J. S. Foster, RCNR	20/5/44	— /5/45
LT	D. B. Harding, RCNR	/5/45	—
Meon			
A/CDR	St. C. Balfour, RCNVR	7/2/44	— 26/3/45
LT	N. W. Adams, RCNVR	27/3/45	— 23/4/45
Merrittonia			
LT	F. K. Ellis, RCNVR	10/11/44	— 5/4/45
LCDR	J. F. Stairs, RCNVR	6/4/45	— 25/4/45
LCDR	R. M. Powell, RCNVR	26/4/45	— 6/5/45
LT	R. J. Keelan, RCNVR	7/5/45	— 11/7/45
Micmac			
LCDR	R. L. Hennessy, DSC, RCN	12/9/45	— 27/3/47
LCDR	J. C. Littler, RCN	28/3/47	— 5/9/47
LCDR	F. C. Frewer, RCN	16/11/49	— 30/11/51
CDR	G. M. Wadds, RCN	14/8/53	— 26/8/54
CDR	J. C. Smyth, RCN	27/8/54	— 1/9/55
CDR	E. T. G. Madgwick, DSC, RCN	2/9/55	— 8/7/56
CDR	L. B. Jenson, RCN	9/7/56	— 4/8/57
CDR	N. Cogdon, RCN	5/8/57	— 13/6/58
CDR	A. B. German, RCN	10/3/59	— 15/12/59
CDR	G. R. Smith, RCN	16/12/59	— 9/2/61
CDR	W. J. Stuart, RCN	10/2/61	— 14/8/62
LCDR	J. M. Cutts, RCN	15/8/62	— 31/3/64
Middlesex			
LT	W. J. Piercy, RCNR	8/6/44	— 5/1/46
LT	J. Butterfield, RCNR	6/1/46	— 15/1/46
LCDR	B. P. Young, MBE, RCN	16/1/46	—
Midland			
A/LCDR	A. B. Taylor, RCNR	17/11/41	— 31/10/43
LT	W. O. O. Barbour, RCNR	1/11/43	— 15/7/45
Milltown			
A/LCDR	J. H. Marshall, RCNVR	18/9/42	— 14/4/43
LT	E. H. Maguire, RCNVR	15/4/43	— 18/9/44
A/CDR	A. H. G. Storrs, RCNR	19/9/44	— 16/10/45
Mimico			
LT	F. J. Jones, RCNVR	8/2/44	— 2/10/44
LT	G. F. Crosby, RCNVR	3/10/44	— 20/11/44
LT	F. J. Jones, RCNVR	21/11/44	— 25/1/45
LCDR	W. R. Stacey, RCNR	26/1/45	— 1/2/45
LT	M. W. Knowles, RCNVR	2/2/45	— 14/2/45
A/LCDR	J. B. Elmsley, RCNVR	15/2/45	— 18/7/45
Minas			
LT	J. C. Barbour, RCNR	2/8/41	— 24/11/41
LT	J. C. Barbour, RCNR	2/12/41	— 13/9/42
LT	W. F. Wood, RCNR	14/9/42	— 17/6/43
LT	J. B. Lamb, RCNVR	18/6/43	— 25/10/44
LT	J. G. Kingsmill, RCNVR	26/10/44	— 1/9/45
LCDR	K. A. Stone, RCN	15/3/55	— 7/11/55
Miramichi			
LT	W. G. Johnstone, RCNR	26/11/41	— 26/10/42
LT	G. H. Matheson, RCNR	27/10/42	— 23/1/44
LT	R. J. Williams, RCNVR	24/1/44	— 21/6/45
SKPR/LT	W. R. Chaster, RCNR	22/6/45	— 24/10/45
Miramichi (2nd)			
LCDR	J. L. Panabaker, RCN	30/7/54	— 11/8/54
LT	D. A. Scott, RCN	12/8/54	— 1/10/54
Miramichi (3rd)			
LCDR	M. A. Considine, RCN	29/10/57	— 8/10/59
LCDR	R. K. Niven, RCN	9/10/59	— 29/6/61
LT	C. Cotaras, RCN	30/6/61	— 16/7/63
LT	D. B. Rogers, RCN	17/7/63	— 28/2/64
Moncton			
LCDR	A. R. E. Coleman, RCNR	24/4/42	— 11/10/42
LT	A. W. Ford, RCNR	12/10/42	— 3/2/44
LCDR	A. T. Morrell, RCNR	4/3/44	— 3/4/44
LCDR	R. J. Roberts, RCNR	4/4/44	— 26/1/45
LT	W. McCombe, RCNR	27/1/45	— 26/6/45
LCDR	C. G. Trotter, RCNVR	21/8/45	— 12/12/45
Monnow			
A/LCDR	L. L. Foxall, RCNR	8/3/44	— 16/7/44
CDR	E. G. Skinner, DSC, RCNR	17/7/44	— 11/6/45
Montreal			
LCDR	R. J. Herman, OBE, RCNR	12/11/43	— 4/7/44
LCDR	S. W. Howell, RCNR	5/7/44	— 26/11/44
A/LCDR	C. L. Campbell, RCNVR	27/11/44	— 26/7/45
Moonbeam			
LT	T. D. Kelly, RCNR	4/12/40	—
CH/SKPR	S. F. Ellis, RCNR	4/1/41	—
LT	W. W. Hackney, RCNR	7/7/42	—
CH/SKPR	E. W. Hannaford, RCNR	15/10/43	—
Moose			
LT	J. Evelyn, RCNR	31/5/40	— 17/10/40
LT	J. H. Langille, RCNR	18/10/40	— 20/7/45
ML 050			
LT	J. W. Braidwood, RCNVR	17/11/41	— 18/4/42
SUB/LT	D. R. Grierson, RCNVR	19/4/42	— 7/6/42
SUB/LT	T. H. Crone, RCNVR	8/6/42	— 25/8/42
LT	J. T. Sharp, RCNVR	26/8/42	— 19/12/43
LT	A. G. Beardmore, RCNVR	10/1/44	— 6/3/44
SUB/LT	R. M. Greene, RCNVR	7/3/44	— 4/4/44
LT	A. G. Beardmore, RCNVR	5/4/44	— 5/12/44
LT	J. J. McLaughlin, RCNVR	21/4/45	— 10/6/45
ML 051			
LT	T. C. Sewell, RCNVR	1/4/42	— 8/10/42
LT	W. H. B. Thomson, RCNVR	14/12/42	— 16/12/43
LT	R. Dickinson, RCNVR	17/12/43	— 8/2/44
LT	R. A. Wyllie, RCNVR	9/2/44	— 2/3/44
LCDR	W. H. B. Thomson, RCNVR	3/3/44	— 26/3/45
LT	D. S. Marlow, RCNVR	27/3/45	— 10/8/45
ML 052			
LCDR	A. D. MacLean, RCNVR	31/10/41	— /12/41
SUB/LT	A. B. Strange, RCNVR	28/2/42	— 16/1/43
ML 053			
LT	C. L. Campbell, RCNVR	17/9/41	— 10/3/42
SUB/LT	S. E. C. Garlick, RCNVR	11/3/42	— 11/5/42
LT	R. P. Baldwin, RCNVR	12/5/42	— 26/2/43
LT	G. M. Shute, RCNVR	27/4/43	— 9/1/44
LT	W. P. Munsie, RCNVR	26/1/44	— 8/1/45
LT	H. D. McFarland, RCNVR	3/5/45	— 13/7/45
ML 054			
SUB/LT	D. D. Morin, RCNVR	17/9/41	— /12/41
LT	S. O. Greening, RCNVR	24/3/42	— 30/3/42
LT	D. G. King, RCNVR	19/4/42	— 29/6/42
LT	W. C. Rigney, RCNVR	29/6/42	— 10/10/42
LT	A. D. Stairs, RCNVR	11/10/42	— 1/11/42
LT	W. C. Rigney, RCNVR	2/11/42	— 27/3/43
LT	H. F. Bartram, RCNVR	22/7/43	— 13/4/44
LT	C. N. Blagrave, RCNVR	14/4/44	— 6/12/44
ML 055			
SUB/LT	C. T. W. Hyslop, RCNVR	29/10/41	— /12/41
LT	F. N. Greener, RCNVR	19/4/42	— 11/12/42
LT	F. N. Greener, RCNVR	7/1/43	— 28/3/43
LT	R. W. Rankin, RCNVR	29/3/43	— 14/1/44
A/LT	J. E. White, RCNVR	15/1/44	— 14/9/44
LT	A. Budge, RCNVR	15/9/44	—
LT	R. G. Spence, RCNVR	25/4/45	— 12/6/45
ML 056			
LT	S. B. Fraser, RCNVR	20/11/41	— 17/12/41
LT	G. P. Manning, RCNVR	11/3/42	— 16/10/42

SUB/LT	G. D. Patterson, RCNVR	17/10/42	— 19/10/43
LT	R. A. F. Raney, RCNVR	20/10/43	— 24/12/44
LT	J. R. Jenner, RCNVR	3/5/45	— 14/6/45

ML 057

LT	R. A. Jarvis, RCNVR	29/10/41	— 12/41
SUB/LT	J. F. Gallagher, RCNVR	17/3/42	— 8/6/43
LT	R. C. Denny, RCNVR	9/6/43	— 22/9/43
SUB/LT	J. A. Davis, RCNVR	23/9/43	— 9/12/43
LT	K. F. Hurst, RCNVR	10/12/43	— 4/5/44
LT	M. O. Beverley, RCNVR	4/5/44	— 26/9/44
LT	C. D. Gillis, RCNVR	27/9/44	— 23/11/44
LT	J. S. Gardiner, RCNVR	2/5/45	— 5/6/45

ML 058

	J. H. G. Bovey, RCNVR	20/10/41	— /12/41
LT	H. K. Hill, RCNVR	1/4/42	— 19/6/42
LT	S. E. C. Garlick, RCNVR	20/6/42	— 14/2/43
LT	G. E. Rising, RCNVR	15/2/43	— 25/1/44
LT	R. Synette, RCNVR	26/1/44	— 26/5/44
LT	J. G. Chance, RCNVR	27/5/44	— 10/7/45

ML 059

LT	H. A. Batey, RCNVR	21/4/42	— 18/10/43
LT	R. Dickinson, RCNVR	19/10/43	— 17/11/43
LT	D. B. Drummond, RCNVR	18/11/43	— 18/8/44
LT	W. B. McTavish, RCNVR	19/8/44	— 7/3/45
LT	K. M. Ross, RCNVR	8/3/45	— 25/6/45

ML 060

LT	H. F. Farncomb, RCNVR	6/9/41	— 17/12/41
SUB/LT	F. K. Ellis, RCNVR	18/12/41	— 17/4/42
LT	J. S. Davis, RCNVR	18/4/42	— 11/2/43
SUB/LT	A. M. Byers, RCNVR	12/2/43	— 10/10/43
LT	R. J. M. Allan, RCNVR	11/10/43	— 15/2/44
SUB/LT	R. M. Greene, RCNVR	16/2/44	— 6/3/44
LT	R. J. M. Allan, RCNVR	7/3/44	— 29/1/45
LT	J. W. MacKenzie, RCNVR	30/1/45	— 13/3/45
LT	R. J. M. Allan, RCNVR	14/3/45	— 17/4/45
LT	G. A. Sweeney, RCNVR	18/4/45	— 20/6/45

ML 061

LT	T. G. Denny, RCNVR	20/10/41	— 17/12/41
LT	S. B. Fraser, RCNVR	18/12/41	— 21/12/41
LT	J. W. Braidwood, RCNVR	22/12/41	— 15/1/42
LT	W. L. Moore, RCNVR	16/1/42	— 17/4/42
LT	G. W. Leekie, RCNVR	18/4/42	— 30/12/42
LT	S. B. Marshall, RCNVR	30/1/43	— 10/10/43
A/LT	E. U. Anderson, RCNVR	11/10/43	— 25/8/44
LT	C. A. Balfry, RCNVR	26/8/44	— 17/1/45
LT	J. A. Barrett, RCNVR	18/1/45	— 19/6/45

ML 062

LT	W. L. Moore, RCNVR	1/4/42	— 7/7/42
LT	H. D. Pepper, RCNVR	8/7/42	— 16/1/43

ML 063

SUB/LT	N. M. Simpson, RCNVR	1/4/42	— 16/1/43

ML 064

LT	T. G. Sewell, RCNVR	20/2/42	— 31/3/42
SUB/LT	N. L. Williams, RCNVR	1/5/42	— 2/10/43
SUB/LT	P. G. D. Armour, RCNVR	3/10/43	— 7/10/43
SUB/LT	N. L. Williams, RCNVR	8/10/43	— 20/2/44
LT	E. G. Jarvis, RCNVR	6/3/44	— 21/4/44
LT	J. G. Chance, RCNVR	22/4/44	— 23/5/44
LT	E. G. Jarvis, RCNVR	24/5/44	— 16/1/45
LT	R. A. F. Raney, RCNVR	17/1/45	— 22/6/45

ML 065

LT	J. J. McLaughlin, RCNVR	1/5/43	— 12/5/43
LT	F. H. B. Dewdney, RCNVR	13/5/43	— 23/11/43
LT	J. F. Stevens, RCNVR	10/1/44	— 25/1/44
LT	J. H. Beeman, RCNVR	26/1/44	— 1/8/44
LT	G. E. McCabe, RCNVR	2/8/44	— 10/2/45
LT	G. E. McCabe, RCNVR	26/2/45	— 4/3/45
LT	W. B. McTavish, RCNVR	5/3/45	— 18/7/45

ML 066

LT	C. F. Draney, RCNVR	6/3/42	— 23/11/42
LT	W. E. W. Snaith, RCNVR	24/11/42	— 10/2/43
CH/SKPR	G. B. McCandless, RCNR	11/2/43	— 3/3/43
LT	W. E. W. Snaith, RCNVR	4/3/43	— 3/7/43
LT	R. R. Maitland, RCNVR	4/7/43	— 12/1/44
LT	J. W. Shaw, RCNVR	13/1/44	— 15/5/44
LT	J. M. Lewis, RCNVR	16/5/44	— 13/6/44
LT	E. S. Blanchet, RCNVR	14/6/44	— 19/6/44
LT	J. M. Lewis, RCNVR	20/6/44	— 20/7/44
LT	W. A. Smith, RCNVR	21/7/44	— 10/9/45

ML 067

SUB/LT	C. C. T. McNair, RCNVR	27/3/42	— 15/6/43
LT	J. F. Beveridge, RCNVR	16/6/43	— 1/11/43
SKPR/LT	G. F. Cassidy, RCNR	2/11/43	— 16/11/43
LT	J. F. Beveridge, RCNVR	17/11/43	— 6/4/44
LT	E. S. Blanchet, RCNVR	7/4/44	— 13/6/44
LT	H. W. Patterson, RCNVR	4/11/44	— 12/7/45
LT	J. M. Ferris, RCNVR	13/7/45	— 12/9/45

ML 068

SKPR/LT	H. E. Young, RCNR	7/3/42	— 28/2/43
LT	E. P. Ashe, RCNVR	29/2/43	— 8/9/43
LT	R. D. Linton, RCNVR	9/9/43	— 30/8/44
LT	J. M. Lewis, RCNVR	31/8/44	— 21/9/44
LT	R. D. Linton, RCNVR	22/9/44	— 27/8/45

ML 069

CH/SKPR	F. W. M. Drew, RCNR	28/3/42	— 15/6/43
LT	R. M. Francis, RCNVR	16/6/43	— 25/10/43
LT	H. W. Patterson, RCNVR	26/10/43	— 19/9/44
LT	E. U. Anderson, RCNVR	20/9/44	— 24/6/45

ML 070

CH/SKPR	G. B. McCandless, RCNR	19/11/42	— 28/11/42
LT	D. F. G. Fladgate, RCNVR	18/1/43	— 22/10/43
LT	F. G. Mitchell, RCNVR	23/10/43	— 21/11/44
LT	R. Muir, RCNVR	22/11/44	— 9/8/45
LT	J. E. E. Richardson, RCNVR	10/8/45	— 18/8/45

ML 071

SKPR/LT	L. S. W. Pusey, RCNR	10/4/42	— 6/2/43
LT	J. E. E. Richardson, RCNVR	7/2/43	— 23/7/43
SKPR/LT	G. F. Cassidy, RCNR	24/7/43	— 15/8/43
LT	J. E. E. Richardson, RCNVR	16/8/43	— 3/3/44
LT	G. E. Devlin, RCNVR	4/10/44	— 5/11/44
LT	E. N. Pottinger, RCNVR	6/11/44	— 11/7/45

ML 072

LT	H. F. Newell, RCNVR	22/11/41	— /12/41
LT	C. L. Campbell, RCNVR	1/4/42	— 18/6/42
LT	D. S. Howard, RCNVR	19/6/42	— 30/4/43
LT	E. G. Jarvis, RCNVR	18/5/43	— 18/11/43
LT	J. A. Davis, RCNVR	14/12/43	— 23/4/44
LT	F. Amyot, RCNVR	24/4/44	— 16/3/45
LT	A. M. C. Kenning, RCNVR	17/3/45	— 5/9/45

ML 073

LT	V. Browne, RCNVR	22/11/41	— /12/41
LT	S. O. Greening, RCNVR	1/4/42	— 17/6/43
LT	J. H. Stevenson, RCNVR	18/6/43	— 19/2/44
LT	R. D. Hayes, RCNVR	20/2/44	— 15/5/45
LT	J. C. Austin, RCNVR	16/5/45	— 28/5/45
LT	R. D. Hayes, RCNVR	29/5/45	— 22/8/45

ML 074

LT	T. G. Denny, RCNVR	21/4/42	— 20/1/43
LT	V. J. Wilgress, RCNVR	21/1/43	— 28/10/43
LT	E. Leyland, RCNVR	29/10/43	— 1/7/45

ML 075

LT	J. G. Humphrey, RCNVR	28/4/42	— 2/5/43
LT	L. J. Wallace, RCNVR	3/5/43	— 27/5/43
LT	T. R. C. Denny, RCNVR	28/5/43	— 31/5/43
A/LCDR	J. M. Todd, RCNVR	1/6/43	— 4/1/44
A/LCDR	J. M. Todd, RCNVR	25/1/44	— 11/10/44
LT	J. D. Lineham, RCNVR	12/10/44	— 8/2/45
LT	C. R. Godbehere, RCNVR	9/2/45	— 16/3/45
LT	J. D. Lineham, RCNVR	17/3/45	— 19/8/45

ML 076

LT	J. Leitch, RCNVR	13/7/42	— 4/4/43
LT	G. R. Brassard, RCNVR	5/4/43	— 8/6/43
LT	T. F. H. Galway, RCNVR	9/6/43	— 21/6/43
LT	W. E. W. Snaith, RCNVR	24/2/44	— 20/7/44
LT	F. B. Pugh, RCNVR	21/7/44	— 19/7/45

ML 077

A/LCDR	J. W. Braidwood, RCNVR	21/4/42	— 7/10/43
SUB/LT	R. Paddon, RCNVR	8/10/43	— 29/10/43
SUB/LT	P. Thomas, RCNVR	30/10/43	— 29/12/43
LT	P. B. C. Samson, RCNVR	30/12/43	— 5/3/44
LT	F. Amyot, RCNVR	6/3/44	— 23/4/44
LT	P. B. C. Samson, RCNVR	24/4/44	— 29/4/45
LT	D. R. Lester, RCNVR	30/4/45	— 19/7/45

ML 078

SUB/LT	J. N. Finlayson, RCNVR	21/4/42	— 11/4/43
LT	G. P. Manning, RCNVR	12/4/43	— 23/4/43
SUB/LT	J. A. Davis, RCNVR	24/4/43	— 5/5/43
LT	D. G. Creba, RCNVR	6/5/43	— 7/10/43
LT	L. O. Storehouse, RCNVR	8/10/43	— 5/5/44
LT	C. H. Adair, RCNVR	6/5/44	— 25/10/44
LT	S. C. Kilbank, RCNVR	26/10/44	— 5/2/45
LT	J. L. Gourlay, RCNVR	24/4/45	— 20/7/45

ML 079

LT	S. B. Fraser, RCNVR	21/4/42	— 3/7/42
LT	H. R. Cruise, RCNVR	4/7/42	— 13/8/43
LT	C. J. Holloway, RCNVR	14/8/43	— 7/11/43
LT	C. A. Balfry, RCNVR	8/11/43	— 15/8/44
LT	J. B. LeMaistre, RCNVR	16/8/44	— 15/12/44
LT	F. J. Johnson, RCNVR	23/4/45	— 11/6/45

ML 080

SUB/LT	J. W. Collins, RCNVR	21/4/42	— 8/9/42
SUB/LT	G. E. Burrell, RCNVR	9/9/42	— 6/10/43
LT	J. E. M. Jones, RCNVR	7/10/43	— 15/12/44
LT	G. E. McCabe, RCNVR	23/4/45	— 31/5/45
LT	J. J. Caya, RCNVR	1/6/45	— 12/7/45

ML 081

LT	F. K. Ellis, RCNVR	21/4/42	— 23/11/42
LT	J. M. Todd, RCNVR	24/11/42	— 31/5/43
LT	T. R. C. Denny, RCNVR	1/6/43	— 8/6/43
LT	J. J. McLaughlin, RCNVR	19/8/43	— 5/10/43
LT	G. C. Brain, RCNVR	6/10/43	— 20/4/44
LT	A. D. Stairs, RCNVR	21/4/44	— 26/11/44
LT	W. J. King, RCNVR	27/11/44	— 14/1/45
LT	A. D. Stairs, RCNVR	23/4/45	— 21/6/45

ML 082

LT	A. B. Strange, RCNVR	21/4/42	— 4/2/43
LT	J. F. Stevens, RCNVR	25/8/43	— 9/1/44
LT	J. F. Stevens, RCNVR	26/1/44	— 25/9/44

ML 083

LT	W. M. Grant, RCNVR	9/5/42	— 10/5/43
LT	M. C. Knox, RCNVR	11/5/43	— 7/10/43
LT	J. R. Akin, RCNVR	8/10/43	— 11/9/44
LT	G. A. Sweeney, RCNVR	12/9/44	— 15/12/44
LT	R. J. M. Allan, RCNVR	23/4/45	— 15/7/45

ML 084

LT	G. E. Cross, RCNVR	4/6/42	— 26/3/43
LT	R. N. McDiarmid, RCNVR	27/3/43	— 16/4/44
LT	J. M. Duck, RCNVR	17/4/44	— 15/12/44
LT	J. C. Mackey, RCNVR	23/4/45	— 22/6/45

ML 085

LT	W. E. D. Atkinson, RCNVR	21/4/42	— 21/10/42
SUB/LT	G. C. Clark, RCNVR	22/10/42	— 7/3/44
LT	J. J. McLaughlin, RCNVR	8/3/44	— 4/4/44
LT	R. M. Greene, RCNVR	5/4/44	— 29/11/44
LT	H. J. Dow, RCNVR	1/5/45	— 4/7/45

ML 086

LT	T. G. Sewell, RCNVR	25/10/42	— 8/2/43
LT	S. C. Robinson, RCNVR	9/2/43	— 2/3/43
LT	T. G. Sewell, RCNVR	3/3/43	— 13/3/43
LT	J. R. Sare, RCNVR	14/3/43	— 21/3/43
LT	G. L. James, RCNVR	22/3/43	— 16/11/43
LT	P. Husoy, RCNVR	17/11/43	— 3/12/44
LT	V. B. Chew, RCNVR	4/12/44	— 31/1/45
LT	P. Husoy, RCNVR	1/2/45	— 7/7/45

ML 087

LT	A. D. Stairs, RCNVR	11/11/42	— 9/1/44
LT	W. G. Finlay, RCNVR	10/1/44	— 6/2/45
LT	V. B. Chew, RCNVR	7/2/45	— 6/3/45
LT	J. C. Austin, RCNVR	7/3/45	— 25/4/45
LT	V. B. Chew, RCNVR	26/4/45	— 8/7/45

ML 088

LCDR	W. L. Moore, RCNVR	10/5/43	— 6/9/43
SUB/LT	J. G. McClelland, RCNVR	7/9/43	— 8/10/43
SUB/LT	R. S. Graves, RCNVR	9/10/43	— 28/10/43
LCDR	W. L. Moore, RCNVR	29/10/43	— 24/11/43
LT	W. G. Cunningham, RCNVR	25/11/43	— 16/8/44
LT	T. M. Kirkwood, RCNVR	17/8/44	— 14/3/45
LT	J. G. W. MacKenzie, RCNVR	15/3/45	— 4/4/45
LT	T. M. Kirkwood, RCNVR	5/4/45	— 25/6/45

ML 089

LT	A. G. Beardmore, RCNVR	26/9/42	— 9/1/44
LT	J. H. Curtis, RCNVR	10/1/44	— 16/3/45
LT	J. A. D. Alguire, RCNVR	17/3/45	— 29/4/45
LT	J. H. Curtis, RCNVR	30/4/45	— 1/7/45

ML 090

LCDR	A. C. Campbell, RCNVR	11/11/42	— 10/5/44
LT	C. A. L. Maase, RCNVR	11/5/44	— 24/1/45
LT	D. A. Dobson, RCNVR	25/1/45	— 6/3/45
LT	C. A. L. Maase, RCNVR	7/3/45	— 13/7/45

ML 091

LT	S. C. Robinson, RCNVR	17/5/43	— 8/10/43
SUB/LT	J. G. McClelland, RCNVR	9/10/43	— 11/11/43
LT	F. H. B. Dewdney, RCNVR	12/11/43	— 7/3/44
LT	R. A. Wyllie, RCNVR	8/3/44	— 22/5/44
LT	E. B. Kendall, RCNVR	23/5/44	— 16/7/45

ML 092

LT	H. J. Brown, RCNVR	28/9/42	— 8/10/43
LT	E. Leyland, RCNVR	9/10/43	— 28/10/43
LT	G. L. Parker, RCNVR	29/10/43	— 1/2/44
LT	R. Dickinson, RCNVR	2/2/44	— 2/7/45

ML 093

LT	D. M. Fraser, RCNVR	2/11/42	— 27/12/42
LT	R. Carfrae, RCNVR	28/12/42	— 1/11/43
LT	A. W. Murray, RCNVR	2/11/43	— 18/4/44
LT	E. G. Arthurs, RCNVR	19/4/44	— 21/1/45
LT	J. C. Austin, RCNVR	22/1/45	— 6/3/45
LT	E. G. Arthurs, RCNVR	7/3/45	— 2/7/45

ML 094

LT	G. Marcil, RCNVR	29/11/42	— 4/3/43
LT	A. P. Morrow, RCNVR	5/3/43	— 7/10/43
LT	C. J. VanTighem, RCNVR	8/10/43	— 11/12/44
LT	C. Carras, RCNVR	12/12/44	— 5/1/45
LT	W. J. Langston, RCNVR	6/1/45	— 6/2/45

ML 095

LT	J. J. McLaughlin, RCNVR	7/7/43	— 18/7/43
LT	H. D. Pepper, RCNVR	19/7/43	— 3/9/43
LT	H. R. Cruise, RCNVR	4/9/43	— 19/9/43
LT	H. D. Pepper, RCNVR	20/9/43	— 21/10/43
LT	N. L. Williams, RCNVR	25/2/44	— 5/1/45
LT	W. J. Langston, RCNVR	6/1/45	— 6/2/45
LT	N. L. Williams, RCNVR	7/2/45	— 1/7/45

ML 096

LT	H. R. Cruise, RCNVR	9/11/42	— 11/8/43
LT	A. M. Harper, RCNVR	12/8/43	— 27/8/43
SUB/LT	R. W. Kettlewell, RCNVR	28/8/43	— 7/11/43
LT	J. M. Lewis, RCNVR	8/11/43	— 16/11/43
LT	T. H. Browne, RCNVR	17/11/43	— 10/1/45
LT	J. H. Morrison, RCNVR	11/1/45	— 9/4/45
LT	W. J. Langston, RCNVR	10/4/45	— 19/4/45
LT	J. H. Morrison, RCNVR	14/5/45	— 1/7/45

ML 097

LT	E. P. Jones, RCNVR	5/1/44	— 15/9/44
LT	J. H. Bailey, RCNVR	16/9/44	— 2/3/45
LT	W. J. Langston, RCNVR	3/3/45	— 9/4/45
LT	J. H. Bailey, RCNVR	10/4/45	— 2/7/45

ML 098

SUB/LT	T. A. Welch, RCNVR	7/11/42	— 18/11/43
LT	E. G. Jarvis, RCNVR	19/11/43	— 4/1/44
A/LCDR	J. M. Todd, RCNVR	5/1/44	— 24/1/44

LT	E. G. Jarvis, RCNVR	25/1/44	— 5/3/44
LT	E. Desrosiers, RCNVR	6/3/44	— 16/3/45
LT	M. L. M. DeMartigny, RCNVR	17/3/45	— 17/4/45
LT	E. Desrosiers, RCNVR	18/4/45	— 25/4/45
LT	J. C. Austin, RCNVR	26/4/45	— 28/4/45
LT	E. Desrosiers, RCNVR	29/4/45	— 16/7/45
ML 099			
SUB/LT	P. G. D. Armour, RCNVR	7/3/42	— 6/11/42
LT	G. M. Moors, RCNVR	7/11/42	— 18/10/43
SUB/LT	P. G. D. Armour, RCNVR	19/10/43	— 9/1/45
LT	J. B. LeMaistre, RCNVR	8/1/45	— 2/7/45
ML 100			
LT	E. G. Scott, RCNVR	8/11/42	— 16/11/43
LT	D. A. Dobson, RCNVR	17/11/43	— 17/12/44
LT	W. G. Lumsden, RCNVR	18/12/44	— 9/1/45
LT	J. R. Jenner, RCNVR	10/1/45	— 7/4/45
LT	D. A. Dobson, RCNVR	8/4/45	— 12/7/45
ML 101			
LT	A. A. MacLeod, RCNVR	20/10/42	— 15/8/43
SUB/LT	C. R. Godbehere, RCNVR		— 11/10/43
LT	G. L. James, RCNVR	17/11/43	— 19/6/44
LT	P. B. Paine, RCNVR	20/6/44	— 20/12/44
LT	F. H. B. Dewdney, RCNVR	25/1/45	— 31/7/45
ML 102			
LT	H. M. Gordon, RCNVR	14/11/42	— 23/4/43
SUB/LT	J. G. W. MacKenzie, RCNVR	24/4/43	— 2/6/43
LT	H. M. Gordon, RCNVR	3/6/43	— 18/10/43
LT	B. C. Heintzman, RCNVR	19/10/43	— 5/7/44
LT	J. K. MacDonald, RCNVR	6/7/44	— 24/6/45
ML 103			
LT	H. A. Agar, RCNVR	18/11/42	— 21/6/43
LT	F. H. Galway, RCNVR	22/6/43	— 6/1/45
LT	W. G. Lumsden, RCNVR	7/1/45	— 26/4/45
LT	J. B. Barbeau, RCNVR	27/4/45	— 8/7/45
ML 104			
LCDR	J. W. Braidwood, RCNVR	8/10/43	— 1/2/44
LT	C. F. W. Cooper, RCNVR	2/2/44	— 3/4/44
LT	J. J. McLaughlin, RCNVR	4/4/44	— 18/2/45
LT	F. H. Galway, RCNVR	19/2/45	— 14/9/45
ML 105			
LT	J. D. Addison, RCNVR	5/9/43	— 29/8/44
LT	W. P. T. McGhee, RCNVR	30/8/44	— 16/9/45
ML 106			
LT	F. B. Pugh, RCNVR	28/8/43	— 3/6/44
LT	C. F. W. Cooper, RCNVR	4/6/44	— 17/2/45
LT	C. N. Blagrave, RCNVR	18/2/45	— 30/8/45
ML 107			
LT	H. P. R. Brown, RCNVR	11/9/43	— 30/8/45
ML 108			
LT	I. L. Campbell, RCNVR	14/8/43	— 19/12/44
ML 109			
LT	J. G. W. MacKenzie, RCNVR	23/8/43	— 22/1/45
LT	J. S. Stephen, RCNVR	23/1/45	— 17/7/45
ML 110			
LT	R. Dickinson, RCNVR		— 18/10/43
LT	H. A. Batey, RCNVR	19/10/43	— 23/6/44
LT	W. B. Bailey, RCNVR	24/6/44	— 23/2/45
LT	J. U. McFall, RCNVR	24/2/45	— 6/3/45
LT	D. A. Dobson, RCNVR	7/3/45	— 7/4/45
SUB/LT	R. R. Peirson, RCNVR	8/4/45	— 29/4/45
LT	W. B. Bailey, RCNVR	30/4/45	— 13/7/45
ML 111			
LT	A. M. Harper, RCNVR	9/9/43	— 5/4/44
LT	C. F. W. Cooper, RCNVR	6/4/44	— 28/5/44
LT	A. M. Harper, RCNVR	29/5/44	— 5/10/44
LT	S. L. Burke, RCNVR	6/10/44	— 6/2/45
LT	P. B. Paine, RCNVR	7/2/45	— 13/7/45
ML 112			
LT	R. C. Denny, RCNVR	25/10/43	— 18/4/44
LT	G. R. Brassard, RCNVR	19/4/44	— 28/12/44
LT	R. M. Greene, RCNVR	29/12/44	— 5/1/45
LT	W. R. Duggan, RCNVR	6/1/45	— 22/2/45
LT	J. E. M. Jones, RCNVR	23/2/45	— 20/3/45
LT	W. R. Duggan, RCNVR	21/3/45	— 16/7/45
ML 113			
LT	C. J. Holloway, RCNVR	8/11/43	— 22/10/44
LT	J. E. M. Jones, RCNVR	21/3/45	— 23/7/45
ML 114			
LT	R. Carfrae, RCNVR	23/11/43	— 8/7/44
LCDR	W. L. Moore, RCNVR	23/10/44	— 26/12/44
LT	W. J. King, RCNVR	27/12/44	— 14/1/45
LT	J. H. Osler, RCNVR	15/1/45	— 28/1/45
LT	G. E. Rising, RCNVR	29/1/45	— 13/2/45
LT	J. H. Osler, RCNVR	14/2/45	— 5/5/45
LT	F. A. Amyot, RCNVR	6/5/45	— 6/6/45
LT	J. H. Osler, RCNVR	7/6/45	— 20/8/45
ML 115			
LT	R. W. Kettlewell, RCNVR	8/11/43	— 7/2/44
LT	C. R. Godbehere, RCNVR	8/2/44	— 4/1/45
LT	C. R. Godbehere, RCNVR	26/3/45	— 8/6/45
LT	F. Amyot, RCNVR	9/6/45	— 25/7/45
LT	C. R. Godbehere, RCNVR	26/7/45	— 13/8/45
ML 116			
LT	E. P. Jones, RCNVR	10/4/44	— 8/9/44
LT	J. D. Addison, RCNVR	9/9/44	— 22/1/45
LT	J. D. Addison, RCNVR	26/3/45	— 31/5/45
LT	G. E. McCabe, RCNR	1/6/45	— 2/9/45
ML 117			
SUB/LT	E. H. Gudewill, RCNVR	17/12/43	— 25/1/44
LT	G. E. Rising, RCNVR	26/1/44	— 26/12/44
LT	J. G. Menzies, RCNVR	27/12/44	— 13/3/45
LT	W. J. King, RCNVR	14/3/45	— 2/4/45
LT	J. G. Menzies, RCNVR	3/4/45	— 19/7/45
ML 118			
LT	V. J. Wilgress, RCNVR	6/11/43	— 7/2/44
LT	W. J. King, RCNVR	3/4/44	— 19/4/44
LT	J. H. Osler, RCNVR	20/4/44	— 8/1/45
LT	W. J. King, RCNVR	11/4/45	— 25/7/45
ML 119			
LT	J. J. McLaughlin, RCNVR	16/11/43	— 7/3/44
LT	F. H. B. Dewdney, RCNVR	8/3/44	— 7/1/45
ML 120			
LT	G. M. Shute, RCNVR	10/1/44	— 19/2/44
LT	J. H. Stevenson, RCNVR	20/2/44	— 21/9/44
LT	W. J. King, RCNVR	22/9/44	— 29/10/44
LT	J. H. Stevenson, RCNVR	30/10/44	— 21/1/45
LT	J. M. Todd, RCNVR	22/1/45	— 26/7/45
ML 121			
LT	R. N. McDiarmid, RCNVR	17/4/44	— 9/1/45
LT	J. G. W. MacKenzie, RCNVR	17/4/45	— 26/7/45
LCDR	J. M. Todd, RCNVR	27/7/45	— 26/8/45
ML 122			
LT	C. K. D. Smith, RCNVR	17/5/44	— 9/10/44
LT	R. T. McKean, RCNVR	10/10/44	— 5/9/45
ML 123			
LT	J. W. Shaw, RCNVR	5/6/44	— 3/7/45
ML 124			
LT	E. S. Blanchet, RCNVR	20/6/44	— 17/8/45
ML 125			
LT	J. E. Kendrick, RCNVR	2/6/44	— 8/6/45
LT	F. J. Fiander, RCNVR	9/6/45	— 13/9/45
ML 126			
LT	R. C. Denny, RCNVR	7/8/44	— 8/11/44
LT	W. H. Davidson, RCNVR	9/11/44	— 12/9/45
ML 127			
LT	J. M. Lewis, RCNVR	25/9/44	— 5/11/44
LT	G. E. Devlin, RCNVR	6/11/44	— 22/11/44
LT	C. K. D. Smith, RCNVR	23/11/44	— 11/9/45
ML 128			
LT	R. K. Baker, RCNVR	4/7/44	— 11/1/45
LT	G. E. Devlin, RCNVR	12/1/45	— 11/9/45
ML 129			
LT	G. L. James, RCNVR	25/9/44	— 30/5/45
LT	E. L. MacDonald, RCNVR	31/5/45	— 3/7/45
Moose Jaw			
LT	F. E. Grubb, RCN	19/6/41	— 8/12/41
LT	H. D. Campsie, RCNR	9/12/41	— 13/2/42
LT	L. D. Quick, RCNR	14/2/42	— 29/8/43
LT	J. E. Taylor, RCNVR	30/8/43	— 6/10/43
LT	L. D. Quick, RCNR	7/10/43	— 3/2/44
LT	H. Brynjolfson, RCNVR	14/3/44	— 12/10/44
LT	A. Harvey, RCNR	13/10/44	— 8/7/45
Morden			
LT	J. J. Hodgkinson, RCNR	6/9/41	— 2/6/43
LT	E. C. Smith, RCNVR	3/6/43	— 14/10/43
LT	W. Turner, RCNR	15/10/43	— 2/1/44
LT	E. C. Smith, RCNVR	3/1/44	— 21/5/44
LT	K. B. Cully, RCNVR	22/5/44	— 18/2/45
LT	F. R. Spindler, RCNVR	19/2/45	— 29/6/45
MTB 459			
LT	C. A. Law, DSC, RCNVR	26/1/44	— 11/9/44
LT	J. H. Shand, RCNVR	12/9/44	— 14/2/45
MTB 460			
LT	D. Killam, DSC, RCNVR	25/2/44	— 1/7/44
MTB 461			
LT	C. A. Burk, DSC, + 2 Bars, RCNVR	28/2/44	— 17/9/44
LT	T. K. Scobie, RCNVR	18/9/44	— 3/2/45
LT	J. R. Cunningham, RCNVR	4/2/45	— 9/2/45
LT	C. V. Barlow, RCNVR	10/2/45	— 14/2/45
MTB 462			
LT	R. J. Moyse, RCNVR	1/3/44	— 28/8/44
LT	J. H. Shand, RCNVR	29/8/44	— 11/9/44
LT	R. Paddon, RCNVR	24/1/45	— 14/2/45
MTB 463			
LT	D. G. Creba, RCNVR	16/3/44	— 7/7/44
MTB 464			
LT	L. C. Bishop, DSC, RCNVR	26/3/44	— 24/2/45
LT	C. V. Barlow, RCNVR	25/2/45	— 6/3/45
LT	L. C. Bishop, DSC, RCNVR	7/3/45	— 9/4/45
MTB 465			
LT	C. D. Chaffey, RCNVR	27/3/44	— 14/2/45
MTB 466			
LT	S. B. Marshall, RCNVR	29/3/44	— 27/7/44
LT	T. K. Scobie, RCNVR	28/7/44	— 17/9/44
LT	S. B. Marshall, RCNVR	18/9/44	— 7/1/45
LT	J. M. Adams, RCNVR	8/1/45	— 14/2/45
MTB 485			
LT	D. G. Creba, RCNVR	31/7/44	— 10/3/45
MTB 486			
LCDR	C. A. Law, DSC, RCNVR	5/8/44	— 24/2/45
LT	C. D. Chaffey, RCNVR	25/2/45	— 3/3/45
LT	T. K. Scobie, RCNVR	4/3/45	— 8/3/45
MTB 491			
LT	C. A. Burk, DSC, + 2 Bars, RCNVR	4/10/44	— 26/1/45
LT	R. J. Moyse, RCNVR	27/1/45	— 10/3/45
MTB 726			
LT	A. P. Morrow, RCNVR	1/2/44	— 22/5/45
MTB 727			
LT	L. R. McLernon, DSC, RCNVR	7/1/44	— 4/4/45
LT	G. D. Pattison, RCNVR	5/4/45	— 21/5/45
MTB 735			
LT	J. W. Collins, DSC, RCNVR	14/2/44	— 2/10/44
LT	J. R. Culley, RCNVR	3/10/44	— 21/6/45
MTB 736			
LT	S. O. Greening, RCNVR	31/3/44	— 17/5/44
LT	G. M. Moss, RCNVR	17/5/44	— 18/5/45
MTB 743			
LT	M. C. Knox, DSC, RCNVR	15/5/44	— 31/5/45
MTB 744			
LT	G. M. Moors, RCNVR	14/2/44	— /5/44
MTB 745			
LT	O. B. Mabee, RCNVR	15/1/44	— 19/5/45
MTB 746			
LT	S. O. Greening, RCNVR	19/5/44	— 20/12/44
LT	G. D. Pattison, RCNVR	21/12/44	— 15/1/45
LT	J. W. Collins, DSC, RCNVR	16/1/45	— 18/5/45
MTB 748			
LCDR	J. R. H. Kirkpatrick, DSC, RCNVR	19/2/44	— 23/5/45
MTB 797			
LT	R. C. Smith, RCNVR	30/12/44	— 12/4/45
LT	R. C. Smith, RCNVR	20/5/45	— 21/5/45
Mulgrave			
LT	D. T. English, RCNR	4/11/42	— 10/10/43
LT	R. M. Meredith, RCNR	11/10/43	— 25/12/44
Nabob			
CAPT	H. N. Lay, OBE, RCN	15/10/43	— 30/9/44
Nanaimo			
LCDR	H. C. C. Daubney, RCNR	26/4/41	— 7/10/41
LT	T. J. Bellas, RCNR	8/10/41	— 20/8/42
LT	E. U. Jones, RCNR	21/8/42	— 10/10/43
LT	J. E. Hastings, RCNR	11/10/43	— 9/10/44
LT	R. C. Eaton, RCNVR	10/10/44	— 2/3/45
LCDR	W. Redford, RCNR	23/3/45	— 28/9/45
Napanee			
LCDR	A. H. Dobson, RCNR	12/5/41	— 8/12/41
LT	S. Henderson, RCNR	9/12/41	— 2/6/44
A/LCDR	G. A. Powell, RCNVR	3/6/44	— 12/7/45
Nene			
LCDR	E. R. Shaw, RCNR	6/4/44	— 11/6/45
New Glasgow			
LCDR	G. S. Hall, RCNR	23/12/43	— 23/7/44
LCDR	T. MacDuff, RCNR	24/7/44	— 29/8/44
LCDR	R. M. Hanbury, RCNVR	30/8/44	— 28/3/45
A/LCDR	E. T. P. Wennberg, RCNVR	29/3/45	— 31/7/45
LT	H. M. Palmer, RCNVR	1/8/45	— 1/11/45
CDR	G. A. LaRue, RCN	30/1/54	— 27/3/55
LCDR	B. C. Hamilton, RCN	28/3/55	— 22/5/56
LCDR	J. W. B. Buckingham, RCN	23/5/56	— 15/11/57
LCDR	A. R. Pickels, RCN	5/5/58	— 6/1/60
LCDR	I. A. Macpherson, RCN	7/1/60	— 13/8/61
LCDR	J. G. Mills, RCN	14/8/61	— 3/3/63
LCDR	J. S. Hertzberg, RCN	4/3/63	— 21/4/64
LCDR	O. J. A. Cavenagh, RCN	22/4/64	— 3/8/65
LCDR	J. I. B. Donald, RCN	4/8/65	— 24/10/65
LT	S. W. Riddell, RCN	25/10/65	— 9/12/65
LCDR	W. R. Vallevand, RCN	10/12/65	— 16/1/66
LCDR	P. E. Simard, RCN	17/1/66	— 1/5/66
LCDR	W. R. Vallevand, RCN	2/5/66	— 8/5/66
LCDR	T. A. Irvine, RCN	9/5/66	— 11/9/66
LCDR	P. E. Simard, RCN	12/9/66	— 30/1/67
New Liskeard			
LT	W. M. Grand, RCNVR	21/11/44	— 15/6/45
LT	W. J. Piercy, RCNR	7/1/46	— 21/2/46
LT	A. H. McDonald, RCN	22/2/46	— 30/4/46
LCDR	J. C. L. Annesley, RCN	1/5/46	— 15/9/46
LCDR	B. P. Young, MBE, RCN	16/9/46	— 11/11/47
LT	I. B. B. Morrow, RCN	12/11/47	— 23/6/49
LT	W. W. MacColl, RCN	24/6/49	— 14/4/51
LCDR	C. E. Coles, RCN	15/4/51	— 14/12/51
LCDR	T. W. Wall, RCN	15/12/51	— 2/3/53
LCDR	R. L. Ellis, RCN	3/3/53	— 6/8/54
LCDR	M. A. Turner, RCN	7/8/54	— 3/6/56

LCDR	G. R. Wood, RCN	4/6/56	— 27/8/57
LCDR	C. H. LaRose, RCN	28/8/57	—

New Waterford

A/LCDR	E. R. Shaw, RCNR	21/1/44	— 23/3/44
A/CDR	W. E. S. Briggs, DSC, RCNR	24/3/44	— 7/7/45
A/CDR	W. E. S. Briggs, DSC, RCNR	13/8/45	— 11/11/45
LCDR	J. M. Leeming, RCNVR	12/11/45	—
LT	J. C. Payne, RCN	9/1/53	— 28/8/53
LCDR	W. S. Blandy, RCN	31/1/58	— 26/10/58
LCDR	I. Butters, RCN	27/10/58	— 17/12/59
LCDR	F. Lubin, RCN	18/12/59	— 14/1/60
LCDR	C. G. Pratt, RCN	15/1/60	— 22/6/61
LCDR	J. H. Wilkes, RCN	23/6/61	— 9/10/62
LCDR	R. C. Brown, RCN	10/10/62	— 28/6/64
LCDR	N. St. C. Norton, RCN	29/6/64	— 31/10/65
LCDR	N. D. Moncrieff, RCN	16/5/66	— 22/12/66

New Westminster

A/LCDR	R. O. McKenzie, RCNR	31/1/42	— 21/6/45

Niagara

A/CDR	E. L. Armstrong, RCN	24/9/40	— 2/7/41
LCDR	T. P. Ryan, OBE, RCN	3/7/41	— 22/2/42
LCDR	R. F. Harris, DSC, RCN	23/2/42	— 4/10/42
A/LCDR	G. H. Davidson, RCN	5/10/42	— 14/10/42
LCDR	R. F. Harris, DSC, RCN	15/10/42	— 9/9/43
A/LCDR	W. H. Willson, RCN	10/9/43	— 5/3/44
LT	J. C. Smyth, RCNR	6/3/44	— 22/6/44
CDR	R. B. Mitchell, RCNR	23/6/44	— 29/6/44
LT	R. N. Smillie, RCNVR	30/6/44	— 18/7/44
CDR	R. B. Mitchell, RCNR	19/7/44	— / /45

Niobe

CDR	W. B. MacDonald, RN	6/9/10	—
LCDR	C. E. Aglionby, RN	20/6/13	—
CAPT	R. G. Corbett, RN	15/8/14	— 1/9/15
A/CDR	P. F. Newcombe, RN	16/10/16	—
CDR	H. E. Holme, RCN	22/12/17	— 1/6/20

Nipigon

LCDR	A. T. Morrell, RCNR	11/8/41	— 14/2/42
A/LCDR	C. A. King, RCNR	15/2/42	— 11/5/42
LT	J. Brock, RCNVR	12/5/42	— 4/10/42
LT	W. J. Piercy, RCNVR	5/10/42	— 28/3/44
LT	W. Turner, RCNR	29/3/44	— 11/4/44
LT	D. R. Baker, RCNVR	12/4/44	— 4/2/45
LT	J. R. Brown, RCNVR	5/2/45	— 13/10/45

Nipigon (2nd)

CDR	D. R. Saxon, DSC, RCN	30/5/64	— 19/5/66
CDR	J. B. Carling, RCN	19/5/66	— 11/9/67
CDR	R. F. Choat, RCN	11/9/67	— 19/12/68
LCDR	O. S. Chorneyko	19/12/68	— 4/2/69
CDR	R. C. Brown	4/2/69	— 31/8/70
LCDR	L. I. MacDonald	31/8/70	— 29/9/70
CDR	A. H. Brookbank	29/9/70	— 19/6/72
CDR	D. A. Avery	19/6/72	— 10/4/74
CDR	J. D. Sine	10/4/74	— 23/5/75
CDR	F. H. Hope	23/5/75	— 1/9/76
CDR	H. L. Davies	1/9/76	— 15/5/78
CDR	R. C. Waller	15/5/78	— 12/6/80
CDR	D. E. Gibb	12/6/80	—

Nootka/Nanoose

LCDR	H. Kingsley, RCN	6/12/38	— 14/5/39
LCDR	K. F. Adams, RCN	15/5/39	— 21/8/39
LCDR	M. A. Wood, RCN	22/8/39	— 13/9/39
LT	A. T. Morrell, RCNR	14/9/39	— 27/9/40
LCDR	W. J. Fricker, RCN	28/9/40	— 28/1/41
LT	J. P. Fraser, RCNR	29/1/41	— 20/7/41
LT	A. M. McLarnon, RCNR	21/7/41	— 2/8/41
LT	J. P. Fraser, RCNR	3/8/41	— 14/9/41
Mate	W. R. Nunn, RCNR	15/9/41	— 15/3/42
CH/SKPR	G. F. Burgess, RCNR	16/3/42	— 13/9/43
SKPR/LT	G. C. Burnham, RCNR	14/9/43	— 29/7/45

Nootka (2nd)

CDR	H. S. Rayner, DSC, RCN	7/8/46	— 17/6/47
LCDR	M. G. Stirling, RCN	18/6/47	— 5/9/47
CAPT	H. F. Pullen, OBE, RCN	6/9/47	— 16/8/48
CDR	A. H. G. Storrs, DSC & Bar, RCN	17/8/48	— 15/8/49
CDR	A. B. F. Fraser-Harris, DSC & Bar, RCN	29/8/50	— 16/9/51
LCDR	C. E. Richardson, RCN	17/9/51	— 14/10/51
LT	F. P. R. Saunders, RCN	15/10/51	— 28/10/51
CDR	R. M. Steele, DSC, RCN	29/10/51	— 16/1/53
LCDR	E. M. Chadwick, RCN	15/12/54	— 4/11/56
CDR	T. S. R. Peacock, RCN	5/11/56	— 31/7/57
LCDR	C. E. Coles, RCN	1/8/57	— 16/8/57
CDR	I. A. McPhee, RCN	17/8/57	— 6/1/59
CDR	R. A. Creery, RCN	7/1/59	— 9/9/61
CDR	S. M. King, RCN	10/9/61	— 8/11/62
CDR	V. J. Murphy, RCN	9/11/62	— 9/4/63
CDR	D. S . Bethune, RCN	10/4/63	— 6/2/64

Noranda

LT	W. R. Nunn, RCNR	15/5/42	— 10/1/43
LT	J. E. Francois, RCNR	11/1/43	— 1/9/44
LT	J. C. K. McNaught, RCNVR	2/9/44	— 17/10/44
LT	R. A. Wright, RCNVR	18/10/44	— 7/11/44
LT	G. E. Gilbride, RCNVR	8/11/44	— 10/7/45

Norsyd

LT	J. R. Biggs, RCNR	22/12/43	— 20/10/44
LT	W. P. Wickett, RCNVR	21/10/44	— 25/6/45

North Bay

LT	B. Hynes, RCNVR	25/10/43	— 29/6/44
LT	J. N. Finlayson, RCNVR	30/6/44	— 11/8/44
A/LCDR	B. Hynes, RCNVR	12/8/44	— 23/1/45
LT	J. W. Radford, RCNR	24/1/45	— 18/2/45
LCDR	A. C. Campbell, RCNVR	19/2/45	— 1/7/45

Oakville

LT	A. C. Jones, RCNR	18/11/41	— 11/5/42
LCDR	C. A. King, DSC, RCNR	12/5/42	— 21/4/43
LT	H. F. Farncomb, RCNVR	22/4/43	— 22/10/44
LT	M. A. Griffiths, RCNVR	23/10/44	— 20/7/45

Ojibwa

LCDR	S. G. Tomlinson, RCN	23/9/65	— 15/11/66
LCDR	J. Rodocanachi, RCN	15/11/66	— 25/8/67
LCDR	J. C. Wood, RCN	25/8/67	— 8/8/69
LCDR	J. E. D. Bell	8/8/69	— 12/7/71
LCDR	C. E. Falstrem	12/7/71	— 1/6/72
LCDR	R. C. Perks	1/6/72	— 14/1/75
LCDR	L. W. Barnes	14/1/75	— 9/3/76
LCDR	W. J. Sloan	9/3/76	— 1/8/77
LCDR	J. T. D. Jones	1/8/77	— 9/7/79
LCDR	K. F. McMillan	9/7/79	— 1/12/79
LCDR	J. M. Ewar	1/12/79	— 30/6/80
LCDR	N. P. Nicolson	30/6/80	—

Okanagan

LCDR	N. H. H. Frawley, RCN	22/6/68	— 18/8/69
LCDR	G. R. Meek	18/8/69	— 5/11/69
LCDR	L. G. Temple	5/11/69	— 22/12/69
LCDR	C. J. Crowe	22/12/69	— 21/12/70
LCDR	H. R. Waddell	21/12/70	— 15/10/71
LCDR	M. Tate	15/10/71	— 8/3/72
LCDR	P. E. Cairns	8/3/72	— 12/6/72
LCDR	C. E. Falstrem	12/6/72	— 7/5/73
LCDR	J. E. D. Bell	7/5/73	— 5/8/74
LCDR	R. C. Hunt	5/8/74	— 1/11/75
LCDR	K. G. Nesbit	1/11/75	— 21/7/77
LCDR	J. M. Ewar	21/7/77	— 6/7/78
LCDR	J. S. Ferguson	6/7/78	— 14/7/80
LCDR	F. Scherber	14/7/80	—

Onondaga

LCDR	G. R. Meek, RCN	22/6/67	— 26/8/68
LCDR	L. G. Temple, RCN	26/8/68	— 4/11/69
LCDR	G. R. Meek	4/11/69	— 23/12/69
LCDR	L. G. Temple	23/12/69	— 29/1/70
LCDR	G. R. Meek	29/1/70	— 31/7/70
LCDR	C. E. Falstrem	31/7/70	— 21/12/70
LCDR	C. J. Crowe	21/12/70	— 1/9/71
CDR	M. Tate	1/9/71	— 15/10/71
LCDR	H. R. Waddell	15/10/71	— 16/6/72
LCDR	P. W. Cairns	16/6/72	— 2/7/74
LCDR	R. C. Perks	2/7/74	— 14/7/75
LCDR	K. G. Nesbit	14/7/75	— 1/11/75
LCDR	R. C. Hunt	1/11/75	— 4/12/75
LCDR	W. J. Sloan	4/12/75	— 15/3/76
LCDR	R. C. Hunt	15/3/76	— 26/7/76
LCDR	W. G. D. Lund	26/7/76	— 19/7/78
LCDR	J. M. Ewan	19/7/78	— 3/12/79
LCDR	K. F. McMillan	3/12/79	— 17/3/81
LCDR	A. B. Dunlop	17/3/81	—

Ontario

CAPT	H. T. W. Grant, DSO, RCN	26/4/45	— 31/12/45
CDR	E. P. Tisdall, RCN	1/1/46	— 4/3/46
CAPT	F. G. Hart, RCN	5/3/46	— 14/6/46
CDR	J. V. Brock, DSC, RCN	15/6/46	— 29/6/47
CAPT	J. C. Hibbard, DSC & Bar, RCN	30/6/47	— 13/7/49
CAPT	H. F. Pullen, OBE, RCN	14/7/49	— 24/8/51
CAPT	E. P. Tisdall, RCN	25/8/51	— 3/3/53
CAPT	D. L. Raymond, RCN	4/3/53	— 14/9/54
CAPT	D. W. Groos, DSC, RCN	15/9/54	— 22/8/56
CAPT	R. P. Welland, DSC & Bar, RCN	23/8/56	— 21/8/57
CAPT	J. C. Littler, RCN	22/8/57	— 31/8/58
CDR	D. G. Padmore, RCN	1/9/58	— 15/10/58

Orangeville

A/LCDR	F. R. Pike, RCNVR	24/4/44	— 16/7/45
A/LCDR	G. A. Powell, RCNVR	17/7/45	— 16/10/45

Orillia

A/LCDR	W. E. S. Briggs, RCNR	25/11/40	— 4/9/42
LT	H. V. W. Groos, RCN	5/9/42	— 13/2/43
LCDR	R. Jackson, RCNR	14/2/43	— 16/4/43
A/LCDR	J. E. Mitchell, RCNVR	17/4/43	— 13/3/44
A/LCDR	J. W. Sharpe, RCNR	8/5/44	— 2/7/45

Orkney

LT	G. L. MacKay, RCNR	18/4/44	— 24/6/44
A/CDR	V. Browne, RCNVR	25/6/44	— 28/3/45
CDR	J. M. Rowland, DSO & Bar, RN	29/3/45	— 21/5/45
LT	N. J. Castonguay, RCNVR	22/5/45	— 2/9/45
LT	H. R. Beck, RCN	19/10/45	— 22/1/46

Oshawa

A/LCDR	J. C. Pratt RCNVR	6/7/44	— 27/5/45
A/LCDR	R. S. Williams, RCNVR	28/5/45	— 28/7/45
LT	J. Kincaid, RCNR	24/10/45	— 26/2/46
LCDR	G. H. Barrick, RCN	11/4/56	— 7/11/58

Ottawa

CAPT	V. G. Brodeur, RCN	15/6/38	— 1/10/38
CDR	C. R. H. Taylor, RCN	2/10/38	— 20/11/38
CAPT	G. C. Jones, RCN	21/11/38	— 1/4/40
CDR	E. R. Mainguy, RCN	2/4/40	— 20/7/41
A/LCDR	A. G. Boulton, RCNVR	21/7/41	— 18/8/41
A/CDR	H. F. Pullen, RCN	19/8/41	— 13/11/41
A/CDR	C. D. Donald, RCN	14/11/41	— 4/7/42
A/LCDR	C. A. Rutherford, RCN	5/7/42	— 13/9/42

Ottawa (2nd)

CDR	H. F. Pullen, RCN	20/3/43	— 8/6/43
CDR	K. F. Adams, RCN	9/6/43	— 6/7/43
CDR	H. F. Pullen, RCN	7/7/43	— 18/5/44
CDR	J. D. Prentice, DSO, RCN	19/5/44	— 9/9/44
LT	E. P. Earnshaw, RCN	10/9/44	— 6/10/44
LCDR	R. J. Herman, OBE, RCN	7/10/44	— 11/10/44
LT	N. Cogdon, RCN	12/10/44	— 4/2/45
A/LCDR	P. D. Budge, DSC, RCN	5/2/45	— 14/7/45
A/LCDR	G. H. Davidson, RCN	15/7/45	— 31/10/45

Ottawa (3rd)

CDR	C. R. Parker, DSC, RCN	10/11/56	— 7/7/58
CDR	W. H. Willson, DSC, RCN	7/7/58	— 28/4/59
CDR	I. B. Morrow, RCN	28/4/59	— 19/8/61
CDR	I. A. MacPherson, RCN	19/8/61	— 25/3/63
LCDR	T. C. Shuckburg, RCN	25/3/63	—
CDR	J. P. Côté, RCN	28/10/64	— 31/7/67
CDR	C. Cotaras, RCN	21/7/67	— 15/7/68
CDR	P. Simard, RCN	15/7/68	— 15/5/70
CDR	M. H. Tremblay	15/5/70	— 7/2/72
LCDR	N. Boivin	7/2/72	— 5/6/73
LCDR	R. L. Burnip	5/6/73	— 14/6/74
LCDR	T. C. Milne	14/6/74	— 30/8/74
CDR	W. J. Draper	30/8/74	— 6/1/77
CDR	L. C. A. Westropp	6/1/77	— 23/1/78
CDR	J. E. D. Bell	23/1/78	— 4/7/80
CDR	E. J. M. Young	4/7/80	—

Otter

LT	D. S. Mossman, RCNR	4/10/40	— 26/3/41

Outarde

LT	H. M. Kennedy, RCNR	4/12/41	— 25/2/42
LT	A. A. R. Dykes, RCNR	26/2/42	— 9/3/42
LT	H. M. Kennedy, RCNR	10/3/42	— 18/5/42
LT	R. Jackson, RCNVR	19/5/42	— 5/2/43
A/LCDR	J. A. Macdonnell, RCNR	6/2/43	— 23/2/44
LT	H. B. Tindale, RCNVR	24/2/44	— 9/3/44
LT	A. C. Jones, RCNR	10/3/44	— 23/8/44
LT	H. B. Tindale, RCNVR	24/8/44	— 24/8/45
LT	J. P. Kieran, RCNR	25/8/45	— 4/10/45

Outremont

A/CDR	H. Freeland, DSO, RCNR	27/11/43	— 11/8/44
LCDR	F. O. Gerity, RCNR	12/8/44	— 5/11/45
LCDR	J. M. Paul, RCN	2/9/55	— 7/5/56
LCDR	P. G. Chance, RCN	8/5/56	— 25/4/57
LCDR	M. O. Jones, RCN	26/4/57	— 8/10/58
LCDR	C. J. Benoit, DSC, RCN	9/10/58	— 12/4/60
LCDR	S. M. King, RCN	13/4/60	— 7/3/61
LCDR	J. A. Fulton, RCN	8/3/61	— 2/9/62
LCDR	J. R. H. Ley, RCN	3/9/62	— 20/6/64
LCDR	R. L. Donaldson RCN	21/6/64	— 7/6/65

Owen Sound

A/LCDR	J. M. Watson, RCNR	17/11/43	— 13/4/45
LT	F. H. Pinfold, RCNVR	14/4/45	— 19/7/45

Parry Sound

A/LCDR	W. J. Gilmore, RCNVR	30/8/44	— 10/7/45

Patrician

LT	G. C. Jones, RCN	1/11/20	— 2/9/22
LT	C. T. Beard, RCN	3/9/22	— 31/10/22
LT	J. E. W. Oland, RCN	1/11/22	— 30/9/24
LT	W. J. R. Beech, RCN	1/10/24	— 14/8/26
LCDR	R. I. Agnew, RCN	15/8/26	— 1/1/28

Patriot

LT	C.T. Beard, RCN	1/11/20	— 2/9/22
LT	G. C. Jones, RCN	3/9/22	— 23/8/23
LT	H. E. Reid, RCN	24/8/23	— 6/10/25
LT	C. R. H. Taylor, RCN	7/10/25	— 4/4/26
LCDR	C. R. H. Taylor, RCN	5/4/26	— 23/10/27

Penetang

A/LCDR	A. R. Hicks, RCNVR	19/10/44	— 22/8/45
LT	E. M. Lutes, RCNVR	23/8/45	— 10/11/45
CDR	B. P. Young, MBE, RCN	1/6/54	— 4/11/54
CDR	V. Browne, RCN	5/11/54	— 13/12/54
LCDR	J. M. Paul, RCN	14/12/54	— 2/9/55
LCDR	A. H. McDonald, RCN	5/1/56	— 25/1/56

Peterborough

LT	J. B. Raine, RCNR	1/6/44	— 19/7/45

Petrolia

LT	P. W. Spragge, RCNVR	29/6/44	— 25/6/45
LT	N. M. Simpson, RCNVR	26/6/45	— 7/8/45
LT	R. H. Ellis, RCNVR	8/8/45	— 11/9/45
LCDR	J. J. Hodgkinson, RCNR	12/9/45	— 8/3/46

Pictou

LCDR	J. L. Diver, RCNR	29/4/41	— 17/8/41
A/LCDR	R. B. Campbell, RCNR	18/8/41	— 4/9/41
LT	A. G. S. Griffin, RCNVR	5/9/41	— 21/8/42
LT	L. C. Audette, RCNVR	22/8/42	— 19/9/42
LT	A. G. S. Griffin, RCNVR	20/9/42	— 14/3/43
LT	P. T. Byers, RCNR	15/3/43	— 19/11/43
A/LCDR	G. K. Fox, RCNVR	20/11/43	— 1/10/44
LT	F. Cross, RCNR	2/10/44	— 12/7/45

Port Arthur

LT	E. T. Simmons, DSC, RCNVR	26/5/42	— 8/7/43

A/LCDR	K. T. Chisholm, RCNVR	9/7/43	— 11/7/45

Port Colborne

LCDR	C. J. Angus, RCNR	15/11/43	— 23/4/45
A/LCDR	M. F. Oliver, RCNR	24/4/45	— 7/11/45

Port Hope

LT	W. Turner, RCNR	30/7/42	— 1/12/42
LT	A. H. Rankin, RCNVR	2/12/42	— 8/4/43
LT	R. K. Lester, RCNVR	9/4/43	— 17/3/44
LT	R. M. Montague, RCNVR	18/3/44	— 17/7/45

Portage

LT	B. P. Young, RCNR	22/10/43	— 19/12/43
A/LCDR	G. M. Kaizer, RCNR	20/12/43	— 4/6/45
LT	J. G. Macdonell, RCNVR	5/6/45	— 13/7/45
LCDR	G. M. Kaizer, RCNR	14/7/45	— 2/8/45
LT	W. E. Williams, RCNR	23/10/45	— 2/11/45
LT	W. R. Aylwin, RCNVR	3/11/45	— 5/2/46
A/LT	W. E. Hughson, RCNR	6/2/46	— 8/4/46
LT	C. J. Benoit, DSC, RCN	9/4/46	— 2/6/46
LT	M. H. Cooke, RCN	3/6/46	— 31/7/46
LT	J. B. Bugden, RCN	12/4/47	— 30/9/47
LCDR	A. H. Rankin, OBE, RCN	24/3/48	— 18/8/48
LCDR	D. M. MacDonald, RCN	12/4/49	— 27/10/49
LT	W. W. MacColl, RCN	28/10/49	— 16/2/50
LT	E. P. Earnshaw, RCN	17/2/50	— 23/6/51
LT	J. H. MacLean, RCN	24/6/51	— 15/3/53
LCDR	A. B. Torrie, RCN	16/3/53	— 25/11/54
LCDR	H. E. T. Lawrence, DSC, RCN	23/4/55	— 25/10/56
LCDR	K. R. Crombie, RCN	26/10/56	— 5/5/57
LCDR	J. A. Farquhar, RCN	6/5/57	— 24/9/57
LCDR	C. W. Fleming, RCN	1/4/58	— 26/9/58

Poundmaker

LCDR	H. S. Maxwell, RCNVR	17/9/44	— 14/4/45
LCDR	J. T. Band, RCNVR	15/4/45	— 19/4/45
LCDR	W. P. Moffat, RCNVR	20/4/45	— 30/5/45
A/LCDR	A. E. Gough, RCNR	31/5/45	— 24/8/45
LCDR	W. P. Moffat, RCNVR	25/8/45	— 25/11/45

Prescott

LT	H. A. Russell, RCNR	26/6/41	— 30/5/42
LT	G. H. Davidson, RCN	31/5/42	— 1/7/42
LT	H. A. Russell, RCNR	2/7/42	— 11/9/42
LCDR	W. McIsaac, RCNVR	12/9/42	— 28/12/44
LT	G. J. Mathewson, RCNVR	29/12/44	— 20/7/45

Preserver

CAPT	B. L. Johnson, DSO, RCNR	11/7/42	— 16/12/43
CDR	G. Borrie, RCNR	17/12/43	— 17/4/45
LCDR	H. C. Walmesley, RCNR	18/4/45	— 18/10/45

Preserver (2nd)

CAPT	M. W. Mayo	30/7/70	— 5/9/72
CAPT	P. J. Traves	5/9/72	— 4/7/74
CAPT	M. Tremblay	4/7/74	— 2/8/75
CAPT	H. W. Vondette	2/8/75	— 6/7/77
CAPT	T. S. Murphy	6/7/77	— 21/7/78
CAPT	J. M. Cumming	21/7/78	— 13/12/79
CDR	T. Heath	14/12/79	— 31/7/80
CAPT	L. J. Cavan	31/7/80	— 3/8/81
CAPT	R. C. Hunt	3/8/81	—

Prestonian

LCDR	I. Angus, RCNVR	13/9/44	— 1/4/45
LCDR	G. N. Downey, RCNR	2/4/45	— 18/7/45
LT	E. M. More, RCNR	19/7/45	— 9/11/45
LCDR	W. C. Spicer, RCN	22/8/53	— 9/6/55
CDR	W. M. Kidd, RCN	10/6/55	— 24/4/56

Prince David

CDR	W. B. Armit, RCNR	28/12/40	— 24/3/41
CDR	K. F. Adams, RCN	25/3/41	— 1/12/41
CAPT	V. S. Godfrey, RCN	2/12/41	— 18/3/42
A/LCDR	T. D. Kelly, RCNR	19/3/42	— 16/4/42
CAPT	V. S. Godfrey, RCN	17/4/42	— 17/4/43
CDR	T. D. Kelly, RCNR	18/4/43	— 1/5/43
CDR	T. D. Kelly, RCNR	23/5/43	— 11/6/45

Prince Henry

CAPT	R. I Agnew, OBE, RCN	4/12/40	— 19/12/41
CAPT	J. C. I. Edwards, RCN	20/12/41	— 31/12/42
CAPT	F. L. Houghton, RCN	1/1/43	— 18/3/43
LCDR	E. W. Finch-Noyes, RCN	19/3/43	— 22/3/43
LCDR	T. K. Young, RCNR	23/3/43	— 23/5/43
CDR	T. D. Kelly, RCNR	24/5/43	— 29/11/43
CDR	K. F. Adams, RCN	30/11/43	— 11/12/43
CAPT	V. S. Godfrey, RCN	12/12/43	— 15/4/45

Prince Robert

CDR	C. T. Beard, RCN	31/7/40	— 7/10/40
CDR	F. G. Hart, RCN	8/10/40	— 21/6/42
A/CAPT	F. L. Houghton, RCN	22/6/42	— 31/12/42
CDR	O. C. S. Robertson, RCN	1/1/43	— 23/3/43
LCDR	E. W. Finch-Noyes, RCN	24/3/43	— 5/6/43
CAPT	A. M. Hope, RCN	6/6/43	— 7/12/44
CAPT	W. B. Creery, RCN	8/12/44	— 19/12/44
CAPT	W. B. Creery, RCN	4/6/45	— 10/12/45

Prince Rupert

LCDR	R. W. Draney, DSC, RCNR	30/8/43	— 31/7/44
A/CDR	C. A. King, RCNR	1/8/44	— 23/10/44
LCDR	R. W. Draney, DSC, RCNR	24/10/44	— 27/8/45
LCDR	J. C. L. Annesley, RCN	24/9/45	— 15/1/46

Protecteur

CAPT	D. R. Hinton	30/8/69	— 13/7/71
CAPT	J. P. Côté	13/7/71	— 24/7/72
CAPT	D. N. Mainguy	24/7/72	— 31/5/74
CAPT	A. M. Brookbank	31/5/74	— 12/2/76
CAPT	J. C. Wood	12/2/76	— 28/7/77
CAPT	L. A. Dzioba	29/7/77	— 4/8/80
CAPT	R. G. Guy	4/8/80	—

Provider

CDR	J. A. Heenan, OBE, RCNR	1/12/42	— 4/5/43
LCDR	W. H. Koughan, RCNR	5/5/43	— 3/7/43
CDR	E. G. Skinner, DSC, RCNR	4/7/43	— 17/11/43
A/CDR	T. Gilmour, RCNR	18/11/43	— 14/2/45
CAPT	L. J. M. Gauvreau, RCN	15/2/45	— 19/11/45
LCDR	D. G. King, RCN	20/11/45	— 22/3/46

Provider (2nd)

CAPT	T. C. Pullen, RCN	28/9/63	— 8/12/64
CAPT	K. H. Boggild, RCN	8/12/64	— 24/8/66
CAPT	D. W. Knox, RCN	24/8/66	— 16/8/67
CAPT	W. J. H. Stuart, RCN	16/8/67	— 5/9/69
CAPT	J. A. Fulton	5/9/69	— 2/8/72
CAPT	F. W. Crickard	2/8/72	— 30/9/74
CAPT	C. H. P. Shaw	30/9/74	— 5/8/76
CAPT	K. M. Young	5/8/76	— 21/7/78
CAPT	R. H. Kirby	21/7/78	— 20/6/80
CAPT	R. L. Donaldson	20/6/80	—

Puncher

CAPT	R. E. S. Bidwell, RCN	10/4/44	— 16/1/46

Qu'appelle

CDR	D. C. Wallace, DSC, RCNR	8/2/44	— 19/4/44
CDR	A. M. McKillop, RN	20/4/44	— 11/7/44
CDR	J. D. Birch, RNR	12/7/44	— 9/9/44
CDR	J. D. Prentice, DSO, RCN	10/9/44	— 4/12/44
CDR	E. L. Armstrong, RCN	5/12/44	— 6/1/45
CDR	E. G. Skinner, DSC, RCN	7/1/45	— 2/4/45
LCDR	I. Angus, RCNVR	3/4/45	— 21/6/45
A/LCDR	W. Davenport, RCNR	22/6/45	— 9/10/45
LT	J. H. C. Bovey, RCN	10/10/45	— 25/11/45
A/LCDR	W. E. Harrison, DSC, RCNR	26/11/45	— 22/3/46
A/LCDR	J. C. L. Annesley, RCN	23/3/46	— 7/4/46
LT	D. Adamson, RCNR	8/4/46	— 27/5/46

Qu'appelle (2nd)

CDR	A. G. Kilpatrick, RCN	14/9/63	— 28/8/65
CDR	H. D. Joy, RCN	28/8/65	— 16/1/67
CDR	R. Ratcliffe, RCN	16/1/67	— 16/12/68
CDR	J. Allan	16/12/68	— 28/7/70
CDR	J. Rodocanachi	28/7/70	— 8/5/72
CDR	R. D. C. Sweeny	8/5/72	— 22/1/73
CDR	J. L. Creech	22/1/73	— 2/7/73
CDR	J. D. Sine	2/7/73	— 14/2/74
CDR	R. F. Choat	14/2/74	— 19/9/75
CDR	K. M. Young	19/9/75	— 4/8/76
CDR	R. H. Kirby	4/8/76	— 25/1/77
CDR	J. M. Chouinard	25/1/77	— 4/10/78
CDR	J. J. Drent	4/10/78	— 28/7/80
CDR	R. J. Luke	28/7/80	—

Quatsino

LT	S. Douglas, RCNR	3/11/41	— 14/12/41
A/LCDR	T. MacDuff, RCN	15/12/41	— 27/5/42
LT	A. E. Gough, RCNR	28/5/42	— 2/4/43
LT	A. H. Gosse, RCNR	3/4/43	— 29/9/43
LT	H. H. Rankin, RCNR	30/9/43	— 22/10/43
LT	A. H. Gosse, RCNR	23/10/43	— 2/1/45
A/LCDR	B. C. Cook, RCNVR	3/1/45	— 26/11/45

Quesnel

LT	J. A. Gow, RCNR	23/5/41	— 4/3/42
LT	A. E. Gough, RCNR	5/3/42	— 3/4/42
LT	J. A. Gow, RCNR	4/4/42	— 16/11/42
LT	M. Smith, RCNR	17/11/42	— 11/4/43
LT	J. M. Laing, RCNR	12/4/43	— 3/7/45

Quinte

LT	C. A. Nicol, RCNR	30/8/41	— 17/1/43
LT	I. B. B. Morrow, RCN	10/11/44	— 26/11/44
SKPR/LT	C. C. Clattenburg, RCNR	27/11/44	— 14/3/45
LT	D. C. MacPherson, RCNVR		— 19/7/45
LT	R. B. Taylor, RCNVR	20/7/45	— 3/8/45
LT	L. McQuarrie, RCNR	7/3/46	— 25/10/46

Quinte (2nd)

LCDR	D. P. Brownlow, RCN	15/10/54	— 23/6/57
LCDR	R. P. Mylrea, RCN	24/6/57	— 2/9/59
LCDR	R. J. Paul, RCN	3/9/59	— 2/8/61
LCDR	G. G. Armstrong, RCN	3/8/61	— 30/7/63
LCDR	R. L. Donaldson, RCN	31/7/63	— 26/2/64

Raccoon

LCDR	J. L. Diver, RCNR	17/5/40	— 17/10/40
LT	F. Roberts, RCNR	18/10/40	— 16/4/41
LT	N. G. Bennett, RCNR	17/4/41	— 22/7/41
LT	D. W. Main, RCNR	23/7/41	— 16/11/41
LT	A. H. Cassivi, RCNR	17/11/41	— 4/12/41
LCDR	J. N. Smith, RCNR	5/12/41	— 7/9/42

Rainbow

CDR	J. D. D. Stewart, RN	4/8/10	— 23/6/11
CDR	W. Hose, RN	24/6/11	— 30/4/17
CDR	H. E. Holme, RCN	1/5/17	— 8/5/17
LCDR	J. H. Knight, RCN	1/7/17	— 21/8/17
CDR	J. T. Shenton, RCN	22/8/17	— 12/5/18
LT	Y. Birley, RCN	13/5/18	— 14/10/19
CAPT	E. H. Martin, CMG, RCN	15/10/19	— 1/6/20

Rainbow (2nd)

LCDR	L. C. Falstrem, RCN	2/12/68	—

Red Deer

LT	A. Moorhouse, RCNR	24/11/41	— 2/2/43
LT	J. A. Mitchell, RCNR	3/2/43	—
LT	D. B. D. Ross, RCNVR	6/6/44	— 2/7/45
SKPR/LT	R. A. Doucette, RCNR	1/10/45	— 30/10/45

Regina

LCDR	R. F. Harris, RCNR	22/1/42	— 23/2/42
LT	R. S. Kelly, RCNR	24/2/42	— 20/10/42
LCDR	H. Freeland, DSO, RCNR	21/10/42	— 3/9/43
LT	J. W. Radford, RCNR	4/9/43	— 8/8/44

Reindeer

LCDR	E. G. Skinner, RCNR	25/7/40	— 17/1/41
LCDR	F. A. Price, RCNVR	18/1/41	— 16/5/41
LT	L. G. Cumming, RCNVR	17/5/41	— 8/7/41
LCDR	F. A. Price, RCNVR	9/7/41	— 31/7/41
LT	L. G. Cumming, RCNVR	1/8/41	— 20/4/42
LT	W. Evans, RCNVR	21/4/42	— 30/4/42
LT	F. J. G. Johnson, RCNVR	1/5/42	— 23/11/42
LT	D. M. Coolican, RCNVR	24/11/42	— 8/2/43
LT	R. G. James, RCNVR	9/2/43	— 19/5/44
LT	J. H. Ewart, RCNVR	20/5/44	— 7/10/44
LT	W. C. Hawkins, RCNVR	8/10/44	— 1/3/45
LT	R. C. Hayden, RCNVR	2/3/45	— 29/4/45
LT	W. C. Hawkins, RCNVR	30/4/45	— 20/7/45

Renard

LCDR	N. V. Clark, RCNR	27/5/40	—
LCDR	D. G. Jeffrey, RCNR	2/10/40	—
Mate	J. H. Maxner, RCNR	28/4/42	—
Mate	H. A. Sowerbutts, RCNR	9/9/42	—

Resolute

LCDR	J. L. Panabaker, RCN	16/9/54	— 14/9/55
LCDR	N. D. Langham, RCN	15/9/55	— 5/8/57
CDR	K. H. Boggild, RCN	6/8/57	— 13/5/58
CDR	A. C. Campbell, RCN	14/5/58	—
CDR	H. J. Hunter, RCN		— 22/3/61
LT	G. W. Garrad, RCN	23/3/61	— 2/1/63
LCDR	M. F. McIntosh, RCN	3/1/63	— 14/2/64

Restigouche

CDR	W. B. L. Holms, RCN	15/6/38	— 25/12/39
CDR	H. N. Lay, RCN	26/12/39	— 23/6/41
LCDR	D. W. Piers, RCN	24/6/41	— 5/6/43
LCDR	D. W. Groos, RCN	6/6/43	— 3/12/44
LCDR	P. E. Haddon, RCN	4/12/44	— 15/4/45
LCDR	R. J. Herman, OBE, RCNR	16/4/45	— 6/10/45

Restigouche (2nd)

CDR	J. W. McDowall, RCN	7/6/58	— 4/8/60
CDR	W. W. MacColl, RCN	4/8/60	— 8/8/62
CDR	B. C. Thillaye, RCN	8/8/62	— 19/5/65
CDR	H. W. Vondette, RCN	19/5/65	— 10/8/66
CDR	R. A. Evans, RCN	10/8/66	— 3/1/68
CDR	P. L. McCulloch, RCN	3/1/68	— 3/8/70
CDR	R. H. Kirby	12/5/72	— 7/9/72
LCDR	R. C. Burnip	7/9/72	— 2/4/73
CDR	R. J. Deluca	2/4/73	— 15/7/75
CDR	C. J. Crowe	15/7/75	— 27/1/77
CDR	R. G. Balfour	27/1/77	— 27/3/77
CDR	C. J. Crowe	27/3/77	— 29/4/77
CDR	H. T. Porter	29/4/77	— 29/7/78
CDR	J. R. Anderson	29/7/78	— 29/9/80
CDR	D. A. Henderson	29/9/80	—

Revelstoke

SKPR/LT	G. Billard, RCNR	4/7/44	— 14/9/44
SKPR/LT	J. E. Moore, RCNR	15/9/44	— 19/2/45
SKPR/LT	J. Craig, RCNR	20/2/45	— 24/4/45
LT	A. B. Plummer, RCNVR	25/4/45	— 15/7/45
SKPR/LT	J. Craig, RCNR	16/7/45	— 6/8/45
LT	A. B. Plummer, RCNVR	7/8/45	— 2/9/45
LCDR	C. A. Binmore, RCN	17/6/52	—
LCDR	C. A. Binmore, RCN	11/6/53	—

Ribble

LCDR	A. B. Taylor, RCNR	24/7/44	— 20/11/44
A/LCDR	A. A. R. Dykes, RCNR	21/11/44	— 11/6/45

Rimouski

LT	J. W. Bonner, RCNVR	27/4/41	— 11/11/41
A/LCDR	A. G. Boulton, RCNVR	12/11/41	— 1/12/42
LT	R. J. Pickford, RCNVR	2/12/42	— 9/9/44
LT	C. D. Chivers, RCNVR	10/9/44	— 17/12/44
LCDR	D. M. MacDonald, RCNVR	18/12/44	— 12/6/45
LT	T. S. Cook, RCNVR	13/6/45	— 24/7/45

Rivière du Loup

LT	R. N. Smillie, RCNVR	21/11/43	— 20/6/44
LT	R. N. Smillie, RCNVR	19/7/44	— 8/1/45
LCDR	F. R. K. Naftel, RCNVR	9/1/45	— 25/1/45
LT	R. D. Weldon, RCNVR	26/1/45	— 2/7/45

Rockcliffe

LT	J. E. Heward, RCNVR	30/9/44	— 28/7/45
A/LCDR	A. E. Gough, RCNR	24/10/45	— 14/1/46
LCDR	J. W. Golby, DSC, RCNR	3/3/47	— 30/3/47
CDR	H. Kingsley, RCN	31/3/47	— 15/10/48
LCDR	J. B. Bugden, RCN	16/10/48	— 3/12/48
CDR	H. Kingsley, RCN	4/12/48	— 25/4/49
LCDR	J. B. Bugden, RCN	26/4/49	— 10/7/49
LCDR	H. R. Beck, RCN	11/7/49	— 6/9/49
A/CAPT	H. Kingsley, RCN	7/9/49	— 21/4/50
CDR	J. S. Davis, RCN	22/4/50	— 15/8/50

Rossland

SKPR/LT	E. E. Kinney, RCNR	15/7/44	— 26/1/45
SKPR/LT	E. E. Kinney, RCNR	1/3/45	— 1/11/45

Rosthern

LT	W. Russell, RCNR	17/6/41	— 20/11/41
CDR	P. B. Cross, RCNVR	21/11/41	— 24/11/42
LCDR	R. J. G. Johnson, RCNVR	25/11/42	— 17/4/44
LT	S. P. R. Annett, RCNVR	18/4/44	— 3/11/44
A/LCDR	R. F. Wilson, RCNVR	4/11/44	— 6/4/45
LT	D. R. Smythies, RCNVR	7/4/45	— 19/7/45

Royalmount

LCDR	J. S. Davis, RCNVR	25/8/44	— 10/5/45
LT	J. H. Dunne, RCNVR	11/5/45	— 8/8/45
LCDR	J. S. Davis, RCNVR	9/8/45	— 17/11/45

Runnymede

A/LCDR	R. C. Chenoweth, RCNVR	14/6/44	— 22/1/45
LT	P. S. Milsom, MBE, RCNVR	23/1/45	— 22/3/45
LCDR	R. C. Chenoweth, RCNVR	23/3/45	— 8/6/45
CDR	C. A. King, DSO, DSC & Bar, RCNVR	9/6/45	— 9/8/45

Sackville

LT	W. R. Kirkland, RCNR	30/12/41	— 5/4/42
LT	A. H. Easton, DSC, RCNR	6/4/43	— 9/4/43
A/LCDR	A. H. Rankin, RCNVR	10/4/43	— 17/5/44
LT	A. R. Hicks, RCNVR	18/5/44	— 17/9/44
LT	C. C. Love, RCNVR	18/9/44	— 5/11/44
LT	J. A. McKenna, RCNVR	6/11/44	— 8/4/46

Saguenay

CDR	P. W. Nelles, RCN	22/5/31	— 6/6/32
CDR	L. W. Murray, RCN	7/6/32	— 22/5/34
CDR	R. I. Agnew, RCN	23/5/34	— 5/5/36
CDR	W. J. R. Beech, RCN	6/5/36	— 29/6/38
LCDR	F. L. Houghton, RCN	30/6/38	— 7/7/39
LCDR	G. R. Miles, RCN	8/7/39	— 21/4/41
LT	P. E. Haddon, RCN	22/4/41	— 7/4/42
A/CDR	D. C. Wallace, RCNR	8/4/42	— 14/1/43
LT	J. W. McDowall, RCN	15/1/43	— 11/3/43
LT	J. H. Ewart, RCNVR	24/8/43	— 17/5/44
LT	W. C. Hawkins, RCNVR	18/5/44	— 6/10/44
A/LT	W. E. Hughson, RCNVR	7/10/44	— 15/4/45
LT	K. P. Blanche, RCNVR	16/4/45	— 30/7/45

Saguenay (2nd)

CDR	G. H. Hayes, DSC, RCN	15/12/56	— 13/3/58
CDR	J. H. G. Bovey, DSC, RCN	31/3/58	— 2/3/59
CDR	D. S . Boyle, RCN	2/3/59	— 14/10/59
CDR	E. M. Chadwick, RCN	14/10/59	— 23/8/61
CDR	H. R. Tilley, RCN	23/8/61	— 22/8/63
CDR	H. H. Plant, RCN	14/5/65	— 13/7/66
CDR	D. A. Avery, RCN	13/7/66	— 23/8/67
LCDR	L. A. Dzioba, RCN	23/8/67	— 15/12/67
CAPT	D. H. P. Ryan, RCN	15/12/67	— 23/1/69
CDR	R. Yanow	23/1/69	— 13/8/70
LCDR	R. Hardy	13/8/70	— 1/11/70
CDR	K. M. Young	1/11/70	—
CDR	D. MacNeil	18/7/72	— 17/6/74
CDR	J. Harwood	17/6/74	— 10/1/75
CDR	J. Luke	10/1/75	— 18/1/77
CDR	C. Milne	18/1/77	— 4/8/78
CDR	J. Goode	4/8/78	— 18/4/80
CDR	A. G. Schwartz	18/4/80	—

St. Boniface

LCDR	J. J. Hodgkinson, RCNR	10/9/43	— 12/5/44
A/LCDR	J. D. Frewer, RCNVR	13/5/44	— 14/4/45
LCDR	J. M. Watson, RCNR	15/4/45	— 25/6/45
LT	C. W. King, RCNVR	26/6/45	— 19/8/45
LCDR	R. N. Smillie, RCNVR	20/8/45	— 29/1/46
LT	H. R. Tilley, RCN	21/3/46	— 26/4/46
SKPR/LT	P. Perrault, RCNR	27/4/46	— 25/9/46

St. Catharines

LCDR	H. C. R. Davis, RCNR	31/7/43	— 14/3/44
LCDR	A. F. Pickard, OBE, RCNR	15/3/44	— 13/12/44
LCDR	J. P. Fraser, RCNR	14/12/44	— 24/5/45
LT	A. B. Swain, RCNVR	25/5/45	— 3/8/45
LCDR	L. C. Audette, RCNVR	4/8/45	— 18/11/45

St. Clair

LCDR	D. C. Wallace, RCNR	24/9/40	— 5/4/42
LCDR	G. O. Baugh, OBE, RCNR	6/4/42	— 11/1/44
LT	J. E. Burnett, RCNVR	8/3/44	— 23/8/44

St. Croix

LT	M. A. Medland, RCN	24/9/40	— 10/10/40
CDR	H. Kingsley, RCN	11/10/40	— 10/12/41
LCDR	A. H. Dobson, DSC, RCNR	6/1/42	— 20/9/43

St. Croix (2nd)

CDR	K. H. Boggild, RCN	4/10/58	— 28/5/59
CDR	W. S. T. McCully, RCN	28/5/59	— 14/3/61
CDR	T. E. Connors, RCN	14/3/61	— 22/7/62
CDR	D. C. Rutherford, RCN	22/7/62	— 31/5/63
CDR	D. M. Maclennan, RCN	31/5/53	— 4/5/64
CDR	J. S. Hertzberg, RCN	4/5/64	— 21/9/66
CDR	J. I. Donald, RCN	21/9/66	— 15/7/68
CDR	J. M. Cumming, RCN	15/7/68	— 31/8/71
LCDR	R. C. Donaldson	31/8/71	— 2/7/73
CDR	T. S. Murphy	2/7/73	— /9/74
CDR	P. E. Simard	/9/74	— 15/11/74

St. Eloi

CH/SKPR	N. H. Pentz, RCNR	15/5/41	—
CH/SKPR	P. E. Blouin, RCNR	1/5/42	—
SKPR	W. I. V. Power, RCNR	31/5/42	—

St. Francis

A/CDR	H. F. Pullen, RCN	24/9/40	— 25/8/41
LT	C. A. Rutherford, RCN	26/8/41	— 3/7/42
LCDR	F. C. Smith, RCNR	4/7/42	— 17/2/43
A/LCDR	H. V. W. Groos, RCN	18/2/43	— 15/11/43
LT	G. L. MacKay, RCNR	16/11/43	— 27/12/43
A/LCDR	J. F. Watson, RCNR	17/1/44	— 11/10/44
SKPR/LT	C. C. Clattenburg, RCNR	12/10/44	— 12/11/44
A/LCDR	J. F. Watson, RCNR	13/11/44	— 11/6/45

Saint John

A/LCDR	R. M. Mosher, RCNR	13/12/43	— 20/2/44
A/LCDR	W. R. Stacey, RCNR	21/2/44	— 18/2/45
LT	C. G. McIntosh, RCNR	19/2/45	— 1/4/45
LCDR	W. R. Stacey, RCNR	2/4/45	— 19/6/45

St. Joseph

LT	A. B. Plummer, RCNVR	24/5/44	— 23/4/45
SKPR/LT	J. Craig, RCNR	24/4/45	— 18/6/45

St. Lambert

LT	R. C. Hayden, RCNVR	27/5/44	— 27/10/44
LT	W. D. H. Gardiner, RCNVR	28/10/44	— 23/6/45
A/LCDR	A. P. Duke, RCNVR	24/6/45	— 20/7/45

St. Laurent

LCDR	R. E. Bidwell, RCN	17/2/37	— 7/12/37
LCDR	A. M. Hope, RCN	8/12/37	— 5/10/39
LCDR	H. G. DeWolf, RCN	6/10/39	— 13/7/40
LT	H. S. Rayner, DSC, RCN	14/7/40	— 18/2/42
LCDR	E. L. Armstrong, RCN	19/2/42	— 13/11/42
LCDR	G. S. Windeyer, RCN	14/11/42	— 19/1/43
CDR	H. F. Pullen, RCN	20/1/43	— 12/3/43
LCDR	G. H. Stephen, DSC, RCNR	13/3/43	— 14/4/44
LCDR	A. G. Boulton, RCNVR	15/4/44	— 7/11/44
LT	M. G. Stirling, RCN	8/11/44	— 7/4/45
LCDR	G. H. Stephen, DSC, OBE, RCNR	8/4/45	— 10/10/45

St. Laurent (2nd)

CDR	R. W. Timbrell, DSC, RCN	29/10/55	— 23/1/57
CAPT	A. G. Boulton, DSC, RCN	23/1/57	— 15/3/58
CAPT	H. L. Quinn, DSC, RCN	15/3/58	— 9/1/59
LCDR	E. Petley-Jones, RCN	9/1/59	— 2/3/59
CDR	M. H. E. Page, RCN	2/3/59	— 29/6/60
CDR	J. B. Fotheringham, RCN	29/6/60	— 10/62
CDR	D. D. Lee, RCN	4/10/63	— 15/9/65
CDR	W. J. Walton, RCN	15/9/65	— 2/2/67
LCDR	B. Hayes, RCN	2/2/67	— 25/8/67
CDR	M. Barrow, RCN	25/8/67	— 11/8/69
CDR	S. W. Riddell	11/8/69	— 7/71
CDR	G. G. Freill	7/71	— 11/72
LCDR	R. L. Burnip	11/72	— 14/6/74

St. Pierre

LCDR	N. V. Clark, OBE, RCNR	22/8/44	— 13/11/44
LCDR	J. A. Tullis, RCNR	14/11/44	— 24/7/45
A/LCDR	A. E. Giffin, RCNVR	25/7/45	— 6/11/45
SKPR/LT	E. L. Ritchie, RCNR	7/11/45	— 22/11/45

St. Stephen

LCDR	C. Peterson, RCNR	28/7/44	— 22/1/45
A/LCDR	R. C. Chenoweth, RCNVR	23/1/45	— 22/3/45
LCDR	N. S. C. Dickinson, RCNVR	23/3/45	— 8/8/45
LT	G. F. Crosby, RCNVR	9/8/45	— 5/9/45
LCDR	A. F. Pickard, OBE, RCNR	17/9/45	— 4/12/45
LT	W. G. Findlay, RCNR	5/12/45	— 30/1/46
LT	E. M. Chadwick, RCN	27/9/47	— 25/8/49
LCDR	G. H. Hayes, DSC, RCN	26/8/49	— 31/8/50

Ste. Thérèse

A/CDR	J. E. Mitchell, RCNVR	28/5/44	— 5/7/45
A/LCDR	A. C. Campbell, RCNVR	6/7/45	— 4/9/45
LT	J. Jackson, RCNVR	5/9/45	— 26/9/45
LT	G. A. MacPherson, RCNVR	27/9/45	— 22/11/45
LCDR	W. F. Potter, RCN	22/1/55	— 3/6/56
LCDR	P. J. Pratley, RCN	4/6/56	— 12/1/58
LCDR	A. R. Pickels, RCN	13/1/58	— 25/4/58
LCDR	J. B. C. Carling, RCN	24/1/59	— 17/8/60
LCDR	A. G. Murray, RCN	18/8/60	— 16/8/62
LCDR	M. A. Martin, RCN	17/8/62	— 2/5/63
LCDR	P. G. May RCN	3/5/63	—
LCDR	K. M. Young, RCN	30/10/64	— 14/9/65
LCDR	P. E. Simard, RCN	15/9/65	— 30/1/67

St. Thomas

LCDR	L. P. Denny, RCNR	4/5/44	— 26/1/45
A/LCDR	B. Hynes, RCNVR	27/1/45	— 20/6/45
LT	J. B. K. Stewart, RCNVR	21/6/45	— 22/11/45

Sans Peur

A/LCDR	W. C. Halliday, RCNR	23/10/39	— 3/6/42
LCDR	T. MacDuff, RCN	4/6/42	— 14/5/43
LCDR	W. Redford, RCNVR	15/5/43	— 9/1/44
LCDR	H. S. MacFarlane, RCNR	10/1/44	— 4/11/45
SKPR/LT	P. Perrault, RCNR	26/2/46	—
LT	D. L. MacKnight, RCN	22/7/46	—

Sarnia

LT	C. A. Mott, RCNR	13/8/42	— 10/2/43
LT	D. I. McGill, RCNVR	11/2/43	— 17/7/43
LT	R. C. Chenoweth, RCNVR	18/7/43	— 12/3/44
LT	H. A. Plow, RCNVR	13/3/44	— 24/6/44
LT	R. D. Hurst, RCNVR	25/6/44	— 9/10/44
LT	R. P. J. Douty, RCNVR	10/10/44	— 21/9/45
LT	D. M. Mossop, RCNVR	22/9/45	— 28/10/45

Saskatchewan

LCDR	G. H. Williams, RN	31/5/43	— 6/7/43
CDR	R. C. Medley, DSO, RN	7/7/43	— 22/3/44
LCDR	E. W. Finch-Noyes, RCN	23/3/44	— 6/4/44
LCDR	A. H. Easton, DSC, RCNR	7/4/44	— 8/8/44
A/LCDR	T. C. Pullen, RCN	25/8/44	— 21/8/45
A/LCDR	F. C. Frewer, RCN	22/8/45	— 28/1/46

Saskatchewan (2nd)

CDR	M. W. Mayo, RCN	16/2/63	— 18/12/64
CDR	M. A. Turner, RCN	18/12/64	— 7/3/66
CDR	P. J. Traves, RCN	7/3/66	— 15/7/67
CDR	N. S. Jackson, RCN	15/7/67	— 23/9/68
CDR	H. Rusk, RCN	23/9/68	— 15/1/70
CDR	N. St. C. Norton	15/1/70	— 9/3/71
LCDR	A. Bajkov	9/3/71	— 2/4/71
CDR	R. F. Gladman	2/4/71	— 6/7/72
CDR	T. S. Hayward	6/7/72	— 9/4/73
LCDR	H. L. Davies	9/4/73	— 31/7/73
CDR	J. Harwood	31/7/73	— 24/5/74
CDR	J. G. Comeau	24/5/74	— 1/9/76
CDR	F. Hope	1/9/76	— 3/8/78
CDR	H. T. Porter	3/8/78	— 3/7/80
CDR	J. D. Sine	3/7/80	—

Saskatoon

LT	J. S. Scott, RCNR	9/6/41	— 15/1/42
LT	J. P. Fraser, RCNR	16/1/42	— 4/2/42
LCDR	C. A. King, DSC, RCNR	5/2/42	— 14/2/42
LT	J. S. Scott, RCNR	15/4/42	— 20/4/42
LT	H. G. Dupont, RCNR	21/4/42	— 11/5/42
LT	J. S. Scott, RCNR	12/5/42	— 9/7/43
LCDR	T. MacDuff, RCNR	10/7/43	— 14/1/44
A/LCDR	R. S. Williams, RCNVR	15/3/44	— 29/5/45
LT	H. R. Knight, RCNR	30/5/45	— 25/6/45

Sault Ste. Marie

LCDR	R. Jackson, RCNVR	24/6/43	— 11/2/44
A/LCDR	A. Moorhouse, RCNR	12/2/44	— 5/7/45
LT	D. Davis, RCNVR	6/7/45	— 28/7/45
LT	A. D. Ritchie, RCNVR	7/9/45	— 12/1/46
LT	A. O. Gray, RCN	7/5/49	— 4/12/49
LT	A. R. Heater, RCNR	5/12/49	— 21/10/51
LCDR	B. T. R. Russell, RCN	22/10/51	— 11/6/53
LT	D. E. Rigg, RCN	12/6/53	— 9/8/53
LT	H. J. Andrews, RCN	10/8/53	— 11/10/54
LCDR	E. T. Coggins, RCN	12/10/54	— 6/12/54
LT	T. Elworthy, RCN	7/12/54	— 10/1/55
LCDR	K. A. Stone, RCN	8/11/55	— 25/10/56
LCDR	R. M. Greene, RCN	26/10/56	— 24/9/57
LCDR	W. V. A. Lesslie, RCN	1/4/58	— 1/10/58

Sea Cliff

LCDR	J. E. Harrington, RCNVR	26/9/44	— 14/6/45

Shawinigan

A/LCDR	C. P. Balfry, RCNR	19/9/41	— 4/1/44
LT	R. S. Williams, RCNVR	5/1/44	— 14/3/44
LT	W. E. Callan, RCNVR	15/3/44	— 4/6/44
LT	W. J. Jones, RCNR	5/6/44	— 24/11/44

Shediac

LT	J. E. Clayton, RCNR	8/7/41	— 22/3/43
A/LCDR	A. Moorhouse, RCNR	23/3/43	— 9/2/44
SKPR/LT	J. B. Cooper, RCNR	10/2/44	— 30/3/44
A/LCDR	T. P. Ryan, OBE, RCNR	31/3/44	— 31/7/44
A/LCDR	P. D. Taylor, RCNVR	1/8/44	— 25/6/45
LT	W. McCombe, RCNR	26/6/45	— 28/8/45

Sherbrooke

LCDR	E. G. M. Donald, RCN	5/6/41	— 2/7/42
LT	J. A. M. Levesque, RCNR	3/7/42	— 29/8/43
LT	R. A. Jarvis, RCNVR	30/8/43	— 30/7/44
LT	D. A. Binmore, RCNVR	31/7/44	— 28/6/45

Sioux

LCDR	E. E. G. Boak, DSC, RCN	21/2/44	— 29/6/45
LCDR	R. A. Webber, DSC, RCN	30/6/45	— 8/11/45
A/LCDR	M. F. Oliver, RCNR	9/11/45	— 27/2/46
CDR	D. W. Groos, DSC, RCN	18/1/50	— 3/7/50
CDR	P. D. Taylor, DSC, RCN	4/7/50	— 9/3/52
LCDR	P. C. Benson, RCN	10/3/52	— 6/5/52
CDR	P. E. Haddon, RCN	7/5/52	— 11/9/53
LCDR	D. R. Saxon, DSC, RCN	12/9/53	— 11/11/53
CDR	A. H. Rankin, OBE, RCN	12/11/53	— 26/9/55
CDR	R. W. Murdoch, RCN	27/9/55	— 27/3/57
LCDR	J. M. Calver, RCN	28/3/57	— 23/5/57
CDR	P. G. Chance, RCN	24/5/57	— 1/7/58
CDR	A. B. C. German, RCN	2/7/58	—

Skeena

CDR	V. G. Brodeur, RCN	10/6/31	— 24/5/32
CDR	G. C. Jones, RCN	25/5/32	— 14/5/34
CDR	J. E. W. Oland, DSC, RCN	15/5/34	— 7/1/36
CDR	H. E. Reid, RCN	8/1/36	— 24/3/37
CAPT	V. G. Brodeur, RCN	25/3/37	— 22/4/38
CDR	H. T. W. Grant, RCN	23/4/38	— 30/11/39
LCDR	E. P. Tisdall, RCN	1/12/39	— 9/3/40
LT	H. S. Rayner, RCN	10/3/40	— 1/4/40
LCDR	J. C. Hibbard, RCN	2/4/40	— 10/12/41
CDR	H. Kingsley, RCN	11/12/41	— 19/5/42
A/LCDR	K. L. Dyer, DSC, RCN	20/5/42	— 28/2/43
A/LCDR	E. E. G. Boak, RCN	1/3/43	— 20/11/43
LCDR	P. F. X. Russell, RCN	21/11/43	— 25/10/44

Skeena (2nd)

CDR	J. P. T. Dawson, RCN	30/3/57	— 20/8/58
CDR	W. M. Kidd, RCN	20/8/58	— 1/10/59
LCDR	G. M. DeRosenroll, RCN	1/10/59	— 5/1/60
CDR	T. H. Crone, RCN	5/1/60	— 22/2/60

CDR	A. L. Collier, RCN	22/2/60	— 11/1/62
CDR	R. M. Leir, RCN	22/1/62	— 10/5/63
CDR	M. A. Martin, RCN	10/5/63	— 26/7/64
CDR	C. J. Mair, RCN	14/8/65	— 29/8/66
LCDR	K. D. Lewis, RCN	29/8/66	— 27/1/68
LT	B. Elson, RCN	27/1/68	— 16/4/68
LCDR	W. G Brown, RCN	16/4/68	— 23/6/69
LCDR	R. Dougan	23/6/69	— 11/8/69
CDR	R. L. Hughes	11/8/69	— 23/7/70
CDR	F. J. Mifflin	23/7/70	— 5/7/72
CDR	N. R. Boivin	15/6/73	— 5/9/75
CDR	J. Chouinard	5/9/75	— 13/5/76
CDR	D. E. Pollard	13/5/76	— 29/5/78
CDR	B. E. Derible	29/5/78	— 7/7/80
CDR	J. G. R. Boucher, OMM	7/7/80	—

Smiths Falls

A/LCDR	P. T. Byers, RCNR	28/11/44	— 8/7/45

Snowberry

LT	R. S. Kelly, RCNR	30/11/40	— 5/2/42
LCDR	P. J. B. Watts, RCNVR	6/2/42	— 21/5/43
LT	J. B. O'Brien, RCNVR	22/5/43	— 9/11/43
A/LCDR	J. A. Dunn, RCNVR	10/11/43	— 24/12/43
LT	J. B. O'Brien, RCNVR	25/12/43	— 14/1/44
LCDR	J. A. Dunn, RCNVR	15/1/44	— 30/4/45
LT	B. T. R. Russell, RCNR	1/5/45	— 8/6/45

Sorel

LT	J. W. Dowling, RCNR	19/8/41	— 22/12/41
LT	A. E. Giffin, RCNVR	23/12/41	— 7/6/42
LT	M. H. Wallace, RCNR	8/6/42	— 14/1/43
LT	P. D. Budge, RCN	15/1/43	— 3/2/43
LT	G. A. V. Thomson, RCNVR	4/2/43	— 19/2/43
LCDR	R. A. S. MacNeil, OBE, RCNR	20/2/43	— 23/11/43
LT	W. P. Wickett, RCNVR	24/11/43	— 13/3/44
LT	J. A. M. Levesque, RCNR	14/3/44	— 24/1/45
LT	C. W. King, RCNVR	25/1/45	— 22/6/45

Spikenard

LCDR	H. G. Shadforth, RCNR	8/12/40	— 10/2/42

Springhill

A/CDR	W. C. Halliday, RCNR	21/3/44	— 23/4/45
LCDR	J. Harding, RCNVR	24/4/45	— 1/12/45

Star XVI

LCDR	T. S. H. Beament, RCNVR	31/3/41	— 19/1/42
LT	J. M. Gracey, RCNVR	20/1/42	— 1/10/44
LT	C. J. Metcalfe, RCNVR	2/10/44	— 31/7/45

Stellarton

LT	R. A. Jarvis, RCNVR	29/9/44	— 19/12/44
A/LCDR	M. G. McCarthy, RCNVR	20/12/44	— 1/7/45

Stettler

LCDR	D. G. King, RCNVR	7/5/44	— 9/11/45
CDR	G. C. Edwards, RCN	27/2/54	— 2/9/55
LCDR	G. R. MacFarlane, RCN	3/9/55	— 9/9/57
LCDR	M. H. Cooke, RCN	10/9/57	— 11/8/59
LCDR	R. A. Evans, RCN	12/8/59	— 8/3/61
LCDR	H. W. Vondette, RCN	9/3/61	— 18/10/62
LCDR	R. F. Gladman, RCN	19/10/62	— 23/8/64
LCDR	T. A. Irvine, RCN	24/8/64	— 8/5/66
LT	S. C. Gould, RCN	9/5/66	— 31/8/66

Stonetown

LCDR	W. P. Moffat, RCNVR	21/7/44	— 20/4/45
A/LCDR	J. T. Band, RCNVR	21/4/45	— 19/8/45
LCDR	G. M. Kaizer, RCNR	20/8/45	— 13/11/45

Stormont

A/LCDR	G. A. Myra, RCNR	27/11/43	— 9/11/45

Stratford

LT	R. M. Meredith, RCNR	29/8/42	— 30/10/42
LT	R. J. C. Pringle, RCNVR	31/10/42	— 3/5/43
LT	W. G. Garden, RCNVR	4/5/43	— 4/8/43
LT	D. W. G. Storey, RCNVR	5/8/43	— 20/12/43
LT	H. A. Ovenden, RCNR	21/12/43	— 21/6/44
LT	R. G. Magnusson, RCNVR	22/6/44	— 1/4/45
LT	J. P. Charbonneau, RCNVR	2/4/45	— 25/4/45
LT	J. M. S. Clark, RCNVR	26/4/45	— 13/6/45
S/LT	G. G. Currie, RCNVR	4/10/45	—

Strathadam

LCDR	H. L. Quinn, DSC, RCNVR	29/9/44	— 6/7/45
LCDR	S. W. Howell, RCNR	7/7/45	— 29/7/45
LCDR	H. L. Quinn, DSC, RCNVR	30/7/45	— 7/11/45

Strathroy

LCDR	W. F. Wood, RCNR	20/11/44	— 27/12/44
LT	H. D. Pepper, RCNVR	28/12/44	— 31/1/45
LT	J. D. Moore, RCNVR	1/2/45	— 12/7/45

Sudbury

LCDR	A. M. McLarnon, RCNR	15/10/41	— 3/5/43
LT	D. S. Martin, RCNR	4/5/43	— 9/1/44
LT	G. L. Mackay, RCNR	10/1/44	— 19/3/44
A/LCDR	J. W. Golby, DSC, RCNVR	20/3/44	— 19/6/45

Suderöy IV

Mate	C. A. Mott, RCNR	7/5/41	— 2/4/42
LT	R. J. C. Pringle, RCNVR	3/4/42	— 24/4/42
LT	C. A. Mott, RCNR	25/4/42	— 9/6/42
LT	C. F. R. Dalton, RCNVR	10/6/42	— 10/8/42
LT	W. McIsaac, RCNVR	11/8/42	— 11/9/42
LT	J. Evelyn, RCNR	12/9/42	— 25/9/42
LT	L. D. Clarke, RCNVR	26/9/42	— 28/2/43
LT	W. Russell, RCNR	1/3/43	— 7/9/43
LT	D. J. Van Bommel, RCNVR	8/9/43	— 5/11/43
LT	D. J. Van Bommel, RCNVR	12/6/44	— 25/7/44
LT	D. J. Van Bommel, RCNVR	13/8/44	— 28/3/45
SKPR/LT	W. H. Crocker, RCNR	29/3/45	— 11/4/45
LT	W. McIsaac, RCNVR	12/4/45	— 31/8/45

Suderöy V

LT	R. M. Meredith, RCNR	2/6/41	— 11/6/42
LT	M. W. Knowles, RCNVR	12/6/42	— 2/11/43
LT	D. E. Francis, RCNVR	3/11/43	— 7/8/45

Suderöy VI

LT	R. J. C. Pringle, RCNVR	19/3/41	— 20/8/41
LT	A. M. McLarnon, RCNR	21/8/41	— 6/9/41
LT	R. J. C. Pringle, RCNVR	7/9/41	— 15/3/42
LT	W. Russell, RCNR	16/3/42	— 2/4/42
LT	R. J. C. Pringle, RCNVR	3/4/42	— 24/4/42
LT	W. Russell, RCNR	25/4/42	— 24/12/42
LT	P. M. MacCallum, RCNVR	25/12/42	— 29/1/43
LT	R. Stark, RCNVR	30/1/43	— 7/11/43
SKPR/LT	W. H. Crocker, RCNR	8/11/43	— 24/11/43
LT	J. C. Smith, RCNR	25/11/43	— 23/2/44
LT	D. I. McGill, RCNVR	24/2/44	— 26/5/44
LT	D. J. Van Bommel, RCNVR	27/5/44	— 11/6/44
LT	D. I. McGill, RCNVR	12/6/44	— 20/12/44
LT	J. S. Barrick, RCNVR	21/12/44	— 8/4/45
SKPR/LT	W. H. Crocker, RCNR	9/4/45	— 26/4/45
LT	J. A. MacKinnon, RCNR	27/4/45	— 10/5/45
LT	J. S. Barrick, RCNVR	11/5/45	— 14/7/45
LT	D. J. Van Bommel, RCNVR	15/7/45	— 4/8/45

Summerside

LCDR	F. O. Gerity, RCNR	11/9/41	— 3/6/43
LT	G. E. Cross, RCNVR	4/6/43	— 31/8/43
LT	G. S. Mongenais, RCNVR	1/9/43	— 15/11/44
LT	F. O. Plant, RCNVR	18/12/44	— 6/7/45

Sunbeam

SKPR	E. W. Hannaford, RCNR	8/5/41	— 27/6/43
CH/SKPR	E. L. Thompson, RCNR	28/6/43	— / /45
LT	J. A. Aldhouse, RCNR	/ /45	—
SKPR/LT	F. J. J. Henderson, RCNR	22/5/45	—

Sussexvale

LCDR	L. R. Pavillard, DSC, RCNR	29/11/44	— 16/11/45
CDR	R. H. Leir, RCN	18/3/55	— 25/8/55
LCDR	J. B. Young, RCN	26/8/55	— 2/1/57
LCDR	E. P. Shaw, RCN	3/1/57	— 23/6/58
CDR	V. J. Murphy, RCN	28/11/58	— 26/4/60
LCDR	H. D. Joy, RCN	27/4/60	— 17/5/62
LCDR	A. N. Turner, RCN	18/5/62	— 26/7/64
LCDR	T. C. Shuckburgh, RCN	27/7/64	— 20/6/65
LCDR	F. W. Crickard, RCN	21/6/65	— 30/11/66

Swansea

A/CDR	C. A. King, DSO, DSC, RCNR	4/10/43	— 29/7/44
CDR	A. F. C. Layard, RN	30/7/44	— 4/11/44
LT	J. T. Band, RCNVR	5/11/44	— 15/4/45
LCDR	G. A. LaRue, RCNVR	16/4/45	— 2/11/45
LT	R. W. Timbrell, DSC, RCN	12/4/48	— 6/2/49
LT	J. P. T. Dawson, RCN	7/2/49	— 11/8/50
LCDR	J. E. Korning, RCN	12/8/50	— 22/1/51
LT	W. A. Manfield, RCN	23/1/51	— 28/2/51
LCDR	J. E. Korning, RCN	1/3/51	— 26/3/52
LCDR	J. R. Coulter, RCN	27/3/52	— 15/8/52
LCDR	W. D. F. Johnston, RCN	14/4/53	— 6/11/53
LCDR	C. H. LaRose, RCN	7/11/53	— 10/11/53
LCDR	J. A. Farquhar, RCN	14/11/57	— 17/2/59
LCDR	G. S. Clark, RCN	18/2/59	— 31/8/60
LCDR	W. E. Clayards, RCN	1/9/60	— 17/7/62
LCDR	B. A. Cartwright, RCN	18/7/62	— 23/1/64
LCDR	D. K. Gamblin, RCN	24/1/64	—

Swift Current

LCDR	A. G. King, RCNR	20/9/41	— 18/4/42
LT	I. H. Bell, RCNVR	19/4/42	— 27/9/42
LT	J. Evelyn, RCNR	28/9/42	— 7/4/44
LT	K. D. Heath, RCNVR	8/4/44	— 13/5/45
LT	J. N. Fraser, RCNVR	14/5/45	— 26/7/45
LT	P. J. Laurence, RCNR	27/7/45	— 23/10/45

Teme

LCDR	D. G. Jeffrey, DSO, RCNR	28/2/44	— 20/2/45
LT	D. P. Harvey, RCNVR	21/2/45	— 4/5/45

Terra Nova

CDR	W. H. Willson, DSC, RCN	6/6/59	— 22/6/60
CDR	C. G. Smith, RCN	22/6/60	— 18/9/62
CDR	J. B. Young, RCN	18/9/62	— 3/4/64
CDR	C. E. Leighton, RCN	3/4/64	— 6/12/66
CDR	N. Brodeur, RCN	6/12/66	— 1/8/68
CDR	J. M. Reid, RCN	1/8/68	— 5/6/71
LCDR	J. Bishop	5/6/71	— 3/8/71
CDR	L. A. Dzioba	3/8/71	— 19/6/74
CDR	J. B. O'Reilly	19/6/74	— 8/1/76
CDR	R. G. Balfour	8/1/76	— 8/2/77
CDR	C. J. Crow	8/2/77	— 25/3/77
CDR	R. G. Balfour	25/3/77	— 29/7/77
CDR	J. D. Large	29/7/77	— 20/6/79
CDR	J. K. Steele	20/6/79	— 18/6/81
CDR	G. J. Eldridge	18/6/81	—

The Pas

LCDR	A. R. E. Coleman, RCNR	21/10/41	— 28/10/41
LCDR	E. G. Old, RCNR	29/10/41	— 14/1/44
LT	R. H. Sylvester, RCNVR	15/4/44	— 9/10/44
LT	J. H. Ewart, RCNVR	10/10/44	— 24/7/45

Thetford Mines

LCDR	J. A. R. Allan, DSC, RCNVR	24/5/44	— 12/6/45
LT	J. M. S. Clark, RCNVR	13/6/45	— 30/6/45
LCDR	J. A. R. Allan, DSC, RCNVR	1/7/45	— 20/7/45
A/CDR	T. Gilmour, RCNR	21/7/45	— 18/11/45

Thorlock

A/LCDR	J. E. Francois, RCNR	13/11/44	— 15/7/45

Thunder

CDR	H. D. Mackay, RCNR	14/10/41	— 25/6/45
LT	A. Moore, RCNR	26/6/45	— 4/10/45

Thunder (2nd)

LCDR	S. Howell, RCN	15/12/53	— 22/12/53
LT	W. N. Holmes, RCN	23/12/53	— 23/2/54
LCDR	J. L. Panabaker, RCN	24/2/54	— 31/3/54

Thunder (3rd)

LCDR	T. F. Owen, RCN	3/10/57	— 27/10/59
LCDR	N. S. Jackson, RCN	28/10/59	— 3/2/62
LCDR	M. Barrow, RCN	4/2/62	— 6/3/64
LT	J. B. Elson, RCN	14/4/67	— /9/67

Tillsonburg

LCDR	W. Evans, RCNVR	29/6/44	— 16/1/45
LT	A. D. Ritchie, RCNVR	17/1/45	— 2/3/45
LCDR	W. Evans, RCNVR	3/3/45	— 9/7/45
LT	G. E. Gilbride, RCNVR	10/7/45	— 4/9/45
LT	F. Angus, RCNVR	5/9/45	— 28/11/45

Timmins

LT	J. A. Brown, RCNR	10/2/42	— 18/8/42
LCDR	A. T. Morrell, RCNR	19/8/42	— 30/8/42
LT	J. M. Gillison, RCNR	31/8/42	— 11/1/43
LT	N. S. C. Dickinson, RCNVR	12/1/43	— 19/3/43
LCDR	J. H. S. MacDonald, RCNR	20/3/43	— 18/4/43
A/LCDR	H. S. Maxwell, RCNVR	19/4/43	— 29/6/44
LT	R. G. James, RCNVR	2/9/44	— 15/12/44
LT	J. Kincaid, RCNR	16/12/44	— 15/7/45

Toronto

LCDR	H. K. Hill, RCNVR	6/5/44	— 17/3/45
LCDR	A. G. S. Griffin, RCNVR	18/3/45	— 17/6/45
A/LCDR	E. B. Pearce, RCNVR	18/6/45	— 27/11/45
LCDR	W. D. F. Johnston, RCN	26/11/53	— 31/8/54
LCDR	A. H. MacDonald, RCN	1/9/54	— 3/1/56
LCDR	G. S. Clark, RCN	4/1/56	— 5/4/56
LCDR	W. W. MacColl, RCN	6/4/56	— 14/4/56

Trail

LT	G. S. Hall, RCNR	30/4/41	— 8/10/43
LT	G. M. Hope, RCNVR	9/10/43	— 20/8/44
LT	D. G. B. Hueston, RCNVR	21/8/44	— 9/10/44
LT	D. J. Lawson, RCNVR	10/10/44	— 17/7/45

Transcona

LT	H. B. Tindale, RCNVR	25/11/42	— 17/1/44
A/LCDR	A. E. Gough, RCNR	18/1/44	— 6/4/45
LT	J. N. Fraser, RCNVR	3/5/45	— 18/5/45
SKPR/LT	H. V. Mossman, RCNR	19/5/45	— 12/6/45

Trentonian

A/LCDR	W. E. Harrison, RCNR	1/12/43	— 30/1/45
LT	C. S. Glassco, RCNVR	31/1/45	— 22/2/45

Trillium

LCDR	R. F. Harris, DSC, RCNVR	31/10/40	— 14/11/41
LT	H. D. Campsie, RCNR	15/11/41	— 8/12/41
SKPR/LT	G. E. Gaudreau, RCNR	9/12/41	— 25/2/42
A/LCDR	P. C. Evans, RCNR	26/2/42	— 24/3/43
LT	R. M. Wallace, RCNVR	25/3/43	— 17/4/43
A/LCDR	P. C. Evans, RCNVR	18/4/43	— 21/5/44
LT	K. E. Meredith, RCNVR	22/5/44	— 27/6/45

Trinity

LCDR	A. H. M. Slater, RCN	16/6/54	— 10/5/56
LCDR	R. C. Thurber, RCN	11/5/56	— 12/12/56
LT	R. C. K. Peers, RCN	13/12/56	— 11/7/57
LT	P. Herdman, RCN	12/7/57	— 21/8/57

Trois-Rivières

A/LCDR	G. M. Kaizer, RCNR	12/8/42	— 11/2/43
LT	J. E. Taylor, RCNVR	12/2/43	— 10/3/43
A/LCDR	G. M. Kaizer, RCNR	11/3/43	— 15/11/43
LT	W. G. Garden, RCNVR	16/11/43	— 12/9/44
LT	R. C. G. Merriam, RCNVR	13/9/44	— 11/12/44
LT	J. M. S. Clark, RCNVR	12/12/44	— 23/4/45
LT	M. D. Gagnon, RCNVR	24/4/45	— 31/7/45

Truro

SKPR/LT	G. A. Myra, RCNR	27/8/42	— 1/8/43
LT	G. D. Campbell, RCNVR	2/8/43	— 27/3/44
LT	E. E. MacInnis, RCNR	28/3/44	— 31/7/45

U 190

LT	K. C. Tryon, RCNVR	25/5/45	— 27/11/45
LCDR	W. F. Hardy, RCNVR	28/11/45	— 17/1/46
LT	J. R. Johnston, RCNR	18/1/46	— 24/7/47

U 889

LT	C. W. Perry, RCNVR	28/5/45	— 27/10/45
LT	J. R. Johnston, RCNVR	28/10/45	— 12/1/46

Uganda/Quebec

CAPT	E. R. Mainguy, OBE, RCN	21/10/44	— 4/7/46
CAPT	K. F. Adams, RCN	5/7/46	— 1/8/47

CAPT	P. D. Budge, DSC, RCN	14/1/52	— 10/9/53
CAPT	E. W. Finch-Noyes, RCN	11/9/53	— 31/7/55
CAPT	D. W. Piers, DSC, RCN	1/8/55	— 8/5/56
CDR	E. S. MacDermid, RCN	9/5/56	— 13/6/56

Ungava

LT	C. Winterbottom, RCNR	5/9/41	— 19/1/42
LT	F. E. Scoates, RCNR	20/1/42	— 8/2/43
LT	D. M. Coolican, RCNVR	9/2/43	— 12/3/44
LT	J. M. Home, RCNVR	13/3/44	— 17/12/44
LT	J. W. Radford, RCNR	18/12/44	— 16/1/45
LT	J. M. Home, RCNVR	17/1/45	— 30/1/45
LT	S. Henderson, RCNR	31/1/45	— 9/4/45
LT	F. K. Ellis, RCNVR	10/4/45	— 16/7/45
LT	F. Cross, RCNR	17/7/45	— 30/10/45

Ungava (2nd)

LCDR	E. J. Semmens, RCN	4/6/54	— 4/5/55
LCDR	R. M. Young, RCN	5/5/55	— 11/4/57
LCDR	T. F. Owen, RCN	12/4/57	— 23/8/57

Valleyfield

LCDR	D. T. English, RCNR	7/12/43	— 7/5/44

Vancouver

LCDR	R. I. Agnew, RCN	1/3/28	— 14/8/28
LCDR	R. W. Wood, RCN	15/8/28	— 4/5/30
LCDR	G. M. Hibbard, RCN	5/5/30	— 19/1/31
LCDR	F. G. Hart, RCN	20/1/31	— 14/12/32
LCDR	L. J. M. Gauvreau, RCN	15/12/32	— 19/12/33
LCDR	F. L. Houghton, RCN	20/12/33	— 30/11/34
LCDR	C. D. Donald, RCN	1/12/34	— 14/5/36
LCDR	E. R. Mainguy, RCN	15/5/36	— 25/11/36

Vancouver (2nd)

LT	P. F. M. DeFreitas, RCNR	20/3/42	— 7/6/43
LCDR	A. T. Morrell, RCNR	8/6/43	— 4/2/44
A/LCDR	A. W. Ford, RCNR	5/2/44	— 9/10/44
LT	G. C. Campbell, RCNVR	10/10/44	— 26/6/45

Vegreville

CDR	F. A. Price, RCNVR	10/12/41	— 19/1/42
LCDR	T. H. Beament, RCNVR	20/1/42	— 11/1/43
LT	T. B. Edwards, RCNR	12/1/43	— 6/11/44
LCDR	A. Sagar, RCN	7/11/44	— 6/6/45

Victoriaville

A/LCDR	L. A. Hickey, MBE, RCNR	11/11/44	— 17/11/45
LCDR	G. B. Wither, RCN	25/9/59	— 4/5/61
LCDR	W. P. Rikely, RCN	5/5/61	— 10/3/63
LCDR	A. J. Norman, RCN	12/12/64	— 8/1/65
LCDR	E. A. Makin, RCN	21/12/66	—

Ville de Québec

LCDR	D. G. Jeffrey, RCNR	24/5/42	— 29/9/42
LT	I. H. Bell, RCNVR	30/9/42	— 11/10/42
LCDR	A. R. E. Coleman, RCNR	12/10/42	— 12/6/43
LT	J. L. Carter, RCNVR	13/6/43	— 12/3/44
LT	C. S. Glassco, RCNVR	13/3/44	— 1/5/44
LCDR	H. C. Hatch, RCNVR	2/5/44	— 6/7/45

Vison

LCDR	R. I. Swansburg, RCNR	5/10/40	— 31/7/41
LCDR	F. A. Price, RCNVR	1/8/41	— 21/11/41
CDR	W. G. Sheddon, RCNR	22/11/41	— 14/4/42
LT	W. E. Nicholson, RCNR	15/4/42	— 4/8/45

Wallaceburg

A/LCDR	F. R. K. Naftel, RCNR	18/11/43	— 2/5/44
LCDR	R. A. S. MacNeil, RCNR	3/5/44	— 9/1/45
A/LCDR	F. E. Burrows, RCNVR	10/1/45	— 21/5/45
LCDR	J. H. G. Bovey, RCNVR	22/5/45	— 16/7/45
LT	R. N. Smillie, RCNVR	17/7/45	— 19/8/45
LT	A. D. Ritchie, RCNVR	20/8/45	— 7/9/45
LT	G. Kelly, RCNVR	23/10/45	— 1/2/46
LCDR	R. M. Steele, RCNR	3/6/46	— 7/10/46
LCDR	J. C. Marston, DSC, RCNR	1/11/50	— 20/12/50
CDR	R. A. Webber, DSC, RCN	21/12/50	— 3/4/51
LCDR	J. H. Maxner, RCN	4/4/51	— 27/9/51
LCDR	I. A. McPhee, RCN	28/9/51	— 21/2/54
LCDR	W. A. Manfield, RCN	22/2/54	— 25/11/54
CDR	F. J. Jones, RCN	14/4/55	— 16/10/55
LCDR	D. S. Bethune, RCN	17/10/55	— 24/9/57

Warrior

CAPT	F. L. Houghton, CBE, RCN	24/1/46	— 17/1/47
COM	H. G. DeWolf, CBE, DSO, DSC, RCN	18/1/47	— 23/3/48

Wasaga

LCDR	W. Redford, RCNR	30/6/41	— 9/3/42
LT	J. B. Raine, RCNR	10/3/42	— 13/5/43
LT	J. A. Dunn, RCNVR	14/5/43	— 17/6/43
LT	J. B. Raine, RCNR	18/6/43	— 22/12/43
LT	J. H. Green, RCNR	23/12/43	— 6/10/45

Waskesiu

LCDR	J. H. S. MacDonald, RCNR	16/6/43	— 4/2/44
LCDR	J. P. Fraser, RCNR	5/2/44	— 13/12/44
A/LCDR	L. D. Quick, RCNR	14/12/44	— 22/10/45

Wentworth

LCDR	S. W. Howell, RCNR	7/12/43	— 4/7/44
LCDR	R. J. C. Pringle, RCNVR	5/7/44	— 15/1/45
A/LCDR	J. B. Graham, RCNVR	16/1/45	— 10/4/45
LT	G. C. Campbell, RCNVR	25/8/45	— 10/10/45

West York

LT	M. Smith, RCNR	6/10/44	— 29/12/44
LCDR	W. F. Wood, RCNR	30/12/44	— 9/7/45

Westmount

A/LCDR	F. G. Hutchings, RCNVR	15/9/42	— 7/12/43
LT	F. H. Pinfold, RCNVR	8/12/43	— 16/3/44
LT	R. L. B. Hunter, RCNVR	17/3/44	— 25/3/45
LT	R. P. Jackson, RCNVR	26/3/45	— 7/7/45

Wetaskiwin

LCDR	G. Windeyer, RCN	17/12/40	— 4/11/42
A/LCDR	J. R. Kidston, RCNVR	5/11/42	— 21/3/44
LT	A. Walton, RCNR	22/3/44	— 6/8/44
A/LCDR	M. S. Duffus, RCNVR	7/8/44	— 15/9/44
LT	A. Walton, RCNR	16/9/44	— 19/6/45

Weyburn

LCDR	T. M. W. Colby, RCNR	26/11/41	— 22/2/43

Whitby

A/LCDR	R. K. Lester, RCNVR	6/6/44	— 16/7/45

Whitethroat

LCDR	B. G. Jemmett, RCNVR	7/12/44	— 26/6/45
SKPR/LT	I. E. Abbott, RCNR	27/6/45	— 6/5/46
LCDR	R. S. Hurst, RCN	17/4/51	— 26/8/51
LCDR	W. E. Williams, RCN	27/8/51	—

Windflower

A/LCDR	J. H. S. MacDonald, RCNR	20/10/40	— 13/10/41
LT	J. Price, RCNR	14/10/41	— 7/12/41

Winnipeg

LCDR	W. D. F. Johnston, RCNR	29/7/43	— 4/4/44
LCDR	R. A. Judges, RCNVR	5/4/44	— 3/9/44

LCDR	G. K. Fox, RCNVR	4/10/44	— 23/7/45
LT	C. F. Usher, RCNVR	10/9/45	— 11/1/46

Wolf

LT	J. A. Gow, RCNR	2/10/40	— 21/4/41
CH/SKPR	J. M. Richardson, RCNR	22/4/41	— 18/9/41
CH/SKPR	A. W. Ogden, RCNR	19/9/41	— 5/10/41
SKPR/LT	W. R. Chaster, RCNR	6/10/41	— 21/4/43
SKPR/LT	G. F. Cassidy, RCNR	22/4/43	— 22/5/43
SKPR/LT	W. R. Chaster, RCNR	23/5/43	— 16/5/45

Woodstock

LT	L. P. Denny, RCNR	1/5/42	— 18/10/42
CDR	G. H. Griffiths, RCN	19/10/42	— 19/1/43
SKPR/LT	J. M. Watson, RCNR	20/1/43	— 16/8/43
LT	C. E. Wright, RCNVR	17/8/43	— 5/10/44
LT	W. McCombe, RCNR	6/10/44	— 27/1/45
LCDR	J. S. Cunningham, RCNVR	17/5/45	— 18/3/46

Yukon

CDR	R. W. J. Cocks, RCN	25/5/63	— 5/7/65
CDR	R. Carle, RCN	5/7/65	— 1/9/66
CDR	S. I. Ker, RCN	1/9/66	— 15/1/68
CDR	P. G. May, RCN	15/1/68	— 12/9/69
CDR	C. H. P. Shaw	12/9/69	— 28/6/71
LCDR	D. Large	28/6/71	— 9/8/71
CDR	C. Cotaras	9/8/71	— 9/8/73
CDR	M. F. MacIntosh	9/8/73	— 1/10/76
CDR	H. Kieran	1/10/76	— 15/5/78
CDR	N. R. Boivin	15/5/78	— 22/5/81
CDR	C. J. Crowe	22/5/81	—

Appendix 5
Naming Of Canadian Warships

Most RCN escort ships were named in a straightforward way for Canadian cities, towns, bays or islands. The 37 in the table below, however, could not be named "verbatim" for the municipalities they commemorated, as to have done so would have caused confusion with similarly-named RCN ships or shore establishments, or with names borne by other Allied warships.

Ship's Name	Place Commemorated	Reason For Circumlocution
Atholl	Campbellton, N.B.	HMS Campbeltown
Beacon Hill	Victoria, B.C.	HMS Victorious
Border Cities	Windsor, Ont.	HMS Windsor
Buctouche	Bathurst, N.B.	HMAS Bathurst
Cape Breton	Sydney, N.S.	HMAS Sydney
Capilano	North Vancouver, B.C.	HMCS Vancouver
Carlplace	Carleton Place, Ont.	abbreviation
Chebogue	Yarmouth, N.S.	HMS Yarmouth
Dunver	Verdun, Que.	HMS Verdun
Eastview	Ottawa, Ont.	HMCS Ottawa (named for the river)
Frontenac	Kingston, Ont.	HMS Kingston
Grou	Point-aux-Trembles, Que.	too long
Hallowell	Picton, Ont.	HMCS Pictou
Inch Arran	Dalhousie, N.B.	HMIS Dalhousie
Kokanee	Nelson, B.C.	HMS Nelson
La Hulloise	Hull, Que.	USS Hull
Lanark	Perth, Ont.	HMAS Perth
Merrittonia	Merritton, Ont.	local preference
Middlesex	London, Ont.	HMS London
Norsyd	North Sydney, N.S.	HMAS Sydney
Orkney	Yorkton, Sask.	USS Yorktown
Portage	Portage-la-Prairie, Man.	too long
Poundmaker	North Battleford, Sask.	HMCS Battleford
Prestonian	Preston, Ont.	HMS Preston
Royalmount	Mount Royal, Que.	HMCS Montreal
Runnymede	York Township, Ont.	HMCS York
Sea Cliff	Leamington, Ont.	HMS Leamington
Stettler	Edmonton, Alta.	HMCS Edmundston
Stone Town	St. Mary's, Ont.	HMS St. Mary's
Stormont	Cornwall, Ont.	HMS Cornwall
Strathadam	Newcastle, N.B.	HMS Newcastle
Sussexvale	Sussex, N.B.	HMS Sussex
Thorlock	Thorold, Ont.	local preference
Trentonian	Trenton, Ont.	USS Trenton
Waskesiu	Prince Albert, Sask.	HMS Prince Albert
Wentworth	Hamilton, Ont.	HMCS Hamilton (named for Hamilton, Bermuda)
West York	Weston, Ont.	HMS Weston

Appendix 6

Pendant Numbers

Pendant numbers make possible the visual identification of ships, especially members of a large class. The number is worn on either side of the fo'c's'le and, usually, on the stern, often displayed as well in the form of flags. During the Second World War the painted-on version was generally seen only in destroyers and smaller ships, except in the USN.

In the list that follows, the Canadian pendants for 1939 to 1945 have been excerpted from much larger lists that included all British and Commonwealth ships; hence the gaps in the series. The only RCN ships affected by a change (1940) in the letter preceding the numerals were *Assiniboine*, *Saguenay*, and *Skeena*, whose letter "D" changed to "I."

RCN pendant numbers having "S," "Z," and the Fishery flag "superior" bore no relation to the RN lists. To make matters even more confusing, many east- and west-coast ships simultaneously bore the same numbers. These may be distinguished in the list by A (Atlantic) and P (Pacific) appended to the ships' names. A further complication arises from the fact that the armed yachts, in particular, were assigned changed numbers at various times.

The letter prefix was no longer displayed after the pendant numbers were revised at the end of 1949. USN-style ship type designations are "understood" in reading these. Thus, HMCS *Preserver* is recognized by her number to be AOR 510.

Pendant Numbers, Wartime

F	56	Prince Robert		08	Bayfield	256	Medicine Hat	
	70	Prince Henry		10	Standard Coaster	257	Vegreville	
	89	Prince David		11	Venosta	258	Grandmère	
	94	Preserver		12	Viernoe	259	Gananoque	
	100	Provider		13	Rayon d'Or	260	Goderich	
				16	Fleur de Lis	261	Kelowna	
G	07	Athabaskan (1st)		21	Canso	262	Courtenay	
	24	Huron		29	Armentières	263	Melville	
	63	Haida		35	Nanoose	264	Granby	
	89	Iroquois		38	Caraquet	265	Noranda	
				46	Festubert	266	Lachine	
H	00	Restigouche		52	Guysborough	267	Digby	
	31	Ottawa (2nd)		64	Comox	268	Truro	
	48	Fraser		69	Ingonish	269	Trois-Rivières	
	49	Margaree		70	Ypres	270	Brockville	
	60	Ottawa (1st)		88	Fundy	271	Transcona	
	61	Gatineau		94	Gaspé	272	Esquimalt	
	69	Qu'Appelle		100	Lockeport	278	Llewellyn	
	70	Saskatchewan		144	Georgian	279	Lloyd George	
	75	Kootenay		146	Cowichan	280	Port Hope	
	83	St. Laurent		148	Malpeque	281	Kenora	
	96	Buxton		149	Ungava	309	Sarnia	
	99	Chaudière		152	Quatsino	310	Stratford	
				154	Nipigon	311	Fort William	
I	04	Annapolis		156	Thunder	312	Kentville	
	18	Assiniboine		159	Mahone	313	Mulgrave	
	24	Hamilton		160	Chignecto	314	Blairmore	
	49	Columbia		161	Outarde	317	Milltown	
	57	Niagara		162	Wasaga	318	Westmount	
	59	Skeena		165	Minas	326	Kapuskasing	
	65	St. Clair		166	Quinte	328	Middlesex	
	79	Saguenay		168	Chedabucto	330	Oshawa	
	81	St. Croix		169	Miramichi	331	Portage	
	93	St. Francis		170	Bellechasse	332	St. Boniface	
				174	Clayoquot	334	Sault Ste. Marie	
J	01	Ross Norman		250	Burlington	336	Wallaceburg	
	03	Suderoy IV		253	Drummondville	337	Winnipeg	
	04	Suderoy V		254	Swift Current	344	Border Cities	
	05	Suderoy VI		255	Red Deer	355	Rockcliffe	

357	Daerwood		106	Edmundston
358	Rossland		110	Shediac
359	St. Joseph		112	Matapedia
364	Coquitlam		113	Arvida
371	Lavallée		115	Lévis (1st)
372	Cranbrook		116	Chambly
373	Revelstoke		118	Napanee
395	Kalamalka		119	Orillia
396	Fort Frances		121	Rimouski
397	New Liskeard		124	Cobalt
480	Alder Lake		125	Kenogami
482	Beech Lake		127	Algoma
484	Cedar Lake		129	Agassiz
486	Elm Lake		131	Chilliwack
488	Hickory Lake		133	Quesnel
489	Larch Lake		136	Shawinigan
492	Pine Lake		138	Barrie
493	Poplar Lake		139	Moncton
494	Spruce Lake		141	Summerside
495	Willow Lake		143	Louisburg (1st)
			145	Arrowhead
			146	Pictou
			147	Baddeck
			148	Amherst
			149	Brandon
			150	Eyebright
			151	Lunenburg
			152	Sherbrooke
			153	Sorel
			154	Camrose
			155	Windflower
			156	Chicoutimi
			157	Dauphin
			158	Saskatoon
			159	Hepatica
			160	Lethbridge
			161	Prescott
			162	Sudbury
			163	Galt
			164	Moose Jaw
			165	Battleford
			166	Snowberry
			167	Drumheller
			168	The Pas
			169	Rosthern
			170	Morden
			171	Kamsack
			172	Trillium
			173	Weyburn
			174	Trail
			175	Wetaskiwin
			176	Kamloops
			177	Dunvegan
			178	Oakville
			179	Buctouche
			180	Collingwood
			181	Sackville
K	03	Dunver	182	Bittersweet
	15	Atholl	191	Mayflower
	101	Nanaimo	194	Fennel
	103	Alberni	198	Spikenard
	104	Dawson	218	Brantford
			220	Midland
			223	Timmins
			225	Kitchener

Fishery Pendant Superior (West Coast)

Pendant Numbers, 1949 onward

74	Onondaga	173	Rockcliffe	218	Cayuga	307	Prestonian
100	Cape Breton (2nd)	174	Oshawa	219	Athabaskan (2nd)	308	Inch Arran
101	Cape Scott	176	Sault Ste. Marie	224	Algonquin (1st)	309	Ste. Thérèse
113	Sackville	177	Winnipeg	225	Sioux	310	Outremont
114	Bluethroat	178	Brockville	226	Crescent	311	Stettler
141	Llewellyn	179	Digby	228	Crusader	312	Fort Erie
142	Lloyd George	180	Granby; Porte St. Jean	229	Ottawa (3rd)	313	Sussexvale
143	Gaspé (2nd)	181	Drummondville	230	Margaree (2nd)	314	Buckingham
144	Chaleur (1st)	182	Kentville	233	Fraser (2nd)	315	New Glasgow
145	Fundy (2nd)	183	Port Hope; Porte St. Louis	234	Assiniboine (2nd)	316	Penetang
146	Comox (2nd)	184	Gananoque; Porte de la Reine	235	Chaudière (2nd)	317	Cap de la Madeleine
147	Cowichan (2nd)	185	Swift Current; Porte Québec	236	Gatineau (2nd)	318	Jonquière
148	Ungava (2nd)	186	Malpeque; Porte Dauphine	256	St. Croix (2nd)	319	Toronto
149	Quinte (2nd)	187	Westmount	257	Restigouche (2nd)	320	Victoriaville
150	Miramichi (2nd)	188	Nipigon	258	Kootenay (2nd)	321	Lanark
151	Fortune	189	Minas	259	Terra Nova	322	Lauzon
152	James Bay	190	Sarnia	260	Columbia (2nd)	323	St. Stephen
153	Thunder (2nd)	191	Kenora	261	Mackenzie	324	St. Catharines
154	Resolute	192	Mahone	262	Saskatchewan (2nd)	400	Bras d'Or (2nd)
156	Chignecto (2nd)	193	Blairmore	263	Yukon	420	Cordova
157	Trinity	194	Milltown	264	Qu'Appelle (2nd)	501	Dundalk
158	Cordova	195	Fort William	265	Annapolis (2nd)	502	Dundurn
159	Fundy (3rd)	196	Red Deer	266	Nipigon (2nd)	508	Provider
160	Chignecto (3rd)	197	Medicine Hat	280	Iroquois (2nd)	509	Protecteur
161	Thunder (3rd)	198	Goderich	281	Huron (2nd)	510	Preserver
162	Cowichan (3rd)	205	St. Laurent (2nd)	282	Athabaskan (3rd)	516	Laymore
163	Miramichi (3rd)	206	Saguenay (2nd)	283	Algonquin (2nd)	531	Whitethroat
164	Chaleur (2nd)	207	Skeena (2nd)	301	Antigonish	780	Loon
168	New Liskeard	213	Nootka	302	Stone Town	781	Cormorant (1st)
169	Portage	214	Micmac	303	Beacon Hill	782	Blue Heron
170	Fort Frances	215	Haida	304	New Waterford	783	Mallard
171	Kapuskasing	216	Huron (1st)	305	La Hulloise		
172	Wallaceburg	217	Iroquois (1st)	306	Swansea		

Appendix 7

Ships by Classes: Principal Dates and Particulars

Key to Builders of Principal Ships

AH	Alexander Hall & Co. Ltd., Aberdeen Scotland	KI	Kingston Shipbuilding Co. Ltd., Kingston, Ont.
AJ	A. & J. Inglis Ltd., Glasgow, Scotland	MI	Marine Industries Ltd., Sorel, Que.
AS	Ailsa Shipbuilding Co. Ltd., Troon, Scotland	MO	Morton Engineering and Dry Dock Co., Quebec City, Que.
BC	Barclay, Curle & Co. Ltd., Glasgow, Scotland	MS	Midland Shipyards Ltd., Midland, Ont.
BL	Blyth Shipbuilding & Dry Dock Co. Ltd., Blyth, U.K.	NN	Newport News Shipbuilding & Dry Dock Co. Ltd., Newport News, Va.
BQ	Bethlehem Shipbuilding Corp. Ltd., Quincy, Mass.	NV	North Van Ship Repairs Ltd., Vancouver, B.C.
BR	Bethlehem Shipbuilding Corp. Ltd., Fore River Yard, Quincy, Mass.	PA	Port Arthur Shipbuilding Co. Ltd., Port Arthur, Ont.
BS	Bethlehem Shipbuilding Corp. Ltd., Squantum, Mass.	PF	Pictou Foundry Co., Pictou, N.S.
BU	Burrard Dry Dock Co. Ltd., Vancouver, B.C.	PM	Palmers Shipbuilding Co. Ltd., Hebburn-on-Tyne, U.K.
CH	Charles Hill & Sons Ltd., Bristol, U.K.	PO	Portsmouth Naval Dockyard, Portsmouth, U.K.
CL	Cammell, Laird & Co., Birkenhead, U.K.	PR	Prince Rupert Dry Dock and Shipyards Co., Prince Rupert, B.C.
CO	Collingwood Shipyards Ltd., Collingwood, Ont.	SD	Smith's Dock Co., South Bank-on-Tees, U.K.
CV	Canadian Vickers Ltd., Montreal, Que.	SH	Swan, Hunter & Wigham Richardson Ltd., Wallsend-on-Tyne, U.K.
DS	Davie Shipbuilding and Repairing Co. Ltd., Lauzon, Que.	SJ	Saint John Dry Dock and Shipbuilding Co. Ltd., Saint John, N.B.
DU	Dufferin Shipbuilding Co. Toronto, Ont.	ST	Seattle-Tacoma Shipbuilding Corp., Tacoma, Wash.
FE	Ferguson Bros. Ltd., Port Glasgow, Scotland	TH	John I. Thornycroft & Co. Ltd., Southampton, U.K.
GD	George T. Davie & Sons Ltd., Lauzon, Que.	UN	Union Iron Works, San Francisco, Calif.
HA	Hall, Russell & Co. Ltd., Aberdeen, Scotland	VB	Vickers-Armstrongs Ltd., Barrow-in-Furness, U.K.
HR	Henry Robb Ltd., Leith, Scotland	VM	Victoria Machinery Depot Co. Ltd., Victoria, B.C.
HW	Harland and Wolff Ltd., Belfast, Ireland	VN	Vickers-Armstrongs Ltd., Newcastle-on-Tyne, U.K.
HX	Halifax Shipyards Ltd., Halifax, N.S.	WH	J. Samuel White & Co. Ltd., Cowes, I.O.W., U.K.
JB	John Brown & Co. Ltd., Glasgow, Scotland	WP	Wm. Pickersgill & Sons Ltd., Sunderland, U.K.
JC	John Crown & Sons Ltd., Sunderland, U.K.	YA	Yarrows Ltd., Esquimalt, B.C.

Particulars — Ships of Part One   1910 - 1939

	Builder	Launched	Displacement	Dimensions	Speed	Crew	Armament
AURORA	H. M. Dockyard, Devonport	30/9/13	3,512	436' x 39' x 14'	25	318	2-6'', 6-4'', 2-3'', 8-21'' TT (4 x II)
CHAMPLAIN	Thornycroft, Southampton	6/3/19	1,087	276' x 27.5' x 10.5'	30	90	3-4'', 1-2 pdr., 4-21'', TT (2 x II)
NIOBE	Vickers, Barrow-In-Furness	20/2/97	11,000	466' x 69' x 26'	15	677	16-6'', 12-12 pdrs., 5-3 pdrs., 2-18'' TT
PATRICIAN	Thornycroft, Southampton	5/6/16	1,004	274' x 27.5' x 10.5'	30	82	3-4'', 1-2 pdr., 4-21'' TT (2 x II)
PATRIOT	''	20/4/16	''	''	''	''	3-4'', 1-2 pdr., 4-21'' TT (2 x II)
RAINBOW	Palmers, Hebburn-On-Tyne	25/3/91	3,600	314.5' x 43.5' x 16.5'	12	273	2-6'', 6-4'', 8-6 pdrs., 4-14'' TT
VANCOUVER	Thornycroft, Southampton	7/12/18	1,087	276' x 27.5' x 10.5'	30	90	3-4'', 1-2 pdr., 4-21'' TT (2 x II)
ACADIA	Swan, Hunter & Wigham Richardson, Newcastle	1913	1,350	170' x 33.5' x 19'	8	59	1-4'', 1-12 pdr.
ALGERINE	H. M. Dockyard, Devonport	6/6/95	1,050	210.5' x 32.5' x 11.5'	12		4-3 pdrs.
CANADA	Vickers-Armstong, Barow	1904	557	206' x 25' x 13'	14	60	2-12 pdrs., 2-3 pdrs.
CARTIER	Swan, Hunter & Wigham Richardson, Newcastle	1910	556	164' x 29' x 13'	12	''	3-12 pdrs.
TUNA	Yarrow & Co., U.K.	1902	124	153' x 15' x 5'	24		1-3 pdr., 2-14'' TT
VENTURE	Meteghan, N.S.	6/37	250	142' x 27' x 14.5'			
CC 1	Seattle Construction & Drydock Co.	3/6/13	313/373	144' x 15' x 11'	13/10	2/16	5-18'' TT
CC 2	''	31/12/13	310/373	152' x 15' x 11'	''	''	3-18'' TT
C. D. 1-100	Various Canadian Builders	1917	99	84' x 19.3' x 10'	9		1-6 pdr.
CH. 14 and 15	Fore River Co., Quincy, Mass.		363/434	150' x 15' x 12'	13/11	4/18	4-18'' TT
CONSTANCE	Polson Iron Works, Owen Sound	1891	185	115' x 19.6' x 11.2'	10	23	
CURLEW	''	1892	''	116.3' x 19.8' x 11.3'	''	''	
FLORENCE	Crescent Shipyard, Elizabeth N. J.	1903	257	144' x 22.5' x 7.5'	12		1-3 pdr.
GALIANO	Dublin Dockyard	1913	393	162.3' x 27' x 13'	11	33	
GRILSE	Yarrow & Co., Glasgow, Scotland	1912	287	202.3' x 18.3' x 9.2'	30	56	2-12 pdrs., 1-14'' TT
GULNARE	C. Connel, Scotstoun	1893	262	137' x 20.5' x 13.6'	10	25	
HOCHELAGA	Hawthorn & Co., Leith	1900	628	192.6' x 27.6' x 14.8'	12		1-12 pdr.
LADY EVELYN	Tranmere, U.K.	1901	483	189' x 26.1' x 9.5'	9		
LAURENTIAN	Cook, Welton & Gemmell, Beverley, U.K.	1902	355	149' x 24' x 11'	11		1-12 pdr.
MALASPINA	Dublin Dockyard	1913	392	162.4' x 27.1' x 13.1'	''	33	1-6 pdr.
MARGARET	Woolston, U.K.	1914	756	182.4' x 32.3' x 15'	15		2-6 pdrs.
PETREL	Polson Iron Works, Owen Sound	1892	192	116' x 22' x 10.3'	10	23	
P.V. I-VII	Various U.S. Builders	1903-1912	258 average	157' x 23' x 12' average	8		1-12 pdr.
SHEARWATER	H. M. Dockyard, Sheerness	10/2/00	980	204' x 33' x 11.5'	12		4-4 pdrs., 4-3 pdrs.
SKIDEGATE	Vancouver, B.C.	1927	15	47' x 13.5' x 5'	8	3/7	
STADACONA	Crescent Shipyard, Elizabeth, N.J.	1899	682	196.4' x 33.5' x 11'	12	62	1-4''
TR 1-60	Various Canadian Builders	1917-1919	275	125' x 23.5' x 13.5'	10		1-12 pdr.

Battle Class Trawlers

	Builder	Launched	Displacement	Dimensions	Speed	Armament
ARLEUX	Canadian Vickers, Montreal	9/8/17	357	130' x 25' x 13'	10	1-12 pdr.
ARMENTIERES	''	11/8/17	''	''	''	''
ARRAS	''	15/9/17	''	''	''	''
FESTUBERT	Polson Iron Works, Toronto	2/8/17	320	130' x 23.5' x 13.5'	''	''
GIVENCHY	Canadian Vickers, Montreal	15/9/17	357	130' x 25' x 13'	''	''
LOOS	Kingston Shipbuilding Co.	27/9/17	357	''	''	''
MESSINES	Polson Iron Works, Toronto	16/6/17	320	130' x 23.5' x 13.5'	''	''
ST. ELOI	''	2/8/17	''	''	''	''
ST. JULIEN	''	16/6/17	''	130' x 23.5' x 13.5'	''	''
THIEPVAL	Kingston Shipbuilding Co.	1917	357	130' x 25' x 13'	''	''
VIMY	Polson Iron Works Toronto	16/6/17	320	130' x 23.5' x 13.5'	''	''
YPRES	''	''	''	''	''	''

Fundy Class Minesweepers

Particulars of Class	Displacement	Dimensions	Speed	Crew	Armament
	460	163' x 27.5' x 14.5'	12	3/35	1-12 pdr.

	Pendant	Builder	Laid Down	Launched	Commissioned	Paid Off	Remarks
COMOX	J64	Burrard D.D. Co., Vancouver	5/2/38	9/8/38	23/11/38	27/7/45	
FUNDY	J88	Collingwood Shipyards Ltd.	24/1/38	18/6/38	1/9/38	''	
GASPÉ	J94	Morton Eng. Co., Quebec City	''	12/8/38	21/10/38	23/7/45	
NOOTKA	J35	Yarrows Ltd., Victoria, B.C.	1/2/38	26/9/38	6/12/38	29/7/45	Renaned NANOOSE, 1943

Particulars — Ships of Part Two   1939 - 1945

Cruisers

	Displacement	Dimensions	Speed	Crew	Armament
ONTARIO	8,800	555' 6'' x 63' x 16' 6''	30	730	9-6'' (3 x III), 10-4'' (5 x II), 6-21'' TT (2 x III)
UGANDA	''	555' 6'' x 62' x 16' 6''	''	''	9-6'' (3 x III), 8-4'' (4 x II), 6-21'' TT (2 x III)

	Pendant	Builder	Laid Down	Launched	Commissioned in RCN	Paid Off	Remarks
ONTARIO	53	HW	20/11/41	29/7/43	26/4/45	15/10/58	Ex-HMS MINOTAUR, 1945
UGANDA	66	VN	20/7/39	7/8/41	21/10/44	13/6/56	Renamed QUEBEC, 1952

Armed Merchant Cruisers

	Displacement	Dimensions	Speed	Crew	Armament
PRINCE DAVID	5,736	385' x 57' x 21'	22	31/386	4-4'' (2 x II), 2-2 pdrs., 8-20 mm
PRINCE HENRY	''	''	''	''	''
PRINCE ROBERT	5,675	''	''	33/405	10-4'' (5 x II), 2-2 pdrs., 6-20 mm

	Pendant	Builder	Launched	Commissioned	Paid Off	Remarks
PRINCE DAVID	F89	CL	1930	28/12/40	11/6/45	Particulars are for PRINCE DAVID and PRINCE HENRY as converted to LSI(M)s; for PRINCE ROBERT as A/A Ship. Original armament as AMCs: 4-6'', 2-3''
PRINCE HENRY	F70	''	''	4/12/40	15/4/45	
PRINCE ROBERT	F56	''	''	31/7/40	10/12/45	

Escort Aircraft Carriers

	Displacement	Dimensions	Speed	Crew	Armament
NABOB	15,390	495' 8'' x 69' 6'' x 25' 5''	18	1,000	2-5'', 16-40 mm (8 x II), 20-20 mm
PUNCHER	14,170	492' x 69' 6'' x 24' 8''	''	''	''

	Pendant	Builder	Laid Down	Launched	Commissioned	Paid Off	Remarks
NABOB	D77	ST	20/10/42	9/3/43	7/9/43	30/9/44	About 20 aircraft carried
PUNCHER	D79	''	21/5/43	8/11/43	5/2/44	16/1/46	About 20 aircraft carried. Canadian-manned but commissioned as RN ships

Destroyers, River Class

	Displacement	Dimensions	Speed	Crew	Armament	Remarks
SAGUENAY, SKEENA	1,337	320' x 32' 6'' x 10'	31	10/171	4-4.7'', 8-21'' TT (2 x IV), 2-2 pdrs.	Modified to: 2-4.7'', 1-3'', 4-21'' TT, 6-20 mm, Hedgehog
ASSINIBOINE, FRASER, MARGAREE, OTTAWA, RESTIGOUCHE, ST. LAURENT	1,375	329' x 33' x 10' 2''	31	10/171	4-4.7'', 8-21'' TT (2 x IV), 2-2 pdrs.	Modified to: 2- or 3-4.7'', 1-3'', 4-21'' TT, 6-20 mm, Hedgehog
KOOTENAY	1,375	329' x 33' x 10' 2''	31	10/171	3-4.7'', 4-21'' TT (1 x IV), 7-20 mm, Hedgehog	
GATINEAU	1,370	329' x 33' 3'' x 10' 10''	31	10/171	3-4.7'', 4-21'' TT (1 x IV), 6-20 mm, Hedgehog	
QU'APPELLE, SASKATCHEWAN	1,405	329' x 33' 3'' x 10' 10''	31	10/171	3-4.7'', 4-21'' TT (1 x IV), 6-20 mm, Hedgehog	2-4.7'' in QU'APPELLE
OTTAWA (2nd)	1,350	323' x 33' x 10' 7''	31	10/171	2-4.7'', 4-21'' TT (1 x IV), 6-20 mm, Hedgehog	
CHAUDIÈRE	1,340	323' x 33' x 9' 11''	31	10/171	2-4.7'', 4-21'' TT (1 x IV), 2-6 pdrs., 6-20 mm, Hedgehog	

	Pendant	Builder	Laid Down	Launched	Commissioned in RCN	Paid Off	Remarks
ASSINIBOINE	D/I18	WH	18/10/30	29/10/31	19/10/39	8/8/45	Ex-HMS KEMPENFELT
CHAUDIÈRE	H99	VN	28/2/35	10/3/36	15/11/43	17/8/45	Ex-HMS HERO
FRASER	H48	VB	1/2/30	29/9/31	17/2/37	28/6/40	Ex-HMS CRESCENT
GATINEAU	H61	SH	23/3/33	29/5/34	3/6/43	10/1/46	Ex-HMS EXPRESS
KOOTENAY	H75	TH	25/6/31	7/6/32	12/4/43	26/10/45	Ex-HMS DECOY
MARGAREE	H49	PM	12/6/31	16/6/32	6/9/40	22/10/40	Ex-HMS DIANA
OTTAWA	H60	PO	12/9/30	30/9/31	15/6/38	14/9/42	Ex-HMS CRUSADER
OTTAWA (2nd)	H31	VB	20/9/34	15/8/35	20/3/43	31/10/45	Ex-HMS GRIFFIN
QU'APPELLE	H69	JB	21/8/33	12/10/34	8/2/44	27/5/46	Ex-HMS FOXHOUND

	Pendant	Builder	Laid Down	Launched	Commissioned in RCN	Paid Off	Remarks
RESTIGOUCHE	H00	PO	12/9/30	30/9/31	15/6/38	6/10/45	Ex-HMS COMET
SAGUENAY	D/I79	TH	27/9/29	11/7/30	22/5/31	30/7/45	
ST. LAURENT	H83	VB	1/12/30	29/9/31	17/2/37	10/10/45	Ex-HMS CYGNET
SASKATCHEWAN	H70	JB	25/7/33	29/8/34	31/5/43	28/1/46	Ex-HMS FORTUNE
SKEENA	D/I59	TH	14/10/29	10/10/30	10/6/31	25/10/44	

Destroyers, Town Class

	Displacement	Dimensions	Speed	Crew	Armament	Remarks
ANNAPOLIS, COLUMBIA, HAMILTON, NIAGARA, ST. CLAIR	1,069	314' 3'' x 30' 6''x 8' 6''	28	10/143	4-4'', 12-21'' TT (4 x III)	Typically modified to: 1-4'', 1-12 pdr., 3-21'' TT, 4-20 mm, Hedgehog
BUXTON, ST. CROIX, ST. FRANCIS	1,190	314' 3'' x 30' 9''x 9' 3''	28	10/143	4-4'', 12-21'' TT (4 x III)	

	Pendant	Builder	Laid Down	Launched	Commissioned in RCN	Paid Off	Remarks
ANNAPOLIS	I04	UN	4/7/18	19/9/18	24/9/40	4/6/45	Ex-USS MACKENZIE
BUXTON	H96	BS	20/4/18	10/10/18	4/11/43	2/6/45	Ex-USS EDWARDS
COLUMBIA	I49	NN	30/3/18	4/7/18	24/9/40	17/3/44	Ex-USS HARADEN
HAMILTON	I24	BR	17/8/18	21/12/18	6/7/41	8/6/45	Ex-USS KALK
NIAGARA	I57	BQ	8/6/18	31/8/18	24/9/40	15/9/45	Ex-USS THATCHER
ST. CLAIR	I65	UN	25/3/18	4/7/18	''	23/8/44	Ex-USS WILLIAMS
ST. CROIX	I81	BQ	11/9/18	31/1/19	''	20/9/43	Ex-USS McCOOK
ST. FRANCIS	I93	''	4/11/18	21/3/19	''	11/6/45	Ex-USS BANCROFT

Destroyers, Tribal Class

Particulars of Class:	Displacement	Dimensions	Speed	Crew	Armament
	1,927	377' x 37' 6'' x 11' 2''	36	14/245	6-4.7'' (3 x II), 2-4'' (1 x II), 4-21'' TT(1 x IV), 4-2 pdrs., 6-20 mm

	Pendant War	Pendant 1949+	Builder	Laid Down	Launched	Commissioned	Paid Off	Remarks
ATHABASKAN	G07		VN	31/10/40	18/11/41	3/2/43	29/4/44	
HAIDA	G63	215	''	29/9/41	25/8/42	30/8/43	22/2/46	Retained. Finally paid off 11/10/63
HURON	G24	216	''	15/7/41	25/6/42	19/7/43	9/3/46	Retained. Finally paid off 30/4/63
IROQUOIS	G89	217	''	19/9/40	23/9/41	30/11/42	22/2/46	Retained. Finally paid off 24/10/62

Destroyers, "V" Class

Particulars of Class:	Displacement	Dimensions	Speed	Crew	Armament
	1,710	362' 9'' x 35' 8'' x 11' 6''	36	14/230	4-4.7'', 8-21'' TT (2 x IV), 4-40 mm, 4-20 mm

	Pendant War	Pendant 1949+	Builder	Laid Down	Launched	Commissioned	Paid Off	Remarks
ALGONQUIN	R17	224	JB	8/10/42	2/9/43	7/2/44	6/2/46	Ex-HMS VALENTINE. Retained. Finally paid off 1/4/70
SIOUX	R64	225	WH	31/10/42	14/9/43	21/2/44	27/2/46	Ex-HMS VIXEN. Retained. Finally paid off 30/10/63

Frigates, River Class

Particulars of Class:	Displacement	Dimensions	Speed	Crew	Armament	Remarks
	1,445	301' 6'' x 36' 7'' x 9'	19	8/133	2-4'' (1 x II), 4-20 mm, Hedgehog	In 1st 15 built: 1-4'', 1-12 pdr.

	War	Pendant 1949+	Builder	Laid Down	Launched	Commissioned	Paid Off	Recommissioned as "Prestonian"	Paid Off (Final)
1942-43 Programme									
BEACON HILL	K407	303	YA	16/7/43	6/11/43	16/5/44	6/2/46	21/12/57	15/9/67
CAP de la MADELEINE	K663	317	MO	5/11/43	13/5/44	30/9/44	25/11/45	7/12/54	15/5/65
CAPE BRETON	K350		''	5/5/42	24/11/42	25/10/43	26/1/46		
CHARLOTTETOWN (2nd)	K244		DS	26/1/43	16/9/43	28/4/44	25/3/47		
CHEBOGUE	K317		YA	19/3/43	17/8/43	22/2/44	25/9/45		
DUNVER	K03		MO	5/5/42	10/11/42	11/9/43	23/1/46		
EASTVIEW	K665		CV	26/8/43	17/11/43	3/6/44	17/1/46		
GROU	K518		''	1/5/43	7/8/43	4/12/43	25/2/46		
JOLIETTE	K418		MO	19/7/43	12/11/43	14/6/44	19/11/45		
JONQUIÈRE	K318	318	DS	26/1/43	28/10/43	10/5/44	4/12/45	20/9/54	23/9/66
KIRKLAND LAKE	K337		MO	16/11/43	27/4/44	21/8/44	14/12/45		
KOKANEE	K419		YA	25/8/43	27/11/43	6/6/44	21/12/45		
La HULLOISE	K668	305	CV	10/8/43	29/10/43	20/5/44	6/12/45	9/10/57	16/7/65
LONGUEUIL	K672		''	17/7/43	30/10/43	18/5/44	31/12/45		
MAGOG	K673		''	16/6/43	22/9/43	7/5/44	20/12/44		
MATANE	K444		''	23/12/42	29/5/43	22/10/43	11/2/46		
MONTREAL	K319		''	''	12/6/43	12/11/43	15/10/45		
NEW GLASGOW	K320	315	YA	4/1/43	5/5/43	23/12/43	5/11/45	30/1/54	30/1/67
NEW WATERFORD	K321	304	''	17/2/43	3/7/43	21/1/44	7/3/46	31/1/58	2/12/66
ORKNEY	K448		''	19/5/53	18/9/43	18/4/44	22/1/46		
OUTREMONT	K322	310	MO	18/11/42	3/7/43	27/11/43	5/11/45	2/9/55	7/6/65
PORT COLBORNE	K326		YA	16/12/42	21/4/43	15/11/43	7/11/45		
PRINCE RUPERT	K324		''	1/8/42	3/2/43	30/8/43	15/1/46		
ST. CATHARINES	K325	324	''	2/5/42	5/12/42	31/7/43	18/11/45		31/8/50
SAINT JOHN	K456		CV	28/5/43	25/8/43	13/12/43	27/11/45		
SPRINGHILL	K323		YA	5/5/43	7/9/43	21/3/44	1/12/45		
STETTLER	K681	311	CV	31/5/43	10/9/43	7/5/44	9/11/45	27/2/54	31/8/66
STORMONT	K327		''	23/12/42	14/7/43	27/11/43	''		
SWANSEA	K328	306	YA	15/7/42	19/12/42	4/10/43	2/11/45	14/11/57	14/10/66
THETFORD MINES	K459		MO	7/7/43	30/10/43	24/5/44	18/11/45		
VALLEYFIELD	K329		''	30/11/42	17/7/43	7/12/43	7/5/44		
WASKESIU	K330		YA	2/5/42	6/12/42	16/6/43	29/1/46		
WENTWORTH	K331		''	11/11/42	6/3/43	7/12/43	10/10/45		
1943-44 Programme									
ANTIGONISH	K661	301	YA	2/10/43	10/2/44	4/7/44	5/2/46	12/10/57	30/11/66
BUCKINGHAM	K685	314	DS	11/10/43	28/4/44	2/11/44	16/11/45	25/6/54	23/3/65
CAPILANO	K409		YA	18/11/43	8/4/44	25/8/44	24/11/45		
CARLPLACE	K664		DS	30/11/43	6/7/44	13/12/44	13/11/45		
COATICOOK	K410		''	14/6/43	26/11/43	25/7/44	29/11/45		
FORT ERIE	K670	312	GD	3/11/43	27/5/44	27/10/44	22/11/45	17/4/56	26/3/65

210

	War	Pendant 1949+	Builder	Laid Down	Launched	Commissioned	Paid Off	Recommissioned as "Prestonian"	Paid Off (Final)
GLACE BAY	K414		''	23/9/43	26/4/44	2/9/44	17/11/45		
HALLOWELL	K666		CV	22/11/43	28/3/44	8/8/44	7/11/45		
INCH ARRAN	K667	308	DS	25/10/43	6/6/44	18/11/44	28/11/45	23/8/54	23/6/65
LANARK	K669	321	CV	25/9/43	10/12/43	6/7/44	24/10/45	15/4/56	19/3/65
LASALLE	K519		DS	4/6/43	12/11/43	29/6/44	17/12/45		
LAUZON	K671	322	GD	2/7/43	10/6/44	30/8/44	7/11/45	12/12/53	24/5/63
LÉVIS (2nd)	K400		''	25/2/43	26/11/43	21/7/44	15/2/46		
PENETANG	K676	316	DS	22/9/43	6/7/44	19/10/44	10/11/45	1/6/54	25/1/56
POUNDMAKER	K675		CV	29/1/44	21/4/44	17/9/44	25/11/45		
PRESTONIAN	K662	307	DS	20/7/43	22/6/44	13/9/44	9/11/45	22/8/53	24/4/56
ROYALMOUNT	K677		CV	7/1/44	15/4/44	25/8/44	17/11/45		
RUNNYMEDE	K678		''	11/9/43	27/11/43	14/6/44	19/1/46		
ST. PIERRE	K680		DS	30/6/43	1/12/43	22/8/44	22/11/45		
ST. STEPHEN	K454	323	YA	5/10/43	6/2/44	28/7/44	30/1/46		
STE. THÉRÈSE	K366	309	DS	18/5/43	16/10/43	28/5/44	2/11/45	21/1/55	30/1/67
SEA CLIFF	K344		''	20/7/43	8/7/44	26/9/44	28/11/45		
STONE TOWN	K531	302	CV	17/11/43	28/3/44	21/7/44	13/11/45		
STRATHADAM	K682		YA	6/12/43	20/3/44	29/9/44	7/11/45		
SUSSEXVALE	K683	313	DS	15/11/43	12/7/44	29/11/44	16/11/45	8/1/55	30/11/66
TORONTO	K538	319	''	10/5/43	18/9/43	6/5/44	27/11/45	26/11/53	14/4/56
VICTORIAVILLE	K684	320	GD	2/12/43	23/6/44	11/11/44	17/11/45	25/9/59	31/12/73
River Class, ex-RN									
ANNAN	K404		HA	10/6/43	29/12/43	13/6/44	20/6/45		
ETTRICK	K254		JC	31/12/41	5/2/43	29/1/44	30/5/45		
MEON	K269		AJ	31/12/42	4/8/43	7/2/44	23/4/45		
MONNOW	K441		CH	28/9/43	4/12/43	8/3/44	11/6/45		
NENE	K270		SD	20/6/42	9/12/42	6/4/44	''		
RIBBLE	K525		BL	31/12/42	10/11/43	24/7/44	''		
TEME	K458		SD	25/5/43	11/11/43	28/2/44	4/5/45		

Frigates, Loch Class

Particulars of Class:	Displacement	Dimensions	Speed	Crew	Armament
	1,435	307' x 38' 7'' x 8' 9''	19	8/133	1-4'', 6-20 mm, Squid

	Pendant	Builder	Laid Down	Launched	Commissioned	Paid Off
LOCH ACHANALT	K424	HR	13/9/43	23/3/44	31/7/44	20/6/45
LOCH ALVIE	K428	BC	31/8/43	14/4/44	10/8/44	11/6/45
LOCH MORLICH	K517	SH	15/7/43	25/1/44	17/7/44	20/6/45

Corvettes, Flower Class

1939-40 Programme

Particulars of Class:	Displacement	Dimensions	Speed	Crew	Armament	
	950	205' 1'' x 33' 1'' x 11' 6''	16	6/79	1-4'', 1-2 pdr., 2-20 mm, Hedgehog in many	

	Pendant	Builder	Laid Down	Launched	Commissioned	Paid Off	Place	Fo'c's'le Extension Place and Date Completed
AGASSIZ	K129	BU	29/4/40	15/8/40	23/1/41	14/6/45	New York City, N.Y.	4/3/44
ALBERNI	K103	YA	19/4/40	22/8/40	4/2/41	21/8/44	Never done; ship was lost	
ALGOMA	K127	PA	18/6/40	17/12/40	11/7/41	6/7/45	Liverpool, N.S.	15/4/44
AMHERST	K148	SJ	23/5/40	4/12/40	5/8/41	16/7/45	Charlottetown P.E.I.	1/11/43
ARROWHEAD	K145	MI	11/4/40	8/8/40	15/5/41	27/6/45	Baltimore, Md.	25/5/44
ARVIDA	K113	MO	28/2/40	21/9/40	22/5/41	14/6/45	''	8/4/44
BADDECK	K147	DS	14/8/40	20/11/40	18/5/41	4/7/45	Liverpool, N.S.	15/11/43
BARRIE	K138	CO	4/4/40	23/11/40	12/5/41	26/6/45	''	17/4/44
BATTLEFORD	K165	''	30/9/40	15/4/41	31/7/41	18/7/45	Sydney, N.S.	31/7/44
BITTERSWEET	K182	MI	17/4/40	12/9/40	15/5/41	22/6/45	Baltimore, Md.	9/11/43
BRANDON	K149	DS	10/10/40	29/4/41	22/7/41	22/6/45	Grimsby, U.K.	16/10/43
BUCTOUCHE	K179	''	14/8/40	20/11/40	5/6/41	15/6/45	Saint John, N.B.	29/1/44
CAMROSE	K154	MI	17/9/40	16/11/40	30/6/41	22/7/45	Pictou, N.S.	15/10/43
CHAMBLY	K116	CV	20/2/40	29/7/40	18/12/40	20/6/45	Liverpool, N.S.	17/3/44
CHICOUTIMI	K156	''	5/7/40	16/10/40	12/5/41	16/6/45	Never done	
CHILLIWACK	K131	BU	3/7/40	14/9/40	8/4/41	14/7/45	Dartmouth, N.S.	10/10/43
COBALT	K124	PA	1/4/40	17/8/40	25/11/40	17/6/45	Liverpool, N.S.	20/7/44
COLLINGWOOD	K180	CO	2/3/40	27/7/40	9/11/40	23/7/45	New York City, N.Y.	14/12/43
DAUPHIN	K157	CV	6/7/40	24/10/40	17/5/41	20/6/45	Pictou, N.S.	5/9/43
DAWSON	K104	VM	7/9/40	8/2/41	6/10/41	19/6/45	Vancouver, B.C.	29/1/44
DRUMHELLER	K167	CO	4/12/40	5/7/41	13/9/41	11/7/45	New York City, N.Y.	15/1/44
DUNVEGAN	K177	MI	30/8/40	11/12/40	9/9/41	3/7/45	Baltimore, Md.	27/12/43
EDMUNDSTON	K106	YA	23/8/40	22/2/41	21/10/41	16/6/45	Halifax, N.S.	3/6/43
EYEBRIGHT	K150	CV	20/2/40	22/7/40	15/5/41	17/6/45	Baltimore, Md.	21/8/43
FENNEL	K194	MI	29/3/40	20/8/40	''	12/6/45	''	6/9/43
GALT	K163	CO	27/5/40	28/12/40	''	21/6/45	New York City, N.Y.	8/5/44
HEPATICA	K159	DS	24/2/40	6/7/40	''	27/6/45	''	8/6/44
KAMLOOPS	K176	VM	29/4/40	7/8/40	17/3/41	27/6/45	Charlottetown, P.E.I.	25/4/44
KAMSACK	K171	PA	20/11/40	5/5/41	4/10/41	22/7/45	Baltimore, Md.	14/3/44
KENOGAMI	K125	''	20/4/40	5/9/40	29/6/41	9/7/45	Liverpool, N.S.	1/10/44
LETHBRIDGE	K160	CV	5/8/40	21/11/40	25/6/41	23/7/45	Sydney, N.S.	27/3/44
LÉVIS	K115	GD	11/3/40	4/9/40	16/5/41	19/9/41	Never done; ship was lost	
LOUISBURG	K143	MO	4/10/40	27/5/41	2/10/41	6/2/43	'' ''	
LUNENBURG	K151	GD	28/9/40	10/7/41	4/12/41	23/7/45	Liverpool, U.K.	17/8/43
MATAPEDIA	K112	MO	2/2/40	14/9/40	9/5/41	16/6/45	Liverpool, N.S.	3/2/44
MAYFLOWER	K191	CV	20/2/40	3/7/40	15/5/41	31/5/45	Baltimore, Md.	14/2/44
MONCTON	K139	SJ	17/12/40	11/8/41	24/4/42	12/12/45	Vancouver, B.C.	7/7/44
MOOSE JAW	K164	CO	12/8/40	9/4/41	19/6/41	8/7/45	Liverpool, N.S.	23/3/44
MORDEN	K170	PA	25/10/40	5/5/41	6/9/41	29/6/45	Londonderry, Ireland	29/1/44
NANAIMO	K101	YA	27/4/40	28/10/40	26/4/41	28/9/45	Never done	

	Pendant	Builder	Laid Down	Launched	Commissioned	Paid Off	Fo'c's'le Extension Place and Date Completed	
NAPANEE	K118	KI	20/3/40	31/8/40	12/5/41	12/7/45	Montreal, Que.	19/10/43
OAKVILLE	K 178	PA	21/12/40	21/6/41	18/11/41	20/7/45	Galveston, Tex.	29/3/44
ORILLIA	K119	CO	4/3/40	15/9/40	25/11/40	2/7/45	Liverpool, N.S.	3/5/44
PICTOU	K146	DS	12/7/40	5/10/40	29/4/41	12/7/45	New York City, N.Y.	31/3/44
PRESCOTT	K161	KI	31/8/40	7/1/41	26/6/41	20/7/45	Liverpool, N.S.	27/10/43
QUESNEL	K133	VM	9/5/40	12/11/40	23/5/41	3/7/45	Pictou, N.S.	23/12/43
RIMOUSKI	K121	DS	12/7/40	3/10/40	26/4/41	24/7/45	Liverpool, N.S.	24/8/43
ROSTHERN	K169	PA	18/6/40	30/11/40	17/6/41	19/7/45	Never done	
SACKVILLE	K181	SJ	28/5/40	15/5/41	30/12/41	8/4/46	Galveston, Tex.	7/5/44
SASKATOON	K158	CV	9/8/40	6/11/40	9/6/41	25/6/45	Pictou, N.S.	1/4/44
SHAWINIGAN	K136	GD	4/6/40	16/5/41	19/9/41	25/11/44	Never done; ship was lost	
SHEDIAC	K110	DS	5/10/40	29/4/41	8/7/41	28/8/45	Vancouver, B.C.	18/8/44
SHERBROOKE	K152	MI	5/8/40	25/10/40	5/6/41	28/6/45	Liverpool, N.S.	22/8/44
SNOWBERRY	K166	DS	24/2/40	8/8/40	15/5/41	8/6/45	Charleston, S.C.	14/5/43
SOREL	K153	MI	24/8/40	16/11/40	19/8/41	22/6/45	Liverpool, N.S.	5/12/42
SPIKENARD	K198	DS	24/2/40	10/8/40	15/5/41	10/2/42	Never done; ship was lost	
SUDBURY	K162	KI	25/1/41	31/5/41	15/10/41	28/8/45	Vancouver, B.C.	10/5/44
SUMMERSIDE	K141	MO	4/10/40	17/5/41	11/9/41	6/7/45	Saint John, N.B.	25/9/43
THE PAS	K168	CO	7/1/41	16/8/41	21/10/41	24/7/45	Never done	
TRAIL	K174	BU	20/7/40	17/10/40	30/4/41	17/7/45	Liverpool, N.S.	23/10/44
TRILLIUM	K172	CV	20/2/40	26/6/40	15/5/41	27/6/45	Boston, Mass.	10/6/43
WETASKIWIN	K175	BU	11/4/40	18/7/40	17/12/40	19/6/45	Galveston, Tex.	6/3/44
WEYBURN	K173	''	21/12/40	26/7/41	26/11/41	22/2/43	Never done; ship was lost	
WINDFLOWER	K155	DS	24/2/40	4/7/40	15/5/41	7/12/41	'' ''	

Flower Class
1940-41 Programme

Particulars of Class:	Displacement	Dimensions	Speed	Crew	Armament
	950	205' 1'' x 33' 1'' x 11' 6''	16	6/79	1-4'', 1-2 pdr., 2-20 mm, Hedgehog in many

	Pendant	Builder	Laid Down	Launched	Commissioned	Paid Off	Fo'c's'le Extension Place and Date Completed	
BRANTFORD	K218	MS	24/2/41	6/9/41	15/5/42	17/8/45	Never done	
DUNDAS	K229	VM	19/3/41	25/7/41	1/4/42	17/7/45	Montreal, Que.	19/11/43
MIDLAND	K220	MS	24/2/41	25/6/41	17/11/41	15/7/45	Galveston, Tex.	25/5/44
NEW WESTMINSTER	K228	VM	4/2/41	14/5/41	31/1/42	21/6/45	Sydney, N.S.	10/12/43
TIMMINS	K223	YA	14/12/40	26/6/41	10/2/42	15/7/45	Liverpool, N.S.	16/10/44
VANCOUVER	K240	''	16/6/41	26/8/41	20/3/42	26/6/45	Vancouver, B.C.	16/9/43

Revised Flower Class
1940-41 Programme

Particulars of Class:	Displacement	Dimensions	Speed	Crew	Armament	Remarks
	1,015	208' 4'' x 33' 1'' x 11'	16	6/79	1-4'', 1-2 pdr., 2-20 mm, Hedgehog in many	First corvettes built with long fo'c's'le

	Pendant	Builder	Laid Down	Launched	Commissioned	Paid Off
CALGARY	K231	MI	22/3/41	23/8/41	16/12/41	19/6/45
CHARLOTTETOWN	K244	KI	7/6/41	10/9/41	13/12/41	11/9/42
FREDERICTON	K245	MI	22/3/41	2/9/41	8/12/41	14/7/45
HALIFAX	K237	CO	26/4/41	4/10/41	26/11/41	12/7/45
KITCHENER	K225	MI	28/2/41	18/11/41	28/6/42	11/7/45
La MALBAIE	K273	''	22/3/41	25/10/41	28/4/42	28/6/45
PORT ARTHUR	K233	PA	28/4/41	18/9/41	26/5/42	11/7/45
REGINA	K234	MI	22/3/41	14/10/41	22/1/42	8/8/44
VILLE de QUÉBEC	K242	MO	7/6/41	12/11/41	24/5/42	6/7/45
WOODSTOCK	K238	CO	23/5/41	10/12/41	1/5/42	27/1/45

Revised Flower Class (Increased Endurance)
1942-43 Programme

Particulars of Class:	Displacement	Dimensions	Speed	Crew	Armament
	970	208' 4'' x 33' 1'' x 11'	16	6/79	1-4'', 1-2 pdr., 2-20 mm, Hedgehog

	Pendant	Builder	Laid Down	Launched	Commissioned	Paid Off
ATHOLL	K15	MO	15/8/42	4/4/43	14/10/43	17/7/45
COBOURG	K333	MS	25/11/42	14/7/43	11/5/44	15/6/45
FERGUS	K686	CO	10/12/43	30/8/44	18/11/44	14/7/45
FRONTENAC	K335	KI	19/2/43	2/6/43	26/10/43	22/7/45
GUELPH	K687	CO	29/5/43	20/12/43	9/5/44	27/6/45
HAWKESBURY	K415	MO	20/7/43	16/11/43	14/6/44	10/7/45
LINDSAY	K338	MS	30/9/42	4/6/43	15/11/43	18/7/45
LOUISBURG (2nd)	K401	MO	11/1/43	13/7/43	13/12/43	25/6/45
NORSYD	K520	''	14/1/43	31/7/43	22/12/43	''
NORTH BAY	K339	CO	24/9/42	27/4/43	25/10/43	1/7/45
OWEN SOUND	K340	''	11/11/42	15/6/43	17/11/43	19/7/45
RIVIÈRE du LOUP	K537	MO	5/1/43	2/7/43	21/11/43	2/7/45
ST. LAMBERT	K343	''	8/7/43	6/11/43	27/5/44	20/7/45
TRENTONIAN	K368	KI	19/2/43	1/9/43	1/12/43	22/2/45
WHITBY	K346	MI	1/4/43	18/9/43	6/6/44	16/7/45

Revised Flower Class (Increased Endurance)
1943-44 Programme

Particulars of Class:	Displacement	Dimensions	Speed	Crew	Armament
	970	208' 4'' x 33' 1'' x 11'	16	6/79	1-4'', 1-2 pdr., 2-20 mm, Hedgehog

	Pendant	Builder	Laid Down	Launched	Commissioned	Paid Off
ASBESTOS	K358	MO	20/7/43	22/11/43	16/6/44	8/7/45
BEAUHARNOIS	K540	''	8/11/43	11/5/44	25/9/44	12/7/45

	Pendant	Builder	Laid Down	Launched	Commissioned	Paid Off
BELLEVILLE	K332	KI	21/1/44	17/6/44	19/10/44	5/7/45
LACHUTE	K440	MO	24/11/43	9/6/44	26/10/44	10/7/45
MERRITTONIA	K688	''	23/11/43	24/6/44	10/11/44	11/7/45
PARRY SOUND	K341	MI	11/6/43	13/11/43	30/8/44	10/7/45
PETERBOROUGH	K342	KI	14/9/43	15/1/44	1/6/44	19/7/45
SMITHS FALLS	K345	''	21/1/44	19/8/44	28/11/44	8/7/45
STELLARTON	K457	MO	16/11/43	27/4/44	29/9/44	1/7/45
STRATHROY	K455	MI	18/11/43	15/6/44	20/11/44	12/7/45
THORLOCK	K394	''	25/9/43	15/5/44	13/11/44	15/7/45
WEST YORK	K369	''	23/7/43	25/1/44	6/10/44	9/7/45

Revised Flower Class (Increased Endurance), ex-RN

Particulars of Class:	Displacement	Dimensions	Speed	Crew	Armament
	970	208' 4'' x 33' 1'' x 11'	16	6/79	1-4'', 1-2 pdr., 2-20 mm, Hedgehog

	Pendant	Builder	Laid Down	Launched	Commissioned	Paid Off	Remarks
FOREST HILL	K486	FE	5/2/43	30/8/43	1/12/43	9/7/45	Ex-HMS CEANOTHUS
GIFFARD	K402	AH	30/11/42	19/6/43	10/11/43	5/7/45	Ex-HMS BUDDLEIA
LONG BRANCH	K487	AJ	27/2/43	28/9/43	5/1/44	17/6/45	Ex-HMS CANDYTUFT
MIMICO	K485	JC	22/2/43	11/10/43	8/2/44	18/7/45	Ex-HMS BULRUSH

Corvettes, Castle Class, ex-RN

Particulars of Class:	Displacement	Dimensions	Speed	Crew	Armament
	1,060	251' 9'' x 36' 8'' x 10'	16	7/105	1-4'', 6-20 mm (2 x II, 2 x I), Squid

	Pendant	Builder	Laid Down	Launched	Commissioned	Paid Off	Remarks
ARNPRIOR	K494	HW	21/6/43	8/2/44	8/6/44	14/3/46	Ex-HMS RISING CASTLE
BOWMANVILLE	K493	WP	12/8/43	26/1/44	28/9/44	15/2/46	Ex-HMS NUNNEY CASTLE
COPPER CLIFF	K495	BL	29/6/43	24/2/44	25/7/44	21/11/45	Ex-HMS HEVER CASTLE
HESPELER	K489	HR	25/5/43	13/11/43	28/2/44	15/11/45	Ex-HMS GUILDFORD CASTLE
HUMBERSTONE	K497	AJ	30/8/43	12/4/44	6/9/44	17/11/45	Ex-HMS NORHAM CASTLE
HUNTSVILLE	K499	AS	1/6/43	24/2/44	6/6/44	15/2/46	Ex-HMS WOOLVESEY CASTLE
KINCARDINE	K490	SD	25/8/43	26/1/44	19/6/44	27/2/46	Ex-HMS TAMWORTH CASTLE
LEASIDE	K492	''	23/9/43	10/3/44	21/8/44	16/11/45	Ex-HMS WALMER CASTLE
ORANGEVILLE	K491	HR	23/7/43	26/1/44	24/4/44	12/4/46	Ex-HMS HEDINGHAM CASTLE
PETROLIA	K498	HW	21/6/43	24/2/44	29/6/44	8/3/46	Ex-HMS SHERBORNE CASTLE
ST. THOMAS	K488	SD	23/6/43	28/12/43	4/5/44	22/11/45	Ex-HMS SANDGATE CASTLE
TILLSONBURG	K496	FE	3/6/43	12/2/44	29/6/44	15/2/46	Ex-HMS PEMBROKE CASTLE

A/S Trawlers, Western Isles Class

Particulars of Class:	Displacement	Dimensions	Speed	Crew	Armament
	530	164' x 27' 8'' x 8' 7''	12	4/36	1-12 pdr., 3-20 mm

	Pendant	Builder	Laid Down	Launched	Commissioned	Paid Off
ANTICOSTI	T274	CO	9/10/41	1/4/42	10/8/42	17/6/45
BAFFIN	T275	''	14/10/41	13/4/42	26/8/42	20/8/45
CAILIFF	T276	''	1/12/41	30/4/42	17/9/42	10/6/45
IRONBOUND	T284	KI	7/10/41	14/1/42	16/10/42	17/6/45
LISCOMB	T285	''	7/1/42	23/3/42	8/9/42	''
MAGDALEN	T279	MI	10/10/41	7/3/42	24/8/42	''
MANITOULIN	T280	''	25/11/41	23/4/42	28/9/42	''
MISCOU	T277	CO	1/12/41	1/6/42	17/10/42	''

Minesweepers, Algerine Class

Particulars of Class:	Displacement	Dimensions	Speed	Crew	Armament
	990	225' x 35' 6'' x 8' 6''	16	8/99	1-4'', 4-20 mm, Hedgehog

	Pendant War	Pendant 1949+	Builder	Laid Down	Launched	Commissioned	Paid Off
BORDER CITIES	J344		PA	26/8/42	3/5/43	18/5/44	15/1/46
FORT FRANCES	J396	170	''	11/5/53	30/10/43	28/10/44	3/8/45
KAPUSKASING	J326	171	''	19/12/42	22/7/43	17/8/44	27/3/46
MIDDLESEX	J328		''	29/9/42	27/5/43	8/6/44	31/12/46
NEW LISKEARD	J397	169	''	8/7/43	41/1/44	21/11/44	8/4/46
OSHAWA	J330	174	''	6/10/42	10/6/43	6/7/44	28/7/45
PORTAGE	J331	169	''	23/5/42	21/11/42	22/10/43	31/7/46
ROCKCLIFFE	J355	173	''	23/12/42	19/8/43	30/9/44	28/7/45
SAULT STE. MARIE	J334	176	''	27/1/42	5/8/42	24/6/43	12/1/46
ST. BONIFACE	J332		''	21/5/42	5/11/42	10/9/43	25/9/46
WALLACEBURG	J336	172	''	6/7/42	17/12/42	18/11/43	7/10/46
WINNIPEG	J337	177	''	31/1/42	19/9/42	29/7/43	11/1/46

Minesweepers, Bangor Class

1939-40 Programme

Particulars of Class:	Displacement	Dimensions	Speed	Crew	Armament
	672	180' x 28' 6'' x 8' 3''	16	6/77	1-4'', 1-3'' or 1-12 pdr., 2-20 mm

	War	Pendant 1949+	Builder	Laid Down	Launched	Commissioned	Paid Off
BELLECHASSE	J170		BU	16/4/41	20/10/41	13/12/41	23/10/45
BURLINGTON	J250		DU	4/7/40	23/11/40	6/9/41	30/10/45
CHEDABUCTO	J168		BU	24/1/41	14/4/41	27/9/41	31/10/43
CHIGNECTO	J160		NV	11/9/40	12/12/40	31/10/41	3/11/45
CLAYOQUOT	J174		PR	20/6/40	3/10/40	22/8/41	24/12/44
COWICHAN	J146		NV	24/4/40	9/8/40	4/7/41	9/10/45
GEORGIAN	J144		DU	10/10/40	28/1/41	23/9/41	23/10/45
MAHONE	J159	192	NV	13/8/40	14/11/40	29/9/41	6/11/45
MALPEQUE	J148	186	''	24/4/40	5/9/40	4/8/41	9/10/45
MINAS	J165	189	BU	18/10/40	22/1/41	2/8/41	6/10/45
MIRAMICHI	J169		''	11/3/41	2/9/41	26/11/41	24/10/45
NIPIGON	J154	188	DU	4/7/40	1/10/40	11/8/41	13/10/45
OUTARDE	J161		NV	15/10/40	27/1/41	4/12/41	24/11/45
QUATSINO	J152		PR	20/6/40	9/1/41	3/11/41	26/11/45
QUINTE	J166		BU	14/12/40	8/3/41	30/8/41	25/10/46
THUNDER	J156		DU	4/12/40	19/3/41	14/10/41	4/10/45
UNGAVA	J149		NV	24/4/40	9/10/40	5/9/41	3/4/46
WASAGA	J162		BU	3/9/40	23/1/41	30/6/41	6/10/45

Bangor Class, ex-RN

Particulars of Class:	Displacement	Dimensions	Speed	Crew	Armament
	672	180' x 28' 6'' x 8' 3''	16	6/77	1-12 pdr., 2-20 mm

	Pendant	Builder	Laid Down	Launched	Commissioned	Paid Off
BAYFIELD	J08	NV	30/12/40	26/5/41	26/2/42	24/9/45
CANSO	J21	''	''	9/6/41	6/3/42	''
CARAQUET	J38	''	31/1/41	2/6/41	2/4/42	26/9/45
GUYSBOROUGH	J52	''	28/5/41	21/7/41	22/4/42	17/3/45
INGONISH	J69	''	6/6/41	30/7/41	8/5/42	2/7/45
LOCKEPORT	J100	''	17/6/41	22/8/41	27/5/42	''

Bangor Class

1940-41 Programme

Particulars of Class:	Displacement	Dimensions	Speed	Crew	Armament
	672	180' x 28' 6'' x 8' 3''	16	6/77	1-4'', 1-3'' or 1-12 pdr., 2-20 mm

	War	Pendant 1949+	Builder	Laid Down	Launched	Commissioned	Paid Off
COURTENAY	J262		PR	28/1/41	2/8/41	21/3/42	5/11/45
DRUMMONDVILLE	J253	181	CV	10/1/41	21/5/41	30/10/41	29/10/45
GANANOQUE	J259	184	DU	15/1/41	23/4/41	8/11/41	13/10/45

	War	Pendant 1949+	Builder	Laid Down	Launched	Commissioned	Paid Off
GODERICH	J260	198	''	''	14/5/41	23/11/41	6/11/45
GRANDMÈRE	J258		CV	2/6/41	21/8/41	11/12/41	23/10/45
KELOWNA	J261		PR	27/12/40	28/5/41	5/2/42	22/10/45
MEDICINE HAT	J256	197	CV	10/1/41	25/6/41	4/12/41	6/11/45
RED DEER	J255	196	''	''	5/10/41	24/11/41	30/10/45
SWIFT CURRENT	J254	185	''	''	29/5/41	11/11/41	23/10/45
VEGREVILLE	J257		''	2/6/41	7/10/41	10/12/41	6/6/45

Bangor Class

1940-41 Programme (diesel)

Particulars of Class:	Displacement	Dimensions	Speed	Crew	Armament
	592	162' x 28' x 8' 3''	16	6/77	1-12 pdr., 2-20 mm

	War	Pendant 1949+	Builder	Laid Down	Launched	Commissioned	Paid Off
BROCKVILLE	J270	178	MI	9/12/40	20/6/41	19/9/42	28/8/45
DIGBY	J267	179	DS	20/3/41	5/6/42	26/7/42	31/7/45
ESQUIMALT	J272		MI	20/12/40	8/8/41	26/10/42	16/4/45
GRANBY	J264	180	DS	17/12/40	9/6/41	2/5/42	31/7/45
LACHINE	J266		''	27/12/40	14/6/41	20/6/42	31/7/45
MELVILLE	J263		''	17/12/40	7/6/41	4/12/41	18/8/45
NORANDA	J265		''	27/12/40	13/6/41	15/5/42	28/8/45
TRANSCONA	J271		MI	18/12/40	26/4/41	25/11/42	31/7/45
TROIS-RIVIÈRES	J269		''	9/12/40	30/6/41	12/8/42	''
TRURO	J268		DS	20/3/41	5/6/42	27/8/42	''

Bangor Class

1941-42 Programme

Particulars of Class:	Displacement	Dimensions	Speed	Crew	Armament
	672	180' x 28' 6'' x 8' 3''	16	6/77	1-4'', 1-3'' or 1-12 pdr., 2-20 mm

	War	Pendant 1949+	Builder	Laid Down	Launched	Commissioned	Paid Off
BLAIRMORE	J314	193	PA	2/1/42	14/5/42	17/11/42	16/10/45
FORT WILLIAM	J311	195	''	18/8/41	30/12/41	25/8/42	23/10/45
KENORA	J281	191	''	''	20/12/41	6/8/42	6/10/45
KENTVILLE	J312	182	''	15/12/41	17/4/42	10/10/42	28/10/45
MILLTOWN	J317	194	''	18/8/41	27/1/42	18/9/42	16/10/45
MULGRAVE	J313		''	15/12/41	2/5/42	4/11/42	7/6/45
PORT HOPE	J280	183	DS	9/9/41	14/12/41	30/7/42	13/10/45
SARNIA	J309	190	''	18/9/41	21/1/42	13/8/42	28/10/45
STRATFORD	J310		''	29/10/41	14/2/42	29/8/42	4/1/46
WESTMOUNT	J318	187	''	28/10/41	14/3/42	15/9/42	13/10/45

Armed Yachts

	Former Name	Pendant	Builder	Launch Date	Displacement	Dimensions	Speed	Crew	Armament	Commissioned	Paid Off
AMBLER	same	Q11/Z32	Tebo Yacht Basin Co., Brooklyn, N.Y.	1922	273	130' x 23' x 10'	9	4/17	3-.303 m.g.	6/5/40	20/7/45
BEAVER	Aztec	S10/Z10	Crescent Shipyard, Elizabeth, N.J.	1902	808	260' x 28' x 13'	12	5/45	1-4''	1/4/41	17/10/44
CARIBOU	Elfreda	S12/Z25	Defoe Shipbuilding Co., Bay City, Mich.	1928	306	142' x 23' x 9'	11	5/35	1-12 pdr.	27/5/40	20/7/45
COUGAR	Breezin' Thru	Z15	Geo. Lawley & Sons, Neponset, Mass.	1916	204	140' x 20' x 10'	10	''	1-6 pdr.	11/9/40	23/11/45
ELK	Arcadia	S05/Z27	Newport News S.B. Co., Newport News, Va.	1926	578	188' x 27' x 11'	11	''	1-4''	10/9/40	4/8/45
GRIZZLY	Machigonne	Z14	Consolidated S.B. Corp., New York, N.Y.	1909	195	140' x 19' x 10'	12	''	1-6 pdr.	17/7/41	17/6/44
HUSKY	Wild Duck	S06/Z13	Defoe Boat & Engine Works, Bay City, Mich.	1930	360	153' x 25' x 10'	10	''	1-4''	23/7/40	3/8/45
LYNX	Ramona	Z07	Newport News S.B. Co., Newport News, Va.	1922	495	181' x 24' x 9'	''	''	''	26/8/40	23/4/42
MOOSE	Cleopatra	Z14	Geo. Lawley & Sons, Neponset, Mass.	1930	263	130' x 22' x 9'	12	''	1-12 pdr.	8/9/40	20/7/45
OTTER	Conseco		Robert Jacob, City Island, N.Y.	1921	419	160' x 25' x 10'	10	''	1-4''	4/10/40	26/3/41
RACCOON	Halonia		Bath Iron Works, Bath, Me.	1931	377	148' x 25' x 10'	11	''	1-12 pdr.	31/12/40	7/9/42
REINDEER	Mascotte	S08/Z08	Newport News S.B. Co., Newport News, Va.	1926	337	140' x 24' x 9'	''	''	1-4''	25/7/40	20/7/45
RENARD	Winchester	S13/Z13	Bath Iron Works, Bath, Me.	1916	411	225' x 21' x 8'	15	''	1-12 pdr., 2-21'' TT	27/5/40	1/8/44
SANS PEUR	same	Z02/Z52	Thornycroft & Co., Southampton, U.K.	1933	856	210' x 30' x 13'	13	5/43	1-4'', 1-12 pdr.	5/3/40	31/1/47
VISON	Avalon	S11/Z30	Pusey & Jones Corp., Wilmington, Del.	1931	422	181' x 24' x 13'	10	5/35	1-12 pdr.	5/10/40	4/8/45
WOLF	Blue Water	Z16	Geo. Lawley & Sons, Neponset, Mass.	1915	320	172' x 23' x 10'	''	5/38	1-12 pdr., 1-2 pdr.	2/10/40	16/5/45

Motor Craft

	Displacement	Dimensions	Speed	Crew	Designed Armament
CMTB.1	32	70' x 20' 4'' x 4' 9''	40	2/8	4-.5'' m.g. (2 x II), 4-18'' TT
S-09	45	70' x 20' x 4' 6''	22		''
"G" TYPE MTBs	44	71' 9'' x 20' 7'' x 5' 8''	39	3/14	1-6 pdr, 2-20 mm (1 x II), 2-18'' TT
"D" TYPE MTBs	102	115' x 21' 3'' x 5' 3''	29	4/28	2-6 pdrs., 2-20 mm (1 x II), 4-18'' TT
"B" TYPE MLs 053-111	79	112' x 17' 10'' x 4' 10''	20	3/14	3-20 mm
"B" TYPE MLs 112-129	''	112' x 17' x 4' 10''	22	''	''

Landing Craft, Infantry (Large)

Displacement	Dimensions	Speed	Crew	Designed Armament
380	158' 6'' x 23' 8'' x 6' 6''	14	2/20	4-40 mm

Auxiliaries

	Displacement	Dimensions	Speed	Crew	Armament	When and Where Built
ADVERSUS	155	112' 3'' x 19' x 11'	12	4/15	1-.303 m.g.	1931, Orillia, Ont.
ALACHASSE	157	116' 4'' x 19' x 11' 3''	''	4/14	''	1931, Sorel, Que.
ANDRÉE DUPRÉ	285	125' x 23' 7'' x 12' 8''	9	4/29		1918, ''
BRAS d'OR	265	124' 6'' x 23' 6'' x 12' 5'	7	4/20		1919, ''
DUNDALK, DUNDURN	950	178' 9'' x 33' 2'' x 13'	11	3/27	1-12 pdr., 2-20 mm	1943, Walkerville, Ont.
EASTORE, LAYMORE	803	176' x 32' x 9'	10		1-4'', 2-20 mm	1944, Brunswick, Ga.
FLEUR de LIS	316	164' 8'' x 21' 1'' x 11' 7'	12	6/30	1-.303 m.g.	1929, Montreal, Que.
FRENCH	226	138' 1'' x 22' 1'' x 10' 8'	11	5/25	1-6 pdr., 1-.303 m.g.	1938, Lauzon, Que.
JALOBERT	378	107' 5'' x 23' x 11' 9''	8	4/16		1911, Kingston, Ont.
LAURIER, MACDONALD	201	113' x 21' x 10' 4''	10	4/25	1-12 pdr., 1-.303 m.g.	1936, Quebec City, Que.
MACSIN	293	125' 2'' x 23' 7'' x 12' 8'	8	3/22		1918, Sorel, Que.
MARVITA, SHULAMITE	121	105' x 20' x 8'	10	2/9		1930, Mahone Bay, N.S.
MASTADON	1,233	210' x 36' 6'' x 13' 9''	6	5/37	1-12 pdr., 2-20 mm	1910, Renfrew, Scotland
MONT JOLI	275	120' 4'' x 24' 6'' x 11' 1'	9	4/29		1938, Meteghan, N.S.
MOONBEAM	589	178' x 33' 6'' x 12'	6	2/18		1913, Lévis, Que.
MURRAY STEWART	234	119' x 26' x 15' 7''	''	2/21		1918, Port Arthur, Ont.
NITINAT	135	99' 5'' x 17' 7'' x 10' 6''	10	3/15	1-.303 m.g.	1939, New Westminster, B.C.
NORSAL	168	122' 4'' x 19' 2'' x 10' 6'	''	3/17	''	1921, Vancouver, B.C.
PRESERVER, PROVIDER	4,670	268' 5'' x 43' 11'' x 17' 8''	''	20/87	1-4'', 2-20 mm	1941-42, Sorel, Que.
RAYON d'OR	342	140' x 24' 1'' x 13'	9	4/31	1-12 pdr.	1912, Beverley, U.K.
REO II	129	96' 1'' x 17' 5'' x 7' 5''	''	4/32		1931, Meteghan, N.S.
ROSS NORMAN	297	131' 8'' x 28' x 12' 6''	10	4/21		1937, Lunenburg, N.S.
SANKATY	459	195' x 38' 2'' x 9' 9''	8	3/39	1-.303 m.g.	1911, Quincy, Mass.
SANTA MARIA	86	67' 5'' x 19' 3'' x 9' 3''	''	1/10	''	1936, Vancouver, B.C.
STANDARD COASTER	150	130' x 22' x 9' 9''	9			1927, Liverpool, N.S.
STAR XVI	249	116' x 23' 9'' x 13' 2''	10	4/25		1930, Oslo, Norway
SUDERÖY IV	252	122' 6'' x 23' 9'' x 10'	9	''		''
SUDERÖY V	''	115' 1'' x 23' 9'' x 13' 2''	''	''		''
SUDERÖY VI	254	121' 9'' x 24' 3'' x 11' 6''	''	''		1929, Middlesbrough, U.K.
SUNBEAM	589	178' x 33' 6'' x 12'	6	2/27		1911, Port Glasgow, N.S.
VENCEDOR	380	146' 10'' x 27' x 14' 6'	''	3/25		1913, Wivenhoe, U.K.
VENOSTA	316	135' 3'' x 23' 5'' x 12' 3''	9	4/28	1-12 pdr.	1917, Selby, U.K.
VENTURE II	510	182' 3'' x 27' 2'' x 10' 3''	12			1925, Leith, Scotland
VIERNOE	273	130' 4'' x 22' x 12' 6''	9	4/28	1-12 pdr.	1914, Selby, U.K.
WHITETHROAT	580	164' x 27' 6'' x 12' 6''	12		1-20 mm	1944, Beverley, U.K.

Particulars — Ships of Part Three   1945 - 1981

Aircraft Carriers

	Displacement	Dimensions	Speed	Armament
BONAVENTURE	16,000	704' x 80' x 25'	24	8-3'' (4 x II), 8-40 mm
MAGNIFICENT	15,700	698' x 80' x 25'	''	6-40 mm (3 x II), 18-40 mm
WARRIOR	13,350	693' 3'' x 80' 4'' x 23'	''	24-2 pdr. (6 x IV), 19-40 mm

	Pendant	Builder	Laid Down	Launched	Commissioned	Paid Off	Remarks
BONAVENTURE	22	HW	27/11/43	27/2/45	17/1/57	1/7/70	Ex-HMS POWERFUL About 30 aircraft carried
MAGNIFICENT	21	''	29/7/43	16/11/44	7/4/48	14/6/57	Ex-HMS MAGNIFICENT About 30 aircraft carried
WARRIOR	31	''	12/12/42	20/5/44	24/1/46	23/3/48	Ex-HMS WARRIOR About 30 aircraft carried

Destroyers, "C" Class

Particulars of Class:	Displacement	Dimensions	Speed	Crew	Armament
	1,730	362' 9'' x 35' 8'' x 11' 6''	31	14/230	4-4.5'', 4-40 mm, 4-20 mm, 4-21'' TT (1 x IV) As revised: (CRESCENT): 2-4'' (1 x II), 2-3'' (1 x II), 2-40 mm, 1 Limbo, homing torpedoes (CRUSADER): 3-4.5'', 6-40 mm, 4-21'' TT (1 x IV)

	Pendant	Builder	Laid Down	Launched	Commissioned	Paid Off	Remarks
CRESCENT	R16/226	JB	16/9/43	20/7/44	10/9/45	1/4/70	Ex-HMS CRESCENT
CRUSADER	R20/228	''	15/11/43	5/10/44	15/11/45	15/1/60	Ex-HMS CRUSADER

Destroyers, Tribal Class (Postwar construction)

Particulars of Class:	Displacement	Dimensions	Speed	Crew	Armament
	2,200	355' 6'' x 37' 6'' x 11' 2''	32	14/245	6-4.7'' (3 x II), 2-4'' (1 x II), 4-2 pdrs. (1 x IV), 6-20 mm, 4-21'' TT (1 x IV) Revised: 4-4'' (2 x II), 2-3'' (1 x II), 4-40 mm, 4-21'' TT (1 x IV), 2 Squid

	Pendant	Builder	Laid Down	Launched	Commissioned	Paid Off
ATHABASKAN (2nd)	R79/219	HX	15/5/43	4/5/46	20/1/48	21/4/66
CAYUGA	R04/218	''	7/10/43	28/7/45	20/10/47	27/2/64
MICMAC	R10/214	''	20/5/42	18/9/43	12/9/45	31/3/64
NOOTKA (2nd)	R96/213	''		26/4/44	7/8/46	6/2/64

Destroyer Escorts, St. Laurent Class

Particulars of Class:	Displacement	Dimensions	Speed	Crew	Armament
	2,263	366' x 42' x 13' 2''	28	12/237	4-3'' (2 x II), 2-40 mm, 2 Limbo, homing torpedoes. As DDHs: 2-3'' (1 x II), 1 Limbo, homing torpedoes, 1 Sea King helicopter

	Pendant	Builder	Laid Down	Launched	Commissioned	Commissioned after conversion to DDH	For Delex	Paid Off
ASSINIBOINE (2nd)	234	MI	19/5/52	12/2/54	16/8/56	28/6/63	1979	
FRASER (2nd)	233	BU	11/12/51	19/2/53	28/6/57	22/10/66	1981	
MARGAREE (2nd)	230	HX	12/9/51	29/3/56	5/10/57	15/10/65	1980	
OTTAWA (3rd)	229	CV	8/6/51	29/4/53	10/11/56	21/10/64	1982	
SAGUENAY (2nd)	206	HX	4/4/51	30/7/53	15/12/56	14/5/65	1979	
ST. LAURENT (2nd)	205	CV	24/11/50	30/11/51	29/10/55	4/10/63		14/6/74
SKEENA (2nd)	207	BU	1/6/51	19/8/52	30/3/57	14/8/65	1981	

Destroyer Escorts, Restigouche Class

Particulars of Class:	Displacement	Dimensions	Speed	Crew	Armament
	2,366	366' x 42' x 13' 6''	28	12/237	4-3'' (2 x II), 2 Limbo, homing torpedoes
GATINEAU, KOOTENAY, RESTIGOUCHE and TERRA NOVA as modified	2,390	372' x 42' x 14' 1''	''	''	2-3'' (1 x II), 1 Limbo, 1 ASROC, 1 Sea Sparrow, homing torpedoes

	Pendant	Builder	Laid Down	Launched	Commissioned	For Delex	Paid Off
CHAUDIÈRE (2nd)	235	HX	30/7/53	13/11/57	14/11/59		23/5/74
COLUMBIA (2nd)	260	BU	1_/6/53	1/11/56	7/11/59		18/2/74
GATINEAU (2nd)	236	DS	30/4/53	3/6/57	17/2/59	1983	
KOOTENAY (2nd)	258	BU	2_/8/52	15/6/54	7/3/59	1984	
RESTIGOUCHE (2nd)	257	CV	15/7/53	22/11/54	7/6/58	1986	
ST. CROIX (2nd)	256	MI	15/10/54	17/11/56	4/10/58		15/11/74
TERRA NOVA	259	VM	14/11/52	21/6/55	6/6/59	1985	

Fast Hydrofoil Escort

	Displacement	Dimensions	Speed	Crew	Armament	Builder	Commissioned	Paid Off
BRAS d'OR (2nd)	180	151' x 21' x 23'	60	4/25	None fitted	Marine Ind. Ltd., Sorel	19/7/68	1/5/72

Submarines
Former U-Boats

Particulars of Class:	Displacement	Dimensions	Speed	Armament	Remarks
	1,120/1,232	252' x 22' x 15'	18/7	6-21'' TT	Original armament included 2-37 mm (1 x II), 4-20 mm (2 x II)

	Builder	Launched	Commissioned in RCN	Paid Off by RCN
U 190	Deschimag A.G. Weser, Bremen, Germany	8/6/42	19/5/45	24/7/47
U 889	''	1944	14/5/45	12/1/46

Patrol Craft, Bird Class

Particulars of Class:	Displacement	Dimensions	Speed	Crew	Armament
	66 full load	92' x 17' x 5' 4''	14	2/19	1-20 mm, Hedgehog

	Pendant	Builder	Launched	Commissioned	Paid Off
BLUE HERON	782	Hunter Boat Works, Orillia	7/5/56	30/7/56	19/11/56
CORMORANT	781	Midland Boat Works, Midland	15/5/56	16/7/56	23/5/63
LOON	780	Taylor Boat Works, Toronto	4/10/54	30/11/55	30/8/65
MALLARD	783	Grew Boat Works, Penetanguishene	30/4/56	16/7/56	2/9/65

Minesweepers, Bay Class

Particulars of Class:	Displacement	Dimensions	Speed	Crew	Armament
	390	152' x 28' x 8'	16	3/35	1-40 mm

	Pendant	Builder	Laid Down	Launched	Commissioned	Paid Off
CHALEUR	144	PA	8/6/51	21/6/52	18/6/54	30/9/54
CHALEUR (2nd)	164	MI	20/2/56	11/5/57	12/9/57	
CHIGNECTO (2nd)	156	''	4/6/51	13/6/52	1/12/53	31/3/54
CHIGNECTO (3rd)	160	GD	25/10/55	17/11/56	1/8/57	
COMOX (2nd)	146	VM	8/6/51	24/4/52	2/4/54	11/9/57
COWICHAN (2nd)	147	DS	20/6/51	12/11/51	10/12/53	31/3/54
COWICHAN (3rd)	162	YA	10/7/56	26/2/57	12/12/57	
FORTUNE	151	VM	24/4/52	14/4/53	3/11/54	28/2/64
FUNDY (2nd)	145	SJ	19/6/51	9/12/53	19/3/54	31/3/54
FUNDY (3rd)	159	DS	7/3/55	14/6/56	27/11/56	
GASPÉ (2nd)	143	''	21/3/51	12/11/51	5/12/53	22/8/57
JAMES BAY	152	YA	16/8/51	12/3/53	3/5/54	28/2/64
MIRAMICHI (2nd)	150	SJ	13/6/52	4/5/54	30/7/54	1/10/54
MIRAMICHI (3rd)	163	VM	2/2/56	22/2/57	29/10/57	
QUINTE (2nd)	149	PA	14/6/52	8/8/53	15/10/54	26/2/64
RESOLUTE	154	KI	29/8/51	20/6/53	16/9/54	14/2/64
THUNDER (2nd)	153	CV	17/5/51	17/7/52	15/12/53	31/3/54
THUNDER (3rd)	161	PA	1/9/55	27/10/56	3/10/57	
TRINITY	157	GD	31/1/52	31/7/53	16/6/54	21/8/57
UNGAVA (2nd)	148	DS	17/12/51	20/5/53	4/6/54	23/8/57

Submarines, Ex-USN

	Displacement	Dimensions	Speed	Crew	Armament	Remarks
GRILSE (2nd)	1,526/2,391	311' 6'' x 27' 3'' x 16' 10''	20/10	7/72	10-21'' TT (originally 1-5'' as well)	Ex-USS BURRFISH
RAINBOW	1,570/2,414	311' 8'' x 27' 4'' x 17'	''	8/74	''	Ex-USS ARGONAUT

	Pendant	Builder	Laid Down	Launched	Commissioned in RCN	Paid Off
GRILSE (2nd)	71	Portsmouth Navy Yard, Portsmouth, N.H.	24/2/43	18/6/43	11/5/61	2/10/69
RAINBOW	75	''	28/6/44	1/10/44	2/12/68	31/12/74

Submarines, "O" Class

Particulars of Class:	Displacement	Dimensions	Speed	Crew	Armament
	1,610/2,410	295' 3'' x 26' 6'' x 18'	12/17	6/62	8-21'' TT (homing torpedoes)

	Pendant	Builder	Laid Down	Launched	Commissioned
OJIBWA	72	H.M. Dockyard, Chatham, U.K.	27/9/62	29/2/64	23/9/65
OKANAGAN	74	''	25/3/65	17/9/66	22/6/68
ONONDAGA	73	''	18/6/64	25/9/65	22/6/67

Destroyer Escorts, Mackenzie Class

Particulars of Class:	Displacement	Dimensions	Speed	Crew	Armament
	2,380	366' x 42' x 13' 6''	28	12/233	4-3'' (2 x II), 2 Limbo, homing torpedoes

	Pendant	Builder	Laid Down	Launched	Commissioned	For Delex
MACKENZIE	261	CV	15/12/58	25/5/61	6/10/62	1985
QU'APPELLE (2nd)	264	DS	14/1/60	2/5/62	14/9/63	1982
SASKATCHEWAN (2nd)	262	VM	29/10/59	1/2/61	16/2/63	1984
YUKON	263	BU	25/10/59	27/7/61	25/5/63	1983

Destroyer Escorts, Annapolis Class

Particulars of Class:	Displacement	Dimensions	Speed	Crew	Armament
	2,400	371' x 42' x 13' 8''	28	12/234	2-3'' (1 x II), 1 Limbo, homing torpedoes, 1 Sea King helicopter

	Pendant	Builder	Laid Down	Launched	Commissioned	For Delex
ANNAPOLIS (2nd)	265	HX	2/9/61	27/4/63	19/12/64	1984
NIPIGON (2nd)	266	MI	5/8/60	10/12/61	30/5/64	1982

Destroyer Escorts, Iroquois Class

Particulars of Class:	Displacement	Dimensions	Speed	Crew	Armament
	3,551	398' x 50' x 14'	30	14/230	1-5'', 1 Limbo, homing torpedoes, 2 Sea Sparrow, 2 Sea King helicopters

	Pendant	Builder	Laid Down	Launched	Commissioned
ALGONQUIN (2nd)	283	DS	1/9/69	23/4/71	3/11/73
ATHABASKAN (3rd)	282	''	1/6/69	27/11/70	30/9/72
HURON (2nd)	281	MI	6/69	9/4/71	16/12/72
IROQUOIS (2nd)	280	''	15/1/69	28/11/70	29/7/72

Arctic Patrol Vessel

	Pendant	Displacement	Dimensions	Speed	Crew	Builder	Laid Down	Launched	Commissioned	Paid Off
LABRADOR	50	6,490 full load	269' x 63' x 26' 8''	11	224	MI	18/11/49	14/12/51	8/7/54	22/11/57

Escort Maintenance Ships

	Pendant	Displacement	Dimensions	Speed	Crew	Builder	Laid Down	Launched	Commissioned	Paid Off
CAPE BRETON (2nd)	100	8,580	441' 6'' x 57' x 20'	11	270	BU	5/7/44	7/10/44	16/11/59	10/2/64
CAPE SCOTT	101	''	''	''	''	''	8/6/44	27/9/44	28/1/59	1/7/70

Operational Support Ships

	Pendant	Displacement	Dimensions	Speed	Crew	Armament	Builder	Laid Down	Launched	Commissioned
PRESERVER (2nd)	510	24,000 full load	555' x 76' x 30'	20	15/212	2-3'', Sea Sparrow	SJ	17/10/67	29/5/69	30/7/70
PROTECTEUR	509	''	''	''	''	''	''	''	7/11/68	30/8/69
PROVIDER (2nd)	508	22,700 full load	551' x 76' x 30	''	11/131	None fitted	DS	21/6/61	5/7/62	28/9/63

Gate Vessels

Particulars of Class:	Displacement	Dimensions	Speed	Crew	Armament
	429 full load	125' 6'' x 26' 4'' x 13'	11	3/20	1-40 mm

	Pendant	Builder	Laid Down	Launched	Commissioned
PORTE DAUPHINE	186	PF	16/5/51	24/4/52	10/12/52
PORTE de la REINE	184	VM	4/3/51	28/12/51	7/10/52
PORTE QUÉBEC	185	BU	15/2/51	28/8/51	19/9/52
PORTE ST. JEAN	180	GD	16/5/50	22/11/50	5/12/51
PORTE ST. LOUIS	183	''	21/3/51	23/7/52	29/8/52

Cormorant (Diving Support Vessel)

Pendant	Displacement	Dimensions	Speed	Crew	Builder	Launched	Commissioned	Remarks
20	2,350	245' x 39' x 16' 6''	14	65	Cantiere Navale Apuania, Marina-Carrara, Italy	1965	10/11/78	Ex-ASPA QUARTO

Cordova (Auxiliary Minesweeper)

Pendant	Displacement	Dimensions	Speed	Crew	Builder	Launched	Commissioned	Paid Off
158	325	136' x 24' 6''x 8'	15	30	H.C. Grebe & Co., Chicago	8/4/44	9/8/52	12/4/57

Cedarwood (Survey Vessel)

Pendant	Displacement	Dimensions	Speed	Crew	Builder	Launched	Commissioned	Paid Off
530	566	166' x 30' 6''x 10'	11	24	Lunenburg, N.S.	1941	22/9/48	19/10/56

Appendix 8
Operational Status Charts

These charts show the assigned command and operational status, by month, for every major warship of the RCN during the Second World War, covering the period from September 3, 1939, to September 2, 1945. The charts comprise, in effect, a detailed capsule history of each of nearly 300 ships.

In order to compress this amount of information into the space available, the assigned command and operational status are represented by combinations of letters and numerals, to a maximum of three per space, arranged in two lines opposite the name of each ship. The top line represents the command or group to which the ship was assigned in each month, while the bottom line shows its operational status.

Referring, for example, to the corvette *Agassiz* for the month of August, 1941, "19N" signifies that the ship was a unit of Escort Group 19 of Newfoundland Escort Force (MOEF), based at St. John's. In the bottom line, "O" signifies that the ship was operational, escorting convoys between St. John's and Iceland.

It will be appreciated that there are limits to the extent to which such a condensation as this can be achieved, but we have done it in such a way as to cause minimum distortion of the ships' histories. This may best be illustrated by two examples:

The corvette *Beauharnois* arrived in Bermuda from Halifax for workups on November 8, 1944, and departed November 30, making two days' passage each way. She is therefore identified operationally that month as "WUB," that being how she was principally employed. Similarly, the frigate *Orkney* left Esquimalt on May 11, 1944, for Halifax, arriving June 8. She is thus shown operationally in May as "O/P," having been on passage most of that month. As the trip took only a month, the symbol appears only once.

Key to Operational Status Charts

NOTE: *In the case of number/letter combinations, the symbol is listed alphabetically by the letter.*

TOP LINE

Symbol	Command	H.Q.
AL	Atlantic Coast Command, unallocated. Ships paid off for long refits or repairs	Halifax, N.S.
AT	Atlantic Coast Command, unallocated. Later N.W. Atlantic Command, unallocated	Halifax, N.S.
AW	America & West Indies Station, unallocated (RN)	Bermuda & Trinidad
A-3	EG A-3, Mid-Ocean Escort Force, Nfld. Command	St. John's, Nfld.
16A	16th EG, RCN. Support group, WEF, local duties	Halifax, N.S.
26A	26th EG, RCN. " " "	"
27A	27th EG, RCN. " " "	"
28A	28th EG, RCN. " " "	"
BH	Bermuda & Halifax Escort Force, unallocated (RN)	Halifax & Bermuda
BP	British Pacific Fleet, unallocated (RN)	Sydney, Australia
4BP	4th Cruiser Sqdn., British Pacific Fleet (RN)	Sydney, Australia
28B	28th Destroyer Flotilla, British Pacific Fleet (RN)	Sydney, Australia
C-1 to C-9	EG C-1 to C-9, RCN (MOEF), Western Approaches Command, Londonderry	Londonderry & St. John's
CA	Commander, Gulf Sea Frontier (USN). For duty in the Caribbean	Miami, Fla.
CK	Combined Operations vessels (RN). In U.K., under Admiralty (RN)	Plymouth & Portsmouth
CM	Combined Operations vessels (RN). In Mediterranean, under C. in C., Med. Fleet	Plymouth & Portsmouth
CN	Commander, North-West Sea Frontier (USN). For duty in Aleutians invasion	Kodiak, Alaska
ES	Commander, Eastern Sea Frontier (USN). For New York-Guantanamo convoys	New York, N.Y.
GE	Gulf Escort Force. For Gulf of St. Lawrence convoys and Quebec-Sydney convoys	Gaspé, Que.
GF	Gaspé Force, unallocated. For Gulf convoys	Gaspé, Que.
GS	St. Lawrence River patrol	Rivière du Loup, Que.
10G	10th EG, Western Approaches Command, Greenock (RN)	Greenock, Scotland
26G	26th EG, Gibraltar Escort Force, Western Mediterranean Fleet (RCN)	Gibraltar
27G	27th EG, " " " "	"
62G	62nd EG, " " " "	"
HA	Halifax Force. For AH-HA (Halifax-Aruba) tanker convoys	Halifax, N.S.
HF	Home Fleet, unallocated (RN)	Scapa Flow
HL	Halifax Local Defence Force. For Western Local escort duties	Halifax, N.S.
HM	Halifax Motor Launch Force	Halifax, N.S.
HN	Halifax Force (for Northern Waters)	Halifax, N.S.
HQ	Halifax Force, for NL-LN (Quebec-Labrador) convoys	Halifax, N.S.
HT	Halifax Tanker Escort Force, for HT-TH (Halifax-Trinidad) convoys	Halifax, N.S.
3-H	3rd Destroyer Flotilla, Home Fleet (RN)	Scapa Flow
10H	10th " " "	"
23H	23rd " " "	"
26H	26th " " "	"
41H	41st EG, Plymouth Command (RN). Ships under F.O.I.C., Milford Haven	Milford Haven, Wales
4-I	4th EG, Iceland Command (RN)	Reykjavik, Iceland
6-L	6th EG, Western Approaches Command, Londonderry. RCN Support Group	Londonderry
9-L	9th EG, " " "	"
11L	11th EG, " " "	"
12L	12th EG, " " "	"
25L	25th EG, Western Approaches Command, Londonderry. RCN support force, 1944-45	"
26L	26th EG, " " "	"

BOTTOM LINE

Symbol	Status or Location of Ship
DL	Used for deck landing training
DP	Nominated for disposal
FDB	For disposal, Shelburne, N.S.
FDC	" Quebec City, Que.
FDE	" Esquimalt, B.C.
FDG	" Louisbourg, N.S.
FDH	" Halifax, N.S.
FDJ	" St. John's, Nfld.
FDL	" London, England
FDN	" Lunenburg, N.S.
FDQ	" Sorel, Que.
FDS	" Sydney, N.S.
FDV	" Vancouver, B.C.
F/O	Fitting out, trials, etc., Canadian yards
FOK	" U.K. yards
ICL	In reserve, Clyde, Scotland
IES	" Esquimalt, B.C.
IFA	" Falmouth, England
IGR	" Grangemouth, England
IHA	" Halifax, N.S.
ILO	" Londonderry, Ireland
IMH	" Milford Haven, Wales
IPT	" Port Talbot, Wales
ISH	" Sheerness, England
ISY	" Sydney, N.S.
IVA	" Vancouver, B.C.
MD	Moored training ship, Digby, N.S.
N/O	Ship non-operational
O	Operational with the Command shown, principally in Canadian waters or North Atlantic, as applicable
OF	Operational, Pacific Ocean (areas beyond west coast of N. America)
OK	Operational, U.K. waters (also includes Gibraltar)
OM	Operational, Mediterranean Sea
O/P	On passage to another operational area (coast to coast or to/from overseas)
OSB	Off station at Bermuda
OSC	Off station in Canadian waters (or acting as local escort in W. Atlantic)
OSK	Off station in U.K.
OSR	Off station in North Russia
OW	Operational in West Indies waters (includes Caribbean and Bermuda area)
P/O	Paid off to Care and Maintenance
RBA	Refit or repairs, Barrow, England
RBB	" Bay Bulls, Nfld.
RBE	" Belfast, Ireland
RBO	" Boston, Mass.
RBT	" Baltimore, Md.
RCA	" Charlottetown, P.E.I.
RCF	" Cardiff, Wales

Symbol	Command	H.Q.
27L	27th EG, Western Approaches Command, Londonderry (RCN)	Londonderry
62L	62nd EG, " " "	"
MG	Mediterranean Fleet, Gibraltar Command, unallocated (RCN)	Gibraltar
1-M	1st Can. Minesweeping Flotilla, Atlantic Coast Command (RCN)	Halifax, N.S.
2-M	2nd " " "	"
9-M	9th EG, Mid-Ocean Escort Force, Western Approaches Command, Londonderry	Londonderry
41M	41st EG, Plymouth Command (RN)	Plymouth
NC	New construction, Atlantic Coast Command. Ship working up	Halifax, N.S.
NF	Newfoundland Escort Force, unallocated (RCN). Mid-ocean escort group	St. John's, Nfld.
NO	Nore Command, unallocated (RN). Under N.O.I.C., Sheerness	Sheerness, Eng.
NP	New construction, Pacific Coast Command. Ship working up	Esquimalt, B.C.
NU	Nore Command, unallocated (RN)	Chatham, England
NW	Newfoundland Local Force, later Newfoundland Force. For local escort duties	St. John's, Nfld.
14N to 25N	14th to 25th EG, Newfoundland Escort Force. Mid-ocean escort groups	St. John's, Nfld.
N-1 to N19	Task Units 4.1.1 to 4.1.19, later 24.1.1 to 24.1.19. Precursors of EG 1 to 19	St. John's, Nfld.
PA	Pacific Coast Command, unallocated	Esquimalt, B.C.
PD	"D" Force under COMNORWESTSEAFRON (USN), Pacific Coast	Dutch Harbor, Alaska
PE	Esquimalt Force, unallocated, Pacific Coast Command	Esquimalt, B.C.
PL	Pacific Coast Command, ships paid off for long refits or repairs	Esquimalt, B.C.
PO	Portsmouth Command, unallocated (RN)	Portsmouth, England
PR	Prince Rupert Force, unallocated, Pacific Coast Command	Prince Rupert, B.C.
PY	Plymouth Command, unallocated (RN)	Plymouth, England
4-P	4th Minesweeping Flotilla, Plymouth Command (RN)	"
8-P	8th Destroyer Flotilla, "	"
10P	10th " " "	"
14P	14th Minesweeping Flotilla, Plymouth Command (RN)	"
16P	16th " " "	"
31P	31st " " "	"
32P	32nd " " "	"
QF	Quebec Force, unallocated	Quebec City, Que
RF	Reserve Fleet (RN) at U.K. ports as shown in bottom line	various
RY	Rosyth Command, unallocated (RN)	Rosyth, Scotland
SH	Shelburne Force, unallocated	Shelburne, N.S.
SI	Based at HMCS Somers Isle (working-up base)	Bermuda
SJ	Saint John N.B. Force, unallocated	Saint John, N.B.
SM	Sydney Force, unallocated	Sydney, N.S.
5-S	5th EG, Newfoundland Command. Mid-ocean support force	St. John's, Nfld.
6-S	6th EG " " " (Renumbered Nov. 21/43 to avoid confusion with C-5)	"
TA	Training ships, Atlantic Coast Command (later N.W. Atlantic Command)	Halifax, Digby & HMCS Cornwallis
TP	Training ships, Pacific Command	Esquimalt, B.C.
US	Ships Refitting in U.S. Yards (RN Command)	Washington, D.C.
14V	14th EG, Western Approaches Command, Liverpool. RN support force	Liverpool, England
WA	Western Approaches Command, C. in C., unallocated (RN)	Liverpool, England
WC	Western Approaches Command, RCN flotilla	Greenock, Scotland
WD	Western Approaches Command, Londonderry, unallocated (RN)	Londonderry
WG	Western Approaches Command, Greenock, unallocated (RN)	Greenock, Scotland
WL	Western Local Escort Force, unallocated (later Western Escort Force)	Halifax, N.S.
WN	Western Approaches Command, Northern Escort Force (RN)	Liverpool, England
WS	Western Support Force, Newfoundland. Support group for mid-ocean convoys	St. John's, Nfld.
WV	Western Approaches Command, Liverpool, unallocated	Liverpool, England
W-1 to W10	Escort Groups W-1 to W-10, Western Local Escort Force (later Western Escort Force)	Halifax, N.S.
4-W	4th EG, Western Approaches Command, Greenock (RN)	Greenock, Scotland
18W	18th Destroyer Flotilla, Western Approaches Command (RN)	Plymouth, England
26W	26th EG, Western Mediterranean Fleet (RCN)	Algiers, Tunisia
27W	27th EG, " "	"

Symbol	Status or Location of Ship	
RCH	Refit or repairs,	Charleston, S.C.
RCL	"	Clyde, Scotland
RCM	"	Chatham, England
RCO	"	Corner Brook, Nfld.
RDA	"	Dartmouth, N.S.
RDH	"	Dalhousie, N.B.
RDU	"	Dunstaffnage, Scotland
RDV	"	Devonport, England
RES	"	Esquimalt, B.C.
RFA	"	Falmouth, England
RGA	"	Galveston, Texas
RGI	"	Gibraltar
RGN	"	Granton, England
RGR	"	Greenock, Scotland
RGY	"	Grimsby, England
RHA	"	Halifax, N.S.
RHT	"	Hartlepool, England
RHU	"	Humber, England
RHY	"	Holyhead, Wales
RIC	"	Hvalfjord, Iceland
RIN	"	Indiantown, N.B.
RLE	"	Leith, Scotland
RLI	"	Liverpool, N.S.
RLN	"	Londonderry, Ireland
RLO	"	London, England
RLS	"	Louisbourg, N.S.
RLU	"	Lunenburg, N.S.
RLV	"	Liverpool, England
RLZ	"	Lauzon, Que.
RMO	"	Montreal, Que.
RNF	"	Norfolk, Va.
RNY	"	New York, N.Y.
RPA	"	Philadelphia, Pa.
RPH	"	Port Hawkesbury, N.S.
RPI	"	Pictou, N.S.
RPL	"	Plymouth, England
RPO	"	Portsmouth, England
RPR	"	Prince Rupert, B.C.
RQC	"	Quebec City, Que.
RRO	"	Rosyth, Scotland
RSB	"	Saint John, N.B.
RSC	"	Scotstoun, Scotland
RSH	"	Shelburne, N.S.
RSN	"	St. John's, Nfld.
RSO	"	Southampton, England
RSS	"	South Shields, England
RSU	"	Sunderland, England
RSY	"	Sydney, N.S.
RTY	"	Tyne R., England
RVA	"	Vancouver, B.C.
TR	Training duties	
TT	Serving as troop transport	
US	Under salvage	
W/U	Working up in Canadian waters	
WUB	Working up, Bermuda	
WUK	Working up in U.K. waters	

Armed Merchant Cruisers

NAME of SHIP	1940						1941												1942												1943								
Built at / Commissioned	July	Aug.	Sep.	Oct.	Nov.	Dec.	Jan.	Feb.	Mar.	Apr.	May	June	July	Aug.	Sep.	Oct.	Nov.	Dec.	Jan.	Feb.	Mar.	Apr.	May	June	July	Aug.	Sep.	Oct.	Nov.	Dec.	Jan.	Feb.	Mar.	Apr.	May	June	July	Aug.	Sep.
PRINCE DAVID Birkenhead Dec.28/40						AT W/U	AT OW	AW OW	AW OW	AW OW	AW OW	AW OW	AW OW	AW OW	AW OW	AW RHA	AW RHA	AW O/P	PA 0	PA 0	PA 0	PA RES	PE 0	PE 0	PE 0	PE 0	CN 0	CN 0	PE 0	PE 0	PE 0	PE 0	PE 0	PL RES	PL RES	PL RVA	PE RVA	PE RVA	PE RVA
PRINCE HENRY Birkenhead Dec.4/40						AT W/U	AT O/P	AW OW	PA OF	PA OF	PA RES	PA RES	PA RES	PA O/P	AW OW	AW OW	AW OSC	AW OSC	AW OW	AW OW	AW OW	AW OW	PE O/P	PE RVA	PE RVA	PE 0	CN 0	CN 0	PE 0	PE 0	PE 0	PE 0	PE RES	PL RES	PL RES	PL RVA	PE RVA	PE RVA	PE RVA
PRINCE ROBERT Birkenhead July 31/40	PA F/O	PA W/U	PA OF	PA OF	PA OF	PA OF	PA OF	PA OF	PA OF	PA OF	PA OF	PA OF	PA OF	PA OF	PA 0	PA RES	PA 0	PA 0	PA 0	PA 0	PA 0	PA 0	PE 0	PE 0	PE 0	PE 0	CN RES	CN RVA	PE RVA	PE RVA	PE RVA	PE W/U	PL 0	PL O/P	PL RCL	PL WUK	PE OM	PE OM	HF OM

Cruisers

NAME of SHIP	1944				1945								
Built at / Commissioned	Sep.	Oct.	Nov.	Dec.	Jan.	Feb.	Mar.	Apr.	May	June	July	Aug.	Sep.
UGANDA Oct.21/44		US RCH	HF O/P	HF OK	4BP O/P	4BP O/P	4BP O/P	4BP OF	4BP OF	4BP OF	4BP OF	4BP OF	PA RES
ONTARIO Belfast Apr.26/45								HF FOK	HF WUK	HF WUK	4BP O/P	4BP OF	4BP OF

Fairmile Depot Ships

NAME of SHIP	1942						1943											
Built at / Commissioned	July	Aug.	Sep.	Oct.	Nov.	Dec.	Jan.	Feb.	Mar.	Apr.	May	June	July	Aug.	Sep.	Oct.	Nov.	Dec.
PRESERVER Sorel July 11/42	AT F/O	AT W/U	NW 0	NW 0	NW 0	NW 0	NW 0	NW 0	NW 0	NW 0	NW 0	NW RSN	NW RSN	NW 0	NW 0	NW 0	NW 0	NW 0
PROVIDER Sorel Dec.1/42						NC W/U	NC RHA	CA OW	CA OW	CA OW	GF RHA	GF 0	GF 0	GF 0	GF 0	GF 0	HM 0	HM O/P

Destroyers

River Class

NAME of SHIP	1939				1940												1941												1942										
Built at / Commissioned	Sep.	Oct.	Nov.	Dec.	Jan.	Feb.	Mar.	Apr.	May	June	July	Aug.	Sep.	Oct.	Nov.	Dec.	Jan.	Feb.	Mar.	Apr.	May	June	July	Aug.	Sep.	Oct.	Nov.	Dec.	Jan.	Feb.	Mar.	Apr.	May	June	July	Aug.	Sep.	Oct.	Nov.
ASSINIBOINE Cowes, I.o.W. Oct.19/39		18W 0	AW O/P	AW OW	AW OW	AW OW	AW OW	AW RHA	AW RHA	AW OSC	AW OSC	AW OSC	BH 0	BH 0	BH 0	BH 0	BH O/P	BH RCF	10G OK	10G OK	10G OK	10G O/P	14N 0	14N 0	14N 0	NF RHA	NF RHA	NF RHA	N17 0	N17 0	N11 0	C-1 0	C-1 0	C-1 0	C-1 0	C-1 0	NF RHA	NF RHA	NF RHA
FRASER Barrow Feb.17/37	AT O/P	AT 0	AW RHA	AW OSC	AW OSC	AW OSC	AW OSC	AW OW	AW OW	WA OK																													
MARGAREE Hebburn Sept.6/40													NU RLO	WN O/P																									
OTTAWA Portsmouth June 15/38	PA RES	PA 0	AW O/P	AW OSC	AW OSC	AW OSC	AW OSC	AW RHA	AW RHA	AW OSC	AW OSC	AW OSC	BH O/P	BH OSK	WC RGR	10G RGR	10G OK	10G OK	10G OK	10G OK	10G OK	NF O/P	NF RHA	NF RHA	NF W/U	N14 0	NF RHA	N11 0	N12 0	NF RBE	NF 0	NF 0	C-4 RHA	C-4 0	C-4 0	C-4 0	C-4 0		
RESTIGOUCHE Portsmouth June 15/38	PA 0	PA 0	AW O/P	AW RHA	AW OSC	AW OSC	AW OSC	AW OSC	AW O/P	WA OK	WA OK	WN OK	WN O/P	WN RHA	BH 0	BH 0	BH O/P	BH OSK	10G OK	10G OK	10G OK	NF O/P	NF RHA	NF 0	NF RHA	N13 0	N13 0	N13 0	NF RGR	NF RGR	NF RGR	C-2 0	NF RCF	A-3 0	NF RSB	NF RSB	C-4 RSB	C-4 0	C-4 0
ST. LAURENT Barrow Feb.17/37	AT O/P	AT 0	AW OSC	AW OSC	AW OSC	AW OSC	AW RHA	AW RHA	AW O/P	WA OK	WA OK	WN OK	WN OK	WN RLV	WC OK	10G OK	10G RGR	10G O/P	WG RHA	WG RHA	WG RHA	10G RHA	16N 0	14N 0	14N 0	N11 0	N11 0	N12 0	N13 0	N13 0	N13 0	NF RHA	NF RHA	NF RHA	NF RHA	C-1 0	C-1 0	C-1 0	C-1 0
SAGUENAY Southampton May 22/31	AT 0	AT OW	AW OW	AW OSC	AW OSC	AW OSC	AW OSC	AW OSC	AW OSC	AW OSC	AW OSC	AW OSC	BH 0	BH O/P	WC OK	10G RBA	10G RBA	10G RBA	10G RBA	10G RBA	10G RBA	NF O/P	15N 0	14N 0	14N 0	NF 0	NF RSB	N15 0	N15 0	NF RSB	NF RSB	C-3 0	C-3 0	C-3 0	C-3 0	C-3 0	C-3 0	C-3 0	NF 0
SKEENA Southampton June 10/31	AT 0	AT 0	AW RHA	AW OSC	AW OSC	AW OSC	AW OSC	AW RSB	AW O/P	WA OK	WA OK	WN OK	WN RLV	WN OK	WC OK	10G OK	10G RHT	10G O/P	WG RHA	WG RHA	WG RHA	10G OSC	24N 0	24N 0	24N 0	N15 0	N15 0	N15 0	N11 0	NF RSB	NF RSB	C-3 0	C-3 0	C-3 0	C-3 0	C-3 0	C-3 0	C-3 0	C-3 0

Town Class

NAME of SHIP	1940				1941												1942												1943										
Built at / Commissioned	Sep.	Oct.	Nov.	Dec.	Jan.	Feb.	Mar.	Apr.	May	June	July	Aug.	Sep.	Oct.	Nov.	Dec.	Jan.	Feb.	Mar.	Apr.	May	June	July	Aug.	Sep.	Oct.	Nov.	Dec.	Jan.	Feb.	Mar.	Apr.	May	June	July	Aug.	Sep.	Oct.	Nov.
ANNAPOLIS S. Francisco Sept.24/40	AT F/O	AT W/U	HX RHA	HX RHA	HX RHA	HX 0	HX RHA	HX RHA	HX RHA	HX 0	HX 0	HX 0	HX 0	HX 0	HX 0	HX 0	HX 0	HX 0	WL 0	WL RSB	WL RSB	WL RSB	WL 0	WL 0	WL 0	WL 0	WL 0	WL 0	WL RHA	WL 0	WL 0	WL 0	WL RDA	WL RDA	W-8 RDA	W-8 RDA	W-8 0	W10 0	W-8 0
COLUMBIA Newport News Sept.24/40	AT F/O	AT W/U	AT 0	AT RHA	WG O/P	WG RDV	WG RDV	4-W OK	4-W OK	NF O/P	20N RSB	20N 0	20N 0	N15 0	N15 0	N15 RHA	NF RHA	NF RHA	WL RHA	WL 0	WL 0	WL 0	WL 0	WL 0	WL 0	WL 0	WL 0	WL 0	WL 0	WL RSB	WL RSB	WL RSB	WL RSB	WL W/U	W-4 0	W-4 0	W-4 0	W-4 0	W-4 0
HAMILTON Quincy, Mass. July 6/41											HX W/U	HX 0	HX 0	HX 0	HX 0	HX 0	HX 0	HX 0	WL RHA	WL RHA	WL 0	WL 0	WL 0	WL 0	WL RHA	WL 0	WL RHA	WS RSN	WS 0	WL 0	WL 0	WL 0	WL 0	WL 0	W-4 0	W-4 0	W-4 0	TA 0	TA 0
NIAGARA Quincy, Mass. Sept.24/40	AT F/O	AT W/U	AT RHA	AT O/P	WG RDV	WG RDV	WG OK	4-W OK	4-W OK	NF O/P	25N 0	25N 0	25N RHA	NF RHA	NF RHA	NF RHA	N13 0	NF RGR	WL 0	WL 0	WL RPI	WL RPI	WL RPI	WL W/U	WL 0	WL 0	WL RHA	WL 0	WL 0	WL 0	WL 0	WL 0	WL 0	WL 0	W-9 RPI	W-9 RPI	W-9 RPI	W10 W/U	W10 0
ST. CLAIR S. Francisco Sept.24/40	AT F/O	AT W/U	AT 0	AT O/P	WG RDV	WG RDV	WG RDV	4-W OK	4-W OK	NF O/P	NF RHA	NF RSB	NF RSB	NF RSB	NF RSB	N14 0	NF RSB	NF 0	WL 0	WL 0	WL 0	WL 0	WL 0	WL RPI	WL RPI	WL RPI	WL RHA	WL 0	WL 0	WL 0	WL 0	WL 0	WL 0	WL 0	W-2 0	W-2 0	W-2 0	W-2 0	W-2 0
ST. CROIX Quincy, Mass. Sept.24/40	AT F/O	AT 0	AT RHA	AT O/P	AT RHA	AT RHA	AT RHA	AT 0	AT 0	AT RSY	HX RHA	21N 0	21N 0	N13 0	N13 0	NF RSB	NF RSB	NF RSB	NF RSB	NF RSB	C-1 0	C-1 0	C-2 0	C-4 0	C-4 0	C-4 0	NF RSB	NF RSB	C-1 0	C-1 0	C-1 0	C-1 0	C-1 0	WL RHA	C-5 RHA	C-5 0	9-M 0		
ST. FRANCIS Quincy, Mass. Sept.24/40	AT F/O	AT W/U	AT 0	AT 0	WG O/P	WG RDV	WG OK	4-W OK	4-W OK	4-I OK	14N O/P	NF RHA	NF RHA	N16 0	N16 0	NF RHA	NF RHA	N12 0	N12 0	C-2 0	C-4 0	C-4 0	C-4 0	C-1 0	C-1 0	C-1 RLN	C-1 0	C-1 RHA	WS RHA	WL RHA	WL RHA	WL W/U	WL 0	C-1 0	C-2 RHA	C-2 0	9-M 0	C-3 0	WL RSH

River Class, 2nd Group

NAME of SHIP	1942		1943												1944												1945								
Built at / Commissioned	Nov.	Dec.	Jan.	Feb.	Mar.	Apr.	May	June	July	Aug.	Sep.	Oct.	Nov.	Dec.	Jan.	Feb.	Mar.	Apr.	May	June	July	Aug.	Sep.	Oct.	Nov.	Dec.	Jan.	Feb.	Mar.	Apr.	May	June	July	Aug.	Sep.
CHAUDIERE Newcastle Nov.15/43													PO RPO	NF WUK	C-2 OK	C-2 0	C-2 0	C-2 0	11L OK	11L OK	11L OK	11L OK	11L OK	11L OK	11L O/P	11L RHA	11L RHA	11L RSY	11L RSY	11L RSY	11L RSY	AT RSY	AT FDS	AT FDS	AT FDS
GATINEAU Wallsend June 3/43								C-2 WUK	C-2 0	C-2 0	C-2 0	C-2 0	C-2 0	C-2 0	C-2 OK	C-2 0	C-2 0	C-2 0	11L OK	11L OK	11L OK	11L RHA	11L RHA	11L RHA	11L RHA	11L RHA	11L RHA	11L RHA	11L F/O	11L WUK	11L OK	AT OK	AT O/P	AT O/P	PA 0
KOOTENAY Southampton Apr.12/43						A-3 WUK	C-5 0	C-5 0	C-5 0	C-5 0	C-5 0	C-5 0	C-5 RHA	C-5 0	C-5 0	C-5 0	C-5 0	C-5 0	11L OK	11L OK	11L OK	11L OK	11L O/P	11L RSH	11L RSH	11L RSH	11L RSH	11L RSH	11L F/O	11L O/P	11L OK	AT O/P	AT TT	AT TT	AT TT
OTTAWA (2nd) Barrow Mar.20/43					WV FOK	A-3 WUK	C-5 0	C-5 0	C-5 0	C-5 0	C-5 0	C-5 RHA	C-5 0	C-5 RHA	C-5 0	C-5 0	C-5 0	C-5 0	11L OK	11L OK	11L OK	11L OK	11L O/P	11L RSB	11L RSB	11L RSB	11L RSB	11L RSB	AT RHA	11L O/P	11L OK	AT O/P	AT TT	AT TT	AT TT
QU'APPELLE Clydebank Feb.8/44																NO FOK	6-L WUK	6-L 0	12L OK	12L OK	12L OK	12L OK	12L OK	11L OK	11L OK	11L RHA	11L RPI	11L RPI	11L RPI	11L RPI	11L RPI	AT RPI	AT W/U	AT 0	AT 0
SASKATCHEWAN Clydebank June 3/43								C-1 WUK	C-3 0	C-3 0	C-3 0	C-3 0	C-3 0	C-3 0	C-3 0	C-3 0	C-3 0	C-3 0	12L OK	12L OK	12L OK	12L OK	12L RSH	11L RSH	11L RSH	11L W/U	11L O/P	14V WUK	14V OK	14V OK	11L OK	AT O/P	AT TT	AT TT	AT TT

Tribal Class

NAME of SHIP	1942		1943												1944												1945								
Built at / Commissioned	Nov.	Dec.	Jan.	Feb.	Mar.	Apr.	May	June	July	Aug.	Sep.	Oct.	Nov.	Dec.	Jan.	Feb.	Mar.	Apr.	May	June	July	Aug.	Sep.	Oct.	Nov.	Dec.	Jan.	Feb.	Mar.	Apr.	May	June	July	Aug.	Sep.
ATHABASKAN Newcastle Feb.3/43				HF WUK	HF WUK	HF RSS	HF RSS	HF RSS	HF RDV	HF RDV	HF RDV	HF RDV	HF RDV	3-H OK	3-H OK	3-H OK	10P OK	10P OK																	
HAIDA Newcastle Aug.30/43										HF FOK	HF WUK	HF WUK	HF WUK	3-H OK	3-H OK	3-H OSR	10P OK	10P OK	10P OK	10P OK	10P OK	10P OK	AT OK	AT RHA	AT RHA	AT RHA	AT O/P	8-P RDV	8-P OK	HF OSR	HF OK	AT O/P	AT RHA	AT RHA	AT RHA
HURON Newcastle July 19/43									HF FOK	HF WUK	HF WUK	HF WUK	HF WUK	3-H OK	3-H OK	3-H OSR	10P OK	10P OK	10P RDV	10P OK	10P OK	10P O/P	AT RHA	AT RHA	AT RHA	8-P RCA	8-P RCA	8-P OK	8-P OK	HF OSR	HF OK	AT O/P	AT RHA	AT RHA	AT RHA
IROQUOIS Newcastle Nov.30/42	HF FOK	3-H WUK	3-H WUK	3-H WUK	3-H OK	3-H OK	HF RDV	HF RDV	HF OK	HF RGR	HF OK	HF OK	HF OK	3-H OK	3-H OK	3-H OSR	3-H RHA	WL RHA	10H RHA	10H OK	10H OK	10H OK	10P OK	10P OK	10P OK	8-P RDV	8-P OK	8-P OK	8-P OK	HF OSR	HF OK	AT O/P	AT RHA	AT RHA	AT RHA

"V" Class

NAME of SHIP	1944											1945								
Built at / Commissioned	Feb.	Mar.	Apr.	May	June	July	Aug.	Sep.	Oct.	Nov.	Dec.	Jan,	Feb.	Mar.	Apr.	May	June	July	Aug.	Sep.
ALGONQUIN Clydebank Feb.28/44	26H FOK	26H WUK	26H OK	26H OK	26H OK	26H OK	26H OK	26H OK	26H OSR	26H OK	23H OK	23H OSR	23H OK	23H OK	23H OK	23H RHA	AT RHA	AT RHA	28B O/P	28B OM
SIOUX Cowes, I.o.W. Mar.5/44		26H FOK	26H WUK	26H OK	26H OK	26H OK	26H OK	26H OK	26H OSR	26H OK	23H OK	23H OSR	23H OK	23H OK	23H OK	23H RHA	AT RHA	AT RHA	AT RHA	AT RHA

(Destroyers / Ships — 1944–1945)

	1944			1945																				
	Oct.	Nov.	Dec.	Jan.	Feb.	Mar.	Apr.	May	June	July	Aug.	Sep.	Oct.	Nov.	Dec.	Jan.	Feb.	Mar.	Apr.	May	June	July	Aug.	Sep.
	PE	PE	O	PE	CK	CK	CK	CK	CK	CK	CM	CM	CM	CM	CM	CM	CM	CM	CM	CM	PA	PA	PA	PA
	RVA	RVA	RVA	O/P	OK	OK	OK	OK	OK	OK	OM	OM	OM	OM	OM	OM	OM	OM	OM	O/P	RES	RES	RVA	RVA
	PE	PE	PE	PE	CK	CK	CK	CK	CK	CK	CM	CM	CM	CM	CM	CM	CM	CM	CM	CK	CK	CK	CK	CK
	RVA	RVA	RVA	O/P	OK	OK	OK	OK	OK	OK	OM	OM	OM	OM	OM	OM	OM	OM	OM	O/P	FDL	FDL	FDL	FDL
	HF	MG	MG	MG	PY	PY	PY	PY	PY	PY	PY	PA	PA	PA	PA	PA	PA	PA	PA	PA	BP	BP	BP	
	OK	OK	OK	OK	OK	OK	OK	OK	OK	OK	O/P	RES	RES	RES	RVA	RVA	RVA	RVA	RVA	W/U	W/U	OF	OF	

	1944													1945								
	Jan.	Feb.	Mar.	Apr.	May	June	July	Aug.	Sep.	Oct.	Nov.	Dec.	Jan.	Feb.	Mar.	Apr.	May	June	July	Aug.	Sep.	
	NW	NW	O	NW	NW	NW	NW	NW	NW	NW	NW	NW	NW	NW	RHA	O	O	O	O	AT	AT	O
	O	O	O	O	O	O	O	O	O	O	O	O	O	O	O	O	O	O	O	O	O	O
	HM	HM	HM	HM	HM	HM	HM	HM	HM	HM	SI	SI	SI	SI	SI	SI	SI	SI	AT	AT	AT	
	OSB	OSB	OSB	OSB	OSB	OSB	OSB	O	OSB	OSB	OW	OSC	OW	OW	OW	OW	OW	OW	O	O	O	

	1943									1944													1945											
	Dec.	Jan.	Feb.	Mar.	Apr.	May	June	July	Aug.	Sep.	Oct.	Nov.	Dec.	Jan.	Feb.	Mar.	Apr.	May	June	July	Aug.	Sep.	Oct.	Nov.	Dec.	Jan.	Feb.	Mar.	Apr.	May	June	July	Aug.	Sep.
	NF	C-3	C-3	C-3	C-3	C-3	C-3	C-1	C-1	C-1	C-1	C-1	C-1	C-1	C-1	C-1	C-1	12L	12L	12L	12L	12L	11L	11L	14V	14V	14V	14V	14V	11L	AT	AT	AT	
	RHA	O	O	RLV	RLV	RLV	RLV	WUK	O	O	O	O	O	O	O	O	O	RSH	RSH	WUB	OK	OK	OK	OK	OK	OK	OK	OK	OK	OK	O/P	TT	FDC	

	C-4	C-4	C-4	C-4	C-4	C-4	C-4	C-3	C-4	C-4	C-4	C-4	C-4	C-4	C-4	C-4	C-4	12L	12L	12L	12L	11L	11L	11L	11L	11L	11L	HX	HX	HX	HX	AT	AT	AT
	0	0	0	0	0	0	0	0	RTY	RTY	RTY	RTY	0	0	0	0	0	OK	OK	OK	OK	OK	RSB	RSB	RSB	RHA	RHA	WUB	0	0	RHA	TT	TT	TT
	C-1	C-1	C-1	C-1	C-1	C-1	C-1	C-1	C-1	C-1	C-1	C-1	C-1	C-1	C-1	C-1	C-1	11L	11L	11L	11L	11L	11L	11L	HX	11L	11L	11L	HX	HX	HX	HX	AT	AT	AT
	0	RHA	0	0	0	0	0	0	0	RDA	RDA	RDA	W/U	0	0	0	0	OK	OK	OK	OK	OK	OK	O/P	RSH	RSH	RSH	WUB	0	RHA	0	TT	TT	TT
	NF	NF	NF	AL	AL	AL	AL	AL	AL	TA	TA	TA	TA	TA	TA	TA	TA	TA	TA	TA	TA	TA	TA	TA	TA	TA	TA	TA	TA	TA	TA	TA	DP	DP	DP
	N/O	RSB	RSB	RSB	RSB	RSB	RSB	MD	MD	MD	MD	MD	MD	MD	MD	MD	MD	MD	MD	MD	MD	MD	MD	MD	MD	MD	MD	MD	MD	MD	MD	MD	DP	DP	DP
	C-3	C-3	C-3	C-3	C-3	C-3	C-3	C-4	C-3	C-3	C-3	C-3	C-3	C-3	C-3	C-3	C-3	12L	12L	12L	12L	11L	11L	AT										
	0	RHA	RHA	RHA	0	0	0	0	0	0	0	0	0	0	0	0	0	RSH	0	OK	OK	OK	OK	OK	OK	OK	N/O							

	1944													1945						
	Dec.	Jan.	Feb.	Mar.	Apr.	May	June	July	Aug.	Sep.	Oct.	Nov.	Dec.	Jan.	Feb.	Mar.	Apr.	May	June	July
	W10	W10	W10	TA	TA	TA	TA	TA	TA	TA	TA	TA	TA	TA	TA	TA	TA	TA	TA	AT
	RSH	0	0	RHA	TR	TR	TR	TR	TR	TR	TR	TR	TR	TR	TR	TR	TR	TR	TR	FDS
	W10	W10	W10	AT	AT	AT	AT	AT	AT	AT										
	0	0	0	RSN	RSN	RSN	RSN	N/O	N/O	N/O										
	TA	TA	TA	TA	TA	TA	TA	TA	TA	TA	TA	TA	TA	TA	TA	TA	TA	TA	AT	AT
	0	TR	TR	TR	TR	RSB	RSB	TR	TR	TR	TR	TR	TR	TR	TR	TR	TR	TR	FDS	FDS
	W10	W10	W10	AT	TA	TA	TA	TA	TA	TA	TA	TA	TA	TA	TA	TA	TA	TA	TA	TA
	0	0	0	RHA	TR	TR	TR	TR	TR	TR	TR	RHA	RHA	RHA	TR	TR	TR	TR	TR	TR
	W10	W10	W10	TA	TA	TA	TA	TA												
	0	P/O	P/C	P/O	TR	RHA	RHA	TR	TR												
	WL	WL	TA	TA	TA	TA	TA	TA	TA	TA	TA	TA	TA	TA	TA	TA	TA	TA	AT	AT
	RSH	RSH	RSH	TR	TR	TR	TR	TR	TR	TR	TR	TR	TR	TR	TR	TR	TR	TR	FDS	FDS

Escort Aircraft Carriers

NAME of SHIP	1943				1944								
Built at / Commissioned	Sep.	Oct.	Nov.	Dec.	Jan.	Feb.	Mar.	Apr.	May	June	July	Aug.	Sep.
NABOB — Tacoma — Sept.7/43	US F/C	US F/O	US RVA	US RVA	US RVA	US W/U	US W/U	US O/P	WG RLV	WG RLV	WG WUK	WG WUK	HF OK
PUNCHER — Tacoma — Feb.5/44					US F/O	US RVA	US RVA	US RVA	US RVA	US O/P	US W/U	US W/U	

NAME of SHIP	1945											
	Oct.	Nov.	Dec.	Jan.	Feb.	Mar.	Apr.	May	June	July	Aug.	Sep.
NABOB	RFR P/O											
PUNCHER	US O/P	WG WUK	WG RCL	WA W/U	HF OK	HF OK	HF OK	HF RCL	WA DL	WA DL	WA DL	RY DL

Frigates
River Class, 1943–1944 Programme

NAME of SHIP / Built at / Commissioned	1944								1945								
	May	June	July	Aug.	Sep.	Oct.	Nov.	Dec.	Jan.	Feb.	Mar.	Apr.	May	June	July	Aug.	Sep.
ANTIGONISH — Esquimalt — July 4/44			NP W/U	NP O/P	NC RHA	NC WUB	16A 0	16A 0	16A 0	16A 0	16A 0	16A 0	16A 0	16A 0	RPI	RPI	RPI
BUCKINGHAM — Lauzon — Nov.2/44							NC F/O	NC RHA	28A WUB	28A 0	28A 0	28A 0	AT 0	AT RLI	AT RLI	AT RSH	RSH
CAPILANO — Esquimalt — Aug.25/44			NP F/O	NP W/U	NP O/P	NC WUB	C-2 0	C-2 0	C-2 0	C-2 0	C-2 0	C-2 0	AT RSH	AT RSH	AT RSH	AT RSH	
CARLPLACE — Lauzon — Dec.13/44							NC F/O	NC RHA	NC RPA	NC WUB	16A 0	16A 0	AT RSB	AT RSH	AT RSH	0	
COATICOOK — Lauzon — July 25/44			NC O/P	NC F/O	NC WUB	NC RHA	27A 0	27A 0	27A 0	27A 0	27A 0	27A 0	AT O/P	PA 0	PA 0	PA RES	
FORT ERIE — Lauzon — Oct.27/44						NC O/P	NC F/O	NC RHA	NC WUB	28A 0	28A 0	28A 0	AT 0	AT RPI	AT RPI	AT RPI	RHA
GLACE BAY — Lauzon — Sept.2/44				NC F/O	NC WUB	NC WUB	C-4 0	C-4 0	C-4 0	C-4 0	C-4 0	C-4 0	C-4 0	AT 0	AT 0	AT 0	
HALLOWELL — Montreal — Aug.8/44				NC F/O	NC RHA	NC WUB	C-1 0	C-1 0	C-1 0	C-1 0	C-1 0	C-1 0	C-1 0	AT 0	AT TT	AT 0	
INCH ARRAN — Lauzon — Nov.18/44							NC F/O	NC RHA	NC WUB	28A 0	28A 0	28A 0	AT 0	AT RSY	AT RSY	AT RSY	RSH
LANARK — Montreal — July 6/44			NC F/O	NC RSH	NC WUB	C-7 0	C-7 0	C-7 0	C-7 0	C-7 0	C-7 0	C-7 0	AT 0	AT RLI	AT RLI	0	
LASALLE — Lauzon — June 29/44	NC F/O	NC F/O	NC RHA	NC WUB	27A 0	27A 0	27A 0	27A 0	27A 0	27A 0	27A 0	AT O/P	PA 0	PA 0			
LAUZON — Lauzon — Aug.30/44			NC F/O	NC O/P	NC F/O	NC WUB	C-6 0	C-6 0	C-6 0	C-6 0	C-6 0	C-6 0	C-6 RLN	AT 0	AT 0	AT 0	
LEVIS — Lauzon — July 21/44			NC F/O	NC RHA	NC WUB	27A 0	27A 0	27A 0	27A 0	27A 0	27A 0	27A 0	AT RLU	AT RLU	AT RLU	RLU	
PENETANG — Lauzon — Oct.19/44						NC F/O	NC RHA	NC WUB	NC RHA	C-9 0	C-9 0	C-9 0	C-9 0	AT TT	AT 0	AT 0	
POUNDMAKER — Montreal — Sept.17/44					NC F/O	NC RHA	NC WUB	C-8 0	C-8 0	C-8 0	C-8 0	C-8 0	AT RLU	AT RLU	AT RLU	AT RHA	
PRESTONIAN — Lauzon — Sept.13/44					NC F/O	NC W/U	NC RHA	NC RHA	28A WUB	28A 0	28A 0	28A 0	AT RHA	AT RHA	AT RHA	0	
ROYALMOUNT — Montreal — Aug.25/44				NC F/O	NC F/O	NC WUB	NC WUB	C-1 0	C-1 0	C-1 0	C-1 0	C-1 0	AT RSY	AT RSY	AT RSY	AT RSY	
RUNNYMEDE — Montreal — June 14/44	NC F/O	NC F/O	NC WUB	C-5 0	C-5 0	C-5 0	C-5 0	C-5 0	C-5 0	C-5 0	C-5 0	C-5 0	PA O/P	PA RVA	PA 0	PA	
ST. PIERRE — Lauzon — Aug.22/44				NC F/O	NC F/O	NC RHA	NC RHA	9-L RHA	9-L RHA	9-L RHA	AT WUB	AT 0	AT RQC	AT RQC	AT RQC	0	
ST. STEPHEN — Esquimalt — July 28/44			NP F/O	NP W/U	NP O/P	NC WUB	C-5 0	C-5 0	C-5 0	C-5 0	C-5 0	C-5 0	C-5 0	AT RDA	AT RDA	AT RDA	
STE. THERESE — Lauzon — May 28/44	NC F/O	NC F/O	NC RHA	NC WUB	AT 0	25L OK	25L OK	25L OK	25L OK	28A 0	28A 0	28A 0	28A 0	AT WUB	AT 0	AT 0	RHA
SEA CLIFF — Lauzon — Sept.26/44					NC F/O	NC F/O	NC WUB	C-3 0	C-3 0	C-3 0	C-3 0	C-3 0	C-3 0	AT RLI	AT RLI	AT RLI	0
STONE TOWN — Montreal — July 21/44			NC F/O	NC RHA	NC WUB	C-8 0	C-8 0	C-8 0	C-8 0	C-8 0	AT 0	AT 0	AT 0	AT RLU	AT 0		
STRATHADAM — Esquimalt — Sept.29/44			NP F/O	NP W/U	NP O/P	NC RHA	25L WUB	25L O/P	25L OK	25L OK	AT OK	AT 0	AT RHA	AT RHA	AT RHA		
SUSSEXVALE — Lauzon — Nov.29/44						NC F/O	NC F/O	NC WUB	NC WUB	26L O/P	26L OK	26L OK	AT RSH	AT RSH	AT RSH	0	
TORONTO — Lauzon — May 6/44	NC F/O	NC RHA	NC WUB	16A 0	16A 0	16A 0	16A RHA	16A RHA	16A RHA	16A RHA	16A RHA	HX 0	HX 0	TA TR	TA TR	AT TR	AT TR
VICTORIAVILLE — Lauzon — Nov.11/44							NC F/O	NC RHA	NC WUB	C-9 0	C-9 0	C-9 0	AT RSB	AT RSB	AT RSB	0	

River Class, 1942-1943 Programme

NAME of SHIP	Built at / Commissioned	1943 Aug	Sep	Oct	Nov	Dec	1944 Jan	Feb	Mar	Apr	May	June	July	Aug	Sep	Oct	Nov	Dec	1945 Jan	Feb	Mar	Apr	May	June	July	Aug	Sep
BEACON HILL	Esquimalt May 16/44										NP W/U	NP O/P	NC RHA	NC WUB	NC O/P	26L OK	26L OK	26L OK	26L OK	26L OK	26L OK	26L OK	26L OK	AT RLI	AT RLI	AT RLI	AT RLI
CAP de la MADELEINE	Quebec City Sept.30/44													NC F/O	NC O/P	NC WUB	NC WUB	C-7 RSN	C-7 RSN	C-7 N/O	C-7 0	C-7 RQC	AT RQC	AT RQC	AT RQC	AT RQC	
CAPE BRETON	Quebec City Oct.25/43			NC F/O	NC F/O	NC RHA	NC W/U	NC O/P	6-L OK	6-L OK	6-L OK	6-L OK	6-L OK	6-L OK	6-L OK	6-L OK	5-L RSH	6-L RSH	6-L RSH	6-L RSH	6-L RSH	6-L RSH	9-L 0	PA O/P	PA RVA	PA RVA	PA RVA
CHARLOTTETOWN	Lauzon Apr.28/44								NC F/O	NC O/P	NC WUB	NC WUB	16A 0	16A 0	16A 0	16A 0	16A 0	16A 0	16A 0	16A 0	16A 0	16A 0	16A 0	16A 0	AT RSY	AT RSY	AT RSY
CHEBOGUE	Esquimalt Feb.22/44							NP W/U	NP O/P	NC RHA	NC WUB	C-1 0	C-1 0	C-1 0	C-1 0	C-1 0	AT N/O	AT P/O	AT IPT	AT IPT	RF IPT	RF IPT	RF IPT	RF IPT	RF IPT	RF IPT	RF IPT
DUNVER	Quebec City Sept.11/43	NC F/O	NC W/U	NC W/U	C-5 0	C-5 0	C-5 0	C-5 0	C-5 0	C-5 0	C-5 0	C-5 0	C-5 0	C-5 0	AT RPI	AT RPI	AT RPI	AT 0	AT RHA	AT WUB	27A 0	27A 0	PA O/P	PA RVA	PA RVA	PA RVA
EASTVIEW	Montreal June 3/44									NC F/O	NC RHA	NC WUB	C-6 0	C-6 0	C-6 0	C-6 0	C-6 0	C-6 0	C-6 0	C-6 0	C-6 0	C-6 RLN	C-6 0	C-6 O/P	AT 0	PA RVA	PA RVA
GROU	Montreal Dec.4/43				NC F/O	NC W/U	NC W/U	6-L O/P	6-L OK	6-L OK	6-L OK	6-L OK	6-L OK	6-L OK	6-L OK	6-L OK	6-L OK	6-L OK	6-L OK	6-L OK	AT RDA	AT RDA	AT RDA	AT RDA	AT RDA	AT RDA	AT 0
JOLIETTE	Quebec City June 14/44										NC F/O	NC F/O	NC WUB	C-1 0	C-1 0	25L N/O	25L RBE	25L RBE	25L RBE	25L RBE	25L RBE	25L RBE	25L RBE	AT WUK	AT O/P	AT WUB	AT RSB
JONQUIERE	Lauzon May 10/44								NC F/O	NC F/O	NC WUB	C-2 0	C-2 0	26L OK	26L OK	26L OK	26L OK	26L OK	26L OK	26L OK	26L OK	26L OK	26L OK	AT OK	AT O/P	AT 0	AT RSB
KIRKLAND LAKE	Quebec City Aug.21/44													NC F/O	NC RHA	NC RHA	NC WUB	NC WUB	16A 0	16A 0	16A 0	16A 0	16A 0	AT RQC	AT RQC	AT RQC	
KOKANEE	Esquimalt June 6/44										NP W/U	NP O/P	NC WUB	C-3 0	C-3 0	C-3 0	C-3 0	C-3 0	C-3 0	C-3 0	C-3 0	C-3 0	C-3 0	C-3 O/P	AT 0	PA RES	PA RES
La HULLOISE	Montreal May 20/44										NC F/O	NC W/U	NC WUB	16A 0	16A 0	25L OK	25L OK	25L OK	25L OK	25L OK	25L OK	25L OK	25L OK	AT RSB	AT RSB	AT RSB	AT RSB
LONGUEUIL	Montreal May 18/44										NC F/O	NC W/U	NC WUB	C-2 0	C-2 0	C-2 0	C-2 0	C-2 0	C-2 0	C-2 0	C-2 0	C-2 0	C-2 0	AT O/P	PA 0	PA RVA	PA RVA
MAGOG	Montreal May 7/44										NC F/O	NC W/U	NC WUB	16A RHA	16A 0	16A 0	AT RQC	AT N/O	AT FDC	AT FDC	AT FDC	AT FDC	AT FDC	AT FDC	AT FDC	AT FDC	AT FDC
MATANE	Montreal Oct.22/43				NC F/O	NC W/U	NC W/U	NC RHA	9-L W/U	9-L O/P	9-L OK	9-L OK	9-L OK	9-L OK	9-L RDU	9-L RDU	9-L RDU	9-L RDU	9-L RDU	9-L RDU	9-L OK	9-L RDU	9-L RDU	9-L WUK	16A O/P	PA 0	PA 0
MONTREAL	Montreal Nov.12/43				NC F/O	NC RHA	NC W/U	NC RHA	C-4 0	C-4 0	C-4 0	C-4 0	C-4 0	C-4 0	C-4 0	26L O/P	26L OK	26L OK	26L OK	26L OK	26L OK	26L O/P	AT RSH	AT RSH	AT RSH	AT RSH	AT 0
NEW GLASGOW	Esquimalt Dec.23/43				NP F/O	NP W/U	NP O/P	NC RHA	NC WUB	C-1 0	C-1 0	C-1 0	C-1 0	C-1 0	26L OK	26L OK	26L OK	26L OK	26L OK	26L OK	26L RRO	26L RRO	26L OK	AT 0	AT 0	AT 0	AT 0
NEW WATERFORD	Esquimalt Jan.21/44					NP W/U	NP O/P	NC W/U	NC WUB	6-L RHA	6-L O/P	6-L OK	6-L OK	6-L OK	6-L OK	6-L OK	6-L OK	6-L OK	6-L OK	6-L OK	6-L OK	6-L OK	6-L OK	AT RLI	AT RLI	AT RLI	AT RLI
ORKNEY	Esquimalt Apr.18/44										NP W/U	NP O/P	NC RHA	NC WUB	16A 0	16A 0	25L 0	25L O/P	25L OK	25L OK	25L OK	25L RDU	25L N/O	AT RLN	AT RLS	AT RLS	AT RLS
OUTREMONT	Quebec City Nov.27/43				NC F/O	NC RHA	NC W/U	6-L O/P	6-L OK	6-L OK	6-L OK	6-L OK	6-L OK	6-L OK	6-L OK	6-L OK	6-L OK	6-L OK	6-L O/P	AT RSY	AT RSY	AT RSY	AT RSY	AT RSY	AT RSY	AT RSY	AT 0
PORT COLBORNE	Esquimalt Nov.15/43				NP W/U	NP O/P	NC RDA	NC WUB	NC RHA	9-L RHA	9-L O/P	9-L OK	9-L OK	9-L OK	9-L OK	9-L OK	9-L OK	9-L OK	9-L OK	9-L OK	9-L OK	9-L OK	9-L OK	AT RLI	AT RLI	AT RLI	AT RLI
PRINCE RUPERT	Esquimalt Aug.30/43	NP F/O	NP W/U	NC O/P	NC W/U	NC RHA	C-3 0	C-3 0	C-3 0	C-3 0	C-3 0	C-3 0	C-3 0	C-3 0	C-3 0	C-3 0	AT 0	AT RLI	AT RLI	AT RLI	AT RLI	AT RLI	27A 0	PA O/P	PA RES	PA RES	PA 0
ST. CATHARINES	Esquimalt July 31/43	NP W/U	NP O/P	NC RHA	C-2 0	C-2 0	C-2 0	C-2 0	C-2 0	C-2 0	C-2 0	C-2 0	C-2 0	C-2 0	C-2 0	C-2 0	AT RSH	AT RSH	AT RSH	AT WUB	AT RHA	AT RHA	AT RHA	AT RHA	AT RHA	AT RHA	AT 0
SAINT JOHN	Montreal Dec.13/43					NC F/O	NC RHA	NC WUB	NC 0	NC RHA	9-L O/P	9-L OK	9-L OK	9-L OK	9-L OK	9-L OK	9-L OK	9-L OK	9-L OK	AT RCF	AT RCF	AT RSB	AT RSB	AT RSB	AT RSB	AT RSB	
SPRINGHILL	Esquimalt Mar.21/44								NP W/U	NP O/P	NC RHA	NC WUB	NC WUB	16A 0	16A 0	16A 0	16A 0	16A 0	16A 0	16A 0	16A 0	16A 0	AT 0	AT RPI	AT RPI	AT RPI	AT RPI
STETTLER	Montreal May 7/44										NC O/P	NC F/O	NC WUB	16A RHA	16A 0	16A 0	16A 0	16A 0	16A 0	16A 0	16A 0	16A 0	16A 0	16A RHA	AT 0	AT RSH	AT 0
STORMONT	Montreal Nov.27/43				NC F/O	NC RHA	NC W/U	NC W/U	NC O/P	9-L OK	9-L OK	9-L OK	9-L OK	9-L OK	9-L OK	9-L OK	9-L OK	9-L OK	9-L O/P	9-L RSH	9-L RSH	9-L RSH	AT RSH	AT RSH	AT RSH	AT RSH	AT 0
SWANSEA	Esquimalt Oct.4/43				NP W/U	NP O/P	NC W/U	NC RHA	9-L RHA	9-L O/P	9-L OK	9-L OK	9-L OK	9-L OK	9-L OK	9-L OK	9-L OK	9-L OK	9-L OK	9-L O/P	9-L RLI	9-L RLI	AT RLI	AT RLI	AT RLI	AT O/S	AT 0
THETFORD MINES	Quebec City May 24/44										NC F/O	NC F/O	NC WUB	NC RHA	AT 0	25L RHA	25L O/P	25L OK	25L OK	25L OK	25L OK	25L OK	25L OK	25L WUB	AT 0	AT 0	AT 0
VALLEYFIELD	Quebec City Dec.7/43					NC F/O	NC RHA	NC WUB	C-1 0	C-1 0	C-1 0																
WASKESIU	Esquimalt June 16/43	NP O/P	NP WUB	5-L 0	5-L 0	6-L 0	6-L OK	6-L OK	6-L OK	6-L OK	6-L OK	6-L OK	6-L OK	6-L OK	6-L RSH	6-L RSH	6-L RSH	6-L RSH	6-L RSH	6-L RSH	6-L WUB	6-L O/P	6-L RSH	AT RES	PA RES	PA RES	PA 0
WENTWORTH	Esquimalt Dec.7/43				NP W/U	NP O/P	NC RSH	NC RHA	NC WUB	NC RHA	C-4 0	C-4 0	C-4 0	C-4 0	C-4 0	C-4 0	C-4 0	C-4 0	C-4 0	C-4 0	C-4 0	AT RSH	AT RSH	AT RSH	AT RSH	AT RSH	AT 0

River Class, ex-RN

NAME of SHIP	Built at / Commissioned	1944 Jan	Feb	Mar	Apr	May	June	July	Aug	Sep	Oct	Nov	Dec	1945 Jan	Feb	Mar	Apr	May	June	July
ANNAN	Aberdeen June 13/44					NC FOK	NC WUK	6-L OK	6-L OK	6-L OK	6-L OK	6-L OK	6-L OK	6-L RLV	6-L RLV	6-L OK	6-L OSC	6-L OK	WA ISH	RF
ETTRICK	Sunderland Jan.29/44	C-1 RHA	C-1 RHA	C-1 RHA	C-1 RHA	C-3 RHA	C-3 WUB	C-3 0	C-3 0	C-3 0	27A 0	27A 0	27A 0	27A 0	27A 0	27A 0	27A O/P	CK RSO	CK RSO	
MEON	Glasgow Feb.7/44		NF RHA	NC RHA	NC W/U	9-L O/P	9-L OK	9-L OK	9-L OK	9-L OK	9-L O/P	27A 0	27A 0	27A 0	27A 0	27A 0	27A 0	27A O/P	CK RSO	CK RSO
MONNOW	Bristol Mar.8/44			NC FOK	NC WUK	C-2 0	C-2 0	C-2 0	C-2 0	9-L OK	9-L OK	9-L OK	9-L OK	9-L OK	9-L OK	9-L OK	9-L OK	9-L OK	9-L OK	RF ISH
NENE	South Bank Apr.6/44				6-L RDA	C-2 RDA	C-2 RDA	C-2 RDA	C-2 WUB	9-L O/P	9-L OK	9-L OK	9-L OK	9-L OK	9-L OK	9-L OK	9-L OK	9-L OK	RF ISH	RF ISH
RIBBLE	Blyth July 24/44							NC FOK	NC WUK	C-4 OK	26L OK	26L OK	26L OK	26L OK	26L OK	26L OK	26L OK	26L OK	RF ISH	RF ISH
TEME	South Bank Feb.28/44		NC FOK	NC FOK	NC WUK	6-L OK	6-L OK	6-L RCF	6-L RCF	6-L RCF	6-L RCF	6-L RCF	6-L RCF	6-L WUK	6-L OK	5-L OK	6-L N/O	RF IFA	RF IFA	RF IFA

Loch Class

NAME of SHIP	Built at / Commissioned	1944 July	Aug	Sep	Oct	Nov	Dec	1945 Jan	Feb	Mar	Apr	May	June	July
LOCH ACHANALT	Leith July 31/44	NC FOK	NC WUK	6-L OK	6-L OK	6-L RHY	6-L OK	6-L OK	6-L OK	6-L OK	6-L OK	6-L OSC	WA OK	RF ISH
LOCH ALVIE	Glasgow Aug.10/44		NC FOK	NC WUK	9-L OK	9-L OK	9-L RLV	9-L OK	9-L OK	9-L OK	9-L OK	9-L OK	RF ISH	RF ISH
LOCH MORLICH	Wallsend July 17/44	NC FOK	NC WUK	6-L OK	6-L RLO	6-L OK	6-L OK	6-L OK	6-L OK	6-L OK	6-L OSC	6-L OK	WA ISH	RF

Corvettes
Flower Class, 1939-1940 Programme

Each ship occupies one row; within a month cell the upper code is the operational area and the lower code (where present) is the base/status. They are shown here as "upper / lower".

NAME of SHIP / Built at	Commissioned	1940 Nov	Dec	1941 Jan	Feb	Mar	Apr	May	June	July	Aug	Sep	Oct	Nov	Dec	1942 Jan	Feb	Mar	Apr	May	June	July	Aug	Sep	Oct	Nov	Dec	1943 Jan	Feb	Mar	Apr	May	June	July	Aug	Sep	Oct	Nov	Dec	1944 Jan
AGASSIZ / Vancouver	Jan.23/41			PA	PA / F/O	PA / W/U	HX / O/P	HX / 0	NF / 0	19N / 0	19N / 0	19N / 0	N13 / 0	N13 / 0	N13 / 0	NF / 0	NF / RLI	NF / RLI	N-2 / RHA	A-3 / 0	A-3 / 0	A-3 / 0	C-3 / 0	C-3 / 0	C-3 / 0	C-3 / 0	C-3 / 0	NF / RLI	NF / RLI	NF / RLI	C-1 / 0	C-1 / 0	C-1 / 0	C-1 / 0	C-1 / 0	C-1 / 0	C-1 / 0	C-1 / 0	C-1 / 0	C-1 / RNY
ALBERNI / Esquimalt	Feb.4/41				PA	PA / W/U	HX / O/P	HX / 0	NF / 0	24N / 0	24N / RQC	24N / OW	N13 / 0	NF / RIC	NF / RIC	NF / RHA	N-1 / RHA	N-1 / 0	N-1 / 0	N-1 / 0	NF / 0	NF / RHA	NF / RHA	NF / RHA	26L / O/P	26L / RLV	26W / OM	26W / OM	26G / OM	62L / O/P	WL / RHA	QF / 0	QF / 0	QF / 0	QF / 0	QF / 0	WL / 0	WL / RLI	WL / RLI	WL / RLI
ALGOMA / Port Arthur	July 11/41									AT	AT / F/O	HX / W/U	N14 / 0	N14 / 0	N14 / 0	N14 / 0	N14 / 0	N-3 / RLI	A-3 / RLI	A-3 / 0	A-3 / 0	NF / RHA	WL / 0	WL / 0	WL / 0	0 / RLI	27L / 0	27L / O/P	27L / OK	27L / OM	27G / OM	27G / OK	27L / O/P	WS / 0	WL / 0	QF / 0	QF / 0	QF / 0	GF / OSK	WL / RLI
AMHERST / Saint John	Aug.5/41										AT	HX / F/O	N16 / W/U	N13 / 0	N13 / 0	N11 / 0	N11 / 0	N11 / 0	C-1 / RLI	C-1 / RLI	NF / 0	NF / 0	C-4 / 0	C-4 / 0	C-4 / 0	C-4 / 0	C-4 / 0	C-4 / 0	C-4 / 0	C-4 / 0	NF / RCA	C-4 / RCA	C-4 / RCA	C-4 / RCA	C-4 / RCA	C-4 / W/U	C-4 / 0			
ARROWHEAD / Sorel	Nov.21/40	AT / F/O	AT / W/U	AT / O/P	AT / RSU	WG / RSU	WG / RSU	WG / WUK	WG / 0	4-I / 0	18N / 0	18N / 0	18N / 0	N12 / 0	N12 / 0	NF / 0	NF / RCH	N17 / RCH	WL / 0	WL / 0	WL / 0	WL / 0	GE / 0	GE / 0	GE / 0	GE / 0	GE / 0	WL / RCH	WL / RCH	WL / RHA	WL / 0	WL / 0	W-7 / 0	W-7 / 0	W-7 / 0	W-7 / 0	W-7 / 0	W-1 / 0	W-1 / 0	W-1 / 0
ARVIDA / Quebec City	May 22/41						AT / F/O	AT / W/U	AT / W/U	SY / 0	23N / 0	N14 / WUK	N14 / 0	N11 / 0	NF / RSB	NF / RSB	NF / RSB	A-3 / 0	A-3 / 0	C-4 / 0	C-4 / 0	C-4 / 0	C-4 / 0	C-4 / 0	NF / RLU	NF / RLU	NF / RSB	NF / RHA	A-3 / 0	C-5 / 0	C-5 / 0	C-5 / 0	C-5 / 0	C-5 / 0	C-5 / 0	C-5 / 0	C-5 / 0	C-5 / 0	C-5 / 0	C-5 / 0
BADDECK / Lauzon	May 18/41						AT / F/O	AT / W/U	NF / 0	HX / RQC	HX / OW	N15 / 0	NF / RIC	RIC / RHA	NF / RHA	NF / RHA	NF / RHA	NF / RHA	NF / RHA	WL / W/U	WL / 0	WL / RHA	WL / O/P	26L / 0	26W / RHA	26W / OM	26W / OM	26G / OM	62G / O/P	62L / RHA	C-4 / 0	C-4 / 0	W-2 / 0	W-2 / RLI	W-2 / RLI	W-1 / RLI	W-1 / RHA	W-1 / W/U		
BARRIE / Collingwood	May 12/41						AT / F/O	AT / W/U	SY / 0	SY / 0	23N / 0	NF / RBE	NF / RBE	NF / WUK	N12 / 0	N12 / 0	N-2 / 0	N-2 / 0	N-2 / 0	WL / RLI	WL / RLI	WL / 0	WL / 0	WL / 0	WL / 0	WL / 0	WL / 0	WL / 0	WL / 0	WL / 0	W-1 / 0	W-1 / 0	W-1 / 0	W-1 / 0	W-1 / 0	W-1 / 0	W-1 / 0			
BATTLEFORD / Collingwood	July 31/41									AT	AT / F/O	AT / W/U	SY / 0	SY / 0	N12 / 0	NF / RLI	NF / RLI	RLI / 0	C-4 / RCF	C-4 / RCF	C-4 / WUK	C-1 / 0	C-1 / 0	C-1 / 0	C-1 / 0	C-1 / 0	C-1 / 0	C-1 / 0	C-1 / RLI	NF / 0	NF / RHA	W-4 / RHA	W-4 / 0	W-4 / 0	W-4 / 0	W-4 / 0	W-4 / 0			
BITTERSWEET / Sorel	Jan.23/41			AT	AT / F/O	AT / W/U	WG / O/P	WG / RTY	WG / RTY	22N / WUK	22N / 0	22N / 0	N11 / 0	N13 / 0	N13 / 0	NF / RCH	NF / RCH	N-3 / 0	A-3 / RLI	A-3 / RLI	A-3 / 0	A-3 / 0	A-3 / 0	A-3 / 0	A-3 / 0	C-3 / 0	C-3 / 0	C-3 / RLI	C-3 / RLI	C-3 / 0	C-3 / 0	C-3 / 0	C-3 / 0	C-3 / 0	C-3 / 0	C-3 / RBT	C-3 / RBT	C-3 / W/U	C-3 / 0	C-3
BRANDON / Lauzon	July 22/41									AT	AT / F/O	AT / F/O	HX / W/U	N15 / 0	NF / RTY	NF / RTY	N-1 / RTY	C-1 / WUK	C-2 / 0	C-2 / 0	C-2 / 0	C-2 / 0	C-2 / RLI	C-2 / RLI	C-4 / 0	C-4 / 0	C-4 / 0	C-4 / 0	C-4 / 0	C-4 / 0	C-4 / 0	C-4 / 0	C-4 / 0	C-4 / RGY	C-4 / RGY	C-4 / RGY	C-4 / W/U	C-4 / 0	C-4	
BUCTOUCHE / Lauzon	June 5/41							AT / F/O	AT / W/U	21N / 0	21N / 0	N12 / 0	N12 / 0	N12 / 0	N12 / 0	N12 / 0	C-2 / RLU	C-2 / RLU	C-2 / RHA	WL / 0	WL / RHA	WL / 0	WL / 0	WL / 0	WL / 0	WL / 0	WL / 0	WL / RSB	W-1 / RSB	W-1 / RSB	W-1 / RSB	W-1 /	W-1 /	W-1 /						
CAMROSE / Sorel	June 30/41							AT / F/O	AT / W/U	AT / 0	HX / 0	N15 / 0	N15 / 0	N15 / RHA	NF / RLU	NF / RLU	C-3 / 0	C-3 / 0	C-3 / 0	WL / 0	WL / 0	27L / OK	27L / OK	27L / RLN	27L / OM	27G / O/P	27G / RPI	27L / RPI	WL / RPI	WL / RPI	5-S / RPI	5-S / W/U	5-S / O/P	6-S / OK	6-L / OK	6-L / OK				
CHAMBLY / Montreal	Dec.18/40		AT / F/O	AT / F/O	HX / W/U	HX / W/U	HX / 0	NF / 0	21N / 0	21N / 0	21N / 0	N14 / 0	N14 / 0	NF / RHA	NF / RHA	NF / RHA	N-2 / 0	NF / OSC	NF / OSC	NF / OSC	NF / OSC	C-1 / 0	C-1 / 0	C-2 / 0	C-2 / RLI	C-2 / RLI	C-2 / O/P	NF / 0	NF / 0	C-2 / 0	C-2 / 0	C-2 / 0	C-2 / 0	C-2 / 0	C-2 / 0	5-S / 0	6-S / 0	6-S / RLI	RLI	
CHICOUTIMI / Montreal	May 12/41						AT / F/O	AT / W/U	SY / 0	SY / 0	N14 / WUK	N13 / 0	N13 / 0	N17 / 0	N17 / 0	N18 / RLI	WL / RLI	WL / 0	WL / 0	WL / 0	WL / 0	WL / 0	WL / 0	WL / 0	WL / 0	WL / 0	WL / 0	WL / RQC	W-1 / RQC	W-1 / RQC	W-1 / 0	W-1 / 0	W-1 / 0							
CHILLIWACK / Vancouver	Apr.8/41					PA / F/O	PA / W/U	PA / O/P	HX / OSC	16N / OSC	16N / 0	16N / 0	N11 / 0	N11 / 0	N14 / RHA	NF / 0	N15 / 0	N-3 / RLI	NF / RLI	C-1 / 0	C-1 / 0	C-1 / 0	C-1 / 0	C-1 / 0	C-1 / 0	C-1 / 0	C-1 / 0	A-3 / RHA	NF / RDA	NF / RDA	NF / RDA	RDA	RDA	RDA / W/U	C-1 / 0	C-1 / 0	C-1 / 0	C-1 / 0	C-1 / 0	C-1
COBALT / Port Arthur	Nov.25/40	AT / F/O	AT / F/O	AT / F/O	HX / W/U	HX / W/U	HX / 0	HX / 0	NF / 0	17N / 0	17N / 0	17N / 0	N12 / 0	N12 / 0	NF / RLI	NF / RLI	C-2 / 0	C-2 / 0	C-2 / 0	WL / 0	WL / 0	WL / 0	WL / 0	WL / 0	WL / 0	WL / 0	WL / 0	WL / RLI	WL / RLI	WL / RPI	W-6 / 0	W-6 / 0	W-6 / 0	W-6 / 0	W-6 / 0	W-6 / 0	W-6 / 0	W-6		
COLLINGWOOD / Collingwood	Nov.9/40	AT / F/O	AT / F/O	HX / W/U	HX / W/U	HX / 0	HX / 0	HX / 0	NF / 0	25N / 0	25N / 0	25N / 0	N11 / 0	N11 / 0	NF / RHA	NF / RHA	N-1 / 0	N-1 / 0	N-1 / 0	A-3 / RLI	A-3 / RLI	A-3 / RHA	A-3 / 0	A-3 / 0	A-3 / 0	C-4 / 0	C-4 / 0	C-4 / RLI	C-4 / RLI	C-4 / RLI	C-4 / 0	C-4 / 0	C-4 / 0	C-4 / 0	C-4 / 0	C-4 / 0	C-4 / 0	RNY	RNY	W/U
DAUPHIN / Montreal	May 17/41							AT / F/O	AT / W/U	SY / 0	SY / 0	23N / WUK	N14 / 0	N14 / 0	N15 / 0	N15 / 0	N15 / 0	N14 / 0	C-4 / RHA	C-4 / RHA	C-4 / 0	C-2 / 0	C-2 / 0	C-2 / 0	C-1 / 0	A-3 / RPI	A-3 / RPI	A-3 / RPI	A-3 / RPI	A-3 / W/U	C-5 / 0	C-5 / 0	C-5 / 0	C-5 / 0	C-5 / 0	C-5 / 0	C-5 / 0			
DAWSON / Victoria	Oct.6/41									PA	PA / F/O	PA / W/U	PA / W/U	PA / 0	PA / 0	PA / 0	PA / 0	PA / 0	PE / 0	PE / 0	PE / 0	PE / 0	CN / 0	CN / RES	PE / RES	PE / 0	PE / 0	PE / 0	PD / 0	PD / 0	PD / 0	PD / RES	PE / 0	PE / 0	PE / 0	PE / RVA	PE / RVA	PE / RVA	PE / RVA	PE
DRUMHELLER / Collingwood	Sept.13/41											AT / F/O	AT / W/U	SY / 0	N14 / 0	N14 / 0	N14 / 0	NF / RSO	NF / WUK	C-2 / 0	C-2 / 0	C-2 / 0	C-2 / 0	C-2 / 0	C-2 / RLI	C-2 / RLI	C-2 / RLI	C-2 / 0	C-2 / 0	C-2 / 0	C-2 / 0	C-2 / 0	C-2 / 0	C-2 / 0	C-2 / 0	C-2 / 0	C-2 / 0	C-2 / RNY	C-2 / RNY	C-2 / RNY
DUNVEGAN / Sorel	Sept.9/41											AT / F/O	SY / W/U	SY / 0	N16 / 0	NF / RHA	N12 / 0	N12 / 0	C-2 / 0	C-2 / 0	C-2 / 0	WL / RLI	WL / RLI	WL / 0	WL / 0	WL / 0	WL / 0	WL / 0	WL / 0	WL / 0	W-8 / 0	W-8 / 0	W-8 / 0	W-8 / 0	W-8 / 0	W-8 / 0	W-8 / RBT	W-8 / RBT	W-8 / WUB	
EDMUNDSTON / Esquimalt	Oct.21/41												PA / F/O	PA / W/U	PA / 0	PA / 0	PA / 0	PA / 0	PE / 0	PE / 0	PE / 0	PE / O/P	WL / 0	WL / 0	WL / RHA	WL / RHA	WL / RHA	WL / RHA	WL / RHA	WL / W/U	5-S / 0	5-S / 0	5-S / 0	5-S / 0	6-S / O/P	6-L / OK	6-L / OK			
EYEBRIGHT / Montreal	Nov.26/40	AT / F/O	AT / W/U	AT / O/P	WG / RSU	WG / RSU	WG / RSU	WG / WUK	4-I / 0	18N / 0	18N / 0	18N / 0	N16 / 0	N16 / 0	NF / RCH	NF / RCH	N14 / 0	N13 / 0	C-3 / 0	C-4 / 0	C-4 / RLV	C-1 / RLV	C-1 / WUK	C-1 / 0	C-1 / 0	C-3 / 0	C-3 / 0	C-3 / 0	C-3 / 0	C-3 / RBT	C-3 / RBT	C-3 / W/U	C-3 / 0	C-3 / 0	C-3 / 0	C-3 / 0	C-3 / 0	C-3 / 0	C-3 / 0	C-3
FENNEL / Sorel	Jan.15/41			AT	AT / F/O	AT / W/U	WG / O/P	WG / RGR	WG / RGR	22N / WUK	22N / 0	22N / 0	NF / RHA	NF / RHA	N11 / WUK	N11 / 0	N11 / 0	N11 / 0	C-1 / 0	C-1 / RNY	WL / RNY	WL / 0	WL / 0	WL / 0	WL / 0	WL / 0	WL / RHA	WL / 0	WL / 0	C-2 / 0	C-2 / RBT	C-2 / RBT	C-2 / W/U	C-2 / 0	C-2 / 0	C-2				
GALT / Collingwood	May 15/41						AT / F/O	AT / W/U	21N / 0	21N / 0	21N / 0	N12 / 0	N15 / 0	N13 / 0	N13 / 0	NF / OSC	NF / RLI	NF / RLI	C-3 / 0	C-3 / 0	C-3 / 0	C-3 / 0	C-3 / 0	C-3 / 0	C-3 / RLI	NF / RHA	NF / W/U	NF / 0	C-1 / 0	C-1 / 0	C-1 / 0	C-1 / 0	C-1 / 0	C-1 / 0	C-1 / 0	C-1 / 0	C-1 / 0	C-1 / 0	C-1 / 0	C-1
HEPATICA / Lauzon	Nov.12/40	AT / W/U	AT / O/P	WG / RCL	WG / RCL	WG / WUK	4-W / 0	4-W / 0	4-I / 0	23N / 0	23N / 0	23N / 0	NF / RHA	NF / RHA	N12 / 0	N12 / 0	C-2 / 0	C-2 / 0	N-1 / 0	N-1 / 0	HT / OW	HA / RHA	GE / 0	GE / 0	HQ / 0	HQ / 0	WL / RNY	WL / RNY	WL / RHA	WL / RHA	WL / 0	W-5 / 0	W-5 / 0	W-5 / 0	W-5 / 0	W-5 / 0	W-5 / 0	W-5 / 0		
KAMLOOPS / Victoria	Mar.17/41					PA / F/O	PA / W/U	PA / W/U	HX / O/P	HX / TR	HX / TR	HX / TR	HX / TR	HX / TR	HX / TR	HX / TR	HX / TR	HX / TR	HX / TR	AT / TR	AT / TR	AT / TR	AT / TR	HX / TR	AT / RLI	AT / RLI	AT / RLI	AT / W/U	RLI / 0	RLI / 0	RLI / 0	C-2 / 0	C-2 / 0	C-2 / 0	C-2 / 0	C-2 / 0	C-2 / 0	C-2 / 0	C-2 / 0	RCA
KAMSACK / Port Arthur	Oct.4/41												AT / F/O	AT / W/U	SY / 0	N13 / 0	N13 / 0	N13 / 0	C-3 / RLI	C-3 / RLI	WL / RHA	WL / 0	WL / 0	WL / 0	WL / 0	WL / 0	WL / 0	WL / RLI	WL / RLI	WL / RHA	C-1 / 0	C-1 / 0	C-1 / 0	C-1 / 0	C-1 / 0	NF / RLI	W-4 / RLI	W-4 / 0	W-4 / 0	W-4 / RBT
KENOGAMI / Port Arthur	June 29/41								AT / F/O	AT / W/U	24N / O/P	24N / 0	N16 / 0	N16 / 0	N16 / 0	N17 / RHA	N17 / RHA	WL / RHA	WL / 0	WL / 0	WL / 0	WL / 0	WL / 0	WL / 0	WL / 0	WL / 0	WL / 0	C-1 / RLI	C-1 / RLI	C-1 / 0	C-1 / 0	C-1 / 0	NF / 0	W-8 / RLI	W-8 / RLI	W-8 / 0	W-8 / 0	W-8 / 0	W-8 / 0	W-8
LETHBRIDGE / Montreal	June 25/41								AT / F/O	AT / W/U	AT / 0	SY / 0	N16 / 0	N16 / 0	N16 / 0	N13 / 0	N14 / 0	N14 / 0	C-4 / 0	C-4 / 0	C-4 / 0	GE / 0	GE / 0	GE / 0	WL / RLI	WL / RLI	ES / W/U	ES / 0	ES / 0	WL / 0	WL / 0	WL / 0	W-3 / RLI	W-3 / RLI	W-3 / RHA	W-3 / 0	W-3 / 0	W-3 / 0	W-3 / 0	W-3 / RSY	RSY
LEVIS / Lauzon	May 16/41					AT / F/O	AT / W/U	HX / W/U	19N / 0	19N / 0																														
LOUISBURG / Quebec City	Oct.2/41												AT / F/O	AT / W/U	SY / 0	SY / OSC	NF / 0	N15 / RHA	NF / RHA	NF / RHA	NF / RHA	NF / RHA	C-3 / 0	C-3 / 0	NF / O/P	25L / RHU	25L / OK	25L / RBE	25L / RBE	25G / OM										
LUNENBURG / Lauzon	Dec.4/41													AT / F/O	AT / W/U	AT / 0	WL / 0	WL / RHA	WL / 0	WL / 0	HN / 0	GE / RLI	25L / RLN	62G / OK	62L / OM	WL / OM	WL / OM	WL / OK	HN / RLV	GE / RLV	25L / RLV	62G / WUK	62L / 0	WL / 0	WL / O/P	5-S / OK	5-S / OK	6-S	6-L	6-L
MATAPEDIA / Quebec City	May 9/41						AT / F/O	AT / W/U	SY / 0	SY / 0	N14 / 0	N14 / 0	N13 / 0	N13 / RPI	N16 / RPI	WL / RPI	WL / 0	WL / 0	WL / 0	WL / 0	WL / 0	WL / 0	WL / 0	WL / 0	WL / 0	WL / 0	WL / RDA	W-5 / RLI	W-5 / RLI	W-5 / RLI	W-5 / RLI	W-5 / 0	W-5 / 0	W-5 / 0	W-5 / 0					
MAYFLOWER / Montreal	Nov.9/40	AT / F/O	AT / F/O	AT / W/U	AT / O/P	WG / RTY	WG / RTY	WG / WUK	4-I / 0	19N / 0	19N / 0	19N / 0	N16 / 0	N16 / 0	NF / RCH	NF / RCH	N-2 / 0	N-2 / 0	A-3 / 0	A-3 / 0	A-3 / 0	A-3 / 0	A-3 / RPI	A-3 / RPI	A-3 / W/U	C-3 / 0	C-3 / 0	C-3 / 0	C-3 / 0	C-3 / 0	C-3 / 0	C-3 / 0	C-3 / 0	C-3 / 0	C-3 / 0	NF / RBT	NF / RBT	C-3	C-3	C-3
MONCTON / Saint John	Apr.24/42																		AT / F/O	AT / W/U	WL / 0	WL / 0	WL / 0	WL / 0	WL / 0	WL / 0	WL / 0	WL / 0	W-5 / 0	W-5 / RDA	W-5 / RDA	W-5 / RDA	W-5 / 0	W-5 / 0	PE / O/P					
MOOSE JAW / Collingwood	June 19/41								AT / F/O	AT / W/U	AT / W/U	NF / 0	NF / WUK	N12 / 0	N12 / 0	N12 / 0	NF / RSB	NF / RSB	NF / RSB	NF / RSB	WL / 0	WL / 0	WL / RHA	27L / O/P	27L / OK	27L / OK	27L / OM	27G / OM	27G / O/P	WL / RHA	QF / 0	QF / 0	QF / 0	QF / 0	GF / 0	GF / 0	WL / RLI			
MORDEN / Port Arthur	Sept.6/41											AT / F/O	AT / W/U	N13 / 0	NF / RGR	NF / RSO	N19 / WUK	N19 / 0	C-2 / 0	C-2 / RLI	HX / RLI	C-2 / 0	C-2 / 0	C-2 / 0	C-2 / 0	C-2 / 0	C-2 / 0	C-2 / RLU	C-2 / RLU	C-2 / W/U	C-2 / 0	9-M / 0	C-2 / 0	C-2 / 0	C-2 / 0	C-2 / RLN	C-2 / RLN			
NANAIMO / Esquimalt	Apr.26/41						PA / F/O	PA / W/U	HX / O/P	HX / 0	HX / RHA	NF / RHA	N16 / 0	N16 / 0	N13 / 0	N13 / 0	N16 / 0	WL / RHA	NF / RHA	WL / 0	WL / 0	WL / 0	WL / 0	WL / 0	WL / 0	WL / 0	WL / 0	W-9 / RLU	W-9 / RLU	W-9 / W/U	W-9 / 0	W-9 / 0	W-9 / 0							
NAPANEE / Kingston	May 12/41						AT / F/O	AT / W/U	SY / 0	SY / 0	N14 / 0	N14 / 0	N14 / 0	N13 / 0	N13 / 0	N12 / RLI	NF / W/U	NF / 0	C-1 / 0	C-1 / 0	C-1 / 0	C-1 / 0	C-1 / 0	C-1 / 0	NF / RMO	C-1 / RMO	C-3 / RMO	C-3 / RMO	C-3 / RHA	C-3 / W/U	C-3 / 0	C-3							
OAKVILLE / Port Arthur	Nov.18/41													AT / F/O	AT / W/U	AT / 0	AT / 0	WL / 0	WL / HA	HA / OW	ES / OW	ES / 0	ES / RHA	ES / RHA	ES / 0	ES / 0	WL / 0	WL / 0	W-7 / RLI	W-7 / RLI	W-7 / 0	W-7 / 0	W-8 / RGA							
ORILLIA / Collingwood	Nov.25/40	AT / F/O	AT / F/O	AT / F/O	HX / W/U	HX / W/U	HX / 0	HX / 0	NF / 0	25N / 0	25N / 0	25N / 0	N14 / 0	N14 / RHA	NF / RHA	NF / RHA	N-1 / 0	C-1 / 0	C-1 / 0	C-1 / 0	C-1 / 0	C-1 / 0	C-1 / 0	C-2 / RLI	C-2 / RLI	C-2 / RLI	NF / 0	NF / 0	C-4 / 0	C-4 / 0	C-4 / 0	C-4 / 0	C-4 / 0	C-4 / 0	C-4 / 0	C-4 / 0	C-4	C-4	C-4	C-4
PICTOU / Lauzon	Apr.23/41						AT / F/O	AT / W/U	NF / 0	21N / 0	21N / 0	21N / 0	N11 / 0	N14 / RHA	N12 / RSN	NF / 0	N16 / RLV	NF / RLV	NF / 0	C-4 / RHA	C-4 / RLI	C-2 / RLI	C-2 / RHA	C-2 / 0	0 / RHA	N/O / RLI	WL / RLI	WL / RHA	WL / 0	C-3 / 0	C-3 / 0	C-3 / 0	C-3 / 0	C-3 / 0	C-3 / 0	C-3 / 0	C-3 / RNY			
PRESCOTT / Kingston	June 26/41								AT / F/O	AT / F/O	HX / W/U	23N / 0	N16 / 0	N16 / 0	N16 / RLI	N11 / RLI	NF / 0	NF / 0	C-4 / RHA	C-4 / RLI	C-4 / RHA	WL / 0	WL / 0	25L / RHU	25L / OK	25L / OK	27L / OK	27G / RHA	27G / RLI	WL / RLI	WL / RLI	5-S / RLI	5-S / RLI	5-S / W/U	6-S / O/P	6-L / OK	6-L			
QUESNEL / Victoria	May 23/41							PA / F/O	PA / W/U	PA / 0	PA / 0	PA / 0	PA / 0	PA / 0	PA / 0	PA / 0	PA / 0	PE / 0	PE / 0	PE / 0	PE / RES	WL / 0	WL / 0	WL / 0	WL / 0	WL / 0	WL / RPI	W-1 / RPI	W-1 / RPI	W-1 / RPI	W-1 / RHA	W-1 /	W-1 /							
RIMOUSKI / Lauzon	Apr.26/41						AT / F/O	AT / W/U	NF / 0	16N / 0	16N / 0	16N / RHA	NF / RHA	NF / RHA	NF / 0	N13 / 0	N13 / 0	WL / 0	WL / 0	WL / 0	WL / 0	WL / 0	WL / 0	WL / 0	WL / 0	WL / RLI	WL / RLI	W-1 / RLI	W-1 / RLI	W-1 / W/U	W-1 / 0	W-1								
ROSTHERN / Port Arthur	June 17/41								AT / F/O	AT / W/U	HX / 0	N15 / WUK	NF / 0	N11 / RHA	NF / RHA	NF / 0	N-2 / RLI	N-2 / RLI	A-3 / 0	A-3 / RHA	A-3 / 0	A-3 / 0	A-3 / 0	A-3 / 0	A-3 / 0	C-5 / RSH	C-5 / RSH	C-5 / RSH	C-5 / W/U	C-5 / 0	C-5 / 0	C-5 / 0	C-5 / 0	C-5 / 0	C-5 / 0	C-5 / 0	C-5			
SACKVILLE / Saint John	Dec.30/41														AT / F/O	AT / W/U	AT / RHA	WL / 0	WL / 0	C-3 / 0	C-3 / 0	C-3 / 0	C-3 / 0	C-3 / 0	C-3 / 0	C-3 / 0	C-3 / 0	NF / 0	NF / RHA	NF / RHA	C-1 / 0	C-1 / 0	C-1 / 0	9-S / 0	C-2 / 0	C-2 / 0	C-2			
SASKATOON / Montreal	June 9/41							AT / F/O	AT / W/U	HX / OW	HX / OW	HX / 0	HX / 0	HX / 0	HX / 0	HX / 0	HX / 0	HX / RHA	HX / RHA	AT / RHA	AT / RHA	AT / RHA	AT / 0	AT / 0	WL / 0	WL / 0	W-8 / 0	W-8 / 0	W-8 / 0	W-8 / 0	W-8 / 0	W-8 / 0	W-8 / 0	W-8 / RPI						
SHAWINIGAN / Lauzon	Sept.19/41											AT / F/O	SY / W/U	SY / 0	N14 / 0	N14 / 0	N14 / 0	C-4 / 0	C-4 / 0	C-4 / 0	HN / RLI	HN / RLI	HN / RHA	HQ / RHA	HQ / 0	WL / 0	WL / 0	WL / 0	WL / 0	WL / 0	W-3 / 0	W-3 / 0	W-3 / 0	W-3 / 0	W-3 / 0	W-3				

Continued

Flower Class, 1939-1940 Programme continued

NAME of SHIP / Built at	Commissioned	1940 Nov.	Dec.	1941 Jan.	Feb.	Mar.	Apr.	May	June	July	Aug.	Sep.	Oct.	Nov.	Dec.
SHEDIAC Lauzon	July 8/41									AT F/O	AT W/U	SY 0	N15 0	N15 0	N15 0
SHERBROOKE Sorel	June 5/41								AT F/O	AT W/U	HX 0	SY 0	N14 WUK	N-1 0	N11 0
SNOWBERRY Lauzon	Nov.30/40	AT F/O	AT F/O	AT W/U	AT O/P	WG RCL	WG WUK	WG 0	4-I 0	15N 0	15N 0	15N 0	N11 0	N11 0	NF RCH
SOREL Sorel	Aug.19/41										AT F/O	AT W/U	SY 0	SY 0	N13 0
SPIKENARD Lauzon	Dec.8/40		AT F/O	AT O/P	WG RSS	WG RSS	WG WUK	WG 0	4-I 0	16N 0	16N 0	16N 0	N11 0	NF RHA	NF RLI
SUDBURY Kingston	Oct.15/41												AT F/O	AT W/U	SY 0
SUMMERSIDE Quebec City	Sept.11/41											AT F/O	AT W/U	SY 0	N14 0
THE PAS Collingwood	Oct.21/41												AT F/O	AT W/U	HX 0
TRAIL Vancouver	Apr.30/41						PA F/O	PA W/U	HX O/P	17N 0	17N 0	17N 0	N11 0	N11 0	N11 0
TRILLIUM Montreal	Oct.31/40	AT F/O	AT O/P	WG RGR	WG RGR	WG WUK	4-W 0	4-W 0	4-I 0	18N 0	23N 0	NF RLU	NF RHA	NF RHA	N14 0
WETASKIWIN Vancouver	Dec.17/40		PA F/O	PA W/U	PA W/U	PA O/P	HX 0	HX 0	NF 0	20N 0	20N RHA	20N 0	N15 0	N15 0	N15 0
WEYBURN Port Arthur	Nov.26/41													AT F/O	AT W/U
WINDFLOWER Lauzon	Oct.20/40	AT F/O	AT O/P	WG RSC	WG RSC	WG WUK	4-W 0	4-W 0	4-I 0	18N 0	23N 0	NF RLI	NF RLI	N12 0	N12 0

NAME of SHIP	1942 Jan.	Feb.	Mar.	Apr.	May	June	July	Aug.	Sep.	Oct.	Nov.	Dec.
SHEDIAC	N15 0	N15 0	N-3 0	A-3 0	A-3 0	A-3 RLI	WL RLI	WL 0	WL 0	WL 0	C-1 0	C-1 0
SHERBROOKE	N12 0	N12 0	N13 0	C-3 0	NF RLU	NF RLU	C-4 0	C-4 0	C-4 0	C-4 0	C-4 0	C-4 0
SNOWBERRY	NF RCH	N17 0	WL 0	WL 0	WL 0	HT OW	HA OW	HA OW	ES 0	ES 0	ES 0	ES 0
SOREL	N17 0	NF RLE	NF RLE	N11 WUK	NF OSC	WL 0	WL 0	WL 0	WL 0	WL 0	WL RLI	WL RLI
SPIKENARD	N15 0	N15 0										
SUDBURY	SY 0	N16 0	WL 0	WL 0	HT 0	HT OW	HA OW	HA OW	ES 0	ES 0	ES 0	ES 0
SUMMERSIDE	N14 0	N14 0	N18 0	WL 0	WL 0	WL 0	GE 0	GE 0	GE 0	26L O/P	26L OK	26W OM
THE PAS	HX 0	HX 0	WL 0	WL 0	HT 0	HT OW	HA OW	HA OW	ES 0	ES 0	ES 0	WL RLI
TRAIL	N13 0	N12 0	N12 0	C-2 RLI	C-2 RLI	HX 0	HN 0	HN 0	HN 0	HQ 0	HQ 0	WL 0
TRILLIUM	N13 0	N13 0	N13 0	C-3 RGA	NF RGA	NF RGA	NF W/U	A-3 0	A-3 0	A-3 0	A-3 0	A-3 0
WETASKIWIN	N15 0	NF RLI	NF RLI	C-3 RLI	C-3 W/U	C-3 0	C-3 0	C-3 0	C-3 0	C-3 0	C-3 0	C-3 0
WEYBURN	AT W/U	AT 0	WL RHA	WL 0	WL 0	WL 0	GE 0	GE 0	GE O/P	25L RLV	62G OM	62G OM
WINDFLOWER												

NAME of SHIP	1943 Jan.	Feb.	Mar.	Apr.	May	June	July	Aug.	Sep.	Oct.	Nov.	Dec.	1944 Jan.
SHEDIAC	C-1 0	C-1 0	C-1 0	C-1 0	NF RLI	NF RLI	W-8 0	W-8 0	W-8 0	W-8 0	W-8 0	W-8 0	W-8 0
SHERBROOKE	C-4 0	C-4 0	C-4 0	A-3 0	NF RLU	NF RLU	W-2 W/U	W-2 0	W-2 0	W-2 0	W-2 0	W-2 0	W-2 0
SNOWBERRY	ES 0	ES 0	ES 0	WL RCH	WL RCH	WL 0	5-S 0	5-S 0	5-S 0	5-S 0	6-S 0	6-L O/P	6-L OK
SOREL	WL RPI	TA TR	TA TR	TA TR	TA TR	TA TR	TA TR	TA TR	C-5 0	C-5 0	WL RHA	WL RHA	WL RDA
SPIKENARD													
SUDBURY	ES RLI	ES RLI	WL 0	WL 0	WL 0	WL 0	W-9 0	W-9 0	W-9 0	W-9 OSK	W-9 0	W-9 0	W-9 O/P
SUMMERSIDE	26W OM	26G OM	62G O/P	WL RSB	WL RSB	WL RSB	QF RSB	QF RSB	QF RSB	QF W/U	NF 0	C-5 0	C-5 0
THE PAS	WL RLI	WL 0	WL 0	WL 0	WL 0	WL 0	W-4 0	W-4 RSH	W-4 RSH	W-4 W/U	W-4 0	W-4 0	W-4 0
TRAIL	WL 0	WL 0	WL 0	WL 0	WL 0	WL 0	W-6 RLU	W-6 RLU	W-6 RHA	W-6 W/U	W-6 0	W-6 0	W-6 0
TRILLIUM	A-3 0	A-3 0	A-3 0	A-3 0	A-3 RBO	C-4 RBO	C-4 W/U	C-4 0	C-4 0	C-4 0	C-4 0	C-4 0	C-4 0
WETASKIWIN	NF RLI	NF RLI	NF RHA	A-3 0	C-5 0	C-5 0	C-5 0	C-5 0	C-5 0	C-5 0	C-5 0	C-5 RGA	C-5 RGA
WEYBURN	62G OM	62G OM											
WINDFLOWER													

Flower Class, 1939-1940 Programme continued

NAME of SHIP	1944 Feb.	Mar.	Apr.	May	June	July	Aug.	Sep.	Oct.	Nov.	Dec.	1945 Jan.	Feb.	Mar.	Apr.	May	June	July
AGASSIZ	C-1 RNY	C-1 RHA	C-1 W/U	W-2 0	W-2 0	W-2 0	W-7 0	W-7 0	W-7 0	W-7 0	W-7 0	W-7 0	W-7 RHA	W-7 RLU	W-7 RLS	W-7 WUB	W-7 0	AT FDC
ALBERNI	WL WUB	W-4 0	W-4 O/P	WD OK	WG OK	WG OK	WG OK											
ALGOMA	WL RLI	AT RLI	AT RLI	C-5 RHA	C-5 WUB	C-5 0	C-5 0	41H OK	41H OK	41H OK	41H OK	41H OK	41H OK	41H OK	41M OK	41H OK	AT O/P	AT FDS
AMHERST	C-4 0	C-4 0	C-4 0	C-4 0	C-4 0	C-4 0	C-4 0	C-4 0	C-8 RLI	C-8 RLI	C-8 RLI	HX WUB	HX 0	C-7 0	HX 0	W-9 0	W-9 0	AT FDS
ARROWHEAD	W-1 0	W-1 0	W-1 RBT	W-1 RBT	W-1 RHA	W-1 WUB	W-1 0	QF 0	QF 0	QF 0	W-8 0	W-8 0	W-8 0	W-8 RHA	W-8 0	W-8 0	WA OK	RF IMH
ARVIDA	C-5 RBT	C-5 RBT	C-5 RHA	W-7 WUB	W-7 0	W-7 0	W-2 0	W-2 0	W-2 0	W-2 0	W-8 0	W-8 0	W-8 0	W-8 0	W-8 RSY	W-8 RSY	W-8 RSY	AT FDC
BADDECK	9-L OSC	9-L O/P	9-L OK	WG OK	WG OK	WG OK	WG OK	NO OK	NO OK	NO OK	NO OK	NO OK	NO OK	NO OK	NO OK	NO OK	AT 0	AT FDQ
BARRIE	W-1 0	W-1 RLI	W-1 RLI	W-1 RLI	W-1 RLI	W-1 RHA	W-1 WUB	W-1 0	W-8 0	W-1 0	W-1 0	W-1 0	W-1 0	W-1 0	W-1 0	W-1 0	W-1 0	AT FDQ
BATTLEFORD	W-4 0	W-4 0	W-3 RSY	W-3 RSY	W-3 RSY	W-3 RSY	W-3 RHA	W-3 WUB	W-3 0	W-3 0	W-3 0	W-3 0	W-3 0	W-3 0	W-3 0	W-3 0	W-3 0	AT FDS
BITTERSWEET	C-3 0	C-3 0	C-3 0	C-3 0	C-3 0	C-3 0	C-3 0	C-3 0	C-3 0	C-3 RPI	HX RPI	HX RHA	HX RHA	HX WUB	HX 0	SY RSY	WA OK	RF IGR
BRANDON	C-4 0	C-4 0	C-4 0	C-4 0	C-4 0	C-4 0	C-4 0	C-4 0	C-6 RLI	C-6 RLI	C-6 RHA	W-7 WUB	W-5 0	W-5 0	W-5 0	W-5 0	W-5 0	AT FDS
BUCTOUCHE	W-1 WUB	W-1 0	W-1 0	W-1 0	W-1 0	QF RPI	QF RPI	QF RPI	W-1 0	W-1 0	W-1 0	W-1 0	W-1 0	W-1 0	W-1 0	W-1 RSY	W-1 RSY	AT FDS
CAMROSE	6-L OK	6-L OK	6-L OK	WG OK	WG OK	WG OK	WG OK	PO O/P	AT RPI	AT RPI	AT WUB	41H OK	41H OK	41H OK	41M OK	41M OK	PY OK	AT FDH
CHAMBLY	6-L RLI	6-L RLI	6-L W/U	C-1 0	C-1 0	C-1 0	C-1 0	C-1 0	C-1 0	C-1 0	C-1 0	C-1 0	C-1 0	C-1 0	C-1 0	C-1 RLS	C-1 FDG	AT FDQ
CHICOUTIMI	W-1 0	W-1 0	W-1 0	W-1 0	W-3 0	W-3 0	W-3 0	TA TR	TA TR	TA TR	TA TR	TA TR	TA TR	TA TR	TA RSY	SY WUB	SY 0	AT FDC
CHILLIWACK	C-1 0	C-1 0	C-1 0	C-1 0	C-1 0	C-1 0	C-1 0	C-1 RSY	C-1 RSY	C-1 RHA	W-8 WUB	W-8 WUB	W-8 0	HX 0	HX 0	HX 0	C-9 0	AT FDS
COBALT	W-6 0	W-6 0	W-5 RLI	W-5 RLI	W-5 RLI	W-5 RLI	W-5 WUB	W-5 0	W-5 0	W-5 0	W-5 0	W-5 0	W-7 0	W-7 0	W-7 0	W-7 0	W-7 0	AT FDS
COLLINGWOOD	C-4 0	C-4 0	C-4 0	C-4 0	C-4 0	C-4 0	C-4 0	C-4 0	C-7 0	C-7 0	C-7 0	C-7 RLI	HX RLI	HX RLI	HX TR	TA RHA	TA TR	AT FDH
DAUPHIN	C-5 0	C-5 0	C-5 0	C-5 0	C-5 0	C-5 0	C-5 0	C-5 RLI	C-5 RLI	C-5 RLI	C-5 WUB	W-7 0	W-7 0	W-7 0	W-7 0	W-7 0	W-7 0	AT FDC
DAWSON	PE 0	PE O/P	AT 0	W-7 0	W-7 0	W-7 0	W-7 0	W-7 0	W-7 0	W-7 0	W-7 0	W-7 RDA	W-7 RDA	W-7 RDA	W-7 WUB	W-7 0	W-7 0	AT FDQ
DRUMHELLER	C-2 0	C-2 0	C-2 0	WG OK	WG OK	WG OK	WG OK	PO OK	PO OK	NO OK	NO OK	NO OK	NO OK	NO OK	NO OK	NO OK	AT 0	AT FDS
DUNVEGAN	W-8 0	W-8 0	W-8 0	W-6 0	W-6 0	W-6 0	W-6 0	W-6 0	W-6 0	W-6 0	W-6 0	W-6 RSH	W-6 RSH	W-6 RSH	W-6 WUB	W-6 0	W-6 0	AT FDQ
EDMUNDSTON	6-L OK	6-L OK	6-L OK	C-1 O/P	C-1 RLI	C-1 RLI	C-1 WUB	C-1 0	C-8 0	C-8 0	C-8 0	C-8 0	C-8 0	C-8 0	C-8 0	C-8 0	AT 0	AT FDC
EYEBRIGHT	C-3 0	C-3 0	C-3 0	C-3 0	C-3 0	C-3 0	C-3 RPI	C-3 RPI	C-3 WUB	W-3 0	W-3 0	W-3 0	W-3 0	W-3 0	W-3 0	W-3 0	WA OK	RF IMH
FENNEL	C-2 0	C-2 0	C-2 0	C-2 0	C-2 0	C-2 0	C-2 RPI	C-2 RPI	C-2 RPI	C-2 WUB	C-2 0	C-1 0	C-1 0	C-1 0	C-1 0	C-1 0	RF ICL	RF ILO
GALT	C-1 0	C-1 RNY	C-1 RNY	W-5 RHA	W-5 WUB	W-5 0	W-5 0	W-5 0	W-5 0	W-5 0	W-5 0	W-5 0	W-5 0	W-5 0	W-5 0	W-5 0	W-5 0	AT FDQ
HEPATICA	W-5 0	W-5 0	W-5 RNY	W-4 RNY	W-4 RHA	W-4 WUB	W-4 0	W-4 0	W-4 0	W-4 0	W-4 0	W-4 0	W-4 0	W-4 0	W-4 0	W-4 0	WA OK	RF IMH
KAMLOOPS	C-2 RCA	C-2 RCA	C-2 RCA	C-2 W/U	C-2 WUB	C-2 0	C-2 0	C-2 0	C-2 0	C-2 0	C-2 0	C-2 0	C-2 0	C-2 0	C-2 0	C-2 0	HX 0	AT FDQ
KAMSACK	W-4 RBT	W-4 RBT	W-4 W/U	W-3 0	W-3 0	W-3 0	W-3 0	W-3 0	W-3 0	W-3 0	W-3 0	W-3 0	W-3 0	W-3 RHA	W-3 RLI	W-3 RLI	W-3 WUB	AT FDH
KENOGAMI	W-8 0	W-8 0	W-8 0	W-6 0	W-6 0	W-6 RLI	W-6 RLI	W-6 RLI	W-6 W/U	W-6 WUB	W-8 0	W-8 0	W-8 0	W-8 0	W-8 0	W-8 0	W-8 0	AT FDS

NAME of SHIP	1944 Feb.	Mar.	Apr.	May	June	July	Aug.	Sep.	Oct.	Nov.	Dec.	1945 Jan.	Feb.	Mar.	Apr.	May	June	July
LETHBRIDGE	W-3 RSY	W-3 RSY	W-3 RHA	W-5 WUB	W-5 RPI	W-5 0	W-5 0	W-5 0	W-5 0	W-5 0	W-5 0	W-5 0	W-5 0	W-5 0	W-5 RSH	W-5 RSH	W-5 TR	AT FDH
LUNENBURG	6-L OK	6-L OK	6-L OK	6-G OK	6-G OK	6-G OK	6-G CK	41H OK	AT RSB	AT RSB	AT RSB	AT WUB	NO OK	NO OK	41M OK	41M OK	PY OK	AT FDH
MATAPEDIA	W-5 RHA	W-5 WUB	W-5 0	W-4 0	W-4 0	W-4 0	W-4 0	W-4 0	W-4 0	GF 0	GF 0	W-4 0	W-4 RHA	W-4 RLI	W-4 RHA	W-4 WUB	W-4 FDC	AT FDC
MAYFLOWER	C-3 W/U	C-3 WUB	C-3 0	WG OK	WG OK	WG OK	WD OK	WD OK	PO OK	PO OK	PO OK	PO OK	PO OK	PO OK	PO OK	PO OK	RF IGR	RF IGR
MONCTON	PE 0	PE 0	PE 0	PE RVA	PE RVA	PE 0	PE 0	PE 0	PE 0	PE 0	PE 0	PE 0	PE 0	PE 0	PE 0	PE 0	PE 0	PA 0
MOOSE JAW	WL RLI	AT RLI	AT W/U	WD O/P	WG OK	WG OK	WG OK	41H OK	41H OK	41H OK	41H OK	41H OK	41H OK	41H OK	41M OK	41H OK	AT 0	AT FDS
MORDEN	C-2 RLN	C-2 0	C-2 0	C-2 0	C-2 0	C-2 0	C-2 0	C-2 0	C-2 0	C-2 0	C-2 RSY	HX RSY	HX RHA	HX WUB	HX 0	W-9 0	W-9 0	AT FDS
NANAIMO	W-9 0	W-9 0	W-9 0	W-7 0	W-7 0	W-7 0	W-7 0	W-7 0	W-7 0	W-7 O/P	PA 0	PA RES	PA RES	PA RES	PA TR	PA TR	PA TR	PA 0
NAPANEE	C-3 0	C-3 0	C-3 0	C-3 0	C-3 0	C-3 0	C-3 0	C-3 RPI	C-4 RPI	C-4 RHA	W-2 WUB	W-2 0	W-2 0	W-2 0	W-2 0	W-2 0	W-2 0	AT FDS
OAKVILLE	W-8 RGA	W-8 RGA	W-8 RHA	W-6 WUB	W-6 0	W-6 0	W-6 0	W-6 0	W-6 0	W-6 0	W-6 0	W-6 0	W-6 0	W-6 0	W-6 RLU	W-6 RLU	W-6 RLU	AT FDS
ORILLIA	C-4 RLI	C-4 RLI	C-4 RLI	W-2 RLI	W-2 RHA	W-2 WUB	W-2 0	W-2 0	W-2 0	W-2 0	W-2 0	W-2 0	W-2 0	W-2 0	W-2 0	W-2 RSN	W-2 N/O	AT FDS
PICTOU	C-3 RNY	C-3 RNY	C-3 0	W-5 WUB	W-5 0	W-5 0	W-5 0	W-5 0	W-5 0	W-5 0	W-5 0	W-5 0	W-5 0	W-5 0	W-5 0	W-5 0	W-5 0	AT FDQ
PRESCOTT	6-L OK	6-L OK	6-L OK	WG OK	WG OK	WG OK	WG OK	PO OK	PO O/P	AT RLI	AT RLI	AT RLI	AT WUB	PO OK	NO OK	NO OK	AT 0	AT FDH
QUESNEL	W-1 WUB	W-1 0	W-1 0	W-1 0	QF 0	QF 0	QF 0	QF 0	QF 0	HX 0	HX RSY	HX RSY	HX WUB	HX 0	HX 0	HX 0	HX 0	AT FDQ
RIMOUSKI	C-3 0	C-3 0	C-3 OK	WG OK	WG OK	WG OK	WG OK	AT O/P	TA TR	AT RLS	AT RLS	AT RLI	AT WUB	AT OK	41M OK	41H OK	PY OK	AT FDH
ROSTHERN	C-5 0	C-5 0	C-5 0	C-5 0	C-5 0	TA TR	TA TR	TA TR	TA TR	TA TR	HX WUB	HX 0	HX 0	HX 0	HX 0	HX 0	HX 0	AT FDS
SACKVILLE	C-2 0	C-2 RGA	C-2 RGA	C-2 RHA	C-2 WUB	C-2 0	C-2 0	TA TR	TA TR	AT RDA	AT RDA	AT RDA	AT RDA	AT RDA	AT RHA	AT RHA	AT RHA	AT RHA
SASKATOON	W-8 RPI	W-8 RPI	W-8 RPI	W-6 WUB	W-6 0	W-6 0	W-6 0	W-6 0	W-6 0	W-6 0	W-6 0	W-6 0	W-6 0	W-6 0	W-6 0	W-6 0	W-6 0	AT FDS
SHAWINIGAN	W-3 0	W-3 RHA	W-3 RLI	W-2 RLI	W-2 RHA	W-2 WUB	W-2 RSH	W-2 0	W-8 0	W-2 0								
SHEDIAC	W-8 0	W-8 0	PE O/P	PE 0	PE RVA	PE RVA	PE 0	PE 0	PE 0	PE 0	PE 0	PE 0	PE 0	PE 0	PE 0	PE 0	PE 0	PA 0
SHERBROOKE	W-2 0	W-2 0	W-2 0	W-7 0	W-7 RLI	W-7 RLI	W-7 RLI	W-7 RHA	W-7 WUB	W-1 0	W-1 0	W-1 0	W-1 0	W-1 0	W-1 0	W-1 0	W-1 0	AT FDS
SNOWBERRY	6-L OK	6-L OK	6-L RBT	W-6 RBT	W-6 RHA	W-6 WUB	AT 0	AT O/P	PO OK	PO OK	PO OK	PO OK	PO OK	PO OK	PO OK	PO OK	RF IGR	RF IGR
SOREL	WL RDA	AT RDA	AT WUB	W-4 0	W-4 0	W-4 RBB	W-4 0	W-4 0	W-4 0	W-4 0	W-4 0	W-4 RHA	W-4 0	W-4 0	W-4 0	W-4 RSY	W-4 RSY	AT FDS
SUDBURY	PE RVA	PE RVA	PE RVA	PE W/U	PE 0	PE 0	PE 0	PE 0	PE 0	PE 0	PE 0	PE 0	PE 0	PE 0	PE RES	PE RES	PE 0	PA 0
SUMMERSIDE	C-5 0	C-5 0	C-5 0	WG OK	WG OK	WG OK	WG OK	41H OK	AT O/P	AT RLI	AT RLI	AT RHA	AT WUB	PO O/P	PO OK	PO OK	AT 0	AT FDS
THE PAS	W-4 0	W-4 0	W-4 0	W-3 0	W-3 0	W-3 0	W-3 0	W-3 0	W-8 RSY	AT RSY	TA TR	TA TR	TA TR	TA TR	TA TR	TA TR	TA TR	AT FDH
TRAIL	W-6 0	W-6 0	W-6 0	W-5 0	W-5 0	W-5 0	W-5 RLI	W-5 RLI	W-5 RLI	W-5 RHA	W-5 WUB	W-4 0	W-4 0	W-4 0	W-4 0	W-4 0	W-4 0	AT FDS
TRILLIUM	C-4 0	C-4 0	C-4 0	C-3 RPI	C-3 RPI	C-3 RHA	C-3 WUB	C-3 0	C-3 0	C-3 0	C-3 0	C-3 0	C-3 0	C-3 0	C-3 0	AT 0	WA OK	RF IMH
WETASKIWIN	C-5 RGA	C-5 RHA	C-5 WUB	C-5 0	C-5 0	C-5 0	C-5 0	C-5 0	C-5 0	W-7 0	W-7 0	W-7 0	W-7 0	W-7 0	W-7 0	W-7 0	W-7 0	AT FDQ

Flower Class, 1940-1941 Programme

NAME of SHIP / Built at / Commissioned	1941 Nov	Dec	1942 Jan	Feb	Mar	Apr	May	June	July	Aug	Sep	Oct	Nov	Dec	1943 Jan	Feb	Mar	Apr	May	June	July	Aug	Sep	Oct	Nov	Dec	1944 Jan	Feb	Mar	Apr	May	June	July	Aug	Sep	Oct	Nov
BRANTFORD — Midland — May 15/42							AT	AT	WL	WL	WL	WL	WL	WL	WL	WL	WL	WL	WL	WL	W-3	W-3	W-3	W-3	W-3	W-3	W-3	W-3	W-3	W-3	W-2	C-3	W-2	W-2	W-2	TA	TA
							F/O	W/U	O	O	O	O	O	O	O	O	O	O	O	O	RQC	RQC	W/U	O	O	O	O	O	O	O	O	O	O	O	RSY	RSY	TR	TR
CALGARY — Sorel — Dec.16/41		AT	AT	AT	WL	WL	WL	WL	WL	WL	WL	WL	WL	27L	27L	27L	27L	27G	WL	WL	5-S	5-S	5-S	5-S	5-S	6-S	6-L	6-L	6-L	6-L	WD	WG	WG	WG	NO	NO	NO
		F/O	W/U	O	O	O	O	O	O	O	O	O	O/P	OK	OK	RCF	RCF	O/P	RHA	O	O	O	O	O	O/P	O	RLI	RLI	RLI	W/U	OK	OK	OK	OK	OK	OK	OK
CHARLOTTETOWN — Kingston — Dec.13/41		AT	AT	AT	WL	WL	WL	WL	GE	GE	GE																										
		F/O	W/U	O	O	O	O	O	O	O	O																										
DUNDAS — Victoria — Apr.1/42						PA	PE	PE	PE	PE	PE	PE	WL	WL	WL	WL	WL	WL	WL	WL	WL	WL	WL	WL	WL	WL	W-7	W-7	W-7	W-7	W-7	W-7	W-5	W-5	W-5	W-4	W-4
						F/O	W/U	O	O	O	O	O/P	O	O	O	O	O	O	O	O	O	O	O	O	O	RMO	RMO	RMO	RMO	RMO	W/U	O	O	O	O	O	O
FREDERICTON — Sorel — Dec.8/41		AT	AT	AT	WL	WL	WL	WL	HA	HA	ES	ES	ES	ES	ES	ES	ES	WL	WL	WL	C-1	C-1	C-1	C-1	C-1	C-1	C-1	C-1	C-1	C-1	C-1	C-1	C-1	C-1	C-1	C-7	C-7
		F/O	W/U	O	O	O	RHA	O	OW	OW	O	O	O	O	O	O	O	RLI	RLI	RLI	RLI	W/U	O	O	O	O	O	O	O	O	O	O	O	O	O	O	RSB
HALIFAX — Collingwood — Nov.26/41	AT	O/P	F/O	W/U	O	O	O	WL	WL	HA	HA	ES	ES	ES	ES	ES	ES	WL	WL	C-3	C-3	C-3	C-3	C-3	C-1	C-1	C-1	C-1	C-1	C-1	C-1	C-1	C-1	C-1	RLU	RLU	RLU
	AT																	RLI	RLI	RLI	RLI	RLI	W/U	RHA	O	O	O	O	O	O	O	O	O				
KITCHENER — Lauzon — June 28/42								AT	AT	AT	WL	27L	27L	27L	27L	27L	27G	WL	WL	5-S	C-5	C-5	C-5	C-5	C-5	C-5	C-5	WG	WG	WG	WG	41H	41H	41H	OK	OK	OK
								O/P	F/O	W/U	O	O/P	RLV	OK	OK	OM	OM	O/P	O	O	O	O	O	RLI	RLI	RLI	WUB	O	OK	OK	OK	OK	OK	OK			
La MALBAIE — Sorel — Apr.28/42						AT	AT	AT	WL	WL	WL	WL	NF	NF	C-3	C-3	C-3	C-3	C-3	C-3	C-3	C-3	C-3	C-3	C-3	C-3	C-3	C-3	C-3	C-3	C-3	C-3	C-3	C-3	C-3	C-3	C-3
						F/O	W/U	O	O	RHA	RHA	RHA	RHA	O	O	O	O	O	O	O	O	O	O	O	O	O	RLI	RLI	RLI	W/U	O	O	O	O	O	O	O
MIDLAND — Midland — Nov.17/41	AT	AT	AT	AT	WL	WL	WL	WL	WL	WL	WL	WL	WL	O	WL	WL	WL	WL	WL	WL	W-2	W-2	W-2	W-2	W-2	W-2	W-2	W-2	W-2	W-2	W-2	W-2	W-2	W-2	W-2	W-2	W-2
	F/O	W/U	O	O	O	O	O	O	O	O	O	O	O	O	RLI	RLI	RHA	RHA	RHA	O	O	O	O	O	O	O	RGA	RGA	RGA	RHA	WUB	O	O	O	O	O	O
NEW WESTMINSTER — Victoria — Jan.31/42			PA	PA	PA	PA	PE	PE	PE	PE	PE	WL	WL	WL	WL	WL	WL	WL	WL	WL	C-5	C-5	C-5	C-5	C-5	C-5	C-5	C-5	C-5	C-5	C-5	C-5	C-5	C-5	C-5	C-5	C-5
			F/O	F/O	W/U	O	O	O	O	O	O/P	RHA	O	O	O	O	O	RSY	RSY	RSY	RSY	RSY	RSY	RHA	W/U	O	O	O	O	O	O	O	O	O	O	O	O
PORT ARTHUR — Port Arthur — May 26/42							AT	AT	AT	WL	WL	26L	26L	26W	26G	62G	WL	WS	5-S	W-9	W-9	W-9	W-9	W-9	W-9	W-9	W-9	WD	WD	WD	WD	PO	PO	PO	OK	OK	OK
							F/O	W/U	O	O	O	O/P	OK	OM	OM	O/P	O	O	O	RLI	RLI	RLI	RLI	RHA	W/U	O	O	OK	OK	OK	OK	OK					
REGINA — Sorel — Jan.22/42			AT	AT	WL	WL	WL	WL	WL	WL	WL	WL	WL	RBE	OK	OM	OM	27G	WL	WL	QF	QF	QF	QF	NF	NF	NF	C-1	C-1	WG	WG	WG	WG				
			F/O	W/U	O	O	O	O	O	O	RHA	O/P	OK	OK	O/P	O/P	O	O	RSY	RSY	RSY	RSY	RPI	RPI	RPI	W/U	O	O	OK	OK	OK						
TIMMINS — Esquimalt — Feb.10/42			PA	PA	PA	PE	PE	PE	PE	PE	PE	WL	WL	WL	WL	WL	WL	WL	WL	WL	W-6	W-6	W-6	W-6	W-6	W-6	W-6	W-2	W-2	W-2	W-2	W-2	W-2	W-2	W-2	W-2	W-2
			F/O	W/U	O	O	O	O	O	O	O	O	O	O	O	O	O	O	O	O	RLI	RLI	W/U	O	O	O	O	O	O	O	RLI	RLI	RLI	RLI	RLI	RLI	RLI
VANCOUVER — Esquimalt — Mar.20/42			PA	PA	PE	PE	PE	PE	CN	CN	PE	PE	PE	PD	PD	PD	PD	PE	PE	PE	PE	PE	PE	PE	PE	PE	W-4	W-3	W-1	QF	QF	QF	W-1	W-1
			F/O	W/U	O	O	O	O	O	O	O	O	O	O	O	O	O	RVA	RVA	RVA	RVA	O	O	O	O/P	O	O	O	O	RCA	RCA	O		
VILLE de QUEBEC — Quebec City — May 24/42							AT	AT	AT	WL	WL	WL	26L	26L	26W	26G	62G	WL	QF	QF	QF	QF	WL	W-2	W-2	W-2	W-2	W-2	AT	AT	WD	41H	41H
							F/O	W/U	O	O	O	O/P	RLV	OM	OM	RGI	RGI	O/P	O	O	O	O	O	RLI	RLI	RLI	RHA	WUB	O	O	C-4	C-4	OK	OK	OK
WOODSTOCK — Collingwood — May 1/42							AT	AT	WL	WL	WL	25L	25L	25L	25L	25L	27G	C-1	C-1	5-S	C-4	C-4	C-4	C-4	C-4	C-4	C-4	C-4	WG	WG	WG	WG	WG	AT	AT	PA
							F/O	W/U	O	O	O/P	RHU	OK	OK	OK	OM	O/P	O	O	RLI	RLI	W/U	O	O	O	O	O	O	OK	OK	OK	OK	OK	RLI	O/P	O

NAME of SHIP	1945 Dec	Jan	Feb	Mar	Apr	May	June	July	Aug	Sep
BRANTFORD	TA / TR	TA / TR	TA / TR	TA / TR	TA / TR	TA / TR	TA / TR	AT / TR		
CALGARY	NO / OK	NO / OK	NO / OK	NO / OK	NO / OK	NO / OK	AT / O	AT / FDC		
DUNDAS	W-4 / O	W-4 / RLI	W-4 / RLI	W-4 / WUB	W-4 / O	W-4 / O	W-4 / O	AT / FDS		
FREDERICTON	C-7 / RSB	HX / WUB	C-9 / O	C-9 / O	C-9 / O	C-9 / O	C-9 / O	AT / FDS		
HALIFAX	C-1 / RHA	HX / WUB	C-9 / O	C-9 / O	C-9 / O	C-9 / O	C-9 / O	AT / FDS		
KITCHENER	41H / OK	41H / OK	41H / OK	41H / OK	41H / OK	41H / OK	AT / O	AT / FDS		
La MALBAIE	C-3 / O	HX / RLS	HX / O	HX / WUB	HX / O	W-9 / O	W-9 / O	AT / FDQ		
MIDLAND	W-2 / O	W-2 / O	W-2 / O	W-2 / O	W-2 / O	W-2 / O	W-2 / O	AT / O		
NEW WESTMINSTER	C-5 / O	C-5 / RSB	HX / RSB	HX / RSB	HX / WU3	SY / O	SY / FDS	AT / FDQ		
PORT ARTHUR	PO / OK	PO / OK	PO / OK	PO / OK	AT / RLI	AT / RLI	AT / RLI	AT / FDS		
REGINA										
TIMMINS	W-2 / O	W-2 / O	W-2 / O	W-2 / O	W-2 / O	W-2 / O	W-2 / O	AT / FDS		
VANCOUVER	W-1 / WUB	W-1 / O	W-1 / O	W-1 / O	W-1 / O	W-1 / O	W-1 / O	AT / FDQ		
VILLE de QUEBEC	41H / OK	41H / OK	41H / OK	41H / OK	41H / OK	41H / OK	AT / O	AT / FDS		
WOODSTOCK	PA / O	PE / O	PE / RES	PE / RES	PE / RES	PE / O	PE / O	PA / O	PA / O	PA / O

Revised Flower Class (I.E.), 1942-1943 Programme

NAME of SHIP / Built at / Commissioned	1943 Oct	Nov	Dec	1944 Jan	Feb	Mar	Apr	May	June	July	Aug	Sep	Oct	Nov	Dec	1945 Jan	Feb	Mar	Apr	May	June	July
ATHOLL — Quebec City — Oct.14/43	NC / F/O	NC / W/U	NC / W/U	NC / RHA	9-L / RHA	9-L / OK	9-L / OK	C-4 / O	C-4 / O	C-4 / O	C-4 / O	C-4 / O	C-4 / O	C-4 / RSY	C-4 / RSY	C-4 / O	C-4 / RHA	C-4 / RHA	C-4 / O	C-4 / O	AT / FDS	
COBOURG — Midland — May 11/44								NC / F/O	NC / F/O	NC / WUB	C-6 / O	C-6 / O	C-6 / O	C-6 / O	C-6 / O	C-6 / O	C-6 / O	C-6 / RHA				
FERGUS — Collingwood — Nov.18/44														NC / F/O	NC / RHA	NC / WUB	C-9 / O	C-9 / O	C-9 / O	C-9 / O	C-9 / O	AT / FDS
FRONTENAC — Kingston — Oct.26/43	NC / F/O	NC / O/P	NC / RHA	NC / W/U	9-L / OSC	9-L / OK	9-L / OK	C-1 / O	C-1 / O	C-1 / O	C-1 / O	C-1 / O	C-1 / O	C-1 / O	C-1 / RLI	C-1 / RLI	C-1 / RHA	C-1 / RHA	HX / WUB	HX / O	AT / FDH	
GUELPH — Collingwood — May 9/44								NC / F/O	NC / F/O	NC / WUB	W-3 / O	W-3 / O	C-8 / O	C-8 / O	C-8 / O	C-8 / O	C-8 / O	C-8 / O	AT / FDQ			
HAWKESBURY — Quebec City — June 14/44								NC / O/P	NC / F/O	NC / WUB	AT / O	C-7 / O	C-7 / O	C-7 / O	C-7 / O	C-7 / O	C-7 / O	C-7 / O	AT / RLI	AT / FDS		
LINDSAY — Midland — Nov.15/43		NC / F/O	NC / O/P	NC / F/O	NC / WUB	AT / O	W-5 / RHA	WD / OK	WG / OK	WG / OK	WG / OK	41H / OK	41H / OK	41H / OK	41H / OK	41H / OK	41H / RDV	41M / RSB	AT / RSB	AT / RSB	AT / RSB	AT / FDS
LOUISBURG — Quebec City — Dec.13/43			NC / F/O	NC / RHA	NC / RHA	NC / WUB	NC / O/P	WD / OK	WG / OK	WG / OK	WG / OK	41H / OK	41H / OK	41H / OK	41H / OK	41M / OK	41M / O/P	AT / RSB	AT / RSB	AT / RSB		
NORSYD — Quebec City — Dec.22/43			NC / F/O	NC / RIN	NC / RIN	NC / RIN	NC / WUB	W-7 / O	W-7 / O	W-7 / O	W-7 / O	W-7 / O	C-2 / O	C-2 / O	C-2 / O	C-2 / O	C-2 / O	C-2 / O	AT / RHA	AT / RHA		
NORTH BAY — Collingwood — Oct.25/43	NC / F/O	NC / O/P	NC / W/U	NC / RHA	9-L / OSC	9-L / OK	9-L / OK	C-4 / O	C-4 / O	C-4 / O	C-4 / O	C-4 / O	C-4 / O	C-4 / RSY	C-4 / RSY	C-4 / O	C-2 / WUB	C-3 / O	AT / O	AT / FDS		
OWEN SOUND — Collingwood — Nov.17/43		NC / F/O	NC / O/P	NC / W/U	9-L / OSC	9-L / OK	9-L / OK	C-2 / O	C-2 / O	C-2 / O	C-2 / O	C-7 / O	C-7 / O	C-7 / O	C-7 / RHA	C-7 / RHA	C-7 / RHA	C-7 / WUB	AT / FDS			
RIVIERE du LOUP — Quebec City — Nov.21/43		NC / F/O	NC / O/P	NC / RHA	NC / WUB	NC / RHA	W-3 / RHA	W-3 / RHA	W-3 / RHA	W-3 / O	W-3 / O	W-3 / O	C-3 / RBE	C-3 / RBE	C-3 / O	C-3 / N/O	C-3 / O	C-3 / O	AT / FDS			
ST. LAMBERT — Quebec City — May 27/44								NC / F/O	NC / F/O	NC / RDA	NC / WUB	C-6 / O	C-6 / O	C-6 / O	C-6 / RBE	C-6 / O	C-6 / O	C-6 / O	O	C-6 / RLN	C-6 / O	AT / FDJ
TRENTONIAN — Kingston — Dec.1/43		NC / O/P	NC / F/O	NC / WUB	NC / O	WD / RHA	WG / OK	WG / OK	WG / OK	41H / OK	41H / OK	41H / OK	41H / OK	41H / OK	41H / OK							
WHITBY — Midland — June 6/44								NC / F/O	NC / F/O	NC / RSH	NC / WUB	C-4 / O	C-4 / O	C-4 / O	C-4 / O	C-4 / O	C-4 / O	C-4 / O	C-4 / O	C-4 / O	AT / FDS	

Revised Flower Class (I.E.), 1943-1944 Programme

NAME of SHIP		1944								1945						
Built at / Commissioned		May	June	July	Aug.	Sep.	Oct.	Nov.	Dec.	Jan.	Feb.	Mar.	Apr.	May	June	July
ASBESTOS			NC	NC	C-2	C-2	C-2	C-2	C-2	C-2	C-2	C-2	C-2	C-2	AT	AT
Quebec City	June 16/44		F/O	F/O	WUB	0	0	0	0	0	0	0	0	0	0	FDS
BEAUHARNOIS						NC	NC	NC	C-3	C-4	C-4	C-4	C-4	C-4	C-4	AT
Quebec City	Sept.25/44					F/O	F/O	WUB	0	0	0	0	0	0	0	FDS
BELLEVILLE							NC	NC	NC	NC	NC	C-5	C-5	C-5	AT	AT
Kingston	Oct.19/44						F/O	RHA	RHA	RHA	WUB	0	0	0	0	FDS
LACHUTE							NC	NC	NC	C-5	C-5	C-5	C-5	C-5	C-5	AT
Quebec City	Oct.26/44						F/O	F/O	WUB	0	0	0	0	0	0	FDS
MERRITTONIA								NC	NC	NC	C-7	C-7	C-7	C-7	AT	AT
Quebec City	Nov.10/44							F/O	F/O	WUB	0	0	0	0	0	FDS
PARRY SOUND					NC	NC	NC	C-7	C-7	C-7	C-7	C-7	C-7	C-7	AT	AT
Midland	Aug.30/44				F/O	F/O	WUB	0	0	0	0	N/0	0	0	0	FDS
PETERBOROUGH			NC	NC	NC	C-6	C-6	C-6	C-6	C-6	C-6	C-6	C-6	C-6	C-6	AT
Kingston	June 1/44		F/O	WUB	0	0	0	0	0	0	0	0	0	RLN	0	FDS
SMITHS FALLS								NC	NC	NC	NC	C-2	C-2	C-2	AT	AT
Kingston	Nov.28/44							F/O	F/O	F/O	RHA	WUB	0	0	0	FDS
STELLARTON						NC	NC	NC	C-3	C-3	C-3	C-3	C-3	C-3	AT	AT
Quebec City	Sept.29/44					F/O	F/O	WUB	RSN	0	0	0	0	0	0	FDS
STRATHROY								NC	NC	NC	NC	HX	HX	HX	HX	AT
Midland	Nov.20/44							F/O	F/O	RSB	RSB	WUB	0	0	0	FDS
THORLOCK								NC	NC	NC	C-9	C-9	C-9	C-9	C-9	AT
Midland	Nov.13/44							F/O	F/O	WUB	0	0	0	0	0	FDS
WEST YORK							NC	NC	NC	NC	C-5	C-5	C-5	C-5	C-5	AT
Midland	Oct.6/44						F/O	F/O	RHA	WUB	0	0	0	0	0	FDS

Revised Flower Class (I.E.), ex RN

NAME of SHIP		1943		1944								
Built at / Commissioned		Nov.	Dec.	Jan.	Feb.	Mar.	Apr.	May	June	July	Aug.	Sep.
FOREST HILL			NC	NC	C-3	C-3	C-3	C-3	C-3	C-3	C-3	C-3
Port Glasgow	Dec.1/43		FOK	WUK	0	0	0	0	0	0	0	0
GIFFARD		NC	C-1	C-1	C-1	C-1	C-1	C-1	C-1	C-1	C-1	C-1
Aberdeen	Nov.10/43	FOK	WUK	0	0	0	0	0	0	0	0	0
LONG BRANCH				NC	NC	WG	C-5	C-5	C-5	C-5	C-5	C-5
Glasgow	Jan.5/44			FOK	WUK	0	0	RSN	0	0	0	0
MIMICO					NC	NC	NC	WG	WG	WG	WG	PO
Sunderland	Feb.8/44				FOK	WUK	WUK	OK	OK	OK	OK	OK

Minesweepers

Bangor Class, 1939-1940 Programme

NAME of SHIP		1941						1942												1943												1944								
Built at / Commissioned		July	Aug.	Sep.	Oct.	Nov.	Dec.	Jan.	Feb.	Mar.	Apr.	May	June	July	Aug.	Sep.	Oct.	Nov.	Dec.	Jan.	Feb.	Mar.	Apr.	May	June	July	Aug.	Sep.	Oct.	Nov.	Dec.	Jan.	Feb.	Mar.	Apr.	May	June	July	Aug.	Sep.
BELLECHASSE							PA	PA	PA	PA	PA	PR	PR	PR	PR	PR	PR	PE	PE	PE	PE	PE	PE	PR	PR	PR	PR	PR	PR	PR	PE	PE	PE	PE	PE	PE	PE	PR	PR	PR
Vancouver	Dec.13/41						F/O	W/U	0	0	0	0	0	0	RPR	0	0	0	0	0	0	RES	0	0	0	0	0	0	0	0	0	0	0	0	0	RES	0	0	0	0
BURLINGTON				AT	AT	HL	HL	HL	HL	HL	HL	HL	GE	GE	GE	GE	GE	GE	GE	SY	WL	WL	WL	WL	WL	W-9	W-9	W-9	W-9	NW	NW	W-9	HL	HL	HL	HL	HL	HL	HL	HL
Toronto	Sept.6/41			F/O	W/U	0	0	0	RDA	0	0	0	0	0	0	0	0	0	0	RLU	RLU	RDA	RDA	RDA	0	0	0	0	0	0	0	0	0	0	0	0	0	RPI	RPI	WUB
CHEDABUCTO				PA	PA	PA	PA	HL	HL	HL	HL	GE	GE	GE	GE	GE	SY	SY	SY	SY	WL	WL	WL	WL	GF	GF	GF	GF	GF	GF										
Vancouver	Sept.27/41			F/O	W/U	O/P	O/P	0	0	0	0	0	0	0	0	0	0	0	0	0	0	RLU	0	RHA	0	0	0	0	0	US										
CHIGNECTO					PA	PA	PA	PA	PA	PA	PA	PA	PE	PE	PE	PE	PE	PR	PR	PR	PR	PR	PE	PE	PE	PE	PE	PE	PE	PE	PE	PE	PE	PE	PE	PE	PE	PR	PR	PR
Vancouver	Oct.31/41				F/O	W/U	0	0	0	0	0	0	0	RES	0	0	0	0	0	0	0	0	0	0	0	0	RES	RES	0	0	0	0	0	0	0	0	0	0	0	0
CLAYOQUOT			PA	PA	PA	HL	HL	HL	HL	HL	HL	HL	GE	GE	GE	GE	SY	SY	SY	HX	HX	HX	HX	HX	HX	SY	SY	SY	SY	SY	SY	TA	TA	TA	TA	TA	TA	TA	TA	TA
Prince Rupert	Aug.22/41		F/O	W/U	O/P	0	0	0	0	0	0	0	0	0	0	0	0	0	0	RHA	RHA	RLI	RLI	RPI	W/U	0	0	0	0	0	0	TR	TR	TR	TR	TR	RLU	RLU	F/O	WUB
COWICHAN		PA	PA	AT	AT	HL	NW	NW	NW	NW	NW	NW	NW	NW	NW	NW	WL	WL	WL	WL	WL	WL	WL	WL	WL	W-6	W-6	W-6	W-6	W-6	W-6	W-6	W-6	32P	32P	31P	31P	31P	31P	31P
Vancouver	July 4/41	W/U	O/P	W/U	0	RHA	0	0	0	0	0	0	0	0	RLI	RLI	0	0	0	0	0	0	0	0	0	0	0	0	RLS	RLS	0	RHA	O/P	OK	OK	OK	OK	OK	OK	OK
GEORGIAN				AT	AT	SY	SY	SY	NW	NW	NW	NW	NW	NW	NW	NW	NW	NW	NW	NW	NW	NW	NW	NW	NW	NW	NW	NW	NW	NW	NW	NW	NW	31P	31P	32P	14P	14P	14P	14P
Toronto	Sept.23/41			F/O	W/U	W/U	0	0	0	0	0	0	0	RHA	0	0	0	0	0	0	0	RSB	0	0	0	0	0	0	RLU	RLU	W/U	0	0	OK	OK	OK	OK	OK	OK	OK
MAHONE				PA	PA	PA	PA	AT	HL	HL	HL	HL	HX	HX	HX	HX	HX	HX	HX	HX	HX	HX	HX	HX	GF	GF	GF	GF	GF	HX	HX	HX	HX	HX	HX	HX	HX	HX	HX	HX
Vancouver	Sept.29/41			F/O	W/U	O/P	O/P	0	0	0	0	0	0	0	0	0	0	0	0	0	RLI	RLI	RHA	0	0	0	0	0	0	0	0	0	RLS	RHA	RHA	RHA	RHA	WUB	0	0
MALPEQUE			PA	PA	PA	HL	SY	SY	HL	HL	NW	NW	NW	NW	NW	NW	NW	NW	NW	NW	NW	NW	NW	NW	NW	NW	NW	NW	NW	NW	NW	NW	NW	32P	32P	31P	31P	31P	31P	31P
Vancouver	Aug.4/41		W/U	O/P	O/P	0	0	0	0	0	0	0	0	0	0	0	0	RLI	RLI	RHA	0	0	0	0	0	0	0	0	RCO	RSY	0	RHA	O/P	OK	OK	OK	OK	OK	OK	OK
MINAS			PA	PA	PA	HL	SY	NW	NW	NW	NW	NW	NW	NW	NW	NW	NW	NW	WL	WL	WL	WL	WL	WL	WL	W-7	W-7	W-7	W-7	W-7	W-4	W-4	W-4	31P	31P	31P	31P	31P	31P	31P
Vancouver	Aug.2/41		W/U	O/P	O/P	0	0	0	0	0	0	0	0	RLU	0	0	0	0	0	0	RHA	0	0	0	RDH	RDH	0	0	0	0	0	0	RHA	O/P	OK	OK	OK	OK	OK	O/P
MIRAMICHI						PA	PA	PA	PA	PA	PA	PR	PR	PR	PR	PE	PE	PE	PE	PR	PE	PE	PR	PE	PE	PE	PE	PE	PE	PE	PE	PE	PE	PR	PR	PR	PR	PR	PR	PR
Vancouver	Nov.26/41					F/O	W/U	0	0	0	0	0	0	0	0	0	0	0	0	RES	RES	0	0	0	0	0	0	0	0	0	0	RES	RES	0	0	0	0	0	0	0
NIPIGON			AT	AT	SY	SY	SY	SY	HL	HL	HL	HL	HX	HX	HX	HX	HX	NW	NW	HX	HX	NW	NW	NW	NW	W-1	W-1	W-1	W-1	W-1	W-1	W-1	W-1	W-1	W-1	AT	AT	HX	HX	HX
Toronto	Aug.11/41		F/O	W/U	W/U	0	0	0	0	RHA	0	0	0	0	0	RLU	RLU	0	0	0	0	0	0	0	0	0	0	0	0	0	0	0	0	RLU	RLI	WUB	0	0	RHA	0
OUTARDE							PA	PA	PA	PA	PA	PA	PR	PR	PE	PE	PE	PE	PR	PR	PR	PR	PR	PR	PE	PE	PE	PE	PR	PR	PR	PR	PR	PR	PE	PE	PE	PE	PE	PE
Vancouver	Dec.4/41						F/O	W/U	0	0	0	0	0	0	RPR	0	0	0	0	0	RES	RES	0	0	0	0	0	0	0	0	0	0	0	0	RES	0	0	0	0	0
QUATSINO						PA	PA	PA	PA	PA	PA	PR	PR	PR	PR	PE	PE	PE	PE	PE	PE	PR	PR	PR	PR	PR	PR	PR	PE	PE	PE	PE	PE	PE	PE	PE	PE	PE	PE	PE
Prince Rupert	Nov.3/41					F/O	W/U	0	0	0	0	0	0	RPR	0	0	0	0	0	0	0	0	0	0	0	RPR	RPR	0	0	0	0	0	0	0	0	0	0	0	0	RES
QUINTE			PA	PA	PA	HL	HL	HL	HL	HL	HL	HL	HX	HX	HX	HX	HX	HX	HX	HX	AL	AL	AL	AL	AL	AL	TA	TA	AT	AT	AT	AT	AT	AT	AT	AT	AT	AT	AT	TA
Vancouver	Aug.30/41		F/O	W/U	O/P	0	0	0	0	0	0	0	0	0	0	0	RLU	RLU	US	US	US	US	US	RPI	RPI	RPI	RPI	RPI	RPI	RPI	RPI	RPI	RPI	RPI	RPI	RPI	RPI	RPI	RHA	TR
THUNDER					AT	SY	SY	SY	HL	HL	HL	HX	HX	HX	HX	HX	SH	SH	SH	SH	SH	HX	HX	HX	SY	SY	SY	SY	SY	SY	SY	HX	HX	31P	32P	32P	4-P	4-P	4-P	4-P
Toronto	Oct.14/41				F/O	W/U	0	0	0	0	0	0	0	0	0	0	0	0	0	0	0	RLI	RLI	0	0	0	0	0	0	0	0	RHA	O/P	OK	OK	OK	OK	OK	O/P	RSY
UNGAVA				PA	PA	HL	HL	HL	HL	HL	HL	HL	HX	HX	HX	HX	HX	HX	HX	HX	HX	HX	HX	HX	GF	GF	GF	GF	GF	GF	HX	HX	HX	HX	HX	HX	SY	SY	SY	SY
Vancouver	Sept.5/41			W/U	O/P	0	0	0	0	0	RHA	0	0	0	0	0	0	0	RLU	RHA	RHA	0	0	0	0	0	0	0	0	0	0	RLS	RLS	0	WUB	0	0	0	0	0
WASAGA		PA	PA	AT	HL	HL	HL	HL	HL	NW	NW	NW	NW	NW	NW	NW	NW	NW	NW	NW	NW	NW	NW	NW	NW	NW	NW	NW	NW	NW	NW	SY	SY	32P	32P	31P	31P	31P	31P	31P
Vancouver	July 1/41	W/U	O/P	W/U	0	RHA	RHA	RHA	0	0	0	0	RHA	0	0	0	0	0	0	0	0	0	0	0	0	RCO	W/U	W/U	0	0	0	0	O/P	OK	OK	OK	OK	OK	OK	O/P

Bangor Class, ex-RN

NAME of SHIP		1942											1943												1944			1944									1945		
Built at / Commissioned		Feb.	Mar.	Apr.	May	June	July	Aug.	Sep.	Oct.	Nov.	Dec.	Jan.	Feb.	Mar	Apr.	May	June	July	Aug.	Sep.	Oct.	Nov.	Dec.	Jan.	Feb.	Mar.	Apr.	May	June	July	Aug.	Sep.	Oct.	Nov.	Dec.	Jan.	Feb.	Mar.
BAYFIELD		PA	PA	PA	PE	PE	PE	PE	PE	PE	PR	PR	PR	PR	PR	PE	WL	WL	HX	HX	HX	HX	HX	HX	HX	HX	31P	31P	31P	31P	31P	31P	31P	31P	31P	31P	31P	31P	31P
Vancouver	Feb.26/42	F/O	W/U	0	0	0	0	0	0	0	0	RPR	0	0	0	O/P	RHA	RBT	0	0	0	0	RHA	W/U	RHA	O/P	OK	OK	OK	OK	OK	O/P	RSB	RSB	O/P	OK	OK	OK	RGY
CANSO			PA	PA	PE	PE	PE	PE	PE	PE	PE	PE	PE	PE	PE	PE	PE	PE	PE	PA	HX	HX	HX	HX	HX	HX	32P	32P	32P	16P	16P	16P	16P	16P	31P	31P	31P	31P	31P
Vancouver	Mar.6/42		F/O	W/U	0	0	0	0	0	0	0	0	0	0	RPR	0	0	RES	O/P	O/P	W/U	0	0	0	0	O/P	OK	OK	OK	OK	OK	O/P	RSB	RSB	O/P	OK	RDV	OK	0
CARAQUET			PA	PA	PE	PE	PE	PE	PR	PR	PR	PR	PR	PR	PE	PE	WL	WL	HX	HX	HX	HX	NW	NW	NW	NW	32P	32P	31P	31P	31P	31P	31P	31P	31P	31P	31P	31P	31P
Vancouver	Apr.2/42		F/O	W/U	W/U	0	0	0	0	0	RPR	0	0	0	0	O/P	RHA	0	0	RBT	W/U	0	0	0	0	O/P	OK	OK	OK	OK	OK	OK	O/P	RLU	RLU	W/U	O/P	OK	OK
GUYSBOROUGH				PA	PE	PE	PE	PE	PE	PE	PE	PE	PE	PE	PE	PE	WL	WL	HX	HX	HX	HX	HX	HX	HX	HX	32P	32P	14P	14P	14P	14P	14P	14P	31P	31P	31P	31P	31P
Vancouver	Apr.22/42			F/O	W/U	0	0	0	0	0	0	0	0	0	0	O/P	RHA	0	0	0	RBT	RBT	W/U	0	0	O/P	OK	OK	OK	OK	OK	OK	OK	OK	OK	O/P	RLU	RLU	O/P
INGONISH					PE	PE	PE	PE	PE	PE	PE	PR	PR	PE	PE	PE	WL	WL	HX	HX	HX	HX	HX	HX	HX	HX	HX	HX	SY	SY	SY	SY	SY	SY	SY	SY	SY	HX	HX
Vancouver	May 8/42				F/O	W/U	0	0	0	0	0	0	0	0	0	O/P	RHA	0	0	0	0	RHA	RBT	RBT	RBT	RNY	RHA	W/U	0	0	0	RSY	RSY	0	0	0	RSB	RSB	RSB
LOCKEPORT					PA	PE	PE	PE	PE	PE	PE	PE	PE	PE	PE	PE	WL	WL	HX	HX	HX	HX	NW	NW	HX	HX	HX	HX	HX	SY	SY	SY	SY	SY	SY	SY	SY	SY	SY
Vancouver	May 27/42				F/O	W/U	0	0	0	0	0	0	0	0	0	O/P	RHA	0	0	0	0	0	0	0	RBT	RBT	RBT	WUB	0	0	0	0	0	0	0	0	0	0	0

(left margin table, continued)

1945

	Oct.	Nov.	Dec.	Jan.	Feb.	Mar.	Apr.	May	June	July
	C-3/O	C-3/O	C-3/O	C-3/RLI	C-3/RLI	C-3/RLI	C-3/WUB	HX/O	HX/O	AT/FDS
	C-1/O	C-1/O	C-1/RLI	C-1/RLI	C-1/WUB	C-1/O	C-1/O	AT/O	AT/O	/FDS
	C-5/O	C-5/O	C-5/O	C-5/O	C-5/O	C-5/O	C-5/O	HX/O	HX/FDH	
	NO/OK	NO/OK	NO/OK	NO/OK	NO/OK	NO/RCM	NO/RCM	NO/OK	NO/O/P	AT/FDS

Castle Class, ex-RN

NAME of SHIP / Built at	Commissioned	Nov.43	Dec.43	Jan.44	Feb.44	Mar.44	Apr.44	May.44	June.44	July.44	Aug.44	Sep.44	Oct.44	Nov.44	Dec.44	Jan.45	Feb.45	Mar.45	Apr.45	May.45	June.45	July.45	Aug.45	Sep.45
ARNPRIOR / Belfast	June 8/44							NC/FOK	NC/WUK	C-1/0	C-1/0	C-1/0	C-1/0	C-1/0	C-1/0	C-1/0	C-1/0	C-1/0	C-1/0	C-1/0	AT/0	AT/RSN	AT/RSN	AT/FDH
BOWMANVILLE / Sunderland	Sept.28/44										NC/FOK	NC/WUK	C-4/0	C-4/0	C-4/0	C-4/0	C-4/0	C-4/0	C-4/0	C-4/0	AT/0	AT/0	AT/0	AT/TR
COPPER CLIFF / Blyth	July 25/44									NC/FOK	NC/FOK	C-6/WUK	C-7/0	C-7/0	C-7/0	C-7/0	C-7/0	C-7/0	C-7/0	C-7/0	AT/O/P	PA/0	PA/0	PA/FDE
HESPELER / Leith	Feb.28/44				NC/FOK	NC/FOK	NC/WUK	C-5/0	C-5/0	C-5/0	C-5/0	C-5/0	C-5/0	C-5/0	C-5/0	C-5/0	C-5/0	C-8/0	C-3/RHA	C-8/RHA	C-8/N/O	AT/RLI	AT/O/P	PA/FDE
HUMBERSTONE / Glasgow	Sept.6/44											NC/FOK	NC/WUK	C-8/0	C-8/0	C-8/0	C-8/0	C-8/0	C-8/0	C-8/0	AT/O/P	PA/O/P	PA/0	PA/FDE
HUNTSVILLE / Troon	June 6/44								NC/FOK	NC/WUK	C-5/0	C-5/0	C-5/0	C-5/0	C-5/0	C-5/0	C-5/0	C-5/0	C-5/0	C-5/0	AT/RHA	AT/RHA	AT/RHA	AT/IHA
KINCARDINE / South Bank	June 19/44								NC/FOK	NC/WUK	C-2/0	C-2/0	C-2/0	C-2/0	C-2/0	C-2/0	C-2/0	C-2/0	C-2/0	C-2/0	AT/0	AT/0	AT/0	AT/FDH
LEASIDE / South Bank	Aug.21/44										NC/FOK	NC/WUK	C-8/0	C-8/0	C-8/0	C-8/0	C-8/0	C-8/0	C-8/0	C-8/0	AT/O/P	PA/O/P	PA/0	PA/FDE
ORANGEVILLE / Leith	Apr.24/44						NC/FOK	NC/WUK	C-1/0	C-1/0	C-1/0	C-1/0	C-1/0	C-1/0	C-1/0	C-1/0	C-1/0	C-1/0	C-1/0	C-1/0	AT/RLI	AT/RLI	AT/RLI	AT/FDH
PETROLIA / Belfast	June 29/44							NC/FOK	NC/FOK	C-4/WUK	C-4/0	C-4/0	C-4/0	C-4/0	C-4/0	C-4/0	C-4/0	C-4/0	C-4/0	C-4/0	AT/0	AT/0	AT/0	AT/RCA
ST. THOMAS / South Bank	May 4/44							NC/FOK	NC/WUK	WD/OK	C-3/0	C-3/0	C-3/0	C-3/0	C-3/0	C-3/0	C-3/0	C-3/0	C-3/0	C-3/0	AT/RHA	AT/RHA	AT/O/P	PA/FDE
TILLSONBURG / Port Glasgow	June 29/44									NC/FOK	NC/FOK	NC/WUK	C-6/0	C-6/0	C-6/0	C-6/0	C-6/0	C-6/0	C-6/0	C-6/0	C-6/RLN	AT/0	AT/0	AT/FDH

(left margin table, continued)

1945

	Oct.	Nov.	Dec.	Jan.	Feb.	Mar.	Apr.	May	June	July	Aug.	Sep.
	PR/0	PR/0	PR/0	PR/0	PE/0	PE/0	PE/0	PE/0	PE/0	PE/0	PE/0	PE/0
	NW/0	NW/0	NW/0	NW/RHA	NW/0	NW/0	NW/0	NW/RSN	NW/0	AT/0	AT/0	2-M/0
	PR/RES	PR/0	PE/0	PE/0	PE/0	PE/0	PR/0	PR/0	PR/0	PR/0	PR/0	PR/0
	TA/TR	HX/0	HX/0									
	31P/OK	31P/OK	31P/OK	31P/OK	31P/O/P	AT/RLU	AT/RLU	AT/RLU	AT/O/P	31P/OK	31P/OK	31P/O/P
	14P/OK	31P/OK	31P/O/P	31P/RLU	31P/RLU	31P/WUB	31P/O/P	31P/RGN	31P/RGN	31P/RGN	31P/OK	31P/OK
	HX/0	HX/0	HX/0	HX/0	HX/0	HX/0	HX/0	HX/0	SY/0	AT/0	AT/0	2-M/0
	31P/OK	31P/OK	31P/OK	31P/OK	31P/OK	31P/O/P	AT/RLI	AT/RLI	AT/O/P	31P/RGN	31P/OK	31P/O/P
	31P/RDA	31P/RDA	31P/W/U	31P/O/P	31P/OK	31P/OK	31P/OK	31P/OK	31P/OK	31P/OK	31P/OK	31P/OK
	PR/0	PR/0	PE/0	PE/0	PE/RES	PE/RES	PE/0	PE/0	PE/0	PE/0	PE/0	PR/0
	HX/0	HX/0	HX/0	HX/0	HX/0	HX/0	HX/RLU	HX/RLU	HX/RLU	HX/W/U	AT/0	1-M/0
	PE/0	PE/0	PE/0	PE/0	PR/0	PR/RES	PE/RES	PE/0	PE/0	PE/0	PR/0	PR/0
	PE/0	PE/0	PR/0	PR/0	PR/0	PR/0	PR/0	PR/0	PR/0	PE/0	PE/0	PE/0
	TA/TR	TA/TR	TA/TR	TA/TR	TA/TR	TA/TR	TA/TR	TA/TR	TA/TR	AT/TR	AT/0	AT/0
	4-P/RSY	31P/O/P	31P/OK	31P/OK	31P/OK	31P/OK	31P/OK	31P/OK	31P/OK	31P/RDV	31P/OK	31P/O/P
	SY/0	GF/0	SY/0	SY/0	HX/0	HX/0	HX/0	HX/RLI	RLI/0	WUB/0	0	1-M/0
	31P/RCA	31P/RCA	31P/RHA	31P/O/P	31P/OK	31P/OK	31P/OK	31P/OK	31P/OK	31P/OK	31P/OK	31P/O/P

(left margin table, continued)

	Apr.	May	June	July	Aug.	Sep.
	31P/OK	31P/OK	31P/CK	31P/RDV	31P/OK	RF/ISH
	31P/0	31P/0	31P/0	31P/0	31P/0	RF/ISH
	31P/OK	31P/OK	31P/OK	31P/OK	31P/OK	RF/ISH
	HX/WUB	HX/0	WA/O/P	RF/ISH		
	SY/0	SY/0	WA/O/P	RF/ISH		

Bangor Class, 1940-1941 Programme (diesel)

NAME of SHIP / Built at	Commissioned	Dec.41	Jan.42	Feb.42	Mar.42	Apr.42	May.42	June.42	July.42	Aug.42	Sep.42	Oct.42	Nov.42	Dec.42	Jan.43	Feb.43	Mar.43	Apr.43	May.43	June.43	July.43	Aug.43	Sep.43	Oct.43
BROCKVILLE / Sorel	Sept.19/42											NC/F/O	NC/W/U	NC/W/U	SY/0	HX/0	WL/0	WL/RSB	WL/0	WL/0	W-3/0	W-3/0	W-3/0	W-3/0
DIGBY / Lauzon	July 26/42										NC/F/O	NC/W/U	SY/0	WL/0	WL/0	WL/0	WL/RHA	WL/0	WL/RLU	WL/RLU	W-5/0	W-5/0	W-5/0	W-5/0
ESQUIMALT / Sorel	Oct.26/42											NC/F/O	NC/W/U	NC/RHA	NC/RHA	NC/RHA	NW/RHA	NW/W/U	NW/0	NW/0	NW/0	NW/0	NW/0	NW/0
GRANBY / Lauzon	May 2/42									AT/W/U	SY/0	SY/0	SY/0	SY/0	WL/0	WL/0	WL/0	WL/RLU	WL/RLU	WL/RHA	WL/W/U	W-3/0	W-3/0	W-3/0
LACHINE / Lauzon	June 20/42								AT/F/O	SY/W/U	SY/RHA	WL/0	WL/0	WL/0	WL/0	WL/0	WL/0	WL/RLU	WL/RLU	WL/RHA	W-6/0	W-6/0	W-6/0	W-6/RDH
MELVILLE / Lauzon	Dec.4/41	AT/F/O	HL/F/O	AT/W/U	AT/W/U	HL/0	HL/0	SH/0	SH/0	SH/0	SH/0	WL/0	WL/0	WL/RLU	WL/RLU	WL/RLU	WL/RHA	WL/RHA	W-5/0	W-5/0	W-5/0			
NORANDA / Lauzon	May 15/42						AT/F/O	AT/W/U	HX/0	HX/0	HX/0	HX/0	HX/0	NW/NW	HX/0	HX/0	WL/0	WL/0	WL/0	WL/0	W-9/RLU	W-9/RLU	W-9/0	W-9/0
TRANSCONA / Sorel	Nov.25/42												NC/F/O	NC/W/U	NC/RHA	NC/RHA	NC/W/U	WL/0	WL/0	WL/0	W-2/0	W-2/0	W-2/0	W-2/0
TROIS-RIVIERES / Sorel	Aug.12/42									NC/F/O	NC/W/U	WL/0	WL/0	NW/0	NW/0	NW/0	NW/0	NW/0	NW/0	NW/0	NW/0	NW/0	NW/0	NW/0
TRURO / Lauzon	Aug.27/42										NC/F/O	NC/W/U	WL/0	WL/0	WL/0	WL/0	WL/0	WL/RHA	WL/0	WL/0	W-4/0	W-4/RLU	W-4/RLU	W-4/W/U

NAME of SHIP	Nov.43	Dec.43	Jan.44	Feb.44	Mar.44	Apr.44	May.44	June.44	July.44	Aug.44	Sep.44	Oct.44	Nov.44	Dec.44	Jan.45	Feb.45	Mar.45	Apr.45	May.45	June.45	July.45	Aug.45	Sep.45
BROCKVILLE	W-3/0	W-3/0	W-3/0	W-3/0	W-3/0	W-3/0	SY/0	SY/0	SY/0	SY/0	SY/0	SY/0	SY/0	SY/RLU	SY/RLU	HX/0	HX/0	SY/0	SY/0	SY/0	AT/FDS	AT/FDH	AT/FDH
DIGBY	W-5/0	W-5/0	W-5/0	W-5/0	W-5/0	W-5/RLU	AT/RLU	AT/RLU	AT/RSH	SY/WUB	SY/0	SY/0	SY/0	SY/0	SY/0	NW/0	NW/0	NW/0	NW/0	AT/FDS	AT/FDH		
ESQUIMALT	NW/0	NW/0	NW/RLU	NW/RLU	NW/0	NW/0	NW/0	NW/0	NW/0	NW/0	HL/RHA	HL/RHA	HL/RHA	HL/0	HL/0	HL/0							
GRANBY	W-3/0	W-3/0	W-3/0	W-3/0	W-3/0	AT/0	SY/RLU	SY/RLU	SY/RLU	SY/RLU	SY/WUB	SY/0	SY/0	SH/0	SH/RSB	HX/0	HX/0	HX/RHA	HX/0	AT/0	AT/FDH	AT/FDH	
LACHINE	W-6/RDH	W-6/W/U	W-6/0	W-6/0	W-6/0	W-6/0	AT/0	AT/0	HX/RHA	HX/RHA	HX/0	HX/0	HX/0	HX/RLU	HX/RLU	HX/W/U	HX/0	HX/0	HL/0	AT/FDB	AT/FDH		
MELVILLE	W-5/0	W-5/0	W-5/0	W-5/0	W-5/0	W-5/0	AT/RLU	AT/RLU	SY/WUB	SY/0	SY/0	SY/0	SY/0	SY/0	SY/0	SY/0	SY/0	SY/0	SY/0	AT/FDS			
NORANDA	W-9/0	W-9/0	W-9/0	W-9/0	W-9/0	W-9/0	SY/0	SY/0	SY/0	SY/0	SY/RLU	SY/RLU	SY/RLU	HX/WUB	HX/0	HX/0	HX/0	AT/FDS	AT/FDH	AT/FDH			
TRANSCONA	W-2/0	W-2/RLU	W-2/0	W-2/0	W-2/0	W-2/0	AT/0	HX/0	HX/0	HX/0	HX/0	W-8/0	HX/0	HX/0	HX/RLU	HX/RLU	HX/RLU	HX/W/U	HX/0	HX/0	AT/FDS	AT/FDH	
TROIS-RIVIERES	NW/RDH	NW/RHA	NW/RSB	NW/0	NW/0	NW/0	NW/0	NW/0	NW/0	NW/RHA	NW/0	NW/0	NW/0	NW/0	NW/0	NW/0	NW/RLU	NW/RLU	NW/WUB	NW/0	AT/FDH		
TRURO	W-4/0	W-4/0	W-4/0	W-4/0	W-4/0	W-4/0	SY/0	SY/0	SY/0	SY/0	SY/0	SY/0	SY/0	SY/RLU	SY/RLU	HX/RLU	HX/W/U	SY/0	SY/0	SY/0	AT/FDS	AT/FDH	

Bangor Class, 1940-1941 Programme

NAME of SHIP	Built at / Commissioned	1941 Oct.	Nov.	Dec.	1942 Jan.	Feb.	Mar.	Apr.	May	June	July	Aug.	Sep.	Oct.	Nov.	Dec.
COURTENAY	Prince Rupert Mar.21/42						PA F/O	PA W/U	PE 0	PE 0	PE 0	PR 0	PR 0	PR RPR	PR 0	PR 0
DRUMMONDVILLE	Montreal Oct.30/41	AT F/O	AT F/O	AT W/U	HL 0	HL 0	HL 0	HL 0	HL 0	GE 0	GE 0	GE 0	GE 0	SY 0	SY 0	SY 0
GANANOQUE	Toronto Nov.8/41		AT F/O	AT W/U	HL 0	HL 0	HL 0	HL 0	HL RHA	HL RHA	HL 0	HL 0	HX 0	GE 0	GE 0	GE 0
GODERICH	Toronto Nov.23/41		AT F/O	AT W/U	HL 0	HL 0	HL 0	HL 0	HL 0	HL 0	HL 0	HL 0	HL 0	HL 0	HL RHA	HX 0
GRANDMERE	Montreal Dec.11/41			AT F/O	AT RPI	AT RPI	AT RPI	AT RPI	AT W/U	SY 0	SY 0	SY 0	SY 0	SY 0	SY 0	SY 0
KELOWNA	Prince Rupert Feb.5/42					PA F/O	PA W/U	PA 0	PR 0	PR 0	PR 0	PR 0	PR RPR	PR 0	PE 0	PE 0
MEDICINE HAT	Montreal Dec.4/41			AT F/O	AT W/U	HL RDA	HL 0	HL 0	HL 0	SY 0	SY 0	SY 0	SY 0	SY 0	SY 0	SY 0
RED DEER	Montreal Nov.24/41		AT F/O	AT W/U	HL 0	HL RHA	HL 0	HL 0	HL 0	HX 0	HX 0	GE 0	GE 0	GE 0	GF 0	GE 0
SWIFT CURRENT	Montreal Nov.11/41		AT F/O	AT W/U	HL 0	HL 0	TA 0	TA 0	TA 0	TA 0	TA 0	TA 0	TA 0	TA 0	TA RHA	TA RHA
VEGREVILLE	Montreal Dec.10/41			AT F/O	AT W/U	HL RLU	HL RLU	HL 0	HL 0	GE 0	GE 0	GE 0	GE 0	NW 0	NW 0	NW 0

NAME of SHIP	1943 Jan.	Feb.	Mar.	Apr.	May	June	July	Aug.	Sep.	Oct.	Nov.	Dec.	1944 Jan.	Feb.	Mar.	Apr.	May	June	July	Aug.	Sep.	Oct.
COURTENAY	PR 0	PR 0	PR 0	PR 0	PR RPR	PR RPR	PE 0	PE 0	PE 0	PE 0	PE 0	PR 0	PR 0	PR 0	PR 0	PR 0	PR 0	PR 0	PE RES	PE 0	PE 0	PE 0
DRUMMONDVILLE	SY 0	WL 0	WL RLI	WL RLI	WL RPI	WL RPI	SY 0	SY 0	SY 0	SY 0	SY 0	SY 0	SY 0	NW 0	NW 0	NW 0	NW RLS	NW RLS	NW RHA	NW WUB	NW WUB	NW 0
GANANOQUE	SY 0	WL 0	WL 0	WL 0	WL RQC	WL RQC	HX W/U	HX 0	HX 0	HX 0	HX 0	HX 0	HX 0	HX 0	HX RHA	HX 0	SY 0	SY 0	SY RCA	SY RCA	SY RCA	SY WUB
GODERICH	HX 0	HX 0	HX RLI	HX RLI	HX RLI	HX 0	HX 0	HX 0	HX 0	HX 0	HX 0	HX 0	HX 0	HX 0	HX 0	HX 0	HX 0	HX 0	HX 0	HX RLU	HX RLU	HX WUB
GRANDMERE	SY 0	WL 0	HX 0	HX 0	HX 0	HX 0	HX RLS	HX RLS	HX RSY	HX W/U	HX 0	HL 0	HL 0	HL 0	HL 0	HL 0	HL 0	HL 0	HL 0	HL 0	HL 0	HL RSY
KELOWNA	PE 0	PE 0	PE 0	PE RES	PE 0	PE 0	PE 0	PE 0	PE 0	PE 0	PE 0	PE 0	PE 0	PE 0	PE 0	PE 0	PE 0	PE RES	PE 0	PE 0	PE 0	PR 0
MEDICINE HAT	SY 0	WL 0	WL 0	WL RLU	WL RLU	WL 0	HX 0	HX 0	HX 0	HX 0	NW 0	NW 0	HX 0	HX 0	HX RHA	HX 0	HX 0	SY 0	SY 0	SY RLU	SY 0	SY 0
RED DEER	SY 0	WL 0	WL RLI	WL RLI	WL 0	WL 0	SY 0	SY 0	SY 0	SY 0	SY 0	SY 0	SY 0	NW 0	NW 0	NW 0	NW RLI	NW RLI	NW RHA	NW WUB	NW 0	NW 0
SWIFT CURRENT	TA RHA	TA 0	HX 0	HX 0	HX 0	GF 0	GF 0	GF 0	GF 0	GF 0	HX 0	HX 0	HX RLU	NW RLU	NW 0	NW 0	NW 0	NW 0	NW 0	NW RHA	NW 0	NW 0
VEGREVILLE	NW 0	NW 0	NW 0	NW 0	NW RLS	NW RLS	NW RLS	NW W/U	NW 0	NW 0	NW 0	NW 0	NW 0	NW O/P	32P OK	32P OK	14P OK	31P OK	31P OK	14P RDV	14P O/P	14P RSY

NAME of SHIP	Nov.	Dec.	1945 Jan.	Feb.	Mar.	Apr.	May	June	July	Aug.	Sep.
COURTENAY	PE 0	PE 0	PE 0	PE 0	PR 0	PR 0	PR 0	PR 0	PR 0	PR 0	PE 0
DRUMMONDVILLE	NW 0	NW 0	NW 0	NW 0	NW 0	NW 0	NW 0	NW 0	AT TT	AT 0	2-M 0
GANANOQUE	SY 0	SY 0	SY 0	NW 0	NW 0	NW 0	NW 0	NW RSY	AT TT	AT 0	2-M 0
GODERICH	HX 0	HX 0	HX RHA	HX RHA	HX 0	HX 0	HX 0	HX 0	AT 0	AT RHA	1-M RHA
GRANDMERE	HL RSY	HL RHA	HX RHA	HX WUB	HX 0	HX 0	HX 0	SY 0	AT 0	AT 0	1-M 0
KELOWNA	PR RES	PR 0	PR 0	PR 0	PE 0	PE 0	PE 0	PE 0	PE 0	PE 0	PE RES
MEDICINE HAT	SY 0	SY 0	SY 0	NW 0	NW 0	NW 0	NW 0	NW 0	AT TT	AT 0	2-M 0
RED DEER	NW 0	NW 0	NW 0	NW 0	NW 0	NW 0	NW 0	NW 0	AT TT	AT 0	2-M RHA
SWIFT CURRENT	NW 0	NW 0	NW 0	NW 0	NW 0	NW 0	NW RHA	NW RDA	AT TT	AT 0	1-M RHA
VEGREVILLE	31P RSY	31P RHA	31P O/P	31P OK	31P OK	31P OK	31P N/O	RF IFA			

Bangor Class, 1941-1942 Programme

NAME of SHIP	Built at / Commissioned	1942 July	Aug.	Sep.	Oct.	Nov.	Dec.	1943 Jan.	Feb.	Mar.	Apr.	May	June
BLAIRMORE	Port Arthur Nov.17/42					NC F/O	NC W/U	NC RHA	NC W/U	WL 0	WL 0	WL 0	WL 0
FORT WILLIAM	Port Arthur Aug.25/42		NC F/O	NC F/O	NC W/U	NC W/U	HX 0	HX RHA	HX RHA	HX 0	HX 0	HX 0	HX 0
KENORA	Port Arthur Aug.6/42		NC F/O	NC W/U	WL 0	WL 0	WL 0	WL 0	WL 0	WL 0	WL 0	WL 0	WL 0
KENTVILLE	Port Arthur Oct.10/42				NC F/O	NC W/U	NC RHA	HX 0	HX 0	HX 0	HX 0	HX RHA	SY RSY
MILLTOWN	Port Arthur Sept.18/42			NC F/O	NC W/U	NC W/U	NC W/U	HX 0	HX 0	HX 0	WL 0	WL 0	GF 0
MULGRAVE	Port Arthur Nov.4/42					NC F/O	NC RHA	NC RHA	HX W/U	HX 0	WL 0	WL 0	WL 0
PORT HOPE	Toronto July 30/42	NC F/O	NC W/U	NC W/U	HX 0	HX 0	HX 0	HL 0	HL RHA	HL 0	HX 0	HX 0	GF 0
SARNIA	Toronto Aug.13/42		NC F/O	NC W/U	NC W/U	NW 0	NW 0	NW 0	NW 0	NW 0	NW 0	NW 0	NW RCO
STRATFORD	Toronto Aug.29/42		NC F/O	NC W/U	NC W/U	NW 0	NW 0	NW 0	NW 0	NW 0	NW 0	NW 0	NW 0
WESTMOUNT	Toronto Sept.15/42			NC F/O	NC W/U	NC W/U	HL RHA	HL RHA	HL RHA	HX 0	HX 0	SY 0	SY 0

NAME of SHIP	1943 July	Aug.	Sep.	Oct.	Nov.	Dec.	1944 Jan.	Feb.	Mar.	Apr.	May	June
BLAIRMORE	W-4 0	W-4 0	W-4 0	W-4 0	W-4 0	W-4 RCO	W-4 RHA	W-4 O/P	31P OK	31P OK	31P OK	31P OK
FORT WILLIAM	NW 0	NW RCO	NW RCO	NW W/U	NW 0	NW 0	NW 0	NW O/P	31P OK	31P OK	31P OK	31P OK
KENORA	W-8 0	W-8 0	W-8 RLI	W-8 RLI	W-8 0	W-8 0	W-8 0	W-8 O/P	32P OK	32P OK	14P OK	14P OK
KENTVILLE	SY RSY	SY 0	SY 0	SY 0	SY 0	HX 0	HX 0	HX 0	HX 0	HX 0	HX RCA	HX RCA
MILLTOWN	GF 0	GF 0	GF 0	GF RLI	HX RLI	HX W/U	HX 0	HX O/P	31P OK	31P OK	31P OK	31P OK
MULGRAVE	W-2 0	W-2 0	W-2 RLS	W-2 RLS	W-2 W/U	W-2 0	W-2 RHA	W-2 O/P	31P OK	31P OK	32P OK	31P OK
PORT HOPE	GF RDH	GF RDH	GF W/U	GF 0	HX 0	HX 0	HX 0	NW 0	NW 0	NW 0	NW 0	NW 0
SARNIA	NW 0	NW 0	NW 0	NW 0	NW 0	NW 0	NW 0	NW 0	NW 0	NW 0	NW 0	NW 0
STRATFORD	NW 0	NW 0	NW RCO	NW 0	NW 0	NW 0	NW 0	NW 0	NW 0	NW 0	NW 0	NW 0
WESTMOUNT	SY 0	SY 0	SY 0	SY 0	SY RLU	SY RLU	SY RHA	HX 0	HX 0	HX 0	HX 0	HX 0

NAME of SHIP	1944 July	Aug.	Sep.	Oct.	Nov.	Dec.	1945 Jan.	Feb.	Mar.	Apr.	May	June	July	Aug.	Sep.
BLAIRMORE	31P OK	31P RDV	31P OK	31P OK	31P OK	31P OK	31P OK	31P OK	31P C/P	31P RLU	31P RLU	31P O/P	31P OK	31P OK	31P OK
FORT WILLIAM	31P OK	31P OK	31P OK	31P OK	31P RDV	31P OK	31P OK	31P O/P	31P RSN	31P RSN	31P RSN	31P O/P	31P OK	31P OK	31P OK
KENORA	14P OK	14P OK	14P OK	14P OK	31P O/P	31P RLI	31P RLI	31P RLI	31P WUB	31P OK	31P OK	31P OK	31P OK	31P RPL	31P O/P
KENTVILLE	HX F/O	HX WUB	HX 0	HX 0	HX 0	HX 0	HX 0	HX RHA	HX 0	HX 0	HX 0	HX 0	AT 0	AT 0	2-M 0
MILLTOWN	31P OK	31P OK	31P RDV	31P OK	31P OK	31P OK	31P OK	31P OK	31P C/P	31P RSB	31P RSB	31P RSB	31P O/P	AT O/P	AT 0
MULGRAVE	31P OK	31P OK	31P OK	31P OK	31P P/O	31P P/O	RF IFA								
PORT HOPE	NW 0	NW 0	NW 0	NW RSB	NW RSB	NW RHA	NW WUB	HX 0	HX 0	HX 0	HX 0	HX 0	AT RHA	AT RHA	1-M 0
SARNIA	NW 0	NW 0	NW RLU	NW RLU	NW WUB	NW WUB	NW 0	HX 0	HX 0	HX 0	HX 0	HX 0	AT 0	AT 0	1-M 0
STRATFORD	NW 0	NW 0	NW 0	NW 0	NW 0	NW RDA	NW RDA	NW 0	NW 0	NW 0	NW RHA	HX RHA	AT RHA	AT RHA	AT FDH
WESTMOUNT	HX 0	HX 0	HX 0	HX 0	HX 0	HX 0	HX 0	HX RLU	HX RLU	HX RLU	HX WUB	HX 0	AT 0	AT 0	1-M 0

Algerine Class

NAME of SHIP	Built at / Commissioned	1943 Aug.	Sep.	Oct.	Nov.	Dec.	1944 Jan.	Feb.	Mar.	Apr.	May	June	July	Aug.
BORDER CITIES	Port Arthur May 18/44										NC O/P	NC F/O	NC WUB	W-2 0
FORT FRANCES	Port Arthur Oct.28/44													
KAPUSKASING	Port Arthur Aug.17/44													NC O/P
MIDDLESEX	Port Arthur June 8/44											NC F/O	NC O/P	NC WUB
NEW LISKEARD	Port Arthur Nov.21/44													
OSHAWA	Port Arthur July 6/44												NC O/P	NC F/O
PORTAGE	Port Arthur Oct.22/43			NC F/O	NC O/P	NC RHA	NC W/U	W-2 0	W-2 0	W-2 0	W-3 0	W-3 0	W-3 0	W-3 0
ROCKCLIFFE	Port Arthur Sept.30/44													
SAULT STE. MARIE	Port Arthur June 24/43	NC O/P	NC WUB	W-9 0	W-9 0	W-9 0	W-9 0	W-9 0	W-9 0	W-9 0	W-7 0	W-7 0	W-7 0	W-7 0
ST. BONIFACE	Port Arthur Sept.10/43		NC F/O	NC O/P	NC W/U	NC W/U	W-5 0	W-5 0	W-5 0	W-5 0	W-4 0	W-4 0	W-4 0	W-4 0
WALLACEBURG	Port Arthur Nov.18/43				NC O/P	NC RHA	NC W/U	W-8 0	W-8 0	W-8 0	W-6 0	W-6 0	W-6 0	W-6 0
WINNIPEG	Port Arthur July 29/43	NC O/P	NC W/U	W-7 0	W-7 0	W-6 0	W-6 0	W-6 0	W-6 0	W-6 0	W-5 0	W-5 0	W-5 0	W-5 RLI

NAME of SHIP	1944 Sep.	Oct.	Nov.	Dec.	1945 Jan.	Feb.	Mar.	Apr.	May	June	July	Aug.	Sep.
BORDER CITIES	W-2 0	W-2 0	W-2 0	W-2 0	W-2 0	W-2 0	W-2 0	W-2 0	W-2 0	W-2 0	AT WUB	AT 0	AT ISY
FORT FRANCES		NC F/O	NC O/P	NC RHA	NC RHA	NC WUB	W-8 0	W-8 0	W-9 0	W-9 0	AT 0	AT 0	AT ISY
KAPUSKASING	NC F/O	NC WUB	NC 0	W-1 0	W-1 0	W-1 0	W-1 0	W-1 0	W-1 RHA	W-1 WUB	AT 0	AT 0	AT ISY
MIDDLESEX	W-3 0	W-3 0	W-3 0	W-3 0	W-3 0	W-3 0	W-3 0	W-3 0	W-3 0	W-3 0	AT RSB	AT RSB	AT 0
NEW LISKEARD			NC F/O	NC O/P	TA TR	NC RHA	NC WUB	W-8 0	W-8 0	W-8 0	AT TR	AT TR	AT TR
OSHAWA	NC WUB	W-6 0	W-6 0	W-6 0	W-6 0	W-6 0	W-6 0	W-6 0	W-6 0	W-6 0	AT 0	AT 0	AT ISY
PORTAGE	W-3 0	W-3 0	W-3 RLI	W-3 RLI	W-3 RHA	W-3 WUB	W-3 0	W-3 0	W-3 0	W-3 0	AT 0	AT 0	AT ISY
ROCKCLIFFE	NC F/O	NC O/P	NC RHA	NC WUB	W-6 0	W-6 0	W-6 0	W-6 0	W-6 0	W-6 0	AT 0	AT 0	AT ISY
SAULT STE. MARIE	W-7 RLI	W-7 RLI	W-7 F/O	W-7 WUB	W-7 0	W-7 0	W-7 0	W-7 0	W-7 0	W-7 0	AT N/O	AT 0	AT ISY
ST. BONIFACE	W-4 0	W-4 RLI	W-4 RLI	W-4 RHA	W-4 WUB	W-4 0	W-4 0	W-4 0	W-4 RHA	W-4 RHA	AT RHA	AT 0	AT 0
WALLACEBURG	W-6 0	W-6 0	W-6 RSY	W-8 RSY	W-8 RSY	W-8 RHA	W-8 WUB	W-8 0	W-8 0	W-8 0	AT N/O	AT TR	AT TR
WINNIPEG	W-5 RLI	W-5 RLI	W-5 RLI	W-5 WUB	W-5 0	W-5 0	W-5 0	W-5 0	W-5 0	W-5 0	AT 0	AT 0	AT ISY

Bibliography

PUBLISHED SOURCES

Abbazia, Patrick *Mr. Roosevelt's Navy: the Private War of the U.S. Atlantic Fleet, 1939-1942.* Annapolis: U.S. Naval Institute, 1975.

Alden, John D. *Flush Decks and Four Pipes.* Annapolis: U.S. Naval Institute, 1965.

Beesly, Patrick *Very Special Intelligence: The Story of the Admiralty's Operational Intelligence Centre 1939-1945.* London: Hamish Hamilton, 1977.

Brice, Martin H. *The Tribals, Biography of a Destroyer Class.* London: Ian Allan, 1971.

Brown, J. D. *Carrier Operations in World War II, Volume 1: the Royal Navy.* London: Ian Allan, 1968.

Chalmers, William S. *Max Horton and the Western Approaches.* London: Hodder & Stoughton, 1954.

Colledge, J. J. *Ships of the Royal Navy, an Historical Index.* (2 vols.) Newton Abbot: David & Charles, 1969-1970.

Dittmar, F. J. and Colledge, J. J. *British Warships 1914-1919.* London: Ian Allan, 1972.

Easton, Alan *50 North: an Atlantic Battleground.* London: Eyre & Spottiswoode, 1963.

Elliott, Peter *Allied Escort Ships of World War II.* London: Macdonald and Jane's, 1977.
Allied Minesweeping in World War 2. Cambridge: Patrick Stephens, 1979.

Gretton, Sir Peter *Convoy Escort Commander.* London: Cassell 1964.
Crisis Convoy: the Story of the Atlantic Convoy HX.231. London: Davies, 1974.

Gröner, Erich *Die Schiffe der Deutschen Kriegsmarine und Luftwaffe 1939-1945.* Munich: Lehmann, 1972.

Herzog, Bodo *U-Boote im Einsatz 1939-1945.* Dorheim: Podzun, 1970.

Hodges, Peter *Tribal Class Destroyers.* London: Almark, 1971.

Jane's Fighting Ships. London: Sampson Low, Marston & Co. Ltd. various editions 1914 to 1980-1981.

Klepsch, Peter *Die Fremden Flotten im 2 Weltkrieg und ihr Shicksal.* Munich: Lehmann, 1968.

Lamb, James B. *The Corvette Navy: True Stories from Canada's Atlantic War.* Toronto: Macmillan, 1977.

Lawrence, Hal *A Bloody War: One Man's Memories of the Canadian Navy 1939-1945* Toronto: Macmillan, 1979.

Lenton, H. T. *British Fleet and Escort Destroyers.* Vols. 1-2, London: Macdonald 1970.
"British Escort Ships." *W.W. 2 Fact Files.* London: Macdonald & Jane's, 1974.

Lenton, H. T. & Colledge, J. J. *Warships of World War II.* London: Ian Allan, 1964.

Lloyd's Register of Shipping. various editions, 1910-1980.

Lund, Paul and Ludlam, Harry *Night of the U-Boats: the Story of Convoy SC-7.* Slough: Foulsham, 1973.

Lynch, Thomas G. *Canada's Flowers: History of the Corvettes of Canada.* Bennington: International Graphics, 1981.

Macintyre, Donald *U-Boat Killer.* London: Weidenfeld & Nicolson, 1956.
The Battle of the Atlantic. London: Batsford, 1961.

Macpherson, Ken R. *Canada's Fighting Ships.* Toronto: Samuel Stevens, 1975.

Mallmann Showell, J. P. *U-Boats under the Swastika.* London: Ian Allan, 1973.

Middlebrook, Martin *Convoy: The Battle for Convoys SC.122 and HX.229.* London: Allen Lane, 1976.

Mitchell, W. H. and Sawyer, L. A. *The Oceans, the Forts & the Parks.* Wartime Standard Ships, Vol. II. Liverpool: Sea Breezes, 1966.

Morison, Samuel Eliot *History of United States Naval Operations in World War II, I, The Battle of the Atlantic, Sept. 1939-May 1943.* Boston: Little, Brown, 1947.
History of United States Naval Operations in World War II, X, The Atlantic Battle Won, May 1943-May 1945. Boston: Little. Brown, 1956.

Poolman, Kenneth: *Escort Carrier 1941-1945.* London: Ian Allan, 1972.

Preston, Anthony & Raven, Alan, "Flower Class Corvettes." *Ensign 3.* London: Bivouac Books, 1973.

Rayner, D. A. *Escort: the Battle of the Atlantic.* London: William Kimber, 1955.

Rehder, Jacob *Die Verluste der Kriegsflotten 1914-1918.* Munich: Lehmann, 1969.

Revely, Henry *The Convoy that Nearly Died: the Story of ONS-154.* London: William Kimber, 1979.

Rohwer, Jürgen *The Critical Convoy Battles of March 1943.* Annapolis: U.S. Naval Institute, 1977.
Die U-Boot-Erfolge der Achsenmachte 1939-1945. Munich: Lehmann, 1968.

Rohwer, Jürgen & Hümmelchen, Gerd: *Chronology of the War at Sea 1939-1945.* (2 vols). London: Ian Allan, 1972-74.

Roskill, Stephen W. *The War at Sea 1939-1945.* (4 vols.) *History of the Second World War.* United Kingdom Military Series. London: H.M. Stationery Office, 1954-1961.
The Secret Capture: the Capture of U-110 London: Collins, 1959.

Schofield, Brian B. *The Arctic Convoys.* London: Macdonald & Jane's, 1977.

Schofield, B. B. & Martyn, L. F. *The Rescue Ships.* Edinburgh: Blackwood, 1968.

Seth, Ronald *The Fiercest Battle: the Story of North Atlantic Convoy ONS.5, 22 April-7 May 1943.* London: Hutchinson, 1961.

Schull, Joseph. *The Far Distant Ships: an Official Account of Canadian Naval Operations in the Second World War.* Ottawa: Department of National Defense, 1952.

Tucker, Gilbert N. *The Naval Service of Canada, Its Official History,* (2 vols.) Ottawa: Minister of National Defense, 1952.

Watts, Anthony: *The U-boat Hunters,* London: Macdonald & Jane's, 1976.

Young, John *A Dictionary of Ships of the Royal Navy of the Second World War.* Cambridge: Patrick Stephens, 1975.

Special Note

Readers interested in a complete bibliography of published material on the Canadian Armed Forces are referred to: *The Canadian Military Experience 1867-1967: A Bibliography* written by Owen A. Cooke of the Directorate of History, National Defence Headquarters, Ottawa: Queen's Printer, 1979.

Journals

Marine News. Journal of the World Ship Society. Kendal: Michael Crowdy, Editor, Years 1946-1981.

Warship International. Journal of the International Naval Research Organization. Toledo: Christopher C. Wright, Editor, Years 1964-1981.

Warships Supplement: Marine News. Journal of the World Ship Society. Kendal: James J. Colledge, Editor, Years 1966-1981.

UNPUBLISHED SOURCES

Directorate of History, Department of National Defence

Naval Service Headquarters, Ottawa, Operations Division.

Daily State 1 — HMC Ships and HM and Allied Ships Operated by RCN Authorities. Feb. 27, 1942 — June 22, 1943

Daily State II — HM and Allied Ships Operating in Canadian Coastal Zones or Refitting in US Ports. Feb. 28, 1942 — June 22, 1943

RCN Weekly State Reports. June 28, 1943 — Feb. 6, 1945 and Jan. 1946 — Dec. 3, 1946

RCN "Ship Movements" Cards. Sept. 3, 1939 — Sept. 3, 1945

"HX" Convoys Binder — Summaries. Sept. 16, 1939 — May 23, 1945

"SC" Convoys Binder — Summaries. Aug. 15, 1940 — May 26, 1945

Weekly Naval Report to Minister. Sept. 21, 1939 — Sept. 6, 1945

RCN Navy Lists. Years 1940 — 1965

Naval Historical Section

Individual "Ship's Files"

RCN Commands — War Diaries

(Reports of Proceedings/Operational War Diary) Halifax, Sept. 1939 —

Sept. 1945; Esquimalt, Sept. 1939 — Sept. 1945; St. John's, July, 1941 — June, 1945

Western Approaches Command — Royal Navy
Western Approaches Monthly News Bulletins, Jan. 1944 — April, 1945 Daily State Reports. July 9, 1944 — July 2, 1945.

Admiralty, Naval Staff, Operations Division
RN "Ship Movements" Binders. Sept., 1939 — Sept., 1945

Admiralty, Historical Section
The "Town" Class Destroyers: the Story of the "Four Stackers". March, 1949

Naval Historical Branch, Ministry of Defence, London
Admiralty, Naval Staff, Operations Division
Pink Lists. Aug. 29, 1939 — July 5, 1948
Admiralty, Naval Staff, Trade Division
Convoy Commodore Binders, Summaries of Atlantic Convoys HG — HX - HXF - JW - KMS - MKS - OA - OB - OG - ON - ONS - OS - PQ - OP - RA - SC - SL. Sept., 1939 - June, 1945
Daily State Reports, Status of North Atlantic Convoys, May, 1941 — Dec., 1941

Public Record Office, Kew Gardens, London
"OB" and "On" Convoys — Reports of Proceedings, ADM File Nos. 199/59, 199/284, 199/582, 199/1141, 199/1145, 199/1147. Years 1940 - 1942

Photo Credits

A majority of the illustrations in this book are from Canadian Forces photographs. Negatives of those taken prior to 1957 are, in general, held by Public Archives of Canada, and more recent ones by the Canadian Forces Photographic Unit, Rockcliffe.

The following photographs were obtained from, or originally taken by, firms or private sources other than the above: *Acadia*, McBride Collection, Maritime Museum of the Atlantic; *Algoma*, Jay Coulter; *Arnprior*, Ministry of Defence, U.K.; *Asbestos*, W. K. Milroy; *Assiniboine*, Bob Petry; *Barrie*, J. F. MacDonald; *Battleford*, U.S. Navy; *Bowmanville*, Ministry of Defence, U.K.; *Brandon*, Imperial War Museum; *Burlington*, P. M. McEntyre; *Carlplace*, R. J. Horne; *Celandine*, D. Trimingham; *Copper Cliff*, Imperial War Museum; *Constance* and *Curlew*, Art Mears; *Diana*, Ministry of Defence, U.K.; *Drumheller*, J. L. Dooley; *Drummondville*, B. A. Earthy; *Edmundston*, M. J. Robertson; *Fergus*, D. Trimingham; *Florence*, Eaton's of Canada; *Forest Hill*, Ministry of Defence, U.K.; *Foxhound*, Imperial War Museum; *Fraser* (1st), James Plomer; *Gananoque*, Bob Petry; *Giffard*, P. L. Robinson; *Glace Bay*, E. W. Finch-Noyes; *Guelph*, R. A. Simon; *Halifax*, D. Trimingham; *Hallowell*, R. G. Pentland; *Hamilton*, John Small; *Humberstone*, R. A. Simon; *Itchen*, J. O. Bayford; *Joliette*, McBride Collection; *Kincardine*, Ruth Markowitz; *La Hulloise*, Imperial War Museum; *Lindsay*, H. A. Agar; *Loch Achanalt*, C. S. J. Lancaster; *Loch Alvie* and *Loch Morlich*, Ministry of Defence, U.K.; *Longueuil*, D. Trimingham; *Louisburg* (1st), Imperial War Museum; *ML 067*, H. W. Patterson; *Manitoulin*, Watson's Studio, Midland; *Matapedia*, Bob Petry; *Melville*, R. W. King; *Merrittonia*, D. Trimingham; *Midland*, E. W. Finch-Noyes; *Mimico*, Ministry of Defence, U.K.; *Monnow*, Imperial War Museum; *Montreal*, C. Zickerman; *Murray Stewart*, James Plomer; *Nanaimo*, W. S. Knapp; *New Liskeard*, Port Arthur Shipbuilding Co.; *New Waterford*, Imperial War Museum; *New Westminster*, B. Trumpour; *Niagara*, Imperial War Museum; *Norsyd*, Larratt Higgins; *North Bay*, W. McMullan; *Orangeville*, Ministry of Defence, U.K.; *Oshawa*, Port Arthur Shipbuilding Co.; *Owen Sound*, P. Hardy; *Parry Sound*, J. W. Bald; *Patrician*, Provincial Archives of B.C.; *Pine Lake*, Watson's Studio, Midland; *Port Hope*, G. Hurrell; *Poundmaker*, R. A. Simon; *Puncher*, Imperial War Museum; *Quesnel*, M. H. Jones; *Quinte*, McBride Collection; *Restless*, R. W. Sandilands; *Ribble*, Imperial War Museum; *Rivière du Loup*, U.S. Navy; *Royalmount*, Bob Petry; *St. Laurent* (1st), C. V. Laughton; *Sans Peur*, McBride Collection; *Sea Cliff*, Donald Warren; *Shediac*, Paul Taylor; *Star XVI*, Bob Petry; *Stellarton*, Joseph Picton; *Stratford*, W. G. Garden; *Strathroy*, HMCS Strathroy Reunion Committee; *Suderöy IV*, R. Stark; *Summerside*, P. M. McEntyre; *Sussexvale*, C. S. J. Lancaster; *Teme*, Imperial War Museum; *Thetford Mines*, L. Gray; *Thorlock*, D. Trimingham; *Tillsonburg*, Imperial War Museum; *Trentonian*, D. Trimingham; *Trillium*, U.S. Coast Guard; *Trois-Rivières*, M. Matheson; *Truro*, W. McMullan; *Tuna*, J. R. Curry; *Vancouver* (1st), U.S. Navy; *Venture*, C. J. Dillon; *Warrior*, James Plomer; *Waskesiu*, E. G. Giles; *Wentworth*, R. J. C. Pringle; *Wetaskiwin*, W. Hemstreet.

The photographs of *Charlottetown (1st)*, *Kitchener*, *Morden*, *Peterborough*, *Portage*, and *Sackville* are from the collection of Ken Macpherson who, to his regret, cannot recall their sources. That of *Porte St. Louis* was taken by himself.

Index